A Companion to
Second-Century Christian
'Heretics'

A Companion to
Second-Century Christian
'Heretics'

Edited by

Antti Marjanen and Petri Luomanen

BRILL

LEIDEN • BOSTON

2008

This book is printed on acid-free paper.

Cover design by: Markku Boberg

Previously published as volume 76 in the Vigiliae Christianae Supplements series (hardback). ISBN 978 90 04 14464 4. Leiden: Brill, 2008

Library of Congress Cataloging-in-Publication Data

A companion to second-century Christian "heretics" / edited by Antti Marjanen and Petri Luomanen.
   p. cm.
   Includes bibliographical references and index.
   ISBN 978-90-04-17038-4 (pbk. : alk. paper) 1. Heresies, Christian. 2. Heretics, Christian—Biography. 3. Church history—Primitive and early church, ca. 30–600. I. Marjanen, Antti. II. Luomanen, Petri, 1961–
   BT1319.C65 2008
   273'.1—dc22

2008026655

ISBN 978 90 04 17038 4

PRINTED IN THE NETHERLANDS

Printed by Printforce, the Netherlands

CONTENTS

Preface vii
Introduction ix

Basilides the Gnostic 1
    Birger A. Pearson

Sethianism 32
    Michael A. Williams

The School of Valentinus 64
    Ismo Dunderberg

Marcion 100
    Heikki Räisänen

Tatian the Assyrian 125
    William L. Petersen

Bardaisan of Edessa 159
    Nicola Denzey

Montanism: Egalitarian Ecstatic "New Prophecy" 185
    Antti Marjanen

Cerinthus 213
    Matti Myllykoski

Ebionites 247
    Sakari Häkkinen

Nazarenes 279
    Petri Luomanen

Jewish Christianity of the *Pseudo-Clementines* 315
    F. Stanley Jones

Elchasaites and Their Book 335
    Gerard P. Luttikhuizen

Notes on Contributors 365

Index of Modern Authors 369
General Index 374

PREFACE

The idea for this publication sprang from an afternoon coffee break in the Department of Biblical Studies at the University of Helsinki. At the table were members of two research groups of the Department: *Early Jewish Christianity* and *Myth and Social Reality in Gnostic and Related Documents*. Both groups work with texts traditionally considered more-or-less heretical. As we chatted together, somehow, rather spontaneously, the idea of a volume focusing on the "other side" of second-century Christianity materialized. It would examine the documents and groups and persons that had been marginalized and denounced as heretical by the emerging "Great Church." After twenty minutes of discussion (and several cups of coffee) a plan was developed to fill an obvious lacuna in current research on the development of early Christianity. A volume was envisioned that would provide an up-to-date description of the most important second-century "heresies" and these movements' leading figures. Although it took several years to convert these plans into reality, the volume in hand suggests that coffee breaks can serve several useful purposes simultaneously.

Although some of the members of the two Finnish research groups (supplemented with Prof. Heikki Räisänen, the leader of their "umbrella organization," the *Research Unit for the Formation of Early Jewish and Christian Ideology*) were already working on some of the topics addressed in the chapters that follow, other topics required reaching outside Finland. We were delighted with the positive responses we received from our foreign colleagues, all experts in their fields, who shared our interest in illuminating the other side of second-century Christianity. We wish to thank them, for this publication would never have seen the light of day without their investment of time and expertise. Special thanks go to Prof. William L. Petersen (Penn State University), one of the editors of the *Supplements to Vigiliae Christianae* series, who not only wrote a contribution to the present volume but who also read the entire manuscript carefully and made helpful suggestions on both content and language.

We also want to express our gratitude to Louise Schouten, Senior Acquisitions Editor of Brill Academic Publishers, and Ivo Romein,

Editor of Brill Academic Publishers, for their help and support in all stages of the editorial process. The responsibility of revising the English of the Finnish contributors was painstakingly borne by Margot Stout Whiting and Gary Denning.

During the time the present volume was under preparation, many of the Finnish contributors of this volume were employed, either for the entire period or in most cases for part of it, by the Academy of Finland and by the Helsinki Collegium for Advanced Studies of the University of Helsinki. These institutions also provided us with technical assistance which has greatly relieved the burden on the editors: Thanks are due to research assistants Perttu Nikander (funded by the Academy of Finland) and Sanna Ingo (Helsinki Collegium for Advanced Studies) for their help in technical editing.

Editors

INTRODUCTION

This collection of essays deals with persons and movements traditionally characterized as heretical. However, as the quotation marks in the title of this volume suggest, the intention is not to map the second-century religious terrain from the viewpoint of the form of Christianity that became dominant and developed into the early Catholic Church. Instead, the idea is to investigate "the other side," by examining the thinkers and movements that were, at the time, embraced by many second-century religious seekers as legitimate forms of Christianity, but which are now largely forgotten, or are known only from the characteristics attributed to them in the writings of their main adversaries.

The task is not easy since much of the crucial firsthand evidence is lost or, at best, waits to be found somewhere in secluded caves, ancient dumping grounds, or in unlisted holdings of papyri. This means that the researcher must try to glean reliable information from the church fathers' polemical writings, their biased descriptions of their adversaries' teaching, and assess it in light of what can be known of these persons' own productions. The problem is that the material for comparison is often extremely scanty.

As a matter of fact, Tatian is the only figure in this volume from whom a complete work exists. Even in his case, the work that has survived is not the one that he is most famous for, the *Diatessaron*, but *Oratio ad graecos*, an apologetic treatise that later served the interest of the Church in Rome very well. Bardaisan's thoughts have to be gleaned from the *Book of the Laws of the Countries* which was composed by one of his students, Philippus. Some fragments of Basilides', Marcion's, Valentinus', and the Montanists' own works have survived in the writings of their adversaries, but no overall picture of their views can be painted on the basis of these fragments alone. Cerinthus' ideas can also be reconstructed only from the polemical, inconsistent, and contradictory writings of the church fathers. If he ever wrote any treatises, no references to his writings have been preserved, apart from rumors which attribute the Gospel of John and the Book of Revelation to him. Although a scholar who aims at a historical-critical reconstruction of the original ideas and teachings of "heretics" like these faces difficulties, the task is by no means impossible. The chapters in this book show that after a careful assessment of the source materials, some distinctive ideas of these alternative second-century Christian movements can be delineated.

The articles in the present collection have been arranged in three partially overlapping thematic clusters: (1) Gnostics, (2) Teachers in the West and in the East, and (3) Jewish Christians. We have also chosen to present teachers and movements that can more squarely be fixed in history before those whose historical character is debated. The thematic arrangement means, however, that there are exceptions to this rule.

The two earliest teachers discussed are Cerinthus and Basilides, who were already active in the late first and early second century. Although Cerinthus may have been active even before Basilides, the collection is opened with the article on "Basilides the Gnostic," followed by two thematically related contributions on Sethianism and Valentinus' school. After Valentinus follow Marcion and Tatian, two teachers who were also active in Rome.

Tatian returned to the East, where his fame was comparable to that of Bardaisan, the great man of Edessa, the center of Eastern Syrian Christianity. The Phrygian prophesy, Montanism, although it also gained influence in Rome and elsewhere in the West, originated in Asia Minor, where it found its greatest support. The same was true with Cerinthus. Since chiliasm has been discussed in connection with both the Montanists and Cerinthus, these two are treated after Bardaisan.

Although Cerinthus was a historical figure, scholars have not been able to agree whether he was a Gnostic or a Jewish-Christian teacher. The chapter in the present collection argues that he was mainly drawing on Jewish ideas. For this reason, and because the heresiologists usually described him as a predecessor of the Jewish-Christian Ebionites, the chapter on him opens the Jewish-Christian section of this volume.

While the information about the history and ideas of Cerinthus, Basilides, Valentinus, Marcion, Tatian, Bardaisan, and the Montanist prophets is meager, there is no doubt about the historicity of these teachers, and a relatively reliable picture of their main ideas can be inferred from the sources available. The situation is different in the case of persons and movements more or less closely tied to Jewish Christianity. Therefore, we have placed the "Gnostics" and the

"Western and Eastern teachers" before the "Jewish Christians" hoping that those who read the articles in that order would be able to form an overall view of the historical circumstances and of current topics in philosophical and theological debates before moving on to the articles—from Cerinthus onwards—that have less first hand evidence available.

The present collection is a selection of "heresies" among which the formative Catholic Christianity found its main adversaries in the second century; but it is clear that it is not a complete collection of the second-century alternative teachers and movements. In addition to the "heresies" listed by the church fathers but not treated in this volume, there were also other movements and teachers who never made their way to the heresiological treatises. Only one such branch of Christianity is discussed in this book: the Jewish Christianity of the *Pseudo-Clementines*. To be sure, Epiphanius obviously had some Pseudo-Clementine writings in his use when he composed his *Panarion* but he attributed them to the Ebionites mixing the data he picked from these texts with all the tales his predecessors had provided about the Ebionites. When studied in its own right, the *Circuits of Peter*, the basic writing behind the *Pseudo-Clementine Homilies* and *Recognitiones*, reveals a type of Jewish Christianity to which Epiphanius' discussion in *Panarion* 30 (the chapter on the Ebionites) hardly does any justice.

The significance of the *Pseudo-Clementines* for the study of Jewish Christianity is comparable to the status of the Nag Hammadi texts in the study of the phenomenon traditionally called Gnosticism. Both the *Pseudo-Clementines* and Nag Hammadi texts provide an important devotees' point of view to religiosity criticized by the church fathers indicating that early Christianity was even more colorful than one would imagine on the basis of the heresiological treatises.

The writers of the articles on Basilides, Sethians and Valentinus' school have made extensive use of the Nag Hammadi texts. Nevertheless, the *Gospel of Thomas* is not discussed in this volume although there is no doubt about its significance in second-century Christianity in general. One reason for this is that the volume focuses on the movements and persons that have been traditionally included among "heresies," and the church fathers did not speak about Thomasine Christians, although they made some reference to the *Gospel of Thomas* in their lists of canonical and non-canonical writings (for instance, Eusebius, *Hist. eccl.* 3.25). Another reason for the omission is that an abundance of literature on *Thomas* and its community is already available.

The fact that Thomasine Christians are not refuted in the heresiologies illustrates very well one of the features that stand out in the present collection as a whole: Teachers and movements were denounced as heretical especially because they were in conflict with the type of Christianity that was gaining the upper hand in Rome in the second half of the second century. Had there appeared a teacher in Rome who based his teaching exclusively on the *Gospel of Thomas*—the same way Alcibiades was drawing on the *Book of Elchasai*—later heresiologists might very well have tried to refute the "Thomasaites," too. The dominance of the Roman viewpoint in heresiological discourse is also exemplified by the fact that Tatian's heretical reputation as one of the chief proponents of Encratism was entertained only in the western heresiologies. Tatian was condemned in the West as a leading proponent of Encratism and expelled from the Roman church. But in the East, Syrian Christianity—which was characterized from the outset by much stronger ascetic tendencies than was Western Christianity—unreservedly accepted him and his harmony of the Gospels, the *Diatessaron*, apparently unaware of (or choosing to ignore) his reputation as a "heretic".

Another characteristic prominent in the following chapters is the proximity of many of the "heretical" ideas discussed in this volume with ideas in the New Testament. Although the teachers who were condemned as "heretics" imported ideas from the outside of the New Testament as well—often from popular philosophy (in which mainstream Christian writers were equally interested)—many of their positions were squarely grounded in the issues with which New Testament authors were also wrestling. For example, Marcion's radical denial of the validity of the Old Testament scriptures can be seen as a logical consequence of Paul's denunciation of the law. On the other hand, it is clear that the views of the conservative Jewish Christians were equally representative of ideas documented in the New Testament. "Possession" Christology, which is linked with Cerinthus and the Ebionites, may very well be one of the oldest Christological models in the New Testament. The central role of prophecy in Montanism has its roots in the proclamation of the Paraclete whom the Johannine Christ promised to send to his followers to teach them the truths his own disciples could not receive in their lifetime. The millenarian kingdom which is part of the teachings of Cerinthus and the Montanists stems from the concluding chapters of the Book of Revelation. Furthermore, ascetism is not an unknown phenomenon in the New Testament. All in all, from the viewpoint of reception history it is often impossible to make any difference between "orthodox" and "heretic" teachers as regards the way they reinterpreted New Testament materials.

Where appropriate, the authors have included an overview of the life and significant publications of the "heretics," along with a description of their theologies and movements. Therefore, this volume can serve as a handbook of the second-century "heretics" and their "heresies." At the same time, however, many of the chapters, written by specialists who wrestle daily with these subjects, offer new perspectives and insights into these issues. In our view, this gives the volume a unique and independent profile and will hopefully also stimulate further research on this fascinating—but often neglected—side of early Christianity.

Petri Luomanen and Antti Marjanen

BASILIDES THE GNOSTIC

Birger A. Pearson

"Basilides the heresiarch was living in Alexandria; from him derive the Gnostics." This is one of the items listed by Eusebius in his *Chronicle* for the sixteenth year of Emperor Hadrian's reign (132 C.E.).[1] This is the only mention in Eusebius' *Chronicle* of any "Gnostics,"[2] if, indeed, that terminology is his. If it is, Eusebius here credits Basilides with being the first "Gnostic," founder, as it were, of what some of us still call "Gnosticism."[3]

That Basilides was a "Gnostic" can hardly be doubted, but he certainly was not the first one. In what follows I shall assess the available sources for Basilides, discuss what I take to be his authentic teachings, and attempt to situate him and his teachings in the context of the history of ancient Gnosticism and in the early history of Alexandrian Christianity. I shall concentrate my discussion on Basilides himself, with only limited attention to what our sources tell us about teachings of his followers (the "Basilidians"). I cheerfully acknowledge here my indebtedness to recent work of scholars more knowledgeable in the subject than I, particularly Winfred Löhr's magisterial

---

[1] *Basilides haeresiarches in Alexandria commoratur. A quo gnostici*; for the text, see R. Helm, ed., *Die Chronik des Hieronymus* (vol. 7 of *Eusebius Werke*; ed. der Kommission für spätantike Religionsgeschichte der deutschen Akademie der Wissenschaften; 2nd ed.; GCS 47; Berlin: Akademie-Verlag, 1956), 201. (Jerome's Latin *Chronicle* is based on that of Eusebius, whose Greek original is lost.) Cf. the Armenian version (A. Schoene, ed. and trans., *Eusebi Chronicorum canonum quae supersunt* [Dublin-Zürich: Weidman, 1967], 1:168): *Basilides haeresiarcha his temporibus apparuit* ("Basilides the heresiarch appeared at this time"). In the Armenian version this is listed for the 17th year of Hadrian's reign, 133 C.E.

[2] On Eusebius' treatment of "Gnostic" heretics see my essay, "Eusebius and Gnosticism," chapter 8 in Pearson, *The Emergence of the Christian Religion* (Harrisburg, Pa.: Trinity Press International, 1997), 147–68.

[3] As is by now well known Michael Williams is encouraging us to drop the term altogether; see Williams, *Rethinking "Gnosticism": An Argument for Dismantling a Dubious Category* (Princeton: Princeton University Press, 1996). For my response to his work, see Pearson, "Gnosticism as a Religion," in *Was There a Gnostic Religion?* (ed. Antti Marjanen; Helsinki: The Finnish Exegetical Society; Göttingen: Vandenhoeck & Ruprecht, 2004).

monograph, *Basilides und seine Schule*,[4] where all of the evidence is collected and discussed, and Bentley Layton's treatment of Basilides in his anthology, *The Gnostic Scriptures*.[5] In choosing to concentrate solely on Basilides himself, I follow Layton's lead.

1. *The Sources*

1.1. *Heresiological Accounts*

The earliest account we have of Basilides' mythological system is that of Irenaeus, *Adversus haereses* 1.24.3–7.[6] Irenaeus situates Basilides in a succession of heretics going back to Simon Magus and Menander. His account is usually thought to be based on Justin Martyr's lost *Syntagma Against All Heresies* (cf. *Apol.* 1.26).[7] Three other patristic accounts are dependent upon Irenaeus: Pseudo-Tertullian, *Adversus omnes haereses* 1.5; Epiphanius, *Panarion* 24, and Filastrius, *Diversarum haereseon liber* 32. It has long been thought that Ps.-Tertullian is based on Hippolytus of Rome's lost *Syntagma Against All Heresies*.[8] While Ps.-Tertullian, Epiphanius, and Filastrius are obviously dependent upon Irenaeus, they have certain deviations from Irenaeus in common, indicating that they used another source beside Irenaeus, presumably Hippolytus' lost *Syntagma*.[9]

A completely different account of Basilides' system is that of Hippolytus, *Refutatio omnium haeresium* 7.20–27.[10] Hippolytus takes pains

---

[4] W. A. Löhr, *Basilides und seine Schule: Eine Studie zur Theologie- und Kirchengeschichte des zweiten Jahrhunderts* (WUNT 83; Tübingen: J. C. B. Mohr [Paul Siebeck], 1996).

[5] B. Layton, *The Gnostic Scriptures* (Garden City, N.Y.: Doubleday, 1987), 417–44. See also Layton, "The Significance of Basilides in Ancient Christian Thought," *Representations* 28 (1989): 135–51.

[6] Latin text in Walther Völker, *Quellen zur Geschichte der christlichen Gnosis* (Tübingen: J. C. B. Mohr [Paul Siebeck], 1932), 44–46; ET in Werner Foerster, *Gnosis: A Selection of Gnostic Texts* (trans. R. McL. Wilson; 3 vols.; Oxford: Clarendon, 1972), 1:59–61, Layton, *Gnostic Scriptures*, 420–25; German summary in Löhr, *Basilides*, 256–57.

[7] See Löhr's discussion, *Basilides*, 257–58, with references to older scholarship.

[8] See e.g. Adolf Hilgenfeld's discussion in Hilgenfeld, *Die Ketzergeschichte des Urchristentums* (1884; repr., Darmstadt: Wissenschaftliche Buchgesellschaft, 1963), 9–15. Hilgenfeld refers to this lost work as Hippolytus I, and Hippolytus' *Refutatio omnium haeresium* as Hippolytus II.

[9] So Löhr, *Basilides*, 273–84.

[10] Greek text in Völker, *Quellen*, 46–56; ET in Foerster, *Gnosis*, 1:62–74; German summary in Löhr, *Basilides*, 284–92.

to show that Basilides based his system on Aristotelian philosophy, in line with his general tendency to attribute heresy to the influence of pagan philosophy.

It is impossible to reconcile Hippolytus' account with that of Irenaeus; one must choose between them, or reject both of them. Since the nineteenth century most scholars have accepted Hippolytus' version as the authentic teaching of Basilides or at least closest to it, with the result that, until rather recently, one could speak of a general consensus of scholarly opinion.[11] That consensus has clearly been broken, thanks to the work of Layton and others, who argue that Irenaeus' account puts us in touch with Basilides himself, and is reconcilable with the unquestionably authentic fragments of Basilides' writings provided by Clement of Alexandria.[12] Löhr, on the other hand, rejects both Irenaeus and Hippolytus as reliable informants on Basilides' authentic teaching.[13] I find myself in agreement with Layton on this issue.

1.2. *Miscellaneous Testimonies*

Löhr has collected fifteen ancient testimonies relating to Basilides and his school, of which eleven deal with the heresiarch himself. Considerable information on Basilides' career can be gleaned from these testimonies (T), but not all of it is reliable.

According to Irenaeus (*Haer.* 1.24.1, T4) Basilides and Saturninus based their teachings on those of Simon Magus and Menander, Basilides teaching in Alexandria and Saturninus in Antioch. An Alexandrian provenance for Basilides is virtually certain, though a sojourn in Antioch cannot be excluded.[14] Less certain is the statement of Hippolytus (*Haer.* 7.27.13, T8) that Basilides studied in Egypt (i.e. outside of Alexandria). That he taught in the Egyptian chora, as reported by Epiphanius (*Pan.* 24.1.1, T13), is highly unlikely. As

---

[11] See Löhr's discussion, *Basilides*, 1–2.

[12] Layton, *Gnostic Scriptures*, 418. It should be noted that Hilgenfeld adopted this position already in 1884 (*Ketzergeschichte*, 195–230). Cf. also Simone Pétrement, *A Separate God: The Christian Origins of Gnosticism* (trans. Carol Harrison; San Francisco: HarperSanFrancisco, 1990), 336–46; and esp. the important article by Robert M. Grant, "Place de Basilide dans la théologie chrétienne ancienne," *REAug* 25 (1979): 201–16.

[13] Löhr, *Basilides*, 255–323.

[14] On the resemblances of Basilides' teachings to those of Saturninus of Antioch, see discussion below.

to the time of Basilides' floruit in Alexandria, Clement's statement
that he taught from the time of the reign of Hadrian (117–138) into
the reign of Antoninus Pius (138–161, *Strom.* 7.106.4–107.1, T5) is
plausible enough. This information accords, too, with Eusebius' testimony, quoted above (T12). Other testimonies, situating Basilides in
Persia (Hegemonius, *Acta Archelai* 67.4) or in Asia Minor (Canon
Muratori, lines 81–85, T9) are certainly wrong, or perhaps refer to
other persons with the same name.[15]

We have already noted that Irenaeus puts Basilides in a line of
succession of heretics going back to Simon Magus. But Basilidian
traditions claim apostolic succession for Basilides instead. Clement
(*Strom.* 7.106.4–107.1, T5) reports a claim made by Basilides that he
had as a teacher one Glaukias, an "interpreter" (Gk. *hermeneus*) of
the apostle Peter. Clement (*Strom.* 7.108.1, T6) also reports that the
Basilidians lay claim to the teachings of the apostle Matthias. Hippolytus
goes further (*Haer.* 7.20.1, T7); he reports that Basilides and his son
Isidore claimed to have received from Matthias secret teachings, presumably of Jesus. None of this can be traced back to Basilides himself. The Peter-Glaukias tradition (whoever Glaukias was) can possibly
be seen as a Basilidian counter to the Peter-Mark tradition current
in Alexandrian ecclesiastical circles.[16] Hippolytus' statement regarding Matthias is chronologically impossible, and is probably a distortion of Clement's statement connecting Basilidian traditions with
Matthias.[17]

According to Agrippa Castor (Eusebius, *Hist. eccl.* 4.7.5–8, T1),
who wrote a refutation of Basilides, Basilides composed 24 volumes

---

[15] Hegemonius refers to a preacher "among the Persians" named Basilides, and
proceeds to quote from one of his books. This is Löhr's fragment 19, on which see
further below. Layton (*Gnostic Scriptures*, 417) surmises that Hegemonius is referring to another person named Basilides. The Canon Muratori refers to "Basilides
of Asia Minor, the founder of the Cataphrygians" (ET in *New Testament Apocrypha*
[ed. W. Schneemelcher; trans. R. McL. Wilson; 2 vols.; rev. ed.; Cambridge: James
Clarke, 1991–1992] 1:36). Was there a Montanist teacher in Asia Minor also called
Basilides? In any case, these testimonies are completely unreliable if they pertain
to Basilides of Alexandria.

[16] So Löhr, *Basilides*, 21–22. That Mark was the "interpreter" of Peter is reported
by Papias of Hierapolis (Eusebius, *Hist. eccl.* 3.39.15). Layton accepts the Glaukias
connection: "In fragment G Basilides writes as a *hermeneus Petrou*, an expositor of
Peter. I see no reason to doubt that Glaucias had earned a reputation as a striking early commentator (*hermeneus*) on a Petrine corpus; Basilides would then have
carried on his master's work" ("Significance of Basilides," 46).

[17] Suggested by Löhr (*Basilides*, 28–29).

on the Gospel. His "prophets" included Barkabbas and Barkoph and others with barbarian names. He taught that Christians can without scruple eat meat sacrificed to idols and deny their faith in times of persecution. Following Pythagoras, he prescribed a five-year period of silence. Agrippa's testimony must obviously be taken with a grain of salt.[18] The only useful information we get from this is that Basilides wrote commentaries on "the Gospel," presumably his *Exegetica*, from which Clement provides three quotations.[19]

Other compositions of Basilides are cited in patristic sources. Origen (*Hom. Luc.* 1, T10) reports that Basilides even dared to write a "Gospel According to Basilides." He also reports (*Enarrat. Job* 21.12, T11) that Basilides composed "odes" comparable to the psalms composed by Valentinus. Origen's report on a "Gospel According to Basilides" is probably nothing more than a distortion of the well-known fact that Basilides had composed a collection of commentaries on "the Gospel."[20] That Basilides composed "odes" is possible, but they are otherwise unattested.[21]

An important testimony relating to Basilides' teaching is provided in Nag Hammadi Codex IX,3: *The Testimony of Truth* (Löhr's T15). We shall return to that text in our discussion of Basilides' mythological system.

1.3. *The Fragments of Basilides*

Löhr's collection of fragments of Basilides and his followers, nineteen of them,[22] supersedes previous collections[23] by virtue of its completeness. Of those nineteen, ten pertain to Basilides himself, five from the fourth book of Clement's *Stromateis* (frgs. 7, 8, 10, 11, 12), two from the fifth book of the *Stromateis* (13, 14), two from homilies

---

[18] According to Löhr (*Basilides*, 9–11) Agrippa's testimony is largely dependent upon Irenaeus' account.

[19] Quotations from Book 23, *Strom.* 4.81.1–83.1, Löhr's fragment 7, Layton's fragment G. A possible quotation from Book 13 is provided by Hegemonius (Löhr's fragment 19), on which see below.

[20] Cf. Löhr's discussion, *Basilides*, 31–34.

[21] According to Löhr, Origen's testimony is "nicht auszuschliessen." Michel Tardieu states flatly that the *Exegetica* of Basilides constitute the only work of his, for all other titles attributed to him are polemical inventions of the heresiologists. See Tardieu, "Basilide le gnostique," in *Dictionnaire des philosophes antiques* (ed. Richard Goulet; Paris: CNRS Éditions, 1994), 2:84–89, esp. 87.

[22] Löhr, *Basilides*, 42–248.

[23] Völker, *Quellen*, 38–44; Foerster, *Gnosis*, 1:74–83.

by Origen (17, 18), and one from Hegemonius' *Acta Archelai* (19). Eight of these are also found in Layton's *Gnostic Scriptures* (frgs. A–H, corresponding to Löhr's fragments 11, 14, 13, 8, 12, 18, 7, and 10). One of the ones omitted by Layton (frg. 17, Origen, *Comm. ser. Matt.* 38) is not really a fragment, but a testimony to Basilides' doctrine of reincarnation, to which we shall return. Löhr's fragment 19, from Hegemonius' *Acta Archelai*, is rejected by Layton as inauthentic. Löhr, on the other hand, argues vigorously for its genuineness.[24] The issues involved pro and con are worth discussing at some length.

Hegemonius' *Acta Archelai* is a fictitious account of a series of doctrinal debates between Archelaus, bishop of a Mesopotamian city called Carchar, and the heresiarch Mani, and is an important document for the study of Manichaeism.[25] It is extant in a Latin translation of the Greek original, now lost but utilized by Epiphanius (chs. 7–13 in *Pan.* 66.25.3–31.8). At one point in the text (ch. 42), Archelaus alleges that Mani stole his doctrine from an earlier teacher named Scythianus, who dictated four books containing the dualistic doctrines adopted by Mani.[26] Mani also got hold of Christian books, and subjected them to a dualistic interpretation based on Scythianus' teaching. Later, Archelaus reports that Mani was not the first one to plagiarize Scythianus' dualistic teaching, and cites another person even before Mani, namely Basilides:

> There was also among the Persians a preacher called Basilides who lived even earlier, not long after the time of our apostles.[27] He was an astute man and had observed that at that time all other areas had been fully studied, so he decided to assert that same dualism that had been present with Scythianus. In short since he had nothing of his own to propound, he challenged his adversaries with the sayings of others. All his books contain some difficult and very abstruse passages. The thirteenth book of his treatises is still extant, and it begins as follows: 'As we are writing the thirteenth book of our treatises the word of salvation will provide for us the necessary and fruitful content. By means of the parable of the rich man and the poor man it demonstrates the source of the nature that comes upon things without a root or a place.' (*Acta Archelai* 67.4–5)

---

[24] Löhr, *Basilides*, 219–49.

[25] In this discussion I utilize the recent translation by Mark Vermes, with introduction by Samuel N. C. Lieu, *Hegemonius, Acta Archelai (The Acts of Archelaus)* (Manichaean Studies 4; Turnhout: Brepols, 2001), based on Beeson's edition.

[26] The titles given, *Mysteries, Capitula, Gospel,* and *Thesaurus,* actually correspond to works produced by Mani himself. See ch. 42.6, pp. 141–42, and Lieu's notes.

[27] Cf. discussion above, and n. 15.

Immediately following this quotation from Basilides, Archelaus continues his disputation, introducing another quotation from Basilides:

> Is this the only subject that the book contains? Does it not contain another topic? And yet, as some people have considered, will you not all be offended by such a book that began in this way. But returning to his subject after an interval of more or less five hundred lines, Basilides says: 'Let us cease from this pointless and idle digression; rather let us investigate what inquiries the barbarians have made about good and evil things, and what opinions they have formed on all these matters. For some of them have said that all things have two beginnings, to which they have associated good and evil, stating that these beginnings themselves are without beginning and unbegotten. In other words there was in the beginning Light and Darkness, which existed of themselves, which were not said to be begotten.' (*Acta Archelai*, 67.6–7)

Archelaus' Basilides continues his account with how Darkness lusted for Light, resulting in an "admixture" that characterizes the current cosmos. The quotation from Basilides concludes as follows: "However, through this very small light, they have been able to produce an image of a creation relating to that admixture that they had received from the light. And this is that creation which we see" (67.11). Archelaus goes on to say that Basilides added to Scythianus' writings the names of demons and other useless gibberish (68.1), arguing that all of Basilides' teachings were dependent upon Scythianus' dualism (68.2). Remarking that "Basilides has stated precisely and briefly the things he had found defined in Scythianus," only promulgating them with more subtle arguments (68.4), Archelaus appeals to his readers to "write against those books that were published by Basilides" (68.5). With that Archelaus concludes his disputation.

What are we to make of this? Can anything Hegemonius purports to quote from Basilides actually be attributed to Basilides of Alexandria? As already noted, Löhr accepts the two quotations as authentic, and argues that they are taken from the thirteenth book of Basilides' *Exegetica*.[28] Now it is conceivable that the first quotation comes from the opening passage of Book 13 of that work, since it clearly refers to the "word of salvation" and to a parable of Jesus, i.e. the parable of the rich man and Lazarus (Luke 16:19–31). An obvious difficulty

---

[28] Foerster (*Gnosis*, 1:74), too, attributes the fragment to the thirteenth book of the *Exegetica*, but suggests that Basilides "probably does not set out his own point of view, but that of others whom he wishes to oppose." That is the only solution possible if one is to accept the fragment's authenticity.

is posed by the enigmatic phrase, "the source of the nature that comes upon things without a root or a place" (*naturam sine radice et sine loco rebus supervenientem unde pullulaverit*). We shall have to return to that problem when we discuss Basilides' doctrine of "nature" (Gk. *physis*).

What about the other quotation on Light and Darkness, which is said to come after around 500 intervening lines? It is important to note that that quotation is said to deal with "another topic" (*alium sermonem*, 67.6). The Light-Darkness dualism propounded in that lengthy quotation clearly has nothing to do with Jesus' parable, and, in fact, presupposes Manichaean doctrine![29] Hegemonius' purpose in having Archelaus quote from Basilides is simply to suggest that Mani depends not only on pagan dualism as expounded by "Scythianus" but on a well-known Christian heretic, whose own heretical doctrines come from the same source. As for "Scythianus," he is clearly a fictitious character.

Thus, while it is conceivable that Hegemonius had access to a quotation from Basilides' *Exegetica*, and that the first quotation in the fragment is genuine, the quotation expounding on Light and Darkness can hardly be attributed to Basilides of Alexandria. And the fact remains that the intended meaning of that first quotation is, at best, obscure.

To conclude this discussion, the seven fragments preserved by Clement constitute those fragments most likely to put us in touch with actual teachings of Basilides. But, as we shall see, even those fragments are open to different interpretations.

2. *Basilides' Mythological and Philosophical System*

As already noted, there is considerable disagreement among scholars regarding the nature of Basilides' mythological system, or even if he had one. Löhr, for example, rejects both of the main heresiological accounts, that of Irenaeus (and those dependent on him) and that of Hippolytus. For him Basilides was simply an early Christian theologian and exegete, though one who was open to contemporary

---

[29] So, correctly, Gerhard May, *Creatio ex Nihilo: The Doctrine of 'Creation out of Nothing' in Early Christian Thought* (trans. A. S. Worrall; Edinburgh: T&T Clark, 1994), 79 n. 84. Löhr, of course, rejects that view (*Basilides*, 233 n. 53).

philosophy, especially Platonism and Stoicism. Löhr therefore plays down the "Gnostic" character of Basilides' teachings.[30] I prefer Layton's approach, and accept Irenaeus' account (*Haer.* 1.23.3–7) as at least partially accurate. To be sure, Irenaeus' account is only an incomplete summary, and, moreover, contains teachings attributed to Basilides' followers as well as those of Basilides himself. As noted by Layton, the attributions made by Irenaeus are important signals ("he says," "they say") which allow us to distinguish between teachings of Basilides himself and those of his followers, though it should also be admitted that some of the teachings attributed to his followers may go back to Basilides himself.

Another issue is posed by Irenaeus' testimony that Basilides and Saturninus based their doctrines on those of Simon and Menander. This would imply a setting in Antioch, where Menander, originally from Samaria, is said to have been active (Justin, *1 Apol.* 26.4), and where Saturninus was based.[31] And it is clear that there are some points in common between what Irenaeus attributes to Saturninus and what he attributes to Basilides. And if Saturninus was an early representative of the "Gnostic sect," as suggested by Layton,[32] some light can be shed on Basilides' teaching by comparison with details found in "Classic Gnostic" texts, of which the *Apocryphon of John* (NHC II,1; III,1; IV,1; BG,2) is clearly the most important.[33] Of course, to the extent that we can shed light on Irenaeus' account

---

[30] Löhr's approach is very similar to that taken by Christoph Markschies to the teachings of Valentinus; see Markschies, *Valentinus Gnosticus? Untersuchungen zur valentinianischen Gnosis mit einem Kommentar zu den Fragmenten Valentins* (WUNT 65; Tübingen: J. C. B. Mohr [Paul Siebeck], 1992).

[31] Epiphanius interprets Irenaeus' testimony to mean that Basilides started out in Antioch, where he and Saturninus (Satornilus) were fellow students, and then went from there to Egypt (*Pan.* 23.1.2; 24.1.1).

[32] Layton, *Gnostic Scriptures*, 159. Layton points out that Irenaeus' brief summary refers to almost all parts of the Gnostic myth and "related topics such as components of the human being, genealogies of humankind, the history of Israel, principles of biblical interpretation, Christology, and ethics" (ibid.). Layton also says (*Gnostic Scriptures*, 417) that Basilides taught a cosmogonic myth "similar to that of classic gnostic scripture." More recently Layton ("Significance of Basilides," 150 n. 17) draws a contrast between Basilides' myth and that of "classic gnostic" (Sethian) writings. He now says that "Basilides' cosmology is not at all Gnostic in the strict historical sense of the name," and argues instead that it is characterized by "integral cosmic monism."

[33] Michael Waldstein and Frederik Wisse, *The Apocryphon of John: Synopsis of Nag Hammadi Codices II,1; III,1; and IV,1 with BG 8502,2* (Nag Hammadi and Manichaean Studies 33; Leiden: E. J. Brill, 1995).

with reference to the fragments of Basilides preserved by Clement, to that extent we are on more solid ground in our reconstruction of Basilides' system.

We have already noted the probability that Irenaeus' account was based on Justin's lost *Syntagma*, which was presumably a doxography of the various heresies known to him. But what was the source of Justin's information on Basilides? And what was its genre? Löhr suggests that the source utilized in the doxography was in the form of an esoteric revelation discourse of the Savior, or perhaps a revelation dialogue (cf. *Ap. John* et al.).[34] I would suggest another possibility, assuming that the source in question is a work of Basilides himself: a learned "disputation," with features of a "sacred discourse" perhaps in an epistolary frame, somewhat akin to the tractate *Eugnostos the Blessed* (NHC III,3; V,1).[35] As we shall see, Basilides' system has some points in common with *Eugnostos*, and it is quite possible that Basilides knew that document. We can further speculate that Basilides' "disputation" served as an introduction to his *Exegetica*. Of course, such speculations take us beyond the limits of our available evidence.

In what follows we shall discuss Basilides' system according to the following topical arrangement: A. theogony; B. cosmogony and cosmology; C. anthropogony and anthropology; D. Christology and soteriology; E. ethical theory and doctrine of providence.

2.1. *Theogony*

Irenaeus opens his account of Basilides' teaching as follows:[36]

> Basilides, so that he may appear to have discovered something higher and more like the truth, vastly extends the content of his own teaching. He presents Nous [Intellect] originating first from the unoriginate Father, and Logos [Word] originating from him, then from Logos Phronesis (Prudence), from Phronesis Sophia (Wisdom) and Dynamis (Power).

---

[34] Löhr, *Basilides*, 264–71.

[35] On the literary genre of *Eugnostos* see Anne Pasquier, *Eugnoste: Lettre sur le Dieu transcendant (NH III,3 et V,1)* (Bibliothéque copte de Nag Hammadi, "Textes" 26; Québec: Les presses de l'Université Laval; Louvain: Peeters, 2000).

[36] *Haer.* 1.24.3, translation in Foerster, *Gnosis*, 1:59, slightly modified, square brackets mine. For the Latin text I use the Rousseau-Doutreleau edition (SC 264).

Thus, Basilides presents as first principles an unengendered Father, and a pentad of emanations from him. It is from Clement that we learn that Basilides actually taught a primal Ogdoad, and he supplies the names for the last two entities in the Ogdoad: "Basilides believes that 'justice' (Gk. *Dikaiosynē*) and its offspring 'peace' (Gk. *Eirēnē*) substantially exist (Gk. *hypostatas*), being arranged inside an octet (Gk. *en ogdoadi*), where they remain."[37] That "Justice" and "Peace" are not simply human virtues, as Löhr suggests, but entities in an Ogdoad of first principles is clear from the immediate context in Clement's account following the reference to Basilides' Ogdoad, where he says, "But it is necessary for us to turn from more philosophical principles (Gk. *apo tōn physikōterōn*) to the more evident ethical principles";[38] he then goes on to quote sayings from the gospels. In Clement's writings the adjective *physikos* (literally "physical") has a special philosophical meaning.[39]

Additional evidence that Basilides taught a primal Ogdoad is provided by one of the tractates in the Nag Hammadi "library" of Coptic Gnostic writings, *The Testimony of Truth* (NHC IX,3). Unfortunately the manuscript is exceedingly fragmentary at crucial points, but here is the evidence from pages 56–57:[40]

/56,1/ he completed the course [of] Valentinus. He himself speaks about the Ogdoad, and his disciples resemble [the] disciples of Valentinus. They on their part, moreover, [. . .] leave the good, [but] they have [worship of] the idols [6 lines are missing] /56,17/ he has spoken [many words, and he has] written many [books . . .] words [ca. 11 lines are missing] [. . . they are] manifest from [the] confusion in which they are, [in the] deceit of the world. /57,1/ For [they] go to that place together with their knowledge [which is] vain. Isidore also, [his son], resembled [Basilides]. He also. . . .

[37] Clem. Alex., *Strom.* 4.162.1, Layton's translation of his fragment A, Löhr's fragment 11, not in Foerster. Layton infers from the verbal adjective ὑποστατάς ("substantially exist") that the entities in Basilides' Ogdoad are called "hypostases" (*Gnostic Scriptures*, 428). Löhr prefers to move the accent, thus yielding a noun: ὑποστάτας (<ὑποστάτης), "supports" (*Basilides*, 165).
[38] My translation, based on Annewies van den Hoek's new edition in the SC series, no. 463 (Paris: Cerf, 2001).
[39] See esp. L. Rizzerio, *Clemente di Alessandria e la "physiologia veramente gnostica": Saggio sulle origini e sulle implicazioni di un'epistemologia e di un'ontologia "cristiane"* (RTAM, suppl. 6; Louvain: Peeters, 1996).
[40] Giversen-Pearson translation in Pearson, ed., *Nag Hammadi Codices IX and X* (NHS 15; Leiden: E. J. Brill, 1981).

Basilides' name appears in the text only on page 57,[41] but the person who is said to have "completed the course of Valentinus" is almost certainly Basilides.[42] His Ogdoad is here compared with that of Valentinus.[43] That Valentinus is mentioned first here simply indicates that the author regards Valentinus as the more important. It is interesting that the author, who may have been a former Valentinian,[44] includes Gnostic teachers among his mainly ecclesiastical opponents, and appears to be familiar with an ecclesiastical doxography of heresy.[45]

It has already been noted that there are basic similarities between Basilides' teaching and that of Saturninus, at least according to Irenaeus' testimony.[46] Basilides' Ogdoad, however, has no counterpart in Saturninus' teaching. Where did he get it? The probable answer to that is that he got it in Alexandria, and probably from a Jewish Gnostic work. At the conclusion of his seminal article on the place of Basilides in ancient Christian theology, Robert Grant suggests that Basilides interpreted theologoumena from the Bible, the Pauline epistles, and the Gospel of John, "en rapport avec un système d'emanations qui était fondé sur quelque autre source." In a footnote, he reports that Jacques-É. Ménard had meanwhile suggested to him that this other source was "la 'Lettre d'Eugnoste,'" now known as *Eugnostos the Blessed* (NHC III,3; V,1), a tractate containing a theology of the transcendent God.[47] I think this observation is right on the mark.

---

[41] Only the last two letters of his name are extant at 57,8, but the restoration is certain on the basis of mention of his son Isidore at 57,6. Löhr includes in his Testimony 15 (*Basilides*, 40–41) only the material on p. 57, and ignores p. 56.

[42] See my notes to the text and translation. See now also Annie and Jean-Pierre Mahé, *Le Témoignage véritable (NH IX,3): Gnose et martyre* (Bibliothéque copte de Nag Hammadi, "Textes" 23; Québec: Les presses de l'Université Laval; Louvain: Peeters, 1996), 198.

[43] Valentinus' Ogdoad is given by Irenaeus, *Haer.* 1.11.1.

[44] I have suggested Julius Cassianus, a former Valentinian, as the author of *Testim. Truth* (Pearson, *Nag Hammadi Codices IX and X*, 118–20).

[45] For a discussion of this passage see Pearson, "Anti-Heretical Warnings in Codex IX from Nag Hammadi," chapter 12 in Pearson, *Gnosticism, Judaism, and Egyptian Christianity* (Minneapolis: Fortress, 1990), 183–93, esp. 192–93.

[46] For a good discussion of these similarities see Pétrement, *Separate God*, 341–43.

[47] Grant, "Place de Basilide," 216 and n. 69. On *Eugnostos* see esp. Demetrios Trakatellis, *The Transcendent God of Eugnostos* (Brookline, Mass.: Holy Cross Orthodox Press, 1991). Especially useful is his retroversion of the Coptic text into Greek, pp. 155–95. That Valentinus, too, knew *Eugnostos* is argued convincingly by Roelof van den Broek, "Jewish and Platonic Speculations in Early Alexandrian Theology:

In Eugnostos' system, the transcendent deity is described as the "unbegotten" "Father of the All" (III,3 71.14–73.3). He is said to contain "the totalities of all totalities," "for he is all mind (Gk. *nous*), thought (*ennoia*) and reflection (*enthymēsis*), thinking (*phronēsis*), reasoning (*logismos*), and power (*dynamis*)," all of these said to be "the sources of all the totalities." "And their whole race even to their end is in the first knowledge (or foreknowledge, Gk. *prognōsis*) of the Unbegotten" (73.6–16).[48]

Though the word Ogdoad does not occur in this context (but see *Eugnostos the Blessed* V,1 14.19), we actually have here an ogdoad consisting of Unbegotten Father, Nous, Ennoia, Enthymesis, Phronesis, Logismos, Dynamis, and Prognosis. Four of these occur in Basilides' Ogdoad: Unbegotten Father, Nous, Phronesis, and Dynamis. Basilides' own four hypostases are derived from scripture or apostolic writings, and thus reflect a "Christianization" of a pre-existing Gnostic system.[49]

The "cosmologico-christological" nature of Basilides' Ogdoad is brilliantly laid out by Grant, and his discussion is of basic importance for understanding Basilides' system. His conclusion is absolutely sound: "The Basilidian Ogdoad is based on a biblical exegesis, as might be expected from the author of the *Exegetica*."[50] The term itself may also derive from early Christian tradition, i.e. speculation on the significance of the "Eighth Day," such as is found in chapter 15 of the (Alexandrian) *Epistle of Barnabas*.[51]

2.2. *Cosmogony and Cosmology*

Irenaeus' account continues as follows:[52]

> from Dynamis and Sophia the powers, principalities, and angels, who are also called the first, and by them the first heaven was made. From their emanation other angels were made, and they made another

---

Eugnostus, Philo, Valentinus, and Origen," in van den Broek, *Studies in Gnosticism and Alexandrian Christianity* (Nag Hammadi and Manichaean Studies 39; Leiden: E. J. Brill, 1996), 117–30, esp. 122–29.

[48] Quoting from Trakatellis' translation and retroversion.

[49] Logos: John 1:1–14. Sophia and Dynamis: 1 Cor 1:24. Dikaiosyne and Eirene: Ps 84(85):11; Heb 7:2. And for Phronesis, shared with *Eugnostos*: Prov 3:19; Jer 10:12. *Eugnostos* itself has been "Christianized" by its expansion into a revelation dialogue of Christ, *The Sophia of Jesus Christ* (NHC III,4; BG,3).

[50] Grant, "Place de Basilide," 211.

[51] Löhr, *Basilides*, 168.

[52] *Haer*. 1.24.3, Foerster's translation.

heaven like the first; and in the same way when other (angels) were made by emanation from them, copies of those who were above them, they fashioned a further, third, heaven. From the third, a fourth group of downward ascending ones, and successively in the same way more and more principalities and angels were made, and 365 heavens. That is why the year has that number of days, in accordance with the number of heavens.

Basilides shares with Saturninus a system of creator-angels. Saturninus posits seven of them (*Haer.* 1.24.1), but Basilides counts 365 groups of angels, each group associated with one of 365 heavens, equal to the number of days in the solar year. Where did he get this detail?

We turn once again to *Eugnostos*, where we find a system quite similar to that of Basilides: 360 powers also associated with the solar year, and equivalent to 360 heavens (III,3 84.1–85.7). The author of *Eugnostos* bases his system of heavens and angels on the Egyptian year of twelve months of thirty days each.[53] Basilides does the same thing, but adds the five "epagomenal" days of the Egyptian calendar, completing the number of days in the solar year.[54] 365 angels also occur in the longer version of the *Apocryphon of John* (II,1 11.12). They are given strange names and are credited with the fashioning of the 365 parts of Adam's "psychic" body (II,1 15.23–19.10).[55] Epiphanius, perhaps wrongly, attributes a similar doctrine to Basilides: "Then, he says, man also has 365 members for this reason, as though one member were assigned to each of the powers" (*Pan.* 24.7.6).[56] Irenaeus attributes to the followers of Basilides the assignment of strange-sounding names to the 365 angels (*Haer.* 1.24.5), presumably meaning the angelic chiefs of the 365 heavens, and this detail may go back to Basilides himself.

---

[53] For a good discussion, see Douglas Parrott's introduction to *Eugnostos* in *Nag Hammadi Codices III,3– 4 and V,1 with Papyrus Berolinensis 8502,3 and Oxyrhynchus Papyrus 1081: Eugnostos and the Sophia of Jesus Christ* (ed. D. M. Parrott; NHS 27; Leiden: E. J. Brill, 1991), 7.

[54] The five epagomenal days were celebrated as birthdays of the gods Osiris, Horus, Seth-Typon, Isis, and Nephthys. See Plutarch, *Is. Os.* 12, and commentary in J. Gwyn Griffiths, *Plutarch's De Iside et Osiride* (Cambridge: University of Wales Press, 1970), 291–308.

[55] This account is said to derive from a "Book of Zoroaster" (19.10). On this passage see R. van den Broek, "The Creation of Adam's Psychic Body in the Apocryphon of John," in van den Broek, *Studies*, 67–85.

[56] Frank Williams' translation in Williams, *The Panarion of Epiphanius of Salamis, Book I (Sects 1– 46)* (NHS 35; Leiden: E. J. Brill, 1987).

The creation of our world is credited to the angels occupying the last heaven in Irenaeus' account:[57]

> But those angels who possess the last heaven, which is the one seen by us, set up everything in the world, and divided between them the earth and the nations upon it. Their chief is the one known as the God of the Jews; because he wished to subject the other nations to his own men, that is, to the Jews, all the other principalities opposed him and worked against him. For this reason the other nations were alienated from his nation.

Saturninus ascribes the creation of the world to seven creator angels (*Haer.* 1.24.1). How many angels of the last heaven there were in Basilides' system is not indicated, but they may have numbered 72, since they are said to have divided up the nations among them, and 72 nations of the world is the traditional number in Jewish lore.[58] We can compare *Eugnostos*, which posits 72 powers: "Thirty-six males and thirty-six females were revealed, so that there are seventy-two powers. Each one of the seventy-two revealed five spiritual (beings), which are the three hundred sixty powers" (III,1 83.13–19).[59]

That the creator-angels' chief, or Archon, is the Jewish God is also a doctrine shared with Saturninus. According to Irenaeus the followers of Basilides refer to him as "Abrasax":[60]

> They arrange the positions of the 365 heavens in the same way as the astrologers (*mathematici*). They accept their principles, and have transferred them to their own brand of doctrine. But the chief of those (365 heavens) is Abrasax, and for this reason (they allege) he has 365 numbers in him (i.e. his name has the numerical value 365).

---

[57] *Haer.* 1.24.4, Foerster's translation.
[58] Pétrement, *Separate God*, 342.
[59] Trakatellis' translation.
[60] *Haer.* 1.24.7; Foerster's translation. $A + B + R + A + S + A + X = 365$. In a secondary addition to the *Acta Archelai* it is reported that Basilides "supposes there are as many gods as there are days in the year, and of these as it were paltry ones he creates one supreme divinity and calls it Mithras, on the basis that by counting up Greek letters Mithras has the number of a year" (Vermes' translation, p. 152). $M + E + I + TH + R + A + S = 365$. See A. M. Di Nola, "Basilide e Basilidiani," *Enciclopedia delle Religioni* (Firenze: Vallecchi, 1970), 1:963–72, esp. 971; cf. Franz Dornseiff, *Das Alphabet in Mystik und Magie* (Leipzig: B. G. Teubner, 1922), 42–43, 105.

This name for a solar deity, frequent on ancient gemstones, was probably not invented by Basilides, as Charles King thought,[61] but may very well have been used by him to refer to the creator Archon.[62] Many of the abrasax gemstones used as amulets couple Abrasax (or Abraxas), usually portrayed as lion-headed with serpentine feet, with Iao (a commonly used form of the divine name YHWH).[63] The name Abrasax occurs frequently in the Graeco-Egyptian magical papyri, often coupled with Iao and/or other names for the Jewish God.[64] The name Abrasax also occurs in other Gnostic texts.[65] A Hebrew etymology has been suggested for the name: 'arba', "four," i.e. the four letters of the sacred Tetragrammaton (YHWH).[66]

Other information on Basilides' Archon is found in one of the Basilidian fragments preserved by Clement:[67]

> Then those around Basilides say in explanation of this verse (Prov 1:7) that the Archon himself, when he heard the utterance of the ministering Spirit, was shocked through what was heard and seen, since he received the glad news beyond (his) hopes, and his shock was called fear, which became the beginning of the wisdom (Prov 1:7) of the distinction of kinds and separation and fulfillment and restoration. For he who is above all sends out (the Spirit), distinguishing not only the world, but also the elect.

While this passage refers not to Basilides himself but to his followers, there is good reason to attribute some of this to Basilides. Compare the following passage from Hippolytus' account:[68]

---

[61] Charles W. King, *The Gnostics and Their Remains, Ancient and Mediaeval* (2nd ed.; New York: Putnam, 1887; repr., Minneapolis: Wizards Bookshelf, 1973), 245.

[62] Both Pseudo-Tertullian (*Haer.* 1.5) and Epiphanius (*Pan.* 24.7.2) report that Basilides gave this name to the supreme deity, but that is clearly wrong.

[63] Some examples are provided in King, *Remains*, pl. C, 2, 3; G, 5; J, 1. For discussion see Campbell Bonner, *Studies in Magical Amulets, Chiefly Graeco-Egyptian* (Ann Arbor: University of Michigan Press, 1950), 134–35. For discussion of the so-called "Gnostic" gems, with rich bibliography, see Peter Zazoff, *Die antiken Gemmen* (Handbuch der Archäologie; München: C. H. Beck, 1983), 349–62; "Abraxas" gems: plate 113,7 (with Iao); 113,8; 114,1 (with Iao); 114,2; 116,4 (with Iao).

[64] See the index to Preisendanz, *PGM.*

[65] *Gos. Eg.* 52.26; 53.9; 65.1; *Apoc. Adam* 75,22; *Zost.* 47.13.

[66] A. A. Barb, "Abrasaxstudien," in *Hommages à Waldemar Deonna* (Collection Latomus 28; Brussels: Latomus, Revue d'études latines, 1957), 67–86, esp. no. 1: "Abrasax und Abracadabra," 67–73.

[67] Clem. Alex., *Strom.* 2.36.1. Foerster's translation of his frg. 15, somewhat modified, Löhr's frg. 4. Layton does not include it in his collection.

[68] *Haer.* 7.16.1–2, Foerster's translation (*Gnosis* 1:70), somewhat modified.

The Archon learned that he was not the God of the universe, but was begotten, and had above him, stored up, the treasure of the ineffable and unnameable non-existent and the Sonship, and he was converted and became afraid, for he perceived what ignorance he was in. This is, he says, the saying: "The Fear of the Lord is the beginning of wisdom" (Prov 1:7). For he (the Archon) began to grow wise under the instruction of the Christ who sits beside him, as he was taught who is the non-existent, what the Sonship, what the Holy Spirit is, how the universe is arranged, and how it will be fully restored.

André Méhat has called attention to certain themes and language that the two texts have in common, and suggests that they both go back to a common source.[69] He argues persuasively that the two texts can be interpreted together, and I would suggest that they both depend on a passage from Basilides' *Exegetica*. While Méhat is especially interested in Basilides' doctrine of *apokatastasis*, the material in common between the texts from Clement and Hippolytus can also provide information on Basilides' teaching concerning the Archon. Note particularly the interpretation given of Prov 1:7 ("the fear of the Lord is the beginning of wisdom"): the Archon sees and hears something mediated by the Spirit sent out by the supreme God, and the result is "fear" or "shock". Especially interesting is the statement in Hippolytus' account that what the Archon learned included the fact that there is a God beyond him. This is reminiscent of the widespread Gnostic topos on the "blasphemy of the demiurge," i.e. the Archon thinking that he is the only God (Isa 46:9 etc.), which brings about a heavenly rebuke, "Man exists and the Son of Man" (e.g. *Ap. John* II,1 14.14–15).[70]

As to the world created by the Archon, Basilides teaches that it is "unique" (Gk. *monogenēs*), relying here on a topos going back to Plato's *Timaeus* (31 ab).[71]

---

[69] A. Méhat, "APOKATASTASIS chez Basilide," in *Mélanges d'histoire des religions offerts à Henri-Charles Puech* (Paris: Presses Universitaires de France, 1974), 365–73, esp. 369.

[70] On this Gnostic topos see esp. Nils Dahl, "The Arrogant Archon and the Lewd Sophia: Jewish Traditions in Gnostic Revolt," in *The Rediscovery of Gnosticism: Proceedings of the International Conference on Gnosticism at Yale, New Haven, Connecticut, March 28–31, 1978* (ed. Bentley Layton; SHR 41; Leiden: E. J. Brill, 1981), 2:689–712.

[71] Clem. Alex., *Strom.* 5.74.3, Löhr's frg. 14, Layton's frg. B. Clement agrees with Basilides but adds that Basilides does not agree with him that "God is one."

2.3. *Anthropogony and Anthropology*

Saturninus includes in his myth an anthropogony according to which the angels created the first human being, but this being could not stand erect until he was endowed from on high with a "spark of life" (Irenaeus, *Haer.* 1.24.1). This anthropogony seems to be a summary of one that is given in greater detail in the *Apocryphon of John* and related texts. Strangely enough, Irenaeus provides no such anthropogony in his account of Basilides' myth, but one is tempted to believe that Basilides' system originally included an account of the creation of Adam. Irenaeus does have Basilides agree with Saturninus that salvation is for the soul only, the body being "by nature corruptible" (*natura corruptibile; Haer.* 1.24.5).

There are fragments from Basilides' writings which suggest that he taught a doctrine of reincarnation, or metempsychosis. One such fragment is found in Origen's *Commentary on Romans*, where he reports that Basilides interprets Paul's statement in Romans 7:9, "I died," to refer to reincarnation. Origen quotes Basilides as saying, "The Apostle explicitly said, 'I lived once without the Law' (Rom 7:9), that is, before I came into this body, I lived in the sort of body that is not under the Law, such as a beast or a bird."[72] Some doubt has been cast upon Origen's quotation, notably by Pierre Nautin, who argues that Origen's statement here, and also in his *Commentary on Matthew*, is dependent on Clement, not on Basilides, whose works Origen never read.[73] Nautin also doubts Clement's attribution to Basilides of the doctrine of reincarnation, and asserts that Basilides taught no such thing.[74] On balance, I do not see any reason to doubt that a Platonizing theologian like Basilides, along with a number of other Gnostic teachers, taught the doctrine of reincarnation.[75]

---

[72] Origen, *Comm. Rom.* 5.1, Foerster's translation of his frg. 5, Löhr's frg. 18, Layton's frg. F.

[73] P. Nautin, "Les fragments de Basilide sur la souffrance et leur interprétation par Clement d'Alexandrie et Origène," in *Mélanges Puech*, 393–404, esp. 401–3. The other passage is Origen, *Comm. Matt.* 38, Löhr's frg. 17, where Origen attributes to Basilides the doctrine that the only punishment for sin is reincarnation of the soul after death.

[74] *Strom.* 4.81.1–83.1, Löhr's frg. 7, Layton's frg. G, Foerster's frg. 4. On that passage see Nautin, "Les fragments," esp. 394–98. For a balanced discussion of Nautin's arguments see Löhr, *Basilides*, 138–44.

[75] In his introduction to his fragment F, on reincarnation, Layton asserts that Origen himself accepted a doctrine of reincarnation, and argues that Origen's polemic ("preposterous and impious fables") "lets us know that the full statement

A matter of some dispute in scholarship is Basilides' doctrine of human nature, and his classification of some people (i.e. Christian Gnostics) as "elect," as over against the rest of humanity who are not. In a discussion of the esoterism of the Basilidians Irenaeus attributes to them the following saying: "And few people can know these things—only one in a thousand, and two in ten thousand."[76] This saying is, no doubt, based on a dominical saying that circulated among the Basilidians and was probably known to Basilides himself. Compare the *Gospel of Thomas* (log. 23): "Jesus said, 'I shall choose you, one out of a thousand, and two out of ten thousand, and they shall stand as a single one.'"[77] Whether or not Basilides knew the *Gospel of Thomas*,[78] there is no doubt that he regarded those "chosen" or "elect" as relatively few in number. But then the question arises as to the basis of divine election. Is it related to the elect person's nature? And if so, in what sense?

Two of the fragments of Basilides quoted and discussed by Clement address this issue, and I quote both of them here:

> "I am a stranger in the land," it says, "and a sojourner among you" (Gen 23:4; Ps 38[39]:12). And thence Basilides understood (the passage) to say that the election (Gk. *eklogē*) is alien to the world, as if it were transcendent by nature (*hyperkosmion physei*).[79]
>
> For if anyone knows God by nature, as Basilides thinks when he understands the exceptional faith as an intellection (*noēsin tēn exaireton pistin*) and as a kingdom (*basileian*), as an acquisition[80] of good things, as an essence worthy to be near the Creator, then he calls faith an essence and not a freedom, a nature and substance, an infinite beauty of an arbitrary creation, but not the rational assent of a free soul.

---

of Basilides' cosmogonic myth included an account of the origin of souls and the cause and mechanism of their reincarnation" (*Gnostic Scriptures*, 438). That may very well be so. But Origen did not teach a doctrine of reincarnation, though he did teach a doctrine of the preexistence of souls, which is not the same thing. See Karl Hoheisel, "Das frühe Christentum und die Seelenwanderung," *JAC* 27/28 (1984/85), 24–46, esp. 41–42.

[76] *Haer.* 1.24.6, Layton's translation.

[77] *NHL* translation. On this and other possible dominical sayings used by the Basilidians see Löhr, *Basilides*, 265–66.

[78] Layton seems to suggest that he did (*Gnostic Scriptures*, 420).

[79] *Strom.* 5.165.3, Layton's translation of his frg. E, modified, Löhr's frg. 12; Foerster's frg. 12.

[80] Here I accept Langerbeck's emendation: κτῆσιν, "acquisition," for κτίσιν, "creation," also followed by Layton. See Hermann Langerbeck, "Die Anthropologie der alexandrinischen Gnosis," in Langerbeck, *Aufsätze zur Gnosis* (Göttingen: Vandenhoeck & Ruprecht, 1967), 38–82, esp. 73.

> Therefore the commandments of the Old and New Testaments are superfluous, if anyone is saved, as Valentinus says, by nature, or if anyone is faithful and elect by nature, as Basilides supposes.[81]

These two fragments present us with a basic problem. They are in indirect discourse, so Basilides is not allowed to speak for himself. What Clement presents of Basilides' position can therefore be taken as polemical distortions, particularly when Basilides is lumped together with Valentinus. Clement holds out for a doctrine of the freedom of the will, as opposed to the determinism presumably espoused by his Gnostic opponents. The phrase "transcendent by nature" could be applied to all human souls, which transcend their physical bodies, which are "corruptible by nature."[82] It should also be remembered that the term "election" is a biblical term used by the apostle Paul (Rom 9:11 etc.). If, indeed, Basilides defined faith as "intellection" (Gk. *noēsis*) he was merely adopting Platonic terminology, and when he used the term "substance" (*hypostasis*), he was using terminology derived from the Epistle to the Hebrews (11:1).[83] The term "kingdom," related to faith, presumably reflects an interiorization of Jesus' teachings concerning God's Kingdom, such as is reflected in logion 3 of the *Gospel of Thomas* ("kingdom within you"). Basilides also would not relate faith to "the Creator" (his "Archon") but to the transcendent God. In short, the available evidence does not allow us to determine with any certainty whether or not Basilides taught a "nature-determinism" like that attributed by Clement to the school of Valentinus.[84]

That Basilides used the term "nature" (Gk. *physis*) is, of course, likely. He may also have speculated on what sort of "nature" lies behind human actions. Here we recall the strange phrase used in the first quotation attributed to Basilides in the *Acta Archelai*: "the source of the nature that comes upon things without a root or a place."[85] In the parable of the rich man and Lazarus, referred to in the context, their respective fates after death were related to what

---

[81] *Strom.* 5.3.2–3, Foerster's translation of his frg. 11, modified, Löhr's frg. 13, Layton's frg. C.
[82] That is the way Layton understands the phrase (*Gnostic Scriptures*, 436).
[83] Langerbeck, "Anthropologie," 74. Langerbeck also relates the term νόησις" to Heb 11:3.
[84] See Löhr's careful discussion of this issue (*Basilides*, 174–90).
[85] See discussion above.

they had done during their lifetimes. The phrase "nature without root," presumably characterizing the rich man, may have been derived from the Lukan version of another parable of Jesus, that of the sower (Luke 8:5–8). In Jesus' explanation to the disciples different types of people are related to the seeds sown on the ground by the sower. Of the group likened to seed falling on rocky ground it is said, "they have no root" (8:13).[86] Unfortunately, there is not enough left of the quotation in *Acta Archelai* for us to learn what Basilides (if that quotation is actually his) taught about the source of the "nature without root," but I consider it likely that he would have argued that the nature "without root" and the "elect" nature have the same source, i.e. God and his providence.

In this respect Basilides apparently differed from Saturninus. Irenaeus explicitly attributes to the latter a different anthropology: "He (Saturninus) was the first to say that two kinds of men had been moulded by the angels, the one wicked, the other good" (*Haer.* 1.24.2) Nothing like that is attributed to Basilides in our extant evidence.

We can conclude this discussion with the observation that whatever kind of "determinism" Basilides might have taught was probably based on the writings of the apostle Paul and other early Christian tradition, and not on any determinist anthropology.[87]

2.4. *Christology and Soteriology*

Basilides' teaching about the creator Archon is followed in Irenaeus' account by teaching relating to the salvation wrought by Christ:[88]

> The unoriginate and ineffable Father, seeing their disastrous plight, sent his first-born Nous—he is the one who is called the Christ—to liberate those who believe in him from the power of those who made the world. To their (the angels') nations he appeared on earth as a man and performed miracles. For the same reason also he did not suffer, but a certain Simon of Cyrene was compelled to carry his cross for him; and this (Simon) was transformed by him (Jesus) so that he was thought to be Jesus himself, and was crucified through ignorance

---

[86] This connection between the two passages is suggested by H.-C. Puech and B. Blatz in their discussion of the "Gospel of Basilides," Schneemelcher, *New Testament Apocrypha*, 1:397–99, esp. 398.

[87] So Langerbeck, "Anthropologie." Of course, his doctrine of providence betrays Stoic influence; see discussion below.

[88] *Haer.* 1.24.4, Foerster's translation.

and error. Jesus, however, took on the form of Simon, and stood by laughing at them. For since he was an incorporeal power and the Nous of the unborn Father, he was transformed in whatever way he pleased, and in this way he ascended to him who had sent him, laughing at them, since he could not be held and was invisible to all.

Basilides shares with Saturninus the doctrine that the savior was sent from on high to liberate people from the power wielded by the creator-angels. Saturninus espouses a docetic Christology: the savior "appeared in semblance as a man" (*putatiue autem uisum hominem* = Gk. *dokēsei de epipephēnenai anthrōpon*; Irenaeus, *Haer.* 1.24.2). Compare Basilides: "he appeared on earth as a man" (*apparuisse eum in terra hominem*), a statement which does not necessarily imply a docetic Christology. What follows in Irenaeus' account is very strange, for Jesus is credited with being a "shape-changer," exchanging shapes with Simon of Cyrene, who turns out to be the one crucified.

I doubt very much that this is what Basilides taught.[89] I suspect that Irenaeus, or his source, has misinterpreted what Basilides taught. Perhaps a clue to how this misinterpretation could have come about can be found in the following passage from the *Second Treatise of the Great Seth* (NHC VII,2):[90]

> For my death which they think happened, (happened) to them in their error and blindness. They nailed their man up to their death. For their minds did not see me, for they were deaf and blind. But in doing these things, they render judgment against themselves. As for me, on the one hand they saw me; they punished me. Another, their father, was the one who drank the gall and the vinegar; it was not I. They were hitting me with the reed; another was the one who lifted up the cross on his shoulder, who was Simon. Another was the one on whom they put the crown of thorns. But I was rejoicing in the height over all the riches of the archons and the offspring of their error and their conceit, and I was laughing at their ignorance. And all their powers I brought into subjection. For when I came down no one saw me. For I kept changing my forms above, transforming from appearance to appearance. And on account of this, when I was at their gates I kept taking their likeness. For I passed them by quietly, and I was

---

[89] Layton accepts the authenticity of Irenaeus' account, and suggests that Basilides might have based his teaching on an ambiguity he found in Mark 15:20–24 ("Significance of Basilides," 145 and 150 n. 25).

[90] *Treat. Seth* 55,30–56,32, Gregory Riley's translation in *Nag Hammadi Codex VII* (ed. B. A. Pearson; Nad Hammadi and Manichaean Studies 30; Leiden: E. J. Brill, 1996), omitting the Greek words supplied in parentheses.

viewing the places, and I did not fear nor was I ashamed, for I was undefiled.

Early interpreters of this passage read it in light of what Irenaeus reports about Basilides, and regarded it as a piece of Basilidian tradition.[91] But the text does not teach the doctrine attributed by Irenaeus to Basilides. What it does say is that the sufferings endured at the crucifixion were not suffered by the real Jesus, but only by the physical body which he inhabited, the creation of the archons, whose crucifixion brought about the archons' own destruction. Those whose faith is centered upon a crucified savior (i.e. "orthodox" Christians) espouse "the doctrine of a dead man" (*Treat. Seth* 60.22). The real Jesus, laughing at the archons' folly, ascended safely into heaven.

Something similar to that was probably Basilides' view. For him, the divine Nous-Christ descended into the human Jesus and displaced his human soul—Basilides probably thought this occurred at Jesus' baptism[92]—and, following Jesus' crucifixion, ascended to the Father who had sent him. That Jesus did in fact suffer is affirmed in a quotation of Basilides preserved by Clement (*Strom.* 4.83.1), a passage to which we shall return.

Irenaeus continues his account as follows (*Haer.* 1.24.4):

> Therefore those who know these things have been set free from the rulers who made the world. It is not right to confess him who was crucified, but him who came in the form of a man and was supposed to have been crucified and was called Jesus and was sent by the Father in order by this dispensation to undo the works of the creators of the world. Thus (he says) if anyone confesses the crucified, he is still a slave, and under the power of those who made the bodies; he who denies (him) has been set free from them, and knows the (saving) dispensation made by the unoriginate Father.

---

[91] See e.g. Frederik Wisse, "The Nag Hammadi Library and the Heresiologists," *VC* 25 (1971): 201–23, esp. 209; cf. Riley's discussion in his introduction to the *Second Treatise of the Great Seth* in Pearson, *Nag Hammadi Codex VII*, 137–38. A similar passage featuring the laughing Jesus at the crucifixion scene is found in the *Apocalypse of Peter* (81.4–24). Michel Tardieu ("Basilide le Gnostique," 89) has suggested that Codex VII as a whole is a Basilidian collection.

[92] The passage preserved by Clement dealing with the fear of the Archon (*Strom.* 2.36.1, discussed above) probably also relates to the scene of Jesus' baptism by John. See Löhr's penetrating discussion (*Basilides*, 62–78). That the Christ descended upon Jesus at his baptism was also affirmed by Cerinthus, according to Irenaeus (*Haer.* 1.26.1).

As already noted, Basilides taught that salvation is for the soul alone and not the corruptible body (Irenaeus, *Haer.* 1.24.5), a doctrine which accords perfectly with his Christology, which attributes suffering and corruption to the human body of Jesus. Salvation, which entails liberation from the power of the creator archons and ascension after death to the Father, is appropriated through knowledge ("those who know these things").

Unlike Valentinus, however, Basilides does not make a strong distinction between faith and knowledge (*gnosis*). This is clear from a fragment already discussed, on the "nature" of the elect (Clem. Alex., *Strom.* 5.165), where faith is posited as "intellection" and a "hypostasis." This can also be seen in Irenaeus' account, where faith and knowledge are virtually equated ("to liberate those who believe in him . . . those who know these things; Irenaeus, *Haer.* 1.24.4).

In addition to his doctrine of the salvation of individuals, Basilides posits an eschatological salvation of the elect as a whole for which he evidently used the term *apokatastasis*, a term which is probably reflected in the Greek adjective *apokatastatikēs* (Clem. Alex., *Strom.* 2.4.1).[93] Valentinian Gnostics used the same term to refer to "the restoration to the Pleroma" (e.g. *Treat. Res.* 44.31–32),[94] but Basilides' doctrine seems to be more influenced by early Christian eschatology—the term occurs in the New Testament at Acts 3:21—and thus is a modification of the "cyclical" use of the term in Graeco-Roman cosmology.[95]

2.5. *Ethical Theory and Doctrine of Providence*

Irenaeus concludes his account of Basilides' own doctrine in the following way:[96]

> Moreover, he says, the prophets came into being through the craftsmen of the world, while the law came specifically through their Archon, who led the people out of the land of Egypt. He enjoined (his followers) not to worry about meat sacrificed to idols, to consider that it

---

[93] Löhr's frg. 4, Foerster's frg. 15, quoted above. Cf. notes 67, 69.

[94] See Malcolm Peel's note to his translation of the *Treatise on the Resurrection* in *Nag Hammadi Codex I (The Jung Codex): Notes* (ed. Harold Attridge; NHS 23; Leiden: E. J. Brill, 1985), 153.

[95] Méhat, "APOKATASTASIS." But Méhat accepts the authenticity of the account in Hippolytus, *Haer.* 7, and bases much of his discussion on that assumption. Cf. Löhr's discussion of the term (*Basilides*, 71–77).

[96] *Haer.* 1.24.5, Layton's translation, modified. Foerster's translation of this passage is unreliable.

is nothing, and to use it without concern. Furthermore, one should consider use of the remaining kinds of behavior and all kinds of pleasure as matters of indifference.

While, as we have seen, Basilides is capable of using and interpreting texts from the Bible, he certainly does not base his ethical theory on Old Testament injunctions. His apparent acceptance of the practice of eating meat sacrificed to pagan gods, universally condemned in "orthodox" circles, could easily have resulted from a reading of Paul's discussion in 1 Corinthians 8, and, moreover, is consonant with a doctrine that regards conventional values as matters of indifference. This certainly reflects Stoic influence, as Layton has convincingly argued.[97]

Irenaeus goes on to attribute to Basilides' followers the use of sorcery and other superstitious practices, and denial of their Christian identity in times of persecution (*Haer.* 1.24.5–6). Such practices cannot be attributed to Basilides himself, any more than the licentious practices attributed to certain Basilidians known to Clement, who, he says, had departed from the teachings of their master (*Strom.* 3.3).

That Basilides took seriously the love commandments of the New Testament is clearly shown in a fragment quoted by Clement:

> But if we, as Basilides himself says, have received as one part of the so-called will of God to love everything (τὸ ἠγαπηκέναι ἅπαντα)—for they relate this word to the All—as a second part to desire nothing and as a third to have nothing, then the punishments also are from the will of God, which it is impious to think.[98]

Basilides here ties the Christian ethic of love to the "will of God," i.e. God's providence. The virtuous person "loves" everything that is ordained by God, even suffering, and is free of both "desire" and "hatred." Reflected here is traditional biblical-Jewish and Christian ethic interpreted from a Stoic philosophical perspective.[99] Clement objects to Basilides' "determinist" perspective, which seems to him to ascribe evil to God.

Basilides' views concerning human suffering and its relation to divine providence can best be seen in three quotations from Book

---

[97] Layton, *Gnostic Scriptures*, 418 and 424 n. i; also "Significance of Basilides," 140–41.

[98] *Strom.* 4.86.1, Foerster's translation of his frg. 15 n. 22, modified, Löhr's frg. 8, Layton's frg. D.

[99] So Löhr, *Basilides*, 152–56; cf. Layton, *Gnostic Scriptures*, 434.

23 of his *Exegetica*, perhaps expanding on 1 Peter 4:12–19.[100] These
quotations are excerpted by Clement in a lengthy passage (*Strom.*
4.81.1–83.1) in which Clement adds his own comments.[101] Referring
to the suffering of Christian martyrs, Basilides says they suffer "because
they have sinned undetected in some other misdemeanors." They
suffer not for actual crimes committed "but because they are Christians.
That encourages them not even to seem to be suffering."

In the second quotation Basilides refers to a child who suffers
though it has not committed any actual sins. Such a child suffers
because "he has sinfulness (τὸ ἁμαρτητικόν) in him." Basilides says, "For
I will say anything rather than call Providence (τὸ προνοοῦν) bad."

In the third quotation the case of the Lord's suffering is treated.
Clement notes that Basilides "speaks about the Lord exactly as if
about a man." Basilides likens the sufferings of Jesus to those of the
little child who suffers not having sinned, adding, "whatever man
you name is man, but God is just. For as someone says, 'Nobody
is free from dirt'" (Job 14:4). While Basilides will not attribute willful sin to Jesus, he does not shrink from ascribing "sinfulness" to
him. It is on that basis that Jesus suffered. We note here, too, that
Basilides does not at all deny that Jesus suffered, as Irenaeus' report
would have it.[102]

Clement adds the comment that Basilides asserts that the soul
punished here has sinned in a previous life, including a Christian
suffering martyrdom. It is to be noted that the reincarnation doctrine actually does not clearly appear in the quotations preserved by
Clement, but it may have occurred in a part of Basilides' text not
quoted.[103]

---

[100] So Layton, *Gnostic Scriptures*, 440; cf. "Significance of Basilides," 146, and n. 16, above.

[101] This is Löhr's frg. 7, Layton's frg. G, and Foerster's frg. 4, from which I quote in what follows.

[102] See discussion above.

[103] That is Layton's assumption (*Gnostic Scriptures*, 440–41; "Significance of Basilides," 140). On frgs. 7 and 8 (Löhr) see now also Paul Schüngel, "Gnostische Gotteslehren: Zum 7. und 8. Fragment des Basilides, zu Valentins 5. Fragment und zwei antiken Kommentaren zu diesem Fragment," *VC* 53 (1999), 361–94, esp. 361–70, 393–94. Schüngel sheds new light on the Platonist background of Basilides' doctrine, but I do not agree with his view that Basilides "lehrt nur einen einzigen Gott, den Gott der jüdischen Tradition" (p. 393).

That Basilides took human sin seriously is also indicated in another passage from Book 4 of Clement's *Stromateis* (4.153.4):[104] "Basilides says that not all sins are forgiven, but only those committed involuntarily or in ignorance." This statement, in indirect discourse, must be put into its context. Clement is referring to sins committed before baptism, which God graciously forgives as though they had never been committed. Clement would have Basilides assert that divine punishment, in the form of suffering, is the consequence of all willful sins, even those committed before baptism.[105]

Strongly influenced by Stoic and Platonic philosophy Basilides asserts his faith in the goodness of divine providence, and the educational value of human suffering. What is remarkable, too, is that Basilides does not shrink from ascribing "sinfulness" to the human Jesus, whose sufferings, moreover, he does not deny. For Basilides, only God is wholly good.[106]

3. *Conclusions: Basilides' Place in the History of Gnosticism and Alexandrian Christianity*

Summarizing now what can be known of Basilides on the basis of our sources, an Alexandrian context for his work is certain. There he taught from 132 on, or perhaps earlier, into the reign of Antoninus Pius, i.e. after 138. His teachings certainly reflect an Alexandrian milieu, for they reflect the influence of Philo and other Hellenized Jewish teachers, Alexandrian Jewish Gnosticism, and Graeco-Roman philosophy, particularly Stoic and Platonic, as taught in Alexandrian schools. So I am inclined to think that Basilides was an Alexandrian from birth, and was educated in Alexandria.

What about Antioch? Justin (the presumed source of Irenaeus' information on Basilides), writing in the mid-second century, places Basilides in Antioch, together with Saturninus. We have noted certain similarities between Basilides and Saturninus in terms of their

---

[104] This is Löhr's frg. 10, Layton's frg. H, and Foerster's frg. 9, from which I quote in what follows.

[105] Here I disagree with the interpretation put forward by Löhr (*Basilides*, 159–65), who attributes to Basilides a teaching more consonant with that of Clement.

[106] On the use of Job 14:4 LXX see Löhr's penetrating discussion of this fragment (*Basilides*, 124–37).

mythological systems. We have also noted differences. I am inclined
to posit a sojourn in Antioch for Basilides. He may very well have
left Alexandria, together with many others, during the revolt of
115–117, an event which seems also to have affected his attitude
toward the Jews and their God. In Antioch he encountered an early
form of the "classic Gnostic" myth, similar to that reflected in Irenaeus'
summary of Saturninus' teaching. Upon his return to Alexandria he
made his own adaptations to that myth on the basis of local Jewish
Gnostic sources, of which *Eugnostos* was probably one, and early
Christian writings as well.

Basilidian gnosis seems not to have taken hold outside of Egypt,
but in Egypt it spread throughout the country and persisted into the
late fourth century, as we know from Epiphanius (*Pan.* 24). Especially
prominent in the early propagation of the Basilidian school was
Basilides' son and pupil, Isidore. Three writings are attributed to
Isidore in the Basilidian fragments we possess: *On the Grown Soul,
Ethics,* and *Expositions of the Prophet Parchor.*[107] The latter title reflects
a tendency among Gnostic authors to attribute esoteric lore to exotic,
"oriental" prophets.

Basilides was a Gnostic. But, more importantly, he was a Christian.
His was a thoroughly "Christianized" form of Gnosticism. Basilides'
education, and his openness to Greek philosophy, is certainly reflected
in his teachings. Indeed, he can truly be said to be the very first
Christian philosopher known to us. He is also the first commentator on writings which became part of the canonical New Testament.
His activity as an exegete, reflecting a long-standing Alexandrian
learned tradition, resulted in his 24-volume *Exegetica,* the only work
which can certainly be attributed to him.

Basilides must certainly have been known to another great Gnostic
Christian teacher, perhaps the greatest, Valentinus, a fellow Alex-
andrian. Valentinus undoubtedly knew and used Basilides' teachings.
But Basilides' influence certainly went beyond "heretical" circles, for,
in a sense, Basilides can be said to be a precursor to other great
Alexandrian teachers, especially Clement and Origen.[108]

---

[107] Löhr's frg. 5, Clem. Alex., *Strom.* 2.112.1–114.2; frg., *Strom.* 3.1–3; frg. 15,
Strom. 6.53.2–5. Some, or perhaps even all, of the other fragments attributed to
Basilidians (Löhr's frgs. 1–4, 9, 16) may also reflect his teachings.
[108] So, rightly, Löhr, *Basilides,* 332.

Finally, it can be said of Basilides that he was not only a learned teacher, but he was also a pastor of souls. Indeed, it is very likely that worship services were part of his school activity. One of the most interesting of the Basilidian fragments deals with the Christian calendar, as it relates to liturgical worship. Clement reports that the Basilidians observe the day of Jesus' baptism, spending the previous night in a vigil of scripture-readings. "They say that it happened in the 15th year of the emperor Tiberius, on the 15th of the month Tybi; others, on the 11th day of the same month."[109] What is of special interest to us is that the 11th of Tybi is equivalent to January 6 in the Julian calendar.[110]

The Basilidian tradition referred to may very well go back to the master himself. If so, Basilides is the first recorded Christian to celebrate what we now refer to as the "Festival of the Epiphany of our Lord."[111] Much more could be known of Basilides had his and other Gnostic "heresies" not been repressed by an ecclesiastical establishment in league with Christian emperors. But what we do know is enough to tell us just how important he was in the development of Alexandrian Christianity.

Bibliography

Attridge, Harold, ed. *Nag Hammadi Codex I (The Jung Codex): Notes.* Nag Hammadi Studies 23. Leiden: E. J. Brill, 1985.

Barb, A. A. "Abrasaxstudien." Pages 67–86 in *Hommages à Waldemar Deonna.* Collection Latomus 28. Brussels: Latomus, Revue d'études latines, 1957.

Bonner, Campbell. *Studies in Magical Amulets, Chiefly Graeco-Egyptian.* Ann Arbor: University of Michigan Press, 1950.

Broek, Roelof van den. *Studies in Gnosticism and Alexandrian Christianity.* Nag Hammadi and Manichaean Studies 39. Leiden: E. J. Brill, 1996.

Dahl, Nils. "The Arrogant Archon and the Lewd Sophia: Jewish Traditions in Gnostic Revolt." Pages 689–712 in vol. 2 of *The Rediscovery of Gnosticism: Proceedings of the International Conference on Gnosticism at Yale, New Haven, Connecticut, March 28–31, 1978.* Edited by Bentley Layton. Studies in the History of Religions 41. Leiden: E. J. Brill, 1981.

---

[109] *Strom.* 1.145.6–146.4, quoting from Foerster's frg. 3, Löhr's frg. 1. The year is derived from Luke 3:1.

[110] See Löhr's discussion, *Basilides,* 43–48. Cf. also my suggestion, above, that Basilides placed the descent of the divine Nous upon Jesus at his baptism.

[111] Cf. Thomas J. Talley, *The Origins of the Liturgical Year* (2nd ed.; Collegeville Minn.: The Liturgical Press, 1991), 119–29, on the Basilidians and subsequent Alexandrian practice.

Di Nola, A. M. "Basilide e Basilidiani." Pages 963–72 in vol. 1 of *Enciclopedia delle Religioni*. Firenze: Vallecchi, 1970.

Dornseiff, Franz. *Das Alphabet in Mystik und Magie*. Leipzig: B. G. Teubner, 1922.

Foerster, Werner. *Gnosis: A Selection of Gnostic Texts*. Translated by R. McL. Wilson. 3 vols. Oxford: Clarendon, 1972.

Grant, Robert M. "Place de Basilide dans la théologie chrétienne ancienne." *Revue des études augustiniennes* 25 (1979): 201–16.

Griffiths, J. Gwyn. *Plutarch's De Iside et Osiride*. Cambridge: University of Wales Press, 1970.

Helm, Rudolf, ed. *Die Chronik des Hieronymus*. Vol. 7 in *Eusebius Werke*. Edited by der Kommission für spätantike Religionsgeschichte der deutschen Akademie. 2nd ed. Die griechischen christlichen Schriftsteller der ersten Jahrhunderte 47. Berlin: Akademie-Verlag, 1956.

Hilgenfeld, Adolf. *Die Ketzergeschichte des Urchristentums*. 1884. Repr., Darmstadt: Wissenschaftliche Buchgesellschaft, 1963.

Hoek, Annewies van den. *Stromate IV, Clément d'Alexandrie*. Sources chrétiennes 463. Paris: Cerf, 2001.

Hoheisel, Karl. "Das frühe Christentum und die Seelenwanderung." Pages 24–46 in *Jahrbuch für Antike und Christentum* 27/28 (1984/85).

King, Charles W. *The Gnostics and Their Remains, Ancient and Mediaeval*. 2nd edition. New York: Putnam, 1887. Repr., Minneapolis: Wizards Bookshelf, 1973.

Langerbeck, Hermann. *Aufsätze zur Gnosis*. Göttingen: Vandenhoeck & Ruprecht, 1967.

Layton, B. *The Gnostic Scriptures*. Garden City, N.Y.: Doubleday, 1987.

———. "The Significance of Basilides in Ancient Christian Thought." *Representations* 28 (1989): 135–51.

Löhr, W. A. *Basilides und seine Schule: Eine Studie zur Theologie- und Kirchengeschichte des zweiten Jahrhunderts*. Wissenschaftliche Untersuchungen zum Neuen Testament 83. Tübingen: J. C. B. Mohr (Paul Siebeck), 1996.

Mahé, Annie and Jean-Pierre. *Le témoignage véritable (NH IX,3): Gnose et martyre*. Bibliothéque copte de Nag Hammadi, "Textes" 23. Québec: Les presses de l'Université Laval; Louvain: Peeters, 1996.

Markschies, Christoph. *Valentinus Gnosticus? Untersuchungen zur valentinianischen Gnosis mit einem Kommentar zu den Fragmenten Valentins*. Wissenschaftliche Untersuchungen zum Neuen Testament 65. Tübingen: J. C. B. Mohr (Paul Siebeck), 1992.

May, Gerhard. *Creatio ex Nihilo: The Doctrine of 'Creation out of Nothing' in Early Christian Thought*. Translated by A. S. Worrall. Edinburgh: T&T Clark, 1994.

Méhat, A. "APOKATASTASIS chez Basilide." Pages 365–73 in *Mélanges d'histoire des religions offerts à Henri-Charles Puech*. Paris: Presses Universitaires de France, 1974.

Nautin, P. "Les fragments de Basilide sur la souffrance et leur interprétation par Clement d'Alexandrie et Origène." Pages 393–404 in *Mélanges d'histoire des religions offerts à Henri-Charles Puech*. Paris: Presses Universitaires de France, 1974.

Parrott, D. M., ed. *Nag Hammadi Codices III,3–4 and V,1 with Papyrus Berolinensis 8502,3 and Oxyrhynchus Papyrus 1081: Eugnostos and the Sophia of Jesus Christ*. Nag Hammadi Studies 27. Leiden: E. J. Brill, 1991.

Pasquier, Anne. *Eugnoste: Lettre sur le Dieu transcendant (NH III,3 et V,1)*. Bibliothéque copte de Nag Hammadi, "Textes" 26. Québec: Les presses de l'Université Laval; Louvain: Peeters, 2000.

Pearson, Birger A. *The Emergence of the Christian Religion*. Harrisburg Pa.: Trinity Press International, 1997.

———. "Gnosticism as a Religion." Forthcoming in *Was There a Gnostic Religion?* Edited by Antti Marjanen. Helsinki: The Finnish Exegetical Society; Göttingen: Vandenhoeck & Ruprecht, 2004.

———. *Gnosticism, Judaism, and Egyptian Christianity*. Minneapolis: Fortress, 1990.

Pearson, Birger A., ed. *Nag Hammadi Codices IX and X*. Nag Hammadi Studies 15. Leiden: E. J. Brill, 1981.
———. *Nag Hammadi Codex VII*. Nag Hammadi and Manichaean Studies 30. Leiden: E. J. Brill, 1996.
Peel, Malcolm L. "NHC I,4: The Treatise on the Resurrection." Pages 137–215 in *Nag Hammadi Codex I (The Jung Codex): Notes*. Edited by Harold Attridge. Nag Hammadi Studies 23. Leiden: E. J. Brill, 1985.
Pétrement, Simone. *A Separate God: The Christian Origins of Gnosticism*. Translated by Carol Harrison. San Francisco: HarperSanFrancisco, 1990.
Preisendanz, K., ed. *Papyri graecae magicae: Die griechischen Zauberpapyri*. Leipzig: B. G. Teubner, 1928–31.
Puech, H.-C., and B. Blatz. "Gospel of Basilides." Pages 397–99 in vol. 1 of *New Testament Apocrypha*. Edited by W. Schneemelcher. Translated by R. McL. Wilson. 2 vols. Rev. ed. Cambridge: James Clarke, 1991–1992.
Rizzerio, L. *Clemente di Alessandria e la "physiologia veramente gnostica": Saggio sulle origini e sulle implicazioni di un'epistemologia e di un'ontologia "cristiane."* Recherches de théologie ancienne et médiévale, supplementa 6. Louvain: Peeters, 1996.
Schneemelcher, W., ed. *New Testament Apocrypha*. Translated by R. McL. Wilson. 2 vols. Rev. ed. Cambridge: James Clarke, 1991–1992.
Schoene, A., ed. and trans. *Eusebi Chronicorum canonum quae supersunt*. Dublin-Zürich: Weidman, 1967.
Schüngel, Paul. "Gnostische Gotteslehren: Zum 7. und 8. Fragment des Basilides, zu Valentins 5. Fragment und zwei antiken Kommentaren zu diesem Fragment." *Vigiliae christianae* 53 (1999): 361–94.
Talley, Thomas J. *The Origins of the Liturgical Year*. 2nd ed. Collegeville, Minn.: The Liturgical Press, 1991.
Tardieu, Michel. "Basilide le gnostique." Pages 84–89 in vol. 2 of *Dictionnaire des philosophes antiques*. Edited by Richard Goulet. Paris: CNRS Éditions, 1994.
Trakatellis, Demetrios. *The Transcendent God of Eugnostos*. Brookline, Mass.: Holy Cross Orthodox Press, 1991.
Vermes, Mark. *Hegemonius, Acta Archelai (The Acts of Archelaus)*. Manichaean Studies 4. Turnhout: Brepols, 2001.
Völker, Walther. *Quellen zur Geschichte der christlichen Gnosis*. Tübingen: J. C. B. Mohr (Paul Siebeck), 1932.
Waldstein, Michael and Frederik Wisse. *The Apocryphon of John: Synopsis of Nag Hammadi Codices II,1; III,1; and IV,1 with BG 8502,2*. Nag Hammadi and Manichaean Studies 33. Leiden: E. J. Brill, 1995.
Williams, Frank, trans. *The Panarion of Epiphanius of Salamis, Book I (Sects 1–46)*. Nag Hammadi Studies 35. Leiden: E. J. Brill, 1987.
Williams, Michael. *Rethinking "Gnosticism": An Argument for Dismantling a Dubious Category*. Princeton: Princeton University Press, 1996.
Wisse, Frederik. "The Nag Hammadi Library and the Heresiologists." *Vigiliae christianae* 25 (1971): 201–23.
Zazoff, Peter. *Die antiken Gemmen, Handbuch der Archäologie*. München: C. H. Beck, 1983.

SETHIANISM

Michael A. Williams

For modern readers the more familiar sons of the biblical Adam and Eve are likely to be Cain and Abel. After all, there you have a classic story of sibling tension, of jealousy and its tragic fruits, of innocence and guilt, of good and evil—or, if not evil in a pure and unmitigated sense, then at least pathetic moral weakness. Less apt to stir much reverberation in modern imagination is what the Book of Genesis has to say about Adam and Eve's other son, Seth, since to most readers of Genesis today Seth probably seems little more than a cipher. He replaces the slain Abel (Gen 4:25); at age 105 he fathers Enosh, lives another 807 years, has other offspring, and dies (Gen 5:6–8). While in the canonical New Testament Cain and Abel are mentioned or alluded to several times, as paradigms of, respectively, wickedness and (persecuted) righteousness, Seth is mentioned exactly once—in a genealogical list in the Gospel of Luke (3:38), as father of Enosh and son of Adam. Not much on which to hang a story.

Yet we know that beginning at least as early as the second century C.E. and for the next few centuries there were religious circles for whom Seth rivaled Christ in importance. Indeed, some of these people essentially identified Christ with Seth, as manifestations of the same divine entity. There were people whose self-image included a remarkable preoccupation with their identity as the offspring or "seed" of Seth. There were those who looked for truth and the key to salvation in holy books containing revelations of the heavenly Seth—the gospel of Seth, so to speak.

The most spectacular evidence for this in modern study came with the discovery in 1945 of the Nag Hammadi Codices,[1] among whose fourth century C.E. manuscripts are copies of several writings in which Seth plays significant roles such as those just mentioned. In

---

[1] For brief background as well as English translation of the Nag Hammadi writings, see James M. Robinson, ed., *The Nag Hammadi Library in English* (3rd rev. ed.; San Francisco: Harper & Row, 1988).

fact, one of the first scholars to work with the Nag Hammadi manuscripts, Jean Doresse, thought that the entire collection might well
have been a part of the library of a "Sethian" sect.[2]

Already as early as the third century C.E. Christian heresiologists
were asserting the existence of heterodox groups they call "Sethians,"
whose alleged myths and doctrines are summarized and attacked as
perversions. These heresiological descriptions of "Sethians" are somewhat problematic in that along with the expected prejudices in viewpoint, there are also some significant disagreements about exactly
what doctrinal or mythic content the "Sethians" are supposed to
have espoused. The lengthy description given by Hippolytus of Rome
(early third century C.E.) of the teaching of the "Sethians" seems to
have little at all to do with what Pseudo-Tertullian, or later, Epiphanius
of Salamis, report of the people they call "Sethians."[3]

As with most labels of this sort, the name "Sethians" was almost
certainly created by critics rather than by devotees, and there was
probably never a group who called *themselves* "Sethians."[4] Devotee-
authored writings such as those from Nag Hammadi so far provide
no evidence for this self-designation.

Nevertheless, what the material from Nag Hammadi does confirm
is that basic elements in some of the heresiological accounts of
"Sethians" were not merely invented by more orthodox Christian
polemicists. If there were not people who actually called themselves
"Sethians," there *were* persons who (1) placed exceptional importance
on their ancestry (whether understood materially or spiritually) as
offspring of Seth and (2) elaborated this theme with mythological
speculation involving variations on an identifiable core of recurrent
mythic patterns, motifs, and cast members.[5] As we will see, the interconnections among these sources are also complex, and scholars have

---

[2] Jean Doresse, *The Secret Books of the Egyptian Gnostics: An Introduction to the Gnostic Coptic Manuscripts Discovered at Chenoboskion* (trans. P. Mairet; New York: Viking Press, 1960), 250–51.

[3] Hippolytus, *Haer.* 5.19.1–22.1; Ps.-Tertullian, *Adversus omnes haereses* 8; Epiphanius, *Pan.* 39.1.1–5.3.

[4] Cf. Frederik Wisse, "Stalking Those Elusive Sethians," in *The Rediscovery of Gnosticism: Proceedings of the International Conference on Gnosticism at Yale, New Haven, Connecticut, March 28–31, 1978* (SHR 41; ed. Bentley Layton; Leiden: E. J. Brill, 1981), 2:562; cf. Clement of Alexandria, *Strom.* 7.108.1–2, who comments on various ways in which sects received their names (after founders; after notable prac-
tices; after doctrinal content, etc.).

[5] From the significant amount of literature on "Sethianism," see especially: John D. Turner, *Sethian Gnosticism and the Platonic Tradition* (Bibliothèque copte de Nag

not entirely agreed about precisely which texts belong within a common "Sethian" tradition with some sort of continuous social history,
and which might merely be writings where jargon has been picked
up and adapted by otherwise socially unconnected individuals or
groups.[6] But complex though they are, the interconnections cannot
be denied, and they are witness to a tradition of mythological and
theological speculation that clearly had a significant impact on the
history of late antique religion. Why was this so, and what are some
of things we know about these people and their religious convictions
and practices?

1. The Biblical Seth in Jewish Speculation

Though there is not much development of the figure Seth in Genesis
itself, Seth does receive further attention in later Jewish literature.
These sources date from over a period of centuries and do not reveal
a uniform tradition but rather a range of exegetical deductions and
speculations.[7] Yet they are helpful in understanding what is encountered in "Sethian" sources from Nag Hammadi and elsewhere. Here
we need provide only a brief summary of examples of the attention
paid to Seth in ancient Jewish texts, in two broad categories: The
special place of Seth as ancestor, and Seth as possessor of special
wisdom.

Hammadi, "Études" 6; Québec: Les presses de l'Université Laval; Louvain: Peeters,
2001) and the extensive literature cited there; various important articles and seminar discussions in Bentley Layton, ed., *The Rediscovery of Gnosticism*, vol. 2; Jean-Marie
Sevrin, *Le dossier baptismal Séthien: Études sur la sacramentaire gnostique* (Bibliothèque copte
de Nag Hammadi, "Études" 2; Québec: Les presses de l'Université Laval; Louvain:
Peeters, 1986); and the seminal argument by Hans-Martin Schenke, "Das sethianische System nach Nag-Hammadi-Handschriften," in *Studia Coptica* (ed. Peter Nagel;
Berliner Byzantinistische Arbeiten 45; Berlin: Akademie-Verlag, 1974), 165–73.
    [6] In addition to other literature cited in this study, see also important discussions
about classification in: Louis Painchaud and Anne Pasquier, eds., *Les textes de Nag
Hammadi et le problème de leur classification: Actes du colloque tenu à Québec du 15 au 10
Septembre 1993* (Bibliothèque copte de Nag Hammadi, "Études" 3; Québec: Les
presses de l'Université Laval; Louvain: Peeters, 1995); Karen L. King, *What is
Gnosticism?* (Cambridge, Mass.: The Belknap Press of Harvard University Press, 2003),
154–69; Bentley Layton, "Prolegomena to the Study of Ancient Gnosticism," in
The Social World of the First Christians: Essays in Honor of Wayne A. Meeks (ed. L. Michael
White and O. Larry Yarbrough; Minneapolis: Fortress, 1995), 334–50.
    [7] See A. F. J. Klijn, *Seth in Jewish, Christian and Gnostic Literature* (NovTSup 46:
Leiden: E. J. Brill, 1977).

It is not surprising that there would be curiosity and speculation about Seth's lineage given the fact that in Genesis Abel is murdered and Cain is portrayed in such a negative light. Indeed, some pre-Christian Jewish writings (such as the *Book of Jubilees* 4.31; 22.12) seem to assume that Abel had no descendants and that the descendants of Cain were killed in the flood of Genesis 6, leaving Seth as the father of all subsequent humankind.[8] Other texts trace the descendants of Seth as one (righteous) line of humanity in conflict with others. The Animal Apocalypse vision in *1 Enoch* symbolically describes Adam as a white bull, and Cain, Abel and Seth as black, red and white bulls, respectively (85.3–9). The descendants of Seth are at first white bulls (Noah, Abraham, Isaac) but then with Jacob they become white sheep that suffer affliction from predatory animals. At the end of the vision a messianic white bull is born who transforms the people into white bulls again (90.37–38), possibly a reference to resurrection. Sethite or Cainite ancestry could be understood by other Jewish writer entirely allegorically, as a typology for virtuous and impious classes of humanity throughout time.[9] In certain Jewish traditions (though exactly how early this began is not certain) the conclusion was drawn that Cain (and sometimes Abel) was not even actually a son of Adam, but was begotten by a lustful angel who impregnated Eve.[10] From this perspective, Adam is the legitimate ancestor only of those who belong to the race of Seth—literally or spiritually, depending on the hermeneutical viewpoint of the source.

Some early Jewish traditions also portray Seth and his descendents as possessors and transmitters of special wisdom. The oldest certainly datable source for this is the first century Jewish historian Josephus—who says that Adam actually had several other children besides Cain, Abel and Seth. According to Josephus, Seth grew up to be virtuous and passed this trait to his children, who lived an idyllic and happy existence, and invented the wisdom of astrological lore. Since Adam predicted that the world would be destroyed once by fire and once by water, the Sethites carved their wisdom in copies on two stelae, one of brick (to withstand fire) and one of

---

[8] See Klijn, *Seth*, 14, 22.
[9] E.g., Philo of Alexandria, *Post.* 40–48.
[10] See Klijn, *Seth*, 3–11, 16; Gedaliahu A. G. Stroumsa, *Another Seed: Studies in Gnostic Mythology* (NHS 24; Leiden: E. J. Brill, 1984), 35–70.

stone (to survive the flood), so that it would be preserved for later humankind.[11] In the *Life of Adam and Eve*, which may contain material going back to the first century C.E., Adam conveys to Seth special revelation that he had seen in an ascent vision (25.1–29.3) as well as other wisdom, and after Adam's death and just before Eve's death, Seth and their other children are told to write on two stelae (brick and stone) everything that they had seen and heard (49.1–50.2).

These and other examples illustrate that the significance of Seth's role and various notions about Sethian ancestry had been subjects of some interesting speculation by the first century C.E. So far scholars have found no clear evidence for specifically "Sethite" sectarian movements during this period. Nevertheless, many of these earlier exegetical traditions find echoes in the more elaborate and distinctive Sethian mythological speculation that begins to be attested at least as early as the second century C.E.

2. *"Sethianism" as a Tradition*

A handful of writings in the Nag Hammadi collection share what are undeniably a set of distinctive features that might be labeled "Sethian," even though there are some variations in their development. These writings are also interlinked by a sufficient amount of other specific content to conclude that there is a common tradition of speculation. Moreover, it appears that at least a few of these writings may reflect the same distinctive ritual practices and therefore could derive from a common sectarian *social* history, though perhaps complex and multi-branched.

2.1. *Example of a "Sethian" Writing: The Holy Book of the Great Invisible Spirit (Gospel of the Egyptians)*

In order to illustrate some of the distinctive features of this tradition we can begin with a look at one of the more important examples. The text with perhaps the most pronounced "Sethian" emphasis is a Nag Hammadi writing entitled *The Holy Book of the Great Invisible Spirit*—which soon after its discovery was referred to as the *Gospel of the Egyptians* due to a phrase found near the ending of one of the

---

[11] Josephus, *Ant.* 1.68–71.

copies of the work, and the latter has unfortunately stuck as the more widely used title. The only two known copies of the *Holy Book* are found among the Nag Hammadi Coptic manuscripts, one in Codex III and one in Codex IV, and although there are differences in detail between them they contain the same major features as far as the present discussion is concerned. Like most all of the writings in the Nag Hammadi cache of manuscripts, these Coptic versions of the *Holy Book* show signs of having been translated from Greek.[12] We can only guess about the date of the original Greek *Holy Book*, but as we will see in a later connection, several considerations favor a dating no later than the early third century C.E.

The *Holy Book* presents itself as a text composed in primordial times by "the great Seth," and hidden away on a high mountain. There it remained for ages, completely unknown to "the prophets and the apostles and the heralds," awaiting to come to light only "at the conclusion of the times and the seasons" (III 68.1–15). In other words, readers are supposed to understand the *Holy Book* as newly available revelation that trumps anything transmitted in Jewish scripture or the writings of Christian apostles and preachers.

The fundamental content of this revelation is a sacred history, beginning with a very elaborate account of (1) the emergence of the divine realm and all its population, including divine Humanity; (2) the appearance of demonic angels who become rulers of the lower, material world; (3) the creation of material humans by these angels in imitation of an image shown to them of the divine Humanity above; (4) the launching of a divine mission to correct the imperfection here below, beginning with the sowing of the seed of divine Humanity ("seed of the great Seth") into material human bodies; (5) the long ages of subsequent struggle, as the demonic powers of this realm persecuted the seed of Seth; and (6) finally the coming of the great Seth in the form of Jesus. After this the *Holy Book* breaks away from the narrative mode, first presenting a sort of catalogue of transcendent entities and their responsibilities, then celebrating the "holy baptism" revealed at the appearance of Jesus, followed by a prayer that would likely have been recited at baptism. Finally there is the

---

[12] Alexander Böhlig and Frederik Wisse, eds., *Nag Hammadi Codices III,2 and IV,2: The Gospel of the Egyptians (The Holy Book of the Great Invisible Spirit)* (NHS 4; Leiden: E. J. Brill, 1975).

frame story claiming Seth's authorship of this writing—though in spite of this fictional authorship Seth is always referred to in the third person in the frame story and elsewhere in the narrative.

The first half of the *Holy Book* contains an account of the emanation of all the entities in the divine realm of "perfection" (Greek: *plēroma*). A brief summary will provide an impression of the rather elaborate mythology in this part of the *Holy Book*, as well as a point of reference for inferring some of the fundamental religious convictions behind this type of literature. Though the myth in the following description may at first seem disconcertingly complex, we will see that there are some basic elements that are not so difficult to delineate:

Everything begins from a single, perfect and absolutely mysterious source, the Invisible Spirit, and then this unity evolves or elaborates itself, into a multiplicity of transcendent entities or powers. That is, divinity is perfectly unified but paradoxically it is at the same time brimming with the abundance of sublime qualities or faculties that constitute perfection. From the Invisible Spirit or ineffable self-begotten Father, a first triad of powers emanates: the Father, Mother (sometimes called "Barbelo")[13] and Son, who emerge from the primordial "Silence" of the self-begotten Father. Rather than implying a second "Father," what seems to be imagined here is a next stage in the elaboration of the original self-begotten Father or Invisible Spirit. Next, each of the three powers in the first triad is expanded into an ogdoad or eight-fold entity. For example, the first ogdoad consists of the Father, thought, word, incorruptibility, eternal life, will, mind, and foreknowledge.

Following the emanation of the first triad and its ogdoads, a second triad of beings appears that seems in some sense to be an image of the Father-Mother-Son triad: A "thrice-male child"; an entity called Youel; and being named Esephech, also called the "child of the child." Somewhat surprisingly, this second triad is subsequently referred to several times as "the *five* seals." The number five is apparently accounted for by adding Youel and Esephech to the *thrice*-male identity of the first member of this triad. (As we will see, the promi-

---

[13] The origin of this name remains debated; see a summary of various theories given by Alastair H. B. Logan, *Gnostic Truth and Christian Heresy: A Study in the History of Gnosticism* (Peabody, Mass.: Hendrickson, 1996), 98–100.

nence of the "five seals" theme is ultimately a function of the ritual agenda of this text that includes an emphasis on a quintuple sealing in baptism.) Following the emanation of the Father-Mother-Son, and then the "five seals," innumerable attendant angels are brought forth as a heavenly chorus giving praise to the prior divine entities.

The next major stage commences with the appearance of a self-begotten Word or Logos, who establishes four eternal realms or "aeons." Then a mysterious power named Mirothoe gives birth to the first Human, Adamas, a transcendent version of the biblical Adam. Since Mirothoe is portrayed as a mother figure, it may be that Logos, Mirothoe, and Adamas are intended to be still a third triadic level that involves a father, mother and son. Adamas himself then asks for a son, and there comes forth a further mother figure, a "power of the great light," who gives birth to four great lights along with the "great incorruptible Seth," son of the incorruptible Human Adamas. Finally, Seth in turn asks for offspring, and another mother entity appears, named Plesithea, who becomes the source for the "seed" or offspring of Seth.

The four great lights generated along with Seth are Harmozel, Oroiael, Davithe and Eleleth, and each is assigned to one of the four eternal realms or aeons established by the self-begotten Logos. Moreover, each of these four lights has a consort (Grace, Perception, Understanding, and Prudence) and an assistant (Gamaliel, Gabriel, Samlo, and Abrasax), and each assistant has a consort (Memory, Love, Peace and Eternal Life). According to the *Holy Book*, the four lights and their four consorts and the four assistants and their four consorts constitute fourth and fifth ogdoads.

The four lights, Harmozel, Oroiael, Davithe and Eleleth, as well as their structural association with Adamas, Seth and the offspring of Seth, are among the distinctive, recurrent elements in Sethian tradition. We learn from a later passage in the *Holy Book* (III 65.12–22) that Harmozel is the location of Adamas and the Self-begotten, Oroiael the location for Seth, Davithe the location for the offspring of Seth, and Eleleth the location for the souls of Seth's offspring.

As bewildering as the account so far may appear to the first-time reader (and the preceding is a simplified summary!), the essential concept is not so difficult to grasp. Beginning with an incomprehensible primal Father we have arrived at a complete and richly populated realm that culminates in ideal Humanity: Seth and his offspring. In other words, Seth in a sense *is* the primal Father in

Human manifestation. Ideal Humanity *is* God's image—is *divine*, essentially.

To this point the narrative has portrayed a scene of perfection without conflict. But the story in the *Holy Book* then moves to the interaction between the divine and material realms. A command comes forth from the realm of the four lights that there be an angel to rule over "Chaos and Hades" (the material cosmos). The manuscripts are damaged here but it appears that there is a continuation of the previously encountered pattern of the appearance of mother figures who give birth to the consecutive levels of offspring. This time the birth-giver is "hylic Sophia" (material Wisdom), from whom comes an angel called Sakla and a consort demon named Nebruel. The notion of Wisdom as divine mediator and agent in the creation of the world was a well-known biblical theme (e.g., Prov 8:22–31) and the subject of widespread speculation in Jewish lore and Christian theology. Variations on a myth in which Wisdom is the mother of a lower cosmic creator or demiurge appear in several important "Sethian" sources, as well as in other traditions such as Valentinian Christianity.[14]

In the *Holy Book*, Sakla and Nebruel generate twelve realms in the material world and twelve angels to administer them. Sakla (whose name in Aramaic means "fool") then utters a foolish boast: "I am a jealous god, and nothing has come into being apart from me!"—a parody of biblical passages such as Deut 32:39.[15] This arrogance is corrected by a divine Voice from on high: "The Human exists, and the Child of the Human," a reference to the heavenly Adamas and Seth. Then, a visible image of this Voice also appears below to Sakla and his angels. From this image, "the first molded form was fashioned" (III 59.8), an allusion to the molding of the first material humans by the creator-angel(s). In other words, the first physical humans were indeed created in the image of God as Genesis states (Gen 1:26–27), but "God" in the form of the spiritual Adamas, the perfect Human archetype in which true divinity (the Invisible Spirit)

---

[14] See George W. MacRae, "The Jewish Background of the Gnostic Sophia Myth," *Novum Testamentum* 12 (1970): 86–101; Nils A. Dahl, "The Arrogant Archon and the Lewd Sophia," in *The Rediscovery of Gnosticism: Proceedings of the International Conference on Gnosticism at Yale, New Haven, Connecticut, March 28–31, 1978* (ed. Bentley Layton; SHR 41; Leiden: E. J. Brill, 1981), 2:689–712.

[15] See also Isa 45:5, 22; 46:9; and Ps 14:1 (= Ps 53:1): "Fools say in their hearts, 'There is no God.'"

manifests itself. However, this molding of the first material humans by the creator-angels is treated as a problem, an imperfection requiring correction.

The correction is set underway by the sowing of the "seed of the great Seth" in the material realm. The imagined story of this process is not so transparent from the sketchy narrative itself, since this section of the *Holy Book* seems to assume and allude to more story than it actually narrates. But the central theme is that populating the cosmos with Seth's offspring is necessary to overcome the imperfection wrought by Sakla and his angels. Why is this the necessary means? Because the fundamental problem to be solved is the incongruity between an imperfect material realm and a perfect spiritual realm, and the perfection of the transcendent spiritual realm is, as we have seen, imagined in *anthropological* terms: The self-expression of God's perfection *is* Humanity—i.e., the Human population of the transcendent realm (the heavenly Adamas, Seth and Seth's offspring, etc.). Therefore the correction of imperfection in the material realm means most of all the correction of an imperfect *humanity*, the "molded" material humanity fashioned by the creator angels. This molded humanity is not perfect, but rather deficient, lacking the spiritual essence of the divine image.

Seth's seed, ideal Humanity, bears the divine image, and so the proliferation of this seed in the world is to lead to a "reconciliation of the world" with the divine.[16] The *Holy Book* alludes to a resulting history of conflict down through the ages between the seed of Seth and the dark forces of evil. The powers of the cosmos sought to persecute the seed, while emissaries from the divine realm guarded and rescued this race. "The prophets and the guardians" (guardian angels) protect the race of Seth through the perils of "the flood" (Gen 6), a conflagration, famines and plagues, and deception by false prophets.

Now one of the most important and interesting questions for the understanding of this and other Sethian sources is the actual mechanism by which the seed of Seth is supposed to have been "sown." The *Holy Book* refers obscurely to the preparation of a "Logos-begotten holy vessel" for the seed of Seth by means of "virgins of the defiled sowing of this aeon." This curious reference might allude to some

---

[16] See *Holy Book (Gos. Eg.)* III 63.9, 16.

sort of virginal conceptions by which Seth's seed was imagined to have been engendered in mortal females down through the ages, though that is not the only possible meaning. The climactic revelatory event is said to have been when the great Seth himself was sent into a "Logos-begotten body ... secretly through the virgin"—i.e., the virgin-born Jesus was none other than Seth himself. This appearance of Seth as Jesus is said to have made possible that the "saints" (Sethian believers) might be begotten by the Holy Spirit through "secret symbols."

Thus, however it is that readers are supposed to understand the mechanism by which the seed of Seth was sown in former generations, the important thing is that in the present time (for the ancient readers) one is begotten as a member of the race of Seth *ritually*, by means of the baptism that is the focus of the last section of the *Holy Book*. The mythology in the first part of the *Holy Book* that established "five seals" in a central position in the transcendent realm is therefore ultimately a function of this ritual agenda, since a rite of "five seals" is involved in, or identical with, the baptism ritual of this text. Initiation by means of the baptismal five seals entails identification with the divine, a quintuple sealing that somehow conveys (or restores) the divine image.

2.2. *Other Texts with Similar Features: Evidence of a Tradition*

The central role played in the *Holy Book* by the myth of the transcendent human family, Adamas, Seth, and Seth's offspring, and the paramount importance placed on belonging to this race of Seth, is a feature found also in several other ancient sources and is our principal point of departure for identifying and describing a "Sethian" tradition. As was mentioned earlier, scholars have debated the precise criteria for defining "Sethianism." The following discussion of some of the more important examples that are usually identified as "Sethian" will illustrate why many researchers feel there is evidence for a common tradition of "Sethian" speculation, but at the same time it will reveal some of the interesting diversity among these sources.

For the *Apocryphon (Secret Book) of John* we have four Coptic manuscripts representing at least two (a longer and a shorter) recensions.[17]

---

[17] Michael Waldstein and Frederik Wisse, eds., *The Apocryphon of John: Synopsis of*

Mythic content similar to that in the *Apocryphon of John* was known to and criticized by the Christian writer Irenaeus of Lyons in the latter half of the second century C.E., which may allow us to date some form of the *Apocryphon of John* as early as the second century. Like the *Holy Book*, the *Apocryphon of John* presents itself as secret revelation, though in this case revelation given by the risen Christ to the apostle John, son of Zebedee. The content of the revelation resembles the basic structure of what was found in the *Holy Book*: (1) an elaborate account of the emanation of entities in the transcendent realm from a completely ineffable primal Invisible Spirit; these include, among others, the enigmatically named "Barbelo" who is the transcendent Mother and first emanation from the Invisible Spirit, and the divine Human family of Adamas and Seth—again associated with the group of four light beings named Harmozel, Oroiael, Davithe and Eleleth; (2) the emergence from Wisdom of lower entities (including a chief named "Ialdabaoth") who become rulers of the material world and who are parodies of the God of the Old Testament; (3) the creation of material humans by these inferior powers; (4) divine initiatives to correct the imperfection below by the infusion of a spiritual identity or "seed" in humanity, and the nurturing of this through revelation; (5) conflicts between the cosmic powers desiring to control and corrupt humanity and divine Providence counteracting those various plots by means of instruments of salvation—above all, by means of revelation such as that in the *Apocryphon of John* about "the race of the perfect Human." The longer recension of the *Apocryphon of John* refers to a sealing with "five seals," possibly a version of the same communal ritual mentioned in the *Holy Book*.

Although both the *Holy Book* and the *Apocryphon of John* share the assumption that Jesus was the latest avatar or manifestation of a transcendent, pre-existent divine revealer, in the *Holy Book* this role of divine revealer who eventually appears as Jesus is condensed in the person of the heavenly "great Seth." The heavenly Seth is portrayed as taking initiative in asking for "guardians" for his seed when these offspring are threatened by the schemes of the lower powers, and finally being sent to rescue the human race. By contrast, in the

Nag Hammadi Codices II,1; III,1; and IV,1 with BG 8502,2 (Nag Hammadi and Manichaean Studies 33; Leiden: E. J. Brill, 1995).

Apocryphon of John Seth is not singled out as the active agent of revelation. He still occupies the same very important structural position
as son of Adamas in the genealogy of divine Humanity, but as such
he is portrayed more as a crucial link in the channel of divine initiative than as the initiator. The Savior who reveals himself to John
does not identify himself as an avatar of Seth, but rather as the
Father, the Mother and the Son—i.e., simply as the one God, who
is without form but might manifest itself in different forms. The latter resembles in certain respects what is known of "modalist" or
"monarchian" Christian theologies of the second and third centuries
C.E. However, the *Apocryphon of John* presents a more mythologically
elaborate, Sethian version of this perspective.

Further important evidence for a Sethian tradition is found in a
very different kind of text. The tractate *Zostrianos*, in Nag Hammadi
Codex VIII, is one of the longest writings in the Nag Hammadi collection although its fragmentary state precludes full knowledge of its
original content.[18] The text gives a lengthy account of an ascent
vision supposedly experienced by a certain Zostrianos, son of Iolaos.
This is presumably the Zostrianos who is claimed by other ancient
sources[19] to have been an ancestor of Er, the visionary famously
depicted toward the end of Plato's *Republic* (614b) as having returned
from death and a visit to Hades to tell about the other world and
how various kinds of souls fare there and are reincarnated. Just as
Er is told in his vision that he is to take the message about what
he sees back to the realm of living humans, so also Zostrianos is
told during his visionary ascent that he is to return to preach about
what he sees in order to "save those who are worthy" (*Zost.* 4.15–17).
Thus, unlike the narratives in the *Holy Book* or the *Apocryphon of John*
that are accounts of the emanation of the transcendent realm, the
creation of the lower world, and the history of conflict between cosmic powers and one or more divine agents who descend to bring
revelation to humans, *Zostrianos* takes the reader on a visionary ascent
back through the various levels of the transcendent realms. The vision
account does briefly allude to a myth regarding the creation of the

---

[18] Catherine Barry, Wolf-Peter Funk, Paul-Hubert Poirier, and John D. Turner,
Zostrien (NH VIII,1) (Bibliothèque copte de Nag Hammadi, "Textes" 24; Québec:
Les presses de l'Université Laval; Louvain: Peeters, 2000); John Sieber, ed. *Nag
Hammadi Codex VIII* (NHS 31; Leiden: E. J. Brill, 1991).
[19] See Arnobius of Sicca, *Adv. nat.* 1.52.

material world by a lower power who is the offspring of Wisdom (9.1–10.31). However, for the most part what the reader sees, with Zostrianos, is the nature of the transcendent world that underlies perceptible experience in this life.

The structure and population of that transcendent world is a variation of what is found in the *Holy Book* and the *Apocryphon of John*, including at the most transcendent level the Invisible Spirit and Barbelo, and, somewhat further down the ontological hierarchy, the distinctive realms of the four lights, Armozel, Oroiael, Davithe and Eleleth, where dwell the heavenly Adamas, Seth and Seth's offspring. *Zostrianos* also refers to a remarkable number of other mythological names encountered in the *Holy Book*, and it is conceivable that the author may have known the latter writing.[20]

Similar to *Zostrianos* in its focus on visionary experience of the transcendent realm is the *Three Steles of Seth*, from Nag Hammadi Codex VII.[21] The *Three Steles of Seth* purports to record a revelation conveyed by a certain Dositheos, who in a vision had seen the content of three steles supposedly inscribed by the ancient Seth himself—similar to the stele tradition already known to Josephus, as mentioned above. The content of the steles consists of praise offered to a series of transcendent entities, beginning with Adamas in the first stele, then the "male virginal Barbelo" in the second, and finally the Preexistent One in the third stele. Thus the three steles amount to a kind of ascent in praise through ontological levels that, as seen above, are also encountered in other Sethian works. The praise in the first stele begins in the first person singular, as a blessing by "Emmacha Seth" to his father "Ger-Adamas."[22] but interestingly the first-person singular extends only through about the first half of the first stele. After that the praises change to first-person plural ("We bless you . . .") for the remainder of the document. This has led some modern interpreters to conclude that the *Three Steles of Seth*

---

[20] Cf. Barry et al., *Zostrien*, 142.

[21] Birger Pearson, ed., *Nag Hammadi Codex VII* (Nag Hammadi and Manichaean Studies 30; Leiden: E. J. Brill, 1996).

[22] On "Ger-Adamas," cf. the discussion by Howard M. Jackson, "Geradamas, the Celestial Stranger," *NTS* 27 (1981): 385–94. This version of the name of Adamas (see also, e.g., *Zost.* 6.23; 13.6; 51.7; *Melch.* 6.6; *Ap. John* II 8.34–35) may derive from the Semitic *ger*, "stranger." Adamas in the *Three Steles of Seth* is indeed said to be from "another race"—i.e., another ontological category—and Ger-Adamas ("Stranger Adamas") may have alluded to this.

was possibly written to be read in the context of a communal liturgy, perhaps involving even a communal ascent ritual.[23]

The mythology in the *Trimorphic Protennoia* ("First Thought in Three Forms") also contains several of the same core Sethian motifs. There is only one known manuscript of this text, a Coptic version found in Nag Hammadi Codex XIII,[24] but the Coptic almost certainly derives from some Greek original. Some interpreters view the few distinctly Christian features that are present in the surviving text to be later additions and believe that the mythology in the writing could be pre-Christian. Most of the content is in the form of a first-person revelatory discourse by Protennoia, the "First Thought" of the Invisible first principle or parent of all things, and who is also called Barbelo. Therefore, the speaker in this text is God, or God in different forms or modes—as transcendent Father, Mother and Son, for example. The text is actually sectioned by subtitles in the manuscript into three parts. The speaker throughout is First Thought, yet each section contains an emphasis on a different mode of her revelatory speech, moving from the least to most articulate. In the first section we hear primarily of the inarticulate Voice or Sound of First Thought; in the second the emphasis moves to this Voice's appearance as Speech; and in the third it is Voice's specific form as rational Word (Logos).[25] So although the first principle is completely incomprehensible and ineffable, there is a process of self-revelation progressing from the completely transcendent to the increasingly formulated, visible and tangible. This is a familiar theme in many apophatic or negative theologies.

The final appearance of the revealer is in the form of Jesus—though this is explicitly stated only in the last few lines. Most of the writing is far more allusive about the appearances of the revealer. Once again we have an underlying mythic narrative that is assumed rather than fully recounted, and it is clear that this assumed narrative is something similar to elements of what we find also in the *Apocryphon of John*. Some of the same distinctive mythic characters

---

[23] E.g., John D. Turner, "Ritual in Gnosticism," in *Gnosticism and Later Platonism* (ed. John D. Turner and Ruth Majercik; SBL Symposium Series 12; Atlanta: Society of Biblical Literature, 2000), 128–29.

[24] Charles W. Hedrick, ed., *Nag Hammadi Codices XI, XII, XIII* (NHS 27; Leiden: E. J. Brill, 1990).

[25] Cf. the discussion by John Turner in Hedrick, ed., *Nag Hammadi Codices XI, XII, XIII*, 383–84.

(e.g., Barbelo, Ialdabaoth, the four light beings Harmozel, Oroiael, Davithe and Eleleth) and mythemes (e.g., lower creators who snatch power from Wisdom to rule over the cosmos, and who create material humans in the likeness of the divine image) appear in both texts. Also appearing are other important mythic names not mentioned in the *Apocryphon of John* but which are encountered in the *Holy Book* and *Zostrianos*, and with similar roles (e.g., Micheus, Michar and Mnesinous, connected to baptismal waters; an important mother figure Mirothea/Mirothoe). *Trimorphic Protennoia* also gives central significance to a ritual of "five seals."

First Thought triumphantly recounts her redemptive activity in apocalyptic language about the smashing of the constraining domain of the "Tyrant" (Ialdabaoth) and the liberating of the "children of the Light"—i.e., humans—so that their spirits might return to the spiritual realm. First Thought accomplishes this through the revelation of mysteries to humanity, bringing to fruition in them the thought or knowledge of the transcendent realm and the family ("my household"—41.32) to which humans belong.

The very poorly preserved tractate *Melchizedek* in Nag Hammadi Codex IX,[26] contains revelation purportedly given to the mysterious ancient priest Melchizedek who had long been an object of speculation by Jewish and Christian writers.[27] In the Nag Hammadi writing the priest Melchizedek receives knowledge from a revealing angel about the transcendent realm, the origin of the children of Seth, the struggle with wicked spirits, a baptism, and the ultimate victory over the forces of wickedness and death. Then Melchizedek speaks in the first person, offering praise to entities in the divine realm, and speaking of his own role in salvation history. Though most of the manuscript is quite fragmentary, it seems that the ancient Melchizedek is understood to have been an avatar or image of the "true High Priest," the pre-existent Jesus Christ. But then Melchizedek later appears to offer himself as sacrifice in the earthly life and crucifixion of Jesus, in order to destroy Death. The entities in the transcendent

---

[26] Birger A. Pearson, ed., *Nag Hammadi Codices IX and X* (NHS 15; Leiden: E. J. Brill, 1981); Wolf-Peter Funk, Jean-Pierre Mahé, C. Gianotto, eds. *Melchisédek (NH IX,1)* (Bibliothèque copte de Nag Hammadi, "Textes" 28; Québec: Les presses de l'Université Laval; Louvain: Peeters, 2000).

[27] See Gen 14:18; Ps 110:4; Heb 6:19–7:28; and the Qumran text *Melchizedek* (11QMelch), where Melchizedek is a heavenly angelic deliverer who will preside over the eschatological judgment and take vengeance on the forces of evil.

realm include, in addition to Christ, a cast of familiar Sethian names, such as the Mother Barbelo; the four luminaries Armozel, Oroiael, Daveithe and Eleleth; and the immortal Ger-Adamas and Seth and his seed.

It is hard to know the precise relationship between the Nag Hammadi writing *Melchizedek* and partly similar teachings reported by heresiologists such as Hippolytus (*Haer.* 7.36), who briefly notes that a certain Theodotus "the money-changer" taught that Melchizedek was a power even greater than Christ, and that the latter was in Melchizedek's image.[28] Epiphanius (*Pan.* 55) significantly elaborates on this by claiming that there was a specific group called "Melchizedekians" who derived from the "Theodotians," and who glorified Melchizedek, saying that access to God is through him, and that humans must make offering to him in order that offering might be made by him on their behalf (55.8.1–3). However, these particular reports lack any reference to the "Sethian" features such as references to Seth or the children of Seth, Adamas, Barbelo, the four luminaries, etc. The essential thing in common with the tractate *Melchizedek* is only the speculation about Melchizedek, his role as transcendent high priest and his relation in this regard to Christ— i.e., speculation that may have derived from the Epistle to the Hebrews or traditions underlying that work. This speculation likely circulated among different circles in the early centuries C.E. and in the case of *Melchizedek*, has been picked up and adapted to a Sethian mythological framework in which now Melchizedek served as another avatar and intermediary of the divine.

In spite of some differences among these writings, it is apparent from the above description that there are also undeniable continuities among them involving distinctive nomenclature and mythic themes that indicate that they are close relatives in the same "genealogical tree" of interpretive tradition.

The list can be expanded to include several other sources that are also closely related, with varying degrees of the same distinctive terminology or nomenclature. For example, very closely related to both *Zostrianos* and the *Three Steles of Seth* in mythological and technical terminology is the tractate *Allogenes* from Nag Hammadi Codex XI, in which a seer called Allogenes (Greek for "Stranger") relates his

---

[28] Cf. also Ps.-Tertullian, *Adversus omnes haereses* 8.

visionary ascent through different ontological levels culminating in a mystical union with the most sublime and ineffable One.[29] Though the name Seth is not found in what survives of this work, the appellation "Allogenes" is known to have been used of Seth in connection with an ascent to the higher realms.[30] Also bearing similarities to this group of texts as well as other "Sethian" works is an untitled tractate in the "Bruce Codex," the conventional designation for a group of Coptic papyri of uncertain date purchased in about 1769 in Upper Egypt by the Scottish traveler, James Bruce. The treatise is a Christian "Sethian" work that describes in systematic fashion the unfolding of the transcendent world and the ordering of material creation, and it contains terminology and special mythic patterns noted in other "Sethian" texts—for example, references to the four luminaries (Eleleth, Daveide, Oroiael, and Harmozel).[31]

The *Hypostasis of the Archons* from Nag Hammadi Codex II contains a myth of origins in which Wisdom creates what becomes an arrogant demiurgical being named Yaldabaoth (also called Samael, "god of the blind," and Sakla, "fool") who then is responsible for creating the material realm and material humans. The text includes a rewritten version of the Garden of Eden story in which the material humans are victimized by their demiurgical creators, though the divine spirit in humans—i.e., the most truly Human element—escapes any harm from these assaults and is passed on in Seth and his sister Norea and their descendants. The text has a prominent role for a revealing angel Eleleth who is said to be one of "the four luminaries" (*Hyp. Arch.* 93.20).

The *Apocalypse of Adam* from Codex V presents revelation allegedly received by Adam and passed on to his son Seth, and foretells the history of humankind and its struggles against the creator god (called "Sakla" at one point), from the age of Adam until the coming and triumph of a final "Illuminator" who rescues the seed of Seth by means of true knowledge and "holy baptism." No mention is made

---

[29] See, e.g, Turner, *Sethian Gnosticism*, 118–22, *et passim*; Karen King, *Revelation of the Unknowable God, with Text, Translation, and Notes to NHC XI,3 Allogenes* (California Classical Library; Santa Rosa, Calif.: Polebridge, 1995).

[30] Epiphanius, *Pan.* 40.7.1–2.

[31] See Carl Schmidt and Violet MacDermot, *The Books of Jeu and the Untitled Text in the Bruce Codex* (NHS 13; Leiden: E. J. Brill, 1978); Charlotte A. Baynes, *A Coptic Gnostic Treatise Contained in the Codex Brucianus (Bruce MS. 96. Bod. Lib. Oxford)* (Cambridge: Cambridge University Press, 1933).

in this writing of any of the "four luminaries," or Barbelo, but some of the other special names found in Sethian texts discussed above do appear—such as Micheu, Michar, and Mnesinous who are also encountered in *Gospel of the Egyptians, Zostrianos* and *Trimorphic Protennoia*. Though inferring connections among texts based merely on shared usage of such *nomina barbara* is notoriously problematic, in this case Micheu, Michar, and Mnesinous are consistently connected with a baptism of some sort.[32] Therefore, combined with the other similarities among these texts, this particular set of names may be stronger evidence of an actual common social history. Interestingly, however, in the *Apocalypse of Adam* Micheus, Michar, and Mnesinous are apparently criticized for having *defiled* baptism in some way, while they are quite positively portrayed in the other Sethian tractates mentioned. This is only one of the indications that whatever social historical connections underlie these writings they were evidently complex and involved more than a single, monolithic sect.

3. *Reconstructing the Social History of Sethianism?*

The preceding discussion has provided some of the examples of the evidence that there did exist a distinctive interpretive tradition that we might label "Sethian." But to what extent is it possible to reconstruct any of the social history of this tradition and its evolution?

Dating the origins of this tradition is the first problem, since, for example, we have no name of a founder with which we might mark its beginnings. The oldest relatively firm evidence for the "Sethian" traditions that are discussed above comes from the second century C.E. Irenaeus of Lyons (ca. 180 C.E.) already criticizes a mythic tradition very close to what is found in the *Apocryphon of John*.[33] Around 260–270 C.E. the philosopher Plotinus argued with opponents who must have been using writings similar in content to *Zostrianos, Three Steles of Seth, Allogenes*, or the untitled tractate in the Bruce Codex.

---

[32] *Apoc. Adam* 84.4–22; *Gos. Eg.* III 64.15–20; *Trim. Prot.* 48.18–21; *Zost.* 6.10–16 (though only Michar and Micheus are mentioned in connection with the "living waters"; Mnesinous does appear in *Zost.* 47,1–4 in another connection). At the very end of *Apoc. Adam* (85.25–31) there seems to be a very prominent role for "Yesseus, Mazareus, [Yesse]dekeus" in connection with baptism or "living water," and this same connection is found in *Gos. Eg.* III 64.9–12 and 66.8–11 (cf. *Zost.* 47.5–6).

[33] Irenaeus, *Haer.* 1.29 and 1.30.

Plotinus's student and biographer Porphyry in fact specifically mentions that these opponents used "apocalypses of Zoroaster and Zostrianos and Nikotheos and Allogenes and Messos" (*Vit. Plot.* 16). In *Allogenes*, the visionary narrates his visions to a certain Messos, and the Bruce Codex refers to visions received by a Nikotheos, among others. Therefore, the evidence from Porphyry provides prima facie evidence that several of these writings were around in some form at least by the early to mid-third century. As mentioned above, the author of *Zostrianos* may have known the *Holy Book of the Invisible Spirit*, and if so then some edition of the *Holy Book* would have been around by the early third century C.E. or before.

Whether or in what form the Sethian traditions in these texts can be dated earlier than the second century C.E. remains a matter of debate:

Scholars who believe that Sethian myths emerged in some form already by the first century C.E., or even earlier, have argued that one can isolate in surviving Sethian writings older layers of tradition.[34] The most commonly employed methodologies have included (a) the identification of potential literary seams that reveal portions of a text that might be secondary; and (b) attempts to distinguish older core myths that might make sense on their own from potentially secondary mythological elements that may have been added. So, for example, surviving manuscripts of the *Apocryphon of John* contain a Christian frame story (Christ appearing to the disciple John) that encases the revelatory discourse and dialogue, but that in principle might be separated from the mythological content itself—and indeed, Irenaeus's description of a closely similar mythology (*Adv. haer.* 1.29; cf. 1.30) contains no mention at all of John or his alleged role in transmitting the myth. Moreover, it has been argued that Christ could also be removed or replaced as the revealer within the mythological narrative and dialogue throughout the rest of the *Apocryphon of John*, and the remaining mythic text would make as much or even more sense.

---

[34] E.g., Hans-Martin Schenke, "The Phenomenon and Significance of Gnostic Sethianism," in *The Rediscovery of Gnosticism: Proceedings of the International Conference on Gnosticism at Yale, New Haven, Connecticut, March 28–31, 1978* (ed. Bentley Layton; SHR 41; Leiden: E. J. Brill, 1981), 2:607–12; Turner, *Sethian Gnosticism*, 127–54; 221–54.

By contrast, other researchers contend that the "Sethianism" of the writings such as those that have been discussed here was a second or early third century C.E. development.[35] According to this view, there is no convincing evidence that the mythological focus on Seth and his seed can be traced back into earliest Christian or pre-Christian Jewish sources, and its presence in such writings as the *Holy Book* and the other texts discussed above is seen to be a "Sethianization" of myths deriving from second century C.E. traditions associated with teachers such as Saturninus, Basilides, or Valentinus. Scholars who take this position tend to view all of these movements, with their typical demotion of the god of Jewish scripture to a lower demiurge, as post-Christian speculations that emerged under the impact of the theologies of writers like Paul or the Gospel of John as well as the influence of Platonic ideas.

Resolving this debate may well be impossible absent the discovery of more and better evidence, and either approach entails a considerable amount of speculative reconstruction. The most extensive attempt actually to chart a hypothetical history of Sethianism is the important research of John Turner,[36] who is essentially aligned with the first of the two general approaches in the debate just mentioned. In Turner's view the "Sethians" as such did first emerge in the second century C.E., but from a fusion of two distinct earlier groups: (a) "Barbeloites," who may have been of Jewish priestly lineage and who practiced ritual baptisms in connection with transcendental visions and revelatory wisdom received from Barbelo, the First Thought of the highest God; and (b) "Sethites," a group of "morally earnest biblical exegetes" who saw themselves as the "seed of Seth" and who touted alleged ancient records recounting revelation given to their ancestor and the history of their seed's enlightenment down through the ages.

According to Turner, the "Barbeloites" probably first amalgamated with Christian baptizing groups, and from such Christianized Barbeloites would have come early core myths underlying the *Apocryphon of John* and the *Trimorphic Protennoia*. Then a further merger of these groups in the later second century with "Sethites" would have resulted

---

[35] E.g., Simone Pétrement, *A Separate God: The Christian Origins of Gnosticism* (trans. Carol Harrison; San Francisco: HarperCollins, 1990); Logan, *Gnostic Truth.*
[36] See especially Turner, *Sethian Gnosticism*, 255–304.

in Christianizing Sethianism, and it would have been this movement that produced the more complete versions of the *Apocryphon of John* and the *Trimorphic Protennoia* actually known to us, as well as other writings such as the *Holy Book of the Great Invisible Spirit*, or the *Apocalypse of Adam*. But Turner thinks that Sethianism then became increasingly estranged from proto-orthodox Christianity in the late second century C.E., and by the third century was universally rejected by Christian heresiologists. These marginalized Sethians were at the same time becoming attracted to contemplative practices in contemporary Platonism, and writings such as the *Three Steles of Seth*, *Zostrianos*, and *Allogenes* would represent this de-Christianized phase of Sethianism. Yet by the middle and late third century Sethians also became alienated from many Platonists, resulting in the polemical attacks by Plotinus and his students against their Platonizing Sethian acquaintances. Finally, Turner suggests that by the fourth century C.E. Sethianism had become increasingly fragmented into various derivative sects and this explains the variety of groups reported by heresiologists such as Epiphanius and others from the fourth century on: Archontics, Borborites, Phibionites, etc., whose alleged teachings often manifest similarities with "Sethian" writings such as those among the Nag Hammadi tractates.[37]

Turner's hypothetical reconstruction is an attempt to create a social-historical narrative that might account for some of the obvious diversity in the surviving Sethian writings. He has especially emphasized the presence of two fundamental types among the Sethian writings: (a) those in which salvation is effected through a series of *descents* by a divine revealer (e.g., *Holy Book of the Great Invisible Spirit*, *Apocryphon of John*, *Trimorphic Protennoia*, *Apocalypse of Adam*, *Hypostasis of the Archons*) and (b) those in which instead the crucial revelatory experience is more a matter of the individual's mystical contemplative *ascent* through supernal realms (e.g., *Zostrianos*, *Allogenes*, *Three Steles of Seth*). The latter type happens to include the writings with many other connections (technical vocabulary, etc.) to the third century philosopher Plotinus and other Neoplatonist figures, while the former involves texts with the larger amount of reinterpreted biblical narrative (i.e., rewritten versions of the creation narrative, the Garden of Eden story, etc.) and sometimes explicitly Christian vocabulary or themes.

---

[37] Epiphanius, *Pan.* 25.2.7–26.13.7; 40.1.1–8.2.

Now on the one hand, something generally similar to the exper-
imentations and interactions that Turner assumes with different religious and philosophical currents must have been characteristic of the
history of Sethian tradition. For example, some of the surviving
Sethian texts do contain explicitly Christian motifs while others manifest little or no uniquely Christian features, and some of the writings
definitely are closely related to the abstract philosophical discourse
and debates of Plotinus's circle.

On the other hand, the discrete stages in Turner's hypothetical
outline of the social history of Sethianism should not be confused
with what was surely a more complex pattern of development. It is
probably unnecessary and unjustified to posit, even hypothetically, a
more or less linear history that moved from an initial fusion with
Christian circles, to an eventual forced migration from activity among
Christian communities, to association with non-Christian Platonist
philosophers, to later alienation also from these Platonists, and then
ultimately to increasing sectarian division. The reality was likely far
more complicated. For instance, it is to be noted that writings such
as *Allogenes, Zostrianos,* and *Three Steles of Seth*—which under the model
above would have originated in a post-Christian phase—have in fact
survived almost exclusively in distinctly Christian books! That is, the
volumes in which these writings are found (Nag Hammadi Codices
VII, VIII and XI) also contain works with very prominently Christian
motifs, and the composition and content of these codices is a part
of the evidence suggesting that the composers and collectors of the
books were fourth century C.E. Christian monastics. In fact, not only
do these writings survive in Christian books, but in at least one
instance—*Allogenes* (and perhaps in a second, *Three Steles of Seth*)—the
inclusion may have been intended to serve a ritual purpose: The
ritual ascent vision in *Allogenes* in Codex XI follows (Valentinian)
Christian ritual texts about baptism and eucharist, so that it is conceivable that for users of this codex the ascent vision in *Allogenes* was
being read as a next step after these rituals.[38] At the very least, all
of this invites more careful thought and explanation if one hypoth-
esizes, as Turner does, that writings such as *Allogenes, Zostrianos* and
Three Steles of Seth were produced by Sethians only after the latter
had been forced to break ties with Christian circles and had joined

---

[38] See Michael Allen Williams, *Rethinking "Gnosticism": An Argument for Dismantling
a Dubious Category* (Princeton: Princeton University Press, 1996), 255–56.

the company of contemporary Platonists. If the fourth century users of codices containing *Allogenes*, *Three Steles of Seth* and *Zostrianos* do not seem to have imagined themselves to have abandoned their Christian ties, could the same have been true also in the third century C.E. for the acquaintances whom Plotinus and Porphyry criticize for composing and using such writings?

We have a few names of specific individuals whom we can connect with some branch of Sethianism, though information about them is too limited to provide much help in fleshing out the social history of the tradition. In referring to the people in Plotinus's circles who were using "revelations of Zoroaster, Zostrianos, Nikotheos, Allogenes and Messos," Porphyry says that they were followers of "Adelphios and Aquilinus," and possessed writings of "Alexander of Libya, Philokomos, Demostratos, and Lydos."[39] It is conceivable that among these names are persons who could have written some of the Sethian tractates that have survived, but at this time we have no way to ascertain this, and we know nothing else about the people in this list. In connection with a group he calls "Archontics," whose reported teachings bear certain similarities to Sethian tractates, the heresiologist Epiphanius mentions two specific individuals in the fourth century who he claims were involved with the sect. A man by the name of Eutaktos is said to have traveled from "Lesser Armenia" (eastern Turkey) to Palestine during the time of Constantine (on a pilgrimage?), and in Palestine he met an old monk named Peter from whom he learned the Archontic teachings. Eutaktos then carried the teaching back to Armenia, made converts among persons even of the senatorial class, which led to more widespread influence of this tradition in that region.[40] Epiphanius also says that the Archontics mention two "prophets" by the names of Martiades and Marsianos, who, like Seth, had experienced ascent visions. The "Bruce Codex" mentions visionaries by the name of Marsanes and Nikotheos, and the very fragmentary writing *Marsanes* from Nag Hammadi Codex X purports to be a revelatory discourse from Marsanes. These three men, Martiades, Nikotheos and Marsanes, therefore may have been famous prophets or seers in the Sethian tradition but if so we know little else about them in social-historical terms.

---

[39] Porphyry, *Vit. Plot.* 16.
[40] Epiphanius, *Pan.* 40.1.1–3; 40.1.8.

We also do not have much certain information about the actual life-styles of producers and readers of Sethian literature. There is evidence that many of them must have been ascetics or at least admired and/or aspired to ascetic practices such as the renunciation of sexuality,[41] but this need not be assumed to have been the case for all writers and readers of these texts. At the other extreme, the most vivid description we have of life-styles of people reportedly associated with Sethian-like mythic traditions comes from the fourth century heresiologist Epiphanius, who paints a picture of outrageous libertine rituals that are likely merely slanderous fictions.[42] It may well be that the majority of the people who were devotees of Sethian teachings in antiquity had day-to-day family lives not unlike those of most of their contemporaries, though they could have seen in the mythology of the serenity of the ideal Human family a model with transformative potential for their own households.[43]

While we have insufficient information to write a true social history of ancient "Sethianism," the surviving evidence does indicate that this tradition had a rather wide-ranging impact in late antiquity. Some version of it seems already to have been viewed by Irenaeus in Gaul in the late second century C.E. as having been the inspiration for Valentinian Christian mythology,[44] which itself exerted widespread attraction and generated both discussion and attack over many generations. As has been mentioned, there was noteworthy interaction between certain Platonizing Sethians and Plotinus and other significant figures within third-century Platonism, and modern scholars have recently begun to uncover evidence that dialogue with Platonizing Sethian acquaintances may even have had a formative influence on certain aspects of Plotinus's thought.[45] The chance discovery of the Nag Hammadi collection has provided important documentation that circles in fourth-century Egypt were still reading

---

[41] E.g., see *Ap. John* II 24,28–31, where sexual desire is planted in humans by the chief archon.

[42] Epiphanius, *Pan.* 25.1.1–26.19.6; see Williams, *Rethinking "Gnosticism,"* 179–84.

[43] Cf. Williams, *Rethinking "Gnosticism,"* 150–60.

[44] Irenaeus, *Adv. haer.* 1.11.1; 1.29.1; see Anne M. McGuire, "Valentinus and the *gnostikē hairesis*: Irenaeus, *Haer.* I.xi.1 and the Evidence of Nag Hammadi," in *Studia Patristica* 18 (ed. E. A. Livingstone; Kalamazoo: Cistercian Press, 1985), 247–52.

[45] See Kevin Corrigan, "Positive and Negative Matter in Later Platonism: The Uncovering of Plotinus's Dialogues with the Gnostics," in Turner and Majercik, eds., *Gnosticism and Later Platonism*, 19–56; Turner, *Sethian Gnosticism*, 407–424.

Sethian writings—along with the other works in these same codices. Epiphanius thought he remembered seeing a group that went by the name "Sethians" in Egypt—though he allows he could have encountered them elsewhere—and the teachings he ascribes to them are similar to teachings in surviving Sethian tractates.[46] As observed above, he also asserts that the apparently related "Archontics" were present not only in Palestine but had spread from there to Armenia, where he asserts that they had a considerable influence even among people from the higher strata of society.

Thus, although the number of its devotees must have been small in relative terms, Sethianism was an interpretive tradition of some importance in the history of late antique spirituality. While the evidence allows us to track a set of identifiable "Sethian" mythic themes, terms and structures that surface with a notable level of continuity over a period of centuries and even geographical areas, "Sethianism" should not be imagined as having been a monolithic sectarian community. Rather, "Sethian" sources are probably best viewed as products from different stages in a complex history of interrelated religious innovations. To be sure, the attention that is given in certain of the writings to distinctive initiation ritual terminology (e.g., baptism, the "five seals")[47] is one form of evidence suggesting that some of the people composing and reading such works did belong to defined sectarian groups with identifiable boundaries. But this was most likely not the case for all. The combination within the Nag Hammadi volumes of Sethian works with other tractates that must have originated from very different traditions is only one example of the variety of interpretive lenses through which Sethian myths were read and re-read.

4. *The Attraction of Sethianism*

That leads naturally to the question: What was the attraction of Sethian mythology and speculation? It is obvious from what has just been said that a complete answer would surely be quite multifaceted, given the diversity of communities and interpreters who adopted and adapted Sethian tradition over a period of centuries. Nevertheless we

---

[46] Epiphanius, *Pan.* 39.1.1–2.
[47] E.g., Sevrin, *Le dossier baptismal Séthien*; Turner, *Sethian Gnosticism*, 238–42.

may summarize in the space remaining a few of the factors that might account for the significant interest in Sethian myth and the considerable energies devoted to its transmission and creative adaptations.

Most of the Sethian sources reflect a preoccupation with the question of human nature and human origins,[48] and what is notable is how humanity is understood in such fundamentally optimistic terms. What it means to be human in the truest sense is a matter of an intimate identification with the transcendent Adam/Adamas and his offspring Seth—i.e., identification with the divine. Sethian sources celebrate the human longing for a remembered perfection, the yearning for a spiritual humanity whose roots stretch back infinitely into the invisible source out of which all reality has poured. Recovery of an awareness of one's membership in this divine family belongs to the essence of salvation in Sethian traditions.

Many are likely to have found attractive a universalism that could be inferred in the mythology of belonging to the seed or race of Seth (or Adamas). Not that this was the only message of universalism in antiquity. Denise Buell has recently discussed a range of examples of the discourse of universalism in early Christianity as well as in Jewish and other Hellenistic-Roman sources.[49] Buell does not discuss Sethian traditions, yet she does make a point that is of fundamental relevance here. Among other things she argues that an alleged "universalism" in early Christian rhetoric should not be set in facile contrast to a Jewish emphasis on ethnicity, since in fact Christian authors also framed identity in terms of race or ethnicity—i.e., belonging to a newly defined *genos* ("family, race"). However, Buell calls attention to Christian authors who found no contradiction in combining this rhetoric of a superior race with the assumption that "others" can be converted to become members of this race. Similarly, although the language of membership in the "race" or "seed" of Seth has often been read as implying a determinism that left no room for individual decision or conversion, this does not in fact seem necessarily to have been the case. The very point of the mythology of "Sethian" lineage, of belonging to Seth's seed or the "race of the Perfect

---

[48] A concern that is perhaps summed up nowhere more succinctly than in *Zost.* 8.5–7: "Why are humans different from one another? In what sense and in what degree are they humans?"

[49] Denise Kimber Buell, "Race and Universalism in Early Christianity," *JECS* 10 (2002): 429–68.

Human" (*Ap. John* II 2.24–25), was arguably to underscore univer-
salizing implications. That is, although not everyone would accept
it, or even come to realize it within the space of one incarnation,
eventual salvation was available in the revealed knowledge and ritual appropriation of one's Human lineage.[50]

Sethian writings also manifest a particular concern to explain age-
old issues surrounding the experience of good and evil. In writing
against his acquaintances whom we know to have been using "Sethian"
writings, Plotinus notes that they complain about the stark economic
disparities in society, the injustices in the distribution of wealth and
poverty, and all of the other unequal circumstances that make life
like nothing more than a sporting match with winners and unlucky
losers (*Enn.* 2.9.9). Epiphanius, also, gives the impression that the
"Sethians" whose teachings he describes were particularly concerned
about "justice"; they asserted that the race of Seth itself was instituted to establish justice and destroy the angelic powers responsible
for the cosmos (*Pan.* 39.2.5).

Sethian mythologies provided explanations for the presence of evil
and injustice that were likely compelling to some people because of
the ways in which these myths distanced divinity from responsibility for moral disorder and any other imperfections in the cosmos,
while at the same time they offered assurance that the divine was
nevertheless intimately involved in and in control of the progress of
events in this life. The Invisible Spirit did not create the material
world, or the imperfect cosmic rulers who did fashion it, or the
morally frail human creatures who struggle so unsuccessfully with
sinful impulses. On the other hand, Sethian traditions frequently
stress in various ways that the divine is present in, or is in control
over, the course of events. Even demiurgical activity by ignorant or
scheming archons can be characterized as something operating by
the "will" of the highest divinity.[51] This can be couched in terms of
the pervasive and saving presence of divine Providence behind the
unfolding of events, offering the reassurance that a benevolent divine
presence oversees the struggle of humans, however much they may
seem caught up in a disordered and unpredictable whirl of cosmic

---

[50] See Williams, *Rethinking "Gnosticism,"* 189–212.
[51] E.g., *Hyp. Arch.* 88.10–11; 88.33–34; 96.11–14; cf. *Ap. John* II 19.18–25; 24.1–3;
Holy Book (Gos. Eg.) III 56.22–57.11 (where the rulership over "chaos and Hades"
by Sakla comes about by a proclamation from the heavenly light Eleleth).

Fate.[52] One can even find statements that sound virtually pantheistic, affirming that the divine dwells within every power and every movement in matter and in all the archons, angels, demons and souls in the cosmos.[53] Scholars have argued with some justification that Sethian texts are often more "dualistic" in their portrait of evil in the cosmos than, say, Valentinian traditions, because many of the Sethian sources paint the demiurge(s) and other cosmic powers as more actively malevolent.[54] Nevertheless, this must be qualified given the assurances also found in some of the same Sethian writings of the secret presence and activity of the divine in the arena of the material world.

This theme of the unseen entrance of the divine into the cosmos, undetected by the powers of evil, was clearly popular in Sethian circles.[55] It was an expression of the conviction that even in a realm where injustice and evil might seem to operate unchecked, the divine Spirit was at work and was invulnerable, and divine values such as truth, justice, love, friendship, or goodness[56] would be vindicated. Myth often provides narrative avenues for thinking about tensions among conflicting values and insights in human experience and arriving at more satisfying resolutions. At least in Western traditions, cosmological myths that include lower-order creators have been one kind of strategy to allow the affirmation of ultimate moral value and order in the face of weak or vulnerable evidence for these in quotidian human experience. Such myths account for *why* life in this world is imperfect and sometimes seemingly chaotic, in spite of a conviction that existence is fundamentally ordered and directed toward a meaningful end. Sethian traditions remain among the classic examples of this interpretive strategy.

---

[52] E.g., *Ap. John* II 30.11–31.25; cf. *Holy Book (Gos. Eg.)* III 42.3; 43.6; 63.21–25; IV 58.23; *Marsanes* 1.24–25; see Williams, *Rethinking "Gnosticism,"* 202–8.

[53] So *Trim. Prot.* 35.12–20; 47.19–22.

[54] E.g., King, *What is Gnosticism?* 159–160, who, however, rightly notes that this general characterization must be qualified in light of the "less radical philosophical monism" of Sethian works such as *Marsanes* or *Allogenes*.

[55] E.g., *Ap. John* II 30.20–21; *Holy Book (Gos. Eg.)* III 63.10–15; *Apoc. Adam* 77.10–15; *Zost.* 4.29–31; 130.10–13; *Trim. Prot.* 47.24–26; 49.6–20; Epiphanius, *Pan.* 40.7.1 (where Seth/"Allogenes" is invisible to the powers of the world after he descends from his vision). Of course, a variety of other writers outside Sethian circles also used similar motifs of divine disguise or deception. To give only a few examples: 1 Cor 2:8; Ign., *Eph.* 19.1–2; *Ascension of Isaiah* 9.15; 10.7–13; Origen, *Hom. Luc.* 3.3–4 (on Luke 1:11); 6.5 (on Luke 1:24–32); cf. Athanasius, *De incarnatione,* 16.

[56] E.g., *Holy Book (Gos. Eg.)* III 60.30–31; 62.20; 68.19–23; *Melch.* 1.17.

Though "Sethianism" never achieved long-term sociological stability to the extent of becoming a highly organized and numerically dominant religious movement, it is notable that persons who must have represented quite a range of social and religious or philosophical connections, over a period of at least two or three centuries, apparently experienced the rediscovery of membership in the family of Seth and Adamas to be in some sense redemptive and profoundly empowering. In the rather astonishingly different adaptations in which many of the same Sethian mythemes were celebrated— from the dense mythic history and baptismal ritual formulas in the *Holy Book of the Great Invisible Spirit* to the more abstract and philosophical ascent visions and speculations of *Allogenes*—we can still behold something of the intensity that this mythological tradition inspired.

Bibliography

Barry, Catherine, Wolf-Peter Funk, Paul-Hubert Poirier, and John D. Turner, eds. *Zostrien (NH VIII,1)*. Bibliothèque copte de Nag Hammadi, "Textes" 24. Québec: Les presses de l'Université Laval; Louvain: Peeters, 2000.

Baynes, Charlotte A. *A Coptic Gnostic Treatise Contained in the Codex Brucianus (Bruce MS. 96. Bod. Lib. Oxford)*. Cambridge: Cambridge University Press, 1933.

Buell, Denise Kimber. "Race and Universalism in Early Christianity." *Journal of Early Christian Studies* 10 (2002): 429–68.

Böhlig, Alexander, and Frederik Wisse, eds. *Nag Hammadi Codices III,2 and IV,2: The Gospel of the Egyptians (The Holy Book of the Great Invisible Spirit)*. Nag Hammadi Studies 4. Leiden: E. J. Brill, 1975.

Corrigan, Kevin. "Positive and Negative Matter in Later Platonism: The Uncovering of Plotinus's Dialogues with the Gnostics." Pages 19–56 in *Gnosticism and Later Platonism*. Edited by John D. Turner and Ruth Majercik. SBL Symposium Series 12. Atlanta: Society of Biblical Literature, 2000.

Dahl, Nils. A. "The Arrogant Archon and the Lewd Sophia." Pages 689–712 in vol. 2 of *The Rediscovery of Gnosticism: Proceedings of the International Conference on Gnosticism at Yale, New Haven, Connecticut, March 28–31, 1978*. Edited by Bentley Layton. Studies in the History of Religions 41. Leiden: E. J. Brill, 1981.

Doresse, Jean. *The Secret Books of the Egyptian Gnostics: An Introduction to the Gnostic Coptic Manuscripts Discovered at Chenoboskion*. Translated by P. Mairet. New York: Viking Press, 1960.

Funk, Wolf-Peter, Jean-Pierre Mahé, and C. Gianotto, eds. *Melchisédek (NH IX,1)*. Bibliothèque copte de Nag Hammadi, "Textes" 28. Québec: Les presses de l'Université Laval; Louvain: Peeters, 2000.

Hedrick, Charles W., ed. *Nag Hammadi Codices XI, XII, XIII*. Nag Hammadi Studies 27. Leiden: E. J. Brill, 1990.

Jackson, Howard M. "Geradamas, the Celestial Stranger." *New Testament Studies* 27 (1981): 385–94.

King, Karen L. *Revelation of the Unknowable God, with Text, Translation, and Notes to NHC XI,3 Allogenes*. California Classical Library. Santa Rosa, Calif.: Polebridge, 1995.

————. *What is Gnosticism?* Cambridge, Mass.: The Belknap Press of Harvard University Press, 2003.

Klijn, A. F. J. *Seth in Jewish, Christian and Gnostic Literature.* Supplements to Novum Testamentum 46. Leiden: E. J. Brill, 1977.

Layton, Bentley. "Prolegomena to the Study of Ancient Gnosticism." Pages 334–50 in *The Social World of the First Christians: Essays in Honor of Wayne A. Meeks.* Edited by L. Michael White and O. Larry Yarbrough. Minneapolis: Fortress, 1995.

Layton, Bentley, ed. *The Rediscovery of Gnosticism: Proceedings of the International Conference on Gnosticism at Yale, New Haven, Connecticut, March 28–31, 1978.* 2 vols. Studies in the History of Religions 41. Leiden: E. J. Brill, 1980–81.

Logan, Alastair H. B. *Gnostic Truth and Christian Heresy: A Study in the History of Gnosticism.* Peabody, Mass.: Hendrickson, 1996.

MacRae, George W. "The Jewish Background of the Gnostic Sophia Myth." *Novum Testamentum* 12 (1970): 86–101.

McGuire, Anne M. "Valentinus and the *gnostikê hairesis*: Irenaeus, *Haer.* I.xi.1 and the Evidence of Nag Hammadi." Pages 247–52 in *Studia Patristica* 18. Edited by E. A. Livingstone. Kalamazoo: Cistercian Press, 1985.

Painchaud, Louis, and Anne Pasquier, eds. *Les textes de Nag Hammadi et le problème de leur classification: Actes du colloque tenu à Québec du 15 au 10 Septembre 1993.* Bibliothèque copte de Nag Hammadi, "Études" 3. Québec: Presses de l'Université Laval; Louvain: Peeters, 1995.

Pearson, Birger A., ed. *Nag Hammadi Codices IX and X.* Nag Hammadi Studies 15. Leiden: E. J. Brill, 1981.

————. *Nag Hammadi Codex VII.* Nag Hammadi and Manichaean Studies 30. Leiden: E. J. Brill, 1996.

Pétrement, Simone. *A Separate God: The Christian Origins of Gnosticism.* Translated by Carol Harrison. San Francisco: HarperCollins, 1990.

Robinson, James M., ed. *The Nag Hammadi Library in English.* 3rd rev. ed. San Francisco: Harper & Row, 1988.

Schenke, Hans-Martin. "Das sethianische System nach Nag-Hammadi-Handschriften." Pages 165–73 in *Studia Coptica.* Berliner Byzantinistische Arbeiten 45. Edited by Peter Nagel. Berlin: Akademie-Verlag, 1974.

————. "The Phenomenon and Significance of Gnostic Sethianism." Pages 588–616 in vol. 2 of *The Rediscovery of Gnosticism: Proceedings of the International Conference on Gnosticism at Yale, New Haven, Connecticut, March 28–31, 1978.* Edited by Bentley Layton. Studies in the History of Religions 41. Leiden: E. J. Brill, 1981.

Schmidt, Carl, and Violet MacDermot. *The Books of Jeu and the Untitled Text in the Bruce Codex.* Nag Hammadi Studies 13. Leiden: E. J. Brill, 1978.

Scott, Alan B. "Churches or Books? Sethian Social Organization." *Journal of Early Christian Studies* 3 (1995): 109–22.

Sevrin, Jean-Marie. *Le dossier baptismal Séthien: Études sur la sacramentaire gnostique.* Bibliothèque copte de Nag Hammadi, "Études" 2. Québec: Les presses de l'Université Laval; Louvain: Peeters, 1986.

Sieber, John, ed. *Nag Hammadi Codex VIII.* Nag Hammadi Studies 31. Leiden: E. J. Brill, 1991.

Stroumsa, Gedaliahu A. G. *Another Seed: Studies in Gnostic Mythology.* Nag Hammadi Studies 24. Leiden: E. J. Brill, 1984.

Tardieu, Michel. "Les livres mis sous le nom de Seth et les Séthiens de l'hérésiologie." Pages 204–210 in *Gnosis and Gnosticism: Papers read at the Seventh International Conference on Patristic Studies (Oxford, September 8th–13th 1975).* Edited by Martin Krause. Nag Hammadi Studies 8. Leiden: E. J. Brill, 1977.

Turner, John D. "Ritual in Gnosticism." Pages 83–139 in *Gnosticism and Later Platonism.* Edited by John D. Turner and Ruth Majercik. SBL Symposium Series 12. Atlanta: Society of Biblical Literature, 2000.

———. *Sethian Gnosticism and the Platonic Tradition.* Bibliothèque copte de Nag Hammadi, "Études" 6. Québec: Les presses de l'Université Laval; Louvain: Peeters, 2001.

Waldstein, Michael, and Frederik Wisse, eds. *The Apocryphon of John. Synopsis of Nag Hammadi Codices II,1; III,1; and IV,1 with BG 8502,2.* Nag Hammadi and Manichaean Studies 33. Leiden: E. J. Brill, 1995.

Williams, Michael Allen. *Rethinking "Gnosticism": An Argument for Dismantling a Dubious Category.* Princeton: Princeton University Press, 1996.

Wisse, Frederik. "Stalking Those Elusive Sethians." Pages 563–78 in vol. 2 of *The Rediscovery of Gnosticism: Proceedings of the International Conference on Gnosticism at Yale, New Haven, Connecticut, March 28–31, 1978.* Edited by Bentley Layton. Studies in the History of Religions 41. Leiden: E. J. Brill, 1981.

THE SCHOOL OF VALENTINUS[1]

Ismo Dunderberg

The school of Valentinus was one of the most significant early Christian groups rejected by representatives of nascent Christian orthodoxy. Irenaeus, bishop of Lyons, wrote already in the 180s a five-volume refutation against Valentinians, now usually called *Adversus haereses* (*Against Heresies*). Irenaeus' major concern was that Valentinians did not form a dissident group of their own but remained within the Church. They confessed, Irenaeus admits, "God the Father" and "our Lord Jesus Christ,"[2] claimed to have "the same doctrine" as other Christians, and resented to being called heretics.[3] They also employed New Testament writings as proof texts for their views.[4] The difference between Valentinians and other Christians was, thus, far from obvious.

Irenaeus' most important goal was to make this difference clear.[5] He wanted to lay bare secret teachings of Valentinians which, in his opinion, ran contrary to Christian faith. Irenaeus constructed his opponents' views in order to show their deviation from what he considered to be the orthodox Christian faith. In so doing, Irenaeus produced the first systematic presentation of the rule of faith (*regula fidei*) that was later used to determine Christian orthodoxy. In addition, his work became a model and major source of information for other anti-Valentinian polemicists, such as Hippolytus of Rome and Tertullian in the early third century, and Epiphanius of Salamis in the fourth.

---

[1] In addition to the editors of this book, I would like to express my heart-felt thanks to Birger Pearson for reading the penultimate draft of this chapter and suggesting some important additions to it.

[2] Irenaeus, *Haer.* 4.33.3.

[3] Irenaeus, *Haer.* 3.15.2.

[4] A sample of Valentinian interpretations of texts in the New Testament is offered by Irenaeus, *Haer.* 1.8.

[5] For Irenaeus' strategy of "making a difference," see now Elaine Pagels, "Irenaeus, 'the Canon of the Truth,' and the *Gospel of John*: 'Making a Difference' through Hermeneutics and Ritual," *VC* 56 (2002): 339–71.

Before the Nag Hammadi Library was found in Upper Egypt in 1945, texts stemming from Valentinian teachers were few, since writings of dissident Christians were actively censored after the nascent orthodox Christianity began to be favored by Roman emperors from the beginning of the fourth century. Only a few fragments from the extensive literary production of Valentinian teachers survived in the works of the early Christian authors who found acceptance by the Church during this period. Already this scanty evidence, however, has demonstrated remarkable deviations from the picture of Valentinianism painted by Irenaeus.

The Nag Hammadi Library brought to light a number of texts written or compiled by Valentinians. These texts bear witness to the continuining popularity of the school of Valentinus in the fourth century, when these texts were copied. They contain little information on the historical development of the school of Valentinus, but the opportunities to assess Valentinian teachings on their own terms have considerably improved due to the new data.

1. *Making a Heretic: Irenaeus' Account of the Valentinians*

Irenaeus' work begins with the so-called "Great Account," which comprises a lengthy presentation of Valentinian theology.[6] This account is no objective description; it is often seasoned with irony and sarcastic remarks. Irenaeus intended to brand his opponents as propagating mere absurdities. This strategy proved effective in years to come. In the introduction to a popular translation of Irenaeus' work in *Ante-Nicene Fathers* from the end of 19th century, it was still affirmed:

> It may be made matter of regret, that so large a portion of the work of Irenaeus is given to an exposition of manifold Gnostic speculations. Nothing more absurd than these has probably ever been imagined by rational beings . . . by giving loose reins to their imagination they built up the most incongruous and ridiculous systems; while, by deserting the guidance of Scripture they were betrayed into the most pernicious and extravagant errors.[7]

---

[6] Irenaeus, *Haer.* 1.1–7.
[7] "Introductory Note to Irenaeus' Against Heresies," *ANF* 1:311.

While this statement bears witness to an uncritical adoption of
Irenaeus' viewpoint, recent scholarship has been more critical in
tracing Irenaeus' tendentiousness embedded in his account of Valentinian theology.[8] The Valentinian "system" described by Irenaeus
is basically his construction and did not exist as such before him.
He pulled together one body of thought from diverse written and
oral sources,[9] but he did not reproduce these sources word for word.
His account is, rather, a summary, or an *epitome*, the purpose of
which was to give to his readers a general outline of the Valentinian
body of thought.[10] While Irenaeus occasionally mentions examples
of diversity in Valentinian views, his general approach tends to give
a more unitarian and systematic picture of Valentinian theology than
it really had.

Moreover, composing a summary is a selective process. It reflects
not only what is found in various sources but also what the composer finds noteworthy in these sources. Since Irenaeus wanted to
distiguish between right and wrong forms of Christianity, he con-
centrated on the issues that, in his view, made this difference clear.
Consequently, his account revolves around two issues. First, there is
a difference in teachings about God. Valentinians did not attribute
the creation of the world to the supreme God but to an inferior and
ignorant creator-God whom they, following Platonic philosophical
tradition, called the demiurge ("craftsman"). Second, Irenaeus emphasizes the Valentinian distinction between "psychic" (from Gr. *psychē*,
"soul") and "pneumatic" (from Gr. *pneuma*, "spirit") human beings.
He employs this distinction to portray Valentinians as an elitist, arrogant, and morally indifferent group who considered themselves spiritual Christians, while ordinary members of the Church belonged to
an inferior class of "psychic" Christians. Irenaeus claims that this
distinction made Valentinian Christians to take liberties that they did
not allow to other members of the Church. This accusation proves
problematic, however, if it is compared to what is said about psychic and spiritual Christians in primary sources. Nevertheless, this

---

[8] For Irenaeus' manner of constructing Valentinian theology, see, above all, Alain
Le Boulluec, *La notion d'hérésie dans la littérature grecque IIe–IIIe siècles* (2 vols.; Paris:
Études augustiniennes, 1985), 1:113–253.

[9] Irenaeus, *Haer.* 1, preface.

[10] For the uses of *epitome*, see H. Gregory Snyder, *Teachers and Text in the Ancient
World: Philosophers, Jews and Christians* (London: Routledge, 2000), 13.

picture of Valentinians suits well Irenaeus' purpose of drawing a clear boundary between them and other Christians.

Irenaeus' "Great Account" begins with Valentinian theories about the origin of the world. The process leading to the creation of the world was set in motion in the divine realm called "fullness" (Gr. *plērōma*). In the beginning, there was only the eternal, incomprehensible and invisible Father in "deep quiet and stillness,"[11] who was accompanied by his thought. The Father's thought is also called "Grace" and "Silence." As the Father decided to "emit from himself the beginning of all things," his decision impregnated his thought, Silence, who gave birth to two other divine qualities, Mind and Truth. Thus begins a chain reaction that finally leads to the creation of the sensible world and the human being. First, new pairs of eternal beings called "aeons" (Gr. *aiōn*, "eternity," also "lifetime," "space of time") were being born from conjugal unions of those beings already in existence. The aeons are personified qualities such as Faith, Hope and Love (cf. 1 Cor 13:13), or Union, Pleasure, and Wisdom. They are divided into male and female ones, and each of them has their own partner of the opposite sex.[12]

Personification of abstract qualities in the Valentinian myth was not unique. In the Hebrew Bible, God's wisdom is portrayed as a separate figure who assisted God in creating the world (e.g., Prov 8). Moreover, it is not clear whether the Valentinians really conceived of the aeons as separate divine beings or whether the aeons were only portrayed as such for the purposes of a cosmogonic tale. At least some Valentinians considered the aeons as qualities and dispositions of the supreme God rather than independent divine beings.

Wisdom (*sophia*) plays a crucial role in the Valentinian cosmogonic tale, but her role is strikingly different from that in Jewish Wisdom Literature.[13] In the Valentinian myth, the aeons have in common their "desire to seek their First-Father." Nevertheless, only Wisdom, the youngest of all aeons, is bold enough to act according to this desire. The consequences are both unexpected and far-reaching. There are two Valentinian versions as to what Wisdom did in the

---

[11] Irenaeus, *Haer.* 1.1.1.

[12] For sexual imagery used by Valentinians in describing the aeons, see now April D. De Conick, "The Great Mystery of Marriage: Sex and Conception in Ancient Valentinian Traditions," *VC* 57 (2003): 316–20.

[13] Irenaeus, *Haer.* 1.2.1–6.

divine pleroma. According to one version, she wanted to understand the Father's greatness. Since this was impossible due to his "unsearchable nature," Wisdom's attempt was doomed to failure. Her failure, in turn, aroused in her emotions that made her weak. In another version, Wisdom wanted to create something on her own, without the consent of her divine spouse. Since her male partner was not involved, Wisdom gave birth to a being devoid of form. In this version, Wisdom's emotions grief and fear were triggered by seeing the formless creature she had made.

In both versions, Wisdom's wrong intention and emotions are removed outside the divine realm.[14] They become substances laying the basis for the creation of the world. Wisdom's intention gave rise to the spiritual substance, and her emotions to the material one. Another, inferior Wisdom is created from these substances. She is also called Achamoth. The name is a pun based upon a Hebrew word *hokhmoth* used of the personified figure of Wisdom in the Hebrew Bible. Achamoth was formless to begin with, but she was provided with a form by the heavenly Christ who visited her from the divine realm. As Christ returned to the pleroma, Achamoth became seized with emotions (grief, fear, and perplexity). Most importantly, however, she has the ability to convert to what is better, to Christ who gave her form. This ability is characteristic of the third substance that now emerges. This substance is called "psychic nature" (*to psychikon*), and it makes conversion possible. Hence the origin of three substances (spiritual, psychic, and material), upon which is built the Valentinian division of humankind into three classes, the spiritual, the psychic, and the material.

While Wisdom in Proverbs assists God in creating the world, the Valentinian Achamoth creates the demiurge, who then creates "the heavenly and earthly things." The demiurge belongs to the middle class of psychic beings; the spiritual substance is not bestowed upon him. The demiurge is also ignorant of the supreme God and the divine realm, and imagines that he is the only God. The ignorant demiurge acts, however, at the instigation of Achamoth and makes use of the three substances that are already in existence. The Valentinian demiurge is not identified with the devil, as the creator-God

---

[14] Irenaeus, *Haer.* 1.4.1–5.

Yaldabaoth is in some Sethian texts.[15] Instead, the devil is part of the demiurge's creation.[16]

The spiritual, psychic and material substances are of different origin and have different determination. The spiritual and material ones are opposites to each other: the former will be saved and the latter will perish no matter what; the former cannot be corrupted, and the latter cannot be saved. The psychic nature lies in the middle, between the two opposites; hence its ability to "go over to that element to which it has an inclination."[17]

All three substances were present in the first human being, Adam. It would seem natural to assume, therefore, that they are bestowed on all other human beings as well. According to Irenaeus, however, this was not the case. He claims that Valentinians divided humankind into three classes, and that neither promotion nor degradation from one class to another was possible. Valentinians held themselves to be the spiritual ones who will be saved in any case due to their nature, while other members of the Church were the psychic ones characterized by ambivalence. Consequently, the latter could be saved only if they were "made steadfast by works and bare faith."[18]

Valentinian teaching as portrayed by Irenaeus excludes, thus, every chance of getting in, or falling away from, the spiritual class. Irenaeus constructs Valentinian theology at this point in a way that fits well his purpose of drawing boundaries, for his portrayal made Valentinianism a far less attractive option to non-Valentinian Christians to whom his work was addressed. The same purpose was served by Irenaeus' claim that the certainty of salvation made Valentinians prone to evil deeds: they had no qualms about eating meat offered to idols, attending pagan festivals and gladiator shows, nor defiling women who have joined them.[19] Moreover, Irenaeus implies that sexual defilement takes place in the Valentinian bridal chamber ritual which "they must always and in every way put into practice."[20]

Irenaeus obviously attempted to make the Valentinian lifestyle as despicable and non-attractive as possible to his audience. It remains

---

[15] On the Sethian demiurge, see Williams' article in this book.
[16] Irenaeus, *Haer.* 1.5.1–6.
[17] Irenaeus, *Haer.* 1.6.1–2.
[18] Irenaeus, *Haer.* 1.6.2.
[19] Irenaeus, *Haer.* 1.6.3.
[20] Irenaeus, *Haer.* 1.6.4.

unclear, however, how reliable his description of Valentinian moral teaching and practice is. Allegations of indifference find no support in the Valentinian texts of the Nag Hammadi Library. Not only do they not encourage licentious behavior, but there are also examples of moral exhortation that are completely absent in Irenaeus. Interestingly, he does mention that there were some Valentinians who tried to live irreproachably. According to Irenaeus, these Valentinians did not fare much better than the licentious ones, for their more ambitious life style only made them irritatingly arrogant![21] In any case, this part of Irenaeus' portrayal shows that his claims about the licentiousness of Valentinians were greatly exaggerated and polemic in nature. In addition, other texts show that the boundary between spiritual and psychic Christians was less fixed in Valentinian theology than Irenaeus would have us to believe.[22]

In spite of its polemical perspective, Irenaeus' account has assumed a dominant position in scholarly presentations of Valentinian theology. Scattered quotations from Valentinian teachers in other patristic sources have usually been interpreted in light of Irenaeus. In recent years, however, primary sources have been increasingly studied on their own terms. Results have been surprising. It has been affirmed that the surviving fragments from Valentinus' own teaching betray no close contact to the Valentinian body of thought described by Irenaeus.[23] Heracleon is another well-known Valentinian teacher whose relationship to Irenaeus' account of Valentinianism has proved remote.[24] Similar problems even pertain to Ptolemy, though it was his disciples from whom Irenaeus solicited information.[25] The way Ptolemy portrays the figure of the demiurge in his *Letter to Flora* is not entirely compatible with Irenaeus' account of the teachings of his followers.

---

[21] Irenaeus, *Haer.* 3.15.2.

[22] Cf. Michel R. Desjardins, *Sin in Valentinianism* (SBLDS 108; Atlanta, Ga.: Scholars Press, 1990), 124–26; Michael A. Williams, *Rethinking "Gnosticism": An Argument for Dismantling a Dubious Category* (Princeton: Princeton University Press, 1996), 189–93, 211–12.

[23] Christoph Markschies, *Valentinus Gnosticus? Untersuchungen zur valentinianischen Gnosis mit einem Kommentar zu den Fragmenten Valentin* (WUNT 65; Tübingen: J. C. B. Mohr [Paul Siebeck], 1992).

[24] Ansgar Wucherpfennig, *Heracleon Philologus: Gnostische Johannesexegese im zweiten Jahrhundert* (WUNT 142; Tübingen: J. C. B. Mohr [Paul Siebeck], 2002).

[25] Irenaeus, *Haer.* 1, preface.

Nevertheless, the Valentinian cosmogonic myth described by Irenaeus was not his own invention. There is multiple attestation for the existence of the basic Valentinian myth, though there is considerable variation in details. Other patristic authors offer slightly different versions of the Valentinian myth which are in part independent of Irenaeus.[26] In addition, the Valentinian *Tripartite Tractate* provides us with a lengthy first-hand account of this myth.

The Valentinian cosmogonic myth was similar both in structure and narrative details to that in the *Apocryphon of John*. Thus, there must have been some affinity between the Valentinian and Sethian cosmogonic myths. The Sethian version seems more archaic; features that were most likely to offend many contemporary groups (both Christians and non-Christian philosophers alike), like the portrayal of the demonic creator-God Yaldabaoth, seem to have been toned down in the Valentinian myth. This suggests that the Sethian version of the myth is earlier. There is, however, no consensus about this issue; some scholars think that the Sethian myth is later than the Valentinian one and based upon it.[27]

In addition, discrepancies in the sources raise the question of continuity in the school of Valentinus. There must have been some reasons for the lumping together of these teachers in ancient sources, but it is more difficult to tell what these reasons were exactly. Irenaeus draws a distinction between the Valentinian public (exoteric) and secret (esoteric) teaching. This distinction has been invoked to account for differences between Irenaeus and primary sources.[28] In so doing, scholars have often too readily taken over Irenaeus' point of view and accepted his account as a disclosure of what Valentinians really taught. Nevertheless, the possibility that Valentinians offered instruction at different levels cannot be discarded altogether. Ptolemy's *Letter to Flora* offers direct evidence for this view of education (see below).

Moreover, Valentinians were regarded by their contemporaries as a school of thought, and they themselves employed terminology

---

[26] Most important variants are reported by Clement (*Exc.*) and Hippolytus (*Haer.*).

[27] Cf. Alastair H. B. Logan, *Gnostic Truth and Christian Heresy: A Study in the History of Gnosticism* (Edinburgh: T&T Clark, 1996), 55; Simone Pétrement, *A Separate God: The Origins and Teachings of Gnosticism* (trans. C. Harrison; San Francisco: Harper San Francisco, 1984), 418–19.

[28] Cf., e.g., Harold W. Attridge, "The Gospel of Truth as an Exoteric Text," in *Nag Hammadi, Gnosticism, and Early Christianity* (ed. C. W. Hedrick and R. Hodgson; Peabody, Mass.: Hendrickson, 1986), 239–55.

related to a school setting.[29] The idea of instruction at different levels
may have come naturally in this context, since in ancient schools of
thought advanced discussion was often confined to insiders.[30] The
setting of a school also provided a forum for learned discussion about
different opinions. This may in part account for the characteristic
diversity of Valentinian theology.

2. *Valentinus*

Irenaeus used the term "the school of Valentinus"[31] and spoke about
his "school (*didaskaleion*) of distinct character."[32] Thus, Valentinus was
from early on considered the founder of an early Christian school
of thought. However, only scattered references to him and his career
have survived in ancient sources. Valentinus most likely originally
came from Egypt, arrived in Rome at the end of 130s, and remained
there for fifteen to twenty years.[33] Unlike Marcion, he was never
expelled from the Roman Christian community.[34] It is even related
that Valentinus ran for the office of the bishop of Rome, but was
defeated by a candidate who had publicly confessed his faith under
persecution.[35] Doubts can be raised as to historical reliability of this
story,[36] but its existence suggests that Valentinus enjoyed some popularity in Rome.

---

[29] For Valentinians as an early Christian school of thought, see Gerd Lüdemann,
"The History of Earliest Christianity in Rome," *The Journal of Higher Criticism* 2
(1995): 112–41, esp. 129; Christoph Markschies, "Valentinian Gnosticism: Toward
the Anatomy of a School," in *The Nag Hammadi Library After Fifty Years: Proceedings
of the 1995 Society of Biblical Literature Commemoration* (ed. J. D. Turner and A. McGuire;
Nag Hammadi and Manichaean Studies 44; Leiden: E. J. Brill, 1997), 436–38;
Anne McGuire, "Valentinus and the *Gnostike Hairesis*: An Investigation of Valentinus'
Position in the History of Gnosticism," (Ph.D. diss., Yale University, 1983), 20–21.

[30] Cf. Ismo Dunderberg, "Valentinian Teachers in Rome," in *Christians as a
Religious Minority in a Multicultural City: Modes of Interaction and Identity Formation in Early
Emperial Rome* (ed. M. Labahn and J. Zangenberg; JSNTS 243; London: T&T Clark,
2004), 157–74.

[31] Irenaeus, *Haer.* 1.30.15.

[32] Irenaeus, *Haer.* 1.11.1. The reference to a school is blurred in Unger and
Dillon's English translation of this passage: "his peculiar system of doctrine."

[33] The dates are based on Irenaeus (*Haer.* 3.4.3), who mentions that Valentinus
was in Rome during the time of three different bishops, Hyginus (136–140), Pius
(140–155) and Anietus (155–166).

[34] Cf. Lüdemann, "The History of Earliest Christianity in Rome," 123.

[35] Tertullian, *Val.* 4.1–2. According to Tertullian, it was Valentinus' resentment
caused by this event that made him invent his heresy.

[36] Cf. Markschies, *Valentinus Gnosticus*, 308.

It is unclear whether Valentinus ever left Rome. Epiphanius claimed that Valentinus was shipwrecked on Cyprus, went mad and became heretic there, but this story is hardly more than a malevolent rumor.[37] It is, nevertheless, possible that Valentinus returned to Egypt at some later point. This would explain the fact that so many quotations from his works are preserved in the *Stromateis* of Clement of Alexandria.

Less than a dozen short passages from Valentinus' writings have survived in the texts of authors accepted in the nascent orthodox church. Even some of these passages are probably not authentic.[38] Although the genuine fragments offer only a very limited glimpse at Valentinus' literary activity, they show that he composed letters, sermons, and poems.[39] Moreover, the fragments clearly demonstrate the Christian profile of Valentinus' teaching. He found important to affirm that it is Jesus who reveals the Father.[40] He also quoted from the Gospel of Matthew;[41] whether he knew other early Christian gospels cannot be known with certainty.[42]

Valentinus' Christian vantage point becomes also visible in his peculiar theory about the divine essence of Jesus:[43]

---

[37] Epiphanius, *Pan.* 31.7.2. For a critical assessment of this passage, see Markschies, *Valentinus Gnosticus*, 331–34.

[38] In my references to Valentinus' fragments, I follow Völker's traditional system. Fragments 1–6 are derived from Clement's *Stromateis* (2.36.2–4 [1]; 2.114.3–6 [2]; 3.59.3 [3]; 4.89.1–3 [4]; 4.89.6–90.1 [5]; 6.52.3–53.1 [6]), and fragments 7–8 from Hippolytus' *Refutatio omnium haeresium* (6.42.2 [7]; 6.37.7 [8]). While these fragments are likely to be authentic, two other passages attributed to Valentinus in the texts of Pseudo-Anthimus (*De Sancta Ecclesia*, 9 [9]) and Photius (*Cod.* 230 [10]) are dubious; cf. Markschies, *Valentinus Gnosticus*. Markschies also suggests that there is still another passage in Hippolytus (*Haer.* 10.13.4) which could possibly be added to the genuine fragments of Valentinus (ibid. 276–90). (An alternate reference system has been proposed by Bentley Layton, *The Gnostic Scriptures* [Garden City, N.Y.: Doubleday, 1987], 229–49, who has arranged the fragments "according to the order of events in the gnostic myth" [p. 229]. The Fragments A-H in Layton correspond to the traditional numbering in the following manner: A = Frag. 7; B = Frag. 9; C = Frag. 1; D = Frag. 5; E = Frag. 3; F = Frag. 4; G = Frag. 6; H = Frag. 2. "Hr" in Layton equals to Frag. 8 in Völker).

[39] Letters: frags. 1–3; sermons: frags. 4 and 6; a poem: frag. 8.

[40] Valentinus, Frag. 2 (H in Layton).

[41] Frag. 2 (H in Layton) contains quotations from Matt 5:18 and 19:17.

[42] If Valentinus was the author of the *Gospel of Truth*, it would follow that he knew the Gospel of John (cf. Layton, *The Gnostic Scriptures*, 251). The attribution of the *Gospel of Truth* to Valentinus is, however, uncertain (see below). As for other early Christian gospels, I find it possible that Valentinus may have known the *Gospel of Thomas*; cf. Dunderberg, "From Thomas to Valentinus: Genesis Exegesis in the Fragment 4 of Valentinus and Its Relationship to the *Gospel of Thomas*," in *Thomasine Traditions in Antiquity* (ed. J. Ma. Asgeirsson, A.D. De Conick, and R. Uro; Nag Hammadi and Manichaen Studies; Leiden: E. J. Brill, forthcoming).

[43] Valentinus, Frag. 3 (E in Layton; trans. Layton with modification).

> He was continent, enduring all things. Jesus practiced divinity; he ate
> and drank in a special way, without excreting his solids. He had such
> a great capacity for continence that the nourishment within him was
> not corrupted, for he did not experience corruption.

From the modern perspetive, speculation about Christ's digestion
may seem odd and Valentinus' solution that Christ ate and drank
but did not defecate may even sound distasteful. Yet in the ancient
Church Valentinus' theory was one attempt to solve a burning theological issue. It was considered a crucial witness for Christ's incarnation that he ate and drank,[44] but it was difficult to reconcile this
idea with the divinity of Jesus. A purely docetic position would have
been that Christ had an ostensible body that needed neither food
nor drink. While this view was rejected by the Church, there were
other theories that came quite close to it. Clement of Alexandria
insisted that Christ "ate not because of his body that was sustained
by the Holy Spirit" but because he wanted to reject the docetic
heresy in advance![45]

Clement and Valentinus shared the idea that Christ had an unusual
body. Paradoxically, Clement's quip at the docetic position is in itself
one step closer to full-blown docetism than Valentinus' teaching. For
unlike Clement, Valentinus did not maintain that Christ's body did
not need nourishment. In addition, Valentinus' claim that Christ did
not defecate was less original in antiquity than it may sound now.
The same claim was made in other sources of Pythagoras.[46] It may
be, thus, that Valentinus' idea of Christ's digestion was based upon
earlier stories about this legendary Greek sage.[47]

Other fragments of Valentinus also bear witness to the influence
of Greek philosophical traditions. Valentinus took over the Platonic
distinction between the eternal model world of ideas and the sensible world based upon that world.[48] This can be seen in Valentinus'
affirmation that the world was created after a model of "the living
eternal realm (aiōn)."[49] His eloquent poem *Harvest* lends, in turn,

---

[44] E.g., Ign., *Trall.* 9; Irenaeus, *Haer.* 3.22.2.

[45] Clement of Alexandria, *Strom.* 6.71.2; cf. Markschies, *Valentinus Gnosticus*, 99.

[46] Diogenes Laërtius, *Philosophoi bioi* 8.19. A similar story was also told of Epimenides (ibid. 1.114).

[47] For the background of Valentinus' view of Christ's digestion in ancient physio-
logy, see De Conick, "The Great Mystery of Marriage," 313–15.

[48] Markschies, *Valentinus Gnosticus*, 182–83.

[49] Valentinus, Frag. 5 (D in Layton).

expression to a Stoic notion of the all-pervasive spirit which keeps all things together like a cosmic bond:[50]

> I see that all is hung up by the spirit,
> I understand that all is carried by the spirit,
> Flesh, hanging from soul,
> Soul, depending on air,
> Air, hanging from aether,
> Fruits that are borne from the depth,
> A babe that is brought forth from the womb.

These teachings of Valentinus betray no attitude of world-rejection, which has often been considered essential to the distinctly gnostic worldview. Although he did not consider the sensible world a perfect place, he taught that the "invisible essence of God" is reflected in this world and makes it "reliable."[51] Valentinus has no qualms about the Stoic idea of a cosmic harmony supported by the all-pervasive spirit. Valentinus' way of using philosophical traditions suggests, therefore, that his worldview was neither very negative nor strictly dualistic.

It is puzzling that the fragments of Valentinus contain no clear links to the Valentinian body of thought described by Irenaeus. There are no references to the figure of Wisdom, to the demiurge, or to the three classes of humankind. Nevertheless, in his teaching about Adam's creation, Valentinus seems familiar with traditions that could be designated as "gnostic." Valentinus described the confusion of the creator angels arising from their observation that there was in Adam "an essence from above" and "the pre-existent human being." This essence made Adam superior to his creators, and they tried to destroy him. Whether they succeeded in their attempt or not remains unclear in the extant fragment.[52] The closest analogy to this interpretation of Genesis is the account of Adam's creation in the *Apocryphon of John*, the key text bearing witness to Sethian views.[53] The close resemblance suggests that Valentinus either knew the *Apocryphon of John* or was familiar with traditions similar to those attested in this text. This affinity could speak in favor of the idea that Valentinus himself was

---

[50] Valentinus, Frag. 8 (Hr in Layton).
[51] Valentinus, Frag. 5 (D in Layton).
[52] Valentinus, Frag. 1 (C in Layton).
[53] *Ap. John* (NHC II,1) 19–21.

the connecting link between Sethians and later Valentinians.[54] Nevertheless, it is impossible to tell how well Valentinus knew Sethian traditions or how crucial they were to his thinking and teaching.

3. *Other Valentinians: Ptolemy, Heracleon, Theodotus and Marcus*

Hippolytus of Rome says that the Valentinians were divided into
two groups due to their differing views about the body of Christ.
The "Italian" faction taught that Christ had a psychic body, which
the spirit entered in his baptism, while the "Eastern" faction opined
that the Savior's body was also spiritual and that he was born from
the Virgin Mary "as through a pipe," without having any physical
contact with her. Ptolemy and Heracleon are identifed as the most
famous representatives of the Italian group.[55] The term "eastern
teaching" occurs also in the full title of the *Excerpts from Theodotus* by
Clement of Alexandria.[56] This suggests that the Valentinian Theodotus
was associated with eastern Valentinianism from early on.

There is even less biographical data related to Ptolemy, Heracleon
and Theodotus than there was concerning Valentinus, but traces of
their texts remain in patristic sources. Ptolemy's *Letter to Flora* is
quoted completely in the anti-heretical compendium written by
Epiphanius;[57] Origen provides us with quotations from Heracleon's
commentary on the Gospel of John; and quotations from Theodotus
can be found in Clement's aforementioned *Excerpts*.[58]

There is an intriguing possibility that the Valentinian Ptolemy
could be identical with the Ptolemy mentioned by Justin Martyr. In

---

[54] This suggestion has been made, but not carefully argued, by Layton, *The Gnostic
Scriptures*, xv–xvi. Irenaeus (*Haer.* 1.11.1) already held a similar view, saying that
Valentinus had "adapted the principles from the so-called Gnostic heresy. . . ."
Irenaeus' subsequent report about this heresy (*Haer.* 1.29–30) is often considered
evidence for a basically Sethian body of thought.

[55] *Haer.* 6.35.5–7.

[56] The full title of this work is *Excerpts from Theodotus and the So-Called Eastern
Teaching at the Time of Valentinus*.

[57] *Pan.* 33.3.1–7.10.

[58] It is not only difficult to determine which parts in Clement's *Excerpts* stem from
Theodotus and which from other Valentinian teachers, but it is also sometimes
difficult to separate Valentinian teachings from Clement's own comments. Casey's
careful assessment of this issue still seems largely valid to me (Robert P. Casey, ed.,
The Excerpta ex Theodoto of Clement of Alexandria [London: Christophers, 1934], 5–16);
some important modifications to it have been made in Menard's edition.

his *Second Apology*, Justin tells about a Christian teacher called Ptolemy who became a martyr, when Urbicus was the prefect of Rome (144–160).[59] Justin's Ptolemy is not associated with the followers of Valentinus nor does Justin make any critical reservations as to Ptolemy's Christian faith. Speaking against the identification of this Ptolemy with the Valentinian Ptolemy is the fact that Valentinians are condemned in Justin's *Dialogue with Trypho*.[60] This work was, however, composed later than *Second Apology*. This leaves the possibility open that, when writing his *Second Apology* (ca. 152 C.E.), Justin either did not yet know exactly what Valentinians taught, or he did not know about Ptolemy's affinity with the school of Valentinus.

Justin's Ptolemy was a teacher of a Roman woman who, after her conversion, wanted to divorce her husband. It is noteworthy that, in his letter addressed to a woman called Flora, the Valentinian Ptolemy touched upon the issue of divorce as well. Ptolemy argued that the law in the Hebrew Bible permitting divorce does not stem from God, but from Moses. In spite of its lesser origin, Ptolemy sees this law justified insofar as its intention is to prevent a greater damage that would follow if divorce were not allowed. This teaching fits well the situation described in Justin, and therefore supports the possibility that the two Ptolemys were the same person.[61]

Ptolemy's *Letter to Flora* is the only surviving document of his writings.[62] Its careful composition demonstrates Ptolemy's skill in literary style. The letter presents itself as instruction addressed to a beginner. It ends with a promise of further teaching—given that the addressee proves worthy of it.[63] The introductory nature of the letter can be

---

[59] *2 Apol.* 2.

[60] *Dial.* 35.

[61] Proponents of the view that the Valentinian Ptolemy is identical with Justin's Ptolemy include, e.g., Lüdemann, "The History of Earliest Christianity," 127–29; Peter Lampe, *From Paul to Valentinus: Christians at Rome in the First Two Centuries* (ed. Marshall D. Johnson; trans. Michael Steinhauser; Minneapolis: Fortress, 2003), 239–40.

[62] Scholars often attribute the Valentinian body of thought in Irenaeus directly to Ptolemy, but this attribution is unwarranted. As was pointed out above, Irenaeus speaks only of his conversations with Ptolemy's disciples. In the Latin version, Irenaeus' account of Valentinian theology ends with the words "thus indeed Ptolemy" (*et Ptolemaeus quidem ita*). Since these words are missing in the extant Greek version of this text, they are likely to be a later gloss; cf. Lüdemann, "The History of Earliest Christianity," 126.

[63] Ptolemy, *Letter to Flora* in Epiphanius, *Pan.* 33.7.9.

seen in its subject matter as well. Ptolemy presents proofs to the
effect that there exists the demiurge who is neither the supreme God
nor the devil, but a figure between them. The demiurge is neither
good nor evil, but, in a rigid manner, righteous and just. Ptolemy's
view about the demiurge is, thus, quite similar to that of Marcion.[64]

To bring his point home, Ptolemy engages in a careful discussion
about the law in the Hebrew Bible. He distinguishes first between
the divine law and human additions to it; the latter go back to Moses
(including the legislation concerning divorce), and to the elders of
Israel. Then Ptolemy goes on to argue that even the divine part of
the biblical law is not entirely perfect. The divine legislation in the
Hebrew Bible is divided into three parts:

(1) the decalogue,
(2) laws based upon retaliation ("an eye for an eye, a tooth for a
    tooth")
(3) ritual laws

It is the second group that proves significant for Ptolemy's argument.
He admits that the good goal of the laws based upon retaliation is
to prevent evil. In actual fact, however, they increase evil. If a mur-
derer receives a death sentence, there will be at the end two mur-
ders instead of one. This shows that the divine legislator who accepted
retaliatory laws was "fooled by necessity." Hence Ptolemy's conclusion that the god giving these kinds of laws cannot be perfect.

Like Valentinus, Ptolemy argued from an emphatically Christian
point of view. He sought proofs for his views from Jesus and Paul;
the latter was "*the* apostle" for Ptolemy. First, Ptolemy pointed out
that Jesus not only accepted the decalogue, but also "fulfilled" it by
demanding more intense observance of it. The fact that the decalogue needs to be fulfilled by Jesus shows, according to Ptolemy, that
even it was not completely perfect. Second, Ptolemy reminds his
audience that Jesus abolished the laws based upon retaliation (e.g.,
Matt 5:38–39). Third, Ptolemy invokes Paul in arguing that ritual
laws in the Hebrew Bible should be interpreted allegorically.

Ptolemy was clearly aware of other contemporary theories about
biblical law.[65] Above all, his study reflects debates about the Hebrew

---

[64] For Marcion's demiurgism, see Heikki Räisänen, "Marcion," in this volume.

[65] For example, the separation of human additions to the law from the divine
legislation is not very crucial for Ptolemy's own argument, but this theory needed

Bible initiated by Marcion in Rome. Ptolemy's *Letter to Flora* is usually taken as a refutation of Marcion's or his followers' views about the Hebrew Bible.[66] Yet Ptolemy, in fact, adopted Marcion's position to a certain degree.[67] The quotations from Matthew show that Ptolemy did not accept Marcion's canon, nor did he demand abandonment of the Hebrew Bible. But Ptolemy's view about the demiurge, whose legislation shows that he is neither good nor evil but merely righteous, is so close to Marcion's position that it must be assumed that Ptolemy took Marcion seriously and showed partial agreement with his ideas.

Heracleon was the author of the earliest commentary on the Gospel of John known to us thus far. He is also called "the most famous in the school of Valentinus,"[68] but no details of his life have survived. A recent study plausibly suggests that Heracleon, like Valentinus, came from Egypt, made a temporary visit in Rome, and then returned to Egypt.[69] The visit in Rome accounts for Heracleon's association with "Italian" Valentinianism in Hippolytus, while his Egyptian provenance can be deduced from the fact that the fragments of his works stem entirely from two Alexandrian authors, Clement and Origen.

A few fragments from Heracleon's commentary on John have survived in Origen's *Commentary on John*. They show Heracleon's great competence in different areas of textual interpretation, such as text criticism, word explanation, analysis of style, and allegorical interpretation.[70] Like Ptolemy, Heracleon assumed the existence of the inferior demiurge and apparently responded to Marcion in his writings.[71] No clear references to the tale of Wisdom's fall are, however, included in the fragments of Heracleon. For him, the real creator who used the demiurge as a tool was Christ, not Wisdom, as in Irenaeus.[72]

---

to be taken into account, since it had been proposed by some Jews and early Christians (cf. Heikki Räisänen, *Paul and the Law* [Philadelphia: Fortress, 1986; orig. 1983], 135, 225–26).

[66] E.g., Lüdemann, "The History of Earliest Christianity," 133–34; Markschies, "Valentinian Gnosticism," 429.

[67] For a more thorough discussion of this issue, see Dunderberg, "Valentinian Teachers," 162–65.

[68] Clement, *Strom.* 4.71.

[69] Wucherpfennig, *Heracleon Philologus*, 360–71.

[70] Wucherpfennig, *Heracleon Philologus*, 44–45.

[71] Cf. Wucherpfennig, *Heracleon Philologus*, 156–58, 178 etc.

[72] Origen, *Comm. Jo.* 6.39; 13.19.

Heracleon's view of the demiurge is surprisingly positive. He saw in the story of the healing of the royal officer's son in John 4:46–54 an allegorical reference to the demiurge asking the Savior for help, as the human being created by the demiurge was about to die.[73] Heracleon's view coincides with the Valentinian idea attested in Irenaeus that the demiurge became the Savior's follower as soon as the latter entered the world.[74]

Heracleon agrees with Irenaeus' account in presupposing the distinction between the spiritual, the psychic and the material essences. Yet these essences do not denote different classes of Christians, but are interpreted in terms of ethnic identity. Heracleon shared with many other early Christian authors the idea that Christians were neither Greeks nor Jews, but formed the third race (tertium genus).[75] Relying on an early Christian text called Kerygmata Petrou, he taught that, while pagans worship the material world and Jews worship the psychic demiurge and his angels, the spiritual ones worship the true Father.[76] The term "the spiritual ones" is used here for "Christians" in general.

The story of the Samaritan woman in John 4:1–42 was interpreted by Heracleon as describing the awakening of the spiritual essence. Heracleon also maintained that spiritual Christians should bring other people to Christ, just like the woman in the story brought other Samaritans to Jesus.[77] It is a matter of debate whether Heracleon considered the three essences predetermined, as one could assume on the basis of Irenaeus' account.[78] In my view, it is not necessary to assume that Heracleon thought in terms of fixed origins of the three classes of humankind. Rather, he reckoned that progress from one group to another is possible. "Like the woman changes to the

---

[73] Origen, Comm. Jo. 13.60.

[74] Irenaeus, Haer. 1.7.4.

[75] For the definition of Christianity in terms of new ethnicity, see Nicola Denzey, "The Limits of Ethnic Categories," in Handbook of Early Christianity: Social Science Approaches (ed. Anthony J. Blasi, Jean Duhaime, and Paul-André Turcotte; Walnut Greek, Calif.: Altamira, 2002), 502–6.

[76] Origen, Comm. Jo. 13.16.

[77] Origen, Comm. Jo. 13.31.

[78] For this debate, see Jeffrey A. Trumbower, Born from Above: The Anthropology of the Gospel of John (HUT 29; Tübingen: J. C. B. Mohr [Paul Siebeck], 1992), 22–30. Trumbower (p. 29) himself sides with those insisting that, in Valentinianism, "the three classes of human beings were fixed . . . . due to their origin."

man", Heracleon affirms, "a voice" can change to "a word."[79] This interpretation (based upon John 1:23) suggests that, in Heracleon's view, the psychic essence is able transform into the spiritual essence.

Theodotus has provided us with a passage that can be found in almost every course book on gnosticism as a summation of what gnostic thinking is all about:[80]

> It is not only baptism that liberates, but also the knowledge (*gnōsis*) of who we were; what we have become;
> where we were, or where we have fallen into;
> where we hasten to; from what we have been redeemed,
> what is birth; what is rebirth.

One central concept in Theodotus' teaching is *to diapheron sperma*, which he employs for Christians. The Greek term is a *double entendre* that means both the "superior seed" and the "separated seed."[81] Theodotus probably played upon both meanings. On the one hand, the divine seed stems from the divine realm; hence its being "superior." On the other, the seed lives now in separation from the divine realm and must be reintergrated into it. The double view of *to diapheron sperma* becomes visible in Theodotus' interpretation of what it means that Jesus is the door (John 10:7, 9):[82]

> Therefore, when he says, "I am the door," he means that "you, who belong to the superior/separated seed (*to diapheron sperma*) will come to the boundary where I am." When he enters himself, also the seed, gathered and brought in by the door, enters with him to the pleroma.

According to Theodotus, the salvation of the divine seed is a crucial event also for Wisdom and the angels, for they can enter the divine realm only after the superior-but-detached-seed has been brought together.[83]

In the light of his excerpts, Theodotus was closer than any other Valentinian teacher mentioned above to the Valentinian body of thought described by Irenaeus. The *Excerpts* contain clear references to the divine pleroma inhabitated by divine couples and presuppose

---

[79] Origen, *Comm. Jo.* 6.20–21; cf. *Gos. Thom.* 114.
[80] Clement, *Exc.* 78.2.
[81] Cf. Elaine Pagels, "Conflicting Versions of Valentinian Eschatology: Irenaeus' Treatise vs. the Excerpts from Theodotus," *HTR* 67 (1974): 35–53, esp. 41.
[82] Clement, *Exc.* 26.1–2; trans. Casey, with modification.
[83] Clement, *Exc.* 35.

a tale of Wisdom that is very similar to that in Irenaeus.[84] However, Theodotus parts company from Irenaeus' Valentinians as regards the distinction between the spiritual and the psychic ones. Theodotus taught that there will be an eschatological marriage feast in which the spiritual and the psychic ones will be joined to each other and made equal to each other. After this reunion, the spiritual essence departs from the souls and enters the pleroma.[85] The spiritual and the psychic are, thus, two separate groups before the marriage feast, but after it there will no longer be any difference between them. From the assembly of the two groups is, then, selected the spiritual essence (*ta pneumatika*)—not the spiritual ones (*hoi pneumatikoi*)—which attains the ultimate salvation. The distinction between "spiritual" and "psychic" was sustained by Theodotus, but it was not related to two different groups of persons, as in Irenaeus, but to two different essences.[86]

Marcus is, in many respects, a special case in the history of Valentinianism.[87] In light of Irenaeus' account, Marcus' teaching was very similar to the Valentinian body of thought, though he tinged it with speculation on letters and their numerical values.[88] Irenaeus portrays Marcus as a magician who attracted men and women, particularly those belonging to upper classes.[89] Irenaeus says that Marcus lured them with tricks performed with cups of wine and made his female adherents to prophesy. Irenaeus also claims that Marcus gathered a fortune from his rich female adherents, gave them love potions, and had sex with them.[90] There was even an early lampoon of Marcus which Irenaeus quotes in his work:[91]

> Marcus, maker of idols, observer of portents,
> Skilled in astrology and in all arts of magic,
> Whereby you confirm your erroneous doctrines.

---

[84] Clement, *Exc.* 21; 32; 34; 35.1.

[85] Clement, *Exc.* 63.

[86] Pagels, "Conflicting Versions," 44–53.

[87] For Marcus, see especially Niclas Förster, *Marcus Magus: Kult, Lehre und Gemeindeleben einer valentinianischen Gnostikergruppe: Sammlung der Quellen und Kommentar* (WUNT 114; Tübingen: Mohr Siebeck, 1999).

[88] Irenaeus, *Haer.* 1.14–16.

[89] Irenaeus, *Haer.* 1.13.3, mentioning women "who are well-dressed and clothed in purple and who are very rich."

[90] Irenaeus, *Haer.* 1.13.3, 5. He also relates a special case of a deacon in Asia Minor whose beautiful wife "was defiled in mind and body by this magician" (*Haer.* 1.13.5).

[91] Irenaeus, *Haer.* 1.15.6 (trans. Unger and Dillon).

Showing wonders to whomever you lead into error,
Showing the works of the apostate Power,
Marvels which Satan, your father, teaches you always
To perform through the power angelic of Azazel,
Using you as the precursor of godless evil.

For the most part, Irenaeus' information about Marcus seems to be nothing more than malevolent rumors.[92] Nevertheless, Marcus and his followers occasioned some confusion in Christian communities of Asia Minor. One reason for the conflict with them was that women were able to assume a more active role in their meetings than in other Christian groups.[93] Marcosians were also more clearly characterized by their distinct rituals than other Valentinians. Notably, Irenaeus did not call the Marcosians a school, like other Valentinians, but a cult society (*thiasos*).[94] He also devoted much attention to describing the extraordinary practices of this group. Some Marcosians performed a deathbed ritual called "redemption" (*apolytrōsis*). In it, the dying were anointed with oil, or a mixture of oil and water, and supplied with the answers they should give the powers and the demiurge and his assistants in the hereafter:[95]

> I am a child of Father, of preexistent Father. I am a child in the pre-existent one. . . . I am returning to my own, whence I came. . . . I am a precious vase, more precious than the female who made you. . . . I know myself, and I know whence I am, and I call upon incorruptible Wisdom who is in Father and who is the Mother of your Mother who had no Father nor a male consort.

This invocation shows that the Valentinian tale of Wisdom was not only an artificial myth (*Kunstmythus*), but there were Valentinian groups in which the knowledge of this tale was considered necessary for salvation, and a special ritual practice was developed to achieve this salvation.

---

[92] Cf. Förster, *Marcus Magus*, 123–25.

[93] This can be inferred from Irenaeus' emphasis on Marcus teaching women to prophesy, and his account that Marcosians commanded "one another to prophesy"—most likely at their banquets where liturgical tasks were distributed by drawing lots in each meeting separately (*Haer.* 1.13.3–4). Cf. Elaine Pagels, *The Gnostic Gospels* (New York: Vintage Books, 1989; orig. 1979), 40; Förster, *Marcus Magus*, 130–31.

[94] Irenaeus, *Haer.* 1.13.4; cf. Förster, *Marcus Magus*, 129.

[95] Irenaeus, *Haer.* 1.21.5 (trans. Unger and Dillon, with modification). Irenaeus points out that not all Valentinians performed a ritual of redemption, and that, among those who did, it was practiced in different ways.

4. In Their Own Words: The Valentinian Texts of the
Nag Hammadi Library

In the Nag Hammadi Library, there are eight texts that are usually classified as Valentinian:[96]

> Prayer of the Apostle Paul (NHC I,1)
> Gospel of Truth (NHC I,3)
> Tripartite Tractate (NHC I,5)
> Treatise on the Resurrection (Letter to Rheginus, NHC I,4)
> Gospel of Philip (NHC II,3)
> (First) Apocalypse of James (NHC V,3)
> Interpretation of Knowledge (NHC XI,1)
> A Valentinian Exposition (NHC XI,2)

These texts have survived only in Coptic copies, but they were most likely originally composed in Greek; the author of the *Gospel of Philip* was also familiar with Syriac (see below). There are limitations as regards the historical value of these texts: their authors cannot be identified; no Valentinian teacher is mentioned in them by name; and they do not contain any accounts of historical events related to the school of Valentinus. An exact dating of these texts is not possible either. They could have been composed any time after 130 C.E. (the beginning of the school) and before 350 C.E. (the approximate date of the Nag Hammadi codices).

In spite of these restrictions, the Valentinian texts of the Nag Hammadi Library offer significant glimpses of Valentinian theology and moral exhortation.

The *Gospel of Truth* is an intriguing text in more than one respect. Irenaeus mentioned that a text with this name was circulated among Valentinians.[97] The *Gospel of Truth* belonging to the Nag Hammadi Library does not bear a title as some other texts in this collection. The title has been given on the basis of the words found at the outset of this text: "The gospel of the truth is a joy for those who have received grace from the true Father."[98] It is possible, however, that

---

[96] Cf., e.g., Desjardins, *Sin in Valentinianism*, 6; Einar Thomassen, "Notes pour la délimitation d'un corpus valentinien à Nag Hammadi," in *Les Textes de Nag Hammadi et le problème de leur classification* (ed. Louis Painchaud and Anne Pasquier; Bibliothèque copte de Nag Hammadi, "Études" 3; Quebec: Les Presses de l'Université Laval, 1995), 243–63. I will refer to the Nag Hammadi texts by giving their title and page numbers in the original codices.

[97] Irenaeus, *Haer.* 3.11.9.

[98] *Gos. Truth* 16.

the text was already known by this title in antiquity, when writings were often identified by their opening words. It has also been suggested that the *Gospel of Truth* was written by Valentinus himself,[99] but this view has not unanimously been accepted by scholars.

The relationship of the *Gospel of Truth* to the Valentinian body of thought described by Irenaeus is not very close. Wisdom, the demiurge, and the three classes of humankind are not mentioned in it. The origin of the world is mentioned only in passing, but it is explained in a manner that runs parallel to Irenaeus' account: As the entirety searched for the Father in vain, ignorance emerged and caused "fear and anxiety." Anxiety then gave rise to error which worked at matter and created "a substitute for truth."[100]

The *Gospel of Truth* puts emphasis on the revelation Jesus brought to humankind. He enlightened those in forgetfulness and darkness, and brought "many back from error."[101] Christ came to call "those whose names he knew in advance," and they possess the knowledge that makes them his followers.[102] Christ's revelation is described with colorful metaphors and seasoned with allusions to the New Testament: "For when they saw and heard him, he let them taste and smell of himself and touch the beloved son, after he had appeared to tell them about the Father. . . ."[103] There are also references to the crucifixion: "He was nailed to a tree and became fruit of the knowledge of the Father."[104] "Jesus appeared, wrapped himself in that book (of the living), was nailed to a piece of wood, and published the Father's edict upon the cross. O, such a great teaching!"[105] Nothing suggests that the author would have considered the suffering of Christ to be ostensible or that someone else would have died on the cross instead of Christ.

Moreover, while Irenaeus complained that the Valentinians were morally indifferent, the author of the *Gospel of Truth* is occupied with moral exhortation:[106]

---

[99] E.g. Layton, *Gnostic Scriptures*, 221–22, 251.
[100] *Gos. Truth* 17.
[101] *Gos. Truth* 18, 22.
[102] *Gos. Truth* 21–22.
[103] *Gos. Truth* 30; cf. 1 John 1:1.
[104] *Gos. Truth* 19, trans. Layton.
[105] *Gos. Truth* 20, trans. Layton.
[106] *Gos. Truth* 32–33, trans. Layton with modifications.

> Speak . . . from the heart, for it is you that are the perfect day, and
> it is within you that there dwells the light that does not set. Speak of
> the truth with those who seek it, and of knowledge in the midst of
> their error. Make steady the feet of those who have stumbled, and
> stretch out your hands to those who are sick. Feed those who are hun-
> gry, and give repose unto those who are weary; and awaken those
> who wish to arise, and get up from your sleep.

The *Tripartite Tractate* is the largest exposition (about 80 pages) of
Valentinian theology known to us. The title of this work stems from
modern scholars and is based upon the fact that, in the Coptic manuscript, the text has already been divided into three different parts
by means of diples (>>>>>). The first part of the *Tripartite Tractate*
(pp. 54–104) consists of a description of the Father, other eternal
divine beings, and the cosmic household (*oikonomia*), to which also
belongs the demiurge and his assistants. The second part offers only
a brief account of the creation of humankind (pp. 104–8). The third
part is again quite extensive. It introduces several focal points of
Valentinian theology, such as views about the Savior, the tripartite
division of humankind, and views about salvation (pp. 108–38).

One feature peculiar to the *Tripartite Tractate* is the idea that the
confusion in the divine realm was occasioned not by Wisdom, but
by Word (*Logos*). Like Wisdom in other Valentinian sources, Word
is portrayed in this text as the real creator of the world who employed
the demiurge as his "hand and mouth."[107] Clearly different from
other Valentinian texts is the characterization of the demiurge and
his assistants by their "lust for power." The latter is, in fact, a central
theme in the whole text. According to it, "lust for power" pervades
the whole sensible world.

The Church is portrayed in the *Tripartite Tractate* as suffering from
hatred and ill-will of those who have power.[108] The Valentinian tripartite division of humankind is in this text related to the portrayal
of the oppressed Church. Those who persecuted Christ and now
persecute the Church are divided into the psychic and the material
ones. Their difference is that the former can convert to Christianity,
while the latter cannot. To which class a human being belongs
becomes clear only when he or she encounters the Savior and either

---

[107] *Tri. Trac.* 101.
[108] *Tri. Trac.* 121–22.

accepts or rejects him.[109] There is no different salvation for the spiritual and the psychic ones; they all will enter the pleroma.[110]

The *Treatise on the Resurrection* offers instruction in the form of a letter; thus it reminds one of Ptolemy's *Letter to Flora*. The text is addressed to a certain Rheginus, who is otherwise unknown, and it deals with views about the resurrection. The resurrection of body is also discussed in the text, but it remains subject to debate whether it is accepted or denied in the text. There is a key passage that has been interpreted in opposing ways:[111]

> Do not doubt resurrection, my child Rheginus. If you were not in flesh, you took on flesh, as you came into the world. Why will you not take on flesh, when you ascend to the eternal realm.

If the sentence "why will you not take on flesh" in this passage is a rhetorical question, the author simply wants to affirm that believers, as a matter of course, will receive a body of spiritual flesh at the resurrection.[112] The sentence can, however, be understood also as a question posed by an imaginary opponent created by the author. In that case, the author himself would argue *against* the resurrection of the body.[113] What makes the latter interpretation difficult is that the Coptic text does not bear clear signs of introducing the opinion of an imaginary opponent at this point. We cannot be sure whether any clearer indications were available in the Greek original of this text.

---

[109] Cf. H. W. Attridge and E. H. Pagels, "The Tripartite Tractate," in *Nag Hammadi Codex I (The Jung Codex): Introductions, Texts, Translations, Indices* (ed. H. W. Attridge; NHS 22; Leiden: E. J. Brill, 1985), 187.

[110] *Tri. Trac.* 123; cf. Attridge and Pagels, "The Tripartite Tractate," 188–89.

[111] *Treat. Res.* 47. For different translations of this passage based upon different interpretations, see Layton, *The Gnostic Scriptures*, 322; Malcolm L. Peel, "The Treatise on the Resurrection," in *Nag Hammadi Codex I (The Jung Codex): Introductions, Texts, Translations, Indices* (ed. H. W. Attridge; NHS 22; Leiden: E. J. Brill, 1985), 153. I am indebted to Mika Hella for pointing out in his Finnish master thesis on the *Treat. Res.* the crucial difference between Layton's and Peel's interpretations.

[112] Cf. Peel, "The Treatise on the Resurrection," 142–43.

[113] Bentley Layton argued for this reading already in his *The Gnostic Treatise on Resurrection from Nag Hammadi* (HDR 12; Missoula, Mont.: Scholars Press, 1979) and it underlies his interpretation of this text in *The Gnostic Scriptures*, 316–24. Layton's translation of the passage quoted above runs as follows: "Do not be doubtful about resurrection, my child Rheginus. Now (you might wrongly suppose), granted you did not preexist in flesh—indeed you took on flesh when you entered this world— why will you not take your flesh with you when you return to the realm of eternity."

However that might be, the author of the *Treatise on the Resurrection* emphasizes the present aspect of salvation. The resurrection can be experienced already in this life: "If you have the resurrection but continue as if you are to die . . . why, then do I ignore your lack of exercise? It is fitting for each one to practice in a number of ways . . .".[114] The passage shows, moreover, that Valentinian instruction was not only concerned with creating a body of thought but also with a certain lifestyle involving exercise and practice (*askēsis*). Unfortunately, there is no description of what kinds of exercises the author had in mind. There are a variety of possibilities. In ancient schools' thought, such exercises could have been either "physical, as in dietary regimes, or discursive, as in dialogue and meditation, or intuitive, as in contemplation. . . ."[115]

The *Gospel of Philip* is neither a narrative account of Jesus (like the gospels in the New Testament), nor a collection of his sayings (like the *Gospel of Thomas*). It is, rather, a collection of teachings stemming from Valentinian Christians and, possibly, from other early Christians. The title already appears in the manuscript, and it is most likely due to the fact that Philip is the only apostle mentioned by name in the text;[116] otherwise he plays no role in it. The *Gospel of Philip* has no apparent thematic arrangement. Only in a few cases do extracts derived from various sources form larger units dealing with one and the same issue. In addition, the text contains teachings that seem contradictory. For example, the authority of the apostles is called upon in some passages,[117] while in some other passages they are considered outsiders to real Christianity.[118] Similarly, the text refutes those insisting upon the physical resurrection and affirms that the earthly body must be stripped off, but it also criticizes those claiming that the body of flesh will not be raised.[119]

The *Gospel of Philip* bears witness to the Valentinian division between the superior and inferior Wisdom: "Echamoth is one thing and Echmoth another. Echamoth is Wisdom simply, but Echmoth is the

---

[114] *Treat. Res.* 49 (trans. Peel).
[115] Pierre Hadot, *What is Ancient Philosophy?* (trans. M. Chase; Cambridge, Mass.: Harvard University Press, 2002), 6.
[116] *Gos. Phil.* 73.
[117] E.g., *Gos. Phil.* 74.
[118] *Gos. Phil.* 55.
[119] *Gos. Phil.* 56–57, 66.

Wisdom of death which is the one which knows death, which is called 'the little Wisdom.'"[120] In this passage, however, Echamoth is identified with the superior Wisdom, while in Irenaeus the inferior Wisdom was called Achamoth. Both names are variants of the word *hokhmoth* employed for the figure of Wisdom in the Hebrew Bible. The name "Echmoth," used for the inferior Wisdom in this passage means in targumic Aramaic and in Syriac "like death"; hence her identification with the "Wisdom of death." There are also other passages in the *Gospel of Philip* offering explanations based upon Syriac terms. The text stems, thus, most likely from Syria.

The *Gospel of Philip* attributes the creation of the world to an inferior creator-God who made it "in error."[121] Nevertheless, like in some other Valentinian sources, it is affirmed in this text that the demiurge will be saved after all.[122] However, neither Wisdom nor the demiurge play any prominent role in the *Gospel of Philip*. Far more central in it are interpretations of Genesis and selected New Testament passages as well as discussion on Christian sacraments.

Five sacraments are mentioned in the *Gospel of Philip*: baptism, anointing, the eucharist, redemption and the bridal chamber.[123] They are collectively called "a mystery", through which "the Lord did everything." In addition, there is a reference to a holy kiss among the perfect.[124] Baptism, anointing and the eucharist were common to most Christians, whereas the redemption and the bridal chamber seem more distinctly Valentinian rituals.[125] Irenaeus describes different ways of how Valentinians performed the redemption. In addition to the Marcosian death-bed ritual that was already mentioned above, the redemption could be the bridal chamber ritual; baptism involving special Hebrew invocations and anointing; or anointing without baptism. Some Valentinians considered the bridal chamber a completely spiritual thing and did not perform any ritual connected to it.[126]

---

[120] *Gos. Phil.* 60, trans. Isenberg.

[121] *Gos. Phil.* 75.

[122] *Gos. Phil.* 84; cf. Irenaeus, *Haer.* 1.7.1.

[123] *Gos. Phil.* 67.

[124] *Gos. Phil.* 58–59; 63–64.

[125] The bridal chamber was not, however, confined to Valentinian groups; it is also mentioned in non-Valentinian texts (*Dial. Sav.* 138; *Exeg. Soul* 132; *Gos. Thom.* 75; *Treat. Seth* 57). Some of them may also refer to the practice of a bridal chamber ritual.

[126] Irenaeus, *Haer.* 1.21.

The *Gospel of Philip* seems to presuppose the practice of the bridal chamber ritual, but there is no description of how it was performed. The text is more concerned with the spiritual interpretation of the bridal chamber. What happens in it is that the separation that took place at creation is removed: ". . . those who have united in the bridal chamber will no longer be separated. Thus Eve separated from Adam because it was not in the bridal chamber that she united with him."[127] The division of humankind into two sexes is considered as a consequence of the fall, while Christ came to rectify its consequences. The unification of those who were separated from each other takes place in the bridal chamber; hence the identification of Christians as "the children of the bridal chamber."[128]

Views about the bridal chamber in the *Gospel of Philip* are congruent with its emphasis on the present aspect of salvation. This emphasis becomes clearly visible in this text's teaching about the resurrection: "Those who say they will die first and then rise are in error. If they do not first receive the resurrection while they live, when they die they will receive nothing."[129] Unlike the *Gospel of Truth*, the *Gospel of Philip* has a clearly docetic view of Christ: Jesus' cry on the cross (Mark 15:34 and parallels) is understood as bearing witness that the heavenly Christ left him before his death: "'My God, my God, why O Lord, have you forsaken me?' It was on the cross that he (Jesus) said these words, for he (the Lord) had departed from that place."[130]

The (First) Apocalypse of James is a revelation dialogue between Christ and James, whom Christ calls his brother, though affirming that they are not brothers "materially."[131] The eastern provenance of this text is suggested by the fact that it mentions Addai, who according to other sources brought Christianity to Edessa.[132] The revelation described

---

[127] *Gos. Phil.* 70, trans. Isenberg.
[128] *Gos. Phil.* 70–71, 73.
[129] *Gos. Phil.* 90, trans. Isenberg.
[130] *Gos. Phil.* 68, trans. Isenberg. A similar Christology was associated with the followers of Ptolemy in Irenaeus (*Haer.* 1.6.1; 1.7.2); cf. Antti Marjanen, "The Suffering of One Who Is a Stranger to Suffering: The Crucifixion of Jesus in the Letter of Peter to Philip," in *Fair Play: Diversity and Conflicts in Early Christianity: Essays in Honour of Heikki Räisänen* (ed. Ismo Dunderberg, Christopher Tuckett and Kari Syreeni; NovTSup 103; Leiden: E. J. Brill, 2002), 488 n. 6.
[131] *1 Apoc. Jas.* 24.
[132] For the provenance and date of *1 Apoc. Jas.*, see Antti Marjanen, *The Woman Jesus Loved: Mary Magdalene in the Nag Hammadi Library and Related Documents* (Nag Hammadi and Manichaean Studies 40; Leiden: E. J. Brill, 1996), 125–29.

in this text takes place on two separate occasions, first prior to the death of Jesus, and then after his resurrection. It is striking that the instruction connected to the Marcosian redemption ritual in Irenaeus appears in this text in a practically identical form,[133] though the ritual itself is not mentioned in it. As in the *Gospel of Philip*, the Christology in the *(First) Apocalypse of James* is docetic: "Never have I suffered in any way, nor have I been distressed. And this people has done me no harm."[134]

Moral exhortation looms large in the *Interpretation of Knowledge*. Unfortunately, the manuscript of this text is poorly preserved: more than half of its contents is either completely missing or badly damaged.[135] Nevertheless, the author of this text casts a situation in which a community is split into two parties, and urges the audience to reconciliation. The parties are engaged in a debate over charismatic gifts, and this has occasioned discord in the community.[136] The author dissuades one part of the audience from being jealous of the gift God has provided to some members of the community: ". . . it is fitting for [each] of us to [enjoy] the gift that he has received from [God, and] that we not be jealous. . . ." If someone has what the author calls "a prophetic gift", others should share it without hesitation.[137] On the other hand, the author addresses the other party of the debate, the spiritually advanced, as well, warning them against regarding lesser members as ignorant.[138]

Like Paul in 1 Corinthians, the author of the *Interpretation of Knowledge* makes use of rhetorical traditions that were characteristic of Greco-Roman concord (*homonoia*) speeches. Their purpose was to put an end to factionalism in society.[139] In them, thus, the city-state was

---

[133] *1 Apoc. Jas.* 33–35.

[134] *1 Apoc. Jas.* 31.

[135] Michel R. Desjardins, "The Interpretation of Knowledge: Introduction," (unpublished manuscript), 13, offers the following calculation: the Coptic text of *Int. Knowl.* consisted originally of ca. 795 lines, of which 202 lines (25%) are now missing, and 153 lines (20%) are severely damaged. The critical edition of this text by John Turner contains a large number of restorations. Although they show the editor's great erudition and command of the subject, they also may lull one into false confidence as to how much can really be known about the contents of the text.

[136] Klaus Koschorke, "Eine neugefundene gnostische Gemeindeordnung: Zum Thema Geist und Amt im frühen Christentum," *ZTK* 76 (1979): 34–35.

[137] *Interp. Know.* 15.

[138] *Interp. Know.* 17.

[139] For concord speeches, see Margaret M. Mitchell, *Paul and the Rhetoric of Reconciliation: An Exegetical Investigation of the Language and Composition of 1 Corinthians*

"portrayed as a body, and strife, discord, or any civil disturbance as a disease that must be eradicated from it."[140] The metaphor of a body is also used in the *Interpretation of Knowledge*:[141]

> Do not accuse your Head because it has not appointed you as an eye but rather as a finger. And do not [be] jealous of that which has been put in the class of an eye or a hand or a foot, but be thankful that you do not exist outside the body.

Like in some other early Christian texts, Christ is identified in this passage with the "head" of the body.[142] The passage possibly recalls Paul's description of body parts squabbling with each other (1 Cor 12:14–26).[143] The *Interpretation of Knowledge* is, however, closer than Paul to the benevolent patriarchalism inherent in concord speeches.[144] The author of this text follows their usual habit of invoking "the body analogy . . . to solidify an unquestioned status hierarchy."[145] Thus, it is pointed out that inferior members, like a finger, should not be jealous of more important members (eye, hand, foot). The former should be thankful that it may exist in the body.[146] In light of the wider context of the *Intepretation of Knowledge*, the purpose of this description is to petrify a clear hierarchy in the community between those who have the prophetic gift and those who have not.[147]

A Valentinian Exposition bears witness to a cosmogonical tale that is strikingly similar to the Valentinian system described in heresiological sources, especially in Hippolytus.[148] It has been concluded that

---

(HUT 28; Tübingen: J. C. B. Mohr [Paul Siebeck], 1991), 20–64; Dale B. Martin, *The Corinthian Body* (New Haven: Yale University Press, 1995), 38–47.

[140] Martin, *The Corinthian Body*, 42.

[141] *Interp. Know.* 18.

[142] Cf. Eph 1:22; 4:15–16; Col 1:18; 2:19; *1 Clem.* 37.5; Ignatius, *Trall.* 11.2.

[143] The relationship between the two passages is not especially close, however. The body members mentioned in them are only partially the same (Paul: foot/hand; ear/eye; eye/hand; head/feet; *Interp. Know.*: head, eye, finger, foot); *Interp. Know.* does not mention the "shameful parts" (1 Cor 12:23–24) at all; and there are no imaginary discussions between body parts in *Interp. Know.* 18, as there were in Paul.

[144] Cf. Martin, *The Corinthian Body*, 38–46.

[145] Martin, *The Corinthian Body*, 94.

[146] As Martin (*The Corinthian Body*, 94–95) has shown, Paul reverses the traditional usage of the body analogy in affirming the necessity of weaker members (1 Cor 12:22–25).

[147] Cf. Koschorke, "Gemeindeordnung," 41–42.

[148] Cf. Elaine Pagels, "A Valentinian Exposition: Introduction," in *Nag Hammadi Codices XI, XII, XIII* (ed. C. W. Hedrick; NHS 28; Leiden: E. J. Brill, 1990), 89–91, 95.

this text "may be placed in the milieu of one of the western, Italic traditions of Valentinian theology."[149] The badly damaged text begins with an account of how the divine realm originated, and then moves on to a tale of Wisdom being dispelled outside the pleroma, and of the demiurge who made a human being "according to his image on the one hand and on the other according to the likeness of those who exist from the first."[150] In addition, the text contains previously unattested Valentinian interpretations of Genesis, including references to Abel and Cain (Gen 4:1–16), the fallen angels (Gen 6:1–6), and the flood (Gen 6:5–8:22).[151] A *Valentinian Exposition* is followed by five supplements which most likely are excerpts from Valentinian sacramental instruction (*On Anointing; On Baptism A; On Baptism B; On the Eucharist A; On the Eucharist B*).

5. *A School of Thought*

Since Irenaeus portrayed Valentinians as a school, it seems likely that this group had some resemblance to ancient schools of thought. The school terminology also appears in some Valentinian texts. The *Gospel of Truth* describes how Christ appeared "in schools (*mma mǎi cbō*)" and "spoke the word as a teacher (*efoei nousah*)."[152] In the *Interpretation of Knowledge*, Christ is called the "teacher of immortality." As such, he is opposed to the figure of "the arrogant teacher." While Christ represents a "living school," the school of the arrogant teacher is confined to the interpretation of writings that only "taught about our death."[153] Moreover, Valentinians placed emphasis on education in their theology. They considered the world a place of instruction that needs to be visited by those coming from above. A human being is made "a dwelling place . . . for the seeds" and "a school . . . for doctrine and for form."[154]

---

[149] Pagels, "A Valentinian Exposition," 105.

[150] *Val. Exp.* 37, trans. Turner.

[151] *Val. Exp.* 38.

[152] *Gos. Truth* 19.

[153] *Interp. Know.* 9.

[154] For Valentinian emphasis on education, see also Irenaeus, *Haer.* 1.6.1; Heracleon, *Frag.* 36 (Origen, *Comm. Jo.* 13.50); *Tri. Trac.* 104; Holger Strutwolf, *Gnosis als System: Zur Rezeption der valentinianischen Gnosis bei Origenes* (FKD, 56; Göttingen: Vandenhoeck & Ruprecht, 1993), 256.

No information has survived on how the school of Valentinus was organized or whether they owned special buildings or rooms for giving instruction. It seems likely that teachers belonging to this school were active in house churches in Rome and other big cities. That Valentinian teachers had a relatively high level of education can be seen, for example, in Valentinus' poetry, Ptolemy's knowledge of rhetoric, and Heracleon's familiarity with the rules of textual interpretation. These qualities were likely to make Valentinian teachers attractive to the educated members of early Christian communities.

In antiquity, education and wealth usually went together. Therefore, it can be also assumed that the educated early Christians were also the wealthy ones who could afford private houses and opened them for the meetings of Christians. The organizational structure of the early house churches was based upon "extended family structures of the Greco-Roman households."[155] The host who invited Christian meetings to his or her house also "assumed major leadership responsibilities," including the recruitment and sustenance of visiting teachers.[156] In consequence, the teachers' success was largely dependent on the impression they were able to make on the hosts. Teachers who were able to demonstrate good education and creative insights were better off in this situation than their less educated competitors.

Ancient schools differed from each other as to how binding they considered traditions stemming from founders or other early teachers of their schools. Valentinian teachers seem to have belonged to those who tolerated different opinions. While Valentinus made use of traditions attested in Sethian texts in addition to Platonic and distinctly Christian ones, Ptolemy accepted to some degree the radical teaching of Marcion. Moreover, Valentinians were ready to discuss their opinions not only among themselves, but also with outsiders. Although Irenaeus claims that Valentinians revealed their real teachings only to the initiated, he also says that he was able to talk with them about their views and had access to their books as well.

On the other hand, as Ptolemy's *Letter to Flora* indicated, Valentinians distinguished between beginners' instruction and the more advanced

---

[155] William L. Lane, "Social Perspectives on Roman Christianity during the Formative Years from Nero to Nerva: Romans, Hebrews, *1 Clement*," in *Judaism and Christianity in First-Century Rome* (ed. K. P. Donfried and P. Richardson; Grand Rapids, Mich.: Eerdmans, 1998), 213.

[156] Lane, "Social Perspectives on Roman Christianity," 211–12.

teaching. A similar distinction is also indicated in the *Gospel of Philip*: "the disciple of God . . . will look at the condition of the soul of each one and speak with him. . . . To the slaves he will give only the elementary lessons, to the children he will give the complete instruction."[157] The idea of two or more levels of instruction was not unusual in ancient schools of thought. Examples can be derived from Origen, Plotinus, Jewish rabbis, and Hermetic writings to the effect that esoteric teaching was often part of advanced philosophical and religious education.[158] The advanced teaching of Valentinians was not, however, necessarily due to their wish to present themselves as mysterious, as Irenaeus insinuates. It may be that they simply thought that some questions could be dealt with only by those having a sufficient education.

6. *What Happened to the Valentinians?*

In Rome, it seems that Valentinians were able to continue teaching for a long time without any disruption in Christian communities. House churches were independent units, and they did not usually pronounce judgments on the views of other early Christian groups. Justin's attack against the Valentinians and other dissidents seems an exception that proves the rule.[159] There is no evidence that Valentinus or any other Valentinian teacher was excommunicated in Rome in the second century. Even Irenaeus' attack against the Valentinians did not change the situation immediately. Victor, Bishop of Rome (189–199), still had a Valentinian presbyter called Florinus as his assistant.[160]

While some Valentinian Christians remained within the ordinary Christian church, others began to drift apart from it at the turn of the third century. The followers of Marcus differed from other Christians more clearly than Valentinians in general. One sign of their greater distance to other Christians was that Marcosians who

---

[157] *Gos. Phil.* 81, trans. Isenberg.
[158] For evidence, see Dunderberg, "Valentinian Teachers in Rome," 166–68.
[159] Cf. Lampe, *From Paul to Valentinus*, 385–96.
[160] Irenaeus had to urge Victor to read Florinus' writings and to get rid of them (*Frag. syr.* 28). For Florinus, see also Eusebius, *Hist. eccl.* 5.20.4; Lampe, *From Paul to Valentinus*, 389–90.

decided to return to the ordinary Christian community were subjected to public confession in the latter. This practice indicates a
clear barrier drawn between Marcosians and other Christians. In
reality, however, even this boundary was less fixed.[161] As Irenaeus
mentions, "some of the most faithful women, who have the fear of
God and could not be deceived," had visited meetings led by Marcus.[162]
Irenaeus also complains that there are some who "waver between
both courses," being "neither outside nor inside."[163] It was only later,
at the turn of the third century, that Marcosians clearly formed a
church of their own. This development can be seen in Hippolytus
who says that Marcosians had their own bishop who performed the
redemption.[164]

The situation of Valentinians and other dissident Christians wors-
ened dramatically at the beginning of the fourth century, as Constantine
the Great made Christianity the privileged religion in the Roman
empire. From this point on, the orthodox Christians could lean on
authority and the financial support of emperors in their battle against
heretics, to whom Valentinians were included. Constantine's laws
from 326 prohibited heretics from owning properties used for common meetings.

While restrictions on their ownership were not always followed,
heretics became outlaws in the Roman empire. Their meetings were
forbidden in the laws of Theodosius.[165] Books written by the heretics
were censored, which explains the fact that Valentinian writings have
survived only under special circumstances. In addition, emperors tolerated orthodox hooliganism. This can be seen well in the correspondence between Ambrose, Bishop of Milan, and the emperor
Theodosius I from 388 C.E. As Christians had burned down a Jewish
synagogue, the emperor had ruled that its rebuilding should be paid
for by the Church. Ambrose wrote a letter of complaint to the
emperor in which he also mentions Valentinians, whose church furious
monks had burned down earlier.[166] If Christians should pay for the

---

[161] Cf. Förster, *Marcus Magus*, 402.
[162] Irenaeus, *Haer.* 1.13.4.
[163] Irenaeus, *Haer.* 1.13.7.
[164] Hippolytus, *Ref.* 6.41.4–5; cf. Förster, *Marcus Magus*, 155.
[165] Eusebius, *Vit. Const.* 3.64–65; *Cod. Theod.* 16.5.6; cf. Klaus Koschorke, "Patristische
Materialien zur Spätgeschichte der valentinianischen Gnosis," in *Gnosis and Gnosticism*
(ed. M. Krause; NHS 17; Leiden: Brill, 1981), 124–25, 134–35.
[166] The Valentinian church is often located in Callinicum on the basis of Ambrose's

rebuilding of the synagogue, Ambrose argues, they should also pay for the rebuilding of the Valentinian church. The latter is, however, out of question, for it is impossible for the Church to support heretics. Hence Ambrose's conclusion: the Church should not be burdened with the rebuilding of the destroyed synagogue either. Ambrose's argument proved effective: Theodosius took back his decision and freed the church from reimbursement for the burned synagogue.[167]

Although hooliganism by orthodox Christians was now allowed, Valentinians held out surprisingly long. New stipulations against them were still made in the canons of the second synod of Trulla, held in 692 C.E.[168] It seems likely that, even at this late stage, there were still some Valentinians against whom such regulations were considered necessary. After this date, all traces of them disappear.

Bibliography

Attridge, Harold W. "The Gospel of Truth as an Exoteric Text." Pages 239–55 in *Nag Hammadi, Gnosticism, and Early Christianity*. Edited by C. W. Hedrick and R. Hodgson. Peabody, Mass.: Hendrickson, 1986.

Attridge, Harold W., and Elaine H. Pagels. "The Tripartite Tractate." Pages 159–337 in *Nag Hammadi Codex I (The Jung Codex): Introductions, Texts, Translations, Indices*. Edited by H. W. Attridge. Nag Hammadi Studies 22. Leiden: E. J. Brill, 1985.

Casey, Robert Pierce, ed. *The Excerpta ex Theodoto of Clement of Alexandria*. London: Christophers, 1934.

De Conick, April D. "The Great Mystery of Marriage: Sex and Conception in Ancient Valentinian Traditions." *Vigiliae christianae* 57 (2003): 307–42.

Denzey, Nicola. "The Limits of Ethnic Categories." Pages 489–507 in *Handbook of Early Christianity: Social Science Approaches*. Edited by Anthony J. Blasi, Jean Duhaime, and Paul-André Turcotte. Walnut Greek, Calif.: Altamira, 2002.

Desjardins, Michel R. "The Interpretation of Knowledge: Introduction." (Unpublished manuscript.)

———. *Sin in Valentinianism*. Society of Biblical Literature Dissertation Series 108. Atlanta, Ga.: Scholars Press, 1990.

Dunderberg, Ismo. "From Thomas to Valentinus: Genesis Exegesis in the Fragment 4 of Valentinus and Its Relationship to the *Gospel of Thomas*." In *Thomasine Traditions in Antiquity*. Edited by J. Ma. Asgeirsson, A. D. De Conick, and R. Uro. Nag Hammadi and Manichaean Studies. Leiden: Brill, forthcoming.

———. "Valentinian Teachers in Rome." Pages 157–74 in *Christians as a Religious Minority in a Multicultural City: Modes of Interaction and Identity Formation in Early Imperial Rome*. Edited by M. Labahn and J. Zangenberg. Journal for the Study of the New Testament: Supplement Series 243. London: T&T Clark, 2004.

---

letter. He mentions, however, only that the burned synagogue was there; where the Valentinian church was is not stated in the letter.

[167] Ambrosius, *Ep*. 40–41; cf. Koschorke "Patristische Materialien," 124, 133.

[168] Koschorke, "Patristische Materialien," 125.

Förster, Niclas. *Marcus Magus: Kult, Lehre und Gemeindeleben einer valentinianischen Gnostikergruppe: Sammlung der Quellen und Kommentar.* Wissenschaftliche Untersuchungen zum Neuen Testament 114. Tübingen: Mohr Siebeck, 1999.

Hadot, Pierre. *What is Ancient Philosophy?* Translated by M. Chase. Cambridge, Mass.: Harvard University Press, 2002.

Koschorke, Klaus. "Eine neugefundene gnostische Gemeindeordnung: Zum Thema Geist und Amt im frühen Christentum." *Zeitschrift für Theologie und Kirche* 76 (1979): 30–60.

———. "Patristische Materialien zur Spätgeschichte der valentinianischen Gnosis." Pages 120–39 in *Gnosis and Gnosticism.* Edited by M. Krause. Nag Hammadi Studies 17. Leiden: E. J. Brill, 1981.

Lampe, Peter. *From Paul to Valentinus: Christians at Rome in the First Two Centuries.* Edited by Marshall D. Johnson. Translated by Michael Steinhauser. Minneapolis: Fortress, 2003.

Lane, William L. "Social Perspectives on Roman Christianity during the Formative Years from Nero to Nerva: Romans, Hebrews, *1 Clement.*" Pages 196–244 in *Judaism and Christianity in First-Century Rome.* Edited by K. P. Donfried and P. Richardson. Grand Rapids, Mich.: Eerdmans, 1998.

Layton, Bentley. *The Gnostic Scriptures.* Garden City, N.Y.: Doubleday, 1987.

———. *The Gnostic Treatise on Resurrection from Nag Hammadi.* Harvard Dissertations in Religion 12. Missoula, Mont.: Scholars Press, 1979.

Le Boulluec, Alain. *La notion d'hérésie dans la littérature grecque IIe–IIIe siècles.* 2 vols. Paris: Études augustiniennes, 1985.

Logan, Alastair H. B. *Gnostic Truth and Christian Heresy: A Study in the History of Gnosticism.* Edinburgh: T&T Clark, 1996.

Lüdemann, Gerd. "The History of Earliest Christianity in Rome." *The Journal of Higher Criticism* 2 (1995): 112–41.

Marjanen, Antti. "The Suffering of One Who Is a Stranger to Suffering: The Crucifixion of Jesus in the Letter of Peter to Philip." Pages 487–98 in *Fair Play: Diversity and Conflicts in Early Christianity: Essays in Honour of Heikki Räisänen.* Edited by Ismo Dunderberg, Christopher Tuckett and Kari Syreeni. Novum Testamentum Supplements 103. Leiden: E. J. Brill, 2002.

———. *The Woman Jesus Loved: Mary Magdalene in the Nag Hammadi Library and Related Documents.* Nag Hammadi and Manichaean Studies 40. Leiden: E. J. Brill, 1996.

Markschies, Christoph. "Valentinian Gnosticism: Toward the Anatomy of a School." Pages 401–38 in *The Nag Hammadi Library After Fifty Years: Proceedings of the 1995 Society of Biblical Literature Commemoration.* Edited by J. D. Turner and A. McGuire. Nag Hammadi and Manichaean Studies 44. Leiden: E. J. Brill, 1997.

———. *Valentinus Gnosticus? Untersuchungen zur valentinianischen Gnosis mit einem Kommentar zu den Fragmenten Valentin.* Wissenschaftliche Untersuchungen zum Neuen Testament 65. Tübingen: J. C. B. Mohr (Paul Siebeck), 1992.

Martin, Dale B. *The Corinthian Body.* New Haven: Yale University Press, 1995.

McGuire, Anne. "Valentinus and the *Gnostike Hairesis*: An Investigation of Valentinus' Position in the History of Gnosticism." Ph.D. diss., Yale University, 1983.

Mitchell, Margaret M. *Paul and the Rhetoric of Reconciliation: An Exegetical Investigation of the Language and Composition of 1 Corinthians.* Hermeneutische Untersuchungen zur Theologie 28. Tübingen: J. C. B. Mohr (Paul Siebeck), 1991.

Pagels, Elaine H. "Conflicting Versions of Valentinian Eschatology: Irenaeus' Treatise vs. the Excerpts from Theodotus." *Harvard Theological Review* 67 (1974): 35–53.

———. *The Gnostic Gospels.* New York: Vintage Books, 1989 (orig. 1979).

———. "Irenaeus, 'the Canon of Truth,' and the *Gospel of John*: 'Making a Difference' through Hermeneutics and Ritual." *Vigiliae christianae* 56 (2002): 339–71.

———. "A Valentinian Exposition: Introduction." Pages 89–105 in *Nag Hammadi Codices XI, XII, XIII.* Edited by C. W. Hedrick. Nag Hammadi Studies 28. Leiden: E. J. Brill, 1990.

Peel, Malcolm L. "The Treatise on the Resurrection." Pages 123–157 in *Nag Hammadi Codex I (The Jung Codex): Introductions, Texts, Translations, Indices.* Edited by H. W. Attridge. Nag Hammadi Studies 22. Leiden: E. J. Brill, 1985.

Pétrement, Simone. *A Separate God: The Origins and Teachings of Gnosticism.* Translated by C. Harrison. San Francisco: HarperSanFrancisco, 1984.

Räisänen, Heikki. *Paul and the Law.* Philadelphia: Fortress, 1986 (orig. 1983).

Snyder, H. Gregory. *Teachers and Texts in the Ancient World: Philosophers, Jews and Christians.* London: Routledge, 2000.

Strutwolf, Holger. *Gnosis als System: Zur Rezeption der valentinianischen Gnosis bei Origenes.* Forschungen zur Kirchen- und Dogmengeschichte 56. Göttingen: Vandenhoeck & Ruprecht, 1993.

Thomassen, Einar. "Notes pour la délimitation d'un corpus valentinien à Nag Hammadi." Pages 243–63 in *Les Textes de Nag Hammadi et le problème de leur classification.* Edited by Louis Painchaud and Anne Pasquier. Bibliothèque copte de Nag Hammadi, "Études" 3. Quebec: Les Presses de l'Université Laval, 1995.

Trumbower, Jeffrey A. *Born from Above: The Anthropology of the Gospel of John.* Hermeneutische Untersuchungen zur Theologie 29. Tübingen: J. C. B. Mohr (Paul Siebeck), 1992.

Williams, Michael A. *Rethinking "Gnosticism": An Argument for Dismantling a Dubious Category.* Princeton: Princeton University Press, 1996.

Wucherpfennig, Ansgar. *Heracleon Philologus: Gnostische Johannesexegese im zweiten Jahrhundert.* Wissenschaftliche Untersuchungen zum Neuen Testament 142. Tübingen: Mohr Siebeck, 2002.

MARCION

Heikki Räisänen

Some years ago, the reaction of a distinguished "common reader" of the Bible to the use made of the Old Testament in a sermon provoked a noteworthy debate in the Lutheran church of Finland. In his memoirs, Mauno Koivisto, former President of the Republic, criticised a bishop who had defended the rights of refugees by quoting a verse from the Pentateuch. The President said that he found it dishonest to pick one emblematic humane sentence from the "books of Moses," since elsewhere "the same Moses" gives extremely brutal commands. The President referred to the story in Num 31:14–20, in which Moses gets angry at his troops who, returning from a revenge campaign that was ordained by the Lord, have allowed the women and children of Midian to live. Moses orders the troops to kill "all males among the little ones" as well as "every woman who has known man by lying with him." In distinct contrast, the Israelite soldiers are advised to keep alive for themselves all those young girls who are still virgins.

Another top politician continued this discussion in the press, likewise wondering whether one is allowed to "select from Moses" passages which correspond to our modern views of justice. Is this honest, he asked, as in so many cases men and women are killed without any mercy at all, or when whole peoples and cities are destroyed? Is not our moral integrity threatened, if we pick and choose particular passages from "Moses," forgetting meanwhile those divine orders which seem outdated and unjust? These well-meant critical questions evoked less-than-polite comments from theological quarters.

1. The Great Rival of the Orthodox Church

A debate like this reminds one of Marcion, a second-century Christian dissenter, who was also morally offended by numerous Old Testament passages—and whose ideas were likewise rudely rejected by the orthodox. His conclusion was that the church had to get rid of such a book. This conflict with the orthodox resulted in Marcion's founding a church of his own which for centuries was a real challenger to the emerging Catholic church. Marcion's church flourished in the latter half of the second century; only after 200 C.E. did the Catholics definitely gain the upper hand.[1] "For many in the second century, whether Christian believers or outside observers, the word 'Christianity' would have meant 'Marcionite Christianity.'"[2] Although Marcion's church already faded in the West before the time of Constantine, it remained strong for centuries in the East. Before Constantine, the Roman state did not distinguish between orthodox and heretic; Catholic and Marcionite Christians died side by side in religious persecutions. Constantine, however, having put an end to these persecutions, soon took action against "heretical" Christians. In the times of his successors, the state and mainstream church joined forces in order to destroy rival congregations. It was not easy. As late as the fifth century, a Syrian bishop boasted of converting no less than eight Marcionite villages—thousands of people—to the true faith. In the East, traces of Marcionite groups are found in Arabic sources as late as the 10th century.[3]

Marcion was felt to be a real danger by mainstream church. Orthodox theologians wrote countless works to refute the teachings of this "wolf of Pontus" and "first-born of Satan." Marcion wrote a work called *Antitheses*, and produced a revised edition of Luke's gospel and Paul's letters. None of his work has survived; our information about it comes solely from his opponents. The main source is the thorough refutation of Marcion's teachings written by Tertullian (*Adversus Marcionem*).[4]

The most important study of Marcion remains the comprehensive work by Adolf von Harnack (first edition, 1921; the enlarged second edition of 1924 was reprinted in 1996).[5] Harnack also presents most

---

[1] Gerhard May, "Markion/Markioniten," *RGG* (4th ed.) 5:834.

[2] Stephen G. Wilson, *Related Strangers: Jews and Christians 70–170 C.E.* (Minneapolis: Fortress, 1995), 208.

[3] Marco Frenschkowski, "Marcion in arabischen Quellen," in *Marcion und seine kirchengeschichtliche Wirkung/Marcion and His Impact on Church History* (ed. Gerhard May and Katharina Greschat; Berlin: Walter de Gruyter, 2002), 39–63.

[4] The edition and translation used is *Tertullian, Adversus Marcionem* (ed. and trans. Ernest Evans; Oxford Early Christian Texts; Oxford: Oxford University Press, 1972).

[5] Adolf von Harnack, *Marcion: Das Evangelium vom fremden Gott. Eine Monographie zur Geschichte der Grundlegung der katholischen Kirche. Neue Studien zu Marcion* (Darmstadt: Wissenschaftliche Buchgesellschaft, 1996). Page numbers marked with an asterisk (*) refer to the appendices (Beilagen) where the source material is collected.

of the available source material, gleaned from a number of patristic sources. Subsequent research has provided corrections on individual points,[6] and Harnack's impressive overall picture hasn't gone unchallenged either.[7] It is agreed that Harnack was right in emphasising (more than anybody else had done) Marcion's historical significance, but it is also becoming clear that he drew too modern a picture, presenting Marcion as a precursor of Luther—and of Harnack himself.[8]

2. *Marcion's Life*

The story of Marcion may evoke the gospel story of Jesus' encounter with a rich man. As is well known, Jesus' demand "go and sell everything and follow me" caused the rich man in question to go away grieving. Marcion, however, was a well-to-do businessman who did not turn away. Even if he did not sell all of his possesions,[9] he invested them in the cause of the gospel. Marcion himself led an ascetic life, which he also required of his adherents.

Marcion was a shipowner (or overseas merchant)[10] from Pontus, according to Epiphanius from Sinope at the Black Sea. Sinope was an important Greek port, which had also been the home town of the famous Cynic philosopher, Diogenes. Jewish communities had long existed in Pontus. Aquila, the co-worker of Paul, came from Pontus (Acts 18:2), as did his later namesake, the proselyte Aquila, who became known as translator of the Hebrew Bible (and was actually a contemporary of Marcion).[11] We will see that Marcion seems to have had connections with Jewish teachers.

---

[6] See, e.g., Barbara Aland, "Marcion (ca. 85–160)/Marcioniten," *TRE* 22 (1992), 98–99.

[7] See now the important congress volume Gerhard May and Katharina Greschat, eds., *Marcion und seine kirchengeschichtliche Wirkung/ Marcion and His Impact on Church History* (Berlin: Walter de Gruyter, 2002).

[8] Cf. Gerhard May, "Marcion ohne Harnack," in May and Greschat, *Marcion*, 6–7; Wolfram Kinzig, "Ein Ketzer und sein Konstrukteur: Harnacks Marcion," ibid. 271–73.

[9] Some scholars assume, however, that Marcion did sell his ship to be able to give a donation to the Roman church.

[10] Regarding Marcion's occupation, see Gerhard May, "Der 'Schiffsreeder' Markion," *Studia Patristica* 21 (ed. E. A. Livingstone; Leuven: Peeters, 1989), 142–53.

[11] According to Epiphanius, he, too, was of Sinope.

Marcion was born towards the end of the first century, possibly around the year 85 C.E. One tradition[12] has it that his father was the Bishop of Sinope. This is not impossible,[13] though Tertullian, in his comprehensive refutation (which does contain hints at Marcion's background), does not seem to know of any such thing. The same tradition further claims that Marcion was expelled from the congregation by his own father. The reason suggested is fanciful: Marcion is said to have seduced a young girl. This allegation is merely a historicised allegory: Marcion corrupted the pure church through his teaching. Should the information concerning the expulsion be correct, the reason must have been of a doctrinal nature.[14] Yet, in that case Marcion would have been considered a dangerous heretic indeed, and it is hard to believe that the congregation of Rome—by which Marcion was heartily welcomed—would have been wholly ignorant of the matter. Modern scholars are increasingly inclined to reject as unreliable all information concerning Marcion's life prior to his arrival in Rome.[15] Even Tertullian seems to have no knowledge of his earlier activities.

Whatever his background, around the year 140 C.E. Marcion sailed to Rome in a ship of his own. He joined the local congregation there and bestowed it with the tremendous sum of 200,000 sesterces (Tertullian, *Praescr.* 30). Inner-Christian diversity flourished in Rome at that time. Christians were divided into relatively independent "house churches" that congregated in private homes; in these small circles diverse opinions were both held and expressed. Among the more critical members of the Roman church were intellectuals such as Cerdo, Valentinus and Ptolemy. Gradually, however, Marcion became a matter of growing concern for the brothers. The

---

[12] The most important source here is the so-called "Pseudo-Tertullian," who is supposed to have used a lost work (called *Syntagma*) by Hippolytus.

[13] 1 Peter 1:1 presupposes that there were Christians in Pontus at the end of the first century (at the latest); this is confirmed by the famous letter to emperor Trajan by Pliny, the governor of Pontus and Bithynia, in which he asks how to handle the Christians (*Ep. Tra.* 10.96).

[14] Thus Harnack, *Marcion*, 23–26, who thinks that, expelled from Sinope, Marcion embarked upon a "propaganda trip" to Asia Minor, eventually ending up in Rome.

[15] See, e.g., Jürgen Regul, *Die antimarcionitischen Evangelienprologe* (Vetus Latina: Aus der Geschichte der lateinischen Bibel 6; Freiburg: Herder, 1969), 177–95; May, "Schiffsreeder," 150; May, "Marcion," 834–35; Aland, "Marcion," 90–91. For a different view, see Gerd Lüdemann, *Heretics: The Other Side of Early Christianity* (trans. John Bowden; London: SCM, 1996), 295–96 n. 513.

situation became critical when, after a few years, Marcion challenged the Roman presbyters to discuss his interpretation of the faith. It can be surmised that he had used these years for his text-critical work, which meant to disclose the original message of Christianity. Patristic sources (e.g., Tertullian, *Marc.* 1.2) claim that he had close connections with the Syrian gnostic Cerdo, who may have influenced his views. This assertion is, however, dubious.[16]

The discussions, in which Marcion set forth his doctrine of two gods, led to a break between himself and the Roman congregation in the year 144;[17] the money donated by Marcion was returned.[18] Marcion did not give in, but instead founded a community of his own, whose organisation and functions were rather like those of the mainstream church, and started a large propaganda campaign (which was no doubt considerably aided by the economic means at his disposal). His message found a wide echo within Christianity. Perhaps a decade later, Justin Martyr rhetorically complained in his *First Apology* (26.5–6) that Marcion's error had spread all over humankind. Tertullian, for his own part, noted at the end of the century that "Marcion's heretical tradition has filled the whole world" (*Marc.* 5.19). The exact date that Marcion died is not known. It is assumed that he was not active in his church for more than approximately fifteen years after the break with Rome.[19]

---

[16] For a recent critique of it, see David W. Deakle, "Harnack & Cerdo: A Reexamination of the Patristic Evidence for Marcion's Mentor," in May and Greschat, *Marcion*, 177–90.

[17] The date is based on a statement by Tertullian (*Marc.* 1.19): the Marcionites of his time held that the break had occurred 115 years and six and a half months after Jesus' appearance in the fifteenth year of Tiberius (29 C.E.). R. Joseph Hoffmann, *Marcion: On the Restitution of Christianity: An Essay of the Development of Radical Paulinist Theology in the Second Century* (American Academy of Religion, Academy Series 46; Chico: Scholars Press, 1984) dates Marcion's activity in a considerably earlier time, but his attempt has been generally rejected (see, e.g., Aland, "Marcion," 90).

[18] It is not quite certain whether Marcion was expelled or whether he himself chose to go his own way. The return of his money favours the former alternative.

[19] According to Tertullian (e.g. *Praescr.* 30), Marcion lived during the emperor Antoninus Pius (138–161), whereas Clement of Alexandria (*Strom.* 7.17) states that he was no longer alive during the time of Marcus Aurelius (161–180). A legend told by Tertullian says that on his death-bed Marcion repented and asked for admission to the Catholic church. This is wholly incredible.

3. *The Outline of Marcion's Thought World*[20]

Marcion was not a philosopher or a systematic theologian, but for the most part a "biblicist" who pondered upon texts. The only direct quotation from his work that we have (if it is genuine) is the opening of the *Antitheses*. In it, the gospel is programmatically praised in a manner which suggests that Marcion's theological conviction was based on an experience of grace as a gift: "Oh fullness of wealth, folly (cf. 1 Cor 1:18), might, and ecstasy, that no one can say or think anything beyond it, or compare anything to it!"[21]

Marcion's thought world is based on his literal understanding of the Bible, although his final conclusions differ drastically from any biblical lines of thought. He subjected the Bible (i.e., what Christians call the "Old Testament") to a rigorous criticism. To be sure, the allegorical interpretation of biblical passages which were offensive, if taken literally, can be construed as an implicit criticism, and allegorical exegesis was routinely practised in most Christian circles, as well as in certain Jewish ones. Marcion, however, rejected allegory and was explicit in his criticism.

Marcion concluded that the Old Testament God could not be the Father of Jesus. The Old Testament speaks of a creator whose foremost quality is "righteousness" according to the principle of retaliation: "an eye for an eye." He is a harsh ruler, whose characteristics include passion for war and a thirst for blood. Therefore, Marcion said, this God resembles a tree that produces bad fruit. Jesus' simile of a good and a bad tree (Luke 6:43) was indeed Marcion's point of departure for these discussions, which led to his break with Rome. The imperfection of the creator is shared by his creation. According to the principle of retaliation, most people face judgment and perdition in the afterlife.

But, claims Marcion, suddenly and unexpectedly (not anticipated by any prophecies), in the fifteenth year of Tiberius, an unknown God appeared, who was pure goodness. He came in the form of his Son Jesus (there are in Marcion's Christology features of "modalism": the one God takes on different "modes" in different connections), in

---

[20] For general accounts, see Harnack, *Marcion*; Hoffmann, *Marcion*; Aland, "Marcion."
[21] The quotation has been preserved by an unknown Syriac author; see Harnack, *Marcion*, 256*.

the words of the apostle (Rom 8:3) "in the likeness of flesh" (*Marc.*
1.19.2). Jesus could not be a real human being,[22] since the humans
made by the creator are imperfect. He taught people goodness,
exhorting them to overcome the law of righteousness with love. While
the God of the Old Testament stood for the law, the new God represented the gospel. The separation of law and gospel was indeed
the cardinal point of Marcion's theology. Faith meant the acceptance of this God's offer of goodness. This God does not judge anybody except "passively" by allowing the godless to remain in their
error (*Marc.* 1.25–26).

According to Marcion, the creator did not recognise this God, but
had him crucified and sent him to Hades. There, however, Christ
continued his redemptive work. He bought free from the power of
death people who had belonged to the creator. In Hades, a stun-
ning version of Paul's "justification of the ungodly" took place. The
impious of the Old Testament—Cain, Korah and his company, the
Sodomites, the Egyptians—believed and were redeemed. By contrast,
Israel's pious ancestors from Noah and Abraham onward were too
closely bound up with their creator to be able to accept Christ's
invitation.[23] They imagined that the creator was yet once more tempting them with error, as he had done so many times, so they did
not respond to Jesus (Irenaeus, *Haer.* 1.27.3). But for this they are
pitied, rather than blamed, by Marcion.

Marcion found that there were many disgusting things in the created world (insects, for instance!). His overall hostility to matter took
expression in asceticism, and the Marcionites did not marry. Anything
"fleshly" was detested by Marcion. Sexual intercourse, even in marriage, was seen as no better than fornication. In second century
Christianity, such an attitude was not unheard-of; it represented one
fairly popular trend of the time. Fasting was abundant in Marcion's
congregations; strict dietary regulations were observed. Contemporary
Christian authors routinely revel in scourging the alleged immoral-

---

[22] Marcion inferred from Luke 11:27–28 that Jesus was not born of a woman.
Jesus was a being similar to the angels who had visited Abraham (*Marc.* 3.9.) One
should note that neither modalism nor docetism had been officially condemned during Marcion's time.
[23] Marcion concluded from the story of the Rich Man and Lazarus (Luke 16:19–31)
that Abraham still dwelt in Hades (not in Heaven) during Jesus' life-time (*Marc.*
4.34).

ity of their adversaries, but no such accusation is ever raised against
Marcion or his church. In Marcion's church, stern morality combined with a readiness for martyrdom. At best, opponents could
claim that Marcion's belief in a God, who in his goodness does not
punish wrong-doers, *ought* to have led to libertinism. Marcion's reply
to such theorising is, like Paul's (cf. Rom 6:1, 15), a terrified *absit,
absit* ("by no means!"; *Marc.* 1.27). The morality was connected with
a willingness to martyrdom; even Marcion's church had plenty of
blood witnesses. In several stories it is told how orthodox and Marcionite martyrs die side by side. Evidently asceticism, fasting and
martyrdom were programmatic expressions of defiance against the
creator and his creation.

The much-debated issue of whether or not Marcion was a gnostic is largely a question of definition. Gnosticism was not a mono-
lith; recently doubts have been expressed regarding the usefulness of
the term altogether.[24] Marcion's notion of an inferior creator God,
his negative view of the world and corporeality, and his criticism of
the Old Testament come close to views commonly considered "gnostic," but other views of his do not. Marcion acknowledges no divine
spark in man; man is not akin to the Redeemer. Salvation does not
consist in the return of the dispersed elements to the divinity, but
in freedom from the creator's law. Actually faith is emphasised more
than insight or knowledge by Marcion. Even his docetism is incomplete: Christ suffers and dies. The roots of Marcion's theology are
in Paul's thought. Perhaps one can speak of "a brand of Paulinism
already open to gnostic influence."[25]

4. *Marcion's Criticism of the Bible*

For mainstream expositors, the Old Testament was, for the most
part, important as a collection of alleged predictions and promises
about Jesus, which were "discovered" in the Old Testament through

---

[24] See in particular Michael Allen Williams, *Rethinking "Gnosticism": An Argument
for Dismantling a Dubious Category* (Princeton: Princeton University Press, 1996).
[25] Wilson, *Strangers*, 214. Christoph Markschies turns the tables and suggests that
full-blown Valentinian Gnosticism (which emphasised the unity of the Divinity) may
have been a *reaction* to Marcion's dissociation of two gods! "Die valentinianische
Gnosis und Marcion—einige neue Perspektiven," in May and Greschat, *Marcion*,
159–75.

the use of allegorical and typological devices. Allegorising also helped one to side-step various difficulties caused by many biblical passages, if they were to be understood literally. By contrast, Marcion read the Old Testament in a literal way, and abstained from explaining away the difficulties. His suspicion of allegory was indeed "a mark of uniqueness in that age."[26]

On the other hand, Marcion regarded the text of the Old Testament in itself as reliable. Unlike the extant gospels and Pauline letters, it was not corrupt; no secondary additions had been made to it (as Ptolemy was to claim in his *Letter to Flora*). The Old Testament was a trustworthy account of the past and even of the future of the Jews; they had reason to expect the Messiah (who was *not* identical with Marcion's Christ) promised to them by Scripture. Yet the contents of the book were subjected to harsh criticisms by Marcion. He pointed out one contrast after another between the two gods.[27] For instance:

- The creator is "a judge, fierce and warlike." "Joshua conquered the holy land with violence and cruelty; but Christ prohibits all violence and preaches mercy and peace . . ."
- The creator commanded the Israelites to leave Egypt with shoes on their feet, a staff in their hand, and a sack on their shoulders, and to take with them the gold and silver of Egypt; Christ sent his disciples into the world without shoes, knapsack, extra clothes or money (Tertullian, *Marc.* 2.21).
- The creator says: love the one who loves you and hate your enemy; Christ says: love your enemies.
- "The prophet of the creator" (Joshua) stopped the sun so that it would not set before the people had revenged their enemies (Josh 10:12–14); the Lord says, "Do not let the sun go down on your anger" (Eph 4:26).
- The prophet of the creator (Moses) stretched out his arms toward God in order to kill many in war (Ex 17:11–13); the Lord stretched out his hands (on the cross) to save people.

Marcion seized on every opportunity to point to a contrast—or to construct one. Christ said: "Let the children come to me." By contrast, the prophet of the creator invited wild bears from the forest

---

[26] E. C. Blackman, *Marcion and His Influence* (London: SPCK, 1948), 116.
[27] Documentation in Harnack, *Marcion*, 272*, 273*, 281*, 282*.

to tear up children—some boys who had mocked Elisha for being bald-headed (2 Kgs 2:22, 24; Tertullian, *Marc.* 4.23–25).

Marcion even pays attention to what might be called the "human rights of the Canaanites" in his ironical comment: "Good indeed is the God of the law who envied the Canaanites to give to the Israelites their land, houses they had not built and olive trees and fig trees they had not planted."

Marcion criticises the creator God for acting in a self-contradictory manner. The creator prohibits work on the Sabbath, but tells the Israelites to carry the ark around Jericho (to make the walls of the town collapse) for eight days in a row (i.e., even on a Sabbath [Tertullian, *Marc.* 2.21]). He forbids images, yet tells Moses to make a bronze serpent. He requires sacrifices and then rejects them; he elects people and then repents of his choices. He creates darkness and evil (Jes 45:7; Tertullian, *Marc.* 2.14), sends disasters—and then repents of them. Marcion identified the creator with the evil tree that produces evil fruit, mentioned by Jesus, and assumed that there absolutely had to be another God to correspond to the good tree.

Of course, Marcion was very one-sided in his scathing criticisms. He took up the dark sides, contradictions and problems with the Old Testament, paying no attention to the large amount of other materials which reflect a more profound, less narrow image of God. Tertullian, though weak in his answers to the criticisms just mentioned, presents a wealth of material in which the creator shows his concern for the poor, or even demands of love for one's enemies (*Marc.* 4.14–16). Yet, to Marcion goes the credit for not explaining away the moral problems raised by the Old Testament. His reaction resembles the reaction of radical feminists to a Bible experienced as hopelessly patriarchal—and also the reaction of many common readers of the Bible. Marcion read the Old Testament with common sense, and exposed a problem which lay dormant in the basics of Christianity: it had adopted a scripture, the contents of which partly refuted its own teachings.

5. *The Problem of Continuity in Marcion's Sources*

The key to the contrast between the old and new order was derived from Paul, in particular, from his letter to the Galatians. If Marcion's picture of Paul is one-sided, it is no wonder, because Galatians is one-sided, especially when compared to Paul's letter to the Romans. Even in modern scholarship, one's overall picture of Paul depends on whether Galatians is read in light of Romans, or vice versa. In Galatians, Paul speaks in a negative tone regarding Old Testament law; he even obliquely suggests that it may not stem from God at all (Gal 3:19–20). Paul equates Torah with the (demonic?) "elements of the world" (Gal 4:3–5) and the holy Jewish rite of circumcision with castration (Gal 5:12).[28] A scholar of the Jewish-Christian relations notes that "we are not really very far here from Marcion's radical solution"; Marcion "did no more than push the apostle's thought to its logical conclusion."[29] In Romans, Paul is at pains to find more continuity between the law and his gospel, although a good deal of ambiguity remains.

Although Paul struggled until the end of his life to maintain some form of continuity between his old and new faith, and although he always wanted to remain a Jew, he did state that Christ put an end to the law (Rom 10:4), and said that Jesus had liberated the believers from its curse (Gal 3:13). Paul even stopped consistently observing the food regulations required by the law (or at least part of them, when he was in a non-Jewish environment). These dietary laws were fundamental to Jewish identity, since they had been ordained by God in the Holy Scripture. Nevertheless, Paul, hard-pressed between the sacred tradition and his new faith, was still struggling to find a solution to his dilemma. Marcion, on the other hand, a few generations later, coolly drew his own logical conclusion: an order that loses its validity can hardly have been divine to begin with (that is, not ordained by the true, "alien" God). For God, of course, cannot change his mind. Marcion's conclusion thus paralleled the inference that Paul's Jewish contemporaries[30] drew from Paul's practice: for them, the apostle was an apostate from Judaism.

One of the oddest things about Paul's view of the law was the connection he established between the law and *sin*: that the law can increase or even engender sin, and in fact this is its very purpose

---

[28] Cf. Kari Kuula, *The Law, the Covenant and God's Plan 1: Paul's Polemical Treatment of the Law in Galatians* (Publications of the Finnish Exegetical Society 72; Helsinki: The Finnish Exegetical Society; Göttingen: Vandenhoeck & Ruprecht, 1999).

[29] Marcel Simon, *Verus Israel: A Study of the Relations between Christians and Jews in the Roman Empire (135–425)* (Oxford: Oxford University Press, 1986), 74.

[30] According to Luke (Acts 21:21), even many Jewish Christians.

(Rom 5:20; 7:7). Marcion seized on this assertion: according to him, what is wrong with the law is that it was established in order to arouse and even exuberantly nurture the sin which, prior to it, did not exist. Thus, Marcion asserted, the law *is* sin (Origen, *Commentary in Romans* 4.4; 3.6). The good God puts an end to the law in his goodness; the false apostles try to put it into force again (cf. Gal 2:18).

Harnack found that Marcion's radical step was actually *smaller* than the one taken by Paul; in effect, Paul had already put an end to the Jewish God's order of salvation. Marcion only needed to complete a line of thought which had remained unfinished in Paul.[31] To Harnack's way of thinking, this assessment is connected with the notion, typical of his age, that Judaism was a legalistic religion composed primarily of externals. This view is now dead and buried. But Harnack's assessment of Paul's relation to Judaism remains sound, although it can no longer be deemed a compliment to Paul. Not surprisingly, a Jewish scholar who reflects on Paul's talk of "the curse of the law" and the slavery of humans under it finds that Paul has in effect "somewhat demonised the God of Israel."[32]

Judaism underlined the covenant which God had, in his grace, made with Israel. It was merely the grateful response of humans to observe the law set down by this merciful God. If obedience to the covenant law was subsequently replaced by faith in Jesus as the Messiah (whose followers largely rejected observance of the law, for instance, its food regulations), the faith of the fathers seemed null and void. The right relationship to God could be based *either* on God's eternal covenant to which belonged the observance of his law, or else on God's alleged new action in Jesus, whose followers gave up the law. It was very difficult to combine both convictions, although Paul did attempt something to that effect.

The problem of discontinuity is found in other first-century sources, too. The Epistle to the Hebrews states brusquely that the law of the "old covenant" has been abolished—and that this law (which is in this epistle crystallised as the cultic law concerning sacrifices) was "weak" and "useless" from the start (Heb 7:12, 18–19). The author does not pause to ask why God should have set forth such a useless

---

[31] Harnack, *Marcion*, 202–3.
[32] Jon Levenson, "Is There a Counterpart in the Hebrew Bible to New Testament Antisemitism?" *JES* 22 (1985): 247.

law in the first place. It is not a far step from here to Marcion. The Gospel of John further leans towards Marcion's views, in that the Jews who appeal to Moses are there lumped together as children of the devil (John 8:44), even though, as we shall see, Marcion's anger is *not* directed at the Jews personally. In John's view, all "shepherds" before Jesus were "thieves and robbers" (John 10:8)—apparently even Moses.[33]

Of course, Marcion's concept of two gods was unacceptable in a monotheistic context. But the theology of Paul and others implied a no less offensive idea: the one and only God had, despite his own repeated affirmations to the contrary, changed his mind. It was clear to Marcion at least that God could not genuinely display such instability. This was equally clear to Marcion's critics, who resorted to a very different solution to the problem. While Marcion posited the existence of two different gods, his critics drastically resorted to reinterpreting the Old Testament for their own ends. God did not change his mind; his unchanged plan had simply been misunderstood. Tertullian emphasises his opposition to Marcion by saying that a novelty must be heresy, "precisely because that has to be considered truth which was delivered of old and from the beginning" (*Marc.* 2.1.6). This claim, from our current perspective, comes close to self-condemnation.

The orthodox Fathers tried to deny any dichotomy between law and gospel in Paul's teaching. Yet it could not be denied that parts of the law (at least its "ritual" parts) *had* been abolished in Christianity (largely as a consequence of Paul's mission). Admitting this and trying to refute Marcion, Tertullian explained that this was all right. In fact, one ought to have known that this had to happen, for the creator had long ago taught this very thing through his prophets. "The old things have passed away, and behold they are new things which I now make" (Isa 43:19); "renew for yourself a new fallow; be circumcised in the foreskins of your heart" (Jer 4:3–4); "your new moons and sabbaths, and the great day, I cannot abide: your appointed days and your fasting, and your feast days, my soul hates" (Isa 1:14). The artificiality reaches its peak in Tertullian's interpretation of Psalm 2 (Ps 2:3): "by exchanging the obligations and burdens of the law for the freedom of the gospel," the apostles "were doing

---

[33] On the similarities between the gospel of John and Marcion see Regul, *Evangelienprologe*, 165–76.

as the psalm advised, 'Let us break their bonds asunder and cast their yoke from us'" (*Marc.* 3.22.3). It does not bother Tertullian that in Psalm 2, this "advice to the apostles" is presented as the counsel of the kings of the earth "against the Lord and his anointed."

Christ "has been foretold of all down the ages," for "with God nothing is unexpected." Christ's work of salvation "required preparatory work in order to be credible" (*Marc.* 3.2.4). Yet in the law, Christ was preached "under a figure, which is why not all the Jews were capable of recognising him" (*Marc.* 5.13.15).

According to the orthodox Fathers, God had not changed his plans; the alleged changes resulted from people having misunderstood those plans. Justin explains that the "ritual" commands of the Old Testament were given in order to discipline the Jews, who were an exceptionally sinful people and therefore in need of especially strict control (*Dial.* 19.6–20.1). In addition, the command of circumcision had a special purpose: according to Justin, it was meant to assist the Romans in identifying Jews in order to punish them (*Dial.* 16.2). Marcion put forward a radical proposal, but he certainly did not create the problem of continuity and discontinuity. It was inherent in the basis of Christianity.

6. *Marcion's New Scripture*

Marcion completely rejected the Old Testament. He replaced it with the writings which he considered to be the genuine founding documents of Christianity: the ten letters of Paul[34] and one gospel. Marcion believed that Paul's mention of "my gospel" referred to a specific written document. Of the writings known to Marcion, Luke's gospel apparently came closest to fitting the picture.

In itself, Luke's gospel, which stresses a certain continuity between the old covenant and the new, did not fit very well with Marcion's view.[35] In Paul's letters, too, a good deal of continuity with the traditions of Israel is found alongside discontinuity. Marcion had to

---

[34] The Pastoral Epistles and Hebrews are missing. It seems, however, that a collection of ten letters existed prior to Marcion, so he did not create it: Ulrich Schmid, *Marcion und sein Apostolos: Rekonstruktion und historische Einordnung der marcionitischen Paulusbriefausgabe* (ANTF 25; Berlin: Walter de Gruyter, 1995), 284–96.

[35] In fact, the gospel of John would have suited Marcion better; cf. Regul, *Evangelienprologe*, 165–76. Regul concludes that Marcion did not know this gospel, at least not as an authoritative work.

assume that both the gospel and the letters contained Judaising additions made by the false apostles of the creator. It was Marcion's self-
appointed task to purify these texts from such distortions.

Marcion thus believed that a great conspiracy against God's truth
had existed in the early church.[36] In fact the opening chapters of
Galatians showed that there had been violent quarrels concerning
Paul's gospel; Paul and Peter had been involved in a vehement
conflict with each other (Gal 2). Why should such battles not have
left traces in the extant letters of Paul, and in other texts? The only
true gospel, Marcion posited, was the one that Paul had received
directly from Christ (Gal 1). How Marcion conceived that this happened remains unclear.[37]

Marcion is believed to have personally omitted much from the
texts of Paul and Luke that did not suit his view of the character
of the true gospel. Actually, rather little is known about the wording of Marcion's New Testament;[38] the main sources, Tertullian and
Epiphanius, seldom quote verbatim the specific text of Marcion they
are criticising. Recent research is inclined to assume that Marcion
handled his texts in a more conservative way than has generally
been thought.[39] Harnack was forced to admit that Marcion indeed
preserved a lot of material that does not sit easily with his own doctrine, and that one might have expected him to omit. Whatever he
did or did not omit, however, Marcion seems *not* to have *added* anything worth mentioning to the texts. Some slight verbal changes
made by him are known to exist, but they are hardly different from
those variants with which the textual history of the New Testament

---

[36] Harnack, *Marcion*, 35.

[37] Some of Marcion's pupils presuppose that Paul was given a book by the risen
Christ, others think that Paul himself wrote the gospel. Ibid. 39, 345*. Marcion did
not provide his own gospel with an author's name (say, Luke).

[38] Harnack still tried to reconstruct the wording of Marcion's new Bible; recent
scholarship has not followed him.

[39] Regarding the gospel, see David Salter Williams, "Reconsidering Marcion's
Gospel," *JBL* 108 (1989): 477–96; see also Joel Delobel, "Extra-Canonical Sayings
of Jesus: Marcion and Some 'Non-received' Logia," in *Gospel Traditions in the Second
Century: Origins, Recensions, Text, and Transmission* (ed. W. L. Petersen; Christianity and
Judaism in Antiquity 3; Notre Dame, Ind.: University of Notre Dame Press, 1989),
105–116. Regarding the letters, see Schmid, *Marcion*. The few lengthy passages
omitted by Marcion were concerned with three themes: Abraham as the father of
the believers; Israel and the promises given to it as the foundation of the church;
Christ as the mediator of creation. In addition, the talk of judgment according to
deeds (Rom 2:3–11) was apparently deleted.

is replete (*all* copyists changed to some extent the text they copied, partly involuntarily, partly with intention).

The lack of Marcion's additions to the text testifies to the sincerity of his intentions: he merely wanted to restore the original uncorrupted wording. Such a "philological" aim is best served by limiting oneself to eliminating alleged additions; making additions of one's own would only undermine the credibility of the enterprise. Marcion never composed a new gospel, though a multitude of apocryphal gospels that gave free rein to fantasy appeared in his time. He did not appeal to the Spirit (as John did when he freely refashioned the speeches of Jesus) nor did he claim to have found hidden documents (as the Deuteronomistic historiographer responsible for 1 Kgs 22 once did). In his handling of texts Marcion even seems much more conservative than Matthew or Luke, who thoroughly edited Mark and Q, and, besides omitting material, also added or even created new stories (Luke in particular). Compared to the authors of his own time, Marcion handled the text of his gospel with much more delicacy than, say, the author(s) of the Alexandrian revision of Mark (the so-called "Secret Mark") or the author(s) of the final version of the *Gospel of Thomas*.

In Marcion's time no New Testament canon existed; there was nothing even resembling an agreed-upon list of particularly authoritative or normative writings. To be sure, almost all (if not all) writings which were to constitute the canon were in existence and in use. But Marcion's "Bible" (one gospel plus the Pauline corpus), which replaced the Old Testament in his congregations, was the first clearly defined New Testament (though this name was not yet used). Many scholars indeed think that it was Marcion who created the idea of a New Testament.[40] His work challenged orthodox opponents to make a canon of their own. In order to preserve their Scripture (the Old Testament) and to defeat Marcion with his own weapons, they had to provide the Old Testament with a "supplement" that was more comprehensive than Marcion's selection. Other scholars think that a New Testament would have been formed one way or the other, yet even on this basis Marcion's work accelerated

---

[40] Harnack, *Marcion*; John Knox, *Marcion and the New Testament: An Essay in the Early History of the Canon* (Chicago: The University of Chicago Press, 1942); Hans Freiherr von Campenhausen, *The Formation of the Christian Bible* (trans. J. A. Baker; 2d ed.; Philadelphia: Fortress, 1984); May, "Markion," 835.

the ensuing development of canon formation (which was already in progress). Due to the paucity of sources, however, such questions are difficult to answer for certain,[41] but one wonders whether Marcion's radicalised Paulinism could have had the success it had, unless Paul's letters already had an acknowledged status in many existing parts of Christendom.

7. Marcion and the Jews

Marcion is often portrayed by scholars as an enemy of the Jews, sometimes even as the worst Antisemite of antiquity.[42] This view needs to be thoroughly revised.[43] To be sure, Judaism was, for Marcion, an inferior religion. No doubt this is a condescending view, but does it follow that Marcion was hostile towards Jews? Unlike so many "orthodox" church fathers, Marcion does *not* blame the Jews for killing Jesus. The death of Jesus, after all, was to be blamed on the imprudent creator.

Tertullian indeed complains that Marcion had formed "an alliance with the Jewish error" (*Marc.* 3.6.2), "borrowing poison from the Jew" (3.8.1); "for from the Jew the heretic has accepted guidance . . ., the blind borrowing from the blind, and has fallen into the same ditch" (3.7.1). Marcion conceded to the Jews that Jesus could not be their long-awaited Messiah; their Messiah was to be a warrior and a liberator. Isaiah's "Emmanuel" would "take up the strength of Damascus and the spoils of Samaria against the kings of the Assyrians" (Isa 8:4; Tertullian, *Marc.* 3.12.1). Marcion believed that this Jewish Messiah warrior would still come to establish a temporary earthly kingdom for his people (Tertullian, *Marc.* 3.6.1–2), regathering them out of dispersion (3.21.1). This Messiah "promises the Jews their former estate, after the restitution of their country, and, when life has run its course, refreshment with those beneath the

---

[41] Wilhelm Schneemelcher, "Bibel III," *TRE* 6 (1980).

[42] For examples, see Heikki Räisänen, *Marcion, Muhammad and the Mahatma: Exegetical Perspectives on the Encounter of Cultures and Faiths* (London: SCM, 1997), 64.

[43] It is another matter that anti-Semitic circles in the Third Reich misused him (and Harnack's book on him) for their purposes. See Achim Detmers, "Die Interpretation der Israel-Lehre Marcions im ersten Drittel des 20. Jahrhunderts: Theologische Voraussetzungen und zeitgeschichtlicher Kontext," in May and Greschat, *Marcion*, 287–92.

earth, in Abraham's bosom" (3.24.1), and Marcion accepts this. To be sure, Christians had been personally warned of this Messiah of the creator by Jesus (Luke 21:8; Tertullian, *Marc.* 4.39).

With that in mind, can Marcion really be regarded as an enemy of the Jews? Do not his "orthodox" opponents seem more anti-Jewish in comparison? Marcion was simply a catalyst. He forced Tertullian and others to pose the question with new seriousness: If, as is agreed, parts of the law are to be abandoned, how can one take seriously the God who made such an inferior arrangement in the first place? How can one avoid criticisms by the Jews on one hand (to the effect that the Christians have transgressed God's will in giving up his law) and Marcion's conclusion on the other (a God who gives an inferior law is himself inferior, and thus not a true God after all)?[44]

Tertullian's answer is representative and clear: since the giver of the law cannot (by definition) be criticised, the blame is transferred to the people who cling to this law. The Old Testament law was deficient and had to be replaced, yet this was not the fault of God, but of the Jews. Here are some examples given by Tertullian (*Marc.* 2.18.1–3; 2.19.1):

- The law of retaliation (*ius talionis*, "eye for an eye") had to be given because "to that stiff-necked people, devoid of faith in God, it seemed a tiresome thing, or even beyond credence" to expect vengeance from God.
- When the law "places restraint upon certain foods," it is "advice on the exercise of self-restraint"; and in doing so, "a bridle was put upon that gluttony which, while it was eating the bread of angels, hankered after the cucumbers and pumpkins of the Egyptians."
- The explanation for "the burdensome expense of sacrifices and the troublesome scrupulosities of services and oblations" is this: "when the people were prone to idolatry and transgression, God was content to attach them to his own religion by the same sort of observances in which this world's superstition was engaged."
- The law has made all manner of regulations in order "to tame the people's hardness, and smooth down with exacting obligations their faith as yet unpractised in obedience."

---

[44] What follows could be documented by a large number of patristic sources, but here it seems proper to precisely use Tertullian's *Adversus Marcionem*.

By that rationale, the law is nothing more than a burden, given for discipline; its individual parts are comparable to superstitious practices in the pagan world.

In contrast to such views, Marcion's own criticism "focuses almost exclusively on the god and the scriptures of Judaism and says little of Jews as such." It was among his orthodox opponents that "the focus shifted from the god of the Jews to the Jews themselves."[45]

Catholic Christianity wrenched the Scripture from the Jews, reinterpreting it to fit its own experience. Covenantal symbols were appropriated by way of spiritualising interpretation: actual circumcision was replaced with the circumcision of the heart, observance of the law with obedience to moral commands. Precisely because it was asserted that the Old Testament had already spoken of Jesus, the continuing existence of Judaism as a religion with rival claims to Scripture was felt to be a threat to Christian identity. For unlike old Simeon in the Lukan infancy narrative, Judaism refused to be dismissed in peace when Jesus entered the scene. In due time, the threat of Judaism was ultimately repressed by violent means. Marcion's identity, by contrast, was not threatened by the continued existence of Judaism.

Marcion represented an extreme position: he believed that there was no connection between Judaism and Christianity. This view is historically impossible. Marcion denigrated Judaism. He picked one side of the Pauline legacy and radicalised it to the extreme. His orthodox opponents developed the other side of this legacy; but their way of establishing continuity was also arbitrary, both from the Jewish and from an historical point of view.

Perhaps unexpectedly, with regard to practical consequences, the exclusive view of Marcion seems less harmful. Where Catholic Christianity took the symbols and attacked the people, Marcion "attacked the symbols but left the people alone."[46] Stephen Wilson hits the nail on the head:

> It is clear that both the Marcionite and the Catholic position involve a denigration of Judaism ... I would not like to be found defending either view of Judaism. However it might be argued that the one which more obviously belittles Jewish symbols was, ironically, in practice the

[45] John Gager, *The Origins of Anti-Semitism: Attitudes Toward Judaism in Pagan and Christian Antiquity* (New York: Oxford University Press, 1983), 172.
[46] Wilson, *Strangers*, 221.

lesser of two evils . . . Judaism is the loser in either case. Whether the Marcionite position, had it prevailed, would have led to the same sad consequences as the view of its opponents is hard to say. But it is worth a moment's reflection.[47]

8. *The Church of Marcion*

The rapid expansion and tenacious persistence of Marcion's church was mentioned at the beginning of this article. The vitality of this church is truly astonishing, since membership in it was not inherited, due to the celibacy of the Marcionites, but resulted from ongoing adult conversions. Clearly, the conditions had to be very favourable to Marcion's message. Apparently, a large part of baptised Christians, especially in the east, were immediately drawn towards his teaching. As Walter Bauer suggests, "What had dwelt in their inner consciousness in a more or less undefined form until then, acquired through Marcion the definite form that satisfied head and heart."[48]

The organisation and rites of Marcionite congregations resembled those of the "Catholic," although the gatherings were open to everyone, including Gentiles. As late as the fourth century, Bishop Cyril of Jerusalem found it necessary to warn members of his church that they might land in a Marcionite building, if while in a foreign town they merely inquired after a "church," without specifying what church they wanted (*Catechesis* 18.26).

After the death of its founder, room opened up in Marcion's church for different schools of thought. Marcion's teaching was taken in somewhat dissimilar directions by different followers. His most independent and important pupil was Apelles, who taught in Alexandria and Rome, developing a philosophical system for the thoughts of his mentor.[49] Unlike Marcion, Apelles assumed that there was only one

---

[47] Stephen G. Wilson, "Marcion and the Jews," in *Anti-Judaism in Early Christianity 2: Separation and Polemic* (ed. Stephen G. Wilson; Waterloo: Wilfrid Laurier University Press, 1986), 58.

[48] Walter Bauer, *Orthodoxy and Heresy in Earliest Christianity* (trans. a team from the Philadelphia Seminar on Christian Origins; ed. Robert A. Kraft and Gerhard Krodel; Philadelphia: Fortress, 1971), 194. With reference to this famous statement of Bauer, Jürgen Regul compares Marcion's impact to that of the German theologian Eugen Drewermann in our time ("Die Bedeutung Marcions aus der Sicht heutiger kirchlicher Praxis," in May and Greschat, *Marcion*, 294).

[49] See Harnack, *Marcion*, 177–96, 404*–20*; Katharina Greschat, *Apelles und Hermogenes: Zwei theologische Lehrer des zweiten Jahrhunderts* (Supplements to Vigiliae Christianae 48; Leiden: E. J. Brill, 2000).

"basic principle," the good God. Even the demiurge was an angel of this God, being the highest of his creatures. Apelles continued Marcion's critical scrutiny of the Old Testament, devoting at least 38 books to the examination of its contradictions and incredible features. He went much further than Marcion, for whom the Old Testament, even if morally inferior, was a historically trustworthy book. For Apelles, the Old Testament was full of fairy-tales and lies,[50] and was not worthy to be attributed even to the demiurge. The Old Testament was the work of *another* angel, a fiery spirit of deceit, who spoke to Moses from the burning bush. This evil angel was the God of Israel (and of those Christians who believed in Israel's God). In Apelles' interpretation, then, the Old Testament God well-nigh became a satanic figure. Marcion's own view was different.

9. *The Challenge of Marcion*

In his book on Marcion, Harnack presented a famous assessment of the Church's relation to the Old Testament:

> To reject the Old Testament in the second century was a mistake which the Church rightly repudiated; to retain it in the sixteenth century was a fate which the Reformation could not yet avoid; but to continue to keep it in Protestantism as a canonical document after the nineteenth century is the consequence of religious and ecclesiastical paralysis.[51]

Harnack's main point in this much-criticised dictum is generally missed. Scholars have been content with noting that his judgment was influenced by his inadequate view of Judaism, typical of his time,[52] which is undoubtedly correct. Yet, it is no less important to pay attention to the context of the passage. Harnack was referring to the sad influence of parts of the Old Testament in Christian history. Allegorical interpretation had once helped to side-step the most problematic parts, but the "Scripture alone" principle elevated the literal meaning of the Old Testament onto a pedestal; in the Calvinist

---

[50] Origen has preserved information concerning the criticisms directed by Apelles, for instance, at the stories of the Flood (how could the elephants be accommodated in the ark?) and Paradise (Adam did the right thing in wanting knowledge of good and evil); see Harnack, *Marcion*, 412*–18*.

[51] Ibid., 217.

[52] E.g. Blackman, *Marcion*, 122; Wilson, *Strangers*, 209.

branch of Protestantism, in particular, the Old Testament was in practice put on the same (if not higher) level as the New Testament. The Christian usurpation of the Old Testament now backfired, when what might be called its sub-Christian—or sub-Jewish, for that matter—features broke through. Harnack writes:

> "If Marcion had reappeared at the time of the Huguenots and Cromwell, he would have met at the very centre of Christianity the warlike God of Israel whom he abhorred."[53] The churches are afraid of a break with the tradition, but they "disregard the much more fatal consequences which continually follow from the preservation of the Old Testament as a holy and therefore inerrant scripture."[54]

What Harnack wished—and here he differed from his hero, Marcion—was not a rejection of the Old Testament, but an elimination of its canonical status and a critical sifting of its contents. Knowledge of what Harnack considered "the truly edifying passages" of the Old Testament remained important even according to him.[55]

"The tree is known by its fruits." Marcion applied this principle to the Old Testament God. Scholars of the effective history of the Bible are beginning to apply it to the book. One does not conclude that there must be two or more gods, but might deduce that holy scriptures can be a curse as well as a blessing.

The effective history of the Old Testament demonstrates how dangerous it has been as a holy book, or as even part of such. Appeals to its stories have served to justify violence; the crusades, the annihilation of Native Americans and the denial of civil rights to Palestinians are only the tip of the iceberg. Marcion can be regarded as a pioneer of moral criticism of the Bible, which seems to be an inevitable task these days.

It should be made clear in this connection that the criticism of cruel passages in the Old Testament does *not* necessarily imply anti-Judaism (Harnack, for one, was a *critic* of anti-Semitism in his environment). Criticism of such passages is also presented by Jewish scholars. Moreover, there is no reason to limit such criticism to the Old

---

[53] Harnack, *Marcion*, 220. This sentence is disregarded even by Kinzig, "Ketzer," 265–67 in his attempt to sketch the background and development of Harnack's view of Marcion and the Old Testament. Detmers does quote it, connecting Harnack's view with the crisis experience of World War One; "Interpretation," 280–83.

[54] Harnack, *Marcion*, 222.

[55] Ibid., 222–23.

Testament. If foreign nations are demonised in parts of the Old Testament, the same tradition of destructive intolerance continues in those New Testament passages which declare non-Christian Jews to be children of the devil (John 8:44) or the "Synagogue of Satan" (Rev 2:9; 3:9). And the usurpation of the Old Testament which is so clear in the church fathers—the dangerous claim to continuity which the obstinate Jews do not perceive—goes back to the New Testament itself.

Nevertheless, it is surely unrealistic to think that the churches could change the contents of their canon. Nor should Marcion be followed in his attempt to purge the New Testament by way of a fictitious reconstruction of its original message. It will not do to remove (or even to tone down) the anti-Jewish passages of the New Testament, or the anti-Canaanite passages of the Old. One should take the more difficult route of coming to terms with one's canon as it is, with all the fruits it has borne. One has to be critical and consciously selective. True, Christians have always been selective in their treatment of the Bible. Yet the fact that educated lay readers like the Finnish President Koivisto are upset when they notice selectivity that is actually practised, demonstrates that the critical process should be made open and plain. Marcion's answers can be rejected, but his questions cannot be evaded.[56]

Bibliography

Aland, Barbara. "Marcion (ca. 85–160)/Marcioniten." Pages 89–101 in vol. 22 of *Theologische Realenzyklopädie*. Edited by Gerhard Krause and Gerhard Müller. Berlin: Walter de Gruyter, 1992.

Bauer, Walter. *Orthodoxy and Heresy in Earliest Christianity*. Edited by Robert A. Kraft and Gerhard Krodel. Translated by a team from the Philadelphia Seminar on Christian Origins. Philadelphia: Fortress, 1971.

Blackman, E. C. *Marcion and His Influence*. London: SPCK, 1948.

Campenhausen, Hans Freiherr von. *The Formation of the Christian Bible*. Translated by J. A. Baker. 2nd ed. Philadelphia: Fortress, 1984.

Deakle, David W. "Harnack & Cerdo: A Reexamination of the Patristic Evidence for Marcion's Mentor." Pages 177–90 in *Marcion und seine kirchengeschichtliche Wirkung/ Marcion and His Impact on Church History*. Edited by Gerhard May and Katharina Greschat. Berlin: Walter de Gruyter, 2002.

---

[56] Regul ("Bedeutung," 308–11) agrees, though writing more clearly from a church perspective.

Delobel, J. "Extra-Canonical Sayings of Jesus: Marcion and Some 'Non-received' Logia." Pages 105–116 in *Gospel Traditions in the Second Century: Origins, Recensions, Text, and Transmission*. Edited by W. L. Petersen. Christianity and Judaism in Antiquity 3. Notre Dame, Ind.: University of Notre Dame Press, 1989.

Detmers, Achim. "Die Interpretation der Israel-Lehre Marcions im ersten Drittel des 20. Jahrhunderts: Theologische Voraussetzungen und zeitgeschichtlicher Kontext." Pages 275–92 in *Marcion und seine kirchengeschichtliche Wirkung/Marcion and His Impact on Church History*. Edited by Gerhard May and Katharina Greschat. Berlin: Walter de Gruyter, 2002.

Frenschkowski, Marco. "Marcion in arabischen Quellen." Pages 39–63 in *Marcion und seine kirchengeschichtliche Wirkung/Marcion and His Impact on Church History*. Edited by Gerhard May and Katharina Greschat. Berlin: Walter de Gruyter, 2002.

Gager, John G. *The Origins of Anti-Semitism: Attitudes Toward Judaism in Pagan and Christian Antiquity*. New York: Oxford University Press, 1983.

Greschat, Katharina. *Apelles und Hermogenes: Zwei theologische Lehrer des zweiten Jahrhunderts*. Supplements to Vigiliae Christianae 48. Leiden: E. J. Brill, 2000.

Harnack, Adolf von. *Marcion: Das Evangelium vom fremden Gott. Eine Monographie zur Geschichte der Grundlegung der katholischen Kirche. Neue Studien zu Marcion*. Darmstadt: Wissenschaftliche Buchgesellschaft, [1924] 1996.

Hoffmann, R. Joseph. *Marcion: On the Restitution of Christianity: An Essay on the Development of Radical Paulinist Theology in the Second Century*. American Academy of Religion, Academy Series 46. Chico: Scholars Press, 1984.

Kinzig, Wolfram. "Ein Ketzer und sein Konstrukteur: Harnacks Marcion," Pages 253–74 in *Marcion und seine kirchengeschichtliche Wirkung/Marcion and His Impact on Church History*. Edited by Gerhard May and Katharina Greschat. Berlin: Walter de Gruyter, 2002.

Knox, John. *Marcion and the New Testament: An Essay in the Early History of the Canon*. Chicago: The University of Chicago Press, 1942.

Kuula, Kari. *The Law, the Covenant and God's Plan. Volume 1: Paul's Polemical Treatment of the Law in Galatians*. Publications of the Finnish Exegetical Society 72. Helsinki: The Finnish Exegetical Society; Göttingen: Vandenhoeck & Ruprecht, 1999.

Levenson, Jon. "Is There a Counterpart in the Hebrew Bible to New Testament Antisemitism?" *Journal of Ecumenical Studies* 22 (1985): 242–260.

Lüdemann, Gerd. *Heretics: The Other Side of Early Christianity*. Translated by John Bowden. London: SCM, 1996.

Markschies, Christoph. "Die valentinianische Gnosis und Marcion—einige neue Perspektiven." Pages 159–75 in *Marcion und seine kirchengeschichtliche Wirkung/Marcion and His Impact on Church History*. Edited by Gerhard May and Katharina Greschat. Berlin: Walter de Gruyter, 2002.

May, Gerhard. "Marcion ohne Harnack," Pages 1–7 in *Marcion und seine kirchengeschichtliche Wirkung/Marcion and His Impact on Church History*. Edited by Gerhard May and Katharina Greschat. Berlin: Walter de Gruyter, 2002.

——. "Markion/Markioniten." Pages 834–836 in *Religion in Geschichte und Gegenwart* 5. 4th ed., 2002.

——. "Der 'Schiffsreeder' Markion." Pages 142–53 in *Studia Patristica* 21. Edited by E. A. Livingstone. Leuven: Peeters, 1989.

May, Gerhard and Katharina Greschat, ed. *Marcion und seine kirchengeschichtliche Wirkung/Marcion and His Impact on Church History*. Berlin: Walter de Gruyter, 2002.

Regul, Jürgen. *Die antimarcionitischen Evangelienprologe*. Vetus Latina: Aus der Geschichte der lateinischen Bibel 6. Freiburg: Herder, 1969.

——. "Die Bedeutung Marcions aus der Sicht heutiger kirchlicher Praxis." Pages 293–311 in *Marcion und seine kirchengeschichtliche Wirkung/Marcion and His Impact on Church History*. Edited by Gerhard May and Katharina Greschat. Berlin: Walter de Gruyter, 2002.

Räisänen, Heikki. *Marcion, Muhammad and the Mahatma: Exegetical Perspectives on the Encounter of Cultures and Faiths.* London: SCM, 1997.

Schmid, Ulrich. *Marcion und sein Apostolos: Rekonstruktion und historische Einordnung der marcionitischen Paulusbriefausgabe.* Arbeiten zur neutestamentlichen Textforschung 25. Berlin: Walter de Gruyter, 1995.

Schneemelcher, Wilhelm. "Bibel III." Pages 22–48 in vol. 6 of *Theologische Realenzyklopädie.* Edited by Gerhard Krause and Gerhard Müller. Berlin: Walter de Gruyter, 1980.

Simon, Marcel. *Verus Israel: A Study of the Relations between Christians and Jews in the Roman Empire (135–425).* Oxford: Oxford University Press, 1986.

Tertullian. *Adversus Marcionem.* Books I–V. 2 vols. Edited and translated by Ernest Evans. Oxford Early Christian Texts. Oxford: Clarendon Press, 1972.

Williams, David Salter. "Reconsidering Marcion's Gospel." *Journal of Biblical Literature* 108 (1989): 477–96.

Williams, Michael Allen. *Rethinking "Gnosticism": An Argument for Dismantling a Dubious Category.* Princeton: Princeton University Press, 1996.

Wilson, Stephen G. "Marcion and the Jews." Pages 45–58 in *Anti-Judaism in Early Christianity 2: Separation and Polemic.* Edited by Stephen G. Wilson. Studies in Christianity and Judaism 2. Waterloo: Wilfrid Laurier University Press, 1986.

———. *Related Strangers: Jews and Christians, 70–170 C.E.* Minneapolis: Fortress, 1995.

TATIAN THE ASSYRIAN[1]

William L. Petersen

About 1195 C.E., Michael the Syrian, Patriarch of Antioch from 1166 until his death in 1199, penned the following description of Tatian:

> [Tatian] became inclined to the blasphemy of the followers of Saturnilos [*sic*] and Marcion, . . . like the followers of Valentinos. He acted stupidly and spoke of invisible aeons, and he called legitimate marriage adultery. And he collected and mixed a gospel and he called it Diatessaron . . . And from him the heresy of the Encratites[2] sprang up. And there were tracts in which he was showing that Christ was from the seed of David.[3] (*Chronicle* VI.5)

Almost exactly a century later, in 1299, a former Metropolitan of Nisibis, 'Abd Iso' bar Berika (Metropolitan, 1290–1291; *obit.* 1318), recorded his understanding of Tatian and his activities in these words:

---

[1] A semester's release from teaching duties was provided by a fellowship from the Institute for the Arts and Humanities at The Pennsylvania State University; it is gratefully acknowledged. The author also wishes to thank Prof. C. Scholten (Cologne) for his helpful comments and suggestions, especially of literature.

[2] "Encratism" means "restraint, abstention, self-control," and broadly refers to those early Christians who rejected sexual relations, meat, and wine; see the article by H. Chadwick, "Enkrateia," *RAC* 5:343–65. There is an excellent, nuanced examination of Encratism by Gilles Quispel, "The Study of Encratism: A Historical Survey," in *La Tradizione dell'Enkrateia: Motivazioni ontologiche e protologiche* (ed. U. Bianchi; Rome: Edizioni dell'Ateneo, 1985), 35–81, esp. 46–73, which traces its influence on earliest Greek, Aramaic (Jewish), and Latin Christianity; it also explores the psycho-social dimensions of the movement.

The classic studies of asceticism in the East are those of Arthur Vööbus: *Celibacy: A Requirement for Admission to Baptism in the Early Syrian Church* (PETSE 1; Stockholm: Estonian Theological Society in Exile, 1951), and his magisterial *The History of Asceticism in the Syrian Orient* (3 vols.; CSCO 184, 197, 500; Louvain: Peeters, 1958, 1960, 1988), esp. 1:31–61, which has sections on Tatian, Marcion, Valentinus, etc.

A broader, more popular treatment (which includes discussions of Encratism and of Tatian) is P. Brown, *The Body and Society: Men, Women, and Sexual Renunciation in Early Christianity* (New York: Columbia University Press, 1988).

[3] J.-B. Chabot, ed., *Chronique de Michel le Syrien* (vol. 4; Paris: Leroux, 1910), 108–109. Unless otherwise noted, all translations are those of the author (there is a French translation in Chabot, vol. 1 [Paris: Leroux, 1924], 180–181).

> Tatian, a certain philosopher, collected the sense of the words of the Evangelists with his skill, and understood in his mind the intention of their divine books; he collected one wonderful Gospel from the four of them, which he called Ditessaron [*sic*] in which, with all carefulness, he preserved the exact order of those things that were spoken and done by the Savior.[4] (*Nomokanon*)

Both of these writers are respected, highly-placed, presumably well-informed figures in the Syrian church. Nevertheless, their opinions of Tatian diverge markedly. Who was Tatian and what—if any— were his "heresies"?[5] This study will attempt to answer these questions in five sections. First we will identify Tatian's literary remains; these will be used to construct his biography in section 2. In section 3 we will examine his personality; in section 4 we will present the charges against him, and see how well they fit. Finally, in section 5 we will examine the reception of Tatian in both the East and the West, and reflect on his status.

1. *Tatian's Literary Remains*

Tatian is best known to scholars today because of the *Diatessaron*, a gospel harmony.[6] As best we can reconstruct its text today, the *Diatessaron* was a woven from the texts of Matthew, Mark, Luke and John, and, perhaps one or more extra-canonical sources.[7] Instead of

---

[4] A. Mai, ed., *Scriptorum veterum nova collection e vaticanis codicibus edita* (vol. 10, part 1; Rome: Burliaeum, 1838), 191 (text), 23 (Latin translation).

[5] The nomenclature of "orthodoxy" and "heresy" is, as has been often pointed out, anachronistic in this period, for the lines separating the two were not clearly drawn and would change over time. See the discussion *infra*, commencing with the second paragraph in section 4.

[6] On the Diatessaron, see William L. Petersen, *Tatian's Diatessaron: Its Creation, Dissemination, Significance, and History in Scholarship* (Supplements to Vigiliae christianae 25; Leiden: E. J. Brill, 1994).

[7] There are passages in the *Diatessaron* that find parallels in "extra-canonical" gospels. Whether Tatian employed a "fifth source" (i.e., an extra-canonical document) alongside the four (canonical) gospels, or whether, at the time Tatian composed the *Diatessaron*, the (proto-)canonical gospels contained material which was later excised and classified as "extra-canonical," is impossible to determine, given our present knowledge of the texts. An example of the problem is the "fire" or "light" in the Jordan River when Jesus is baptized. It is found in the "Hebrew Gospel," and in the *Diatessaron*; but it also crops up in two Vetus Latina manuscripts (MSS *a* and *g¹*) of the Gospel of Matthew. Whence did Tatian obtain the reading? From a ver-

two virgin birth accounts, the *Diatessaron* contains only one—subtly harmonized from the Matthean and Lucan accounts; instead of four crucifixion accounts, the *Diatessaron* contains only one—woven from at least the four canonical accounts.

Unfortunately for us, no direct copy of the *Diatessaron* exists today. Rather, the researcher is confronted with a confusing array of what are termed "witnesses" to the *Diatessaron*, meaning that here and there—but not consistently—their text *may* offer readings from the ancient *Diatessaron*. These witnesses take various forms: some are in the form of brief quotations or lemmata, apparently from the *Diatessaron* (e.g., the lemmata in the commentary of Ephrem Syrus, apparently written on the text of a *Diatessaron*; some of the gospel quotations of the Syrian church father Aphrahat); others are in the form of translations made from Syriac copies of the *Diatessaron* (e.g., the Arabic Harmony); others are "new" harmonies—that is, harmonies whose sequence of harmonization is new, but whose text sometimes shows agreements with variants found in other Diatessaronic witnesses (e.g., the Persian Harmony); finally, we have revised translations of revised translations of a *Diatessaron* (e.g., the Old High German Harmony, which rests on a Latin base; this Latin base was, however, a translation from, presumably, the Syriac, which is probably the language in which the *Diatessaron* was composed). In date, these witnesses range from the fourth century to the sixteenth, and in geography they range from northern Europe to Egypt, and from the Low Countries east to China. It is from the occasional conjunction of several of these witnesses, all deviating from the standard Greek gospel text in the same manner, that scholars reconstruct the *Diatessaron*'s text.

For our purposes, however, the *Diatessaron* is of limited importance. Although it is the work for which Tatian is best known today, its genre—a gospel harmony—precludes any biographical information about Tatian. And while we will refer to some of its variants when reconstructing Tatian's own theological preferences, the number of such instances is very small.

---

sion of Matthew that had the variant, or from the "Hebrew Gospel"? See further Petersen, *Tatian's Diatessaron*, in the index, s.v. "Diatessaron, 'fifth source'."

Although the titles of six of Tatian's prose works have been trans-mitted,[8] only one survives: his *Oratio ad graecos*.[9] This apology[10] has three aims. First, it pleads for pagan tolerance of Christians; second, it seeks to defend Christianity by castigating everything Greek; third, it presents a chronology of the ancient world, demonstrating the superiority of Christianity to Greek culture by "proving" that Moses is older than Homer (Tatian employs the then-accepted idea that the antiquity of a tradition was equivalent to its truth; therefore, since Moses antedates Homer, Christianity [via Moses] must be supe-rior to Greek culture [via Homer]).[11]

For our purposes, the *Oratio* is valuable for its biographical asides and theological assertions. Although the biographical comments are few, they are our only direct contact with Tatian. The *Oratio* is also valuable for the psychological insight it affords us: we can gather a sense of the man from how he wrote, argued, and presented himself.

In what follows our procedure will be to take information gleaned from the *Oratio* and collate it with the reports transmitted by the

---

[8] The titles of the five lost (or, in one case, perhaps never-written) works are: *On Animals* (mentioned by Tatian himself, *Or.* 15.2 [*Tatian, Oratio ad graecos and Fragments* (ed. M. Whittaker; OECT; Oxford: Clarendon, 1982), 30]); *On Perfection according to the Savior* (mentioned by Clement of Alexandria, *Strom.* 3.12 [81.1] [*Clemens Alexandrinus, II. Stromata* (ed. O. Stählin and L. Früchtel; GCS 52; 15, for the first edition; third edition; Berlin: Akademie-Verlag, 1960), 232]); *Problems* and a treatise *On the Six Days of Creation* (both mentioned by Eusebius [quoting Rhodon], *Hist. eccl.* 5.13 [*Eusèbe de Césarée, Histoire ecclésiastique: Livres V–VII* (ed. G. Bardy; SC 41; Paris: Cerf, 1955), 42–44]). Tatian says he intends to write a treatise *To those who have propounded ideas about God* (*Or.* 40.2 [Whittaker, 73]), but whether he ever did so is unknown.

[9] Various editions exist; among the most significant are: J. C. Th. Otto, *Corpus apologetarum christianorum saeculi secundi* (vol. 6; Jena: Mauke, 1851); E. Schwartz, *Tatiani Oratio ad Graecos* (TU 4.1; Leipzig: J. C. Hinrichs, 1888). We cite from the most recent edition: *Tatian, Oratio ad graecos and Fragments* (ed. Whittaker).

[10] For a discussion of the genre of the *Oratio*, see Petersen, *Tatian's Diatessaron*, 73 n. 120. The enactment of certain laws hostile to Christians, and the attacks on Christians occasioned by these laws, seem to have prompted Tatian to compose the *Oratio*: "*Why, men of Greece, do you want to cause society to come to blows with us?* If I refuse to take part in some people's normal activities, *why should I be hated as if I were utterly loathsome?*" (*Or.* 4.1 [Whittaker, 9]); "So drop all your nonsense and *be done with this criminal hatred of us*" (*Or.* 9.4 [Whittaker, 19]); "For this reason I also *condemn your legislation*" (*Or.* 28.1 [Whittaker, 53]).

[11] On the disputes over whose "history" and philosophy were more ancient, see A. J. Droge, *Homer or Moses? Early Christian Interpretations of the History of Culture* (HUT 26; Tübingen: J. C. B. Mohr [Paul Siebeck], 1989), and P. Pilhofer, *Presbyteron kre-itton: Der Altersbeweis der jüdischen und christlichen Apologeten und seine Vorgeschichte* (WUNT 2.39; Tübingen: J. C. B. Mohr [Paul Siebeck], 1990), esp. 253–60 for Tatian (cp. the review of Pilhofer by C. Scholten, *JAC* 34 [1991]: 184–87).

early church fathers—mainly Irenaeus—to create, first, a biography of Tatian, then a sketch of his personality, and finally the outlines of his theology.[12]

2. Tatian's Biography

One of the few things we know about Tatian is where he was born, for in the *Oratio ad graecos* he says he was born "in the land of the Assyrians."[13] Tatian must have come from a family of means, for he had the leisure to wander the ancient world, sampling various philosophic schools searching for "truth."[14] This impression is reinforced by his assertion that "I do not boast of my good birth."[15] We know nothing of Tatian's youth and education. Although he knows Greek well, his style is—despite its superficial polish—often awkward and inelegant,[16] suggesting that it was not his first language.

At some point, however, Tatian left his Assyrian home and set out—as many young men of means did[17]—to explore the world, searching for "truth." This intellectual journey was primarily through Greek religion and philosophy, and much of it was, therefore, almost certainly in Greece.[18] This is suggested not only by his familiarity

---

[12] Martin Elze, *Tatian und seine Theologie* (Forschungen zur Kirchen- und Dogmengeschichte 9; Göttingen: Vandenhoeck & Ruprecht, 1960), is the only study of Tatian's theology; see esp. Chap. 6, "Tatian in der Überlieferung."

[13] *Or.* 42.1 (Whittaker, 77); in this period, "Assyria" extended from the Armenian mountains (N) to Ctesiphon (S), and from Media (E) to the Tigris (W); in common usage, it often referenced Syria, in general (including Samosata, Hierapolis, etc.). See Petersen, *Tatian's Diatessaron*, 68.

[14] Tatian wonders "by what means I could discover the truth" (*Or.* 29.1 [Whittaker, 54]); after his conversion to Christianity, he labels himself "the herald of truth" (*Or.* 17.1 [Whittaker, 35]).

[15] *Or.* 11.1 (Whittaker, 23).

[16] For example, Whittaker remarks that "He uses antithesis and chiasmus, often forced, to such an extent that they are apt to become tedious. . . . His short rhythmical cola standing alone in question and answer have a vivid effect, but when they are combined in longer periods they tend to become turgid and obscure" (xiv).

[17] A marvelous parallel is Lucian's account of "The Passing of Peregrinus," in *Lucian* (ed. A. M. Harmon; vol. 5; LCL; Cambridge: Harvard University Press, 1962), 1–51. It tells of Peregrinus, a Cynic, who became a Christian, then returned to Cynicism, and then, finally, enamored of Hindu ideas, immolated himself near Olympia. Peregrinus' wealth is mentioned in chap. 14 (pp. 14–17); upon his father's death, it turns out to be less than expected, but still sufficient to support him in the manner to which he was accustomed.

[18] While one cannot absolutely exclude the possibility that Tatian's experience of

with Greek culture, especially its religions and philosophies, but also from his statement that this familiarity came "not from second-hand knowledge, but after much travel. I followed your [Greeks'] studies and came across many devices and many notions, and finally I spent time in the city of the Romans. . . ."[19] He explicitly mentions participating in Greek religious rites: "when I had seen these things and had also taken part in mysteries. . . ."[20] Tatian's restless spirit, however, was not satisfied by any of the offerings of Greek civilization. Eventually—after what must have been a considerable interlude, given the knowledge and experience of Greek culture he amassed— Tatian "spent time in the city of the Romans," Rome.

Where and how Tatian came in contact with Christianity is unclear. It was certainly after his long sojourn through Greek philosophy and religion, for he compares "Christian" writings with Greek philosophy: "I happened to read some barbarian ["Christian"] writings, older by comparison with the doctrines of the Greeks, more divine by comparison with their errors."[21] These "barbarian writings" appear to have been the Septuagint, for Tatian is impressed by their "lack of arrogance in the wording, the artlessness of the speakers, the easily intelligible account of the creation of the world, the foreknowledge of the future, the remarkable quality of the precepts and the doctrine of a single ruler of the universe."[22] These artless, barbarian writings led Tatian to convert to Christianity.

In passing one should note that Tatian's conversion (at least as he describes it) is essentially an intellectual exercise, not a charismatic experience. He is not evangelized; there is no catharsis; there is no emotion involved. We do not know where this conversion took place, or when. It may well have been in Rome, however, for Tatian writes that it was

> . . . when I had seen these things and had also taken part in mysteries . . . and found that among the Romans their Zeus Latiaris took

---

things Greek occurred in a strongly Hellenized area outside of Greece (such as Alexandria or Antioch), this seems unlikely, for his geographic trajectory—which begins in "Assyria," passes through a "Greek" interlude, and then ends up in Rome—would quite logically pass through Greece and Athens, especially given Tatian's interest in philosophy.

[19] *Or.* 35.1 (Whittaker, 65).
[20] *Or.* 29.1 (Whittaker, 53).
[21] *Or.* 29.1 (Whittaker, 55).
[22] *Or.* 29.2 (Whittaker, 55).

pleasure in men's gore and blood..., when I was by myself I began to seek by what means I could discover the truth. While I was engaged in serious thought I happened to read some barbarian writings....[23] (*Or.* 29.1)

The fact it was *after* Tatian had learned how *Roman* rites were (in his view) as depraved as Greek rites that he began his explorations into the "barbarian" writings of the Septuagint suggests—but does not demand[24]—that Tatian was in Rome (or at least Italy) when he began casting about for a new religion. We may presume that his conversion marked the end of his sampling of the various pagan philosophies and religions.

Although Tatian does not mention it, Irenaeus (and later sources, dependent upon Irenaeus) states that Tatian was a pupil of Justin Martyr.[25] In the *Oratio*, Tatian twice mentions Justin; both references are positive, but brief and opaque.[26] Tatian's failure to mention Justin in connection with his conversion suggests that their acquaintance began *after* that event. Since Justin is usually presumed to have arrived in Rome about 150[27] and was martyred there between 163 and 168,[28]

---

[23] Whittaker, 53–55.

[24] It is possible, for example, that Tatian learned of the Roman rituals while still in Greece.

[25] Irenaeus, *Haer.* 1.28.1 (*Irénée de Lyon, Contre les hérésies: Livre I, tome II* [ed. A. Rousseau and L. Doutreleau; SC 264; Paris: Cerf, 1979], 356); the tradition is also found in Eusebius; Victor of Capua's preface to Codex Fuldensis; Isho'dad of Merv; Agapius of Hierapolis, in his *Kitab al-'Unwan* (which appears dependent upon Irenaeus, *apud* Eusebius); Dionysius bar Salibi (dependent upon Isho'dad of Merv); Michael the Syrian (appears dependent upon Irenaeus, *apud* Eusebius). For the text and full references for these *testimonia*, see Petersen, *Tatian's Diatessaron*, 46, 52, 57, 59, 61.

[26] Nothing in either reference confirms that Justin was Tatian's teacher, or even confirms personal contact: "The most admirable Justin..." (*Or.* 18.2 [Whittaker, 37]); "[Crescens] set about involving Justin—as he did me too—in the death penalty..." (*Or.* 19.1 [Whittaker, 39]). A description of the Crescens–Justin clash is found in Justin's *Second Apology* 3.1–7 (*Die ältesten Apologeten* [ed. E. J. Goodspeed; new printing (orig. 1914); Göttingen: Vandenhoeck & Ruprecht, 1984], 80–81), and in Eusebius, *Hist. eccl.* 4.16 (*Eusèbe de Césarée, Histoire ecclésiastique: Livres I–IV* [ed. G. Bardy; SC 31; Paris: Cerf, 1952], 190–92).

[27] This date should be understood as the midpoint of a range, and is derived from the date of Justin's *First Apology*, which is usually fixed to about 151; see, e.g., Leslie W. Barnard, *Justin Martyr: His Life and Thought* (Cambridge: Cambridge University Press, 1967), 5–8, esp. 19.

[28] According to the "The Martyrdom of Saints Justin...," Justin was martyred under the Prefect Junius Rusticus (Prefect from 163 to 168 [cp. H. Musurillo, ed., *The Acts of the Christian Martyrs* (Oxford: Oxford University Press, 1972), 43 n. 1]); many writers (e.g., Johannes Quasten, *Patrology* [vol. I; Utrecht: Spectrum, 1950],

Tatian's association with him must have been in the 150s or early 160s.[29]

That Tatian and Justin eventually found each other is not surprising. The most obvious reason would have been that the Christian community in Rome, though growing, was still relatively small. But there were other reasons as well, embedded in the lives of the two men. Both were from the East (Justin from Sechem/Flavia Neapolis; Tatian from Assyria); both styled themselves "philosophers"; both converted to Christianity through an intellectual process, not a charismatic event.[30]

Irenaeus goes on to report that after Justin's death Tatian and the Roman Christian community had a falling out. (The specific charges that led to this split will be discussed below, in section 4.) It was then, according to Irenaeus, that Tatian "separated from the church." In his *Chronicon*, Eusebius reports that Tatian was expelled from Roman congregation in 172 C.E.,[31] but we do not know whence he obtained this date. Eusebius' report is, however, as reasonable as any other, since Justin's died in or before 168.

After Justin's death, Tatian set up his own school in Rome.[32] Tatian's status as a teacher and his school seem to have played a role in his separation from the church, for Irenaeus notes that Tatian, "exalted at the prospect of being a teacher, and puffed up as if he were superior to everyone else, he created a unique doctrine."[33] Eusebius repeats this tradition, but adds the name of one of Tatian's pupils, a man named Rhodon, who became a noted Christian opponent of Marcion.[34] Eusebius also remarks that "early in his life"

---

197) pick the midpoint of Rusticus' prefecture, and suggest Justin's death took place "probably in 165."

[29] This assumes—as was almost certainly the case—that their contact was in Rome.

[30] Another reason may be that a late report describes Justin as a rigorous ascetic; see *infra*, n. 47.

[31] Eusebius, *Chron.*, *ad ann. cit.* (*Eusebius Werke VII: Die Chronik des Hieronymus*, [ed. R. Helm; 2nd ed.; GCS 47; Berlin: Akademie-Verlag, 1956], 206).

[32] The venue is not only logical, but explicitly stated by Eusebius, *Hist. eccl.* 5.13.8 (ed. Bardy; SC 41, 44).

[33] Irenaeus, *Haer.* 1.28.1 [Rousseau and Doutreleau, 356].

[34] See Eusebius, *Hist. eccl.* 5.13.1 (Bardy; SC 41; 42); Jerome, dependent upon Eusebius, also mentions Rhodon (*Vir. ill.* 37 [*Gerolamo, Gli uomini illustri* (ed. A. Ceresa-Gastaldo; Biblioteca patristica 12; Florence: Nardini, 1988), 132–135]).

Tatian "was trained in the learning of the Greeks and gained no small repute in it."[35]

We do not know how long Tatian remained in Rome after his break with the Christian congregation there, and our principal sources (Tatian, Irenaeus, Eusebius) are silent. Given his apparent success there, we might assume that Tatian remained in the capital for some years, continuing his dispute with the church, advancing his views through his school, and earning his living as a teacher. Eventually, however, it appears that Tatian left Rome. We have only one source for Tatian's life after his separation from the church: Epiphanius. Since Epiphanius' reports are usually second-hand and sometimes garbled, they cannot be accepted uncritically. He reports that Tatian left Rome, returned to the East, and founded a school in "Mesopotamia." He mentions Antioch of Daphne (Antioch on the Orontes, in Syria), Celicia, and Pisidia as places where Tatian's doctrines were well-received.[36]

Whether Tatian went to Mesopotamia, as Epiphanius reports, or somewhere else, has been disputed. Edessa—the cradle of Syrian Christianity, with which the *Diatessaron* is so strongly linked—has been suggested, as have Asia Minor (proposed because of the reported popularity of Tatian's teachings in Celicia and Pisidia), Assyria, Adiabene, and Arbela.[37] All these suggestions remain nothing more than guesses, however, for other than Epiphanius, our sources are silent. We know nothing of Tatian's death; he simply disappears from the pages of history.

Using what we have recounted above, let us now attempt to construct a timeline for Tatian's life. Justin seems to have arrived in

---

[35] Eusebius, *Hist. eccl.* 4.16.7 (Bardy; SC 31; 192).

[36] *Pan.* 1.46.1.6 (*Epiphanius, Panarion haer. 34–64* [ed. K. Holl and J. Dummer; 2nd ed.; GCS; Berlin: Akademie-Verlag, 1980], 204). Another father, Hippolytus, remarks that "Saturnilus . . . spent his time in Antioch of Syria" (*Haer.* 7.28.1 [*Hippolytus, Refutatio omnium haeresium* (ed. M. Marcovich; PTS 25; Berlin: Walter de Gruyter, 1986), 302]); this raises two intriguing questions. (1) Is Epiphanius' report based on fact, or is it based on an inference that since Saturnilus/Saturninus had been active in the area of Antioch, and since Tatian was a follower of Saturninus, therefore Tatian's ideas would/must have been well-received there? (2) Alternatively, assuming Epiphanius' report is based on fact, one then must wonder whether the popularity of Tatian's teaching in this area was due—at least in part—to the inhabitants' familiarity with Saturninus' teachings?

[37] For the scholarly proponents of each, and their reasons, see Petersen, *Tatian's Diatessaron*, 71–72.

Rome about 150, and we must allow some years for Justin to establish himself and earn his reputation before he and Tatian meet. If
one allows five years for Justin to launch his own career, then one
might presume Tatian and Justin met sometime between 155 and
160. Tatian's conversion occurred prior to his contact with Justin;
this suggests his conversion occurred between roughly 150 and 155.
And before that, as we have seen, Tatian spent considerable time—
probably about a decade—among the Greeks. That sojourn, then,
would have begun about 140 or 145. It is difficult to imagine Tatian's
excursion among the Greeks beginning before he had reached his
majority; if he were about twenty years old when he left home in
search of "truth," then one might suggest he was born in the 120s,
probably near the middle of that decade.

Our reports tell us that after Justin's death, Tatian remained in
Rome for some years, establishing his own school (in which Rhodon
was a pupil). Eventually, however, he was expelled from the Roman
congregation; that event occurred in 172, if one accepts Eusebius'
dating. After his separation from the church, he probably lingered
in Rome for a few years before, eventually, setting out to find a
more receptive audience. If Epiphanius is correct in reporting that
he returned to the East, then he probably left Rome about 175 or
177. Once back in the East (Mesopotamia?), he set up another school;
he probably died between 185 and 190, roughly sixty-five or seventy
years of age.

3. Tatian's Personality

> I have no desire to rule, I do not wish to be rich; I do not seek com-
> mand, I hate fornication, I am not driven by greed to go on voy-
> ages ... I do not boast of my good birth.[38] (*Or.* 11.1)

Two things stand out. First, Tatian is self-absorbed (consider his
repeated use of the first person); second, any reader—ancient or
modern—is struck by his hauteur. This is of more than passing interest, for recall that Irenaeus criticized Tatian for becoming "exalted
at the prospect of being a teacher, and puffed up as if he were supe-

---

[38] Whittaker, 21–23.

rior to everyone else."[39] Irenaeus' charge would seem to be confirmed from Tatian's own pen.

Other passages in the *Oratio* reinforce the idea that Tatian had a high opinion of himself and his discernment. They also reveal an unpleasant, rigid, uncompromising personality. Although a detailed examination of the *Oratio* is beyond the scope of this chapter, much of the tract can be characterized as a scathing, scalding, sarcastic attack on anything Greek. Their philosophers? Rubbish. Their art? Garbage. Their religions? Obscene. Two examples will suffice to make the point:

> What that is distinguished have you [Greeks] produced by your phi-
> losophizing? Who among the real enthusiasts is innocent of self-dis-
> play? Diogenes by boasting of his tub prided himself on his self-sufficiency;
> he ate raw octopus, was seized with pain, and died of an internal
> obstruction because of his intemperance. Aristippus, walking about in
> a purple robe, abandoned himself to luxury under a cloak of respectabil-
> ity. Plato, while philosophizing, was sold by Dionysius because of his
> gluttony. Aristotle, too, after ignorantly setting a limit for providence
> and defining happiness in terms of his own pleasures, used to fawn in
> a very uncultured way on that wild young man Alexander [the Great]
> who, in true Aristotelian fashion, shut his own friend up in a cage,
> because he refused to prostrate himself....[40] (*Or.* 2.1–2)

> With us [Christians] there is no desire for false glory, nor do we employ
> subtleties of doctrine. Withdrawn from public and earthly talk, obedi-
> ent to God's commands and following the law of the incorruptible
> Father, we reject all that is based on human opinion;.... We do not
> lie when we speak; but it would be a good thing if there were an end
> to your [the Greeks'] persistent disbelief. Otherwise let our case be
> vindicated by God's judgment. You may laugh now, but you will weep
> later.[41] (*Or.* 32.1–2)

Tatian seems unable to modulate his tone. He is in "attack mode" all the time. No quarter is given. Everything is black or white: Tatian is correct, while everyone else—Diogenes, Plato, Aristotle—is wrong and bound for damnation. Self-doubt, subtlety, and critical reflection are unknown to him. He is cock-sure of himself, an evangelist pouring on the brimstone. It is worth noting that his certainty and intolerance

---

[39] Irenaeus, *Haer.* 1.28.1 (Rousseau and Doutreleau, 356).
[40] Whittaker, 5.
[41] Whittaker, 59.

may have brought him into conflict with other equally-ardent Christians in Rome, whose views might have differed.[42]

That Tatian was strong-willed, intolerant, and adopted a "scorched earth" policy against opponents, should not be surprising. Such a psychological profile is common among charismatic leaders and religious figures of note. A wag once remarked that the three people in history he would *least* like to have met were St. Paul, Augustine, and John Calvin. All of them have something of these same characteristics: arrogance (albeit sometimes cloaked in mock humility), overweening self-confidence, a razor-sharp tongue, and a supreme confidence (despite private moments of doubt) in their calling as God's messenger to humanity.

Not surprisingly, Tatian's intellectual makeup was influenced by his personality, and vice-versa. Many "seekers of truth," however, eventually come to the realization that truth does not exist, or that it is dependent upon what *they* want to be true at a given time and place, or in a given circumstance.[43] No such realization seems to have dawned on Tatian. He seems to have remained (as best we can tell [recall that our sources fail us towards the end of his life]) engaged in his stubborn quest, rather like the person who changes religions every few years, convinced that the *next* religion to which he converts will be the "right" one—or at least a "better fit." Tatian's youthful promenade through a series of religions and philosophies supports this analysis. And although Christianity eventually seems to have afforded him some stability, recall that he was expelled from the Roman congregation for teaching "he created [*his own*] unique

---

[42] We know there were a wide variety of Christian viewpoints in Rome at this time, all equally legitimate, and, therefore, requiring toleration and tact. An example is the Quartodeciman Controversy. Near the end of his life, the aged bishop of Smyrna, Polycarp, traveled to Rome, to meet with Anicetus, the bishop of Rome, to discuss their different ways of celebrating Easter and their different dates for Easter (their meeting probably took place in 154 or 155). Agreeing that both were the recipients of ancient traditions, the two bishops, in the end, agreed to disagree and, as a sign of respect for Polycarp and the Quartodecimans, Anicetus provided Polycarp with a church in which he might celebrate the Quartodeciman Easter. See William L. Petersen, "Eusebius and the Paschal Controversy," in *Eusebius, Christianity, and Judaism* (ed. H. Attridge and G. Hata; Detroit: Wayne State University Press, 1992), 311–25.

[43] The malleable nature of "religious truth" is patently obvious to anyone observing a religion from the outside. In Christianity one may point to the inconsistent, changing views of women, lending at interest, Jews, homophiles, science, slavery, etc.

doctrine" (so Irenaeus), and then proceeded to set up *his own* school
(obviously teaching *his own* version of Christianity) back in the East.
It would seem that, in the end, the only religion Tatian found acceptable was *his own* version of Christianity.[44]

Finally, one must also remark on a certain prudishness or sobriety that seems to have been part of Tatian's makeup. It may well
be related to Tatian's Encratism.[45] Tatian seems to embrace a rather
simple life: he rejects luxury, power, and wealth ("I have no desire
to rule, I do not wish to be rich; I do not seek command . . . I am
not driven by greed to go on voyages . . ."), and it is not difficult to
discern a bias against the erotic: "I hate fornication. . . ." Elsewhere
he describes his revulsion at Greek (mystery?) religious rites, led by
"effeminate," "male-screwing" officiants, rites which "busily encouraged wrong-doing."[46] Compared with the culture that surrounded
him—one that glorified voluptuousness and eroticism (both in the
bedroom and in the arena)—Tatian seems something of a prude.[47]
A pre-existent Puritan, it is striking that Tatian never once exposes
a "soft" spot for the common things of life: a spouse, a child, love,
desire, affection, empathy, companionship, sorrow at the loss of someone, love of the beautiful person or object. All these are conspicuous by their absence from the *Oratio*. There are no "bridal chamber"
metaphors, there is no indication that Tatian ever "so loved" anything. Rather, all he displays is a hard, brittle façade, overly (exces-
sively?) cerebral, incapable of enjoying (or not interested in?) the
"good" things of life: wine, women (or men) and song. There appears

---

[44] While it is true that every religious person, to some degree or other, "creates"
his or her own internalized, personalized faith, most religious people do not pur-
sue this goal so zealously or systematically that they end up estranging themselves
from their co-religionists (as Tatian did), and founding their own sect. It is of
more than passing interest that, in contrast to the mild-mannered (if a bit dim-wit-
ted) Justin and the irenic Irenaeus, Tatian finds a parallel in his slightly-younger
contemporary, Tertullian, who was another "authoritarian personality," who also
wrote invective, and who was also excommunicated by the "Great Church," and
who also is reported to have founded his own sect, the "Tertullianists."

[45] On Encratism, see the definition and literature *supra*, n. 2.

[46] *Or.* 29.1 (Whittaker, 53).

[47] It is, perhaps, significant that Epiphanius reports that Justin lived a life of "rigorous asceticism" (*Pan.* 1.46.3; *The Panarion of Epiphanius of Salamis: Book I: Sects 1–46*
(trans. F. Williams; Nag Hammadi and Manichaean Studies 35; Leiden: E. J. Brill,
1997), 348]). However, the report is late, and Epiphanius is often unreliable. If the
report were correct, however, it would be one more parallel between Tatian and
Justin: both would have had strong ascetic tendencies.

to be something of a disjunction in the man: while he is supremely self-confident in his religious and philosophic views, he also seems, ultimately, ill-at-ease in his own skin. And, once again, we must note that this behavior pattern is well-known among religious figures of note: our maladjusted, religion-swapping, invective-hurling trinity of St. Paul, Augustine, and Calvin immediately springs to mind.

4. *The Charges Against Tatian*

All of the descriptions as to why Tatian was separated from the Roman church—including the accusations of heresy—ultimately go back to Irenaeus. There are four charges. The first we have already dealt with: Tatian's pride at being a teacher, and his high opinion of himself. That need not detain us now, for whatever it is, it is not a heresy.

Before examining the three remaining charges against Tatian, we must underscore two points that have become commonplaces in examinations of the theologies of the early church. First, there was no "theology" of the early church; rather, there were "theologies." There were no universal standards during this period;[48] the canon had not been set, and no gospels were universally recognized as authoritative.[49] What Jesus was (just a man; an angel; a demiurge or "lesser power" in heaven; God himself) was still undecided. Second, and following from this first point, it is, therefore, anachronistic to speak of "orthodoxy" and "heresy" in this period. This has been understood by many—but not all—writers since at least the time of Walter Bauer, whose *Orthodoxy and Heresy in Earliest Christianity*[50] high-lighted the problem. Towards the end of the second century we

---

[48] The Quartodeciman Controversy (see *supra*, at n. 42) is one example; the virtually simultaneous excommunication (in Alexandria) and ordination (in Caesarea) of Origen is another.

[49] Tatian's *Diatessaron* may well have been an attempt to create a single new, authoritative gospel, an attempt that was, at least in Syria, apparently successful for over two hundred years (see *infra*, n. 52). The canon would not be universally agreed upon until the Quinisextine (or Trullan) Synod, in 692 C.E. All earlier conciliar decisions (Hippo Regius [393], Carthage [397], etc.) were not universally recognized. See also our remarks *supra*, n. 42.

[50] Walter Bauer, *Orthodoxy and Heresy in Earliest Christianity* (eds. Robert A. Kraft and Gerhard Krodel; trans. a team from the Philadelphia Seminar on Christian Origins; Philadelphia: Fortress, 1971).

have, at most, the very first beginnings of what early church historians call the "great church"[51] in the Latin West and Alexandria; but what was happening in Greece, Anatolia, Syria and Palestine was very different, and remains even today largely uncharted.[52] Only in retrospect can one speak about "orthodoxy" and "heresy" in this period, for the norms by which such judgments are made were local, in flux, and would later be revised.

With this warning fresh in minds, let us look at the first of the three theological charges Irenaeus brings against Tatian: Encratism.[53]

As prologue, it must be pointed out that Encratism is a poorly-defined movement, with no clear boundaries. The name "Encratism" comes from the Greek word *egkrateia*, meaning "restraint of one's emotions, impulses, or desires, self-control." Considered a virtue by Greek writers, this concept manifested itself in various forms, both in Jewish thought in the Hebrew Bible, in the intertestamental period in Palestine, and in the secular world at large. To understand the charge against Tatian, one must understand something of this larger background.

In the Graeco-Roman world at large, ascetic practices, such as vegetarianism, were a part of various religions and philosophies, Pythagoreanism being one example;[54] chastity, too, was an integral

---

[51] On this term, see William H. C. Frend, *The Rise of Christianity* (Philadelphia: Fortress, 1984), 230 (and the note, on 260); the term originates—ironically enough—with the pagan philosopher Celsus; see Frend, *Rise*, 194; the phrase is in a fragment of Celsus, preserved in Origen's *Contra Celsum*, 5.59 (*Origen, Contra Celsum* [trans. H. Chadwick; Cambridge: Cambridge University Press, 1953], 310), about 178 C.E. (Chadwick [ibid., xxviii] dates Celsus' *Alethes logos* to between 177 and 180). In modern scholarship, it connotes the emerging lines of thought and praxis that would, eventually (and perhaps with further revision and modification), become "normative" and later be recognized, in retrospect, as "orthodox."

[52] Each geographic area must be examined separately, as Bauer does; Frend follows the same geographic approach (Frend, *Rise*, 142–47). An example of this geographic "particularism" concerns Tatian's *Diatessaron*, which apparently became the standard gospel of the Syrian church from its introduction (in the 180s?) down through the early fifth century: around 425, bishops Rabbula of Edessa and Theodoret of Cyrrhus took steps to replace the *Diatessaron* with the separated gospels (see Petersen, *Tatian's Diatessaron*, 41–44).

[53] Cf. the definition and references *supra*, n. 2.

[54] See, e.g., "Pythagoras," section C.2 ("Praktische Lehren, Lebensregeln, Tabus"), in *Paulys Real-Encyclopädie der classischen Altertumswissenschaft: Neue Bearbeitung, Band 24* (ed. G. Wissowa, W. Kroll, et al.; Stuttgart: Druckenmüller, 1963), coll. 192–97; K. Algra, J. Barnes, J. Mansfeld, et al., eds., *Cambridge History of Hellenistic Philosophy* (Cambridge: Cambridge University Press, 1999), 787; see also R. M. Grant's very helpful "Dietary Laws Among Pythagoreans, Jews, and Christians," *HTR* 73 (1980): 299–310.

component of certain groups, such as the Virgins of Vesta, in Rome.[55] Within Judaism such ideas were also known, and from an equally early date. The Nazirite vow—which entailed eschewing "wine and strong drink," any contact with corpses (even those of family members), and cutting of the hair—meant separating one's self from society.[56] Moving nearer to the beginning of the Christian era, we find the Essenes of Qumran following a lifestyle that can only be described as ascetic, monastic and (for at least one group of Essenes) celibate.[57] While wine and meat are apparently permitted, the community embraces poverty and severe self-discipline. Another pre-Christian example is John the Baptist, whose clothing, diet, and withdrawn life in the wilderness indicate an ascetic lifestyle.[58]

With the arrival of Christianity, certain of these motifs carried over into the New Testament. The depiction of Jesus as an itinerant, apparently celibate teacher of wisdom who embraces poverty, is congruent with the streams of thought we have seen in both pagan and Jewish predecessors. Jesus also speaks approvingly of those "who have made themselves eunuchs for the sake of the kingdom of heaven" (Matt 19:12). Paul's advocacy of celibacy (1 Cor 7:1, 6–8, 25–28, 38) as the "better" state—and thereby relegating marriage to a lesser, secondary position—is well-known.[59]

There is, then, evidence in the New Testament itself which shows that Christianity, from the very beginning, had certain ascetic—and, therefore, Encratitic—tendencies. We also have evidence that such

---

[55] See s.v. "Vesta, D.5: *virgo* nicht *mater familias*," in *Paulys Real-Encyclopädie der classischen Altertumswissenschaft: Neue Bearbeitung, Band 8A.2* (ed. G. Wissowa and W. Kroll, et al.; Stuttgart: Druckenmüller, 1958), coll. 1724–44.

[56] The prescriptions of the Nazirite vow are found in Numbers 6:1–21; see also the story of Samson, who was "a Nazirite to God from birth," in Judges 13–16; cp. Amos 2:11–12.

[57] See any of the standard introductions to the Essenes and Qumran. The celibacy of the Essenes is explicitly mentioned, independently, by Josephus, *B.J.* 2.120 (2.8.2) (*Jospehus, The Jewish War: Books I–II* [ed. H. St. J. Thackeray; LCL 203; Cambridge, Mass.: Harvard University Press, 1927], 368–369) and Pliny the Elder, *Nat.* 5.15 (5.71) (*Pliny, Natural History: Vol. II: Libri III–VII* [ed. H. Rackham; LCL 352; Cambridge, Mass.: Harvard University Press, 1969], 276–277); their simple life-style is well-illustrated in their *Rule of the Community* (1QS).

[58] Cf. Matt 3:1–6.

[59] See the literature *supra*, n. 2. For reports of asceticism and celibacy among the very earliest Judaic Christians (and some Jews), see Epiphanius (all references are from *Epiphanius, Ancoratus und Panarion 1–33* (ed. K. Holl; GCS 25; Leipzig: J. C. Hinrichs, 1915), Pan. 1.30.2.6 (Ebionites: 334–335); 1.19.1.7 (Ossaeans: 218); 1.16.1.2 (Pharisees: 210); 1.15.1.7 (Scribes: 209); 1.13.1.1 (Dositheans: 205–206).

ideas were put into practice by early Christians. This is not only evident from the communistic lifestyle adopted by the primitive Jerusalem church (Acts 2:44–45; 4:32, 34–37; 5:1–11), but also from a request by a young Christian in Alexandria to the Roman governor there, Felix, that he be permitted to have himself castrated, presumably in order emulate Jesus' words in Matt 19:12.[60] Such ideas extended even into later Christianity, especially in the East, where celibacy was a requirement for baptism in some Christian communities.[61] Obviously, with such a rich background—in secular society at large, in Graeco-Roman philosophy and religion, and in Judaism—it is difficult to trace the precise contours of Christian Encratism in the first two centuries. In a period of geographic, cultural and theological balkanization, and without any strong central authority or standard of reference, it undoubtedly took on various forms in various locales at various times, even as it does today.

Writing about 185 C.E., Irenaeus is the first Christian writer to report that Marcion ($fl.$ 140) and Saturninus ($fl.$ 140 [?]) held that "marriage was corruption and fornication."[62] Slightly later (ca. 190 [?]) and apparently independently, Clement of Alexandria levels the same charge at Marcion.[63] Still later, Hippolytus of Rome (ca. 225) says that Marcion "prevents marriage, begetting children, [and advocates] avoiding meats."[64] Of Saturninus, Hippolytus says he "affirms that marriage and procreation are from Satan";[65] the followers of Saturninus, says Hippolytus, "abstain from living things."[66]

Hippolytus is very instructive concerning the background of these ideas.[67] He states that Marcion was (or had been) a follower of the

---

[60] The episode is related by Justin, *1 Apol.* 19.2–3 (*Die ältesten Apologeten*, 45); Felix refused permission, upon which Justin relates that "the youth remained single." One is reminded of Origen's reportedly-successful attempt to have the same mutilation performed on himself, in the same city, near 198 C.E. (recounted in Eusebius, *Hist. eccl.* 6.8.1–3 [SC 41, pp. 95–96]). Cp. Epiphanius' report that the early Ebionites were celibate (*Pan.* 1.30.2.6 [ed. Dindorf, Vol. 2, p. 91]).

[61] See the literature *supra*, n. 2.

[62] Irenaeus, *Haer.* 1.28.1 (Rousseau and Doutreleau, 356–357).

[63] *Strom.* 3.3.1–3 [12.1–3] (Holl and Dummer; GCS; pp. 200–201).

[64] Hippolytus, *Haer.* 7.30.3 (Marcovich, 312).

[65] Hippolytus, *Haer.* 7.28.7 (ibid., 304).

[66] Hippolytus, *Haer.* 7.28.7 (ibid.).

[67] What follows is an interesting example of how ancient ideas reached early Christians via intermediaries: here, Marcion need not have known Pythagoras' ideas directly (although he probably did), for Pythagoras influenced Empedocles, and Marcion (as per Hippolytus) was a devotee of Empedocles.

teachings of Empedocles (fifth cent. B.C.E.; born in Agrigento, Sicily).[68] Empedocles taught abstinence from meat; in this, Empedocles may have been influenced by Pythagoras (6th cent. B.C.E.) and Orphism (which, presumably, antedates Pythagoras), both of which also advocated avoiding meat.

Irenaeus, our oldest source of the charge of Encratism against Tatian, expresses his complaint in these words:

> . . . the ones called Encratites, issuing from Saturninus and Marcion, preached abstinence from marriage . . . and they have introduced [dietary] abstinence from what they call "living things". . . . They likewise deny the salvation of him who was the first formed [Adam]. But this last idea was recently invented among them, when a certain Tatian first introduced this blasphemy. He was an *auditor* of Justin. . . . and exalted at the prospect of being a teacher, and puffed up as if he were superior to everyone else, he created a unique doctrine. Like those who follow Valentinus, he expounded an account of invisible Aeons; and like Marcion and Saturninus, he said marriage was corruption and fornication. But denying the salvation of Adam was his own doing.[69] (*Haer.* 1.28.1)

The charges say nothing about abstaining from wine. The idea that Tatian was a teetotaler first appears in Jerome (ca. 385): "Tatian . . . assert[ed] that wine should not be drunk."[70] Whether Jerome's tradition is reliable, or whether he simply inferred it from earlier descriptions of Encratism, is unknown. The basis for making such an inference dates back to at least Clement of Alexandria (ca. 200) who, after a long discussion of the dangers of wine, nevertheless defends its consumption by citing the description of Jesus as being "a glutton and a wine-bibber" (Matt 11:19), saying: "Let this be held fast by us against those that are called Encratites."[71]

---

[68] Hippolytus, *Haer.* 7.30.1 (Marcovich, 34).

[69] Eds. Rousseau and Doutreleau, 354–357.

[70] Jerome, *Comm. Am.* 1.12 (*S. Hieronymi Presbyteri Opera: Pars I.6*; CCSL 76; Turnhout: Brepols, 1969), 239.

[71] *Paed.* 2.2.33.1 (*Clemens Alexandrinus. I. Protrepticus und Paedagogus* [ed. O. Stählin and U. Treu; third revised ed.; GCS 12; Berlin: Akademie-Verlag, 1972], 176). Slightly later (ca. 225), Hippolytus of Rome, *Haer.* 8.20.1 (Marcovich, 399) also mentions that Encratites avoid alcoholic beverages (they are "water-drinkers"). It should also be pointed out that there seems to be a rather well-known (almost proverbial?) linkage in antiquity between avoiding wine and meat: elsewhere, Clement of Alexandria quotes Androcydes against consuming both meat and wine: "Wine and indulgence in meat make the body strong but the soul more sluggish," *Strom.* 7.33.7 (*Clemens*

In the final analysis, then, there appear to have been various forms of Encratism; indeed, Irenaeus' charge indicates three stages of evolution: the core seems to be a denunciation of marriage (so Saturninus and Marcion); to this "they have introduced" vegetarianism (no mention of alcohol); and, finally, Tatian added (to this already-existing system) the idea that Adam would not be saved. Owing to the diffuse nature of Encratism in this period, we cannot be dogmatic about Tatian's attitude towards alcohol. It seems likely that he—like many (most?) other Encratites—avoided it, but no one before Jerome explicitly makes this claim for Tatian.

Neither the rejection of marriage nor the rejection of meat is unique. As we have seen, Hippolytus reports that Marcion also scorned marriage and advocated abstinence from meat. Before Marcion, the denigration of marriage is also found in the New Testament itself: recall that Paul says the person who remains celibate has done a "better thing" than the person who marries, and that Jesus' statement about "those who make themselves eunuchs for the sake of the kingdom of heaven" was taken at face value by some, who hastened to their surgeons.[72] Before Marcion, the rejection of meat is also found in Marcion's favorite philosopher, Empedocles, as well as in other older Greek schools.[73]

In the course of being appropriated by later writers (both ancient and modern), Irenaeus' report has been corrupted. According to Eusebius, for example, Tatian is the Encratite's "first leader."[74] This cannot be squared with his source, Irenaeus, who only attributes to Tatian the invention of the idea that Adam will not be saved; Tatian added this to the Encratites' preexisting aversions to marriage and meat, in order to create his own "different" system.[75]

Alexandrinus III: Stromata Buch VII und VIII. (ed. O. Stählin, L. Früchtel and U. Treu; GCS; Berlin: Akademie-Verlag, 1970), 130, here quoted after the ET of Grant, "Dietary Laws," 301–2.

[72] Cp. supra, n. 60.

[73] See supra, n. 68.

[74] Tatian's position as a heresiarch is, after Eusebius, repeated by Rufinus (in his Latin translation of Eusebius' Hist. eccl. [ed. Th. Mommsen; in Schwartz; GCS 9/3; Leipzig: J. C. Hinrichs, 1909), 393]); Jerome (Vir. ill. 29 [ed. Ceresa-Gastaldo], 124–125); Michael the Syrian (in his Chronicle, 6.5 [ed. Chabot; vol. IV; 108–109 (text); vol. I, 180–181 (translation)]), and Bar Hebraeus (in "The Candelabra of Holiness..." [ed. F. Nau, PO 13.2 (Paris: Firmin-Didot, 1916), 254–255]). This erroneous claim is still frequently repeated today: cp. Whittaker, x.

[75] Cp. Irenaeus, Haer. 1.28.1; and 3.23.8 (Irénée de Lyon, Contra les Hérésies: Livre

Is there confirmation of the charge of Encratism in Tatian's œuvre, and if so, where, and how much?

When discussing Tatian's biography and his *Oratio ad graecos*, we alluded to Tatian's prudishness, and provided the references.[76] He abhors the blood, gore and slaughter of the spectacles and certain religious rites; he dislikes effeminate homosexual behavior, and he never mentions women. At the same time he avoids discussion of anything domestic: children, love, marriage (or even a paramour), affection, family, home and hearth. From this we can conclude that a certain prudishness, congenial with Encratism, is found in the *Oratio*. But the evidence for this conclusion is implicit rather than explicit. For example, when sexual or erotic themes are mentioned, they are always placed in a negative light; but there is no explicit condemnation of marriage. Similarly, although alcohol does not figure in the *Oratio*, it is clear that the (potential) loss of control it offers, and the possibility of licentious behavior that might follow consumption, would not meet with Tatian's approval. And although Tatian condemns sacrifices—which presumably included meat offerings—he does not explicitly enjoin the eating of meat in the *Oratio*. Therefore, although one must conclude that the *Oratio* is not overtly Encratite, and cannot be called an Encratite tract, it is, nevertheless, entirely compatible with an Encratite worldview.

The *Diatessaron* is a bit of a different story, however, albeit a rather confusing one. The first problem is, as noted previously, the reconstruction of the *Diatessaron*'s text from among the many witnesses, in their very divergent languages. All of the witnesses come from different periods and places, and each has, of course, its own unique transmission history.

Over the years, four scholars (H. J. Vogels, D. Plooij, A. Vööbus, and L. Leloir) have noted a total of thirteen places in Diatessaronic witnesses where variants occur that might be Encratite. Your author has collected and published these variants elsewhere.[77] Unfortunately, most of the variants are usually found in only a single Diatessaronic witness, making it impossible to know whether the variant is gen-

---

III, tome II [ed. A. Rousseau and L. Doutreleau; SC 211; Paris: Cerf, 1974], 466–467): [discussing Adam] "But this [belief] he [Tatian] devised himself, so that by initiating something new, different from the rest, [and] speaking emptily, he might gain for himself hearers empty of faith, he sought to be regarded as a teacher...."

[76] See *supra*, nn. 45 to 47.
[77] Petersen, *Tatian's Diatessaron*, 76–82.

uinely Diatessaronic, or merely a variant that arose in the trans-mission-history of that particular witness. For example, in Ephrem's *Hymn on the Resurrection of Christ*, Leloir noted that when quoting Matt 11:19, which speaks of the Son of Man drinking and being a "wine-bibber," Ephrem reproduces only the part about the Son of Man drinking, and omits "wine-bibber." There are, however, many other possible explanations for this omission: Ephrem may have dropped the word for metrical reasons; Ephrem himself—and not Tatian—may have wished to avoid mention of "wine-bibber" here; Ephrem may have cited the text from memory and simply forgotten the word. Leloir's case is weak not just because the reading is found in only one source, but also because other—and perhaps better—explana-tions lie at hand. The lesson any would-be researcher should learn from this example is that not every Encratite-friendly variant in a Diatessaronic witness can be traced back to Tatian's pen.

This raises the question of how one might, in a more reliable manner, go about detecting readings which stem from the *Diatessaron itself*, as distinct from readings which arose in the transmission-his-tory of a particular Diatessaronic *witness*. Elsewhere, your author has published a set of criteria which help separate those readings which have a high likelihood of being Diatessaronic from those which do not. The likelihood that a variant comes from the *Diatessaron* is increased if the variant occurs in *multiple* witnesses (not just one), that are geographically diversified: the identical variant should occur in at least one Eastern witness and one Western witness.[78] Three of the thirteen readings meet these criteria; therefore, they deserve men-tion here.

At Luke 2:36, H. J. Vogels noticed that a slight change in the text made the passage congenial with Encratite values. While the standard Greek of Luke says that "Anna . . . was of a great age, hav-ing lived with her husband seven years *from* her virginity," no fewer than three Diatessaronic witnesses—one in the East, and two in the West—read: "Anna remained seven years a virgin *with* her husband."[79] Anna's marriage is transformed into the Encratite ideal: *un mariage blanc*.

---

[78] This is an abbreviated expression of the criteria; because the matter is very complex and beyond the realm of this study, the interested reader is referred to the full discussion in Petersen, *Tatian's Diatessaron*, 373–424.

[79] For the full texts, references, and discussion, see Petersen, *Tatian's Diatessaron*, 80–81.

The second variant with multiple, bilateral support is found at Matt 1:24. Here, instead of having the text say Joseph "took" Mary, a total of five Diatessaronic witnesses (three in the East and two in the West) state that Joseph "guarded" Mary—avoiding the whole idea of marriage.[80]

Although the third and final reading has multiple support, it must remain doubtful, because it is an omission. At Matt 1:19, three Diatessaronic witnesses (one in the East, and two in the West) omit the words "the husband"; Vööbus suggested this change was Encratite-inspired. However, since the reading is an omission (whose genesis in each individual witness may be different), there is no way to know whether it is Diatessaronic or not.

Let us now turn to the second theological charge Irenaeus levels, namely, that Tatian, "like those who follow Valentinus, expounded an account of invisible Aeons." The mention of "aeons" and "Valentinus" means that Irenaeus is, in essence, calling Tatian a Gnostic. It is probable that this more general charge is related to Irenaeus' more specific allegation that Tatian invented the idea that Adam—the first man—would not be saved, for "Adam"-speculation figures prominently in many Gnostic systems.[81]

By the time of Irenaeus, a charge of Gnosticism was something of a catch-all libel with which to defame an ecclesiastical foe; a certain skepticism is, therefore, warranted. On the other hand, however, there are clear signs of Gnosticism in Tatian's *Oratio*. Among other markers, Tatian's account of creation clearly places an intermediary—a "demiurge" in Gnostic terminology—between God and the creation.

According to Tatian, only "God" is "in the beginning" (*Or.* 5.1). Later, "by partition," the "Word" comes into being from "God" (whom Tatian also calls "the Father"). The "Word" is the "firstborn" of God. God is the "power" of the "Word."

---

[80] The same description—and word—is found in the apocryphal *Protevangelium Iacobi*, 9.1; 9.3; 13.1 (*La forme la plus ancienne du Protévangile de Jacques* [ed. É. de Strycker; SH 33; Brussels: Société. des Bollandistes, 1961], 106, 108, 122). One must, therefore, entertain the possibility that this variant may not reflect Tatian's ideas, but those of the author of the *Protevangelium*.

[81] See s.v. "Adam," in the index of James M. Robinson, ed., *The Nag Hammadi Library in English* (Leiden: E. J. Brill, 1977); see also Irenaeus' description (*Haer.* 1.30.7–14) of the Ophites and Sethians, which is separated from his discussion of Tatian (*Haer.* 1.29) by only a single intervening chapter.

After a digression on resurrection (*Or.* 6), Tatian resumes his theogony (*Or.* 7); new terms are introduced without definition or explication. The "celestial Word" (presumably, the "Word" discussed in *Or.* 5, and described there as the "firstborn") is now described as having been "made" from two elements: "spirit from the Spirit[,] and Word from [the] power of the Word" (*Or.* 7.1). This suggests that Tatian understood God the Father as having two aspects— "spirit" and "word"—from which the "firstborn" Word was "made" ("by partition" ?). Then comes the generation of angels: "before the Word made man, he created angels." Note this very important point: the angels and man are created by "the Word," not by God the Father.

"Then," says Tatian, "came one who was cleverer than the rest because he was firstborn, and men and angels followed along with him, and proclaimed as god the traitor to God's law; and so the power of the Word banished the arch-rebel and his followers from life with him" (*Or.* 7.2). This arch-rebel appears to be—although it is not made explicit—the "firstborn" angel; this rebellious angel is "proclaimed as god" by humans and the angels who follow him. This rebellious angel and his followers are "banished" from life with the "power of the Word"—that is, they are banished from heaven, for that is where the "power of the Word" dwells. This is the point at which humanity—which is itself composed from "two different kinds of spirits, one of which is called soul, but the other [spirit] is greater than the soul; it is the image and likeness of God" (*Or.* 12.1)— becomes mortal. This change comes about because of the departure of the "more powerful spirit"—the "image and likeness of God"— from humans (*Or.* 7.3; cp. 12.1); we fallen humans are left with only the lesser "spirit," the "soul." The "firstborn" rebellious angel becomes "a demon, along with those who had followed his example."

Tatian's account clearly places an intermediary, a demiurge, between God "the Father" and the created orders of men and angels. The creating is not done by God "the Father," but by "the firstborn" of God, namely "the (celestial?) Word." One of the problems Gnosticism set out to solve was the problem of evil: how could God, who is totally good,[82] create a world as defective and evil as ours? The

---

[82] Following Greek philosophy, God is pure goodness; this view is, of course, inconsistent with the view of the Hebrew Bible, where God is, directly, the cause of evil (cf. 1 Sam 16:14 and 19:9). Christianity has formally adopted the Greek

answer was to interpose an intermediary—a demiurge—between the totally good supreme God and our created world. In such systems, it is the demiurge—in Tatian's case, "the Word"—that does the creating, not God "the Father."

Confirmation that Gnostic motives are at work here is found in the fact that elsewhere in the *Oratio*, Tatian condemns Zeno because "he portrays God as creator of evil."[83] Zeno's depiction would indeed have been anathema to a Gnostic, who sought to defend God against the charge of creating evil. Further confirmation comes from Clement of Alexandria, who quotes fragments of Tatian's lost works. Writing within a decade or two of Tatian's death, Clement remarks that "[Tatian] would do away with the law, as originating from *another God*."[84] In other words, the Law did not come from the supreme deity, God "the Father," but from another heavenly creature, probably (on the basis of the theogony found in the *Oratio*) the "Word"— thus preserving the perfection of God "the Father."

Yet another element of Gnosticism is in evidence in Tatian's theogony. Recall that he describes the "celestial Word" as infused with or constituted out of two constitutive elements, "spirit" and "word"—both of which must come from (or be part of) the only other existing "thing," namely, the supreme deity, "God." The creation or constituting of a new thing from two antecedent objects, whose genders are opposites, is redolent of the Gnostic idea of syzygies (the union of pairs or opposites). A male principle (here, the masculine "word"/logos, in Greek) and a feminine principle (the feminine "spirit"/*ruach*, in Hebrew and Syriac[85]) combine to animate the new "celestial Word."[86]

---

philosophical view—but has also formally adopted the Hebrew Bible as part of its canon. It has never satisfactorily reconciled these two utterly incompatible world views.

[83] *Or.* 3.2 (Whittaker, 7).

[84] Clem. Alex, *Strom.* 3.82.3 (ed. Stählin and Früchtel; GCS 52; 233; ET: *Alexandrian Christianity* [trans. J. E. L. Oulton and H. Chadwick; LCC 2; Philadelphia: Westminster, 1954], 78, emphasis added).

[85] The idea of a feminine (holy) spirit is known in early Christianity, and derives from the Semitic languages, where "spirit" is a feminine noun. Tatian's Oriental heritage (viz., his awareness of the feminine gender of "spirit" in the Semitic languages) may shape his language and thinking here. See, for example, the well-known quotation from the "Gospel of the Hebrews" preserved in Origen, *Comm. Jo.* 2.12, etc. (readily available in *New Testament Apocrypha* [ed. W. Schneemelcher; trans. R. McL. Wilson; 2 vols.; rev. ed.; Cambridge: James Clarke, 1991–1992]), 1:177. See also *Ap. John.* 9 (Robinson, *The Nag Hammadi Library*, 103).

[86] In conversation with your author, Prof. Gilles Quispel (Utrecht) listed six mark-

In addition to these rather obvious features suggestive of Gnostic ideas, Robert M. Grant has noted certain expressions in the *Oratio*, which suggest contact with Valentinian Gnosticism. The most convincing of these, in your author's opinion, is Tatian's characterization of demons as robbers who deceive souls abandoned by the divine Spirit (*Or.* 14.1). According to Grant, this "closely resembles" the beliefs of the Valentinian Theodotus (as described by Clement of Alexandria, *Exc.* 72.2).[87]

Because of its genre (a gospel harmony), Tatian's only other extant work, the *Diatessaron*, offers no evidence either for or against Tatian's Gnosticism. Indeed, the most "Gnostic" passages in the *Diatessaron* are its excerpts from the Gospel of John.

The third and final theological charge Irenaeus levels at Tatian is his "denial of Adam's salvation"; according to Irenaeus, Tatian is the originator of this idea. Curiously, none of the early sources offer a description of this distinctively Tatianic belief. Only when we reach Epiphanius (ca. 375) do we find a discussion.

Epiphanius begins his critique of Tatian by arguing against intermediaries (demiurges) in creation: there is, says Epiphanius, only one first principle. Adam was created by this first principle, not some lesser divine being (recall Tatian's statement in the *Oratio* that both men and angels were created by the "Word"). Since Adam, along

---

ers he has found helpful in identifying Gnostic systems and texts in this period; to the best of your author's knowledge, this is the first time they have been published. (1) An intermediary in creation (evident here); (2) a radical dualism (including what we find here: a system of syzygies in which opposites unite to create new beings); (3) an androgynous supreme deity (while not explicit here, it cannot be precluded, and may be philosophically implicit in Tatian's system [God is "spirit" (feminine) and "word" (masculine) ?]); (4) a highly developed angelology (not in evidence here, for despite Tatian's mention of angels, his account is no more elaborate than that found in Genesis); (5) the possibility for the true Gnostic to achieve mystical union with the divine (not found here); and (6) a hierarchical system of belief including secret teachings (not evident here).

The definition of "Gnosticism" is, of course, a much-disputed problem: cp., for example, the discussions of J. Holzhausen, "Gnostizismus, Gnosis, Gnostiker: Ein Beitrag zur antiken Terminologie," *JAC* 44 (2001): 58–74, or K. L. King's recent *What is Gnosticism?* (Cambridge, Mass.: The Belknap Press of Harvard University Press, 2003), or C. Scholten's "Probleme der Gnosisforschung: Alte Fragen–neue Zugänge," *Comm* 26 (1997): 481–501.

[87] R. M. Grant, "The Heresy of Tatian," *JTS* 5 (1954): 62–68; here 63. For Clement: *Clément d'Alexandrie, Extraits de Théodote* (ed. F. Sagnard; new printing [orig. 1948]; SC 23; Paris: Cerf, 1970), 194–197; or ed. Stählin, Früchtel and Treu; GCS; 130.

with everything else, was created by God, then—argues Epiphanius—it follows that Adam, like the rest of creation, can be saved.

Behind this polemic against Tatian, we can begin to detect, perhaps, the outline of Tatian's theology of Adam. Although Adam does not figure in the *Oratio*, certain features of Tatian's cosmology and anthropology allow one to conjecture the role Adam played in Tatian's system.

We have already seen that, according to Tatian, man was created by an intermediary, the "Word," and that, before the Fall, man possessed two spirits, one inferior (the "soul") and one more divine ("the image and likeness of God"):

> We have knowledge of *two* different kinds of *spirits, one of which is called soul,* but *the other is greater than the soul; it is the image and likeness of God.* The *first men were endowed with both,* so that they might be part of the material world, and at the same time [be] above it.[88] (*Or.* 12.1)

At the Fall, the higher spirit, "the image and likeness of God," departed, precluding man's participation in the heavenly world. We were left with only the lower "soul," which gave us participation only in "the material world."

Within his system, Tatian must have placed Adam among "the first men," who possessed both types of spirit; we, however, are descendents of the fallen Adam. We possess only the "lower" of these two spirits, the soul. This is perishable: "The soul, men of Greece, is not in itself immortal but mortal; yet it also has the power to escape death" (*Or.* 13.1). This raises the question: How does our soul—how do *we*—escape death? Tatian's answer smacks of Pelagianism and predestination. God, for his part, sent his spirit to reveal the path to salvation to certain right-acting men: "God's spirit *is not given to all,* but dwelling among *some who behaved justly* . . . it revealed by predictions . . . what had been hidden" (*Or.* 13.3);[89] the properly religious man, for his part, "advance[s] far beyond his humanity toward God himself" (*Or.* 15.2).[90] The Pelagianism (before Pelagius!) is visible in *our* need to "behave justly" and to "advance . . . beyond [our] humanity toward God"; the predestination is visible in the fact that "God's spirit is not given to all."

---

[88] Whittaker, 23, emphasis added.
[89] Whittaker, 27.
[90] Whittaker, 31.

The key to salvation in Tatian's system is *gnosis*, "knowledge": a human soul will "not die, even if it is dissolved for a time, *if it has obtained knowledge of God*" (*Or.* 13.1).[91] Therein lies the explanation of Adam's predicament, and why Tatian argued Adam would not be saved: although Adam *had* had the knowledge of God, he—through free will[92]—rejected it. This rejection resulted in the Fall: Adam's loss of "the image and likeness of God" (which is not flesh, and should not be confused with our bodies).[93] Unlike Adam, who enjoyed the prelapsarian idyll, we have never enjoyed this perfect "dual" life (in which we would have consisted of both a "soul"—which animates us in the physical world—*and* a "spirit [which is] the image and likeness of God"—which allows us to "live" in the celestial realms, enjoying intercourse with God, the Word, and the angels). And although *we* never rejected "the image and likeness of God" (that is, the "higher" soul or "spirit"), *Adam* did. Hence, *we* have the opportunity to regain what we lost through *Adam's* rejection—not *our* rejection: "*We* ought now to search for what we [as a race] once had [in Adam] and have lost, and link the soul to the Holy Spirit and busy ourselves with the union ordained by God."[94] Adam, however, does not have this opportunity, for he once enjoyed that blissful, pre-Fall state of union, and rejected it. Therefore, he does not get a second chance. We, however, are to be allowed *our* chance, our *first* chance.

Surveying the above evidence, one may conclude that Irenaeus' four allegations against Tatian appear well founded. His first charge, that Tatian become puffed up with pride when he took on the role of teacher and thought himself superior to others, seems reasonable, given the pride we have seen displayed in the *Oratio*, and his categorical condemnation of everything Greek. Nuance, tact and fine discriminations are not familiar to Tatian. Second, although the *Oratio* gives no explicit clues, there are potentially a very few passages in the *Diatessaron* which appear sympathetic to Encratism. Although Irenaeus mentions only an aversion to marriage and meat, it is not

---

[91] Whittaker, 27, emphasis added.

[92] For Tatian, free will is what did us in. While both men and angels have free will (*Or.* 7.1 [Whittaker, 13]), both have failed to exercise it wisely: "Free will has destroyed us" (*Or.* 11.2 [Whittaker, 23]).

[93] "Now the perfect God is fleshless, but man is flesh" (*Or.* 15.2 [Whittaker, 31]).

[94] *Or.* 15.1 ([Whittaker, 29], emphasis added).

unreasonable to assume that Tatian avoided wine, as well. Third, there are clear signs in the *Oratio* of Gnostic tendencies. Tatian appears to subscribe to belief in an intermediary in creation, a system of syzygies, and salvation through knowledge of God.[95] Thus, Irenaeus' claim that Tatian was a follower of Marcion and Valentinus, and believed in a system of invisible aeons, seems well founded. Finally, regarding Irenaeus' fourth charge, the denial of Adam's salvation, we have suggested that it can be inferred from a close reading of the theology of the *Oratio*. Adam once enjoyed bliss with God, but rejected the part of him that was "the image and likeness of God"; having made that choice, Adam has forever condemned himself, and will not be saved because of his free-will choice.

It is important to note, however, that our methodology in this chapter has been to use the Patristic reports as a guide for sifting through Tatian's writings. Our points for comparison come from Irenaeus; using these, we have then sought corroboration in Tatian's *œuvre*. If, however, none of the Patristic reports about Tatian survived, and one read the *Diatessaron* and the *Oratio* without any knowledge of Tatian, then only two of Irenaeus' charges would be recognizable. First, a reader of the *Oratio* would quickly conclude that Tatian was an arrogant, prideful controversialist. Second, one would certainly label him a Gnostic; too many Gnostic ideas percolate through the *Oratio* to deny such tendencies.[96] But there is no immediately apparent evidence to support Irenaeus' two other charges, namely, that Tatian was an Encratite, or he denied Adam's salvation.

5. *Tatian, a Heretic?*

One of the more unusual aspects of Tatian's reception is the enormous difference between the East and the West. In the West, for

---

[95] One of the more remarkable things about the *Oratio* is that the words "Christ" or "Jesus" never occur. Tatian's theology is absolutely non-Christocentric. There is a parallel for this lack of interest in Jesus/Christ: Theophilus of Antioch's *Ad Autolycum* also fails to use either word. This non-Christocentrism may be part of a primitive Hellenistic theology in which Jesus' role was minimized, and one focused on the *logos* and God instead. Cp. William L. Petersen, "The Genesis of the Gospels," in *New Testament Textual Criticism and Exegesis* (ed. A. Denaux; BETL 161; Leuven: Peeters, 2002), 55–56.

[96] It must be pointed out, however, that the Gnostic ideas found in the *Oratio* are very tame and "non-mythological," especially when compared with the elaborate systems of other Gnostic teachers (e.g., Basilides [as per Irenaeus, *Haer.* I.24.3–7]) or found in Gnostic tracts (e.g., the *Apocryphon of John*).

example, he is called an "Assyrian"; in the East, however, he is called a "Greek." In the West, he is known by name from the late-second century onwards, beginning with Irenaeus. In the East, however, his name is unrecorded in our sources until it first appears in a Syriac translation of a Western work, Eusebius' *Historia ecclesiastica*. In the West, he is known from the outset as a heretic. In the East, however, that word is not applied to him by any original Eastern work[97] until the tenth century. In the West, Tatian's literary reputation rests solely on his apologetic writings, which are even praised by Clement of Alexandria and Eusebius;[98] the *Diatessaron* remains unmentioned until Eusebius names it; the first physical evidence of a Diatessaron in the West occurs ca. 546, when Bishop Victor of Capua stumbles across a gospel harmony manuscript, *sans* title, *sans* author, and orders a copy made—that copy is our Latin Codex Fuldensis. In the East, however, Tatian's literary reputation derives solely from his *Diatessaron*, which was apparently the standard gospel used in many Syrian churches until the early fifth century; Tatian's apologetic works are passed over in silence (or mentioned *en passant*). While St. Paul spoke of being a "Greek to the Greeks, and a Jew to the Jews," Tatian achieved an even more remarkable feat: to the Greeks he was an Oriental, and the Orientals he was a Greek.

As noted above, Tatian's reputation as a heretic was established early by Irenaeus, and was transmitted without dispute by the many later Western writers we have cited previously in this chapter: Tertullian, Hippolytus, Eusebius, Epiphanius, Jerome, etc. While his apologetic works and chronological demonstration earned praise, his Gnosticism and Encratism were insuperable stumbling blocks: he could not be considered orthodox.

In the East, however, the situation was very different. While the anonymous fourth-century Syriac translation of Eusebius' *Historia ecclesiastica* reproduces Eusebius' account of Tatian's separation from the Roman church,[99] it would be centuries before a source *originally*

---

[97] This phrasing is used to exclude the Syriac translation of Eusebius' *Hist. eccl.* (see n. 99).

[98] Both commend Tatian's chronology (found in the *Oratio*), which "proved" the superior antiquity of Moses over Plato: cp. Clem. Alex., *Strom.* 1.21 [101.2] (ed. Stählin and Früchtel; GCS 52, 64); Eusebius, *Hist. eccl.* 4.29.7 (Bardy, 214).

[99] This is the oldest reference to Tatian in an Oriental language (W. Wright and N. McLean, eds., *The Ecclesiastical History of Eusebius in Syriac* [Cambridge: Cambridge University Press, 1898]). The oldest (Syriac) manuscript of this translation dates from 462 C.E. (cf. *Eusebius Werke II. Die Kirchengeschichte*, Teil 3 [ed. E. Schwartz;

composed in the East does so. Indeed, it seems that it is not until
about 942 that Agapius of Hierapolis, in his Arabic *Kitab al-ʿUnvan*
(*Universal History*), becomes the first Eastern writer to call Tatian a
heretic. Later, obviously following Irenaeus, Michael the Syrian (d.
1199; quoted in the introduction to this chapter), also classes Tatian
among the heretics; so does Bar Hebraeus (*fl.* 1280), who links him
with Encratism and Gnosticism. But between the Syriac translation
of Eusebius and Agapius of Hierapolis, there is a long list of Oriental
luminaries who write of Tatian only in positive terms. The oldest
reference to Tatian in a work originally composed in an Oriental
language[100] appears to be in Theodore bar Koni's *Liber scholiorum*,
composed in 791; even at this late date, Tatian is called "the Greek,"
and there is no mention of Encratism, Valentinus, Marcion, or heresy.
Instead, Theodore's description simply focuses on the *Diatessaron* and
its composition. Similar references[101] are found in Ishoʿdad of Merv
(*fl.* 860); Ishoʿ bar Ali (*fl.* 890);[102] Moses bar Kepha (d. 903)—who
calls him "Tatian the Greek"; ʾAbuʾl Hasan bar Bahlul (latter half
of tenth cent.)—who suggests Tatian composed the *Diatessaron* in
Alexandria, and was a bishop (!); the *Chronicle of Seʿert* (written in
Arabic shortly after 1036)—which also speaks of "Tatian the Greek";
Dionysius bar Salibi (d. 1171)—who places composition of the
Diatessaron in Alexandria, and also calls Tatian a bishop; and ʿAbd
Isoʿ bar Berika (d. 1318)—who speaks glowingly of Tatian as "a certain philosopher" and gospel harmonist (his remarks were quoted at
the beginning of this chapter). None of these writers mentions Tatian's
expulsion from the Roman church or his links with heresy. What
can explain this?

Three reasons may be suggested. First, Tatian was the composer
of the *Diatessaron* which was, apparently, the form in which the gospels

---

GCS 9/3; Leipzig: J. C. Hinrichs, 1909], xli). Note, however, that this is a *translation* of the Greek *Hist. eccl.*, and not, therefore, an *original work* composed in the
East.

[100] And so distinguished from the oldest mention in a translation into an Oriental
language (see *supra*, n. 99).

[101] For the actual texts describing Tatian, bibliography, and discussion of all the
Eastern authors mentioned in this paragraph, see Petersen, *Tatian's Diatessaron*, 51–67.

[102] One manuscript of bar Ali's lexicon, which contains a reference to Tatian
and the *Diatessaron*, closes the entry with a sentence stating that Tatian was anathematized because the *Diatessaron* omitted the genealogy of Jesus; but because this
sentence is not found in other manuscripts of bar Ali's lexicon, it is presumed to
be a later addition (see Petersen, *Tatian's Diatessaron*, 53–54).

first circulated in Syriac. As such, the *Diatessaron* occupied an extremely prestigious and revered place in this history of Eastern Christianity.[103] Not only did it influence all later vernacular translations in Syriac, but also, indirectly, all other vernacular translations made from (or influenced by) the Syriac (e.g., the Armenian, Georgian, and Arabic versions). Because of this, it would have been embarrassing to classify Tatian as a heretic; it would be as if the Roman Catholic Church said the Vulgate had been translated by Valentinus. Second, the issues which were at stake here—namely, ascetic practices, theological issues relating to creation, and Adam—were of (greater) moment in the West, not the East. In the West, issues of authority (and the product of authority, namely, unity) were of primary concern. In the East, however, always Balkanized by language and by small city-states, authority and unity were of lesser concern; in the East, *Christology* was the matter of primary concern, due to the prevalence of "low" Christologies among Judaic Christians. Tatian's Christology—the "litmus test" of "orthodoxy" in the East—seems to have been within the bounds of orthodoxy; therefore, from the perspective of the Eastern church, he did not arouse suspicions. And his Gnostic speculation—which was the primary marker of heresy in the West, especially in Rome (which became the home of both Marcion and Valentinus)—was not a "red flag" in the East. Unlike the West, the East had long been familiar with Greek philosophy; it also enjoyed proximity to and familiarity with Oriental religions (e.g., Zoroastrianism, Hinduism, Judaism, etc.); the East was a place where speculation about the cosmos and the symbolic (as opposed to a literal) understanding of such conjectures was normative. Third and finally, Tatian's Encratism was complementary to the profound ascetic streak already present in the East.[104] Here again, Tatian—either because of his birth, or because of his personality—seems to have been more in tune with the East than the West. In short, the issues that burned with such

---

[103] The *Diatessaron*'s preeminence extended into the early fifth century: the imported Greek bishop Theodoret, who occupied the see at Cyrrhus from 423 to 457, confiscated "more than two hundred copies" of the *Diatessaron* from among the 800 churches in his diocese, where he found the gospel harmony "in reverential use." At the same time, Rabbula of Edessa issued a canon requiring that copies of the "separated" gospels should be kept in all churches; presumably this canon was needed because the churches were using the *Diatessaron*. See Petersen, *Tatian's Diatessaron*, 41–45, for the texts and details of these reports.

[104] Cf., e.g., the studies by Vööbus and Brown (cited *supra*, n. 2).

intensity in Rome did not generate much heat in Edessa or Nisibis. Or, as Arthur Vööbus put it more than fifty years ago, "Tatian's rigid and severe asceticism perplexed the Roman congregation;" nevertheless, "that which was abominable to the Western mind was welcome to the taste of the passionate psyche of Syrians who turned their devotion to the Christian message" as proclaimed by the Encratite, Tatian.[105]

In the final analysis, then, Tatian can be seen—as have been numerous "heretics" throughout the history of Christianity—as simply a victim of time and place: where and when he was active. We have already pointed to other such cases, including the virtually simultaneous excommunication and ordination of Origen, and the rival Easter celebrations of Anicetus and Polycarp.[106] Had Tatian been active only in the East, then he probably would not be known as a heretic.[107] There is one more factor that must be mentioned as well: heresy is frequently not only a question of theology, timing, and location; it is also a matter of personality and presentation. And Tatian's personality seems, in no small measure, to have contributed to his problems with the church in Rome.

Bibliography

Algra, K., J. Barnes, and J. Mansfeld, et al., eds. *Cambridge History of Hellenistic Philosophy*. Cambridge: Cambridge University Press, 1999.

Bar Hebraeus. "The Candelabra of Holiness . . ." Edited by F. Nau. Patrologia orientalis 13.2. Paris: Firmin-Didot, 1916.

Bardy, G., ed. *Eusèbe de Césarée, Histoire ecclésiastique: Livres I–IV*. Sources chrétiennes 31. Paris: Cerf, 1952.

Barnard, Leslie W. *Justin Martyr: His Life and Thought*. Cambridge: Cambridge University Press, 1967.

Bauer, Walter. *Orthodoxy and Heresy in Earliest Christianity*. Edited by Robert A. Kraft and Gerhard Krodel. Translated by a team from the Philadelphia Seminar on Christian Origins. Philadelphia: Fortress, 1971.

---

[105] Vööbus, *Celibacy: A Requirement*, 17.

[106] See *supra*, nn. 42 and 48.

[107] It is hard to imagine Tatian's Encratism causing him problems in the East in the late-second century. Even his Gnostic teachings probably would have caused little difficulty in a region that welcomed Bardaisan at about the same time (although there are differences, there also are similarities between Tatian's and Bardaisan's theologies: according to H. J. W. Drijvers, Bardaisan regarded the "First Word [as the force] which formed the world," and claimed that "salvation consists in knowledge" [*Bardaisan of Edessa* (Assen: van Gorcum, 1966), 220–221]).

Brown, P. *The Body and Society: Men, Women, and Sexual Renunciation in Early Christianity.* New York: Columbia University Press, 1988.

Ceresa-Gastaldo, A. *Gerolamo, Gli uomini illustri.* Biblioteca patristica 12. Florence: Nardini, 1988.

Chabot, J.-B., ed. *Chronique de Michel le Syrien.* Vol. 4. Paris: Leroux, 1910.

Chadwick, H. "Enkrateia." Pages 343–65 in vol. 5 of *Reallexikon für Antike und Christentum.* Edited by Theodor Klauser, Ernst Dassmann, and Georg Schöllgen. Stuttgart: Anton Hiersemann, 1962.

Chadwick, H., trans. *Origen, Contra Celsum.* Cambridge: Cambridge University Press, 1953.

Drijvers, H. J. W. *Bardaisan of Edessa.* Assen: van Gorcum, 1966.

Droge, A. J. *Homer or Moses? Early Christian Interpretations of the History of Culture.* Hermeneutische Untersuchungen zur Theologie 26. Tübingen: J. C. B. Mohr (Paul Siebeck), 1989.

Elze, Martin. *Tatian und seine Theologie.* Forschungen zur Kirchen- und Dogmengeschichte 9. Göttingen: Vandenhoeck & Ruprecht, 1960.

Frend, William H. C. *The Rise of Christianity.* Philadelphia: Fortress, 1984.

Goodspeed, E. J., ed. *Die ältesten Apologeten.* New printing (orig. 1914). Göttingen: Vandenhoeck & Ruprecht, 1984.

Grant, R. M. "Dietary Laws Among Pythagoreans, Jews, and Christians." *Harvard Theological Review* 73 (1980): 299–310.

———. "The Heresy of Tatian." *Journal of Theological Studies* 5 (1954): 62–68.

Harmon, A. M., ed. *Lucian.* Vol. 5. Loeb Classical Library. Cambridge: Harvard University Press, 1962.

Helm, R., ed. *Eusebius Werke VII: Die Chronik des Hieronymus.* 2nd ed. Die griechischen christlichen Schriftsteller der ersten Jahrhunderte 47. Berlin: Akademie-Verlag, 1956.

Holl, K., ed. *Epiphanius, Ancoratus und Panarion 1–33.* Die griechischen christlichen Schriftsteller der ersten Jahrhunderte 25. Leipzig: J. C. Hinrichs, 1915.

Holl, K., and J. Dummer, eds. *Epiphanius, Panarion haer. 34–64.* 2nd ed. Die griechischen christlichen Schriftsteller der ersten Jahrhunderte. Berlin: Akademie-Verlag, 1980.

Holzhausen, J. "Gnostizismus, Gnosis, Gnostiker: Ein Beitrag zur antiken Terminologie." *Jahrbuch für Antike und Christentum* 44 (2001): 58–74.

Jerome. *S. Hieronymi Presbyteri Opera: Pars I.6.* Corpus Christianorum: Series latina 76. Turnhout: Brepols, 1969.

King, Karen L. *What is Gnosticism?* Cambridge, Mass.: The Belknap Press of Harvard University Press, 2003.

Klauser, Theodor, Ernst Dassmann, and Georg Schöllgen, eds. *Reallexikon für Antike und Christentum.* Stuttgart: Anton Hiersemann, 1950–.

Mai, A., ed. *Scriptorum veterum nova collectio e vaticanis codicibus edita.* Vol. 10, part 1. Rome: Burliaeum, 1838.

Marcovich, M., ed. *Hippolytus, Refutatio omnium haeresium.* Patristische Texte und Studien 25. Berlin: Walter de Gruyter, 1986.

Musurillo, H., ed. *The Acts of the Christian Martyrs.* Oxford: Oxford University Press, 1972.

Otto, J. C. Th. *Corpus apologetarum christianorum saeculi secundi.* Vol. 6. Jena: Mauke, 1851.

Oulton, J. E. L., and H. Chadwick, trans. *Alexandrian Christianity.* Library of Christian Classics 2. Philadelphia: Westminster, 1954.

Petersen, William L. "Eusebius and the Paschal Controversy." Pages 311–25 in *Eusebius, Christianity, and Judaism.* Edited by H. Attridge and G. Hata. Detroit: Wayne State University Press, 1992.

———. "The Genesis of the Gospels." Pages 33–65 in *New Testament Textual Criticism and Exegesis.* Edited by A. Denaux. Bibliotheca ephemeridum theologicarum lovaniensium 161. Leuven: Peeters, 2002.

———. *Tatian's Diatessaron: Its Creation, Dissemination, Significance, and History in Scholarship.* Supplements to Vigiliae Christianae 25. Leiden: E. J. Brill, 1994.

Pilhofer, P. *Presbyteron kreitton: Der Altersbeweis der jüdischen und christlichen Apologeten und seine Vorgeschichte.* Wissenschaftliche Untersuchungen zum Neuen Testament 2.39. Tübingen: J. C. B. Mohr (Paul Siebeck), 1990.

Quispel, Gilles. "The Study of Encratism: A Historical Survey." Pages 35–81 in *La Tradizione dell'Enkrateia: Motivazioni ontologiche e protologiche.* Edited by U. Bianchi. Rome: Edizioni dell'Ateneo, 1985.

Rackham, H., ed. *Pliny, Natural History: Vol. II: Libri III–VII.* Loeb Classical Library 352. Cambridge, Mass.: Harvard University Press, 1969.

Robinson, James M., ed. *The Nag Hammadi Library in English.* Leiden: E. J. Brill, 1977.

Rousseau, A., and L. Doutreleau, eds. *Irénée de Lyon, Contre les hérésies: Livre I, tome II.* Sources chrétiennes 264; Paris: Cerf, 1979.

———. *Irénée de Lyon, Contre les hérésies: Livre III, tome II.* Sources chrétiennes 211. Paris: Cerf, 1974.

Sagnard, F., ed. *Clément d'Alexandrie, Extraits de Théodote.* New printing (orig. 1948). Sources chrétiennes 23. Paris: Cerf, 1970.

Schneemelcher, W., ed. *New Testament Apocrypha.* Translated by R. McL. Wilson. 2 vols. Rev. ed. Cambridge: James Clarke, 1991–1992.

Scholten, C. "Probleme der Gnosisforschung: Alte Fragen—neue Zugänge." *Communio* 26 (1997): 481–501.

———. Review of P. Pilhofer, *Presbyteron kreitton: Der Altersbeweis der jüdischen und christlichen Apologeten und seine Vorgeschichte. Jahrbuch für Antike und Christentum* 34 (1991): 184–87.

Schwartz, E. *Tatiani Oratio ad Graecos.* Texte und Untersuchungen 4. Leipzig: J. C. Hinrichs, 1888.

Schwartz, E., ed. *Eusebius Werke II. Die Kirchengeschichte.* Teil 3. Die griechischen christlichen Schriftsteller der ersten Jahrhunderte 9/3. Leipzig: J. C. Hinrichs, 1909.

Stählin, O., and L. Früchtel, eds. *Clemens Alexandrinus, II. Stromata.* Die griechischen christlichen Schriftsteller der ersten Jahrhunderte 52; 15. Berlin: Akademie-Verlag, 1960.

Stählin, O., L. Früchtel, and U. Treu, eds. *Clemens Alexandrinus III: Stromata Buch VII und VIII.* Die griechischen christlichen Schriftsteller der ersten Jahrhunderte. Berlin: Akademie-Verlag, 1970.

Stählin, O., and U. Treu, eds. *Clemens Alexandrinus. I. Protrepticus und Paedagogus.* Third revised edition. Die griechischen christlichen Schriftsteller der ersten Jahrhunderte 12. Berlin: Akademie-Verlag, 1972.

Strycker, É. de, ed. *La forme la plus ancienne du Protévangile de Jacques.* Subsidia hagiographica 33. Brussels: Société des Bollandistes, 1961.

Thackeray, H. St. J., ed. *Josephus, The Jewish War: Books I–II.* Loeb Classical Library 203. Cambridge, Mass.: Harvard University Press, 1927.

Vööbus, Arthur. *Celibacy: A Requirement for Admission to Baptism in the Early Syrian Church.* Papers of the Estonian Theological Society in Exile 1. Stockholm: Estonian Theological Society in Exile, 1951.

———. *The History of Asceticism in the Syrian Orient.* 3 vols. Corpus scriptorum christianorum orientalium 184, 197, 500. Louvain: Peeters, 1958, 1960, 1988.

Whittaker, M., ed. *Tatian, Oratio ad graecos and Fragments.* Oxford Early Christian Texts. Oxford: Clarendon, 1982.

Williams, F., trans. *The Panarion of Epiphanius of Salamis: Book I: Sects 1–46.* Nag Hammadi and Manichaean Studies 35. Leiden: E. J. Brill, 1997.

Wissowa, G., and W. Kroll, et al., eds. *Paulys Real-Encyclopädie der classischen Altertumswissenschaft: Neue Bearbeitung, Band 8A.2 & 24.* Stuttgart: Druckenmüller, 1958–63.

Wright, W., and N. McLean, eds. *The Ecclesiastical History of Eusebius in Syriac.* Cambridge: Cambridge University Press, 1898.

BARDAISAN OF EDESSA

Nicola Denzey

1. *Introduction*

Like many of the other "heretics" in this volume, we know of
Bardaisan of Edessa (154–222 C.E.) only through the voices of others. Most of these voices come from opponents of later centuries,
and so modern scholars face the difficult task of recreating an authentic voice and doctrine from a web of misrepresentations, rumors,
and inaccuracies. Yet we are also fortunate enough to have an original work not of Bardaisan (sometimes spelled "Bardesanes," the
Greek version of his name), but of his student Philippus, in which
Bardaisan is featured as chief interlocutor in a dialogue against his
pupil and intellectual sparring-partner Awida. This dialogue, entitled
On Fate or (as it is more commonly known) the *Book of the Laws of
the Countries* (BLC) survives in a single Syriac manuscript, B. M. Add.
14.658, first published in the modern era by W. Cureton in 1855.[1]
It was possibly written originally in Greek or, more likely, in Syriac.
On one level, this Hellenistic-style dialogue is a form of ethnographic
literature, in which Philippus was able to show off his teacher's knowledge of other cultures' laws, religions, and traditions. More unusual
than the BLC's ethnography, however, is its elaborate philosophical
discussions on the influence of astrology and the power of Fate. The
work reveals an active interest in astral fatalism which is nowadays
generally (and erroneously) believed to have been rendered inap-
propriate, even moot, within a Christian worldview. Because of the
potent testimony of the BLC, Bardaisan stands apart as a "Christian
astrologer" of the second century, although as we shall see, this perception must be properly understood by placing him in relation to
a broader socio-cultural context.

---

[1] W. Cureton, *Spicilegium syriacum* (London: Rivingtons, 1855). It is not clear
whether or not the BLC is the same dialogue entitled "On Fate" which Bardaisan
wrote and dedicated to the emperor Antoninus (either Antoninus Pius or, more
likely, his son Marcus Aurelius), according to Eusebius of Caesarea (*Hist. eccl.* 4.30;
Praep. ev. 6.9).

Since the BLC is not Bardaisan's own but the work of his student, Philippus, debates have raged over the degree to which we
can understand it as indicative of Bardaisan's thought. Fortunately,
we have a second, major source for Bardaisan's system in the work
of a later Syrian Christian, Ephrem (306–373 C.E.). Ephrem (sometimes called Ephrem Syrus or "Ephrem of Syria"), a proponent of
orthodoxy in the fourth century, composed elaborate, polemical prose
and even hymns against Bardaisan's teachings.[2] If nothing else, these
works tell us that Bardaisan's legacy was still influential and threatening over a century after his death. When we are fortunate, the
work of Ephrem can sometimes corroborate and confirm ideas we
find in the BLC. So, too, do fragments of sources and notices from
other proponents of Christian orthodoxy, some of whom are familiar to readers of this volume from other chapters in this volume:
Eusebius of Caesarea (ca. 260–341 C.E.) and Epiphanius of Salamis
(315–403 C.E.), to name only two. Others, such as Agapius of
Mabbug (tenth century), Theodore bar Koni (ninth century), and
Michael Syrus (1166–1199) were much later historians, chroniclers
and theologians of the Syrian Orthodox church. The information in
this chapter has been assembled from all these sources which, taken
together, form our most reliable portrait of Bardaisan. Whenever
possible, I have also endeavored to show the moments where these
sources disagree, and to explore what might have been at stake in
the manner in which they chose to present their arguments concerning Bardaisan.

We possess solid knowledge of only a small portion of Bardaisan's
entire philosophical and religious system. Still, our best reconstruction reveals Bardaisan's Christian theology to be cohesive and congruent with other spiritual traditions and trajectories of his day,
naturally at home in the Hellenized world of northern Mesopotamia
of the late second century.[3]

---

[2] For critical editions of Ephrem's works, see Edmund Beck, ed., *Des Heiligen
Ephraem des Syrers Hymnen Contra Haereses* (CSCO, Scriptores Syri. 76 (Text), 77
(Translation): Louvain: L. Durbecq, 1957) and C. W. Mitchell, *S. Ephraim's Prose
Refutation of Mani, Marcion and Bardaisan* (2 vols.; London: Williams and Norgate,
1912–1921). For the sake of simplicity, I have abbreviated references to Beck's translation of Ephrem's *Hymns Against Heresies* as "Ephrem, *CH*" followed by the hymn
and line number in Beck; accordingly, abbreviated references to Mitchell's translation of Ephrem's *Prose Refutations* are listed in these footnotes as "Ephrem, *PR*" followed by the volume number and page number in Mitchell's edition.
[3] The late scholar Han Drijvers devoted the better part of his life to recon-

2. Bardaisan's World: Edessa in the Second Century

Modern Sanliurfa is a dusty city on Turkey's southern border with Syria. Tributaries of the mighty Euphrates river trickle through the city, but here the desert feels close, with Bedouin shepherds herding flocks of goats through the livestock markets and the smell of grilled lamb rendering the air aromatic and smoky. Before the Second World War, Sanliurfa was simply known as "Urfa"—the name under which it remains on many maps—but it won its title "Sanli," or "honored," for its brave resistance during the Turkish War of Independence (1919–1922). It still has the feel of a frontier town. Today, almost all traces of the ancient city of Edessa have been erased, built over in the building campaigns of much later times. Edessa the Christian city vanished under its Muslim colonists, who built soaring, elegant shrines, mosques and madrashes over the footprint of an ancient city.

In the second century C.E., Edessa was already ancient. A main station on the Silk Road to China, it was identified with Ur, the ancient birthplace of Abraham, and was an important city of the Hurrians in the second millennium B.C.E. By the time that Bardaisan gathered his students in the city, Seleucos I Nicator had long before transformed the kingdom of Osrhoene into Edessa, a *polis* with all that that entailed, including access for its citizens to a Greek education with a rich philosophical, aesthetic and political heritage. Still, the Greek influence was perhaps not the dominant form of culture; in the first half of the second century of the Common Era, an Armenian dynasty ruled Edessa; by Bardaisan's time in the second half of the century, it had been replaced by a Parthian dynasty. Edessa was also part of the Roman Empire, engulfed by the Roman expansion eastward that dominated the second century. Romanization in Edessa meant Roman dress, a cultivated style, and a certain type of cosmopolitanism born from the presence of soldiers from across the Empire. But Edessa was as far conceptually from Rome as it

---

structing Bardaisan's life. His publications on Bardaisan are considerable, and this chapter owes a deep debt to his scholarship. All English translations of Bardaisan's *Book of the Laws of the Countries* (BLC) I have taken from Drijvers' critical edition of the Syriac text: Bardaisan of Edessa, *The Book of the Laws of Countries: Dialogue on Fate of Bardaisan of Edessa* (trans. H. J. W. Drijvers; Assen: Van Gorcum, 1965). The footnote form marks the title of the work (BLC) followed by the page numbers of Drijvers' English translation of facing-page Syriac text.

was geographically—its culture was flavored by Parthia and Armenia, by the Syriac language rather than by Greek or Latin, and by the presence of the desert and more constant contact with Persia and India than with the city of Rome.

Edessa itself was in Bardaisan's day predominantly a pagan city, with traditional forms of religion remaining in place well into Late Antiquity.[4] Surrounded by desert, Edessa's high degree of urbanism necessitated that Christians, pagans and Jews would have had to interact closely with one another. Strolling through the streets of the city, you could take your pick of places to worship: shrines to the goddess Dea Syria, to Baal, or to the ancient Semitic triumvirate of Attis-Atargatis-Nebo, with their elaborate décor and gilded images of the deities. There were astrological temples set up to Marilaha, the local deity who ruled the cosmos through the seven planets. If you were Jewish, you could find a number of synagogues to frequent; the Jewish community in Edessa was also ancient. The Edessan King Abgar VII bar Isates (109–116 C.E.) hailed from the royal house of Adiabene, which had converted to Judaism. His conversion bears witness to the level of prestige which the Jews of Edessa held. They may have communicated with the substantial Jewish community of Babylon, who were by the second century of the Common Era assembling the Babylonian Talmud which is still central to modern Judaism today.

Christianity had come early to Edessa, apparently from farther East, perhaps from Adiabene. The early Christian texts that we have from this area—the *Odes of Solomon*, the *Syriac Didascalia*, and the Pseudo-Clementine literature[5]—many scholars classify as "Jewish-Christian" to characterize their profound connection with Jewish scriptures and thought-worlds. But this classification sometimes leads us to forget the fact that, in the second century, there *was* no dominant form of Christianity—neither in Edessa nor in any other urban

---

[4] H. J. W. Drijvers, *Cults and Beliefs at Edessa* (EPRO 82; Leiden: E. J. Brill, 1980); H. J. W. Drijvers, "The Persistence of Pagan Cults and Practices in Christian Syria," in *East of Byzantium: Syria and Armenia in the Formative Period* (eds. N. Garsoian et al.; Washington, D.C.: Dumbarton Oaks, 1982), 35–43; H. J. W. Drijvers, "Jews and Christians at Edessa," in *History and Religion in Late Antique Syria* (ed. Han J. W. Drijvers; Aldershot, Hampshire, United Kingdom: Variorum, 1995), 89.

[5] On the Christians who produced and used the Pseudo-Clementine Literature, see Jones in this volume.

center in the Roman Empire. Instead, various Christian groups met in relative isolation from one another, each holding separate and often distinct theologies. Accordingly, Christians in Edessa practiced a variety of forms of Christianity, some more aligned with Judaism than others. Many Christian communities in Edessa followed the teachings of influential Eastern Christians, particularly Tatian[6] or Marcion,[7] who sought to distance Christianity from its Jewish origins. Others were adherents of hybrid Christian sects which eventually died out, such as the Quqites or the Audians. Like the philosophical study groups they so closely resembled, all these Christian groups met in private residences, as yet without public worship spaces of their own. Where Bardaisan fit into these circles remains unclear, but he was aligned neither with Marcion nor with Tatian, and the brand of Christianity he developed in Edessa, as best as we can see, owed less to Judaism and Jewish Christianity than it did to pagan philosophical traditions, particularly Stoicism.

3. A Brief Biography of Bardaisan

Bardaisan had, most likely, a gentile background; he is called, at various times and in various sources, Parthian, Armenian, Syrian and Mesopotamian. His name, in Syriac, indicates that he was native to Edessa, born along the banks of the Daisan river which runs through the city. The *Chronicon Edessenum* provides us with the date and year of his birth as the 11th of July of 465 of the Seleucid era, or 155 C.E.[8] Given the education of a relatively high-born aristocrat, he took his place among the ranks of Edessa's more privileged. Bardaisan spent much of his life at the court of the Parthian King Abgar VIII the Great (179–214 C.E.), where he passed his days like a good country gentleman. The famed Christian chronographer Julius Africanus (160–240 C.E.) encountered the courtier-scholar Bardaisan honing his skills at archery and composing lengthy philosophical, religious and ethnographic treatises.[9] Bardaisan was compendious in

---

[6] For Tatian, see Petersen in this volume.

[7] For Marcion, see Räisänen in this volume.

[8] I. Guidi, *Chronicon Edessenum* (vol. 1 of *Chronica Minora*; ed. E. W. Brooks and J.-B. Chabot: CSCO, Scriptores Syri, Series Tertia, 4; Paris: E Typographeo Reipublicae, 1903–1905).

[9] Julius Africanus, *Cestes* 1.20 (J. R. Vieillefond, *Les 'Cestes' de Julius Africanus: Étude*

his knowledge and curious, as learned in the Brahmanic philosophical traditions of India as in Greek Platonism.

Whether or not Bardaisan married remains unknown, although certain traditions record that he had a son, Harmonius, who continued his teachings.[10] It seems consistent that he, unlike his fellow Syrian Tatian, did not espouse a life of chastity and asceticism. Ephrem is outraged at Bardaisan's positive view of sexual intercourse as purification (particularly for women, for whom such purification lessens sin, according to Michael Syrus' report of Bardaisan's teachings). As for Harmonius, Greek historians of the Church assert that he composed hymns in Syriac and arranged them for vocal performance. Indeed, a tradition exists that Ephrem Syrus' renowned *Hymns Against Heresies* were Ephrem's own lyrics set to Harmonius' music and meter.[11] More reliable is Ephrem's testimony that it was Bardaisan himself, and not his son, who composed hymns and poetry which became famous in his day and which were preserved, at least in part, for their beauty.[12] Some scholars have surmised that Bardaisan was the author of other Edessan Christian hymnic material such as the *Odes of Solomon* and the "Hymn of the Pearl" from the Apocryphal *Acts of Thomas*; however, there is no secure reason for this to be anything more than mere conjecture.[13] We do not know when, or why, Bardaisan chose to convert to Christianity.

We are left with two opposing traditions about his career in the Church. According to Eusebius of Caesarea and Didymus the Blind (313–398 C.E.), Bardaisan at first joined the Valentinians,[14] but left them to become a priest in the mainstream church.[15] Later orthodox chroniclers such as Theodore bar Koni and Agapius of Mabbug

---

sur l'ensemble des fragments avec édition, traduction et commentaires. [Publications de l'Institut Français de Florence, 1st ser., 20; Paris: Sansoni, 1970]).

[10] Michael Syrus names three sons: Abgarus, Hasdu and Harmonius. See the edition of J.-B. Chabot, *Chronique de Michel le Syrien* (Brussels: Culture et Civilisation, 1963), 1:109.

[11] Sozomen, *Hist. eccl.* 3.16.

[12] Ephrem, *PR* (Mitchell, 2:106).

[13] On Bardaisan as the author of the *Odes of Solomon*, see William Romaine Newbold, "Bardaisan and the Odes of Solomon," *JBL* 30 (1911): 161–204. For a commentary on Bardaisan's relationship to the *Acts of Thomas*, see Drijvers, *Bardaisan of Edessa* (Studia Semitica Neerlandica; Assen: Van Gorcum, 1966), 211–12.

[14] For Valentinians, see Dunderberg in this volume.

[15] Eusebius, *Hist. eccl.* 4.30; Epiphanius, *Pan.* 56; Didymus the Blind, *Psalmenkommentar (Tura-Papyrus)* (ed. A. Gesché and M. Gronewald; Papyrologische Texte und Abhandlungen 8; Bonn: Habelt, 1969), 3: 182–84.

reversed the order of events, making Bardaisan the priest "go over to the other side," to end his life as a Valentinian.[16] Theodore bar Koni remarks that after Bardaisan was baptized and trained in the holy scriptures, he was ordained to the priesthood but left the church when his ambitions to be elevated to the episcopacy were not recognized.[17] Agapius' account is still more detailed:

> As [Bardaisan] was walking along the streets of Edessa and was passing by the church built by the apostle Addai, he heard the bishop of Edessa preaching the scriptures to the people. Bardaisan, reflecting of the matter, decided to acquaint himself with the Christian mysteries. . . . The bishop (eventually) instructed him in the Christian faith, baptized him, made him a deacon, and gave him a position in the church.[18]

All these traditions about Bardaisan's conversion and career are probably apocryphal, however; he himself says nothing about them. There are, however, interesting connections (however tenuous) between Bardaisan's theology and Valentinianism; whether these are because he learned them from Valentinus or Valentinus' school, or whether they are simply products of second-century philosophical speculation is difficult to say. We will have the opportunity to examine Bardaisan's similarities with Valentinianism presently.

We do not know much about the end of Bardaisan's life. In 216 C.E., the Roman emperor Caracalla put an end to Edessa's relative political autonomy. Edessa's King Ma'nu IX was murdered, his two sons taken to Rome as political prisoners. During the ensuing persecutions of Edessan Christians, Bardaisan was most likely exiled to Armenia, to the stronghold of Ani. There, he spent his days writing, among other learned treatises, long ethnographic and historical accounts of India and Armenia. We do not know where, nor when, Bardaisan died; our best guess is around 222 C.E., in Armenia.

4. Philosophy

However he came to the Christian faith, Bardaisan's understanding of the world as a Christian does not appear to have fundamentally

---

[16] See Sebastian Brock, "Didymus the Blind on Bardaisan," *JTS* 22 (1971): 530–31.

[17] Theodore bar Koni, *Liber scholiorum* (ed. A. Scher; CSCO, Scriptores Syri, Series Secunda, 65–66; Paris: E Typographeo Reipublicae, 1910–1912), 2:24–26.

[18] Agapius of Mabbug, *Kitâb al 'unwân*; quoted in Brock, "Didymus the Blind on Bardaisan," 531.

differed from that which he had gleaned from his Greek philosophical training. Like others of his day, Bardaisan explored basic philosophical questions with his students: How was the world created? Of what was the soul composed, and what was its destiny? Was there such a thing as evil? How could we act in accordance with the Good? Was there such a thing as free will? If God had created the world good, after all, why then did evil exist, and why did people do evil things? And why did evil befall good people—did this not suggest that God was not all powerful? At the heart of these questions lurked the complex and confusing relationship between God's providential care and human free will—an issue deemed by classicist John Dillon as "perhaps the most burning philosophical and spiritual issue . . . in second-century Platonism."[19] This problem, in fact, had already been anticipated by the "Platonizing, dualistic mystical Stoic" philosopher Posidonius in the second century B.C.E., who had declared that God was not identical with Nature and Fate. This formulation was to lie dormant in philosophical thought for over two centuries until it became central once again among Christian study groups of the second century such as the one which Bardaisan led in Edessa.

Like most of the so-called "heretics" of the second century, then, Bardaisan was deeply conversant with Greek philosophical traditions. In his day, the study of Platonism was experiencing a Renaissance (scholars of today call this period *Middle Platonism* to distinguish between the *Platonism* of the ancient Greek world and the *Neoplatonism* of Late Antiquity). Bardaisan engaged in the textual studies and polemical treatise-writing against one's philosophical opponents that was *de rigueur* for a man of his status; he composed a treatise against the Platonists—specifically against the prominent philosopher Albinus (ca. 152 C.E.), a fellow Syrian—entitled *Of Domnus*, which focused on the difference between corporeal and incorporeal bodies.[20]

Besides Platonism, Stoicism was also popular in the Eastern Roman Empire. One of the most prolific and respected Stoic thinkers, Posidonius, hailed from Apamea not far to the south of Edessa. It is little surprise, then, that Bardaisan shows such clear affinities with

---

[19] John Dillon, "Plutarch and Second-Century Platonism," in *Classical Mediterranean Spirituality* (ed. A. H. Armstrong; New York: SCM Press, 1989), 225–26.
[20] Mitchell, *S. Ephraim's Prose Refutation of Mani, Marcion and Bardaisan*, 2:III.

Stoic positions on the nature of fate and the role of human free will. Stoicism was renowned in antiquity for the prominence it afforded to astrology. Of all the ancient Greek schools, citizens of the second century believed that it emphasized a relentless astral fatalism, in which humans were wholly powerless under the influence of the stars. Often quoted, for instance, was a famous statement attributed to the ancient Stoic philosopher Chrysippus (c. 281–208 B.C.E.): "Everything happens according to fate (*kath' heimarmenēn de . . . ta panta ginesthai*)."[21]

By the second century, the idea that the Stoics had posited a thoroughgoing determinism had permeated Platonist circles. Most Platonists of the second century were quick to criticize Stoic determinism for what they perceived as its significant philosophical limitations. Since the early Stoics had been unwilling to assign to God anything other than the Good, any evil that befell humans could not be reconciled with an essentially beneficent cosmic economy. For later Stoics, the solution was simple: they simply shifted the problem of good and evil from the field of physics to the field of ethics, in other words, to human emotions and actions.[22] The Middle Platonists adopted this solution. Responsibility for evil lay not within fate, but within human action and responsibility, since human will was perceived as essentially autonomous. Indeed, Bardaisan's own teachings about fate, as we shall see, move in a similar direction.

Bardaisan's immediate community of believers very much resembled the Stoic or Middle Platonist schools of philosophy common in the first and second centuries. Ephrem reports that they met in caves, where they sang hymns and studied and expounded various writings, including Bardaisan's own.[23] These treatises, now lost, bore titles such as the *Book of the Chaldeans* and the *Book about the Signs of the Zodiac*.[24] It is not clear what other writings, besides Bardaisan's, might have been studied. According to Epiphanius (*Pan.* 9), Bardaisan made use of the Law and the Prophets, the Old and New Testaments and

---

[21] Chrysippus, *Peri Heimarmenēs* 915; excerpted in *Stoicorum Veterum Fragmenta* (ed. H. von Arnim; 4 vols.; Leipzig: Teubner, 1903–1924), 2:265.

[22] For a summary of Stoic ethics, see William Chase Greene, *Moira: Fate, Good and Evil in Greek Thought* (New York: Harper & Row, 1944), 340–54; Charlotte Stough, "Stoic Determinism and Moral Responsibility," in *The Stoics* (ed. John Rist; Berkeley: University of California Press, 1978) 203–32.

[23] Ephrem, *CH* 1.17.18.

[24] BLC 51; Ephrem, *CH* 1.14.18.

some of the Apocrypha—in other words, he drew on the same collection of scriptures as did many other Christians of the century.

5. *Cosmology*

Back in 1920, the Italian scholar Levi della Vida noted that Bardaisan's
cosmology, such as it can be discerned from our extant documents,
does not contain a single Christian element.[25] Rather than using this
as a powerful argument that Bardaisan could not have been Christian,
della Vida reasons that since Bardaisan was considered to be Christian
by tradition, this paradox is reason enough to consider the tradition
to be authentic. In other words, later Christians would have had no
reason to consider Bardaisan a Christian—and a heretical Christian
at that—unless he had considered himself (and been considered)
Christian by his contemporaries. Still, it is important to emphasize
that Bardaisan appears to have drawn his philosophy directly from
Graeco-Roman precedents, without adding to it anything more than
the most superficial Christian veneer. Nevertheless, since Christian
doctrine was still inchoate in the second century, there were no parameters which had as yet been established between "pagan" and
"Christian" physics and metaphysics and thus no parameters to trans-
gress. For this reason, Bardaisan understood himself as "Christian"
following a set of criteria very different from those which delineated
Christians even a century later; Bardaisan lacked a Christian cosmology because, in second-century Edessa, such a category had not
yet been developed.

To address any protological or cosmological questions that would
have been deliberated within a philosophical study circle of the second century, an educated Christian would likely have turned first to
the Book of Genesis—the only canonical work from the Judeo-
Christian tradition to explicitly address the question of the origin of
the world. Unfortunately, Genesis' creation myth offers far less of a
satisfying "scientific" model for protology than Greek philosophical
works. Accordingly, if the book of Genesis had any direct influence
on Bardaisan's understanding of the creation of the world, it is

---

[25] G. Levi della Vida, "Bardesane e il dialogo delle leggi del paesi," *Rivista di
studi filosofici e religiosi* 1 (1920), 399–430, esp. 425.

difficult to discern from his teachings. Instead, Bardaisan—like so many of his Christian contemporaries—turned to ancient tractates on the nature of the cosmos. Foremost among these Greek texts was Plato's *Timaeus*, which offered an explanation for the creation of the world that was at once monotheistic and "scientific." From the *Timaeus* Bardaisan likely took the idea that the cosmos had been created from pre-existent matter by a demiurgical figure, who also formed the seven planets (Mercury, Mars, Venus, Jupiter, Saturn, Earth, and the Moon). At the creation of the world, these planets were assigned their fixed paths through the heavens and each given a part in the governing of the cosmos. We find this same idea expressed in numerous other works of the second century, whether Middle Platonist, Stoic, or Christian.

Like his contemporary, Valentinus, Bardaisan taught that the four fundamental elements of Stoic physics—wind, water, fire, and light—were combined with each other in different balances and measures to create the different constituents of the world.[26] This teaching was not unusual in Middle Platonist circles of Bardaisan's day. In his treatise *On the Face of the Moon*, for instance, Plutarch (45–125 C.E.) observed that the initial disorder and separation of the higher cosmic elements caused them to avoid each other in disarray.[27] Bardaisan also borrowed from the teachings of the early Greek philosopher Democritus a sort of proto-atomic theory which posited that the elements' atomic structure allowed them to be mixed in an infinite number of combinations.[28]

In Bardaisan's physics, matter is pre-existent; God did not create matter but rather ordered it. This view was anathema to later Christians, who preferred the Genesis account in which God creates as well as orders; thus, according to later Christian formulations, there was a time in which God was, but the universe was not—a concept that Greeks and Romans would have found absurd. Matter's origin was not a topic of penetrating analysis in ancient debate; more interesting to second-century philosophers was the question of matter itself. In his treatise against Albinus, Bardaisan emphasized that the four fundamental elements were themselves corporeal; that is to

---

[26] Ephrem, *PR* (Mitchell, 2:106). Drijvers, *Bardaisan of Edessa*, 136–42.
[27] Plutarch, *Fac.* 926F–927A.
[28] Ephrem, *PR* (Mitchell, 1:106).

say, they were composed of substance or matter. The implications of this for Christian theology were important: if the basic building blocks of the cosmos were material, even things as subtle as thoughts, or emotions, or even the human soul, were likewise material. If they were material, too, they were also contingent and mutable; they could be generated but also dissolved. Taken as a whole, Bardaisan's doctrine of matter most likely derives, like most elements of his philosophy, from the *Timaeus*.[29]

6. *Christology and Theology*

Bardaisan was a strict monotheist—more properly, a monist—which was in keeping with both his Christian convictions and his Greek philosophical background. Using terms drawn from Stoicism and Platonism, Bardaisan understood God to be a single principle, identical with the hypostasis known as the Good. The BLC opens with Bardaisan's opponent, Awida, posing an intellectual challenge in Marcionite terms: "If God is One, as you say He is, and He has created humankind intending you to do what you are charged to, why did He not create humankind in such wise that they could not sin, but always did what is right? Thereby His desire would have been fulfilled" (BLC 5). The thrust of the BLC is that although God is all powerful and all Good, He had delegated out the creation and the administration of the world to the seven planetary beings. This process of delegation could explain the origin of sin and defect in the world without attributing it to God. This strategy, too, is reminiscent of the *Timaeus*, where the Demiurge divides up the administration of the cosmos among the seven, planetary "young gods." Again, the teaching of a demiurgical figure working in concert with lesser deities or rulers is not particularly unusual within second-century Middle Platonist or Stoic teachings, many of which drew their authority from Plato's teachings. We even find the same theme expressed in the Christian cosmogonic myths preserved in the Nag Hammadi library, including the *Apocryphon of John* and *On the Origin of the World*.

---

[29] See in particular Plato, *Tim.* 52D–53B on the nature and constituency of matter.

Ephrem's hymns record a Bardesanite teaching about a Father of Life and a Mother of Life, who together brought forth a Son.[30] It is unclear how this Trinitarian scheme fits into Bardaisan's comprehensive, monadic theology, but these figures could have been part of a mythological or poetic system to be understood symbolically or allegorically. Certainly Bardaisan was not alone among ancient Christians in considering the second person of the Trinity to be female. What evidently bothered Ephrem more was Bardaisan's use of sexual metaphors to describe the creation of the world.[31] Within this Bardesanite Trinity, the Son is also termed the Word (or Logos) of Thought. Our early sources indicate that this Word of Thought was akin to the creative, dynamic Nous or "Divine Mind" of Platonism. According to Theodore bar Koni, Bardaisan also termed the Logos of Thought the "wind of the heights" or the *pneuma*, pointing us, perhaps, to the creative agency of the *pneuma* or "Spirit of God" in Gen 1:2: "And the Spirit of God moved upon the face of the waters."

Bardaisan also seems to have tapped into Jewish sapiential teachings concerning Wisdom as God's co-agent at Creation, as we find in Prov 8:22–31 (particularly 8:29b–30: "When [God] traced the foundations of the earth, I was beside him"). In the BLC, the hypostasized figure of Wisdom appears alongside God, bestowing power to the planets which they, in turn, exercise to control human existence. Still, Philippus was careful to note the contingent, limited powers of any figure subordinate to God: ". . . this power is in the possession of God, the angels, the Rulers, the Guiding Signs, the elements, humankind and the animals. Yet to each of these orders I have named power is not given over everything. For he who has power over everything is One" (BLC 29).

But what about the creative power of Bardaisan's Logos of Thought? Moses bar Kepha and Iwannis of Dara record that in Bardaisan's system, the Logos of Thought is Christ, but our earlier sources (particularly Ephrem) never draws this connection, leading the Bardaisan scholar Han Drijvers to suggest that the identification was a later addition.[32] In fact, we have no reliable Christology whatsoever that derives directly from Bardaisan or a Bardesanite. There is no

---

[30] Ephrem, *CH* 55.10.
[31] Ephrem, *CH* 55.2.
[32] Drijvers, *Bardaisan of Edessa*, 101, 110.

mention of Jesus Christ—or even a Redeemer figure—in the BLC.

Bardaisan came under fire by some later theologians, who insisted that he had asserted a docetic christology. A benchmark of *docetism* was the conviction that Christ did not suffer on the cross—a belief attributed to both Valentinus and Bardaisan, although again, without a great deal of reliability.[33] The late fifth-century theologian Philoxenus of Mabbug (450–522 C.E.) comments, "Valentinus and Bardaisan aver, that the Logos caused a body to descend for it from heaven and that its incarnation did not take place through Mary."[34] A hymn of Ephrem, too, lampoons the followers of Bardaisan, who sing,

> Something flowed down from the Father of Life
> And the Mother became pregnant with the mystery
> Of the fish and bore him,
> And he was called the Son of Life.[35]

Finally, Michael Syrus records that Bardaisan taught that "our Lord was clothed with the body of an angel, and Mary clothed a soul from the world of light, who enveloped himself in the shape of a body."[36]

Conversely, Ephrem maintained that Bardesanites "called our Lord a child that was produced by two through sexual union"—quite the opposite of docetism, but in keeping with Bardaisan's apparently positive assessment of human sexual activity and rejection of ascetic behavior. Docetism, too, sits only very awkwardly within any philosophical system that does not reject the flesh as inherently sinful or defective. It seems most likely, then, that Bardaisan—despite the words of his later opponents—was not himself a docetist, although he seems to have espoused a high christology with his teaching on a "Logos of Thought." Whether or not Bardaisan understood this Logos of Thought as having incarnated into the body of Jesus of Nazareth—in other words, whether or not Bardaisan thought that Jesus Christ was the Messiah—remains for us an unanswered question.

---

[33] R. Draguet, "Pièces de polémique antijulianiste," *Muséon* 44 (1931): 255–317, esp. 267.

[34] *Les hérésies Christologiques d'après Philoxène de Mabboug (Xenia) et Bar Hébraeus* (ed. F. Nau; PO 13; Paris: Firmin-Didot, 1919), 248.

[35] Ephrem, CH 55 Strophe 1.

[36] Chabot, *Chronique de Michel le Syrien*, 1:109.

7. *Anthropology*

In accordance with the principles of second-century philosophy, Bardaisan maintained that humans were aggregate beings, composed of different types of materials, each of which was governed or controlled by a different agent. According to Agapius of Mabbug and Michael Syrus—two later Syrian Christian opponents—Bardaisan taught that there was a direct relationship between the parts of the body and the planets: the mind of humans come from the Sun, the bones from Saturn, the veins from Mercury, the flesh from Jupiter, the hair from Venus, the skin from the moon.[37] Such teachings were common in Bardaisan's world. Medical writers of the imperial era frequently divided the human body into seven components—an innovation perhaps traced back to the ancient philosopher Posidonius. But a variety of religious writings also contain the idea that the human body is directed by the seven planets, or by seven hypostasized deities. Theodore bar Koni, for instance, reproduces a fragment of an *Apocalypse of John* preserved by Audius. The order of creation for the soul runs: "My Wisdom made the flesh, and Understanding made the skin, and Elohim made the bones and my Kingdom made the blood. Adonai made the nerves and Anger made the flesh, and Thought made the Marrow."[38] These order lists all apparently derive from the *Timaeus* 73–76, where the seven young planetary gods order the seven soul-components of the primordial human.

Following a Neo-Pythagorean idea prevalent in philosophical circles of the second century, Bardaisan in the BLC distinguishes spirit from soul: "The spirits undergo changes while descending to the soul, and the souls while descending to the bodies. . . . The body, then, is led by its natural constitution, while the soul suffers and receives impressions together with it" (BLC 33). The spirit, then, has a divine origin and as such, remains ontologically free, even when

---

[37] Agapius of Mabbug, *Kitab al ʿunwan*, 7.4. For more, see Drijvers, "Bardaisan of Edessa and the Hermetica: The Aramaic Philosopher and the Philosophy of His Time," *Vooraziatisch-egyptisch Genootschap "Ex Oriente Lux", Jaarbericht* 21 (Leiden: Ex Oriente Lux, 1970), 200.

[38] Michael Waldstein and Frederik Wisse, eds., *The Apocryphon of John: Synopsis of Nag Hammadi Codices II,1; III,1; and IV,1 with BG 8502,2* (Nag Hammadi and Manichaean Studies 33; Leiden: E. J. Brill, 1995), 194.

combined in the triad spirit-soul-body. The soul, by contrast, is subject to astral and planetary destiny, so that the horoscope which each person receives at the moment of birth is essentially binding, but only to one component of the spirit-soul-body triad. The body, as the third component, is subject not to Fate but to Nature, which determines physical characteristics such as height, hair, eye color, and even length of life (BLC 33–37). Together, Drijvers notes, the triadic microcosm of the body complements a triadic microcosm of the cosmos: ". . . the triad freedom, outward fortunes and nature, corresponds with the triad spirit, soul and body."[39] Such triads were frequently developed in Greek philosophy; this idea of a body-soul-mind triad ruled by nature, fate, and freedom Bardaisan and Philippus gleaned directly from Middle Platonism.

All our sources agree that Bardaisan rejected the doctrine of bodily resurrection.[40] Since the body was material and therefore corruptible, it was unthinkable and absurd in a Graeco-Roman philosophical context that the flesh itself could resurrect. Instead, Bardaisan argued that the Resurrection would provide a "spiritual body." This perspective is, like most aspects of Bardaisan's theology, not atypical of second century Christianity; Valentinus and others also apparently taught a similar doctrine. Bardaisan and his contemporaries could find scriptural support for this concept in Paul's teachings on the nature of the resurrection body in 1 Cor 15:44. At death, Bardaisan held, the spirit and soul were released from the fetters of the body, to ascend upward to unite with the source of their origin, in the "Bridal Chamber of Light."[41] This expression bears remarkable similarities to the eschatological "Bridal Chamber" of Valentinianism, mentioned in sources as diverse as the *Gospel of Philip* (NHC II,3), the *Dialogue of the Savior* (NHC III,5), the *Second Treatise of the Great Seth* (NHC VII,2), and the *Teachings of Silvanus* (NHC VII,4). We also find the expression on Christian funerary epitaphs from the high Empire. In 1974, Gilles Quispel published a famous epitaph of a second-century Roman woman by the name of Flavia Sophe, which clearly expresses a belief that the soul will return to its source in the eschatological Bridal Chamber:

---

[39] Drijvers, *Bardaisan of Edessa*, 219.
[40] For the basic text, see Ephrem, *PR* (Mitchell 2:102, 66).
[41] Ephrem, *PR* (Mitchell 2:77, 32–40).

You who have yearned for the paternal light, sister and spouse, my Sophe,
Anointed in the baths of Christ with incorruptible, holy oil,
you hastened to look upon the divine faces of the aeons,
The great angel of the great council, the true son,
as you enter the bridal chamber, ascending
[immortal] to the bosom of the father.[42]

Whether Valentinus was the originator of the term "Bridal Chamber of Light," which Bardaisan then borrowed from him directly, or whether the term was by the second century part of the religious *koine* of the Empire is unclear; the latter, however, seems more likely, given its attestation in a variety of sources.

Aside from Ephrem's single reference to this "Bridal Chamber of Light," Bardaisan's system, such as it reaches us today, lacks a developed eschatology as well as an explicit soteriology. The only reference to a Bardesanite doctrine of redemption is from Ephrem, who claimed that Bardaisan believed that souls could return to their source if they received the Christ's teaching. This instruction could remove the effects of Adam's sin, which had not caused death but made the soul's return to the Bridal Chamber of Light impossible until Christ taught humans to exercise free will in order to act in the direction of the Good.[43]

8. *Astrology*

No study of Bardaisan can be complete without some comments on his relationship to astrology. The BLC constitutes the earliest and best of our numerous Christian anti-astrological treatises composed in the first six centuries C.E. Since the BLC's position on fate is more subtly complex than the outright condemnation we find in subsequent Christian texts, Bardaisan—perhaps unfairly—earned a reputation evident in the works of his later opponents as one who strayed

---

[42] See G. Quispel, "L'inscription de Flavia Sophe," in Quispel, *Gnostic Studies* (2 vols. Istanbul: Nederlands Historisch-Archaeologisch Instituut in het Nabije Oosten, 1974), 1:58. The funerary stele is now on display at the newly opened Epigraphic collection of the Museo Nazionale, Rome.

[43] Ephrem, *PR* (Mitchell 2.77); see also the discussion in H. J. W. Drijvers, "Bardaisan of Edessa and the Hermetica," 205.

where he ought not to have: to understand the workings of the cosmos and the manner in which the cosmos directly or indirectly governed human existence. This chapter endeavors to place Bardaisan
into the broader intellectual context of the second century, to help
us to understand to what degree Bardaisan functioned as an intellectual maverick, introducing astrology and astrological principles into
nascent Christian doctrine.

Reverence for the astral and planetary bodies constituted a potent
and respected component of Roman and Babylonian religiosity.
Within the environs of Edessa during Bardaisan's time there could
be found one of the most elaborate planetary temple sanctuaries in
the Eastern Empire. In the 1950s, the noted archaeologist J. B. Segal
investigated the ruins of Sumatar Harabesi, 50 km southeast of Edessa.
The ruins—dated from inscriptions to 476 of the Seleucidean era,
or 164–165 C.E.—are of seven differently shaped buildings around
a central mountain. Under each building lies a cave with an opening directed towards the central mountain.[44] Were these the under-
ground "caves" where Ephrem reports that Bardaisan met with his
students to teach them the fundamentals of astral religion? Even if
not, this sanctuary would have been well known to Bardaisan as a
sacred place to study and wonder at the beauty and power of the
celestial bodies.

In terms of the ancient branch of philosophy known as astrology,
it must be emphasized that there was no distinction in antiquity
between astrology and astronomy; the "science of the stars" was perceived as a form of scientific knowledge, not pseudo-science or superstition. A learned man such as Bardaisan would have been schooled
in the philosophical underpinnings of astrology, and have written
and discoursed on this science to enhance his reputation as a man
of knowledge. But would an educated Christian have taught astrological doctrine? In other words, was Bardaisan already a Christian
when his disciple wrote the *Book of the Laws of the Countries*? There
is no reason to suppose otherwise. The widely-held perception that
early Christians actively and consistently opposed astrology is largely

---

[44] J. B. Segal, "Pagan Syriac Monuments in the Vilayet of Urfa," *AnSt* 3 (1953):
97–117; J. B. Segal, "The Sabian Mysteries, The Planet Cult of Ancient Harran"
in *Vanished Civilizations: Forgotten Peoples of the Ancient World* (ed. E. Bacon; London:
Thames and Hudson, 1963), 201–20. For the dating, see J. B. Segal, "Some Syriac
Inscriptions of the 2nd and 3rd century A.D.," *BSOAS* 16 (1954): 97–120.

misinformed and over-simplifying.[45] Christians, like Jews and pagans in the Roman Empire, engaged both sides of a lively and impassioned debate concerning the validity—not to mention the true significance—of astrology and astrological prognostication.[46] Before the third or fourth centuries, we find few Christian condemnations of astrology. In the second century, diverse communities of Christians apparently accepted the principles of astrology, even if they considered astrology to be an unjust or contingently administered system. Irenaeus, for instance, reports that the Phibionites and Marcosians revered the Monomoirai or divinities associated with single degrees of the ecliptic;[47] Hippolytus recounts Basilides' doctrine of *climata* (geographical zones given their particular climatic characteristics by particular planetary and stellar configurations), and the Peretae's conviction that the stars were powers of destruction.[48]

Our chief source for Bardaisan's views on astrology remains the BLC. Because the BLC is also, in part, an ethnographic work, Philippus (through the character of Bardaisan) employs a series of arguments known as the *nomima barbarika*, "the laws of foreigners" which outline the customs of various foreign peoples and use these as proof that human culture and customs are powerful enough to override astral and planetary influence. "In all places, every day and each hour," Bardaisan states, "people are born with different horoscopes, but the laws of men are stronger than Fate" (BLC 53). This line of argumentation provided Philippus with the opportunity to display his compendious knowledge of various peoples. We learn various snippets of intriguing lore—some accurate and some the stuff of legends: we learn, for instance, about the Indian practice of suttee, by which Hindu wives are immolated alive with their deceased husbands; that the Germans all die by strangulation, and that when the Medes die, their bodies are thrown to the dogs (BLC 52–53).

---

[45] For a recent survey of Christian astrological sources, see Tim Hegedus, "Attitudes to Astrology in Early Christianity: A Study Based on Selected Sources" (Unpublished Ph.D. diss., University of Toronto, 2000) and my own unpublished Ph.D. dissertation: Nicola Denzey, "Under A Pitiless Sky" (Ph.D. diss., Princeton University, 1998).

[46] On this, see Otto Riedinger, *Die frühchristliche Kirche gegen die Astrologie* (Innsbruck: Wagner, 1956); more generally, see David Amand de Medieta, *Fatalisme et liberté dans l'antiquité grecque* (Amsterdam: A. M. Hakkert, 1973).

[47] Irenaeus, *Haer.* 1.17.1 (1.2.268 Rousseau and Doutreleau).

[48] Hippolytus, *Haer.* 5.15.6 (183.30–39 Marcovich).

Philippus presents his information idealistically and dogmatically—
for example, his statement that all people of Edessa lived "chastely"
(BLC 53) was surely more wishful thinking than reality; remarkably,
however, he also gets a great deal right—particularly when describing Brahmanic or Parthian customs—providing us with some fascinating insights into the way in which citizens of the eastern Roman
Empire delimited and taxonomized various forms of a curiously
different "Other." But these ethnographic details Philippus did not
glean from Bardaisan's ingenuity or empirical experience. Other
ancient authors and texts, including Diodorus of Tarsus (d. 390 C.E.),
the *Quaestiones* of Caesarius, and the *Chronicon* of Georgius Hamartolus,
provided similar examples of foreign cultures. Still, to be generous
to Bardaisan and his school the common thread that ties these texts
to the BLC was probably Stoicism and learned philosophical traditions; we do not know that Bardaisan directly plagiarized these sections of his monologue from any other ancient work.

If Bardaisan knew and accepted some of the basic principles of
astrology, scholars have debated the extent to which he himself was
a practicing astrologer.[49] The BLC contains numerous technical terms
drawn from astrology—the planets sometimes stand in "opposition";
there are "right-handed" beneficent and "left handed" malefic stars;
at midheaven they act against Nature (BLC 37, 41). Clearly, Philippus
had a solid grasp of the fundamentals of ancient astrological theory,
which he more than likely learned from Bardaisan himself. Certainly,
later Christian interpreters emphasized Bardaisan's active role as
astrologer. Ephrem insists that Bardaisan "observed the hour" and
"inquired into the proper times," which is to say, he may have practiced catarchic astrology, a branch of astrological prognostication
which aimed to determine auspicious moments of the day, week or
month to commence an action.[50] Bardaisan also seems to have
affirmed the power of genethlialogy, that is, the casting of horoscopes
from the position of the stars at the morning of birth. As far as tech-

---

[49] See the arguments of Albrecht Dihle, "Astrology in the Doctrine of Bardesanes,"
in *Studia Patristica* 20 (ed. E. A. Livingstone; Louvain: Peeters, 1989), 160–68, and
more recently, F. Stanley Jones, "The Astrological Trajectory in Syriac-Speaking
Christianity (Elchasai, Bardaisan, and Mani)," in *Atti del terzo congresso internazionale
di studi "Manicheismo e oriente Cristiano antico"* (ed. Luigi Cirillo and Alois van Tongerloo;
Manichaean Studies 3; Brepols: International Association of Manichaean Studies in
Conjunction with the Center of the History of Religions, 1997), 183–200.
[50] Ephrem, *CH* 51.13.

nical knowledge goes, the seventh-century chronicler Severus Sebokt reports that Bardaisan was very adept at astrological matters, demonstrating for his disciples that the planets entered into conjunctions one hundred times during the six thousand years which he, like many other Christians, posited for the duration of the world.[51] We have, too, two separate but similar lists dating from the seventh century which list Syriac names for the signs of the zodiac, attributed to Bardaisan's disciples.[52] Still, these names were standard Aramaic terms, and thus not specifically attributable to the Bardaisanites.

In the BLC 27, Bardaisan admits that he had once cherished astrology, but implies that he no longer holds it in the esteem that do the "Chaldeans," a blanket term in antiquity for Babylonian astrologers. Indeed, upon careful reading, one may wonder if Bardaisan and Philippus were really as learned in practical and theoretical astrology as their later critics charged. Many of the technical terms which Bardaisan employs would have been known to any educated person of the second century. Philippus appears not to have any direct knowledge of "Chaldean" astrology, which he erroneously states was identical to Egyptian astrology (BLC 41). Neither should we overestimate Philippus' originality in composing his master's monologue on astrology in the BLC; large chunks of it appear to have been lifted directly from the Peripatetic philosopher Alexander of Aphrodisias' treatise *On Fate* (ca. 200 C.E.). The BLC also bears a strong relationship to Philo's *De Providentia*, particularly Philo's passages on human law overriding Providence.

Still, Bardaisan acquired notoriety in Late Antiquity not because he was known to have been a learned astrologer, but because unlike later dogmatic Christian anti-fate treatises, the BLC never refutes the idea that the planets have an influence on humans.[53] Bardaisan informs Awida that "there exists something which the Chaldaeans call Fate. And not everything happens according to our will" (BLC 31). Rather than rejecting the concept of fate, the *Book of the Laws of the Countries* illustrates its limitations and emphasizes the importance of human free will. Here, however, the BLC adopts a fairly conventional position for a second-century philosopher. In his

---

[51] For the text, see F. Nau, "Notes d'astronomie syrienne," *JA* 16 (1910): 209–28.

[52] Jones, "The Astrological Trajectory," 189.

[53] Jones, "The Astrological Trajectory," 189.

refutation of Stoic tenets, for instance, Bardaisan's near contemporary Justin Martyr (100–165 C.E.) challenges Stoic determinism in
his *Second Apology*: "But neither do we affirm that it is by fate (*kath'
heimarmenēn*) that people do what they do, or suffer what they suffer,
but that each person by free choice (*prohairesis*) acts rightly or sins."[54]
The point of the BLC, similarly, is not to expound on the power
of the stars and planets to rule over human existence, nor to provide practical directions for prognostication or genethlialogy. Instead,
the treatise emphasizes repeatedly that God provided all people with
free will, which they can exercise to help them to rise above fate's
constraints.

Ultimately, the source for Bardaisan's teachings on fate in the
BLC appears to derive in part from Greek philosophical exegesis of
the *Timaeus*. In the *Timaeus*, God creates an essentially good cosmos,
endowed with soul and reason, through his Providence.[55] To con-
front the problem of evil, Plato weaves an elaborate cosmic myth in
which souls are implanted in bodies "according to the dictates of
Necessity."[56] Bodies themselves are subject to negative emotions, but
those who live virtuously may master them. The *Timaeus* also provided justification to understand some form of necessity or fate administered by planetary beings. The planets, therefore, were thought to
have direct influence on the human beings through the mechanism
of fate—an idea originally based upon astrological principles, now
integrated into Graeco-Roman philosophy. Few educated people of
Bardaisan's time would have believed otherwise. What Bardaisan and
Philippus do not say, surprisingly, is that Christ had the power to
annul planetary influence—a perspective we find prevalent in all
other second-century Christian commentaries on astral fatalism. This
omission is striking enough to make us question the degree to which
Bardaisan and his immediate disciples were Christians at all.

9. *Theological Friends and Foes*

In our Late Antique sources, Valentinus was often paired with
Bardaisan. Yet the connections between the two philosophers appears

---

[54] Justin Martyr, *2 Apol.* 7.
[55] Plato, *Tim.* 30B.
[56] Plato, *Tim.* 42B.

to be quite vague, and can more likely be attributed to a common thought-world rather than a direct line of teaching. As Han Drijvers points out, there is in our extant information about Bardaisan no indication that he espoused significant elements of Valentinianism, whether its tripartite anthropology, its elaborate cosmology based on the mythological scaffolding of the Pleroma, its system of emanations, or the myth of a fallen and redeemed Sophia.[57] Bardaisan does not draw upon the writings of the New Testament and deliver sophisticated conceptual exegeses of Paul, as did the Valentinians; indeed, unlike Valentinus, Bardaisan's system bears little sign of having been Christian at all. What the two men clearly shared was a deep familiarity—even an indebtedness—to their Greek philosophical background. This shared background can easily be perceived as some sort of direct, seminal relationship between the two; properly understood, we can understand both figures as interpreters of ancient traditions, working hard to craft a new understanding of the physical cosmos within a Christian purview.

Although it is difficult to ascertain the relationship between Valentinus and Bardaisan as anything more than shallow and circumstantial, Bardaisan's connection to another prominent "heretic" of his time, Marcion, is much less opaque. Unlike Marcion, Bardaisan appears to have accepted the scriptural authority of the Old Testament, as he believed in the inherent philosophical Goodness of the God of the Old Testament. Ephrem reports that Bardaisan criticized Marcion directly: "Two Gods cannot be, for the name . . . is singular, namely God."[58] Evidence, too, for the fundamental intellectual enmity between the two is Awida's opening question to Bardaisan in the BLC, first noted as anti-Marcionite by Theodoret of Cyrus (395–460 C.E.): "If God is One, *as you say He is* . . ." (emphasis added).[59] Intriguingly, in the BLC, Bardaisan directs his speech at "Philippus and Bar Jamna"; this second character, whose name means "Son of the Sea" may refer to Marcion, who was born on the coast of the Black Sea in the town of Sinope.

Finally, there are some interesting points of contact between Bardaisan and Mani. Both men descended from the same Parthian-

---

[57] Drijvers, *Bardaisan of Edessa*, 183–84.
[58] Ephrem, *CH* 3.4.
[59] Theodoret of Cyrus, *Haereticarum fabularum compendium* 1:22.

Iranian culture, as men of noble descent. Both ended their lives in
exile. Both spoke a similar language. Ephrem goes so far as to call
Bardaisan the "Teacher of Mani": "Because Mani was unable to
find another way out, he entered, though unwillingly, by the door
which Bardaisan opened."[60] Among the teachings which Mani took
from Bardaisan, Ephrem states, were those on astrology. But Mani
and Bardaisan disagreed on the ideas of the soul's relation to the
body, as well as in the notion of a Platonic World Soul. Mani differed
from Bardaisan and polemicized against his predecessor; still, their
teachings were similar enough for many followers of Bardaisan to
join Manichaean communities.

As a final note to this section, it should be stated that weighed
against the prevailing "heretics" of the second century—namely
Valentinus and Marcion—Bardaisan actually fared quite well; Han
Drijvers notes that Bardaisan was given a modicum of respect by
some of our most prolific and orthodox Christian historians, including Julius Africanus, Eusebius, Jerome, and Epiphanius. From this,
Drijvers infers that Bardaisan was made a heretic only gradually,
and that orthodoxy arrived relatively late in Syria.[61]

10. *The Bardesanites*

Bardaisan, like Marcion and Tatian, had profound influence on the
religious tenor of Late Antique Edessa. Despite the crisis which the
persecutions of 216 C.E. brought to Edessa, the Bardesanites appear
to have survived as a community. Even in Bardaisan's days, though,
his followers did not espouse a coherent theology, but battled significant
doctrinal differences which are still evident from their hymns. Some,
it appears, joined the Manicheans. Still, two centuries after Bardaisan's
death, Bardesanites comprised a sizable population in the city. They
took their place beside a variety of religious groups, all of which
struggled to find a way to negotiate Edessa's difficult geographical
location in Late Antiquity, sandwiched as it was between the Byzantine
and Sassanid empires.

Bardaisan's adherents survived beyond the fifth century, when they
were subject to extensive persecutions. In an attempt to extirpate all

---

[60] Ephrem, *PR* 1.
[61] Drijvers, *Bardaisan of Edessa*, 185.

traces of paganism and heterodoxy in the city, the bishop Rabbula of Edessa (d. 435) ordered their forcible conversion to "orthodox" Christianity along with the destruction of Bardesanite churches. Remarkably, as late as the seventh century, Jacob of Edessa (633–708) still knows of them. Their interest in astrology and cosmology made them vital links in the transmission of Greek knowledge into Islam. For this interest, Bardaisan and his followers received more notice by later historians and chroniclers than many other "heretics" of second-century Syriac Christianity. For this reason, too, the sole manuscript of the BLC which survives today was copied by an unknown cleric in the sixth or seventh century, to ensure that precious philosophical and cosmological speculation would not be lost forever in the changing fortunes of Empire.

Bibliography

Amand de Medieta, David. *Fatalisme et liberté dans l'antiquité grecque*. Amsterdam: A. M. Hakkert, 1973.

Beck, Edmund, ed. *Des Heiligen Ephraem des Syrers Hymnen Contra Haereses*. Corpus scriptorum christianorum orientalium, Scriptores Syri. 76 (Text), 77 (Translation). Louvain: L. Durbecq, 1957.

Brock, Sebastian. "Didymus the Blind on Bardaisan." *Journal of Theological Studies* 22 (1971): 530–31.

Chabot, J.-B. *Chronique de Michel le Syrien*. Brussels: Culture et Civilisation, 1963.

Chrysippus. *Stoicorum Veterum Fragmenta*. Edited by H. von Arnim. 4 vols. Leipzig: Teubner, 1903–1924.

Cureton, W. *Spicilegium syriacum*. London: Rivingtons, 1855.

Denzey, Nicola. "Under A Pitiless Sky." Ph.D. diss., Princeton University, 1998.

Didymus the Blind. *Psalmenkommentar (Tura-Papyrus): Teil 3: Kommentar zu Psalmen 29–34*. Edited by A. Gesché and M. Gronewald. Papyrologische Texte und Abhandlungen 8. Bonn: Habelt, 1969.

Dihle, Albrecht. "Astrology in the Doctrine of Bardesanes." Pages 160–68 in *Studia Patristica 20*. Edited by E. A. Livingstone. Louvain: Peeters, 1989.

Dillon, John. "Plutarch and Second-Century Platonism." Pages 214–29 in *Classical Mediterranean Spirituality*. Edited by A. H. Armstrong. New York: SCM Press, 1989.

Draguet, R. "Pièces de polémique antijulianiste." *Muséon* 44 (1931): 255–317.

Drijvers, H. J. W. *Bardaisan of Edessa*. Studia Semitica Neerlandica. Assen: Van Gorcum, 1966.

———. "Bardaisan of Edessa and the Hermetica: The Aramaic Philosopher and the Philosophy of His Time." Pages 190–210 in *Vooraziatisch-egyptisch Genootschap "Ex Oriente Lux," Jaarbericht 21*. Leiden: Ex Oriente Lux, 1970.

———. *The Book of the Laws of the Countries: Dialogue on Fate of Bardaisan of Edessa*. Assen: Van Gorcum, 1965.

———. *Cults and Beliefs at Edessa*. Etudes préliminaires aux religions orientales dans l'empire romain 82. Leiden: E. J. Brill, 1980.

———. "Jews and Christians at Edessa." Pages 88–102 in *History and Religion in Late Antique Syria*. Edited by Han J. W. Drijvers. Aldershot, Hampshire, United Kingdom: Variorum, 1995.

———. "The Persistence of Pagan Cults and Practices in Christian Syria." Pages 35–43 in *East of Byzantium: Syria and Armenia in the Formative Period.* Edited by N. Garsoian et al. Washington, D.C.: Dumbarton Oaks, 1982.

Greene, William Chase. *Moira: Fate, Good and Evil in Greek Thought.* New York: Harper & Row, 1944.

Guidi, I. *Chronicon Edessenum.* Vol. 1 of *Chronica Minora.* Edited by E. W. Brooks and J.-B. Chabot. Corpus scriptorum christianorum orientalium, Scriptores Syri, Series Tertia, 4. Paris: E Typographeo Reipublicae, 1903–1905.

Hegedus, Tim. "Attitudes to Astrology in Early Christianity: A Study Based on Selected Sources." Ph.D. diss., University of Toronto, 2000.

Jones, F. Stanley. "The Astrological Trajectory in Syriac-Speaking Christianity (Elchasai, Bardaisan, and Mani)." Pages 183–200 in *Atti del terzo congresso internazionale di studi "Manicheismo e oriente Cristiano antico."* Edited by Luigi Cirillo and Alois van Tongerloo. Manichaean Studies 3. Brepols: International Association of Manichaean Studies in Conjunction with the Center of the History of Religions, 1997.

Levi della Vida, G. "Bardesane e il dialogo delle leggi del paesi." *Rivista di studi filosofici e religiosi* 1 (1920), 399–430.

Mitchell, C. W. S. *Ephraim's Prose Refutation of Mani, Marcion and Bardaisan.* 2 Vols. London: Williams and Norgate, 1912–1921.

Nau, F. "Notes d'astronomie syrienne." *Journal asiatique* 16 (1910): 209–28.

Nau, F., ed. *Les hérésies Christologiques d'après Philoxène de Mabboug (Xenia) et Bar Hébraeus.* Patrologia orientalis 13. Paris: Firmin-Didot, 1919.

Newbold, William Romaine. "Bardaisan and the Odes of Solomon." *Journal of Biblical Literature* 30 (1911): 161–204.

Quispel, G. "L'inscription de Flavia Sophe." Pages 58–69 in vol. 1 of *Gnostic Studies.* 2 vols. Istanbul: Nederlands Historisch-Archaeologisch Instituut in het Nabije Oosten, 1974.

Riedinger, Otto. *Die frühchristliche Kirche gegen der Astrologie.* Innsbruck: Wagner, 1956.

Segal, J. B. "Pagan Syriac Monuments in the Vilayet of Urfa." *Anatolian Studies* 3 (1953): 97–117.

———. "The Sabian Mysteries, The Planet Cult of Ancient Harran." Pages 201–20 in *Vanished Civilizations: Forgotten Peoples of the Ancient World.* Edited by E. Bacon. London: Thames and Hudson, 1963.

———. "Some Syriac Inscriptions of the 2nd and 3rd century A.D." *Bulletin of the School of Oriental and African Studies* 16 (1954): 97–120.

Stough, Charlotte. "Stoic Determinism and Moral Responsibility." Pages 203–32 in *The Stoics.* Edited by John Rist. Berkeley: University of California Press, 1978.

Theodore bar Koni. *Liber scholiorum.* Edited by A. Scher. Corpus scriptorum christianorum orientalium, Scriptores Syri, Series Secunda, 65–66. Paris: E Typographeo Reipublicae, 1910–1912.

Vieillefond, J. R. *Les 'Cestes' de Julius Africanus: Étude sur l'ensemble des fragments avec édition, traduction et commentaires.* Publications de l'Institut Français de Florence, 1st ser., 20. Paris: Sansoni, 1970.

Waldstein, Michael, and Frederik Wisse, eds. *The Apocryphon of John: Synopsis of Nag Hammadi Codices II,1; III,1; and IV,1 with BG 8502,2.* Nag Hammadi and Manichaean Studies 33. Leiden: E. J. Brill, 1995.

MONTANISM: EGALITARIAN ECSTATIC "NEW PROPHECY"

Antti Marjanen

1. *Introduction*

First-century Christianity witnessed considerable prophetic activity and charismatic phenomena (1 Thess 5:20; 1 Cor 11:4, 5; 12:10, 28; 14:3–4; Rom 12:6; Eph 2:20; 3:5; 4:11; Matt 7:22; 10:41; Luke 11:49; Acts 11:27; 15:32; 21:9, 10; 1 Tim 4:14; Rev 2:20; 19:10). With the turn of the century ecclesiastical structures and offices began to gain more permanent forms, while prophetic enthusiasm slackened; but unlike what one might suppose it did not cease altogether. Indeed, the second century saw the rise of a Christian movement in which prophecy gained an extraordinarily outstanding position. The centrality of prophetic activity among these Christians is stressed by the fact that even though later generations knew the movement best as "Montanists,"[1] a name derived from one of its first prophets and leaders, Montanus, the adherents of the movement called it "Prophecy" (Eusebius, *Hist. eccl.* 5.16.4; Clem. Alex., *Strom.* 4.13). Even their opponents knew the Montanists as the "New Prophecy" recognizing the strong prophetic ethos of the movement, albeit emphasizing its difference from the prophets of the apostolic age (Eusebius, *Hist. eccl.* 5.16.4; 5.19.2).

2. *Sources*

Like many other early Christian "heretic" movements, Montanism is mainly known through heresiological sources. In addition to approximately fifteen oracles quoted by the heresiologists[2] and numerous

---

[1] The name "Montanists" appears for the first time in the writings of Cyril of Jerusalem (d. 386) (*Catecheses illuminandorum* 16.8).

[2] For the extant Montanist oracles, see Pierre de Labriolle, *Les sources de l'histoire du Montanisme: Textes Grecs, Latins, Syriaques* (Collecteanea Friburgensia 24; Fribourg: Librairie de l'université; Paris: Ernest Leroux, 1913); Kurt Aland, "Bemerkungen

inscriptions,[3] which are generally considered to be genuine expressions of Montanist proclamation and thinking, as well as the writings of Tertullian in his Montanist period and the *Martyrdom of Perpetua
and Felicitas*,[4] the main evidence of the movement is derived from
anti-Montanist heresiological texts. The most important heresiological sources are Eusebius and Epiphanius who have preserved quotations of late second-century or early third-century anti-Montanist
writers, including Gaius (Eusebius, *Hist. eccl.* 2.25.6–7; 3.31.4), Apollonius
(Eusebius, *Hist. eccl.* 5.18), Serapion of Antioch (Eusebius, *Hist. eccl.*
5.19), and a (most likely pro-Montanist) report from the martyrs of
Gaul cited by Eusebius (*Hist. eccl.* 5.1.3–63)[5] as well as two anonymous authors (Eusebius, *Hist. eccl.* 5.16–17; Epiphanius, *Panarion*
48.1.2–14.2).[6] Other heresiologists who discuss Montanists include:

---

zum Montanismus und zur frühchristlichen Eschatologie," in *Kirchengeschichtliche
Entwürfe: Alte Kirche, Reformation und Luthertum, Pietismus und Erweckungsbewegung* (Gütersloh:
Gerd Mohn, 1960), 143–48; Ronald E. Heine, *The Montanist Oracles and Testimonia*
(Macon, Ga.: Mercer University Press, 1989); Sheila E. McGinn, "The 'Montanist'
Oracles and Prophetic Theology," *Studia Patristica* 31 (ed. E. A. Livingstone; Leuven:
Peeters, 1997), 128–35. Kurt Aland ("Bemerkungen zum Montanismus," 143–48)
has found 25 Montanist oracles or their summaries in the texts of the heresiologists; he regards 16 of them as authentic. Heine (*Montanist Oracles and Testimonia*)
and McGinn ("'Montanist' Oracles," 128–35) consider only 14 of Aland's 16 oracles genuine. They think that numbers 1 and 2 (according to Aland's enumeration),
in which Montanus announces himself as the Father, the Son and the Paraclete/the
Spirit, are secondarily placed in his mouth.
[3] For Montanist inscriptions, see William Tabbernee, *Montanist Inscriptions and
Testimonia: Epigraphic Sources Illustrating the History of Montanism* (North American Patristic Society: Patristic Monograph Series 16; Macon, Ga.: Mercer University Press,
1997).
[4] It has been suggested that at least the final version of the *Martyrdom of Perpetua
and Felicitas* is a result of Montanist redaction; see William Tabbernee, "Remnants
of the New Prophecy," in *Studia Patristica* 21 (ed. E. A. Livingstone. Leuven: Peeters,
1989), 195–97; Christine Trevett, *Montanism: Gender, Authority and the New Prophecy*
(Cambridge: Cambridge University Press, 1996), 176–77.
[5] For the interpretation of the text as an originally Montanist report of the mar-
tyrdoms in Gaul, see Anne Jensen, *God's Self-Confident Daughters: Early Christianity and
the Liberation of Women* (trans. O. C. Dean Jr.; Louisville, Ky.: Westminster John
Knox, 1996), 136–37.
[6] The exact nature and extent of Epiphanius' anonymous source is difficult to
determine (cf. Ronald E. Heine, "The Role of the Gospel of John in the Montanist
Controversy," *SecCent* 6 [1987/88]: 3). According to his own testimony (*Panarion*
48.15.1), Epiphanius uses both written and oral sources in his description of Montanists.
Although he only occasionally quotes his written source and redacts it quite freely
it is most likely that he is employing it in *Panarion* 48.1.2–48.14.2, which concen-
trates more strictly on the presentation of the Phrygians, whereas in 48.14.3 he
introduces the Tascodrugians, which are somewhat artificially connected with the
preceding.

Irenaeus, Clement of Alexandria, Hippolytus, Origen, Pseudo-Tertullian, Firmilian, Cyril of Jerusalem, Didymus of Alexandria, Filastrius, Jerome, and Augustine.[7] A further useful source is an anti-Montanist *Dialogue of a Montanist and an Orthodox*, composed by an anonymous writer in the fourth century.[8]

Even though most of the original Montanist writings have been lost the representatives of the "New Prophecy" evidently produced a great number of their own texts. This is contended both by Eusebius (*Hist. eccl.* 6.20.3) and Hippolytus (*Haer.* 8.19.1). Hippolytus even insists that Montanus, Maximilla, and Priscilla, the first leaders and prophets of the movement, did themselves compose writings (*Haer.* 8.19.1). This is possible but cannot be verified beyond doubt.[9] Another anti-Montanist source that speaks about Montanist writings is the *Chronicle* of Michael the Syrian written in the twelfth century. It relates that when John of Ephesus in the mid-sixth century burnt the Montanist assembly-place and the bones of Montanus, Maximilla, and Priscilla in Pepuza, he incinerated their books as well.[10] Whether the exact course of the events described by Michael the Syrian is historically true is difficult to know. Yet, even if the burning of the books did not happen on this particular occasion, it is feasible that its mention corresponds to the practice of how mainstream Christians dealt with the books of the heretics, in general, and of the Montanists, in particular. In any case, the reference to the Montanist writings confirms the data given by Eusebius and Hippolytus.

In addition to these general references to writings by Montanists, Apollonius knows of the Montanist Themiso who composed a catholic letter "imitating the apostle (= Paul)" (Eusebius, *Hist. eccl.* 5.18.5) and the anonymous presbyter of a book, possibly a collection of the oracles, written by Asterius Urbanus (Eusebius, *Hist. eccl.* 5.16.17).

---

[7] The most important collections of patristic testimonia illuminating the history of Montanism are Labriolle, *Les sources de l'histoire du Montanisme*; Nathanael Bonwetsch, *Texte zur Geschichte des Montanismus* (Kleine Texte für Vorlesungen und Übungen 129; Bonn: A. Marcus und E. Weber, 1914); Heine, *Montanist Oracles and Testimonia*.

[8] For the text, see Labriolle, *Les sources de l'histoire du Montanisme*, 93–108.

[9] However, there is another anti-Montanist source which contends that the first leaders of the Montanist movement composed texts. In the *Dialogue of a Montanist and an Orthodox* it is stated that Priscilla and Maximilla wrote books; see Labriolle, *Les sources de l'histoire du Montanisme*, 107.

[10] For the Syriac text and its English translation, see Tabbernee, *Montanist Inscriptions and Testimonia*, 35–39.

Unfortunately, apart from one oracle by Maximilla, nothing has been preserved from these two works.

Tertullian's works that derive from his Montanist period constitute the largest body of authentic Montanist writings and are thus a valuable source for the Montanist movement.[11] When Tertullian's works are used, one has to take into account, however, that Tertullian himself does not represent the earliest phase of the movement. Neither was he personally familiar with the earliest Montanist prophets, and his view of Montanist theology is colored by his own apologetic tendencies.[12]

3. The First Prophets of the "New Prophecy"

The Montanist oracles and the heresiological sources do not provide us with much data of personal character about the first leaders and prophets of the Montanist movement. If late, clearly fictitious fabrications of a polemical nature to which no scholar has attached any weight are omitted, there is extremely little material one can build upon when one tries to sketch a historical picture of Montanus, Priscilla, and Maximilla.[13] The information of the anonymous presbyter quoted by Eusebius (Hist. eccl. 5.16.7), that Montanus originated from a Mysian village Ardabau, does not say very much because, as stated below, we have no knowledge of the exact location or character of that place. The mention that Montanus was newly converted may be true but that can also be an anti-Montanist fabrication. It was a common Christian truth that a church-leader may not be newly converted because such a person can more easily fall into the trap of the Devil (1 Tim 3:6). Therefore it is no wonder that a heretic like Montanus was portrayed as a man who had been a member of the Christian church only for a short period before he assumed a leadership role and began his non-orthodox prophetic activity (see below).

---

[11] For the identification of the writings of Tertullian's Montanist period, see Trevett, Montanism, 72–73.

[12] So also A. Jensen, God's Self-Confident Daughters, 135; Trevett, Montanism, 66–69.

[13] The claims that the early Montanists were magicians, child-murderers, fornicators, and idol worshippers (e.g. Isidore of Pelusium, Ep. 1.242) were typical expressions of religious polemics without being based on reality.

The fourth-century theologian Jerome states that Montanus was "castrated and emasculated" (*Ep.* 41.4). Based on this characterization, some have speculated that, before his conversion to Christianity, Montanus was a priest of Cybele.[14] This inference is unlikely, however, since the characterization does not occur in any other anti-Montanist writings before Jerome, and it can easily be understood in terms of polemical denigration. The same is probably true with an attempt to see Montanus as a former priest of Apollo; this suggestion is made in the *Dialogue of a Montanist and an Orthodox.*[15]

The claim advanced by Apollonius that Maximilla and Priscilla left their husbands after having become filled with the Spirit (Eusebius, *Hist. eccl.* 5.18.3) may be true. Even Paul consents that Christian women can divorce their (non-believing) spouses (1 Cor 7:11). It is also possible that Maximilla's and Priscilla's husbands divorced their wives when these women became involved in the activities of the new religious movement but in the later polemics the women were made responsible for the event.[16] The fact that, according to Apollonius, the Montanists themselves regarded Priscilla as a virgin (Eusebius, *Hist. eccl.* 5.18.3) may not necessarily indicate that the information about her divorcing her husband was a false defamation, but it may show that after her divorce she practiced continence in an exemplary way.

A relatively early piece of data imparted by the anonymous presbyter of Eusebius (*Hist. eccl.* 5.16.13), according to which Montanus and Maximilla committed suicide, hardly holds true. This is confirmed by the fact that the writer himself considers his information to be unreliable (Eusebius, *Hist. eccl.* 5.16.15). It is simply "gossip." In addition, if it is true that the bones of the early Montanist prophets became an object of veneration, as claimed by Pseudo-Dionysius of Tell-Mahrē and Michael the Syrian,[17] it is unlikely that this would have happened if Montanus and Maximilla had taken their own lives.[18]

---

[14] So e.g., W. H. C. Frend, *The Rise of Christianity* (Philadelphia: Fortress, 1984), 253.

[15] On the text, see Labriolle, *Les Sources de l'histoire du Montanisme*, 103.

[16] See also the discussion below in the section 7.

[17] For the texts and their commentaries, see Tabbernee, *Montanist Inscriptions and Testimonia*, 27–47.

[18] Tabbernee, *Montanist Inscriptions and Testimonia*, 30.

4. *The Origins and Spread of the Montanist Movement*

Montanism originated in Asia Minor, more precisely in the region of Phrygia.[19] The towns or villages that are connected with the beginnings of the movement are Ardabau, Pepuza and Tymion. An anonymous presbyter, who is cited by Eusebius (*Hist. eccl.* 5.16.7) and who addressed his anti-Montanist text to Avircius Marcellus, states that Montanus commenced his preaching activity in a village called Ardabau. There exists no data, however, where the place could be located. Some scholars have even speculated that Ardabau was no real geographical site. Rather it was a symbolic name, which was taken over from the *Fourth Book of Ezra*, in which Ardat, or its variant reading Ardab, refers to a fertile plain where the heavenly Zion is expected to descend (9:26).[20] This suggestion is not very likely, however. The function of Ardat in *4 Ezra* as a lonely place outside of any settlement does not easily match a village or a town in the account of the anonymous presbyter. Furthermore, the presbyter makes no claim that Ardabau be regarded as a location for the heavenly Zion or Jerusalem. On the whole, the links between Ardat of *4 Ezra* and Ardabau of the text of the presbyter are so fragile that nothing can really be built on them. For the time being, Ardabau is deemed to remain an unsolvable puzzle.

Until recent times, Pepuza and Tymion have also created problems for scholars. Despite many efforts, no one has been able to locate them with any degree of certainty.[21] Yet two new archaeological discoveries may signal a turning point in the search for the locations associated with Montanist beginnings.[22] In 1998 the director of the Usak Archaeological Museum in Turkey purchased a mar-

---

[19] This is reflected in the fact that the opponents of the movement can also style it the "Phrygian heresy" (e.g., *Muratorian Canon* 84–85; Origen, *In epistula ad Titum* [for the text, see Labriolle, *Les sources de l'histoire du Montanisme*, 56]; Firmilian [in a letter preserved in Cyprian, *Ep.* 75.7]; Eusebius, *Hist. eccl.* 2.25.6; 5.16.1; 6.20.3; *Vit. Const.* 54; Epiphanius, *Pan.* 48.1).

[20] So Heinz Kraft, "Die altkirchliche Prophetie und die Entstehung des Montanismus." *TZ* 11 (1955): 260; Trevett, Montanism, 25–26.

[21] On past efforts to locate Pepuza and Tymion, see August Strobel, *Das heilige Land des Montanisten: Eine religionsgeographische Untersuchung* (Religionsgeschichtliche Versuche und Vorarbeiten 37; Berlin: Walter de Gruyter, 1980); William Tabbernee, *Montanist Inscriptions and Testimonia*, 27–28, 153–54, 487–88.

[22] William Tabbernee, "Portals of the Montanist New Jerusalem: The Discovery of Pepuza and Tymion," *JECS* 11 (2003): 87–93.

ble slab with an inscription carved on it referring to Tymion. The slab was probably found near the modern Turkish village Susuzören, presumed to be situated near the ancient Tymion.

Two years later, inspired by the former discovery, a group of researchers led by William Tabbernee engaged in field work in the same general area, when they detected a Byzantine monastery in the proximity of the modern village Karayakuplu. According to tentative estimate, William Tabbernee believes that the monastery is the one mentioned in medieval sources and which was built close to ancient Pepuza. Since there are signs of an ancient settlement in the vicinity of the monastery, William Tabbernee and his colleagues have concluded that both Tymion and Pepuza can now be identified. Future archaeological excavations of these sites will show whether the inference proves to be correct.

The activities of the Montanist movement were not confined to Asia Minor.[23] Already during the time of the Roman bishop Eleutherus (174–189) traces of influence from the "New Prophecy" can be detected both in the capital of the Empire and in Gaul (Eusebius, *Hist. eccl.* 5.3.4). The permanent presence of the Montanists in Rome is corroborated by the fact that Gaius, a contemporary of the bishop Zephyrinus (ca. 198–217), wrote a polemical pamphlet in the form of a dialogue against the Montanist Proclus (Eusebius, *Hist. eccl.* 2.25.6; 3.31.4; 6.20.3). There are also signs of the spread of the Montanist movement to Antioch of Syria and to Thrace in the last decade of the second century. This becomes apparent from the letter of Serapion, the bishop of Antioch (190–211), in which he forcefully criticizes the Montanist movement and also states that his colleagues in Thrace agree with his notions (Eusebius, *Hist. eccl.* 5.19.1–3). The most important North African theologian of the time, Tertullian, adopted a Montanist version of Christianity at the very beginning of the third century. This shows that Montanist ideas had also reached the region of Carthage before that, perhaps in the last decade of the second century. Furthermore, it is evident that

---

[23] Besides Ardabau (?), Pepuza, and Tymion, there were Montanists also in Ankyra in Galatia (cf. the anonymous presbyter in Eusebius, *Hist. eccl.* 5.16.4) and probably in Hierapolis (Eusebius, *Hist. eccl.* 5.19.2) at the end of the second century. The early third-century Montanist tomb incriptions found in ancient Temenouthyrai point to the presence of Montanists in that town already in the previous century (see Tabbernee, *Montanist Inscriptions and Testimonia*, 62–76).

Montanism had consolidated its presence in Alexandria by the end
of the second century as well (Clem. Alex., *Strom.* 4.13; 7.17).

Towards the close of the second century the Montanist movement
had thus been widely disseminated throughout the Roman Empire.
Nevertheless, it is still difficult to determine exactly when Montanism
originated. The sources Eusebius is citing do not refer to persons or
events that can be reliably dated. The datable events Epiphanius
mentions in connection with the Montanists are again in seeming
contradiction with each other. He states that Montanus began his
prophetic activity in the nineteenth year of the Emperor Antoninus
Pius, i.e., ca. 157 C.E. (*Pan.* 48.1.1). In another passage Epiphanius
asserts that the Montanist female prophet Maximilla died 290 years
before the writing of *Panarion*, which he dates to 376 (*Pan.* 48.2.7).
If this is true, then Maximilla should have had her active period
before the middle of the 80s. Many scholars have concluded that
Epiphanius is totally mixed up in his calculations and his dates must
be considered unreliable.[24] It is nevertheless possible that the text of
Panarion may have been corrupted in the second passage, and its
original reading was 206 and not 290 years. The first editor of
Epiphanius' work, Karl Holl, has suggested this text correction.[25]
The emendation presupposes that in an earlier phase of the manuscript tradition the year was written with letters instead of numer-
als. When the numbers 206 and 290 are written with letters they
are very similar (206 = sigma+digamma; 290 = sigma+qoppa). If
this assumption is accepted, then the effective period of Maximilla
can be dated back to ca. 170. In light of this, Epiphanius' dates
may be correct, and Montanism originated in the 150s or 160s.

5. *Montanism and the Formative Catholic Church*

The expanding Montanist movement was variously received by the
formative Catholic Church. Eusebius tells us that some Christians in
Gaul presented an approving estimation of the Montanists in the
second half of the second century. They sent a letter to the current

---

[24] So e.g., Trevett, *Montanism*, 29.
[25] Frank Williams mentions it in *The Panarion of Epiphanius of Salamis: Books II &
III (Sects 47–80, De Fide)* (Nag Hammadi and Manichaen Studies 36; Leiden: E. J.
Brill, 1994), 8.

bishop of Rome, Eleutherus (174–189), and asked him to take a positive stand toward the Montanists for the sake of general peace in the church (Eusebius, *Hist. eccl.* 5.3.4). Irenaeus who at the time was a presbyter in the church of Lyons brought the letter to Rome (*Hist. eccl.* 5.4.1–2).

Eusebius' reference indicates that already before the time of Gaius and Proclus the role of the Montanists was a matter of debate. Nevertheless, Eleutherus did not make any negative decision about them. This is shown by the fact that the successor of Eleutherus, Victor (189–199), adopted a positive attitude toward Montanists at the beginning. Victor even issued an edict in which he acknowledged the prophetic gifts of the Montanists and recommended that the Montanist congregations in Asia Minor and in Phrygia be accepted into the Eucharistic fellowship of the Catholic Church (Tertullian, *Prax.* 1). Nevertheless, Victor changed his mind under the influence of Praxeas, a man whom Tertullian vehemently opposed. At the time of Zephyrinus (199–217), successor of Victor, Montanism was officially condemned in Rome.[26] In Antioch and in Asia Minor this happened during the time of Bishop Serapion (190–211).[27]

In the third century the understanding of Montanism was thus transformed from a renewal movement of the Christian church to a heresy. During the following centuries, Montanism lost its support in many places.[28] Both in Rome and in North Africa the movement seemed to have shrunk to nearly nothing in the fourth and fifth centuries.[29] In its birthplace, in Asia Minor, Montanism maintained its position the longest. But even there the movement got into difficulties in the sixth century, when the Eastern emperor Justinian I (482–565) was promulgating laws against Christians whose ideas and doctrines deviated from those of the Catholic Church. Montanism suffered a

---

[26] Trevett, Montanism, 55–56.

[27] On this, see Eusebius, *Hist. eccl.* 5.19.1–4.

[28] On the final phases of the Montanist movement, see Trevett, *Montanism*, 223–32.

[29] Some scholars have assumed that the extreme desire of the Montanists to seek martyrdom also reduced their number significantly. To be sure, "the New Prophecy encouraged readiness to embrace martyrdom and it discouraged flight in persecution" (Trevett, *Montanism*, 128). Still, it is an exaggeration to claim that, despite the fact that they were critical of the second repentance after apostasy, Montanists especially sought to surrender themselves to the authorities to be martyred. For a persuasive argument on this, see William Tabbernee, "Early Montanism and Voluntary Martyrdom," *Colloq* 17 (1985): 33–44; Trevett, *Montanism*, 121–29.

fatal blow when John, bishop of Ephesus (507–589), undertook a systematic persecution against the movement and began to incinerate their writings and churches.[30]

What were the reasons that Montanism was condemned as a heresy? On the whole the reactions of those representing mainstream Christianity to the Montanist movement were not altogether negative. We have noted, for example, that Eusebius makes a reference to Irenaeus carrying a letter from Lyons to Rome that defended Montanist martyrs in Gaul (*Hist. eccl.* 5.4.1–3). In his own writings, moreover, Irenaeus seems to support the Montanists over against those who in their condemnation of Montanism rejected the Gospel of John and the prophetic gift valued by Paul (*Haer.* 3.11.9). Despite his critical view of Montanists, Hippolytus too admitted that the Montanists had acceptable conceptions of God as the Creator, ecclesiology, and Christology (*Haer.* 8.19.2). The third famous heresiologist, Epiphanius, also confirms that there is nothing wrong with the Montanists' view of God, the Trinity, Christ, and the resurrection (*Pan.* 48.1.3–4).[31]

There were voices among mainstream Christians, however, which maintained that the Christology of the Montanists was modalistic (Hippolytus, *Haer.* 8.19.3; Jerome, *Ep.* 41.3). According to the modalistic view, advanced among others by Noetus and Sabellius, God himself was born, suffered, and died as the Son. This accusation was probably applicable only to part of the Montanists, especially to those who lived in Asia Minor.[32] Yet it is noteworthy that they represented a Christological view that was dominant in that geographical area.[33] As far as the doctrine of the Trinity was concerned, even in the third century many Montanists seemed to have kept to the generally accepted view of the relationship between the Father and the Son. This is shown by the fact that Tertullian composed a text

---

[30] Labriolle, *Les sources de l'histoire du Montanisme*, 238; Tabbernee, *Montanist Inscriptions and Testimonia*, 27–47.

[31] Cf. also Filastrius, *Liber de haeresibus* 49.

[32] It is also likely that about 200 C.E. there were two different Montanist groups in Rome, one led by Aeschines representing modalistic Christology and the other led by Proclus espousing mainstream Christology (Pseudo-Tertullian, *Adv. omn. haer.* 7–8); for this, see Peter Lampe, *From Paul to Valentinus: Christians at Rome in the First Two Centuries* (trans. Michael Steinhauser; Minneapolis: Fortress, 2003), 381.

[33] Alistair Stewart-Sykes, "The Original Condemnation of Asian Montanism," *JEH* 50 (1999): 1–22, esp. 3.

against Praxeas, in which he criticizes Praxeas for emphasizing too much the unity of God and for repudiating the early Christian doctrine of the Trinity.

On the whole it seems likely that the opposition against the Montanists was not mainly due to doctrinal reasons. Recently it has been advocated that the greatest divergences of opinion between the Montanist and Catholic Christians had to do with the central position of the prophetic proclamation and the enthusiastic expectation of an imminent end in Montanism.[34] Certainly, Montanism was a prophetic movement and it did emphasize the expectation of an imminent end as one of the important features in its theology, albeit perhaps not as the most important one. Yet this was nothing new as such. First-century and in some respects second-century Christianity provided other examples with similar concerns. Indeed, the Montanists regarded such prophetic figures as their prototypes that were also approved by mainstream Christians, including Agabus, the daughters of Philip, Ammia, and Quadratus (Eusebius, *Hist. eccl.* 5.17.3). Not even the idea that the Holy Spirit spoke through the Montanist prophets was in conflict with the notions of early mainstream Christianity. Neither was the expectation of the imminent end considered to be an issue that should have led to charges of heresy.

The present chapter will attempt to show that it was not the *fact* that Montanists focused on prophetic activity and the expectation of an imminent end that led to a development which eventually placed Montanist communities outside the Catholic Church. Rather, it was the *way* these theological emphases came into expression in Montanism and shaped the power structures in and relationships between various early Christian communities. It is furthermore likely that the requirements the Montanists put on those who joined and stayed in their communities were stricter than the ones presented in mainstream churches, and thus also provoked indignation.

---

[34] D. F. Wright ("Why Were the Montanists Condemned?" *Them* 2 [1976]: 15–22) thinks that the central role the prophetic proclamation played in the Montanist movement was the crucial factor in its condemnation as heresy. According to Walter Burkhardt ("Primitive Montanism: Why Condemned?" in *From Faith to Faith: Essays in Honor of Donald G. Miller* [ed. Dikran Hadidian; Pittsburgh: Pickwick Publications, 1979], 339–56), the most important reason for declaring Montanism a heresy was its expectation of the imminent end.

6. Montanism as a Prophetic Movement

When the anonymous presbyter cited by Eusebius describes the initial appearance of Montanus he depicts his activity as follows:

> At first it is reported in Ardabau that during the time when Gratus
> was the proconsul of Asia one of the newly converted, called Montanus,
> in the immense desire of his soul to strive to be first, let the adver-
> sary enter into himself. He became possessed by a spirit and, being
> overpowered and entranced by this, he suddenly fell into an ecstasy
> and began to speak and utter strange words, really prophesying in the
> way which was against the tradition and the custom of the church
> from the very beginning. (Eusebius, *Hist. eccl.* 5.16.7)

The quotation shows that Montanism was a prophetic movement
from its very beginning. This is confirmed by the Montanists' own
oracles as well as by the testimonies of several anti-Montanist writers.[35] According to the anonymous presbyter quoted by Eusebius, the
proclamation of Montanus and the accompanying women prophets
was highly ecstatic and contained strange and incomprehensible oracles (Eusebius, *Hist. eccl.* 5.16.7–9).[36] This may suggest that, at least
from the perspective of an outsider, the prophetic proclamation of
the early Montanists often had uncontrolled features. In his criticism, the presbyter of Eusebius also refers to an anti-Montanist writer
Miltiades, who rejected the Montanist prophecy, since "a prophet
must not speak in ecstasy" (Eusebius, *Hist. eccl.* 5.17.1). The presbyter agrees. According to him ecstatic prophecy derives from a false
spirit and leads to a proclamation that is nonsensical, indecent, and
strange (Eusebius, *Hist. eccl.* 5.16.9). Firmilian, bishop of Caesarea in

---

[35] For the oracles of the Montanists stressing the prophetic character of the movement, see Tertullian, *Exh. cast.* 10.5; Eusebius, *Hist. eccl.* 5.16.17; Epiphanius, *Pan.*
48.2.4. For Tertullian Montanism was the prophetic movement par excellence (see,
e.g., *Pud.* 21.7). For the testimonia of the anti-Montanists referring to the prophetic
nature of the Montanist movement, see, e.g., Eusebius, *Hist. eccl.* 5.16.4; 5.16.12;
5.17.1–4 (an anonymous presbyter); 5.18.3 (Apollonius); 5.19.2 (Serapion of Antioch);
Epiphanius, 48.3–8; 48.10.3 (probably containing data derived from an anonymous
source); Hippolytus, *Haer.* 8.19.1; Eusebius, *Hist. eccl.* 5.3.4; 5.14; Filastrius, *Liber de
haeresibus* 49; Jerome, *Ep.* 41.1–2. It is even possible that the non-Christian Celsus
was aware of the Montanist movement and of its prophetic nature (see Origen,
Cels. 7.8–9).
[36] It is also possible although not sure that the proclamation of the Montanists
was sometimes incomprehensible because they also spoke in tongues. The verb
xenofōnein, which the presbyter uses to describe Montanus' prophecy, may refer to
glossolalia (so Trevett, *Montanism*, 89–91).

Cappadocia (ca. 230–268), advances a similar opinion. He refers to an anonymous Montanist woman who "in the state of ecstasy announced herself as a prophetess, and acted as if filled with the Holy Ghost," but who was, in Firmilian's view, "moved by the impetus of the principal demons" (in a letter preserved in Cyprian, *Ep.* 75.10).[37]

Epiphanius or his early source is also critical of the way the Montanist prophets presented their prophetic speeches or oracles. But since he remembers that Peter was also said to be in ecstasy when he saw his vision in Cornelius' house (Acts 10:10), it is not the fact that a prophet fell into ecstasy which made the Montanist prophecy unacceptable. Even the true prophets had fallen into ecstasy. Rather, it is an ecstasy that clouds the reason of the prophets that has to be avoided (*Pan.* 48.7.3). A similar distinction is made by Didymus the Blind, who maintains that there are several forms of ecstasy. Divine ecstasy was a matter of sobriety, whereas Montanist ecstasy was a matter of mania (*Frag. 2 Cor.* 5.12). The anonymous presbyter of Eusebius, Epiphanius or his source, and Didymus thus agree that the incomprehensibility and irrationality of prophecy is a sure indication of its falsity, and Montanism represents this kind of prophecy at its worst. It is no wonder that Tertullian feels compelled to defend the Montanist position over against the *psykhikoi*, the mainstream Christians, by insisting that being rapt in the spirit necessarily involves losing one's sensibility (*Marc.* 4.22.5).

Epiphanius has preserved an oracle by Maximilla that says that after her there will no longer be new prophets among Montanists (*Pan.* 48.2.4). Nevertheless, it is probable that the prophetic period did not confine itself to Montanus, Priscilla, and Maximilla, but continued even after the initial phase of the movement. To be sure, the first three prophets were the most important figures of the movement. Still, the anti-Montanist writers mention others also, such as Alcibiades and Theodotus (Eusebius, *Hist. eccl.* 5.3.4), Quintilla (Epiphanius, *Pan.* 49.2.1) as well as two anonymous women prophets, one mentioned by Tertullian (*An.* 9)[38] and the other by Firmilian (in

---

[37] The translation is made by Ernest Wallis and it stems from *Ante-Nicene Fathers* (ed. Alexander Roberts and James Donaldson; 10 vols.; 1885–1887; repr. Peabody, Mass.: Hendrickson, 1994), 5:390–397. The number given to Firmilian's letter in *Ante-Nicene Fathers* is 74.

[38] Tertullian does not explicitly call the woman a prophet but gives us to understand

a letter preserved in Cyprian, *Ep.* 75.10). Apollonius also suggests that there were many Montanist prophets after the three first ones although he fails to mention their names (Eusebius, *Hist. eccl.* 5.18.7–11).

The Montanists thought that Jesus' promise of the Paraclete materialized in the activity of their early prophets (John 14:16–17; 16:7–15).[39] Therefore they believed that their prophets could convey to them teachings that had not been delivered before. Thus, the words of Jesus, recorded in John 16:12–13, were seen to be fulfilled: "I have much more to say to you, more than you can now bear. But when he, the Spirit of truth, comes, he will guide you into all truth. The Spirit will not speak on his own; he will speak only what he hears, and he will tell you what is yet to come" (NIV). Even though the Montanists still clung to the writings of the Old Testament and the apostles they regarded the proclamation and the texts of their own prophets to be equally authoritative. Even Tertullian, who thought that the content of the apostolic *regula fidei* was unchangeable and immutable, used the Paraclete passages to justify changes which were, according to him, useful and necessary in matters of church life and discipline (*Virg.* 1). By referring to the above-mentioned Johannine text, Tertullian can even insist that its realization

---

that she was provided with *charismata reuelationum*, which implies that she was considered to be a prophet. On this, see Walter Bauer, *Rechtgläubigkeit und Ketzerei im ältesten Christentum* (2nd ed., revised by Georg Strecker; Tübingen: J. C. B. Mohr [Paul Siebeck], 1964), 183.

[39] It has been debated whether the notion of the Paraclete as the source of prophetic inspiration among the Montanists characterized the very beginning of the movement in Phrygia (so Trevett, *Montanism*, 62–66) or whether it only developed in Rome some twenty or thirty years later, as Heine has argued ("The Role of the Gospel of John in the Montanist Controversy," 1–19). I think Trevett's position is more plausible since the idea that Montanus, the women prophets, and the other earliest Montanist prophets acted as the mouthpieces of the Paraclete, although not found in the extant Montanist oracles, is set forth or presupposed in various early sources of diverse origin, including Irenaeus (*Haer.* 3.11.9), the report from the martyrs of Gaul quoted by Eusebius (*Hist. eccl.* 5.1.9–10), the early anti-Montanist source of Epiphanius (*Panarion* 48.11.5–8), Tertullian (*Jejun.* 1; *Pud.* 21; *Res.* 11; *Virg.* 1; *Prax.* 1; see also *Mon.* 2; 3), Hippolytus (*Haer.* 8.19.1), Pseudo-Tertullian (*Adv. omn. haer.* 7), Origen (*Princ.* 2.7.3). Cf. also the following later texts: Basil of Caesarea, *Epist.* 188; Jerome, *Epist.* 41.4; Pseudo-Dionysius of Tell Mahrē, *Chron.* Although some later sources suggest (Eusebius, *Hist. eccl.* 5.14; *Discussion of a Montanist and an Orthodox* [see Labriolle, *Les sources de l'histoire du Montanisme*, 97; see also 95]; Didymos, *Trin.* 3.41) that Montanus himself said: "I am the Father, the Son, and the Paraclete," it is less certain (so also Trevett, *Montanism*, 79) but not impossible (so Tabbernee, *Montanist Inscriptions and Testimonia*, 32–33).

in the activities of the Montanist prophets well illustrates a divine strategy against the devil:

> What kind of supposition is it, that, while the devil is always operating and adding daily to the ingenuities of iniquity, the work of God should either have ceased, or else have desisted from advancing? The reason why the Lord sent the Paraclete was, that, since human mediocrity was unable to take in all things at once, discipline should, little by little, be directed, and ordained, and carried on to perfection, by that Vicar of the Lord, the Holy Spirit. (*Virg.* 1)[40]

Catholic Christians sharply criticized this line of reasoning. Apollonius, for example, reproached Themiso for daring to write a catholic letter and place "his empty words" next to those of the Lord, the apostles, and the holy church (Eusebius, *Hist. eccl.* 5.18.5). A new revelation, which made a claim for being more far-reaching than the Old Testament and the apostolic writings, could not be accepted.

Because of its irrational ecstatic character and its claim for greater authority than that of the previous apostolic traditions, the Montanist prophecy was regarded as the work of evil spirits. The anti-Montanist writers cited by Eusebius report several attempts by mainstream bishops to exorcize demons from both Priscilla and Maximilla (*Hist. eccl.* 5.16.16; 5.18.13; 5.19.3).[41] All these endeavors ended without success because of the aid the women prophets received from their own supporters. The Montanists, for their part, considered mainstream Christians to be "prophet-slayers" (cf. Matt 23:34) since these did not approve of their prophetic message (Eusebius, *Hist. eccl.* 5.16.12).

7. *Fasting, Marriage, and the Second Repentance*

Practically speaking, the original sources of the earliest phase of Montanism have vanished, leaving no clear evidence for the content of the prophetic message. Nevertheless, some features in the Montanist teaching had apparently attracted so much attention among Catholic antagonists that they did leave traces in extant anti-Montanist writings. Montanus, Priscilla, and Maximilla obviously demanded that

---

[40] The text is translated by S. Thelwall and the translation is taken from *Ante-Nicene Fathers*, 4:27.

[41] A similar attempt was made with the prophetess mentioned by Firmilian in his letter to Cyprian (Cyprian, *Ep.* 75.10).

their followers fast and at least occasionally eat only dry food and vegetables.[42] To fast and to obey various food regulations was nothing unique as such. This was practiced by many mainstream Christians as well. Neither need we think that the early Montanists would have been especially rigorous in their fasting. Even allowing for some exaggeration, the accusation that the Montanists were known for both gluttony and feasting shows that they were not extreme ascetics (Eusebius, *Hist. eccl.* 5.18.2).[43] It is possible, however, that among Montanists, at least in its earliest phase, fasting and food regulations were practiced as a preparation for prophetic visions. The model for this was gained from Jewish apocalyptic texts (cf. Dan 10:2–3; *4 Ezra* 9:26).[44]

In a later phase, especially in North Africa, the Montanist fasting practices reached more severe forms. Tertullian, who may even have been the promoter of this development, frequently stresses that the Montanists fasted longer and more scrupulously than their mainstream fellow Christians (*Jejun.* 1; *Mon.* 15). Tertullian also emphasizes that whereas Catholic Christianity recommended fasting more or less as a voluntary act of devotion, North African Montanists on their part held it to be obligatory, a sacred duty. For him, fasting is no longer a preparatory step towards a more holy experience but an end in itself. It serves as a Christian discipline that makes a spiritual person pleasing to God. According to Tertullian, fat Christian martyrs appeal to bears and lions, whereas God has a liking for slender Christians who also more easily pass through the narrow gate of salvation and rise to their heavenly abode (*Jejun.* 17).

A widely discussed question in Montanism research has lately been the attitude of the Montanists toward marriage. Especially prominent is the question whether Montanism at its early stage disallowed marriage altogether. Apollonius states that Montanus exhorted his listeners to dissolve their marriages and that Priscilla and Maximilla divorced their husbands after having been filled with the Holy Spirit (Eusebius, *Hist. eccl.* 5.18.2–3). Is this information part of anti-Montanist polemical exaggeration or does Apollonius preserve an authentic piece of historical data? The stand Tertullian adopts toward marriage at

---

[42] This is suggested by Apollonius (Eusebius, *Hist. eccl.* 5.18.2), Hippolytus (*Haer.* 8.19.2), and Tertullian (e.g., *Jejun.* 1).
[43] This is correctly emphasized by Trevett, *Montanism*, 105.
[44] Trevett, *Montanism*, 107.

least clearly diverges from the position Apollonius attributed to early Montanist prophets. In his work *De monogamia*, Tertullian states that only heretics, thus not Montanists, entirely rejected marriage, whereas the *psykhikoi*, i.e., Catholic Christians, approved a second marriage as well. The adherents of the New Prophecy, according to Tertullian, valued celibacy but also regarded marriage as sacred to the extent that a second marriage, either after divorce or the death of one's spouse, was not acceptable (*Mon.* 1; 14; 15; *Pud.* 1; *Marc.* 1.29).

Tertullian's view was nothing unique. Similar notions could be found among Catholic Christians as well (e.g., Epiphanius, *Pan.* 48.9.1). Therefore, it is not certain that his views reflect those of the early Montanists. He himself might have introduced these views into Montanism. Apollonius' notion therefore may well mirror the ascetic rigor of the early Montanist prophets. Montanus could have insisted that the early prophets practiced continence in order that they might completely, without any worries, dedicate their lives to their prophetic task. A Montanist oracle preserved by Tertullian in his work *De fuga in persecutione* suggests this. In it women adherents of the Montanist movement are exhorted to pick up the gauntlet of martyrdom instead of focusing on family life. They are told: "Seek not to die on bridal beds, nor in miscarriages, nor in soft fevers, but to die the martyr's death, that He may be glorified who has suffered for you" (*Fug.* 9).[45] Another item in Apollonius' description of the early Montanists' attitude to marriage, i.e., the reference to Priscilla's and Maximilla's renunciation of their marriages may find its explanation in the fact that both of them were married to non-believing men, nonsympathetic to their Christian conviction. Their marriages then ended in a separation—following the direction of Paul expressed in 1 Cor 7:15.

But if the early Montanists advocated abstinence from marriage, they were not the first Christians to opt for this kind of practice. As Christine Trevett has pointed out,[46] women of the second-century apocryphal Acts are portrayed as having abandoned family life. Without any disapproval, many second- and early third-century Christians are depicted as having satisfied their craving to live continent life. Some have tried to castrate themselves (e.g., an anonymous

---

[45] Translation by S. Thelwall in *Ante-Nicene Fathers*, 4:121.
[46] Trevett, *Montanism*, 110.

Christian mentioned in Justin, *1 Apol.* 29) while others have done it
(Melito, bishop of Sardis, referred to in Eusebius, *Hist. eccl.* 5.24.5;
a Roman presbyter Hyacinthus mentioned in Hippolytus, *Haer.*
9.12.10). Additionally, Marcion as well as Tatian the Assyrian espoused
denunciation of marriage (Irenaeus, *Haer.* 1.28.1).[47]

Thus, it was actually not the encratite stance as such that made
mainstream Christians critical of the Montanist view of sexual morality. Rather, it was the strict espousal of continence coupled with a
severe refusal to forgive those who had failed and needed repentance that increased the disfavor of Montanism among Catholic
Christians. Before his conversion to Montanism even Tertullian had
allowed for one post-baptismal repentance in the case of fornication
(*Paen.* 8).[48] After having become an adherent of the New Prophecy
he assumed a more rigid position: he could no longer accept fornication and a second marriage (*Pud.* 1).

The change in Tertullian's attitude can be accounted for based
on the fact that he joined Montanism in its general negative stance
toward the possibility of a second repentance. Tertullian himself has
preserved a Montanist oracle in which the Paraclete or a prophet
states: "The church has the power to forgive sins; but I will not do
it, lest they commit others withal" (*Pud.* 21).[49] That this text refers
to the question of a second repentance is obvious since it is unlikely
that the oracle wants to deny every act of forgiveness, including the
first one. Even though the denial of a second repentance—especially
in matters, such as various sexual sins, a second marriage, apostasy—was not only confined to the Montanists,[50] it certainly very
much affected the way the Catholic Christians viewed the movement. The harsher the Montanists judged relapsed sinners the more
difficult it was for them to find sympathy within the Christian Church.

---

[47] For Marcion, see Räisänen in this volume; for Tatian the Assyrian, see Petersen
in this volume.

[48] *Pace* Anne Jensen (*God's Self-Confident Daughters*, 149–50), who maintains that the
early Montanists allowed a second repentance but Tertullian introduced a new rigorous practice into Montanism. Nevertheless, her theory does not account for the
clear shift in Tertullian's thinking.

[49] Translation by S. Thelwall in *Ante-Nicene Fathers*, 4:99.

[50] Eusebius refers to a letter written by Dionysius of Corinth to Bishop Palmas,
in which the Corinthian bishop exhorts his colleague to receive to the church some
repentant Christians who had fallen into various sins and who had evidently been
excommunicated (*Hist. eccl.* 4.23.6).

8. *The Expectation of the Imminent End and the New Jerusalem*

It used to be commonplace to assume that the fervent expectation of the imminent and concrete end was one of the most central features of Montanist thought, at least at its earliest stage. Usually scholars linked this with a chiliastic emphasis, according to which the early Montanist prophets waited to see the beginning of a millenarian kingdom in the form of a heavenly Jerusalem descending in Pepuza.[51] Recently, however, new and more sophisticated suggestions have been put forward. Anne Jensen, for example, has argued that Montanism at its early stage was not an apocalyptic movement at all and its representatives did not expect an imminent end, but regarded Pepuza as Jerusalem since it was the place where Jesus appeared to Priscilla in female form.[52] Other scholars maintain that there were allusions to the expectation of the imminent end in Montanist thinking but the apocalyptic and chiliastic features and the role of Jerusalem in the eschatology of the movement changed, developed and gained new nuances in various times and places.[53]

When Montanist eschatology is explored, the first thing that draws attention is the small number of references one finds concerning the expectation of the imminent end and the role of the descending Jerusalem in the earliest sources. Only one of the preserved Montanist oracles seems to speak about the expectation of the end. Epiphanius has recorded the following words from Maximilla: "After me there will no longer be a prophetess but the end (*synteleia*)" (*Pan.* 48.2.4). If the *synteleia* in this sentence means the end of the world, as it frequently does in apocalyptic texts[54] and without exception in the New

---

[51] So, e.g., Aland, "Bemerkungen zum Montanismus," 120–22; Karl Baus, *Von der Urgemeinde zur frühchristlichen Großkirche* (vol. 1 of *Handbuch der Kirchengeschichte*; ed. Hubert Jedin; Freiburg: Herder, 1962), 232; Frederick C. Klawiter, "The Role of Martyrdom and Persecution in Developing the Priestly Authority of Women in Early Christianity: A Case Study of Montanism," *CH* 49 (1980): 253. For more recent studies advocating this view, see Ronald E. Heine, "Montanus, Montanism," *ABD* 4:899–900; Bart Ehrman, *Lost Christianities: The Battles for Scripture and the Faiths We Never Knew* (Oxford: Oxford University Press, 2003), 150.

[52] Jensen, *God's Self-Confident Daughters*, 151–52, 157–58, 160–67.

[53] Cf. e.g., Trevett, *Montanism*, 95–105; Christine Trevett, "Eschatological Timetabling and the Montanist Movement," *Studia Patristica* 31 (ed. E. A. Livingstone; Leuven: Peeters, 1997), 218–24.

[54] See note 56.

Testament (Matt 13:39, 40, 49; 24:3; 28:20; Heb 9:26),[55] then Maximilla's oracle undeniably contains an idea of the imminent expectation of the end.[56] Another interesting text in this regard is the statement of the anonymous presbyter in Eusebius, according to which Maximilla predicted wars and confusion (*Hist. eccl.* 5.16.18). Unless the prediction is simply to be taken to anticipate generally bad times, as the presbyter certainly took it, it could be seen as an expression of the expectation of the end that is accompanied by unpleasant cosmic portents following the style of Mark 13. If both of these texts, the first more certainly than the second, can be taken as indications of the expectation of an imminent end among early Montanists, it must still be noted, however, that neither is linked with a chiliastic view or an idea of the descending heavenly Jerusalem.

The text that has played the leading role in reconstructions of chiliastic Montanist eschatology is an oracle preserved by Epiphanius in *Panarion* 49.3. It describes a dream of Priscilla or Quintilla in Pepuza—Epiphanius himself does not seem to know which of the ladies had the dream and spoke the oracle. At any rate the oracle states: "Christ came to me dressed in a white robe, in the form of a woman, imbued me with wisdom, and revealed to me that this place is holy, and that Jerusalem will descend from heaven here."[57] To be precise, not even this oracle explicitly speaks of a millenarian kingdom. The reference to Jerusalem may also reflect the prediction of chapter 21 in the Book of Revelation, according to which

---

[55] The word is used in the same way also in the Shepherd of Hermas (*Vis.* 3.8.9; *Sim.* 9.12.3).

[56] Jensen (*God's Self-Confident Daughters*, 157–58) claims that only a later interpretation has brought an eschatological connotation into the oracle, thus trying to make Maximilla look ridiculous. Originally the oracle was not meant to say anything more than to predict the end of prophecy in the Montanist movement. Jensen's thesis is not convincing. In addition to the fact that in Christian terminology *synteleia* is often used as an apocalyptic technical term to denote the end of the ages, the same is also true in the Septuagint version of the Book of Daniel and in the *Testaments of the Twelve Patriarchs* (see Erich Grässer, *An die Hebräer: Zweiter Teilband [Hebr 7,1–10,18]* [EKK 17/2; Zürich: Benziger; Neukirchen-Vluyn: Neukirchener Verlag, 1993], 196). Therefore, an assumption of a later eschatological interpretation is clearly a circular argument, motivated by Jensen's desire to prove that an early Montanist oracle *cannot* contain a reference to the expectation of an imminent end.

[57] The translation is derived from Williams, *The Panarion of Epiphanius of Salamis*, 21.

the eternal divine kingdom is expected to descend upon earth in the form of the heavenly Jerusalem.

There is another problem involved in the text. If the person who had the dream was not Priscilla but Quintilla, then the text does not stem from the earliest phase of Montanism but probably dates from a much later period. This is in harmony with the fact that, in another context, when Epiphanius speaks of Pepuza as the place where the heavenly Jerusalem is expected to descend, he seems to presuppose that this is a late idea. He knew Pepuza to be a deserted place. Because of the important role it had served at the beginning of the Montanist movement, it had nevertheless become a site of pilgrimage for Montanists, a place where the eschatological consummation was expected to take place in future (*Pan.* 48.14.1–2).[58] An argument for a late dating of Quintilla's dream and oracle is also the fact that Tertullian, who was aware of a Montanist expectation of the millenarian kingdom, does not say anything about Pepuza as its possible site (*Marc.* 3.24). It is therefore most likely that the idea of Pepuza as the location of the millenarian kingdom or the new Jerusalem only developed after Tertullian.[59] This assumption is confirmed by the information imparted by Apollonius. According to him Montanus himself spoke about Pepuza (and Tymion) as Jerusalem where he invited his adherents to gather together. Still, he does not think that the new Jerusalem was a place for a millenarian kingdom descending from heaven but rather a metaphor for a Montanist center (Eusebius, *Hist. eccl.* 5.18.2).

In light of the extant evidence, we can say that the earliest phase of Montanism included the expectation of an imminent end, which was possibly intensified by general unrest in the eastern part of the Empire. The relatively peaceful reign of Antoninus Pius had ended in 161, and Marcus Aurelius had ascended the throne. Disorders plagued many Roman borders. Parthian troops attacked Romans threatening the provinces in Syria and Asia Minor. Wars had exhausted the resources of the state and caused financial straits in many places. There was also political intrigue, as the Emperor had to

---

[58] It is also possible, as Tabbernee (*Montanist Inscriptions and Testimonia*, 32) has suggested, that the bones of the earliest Montanist prophets were kept and venerated in a Montanist shrine in Pepuza.

[59] This is rightly emphasized by Trevett, *Montanism*, 98.

defend himself against Syrian pretenders. Alongside wars, a plague had spread into wide areas and reaped a grim harvest. During the time of Commodus (180–192), successor to Marcus Aurelius, the situation became even worse. In the face of these events, it is no wonder that the Montanists in Asia Minor also joined the proclaimers of the imminent end and elicited a response among the people.[60]

Although there is no direct evidence for it, it cannot be ruled out that some early Montanist teachers included chiliastic emphases in their proclamation. This is suggested by the fact that the Montanists were well aware of the chiliastic speculations since they knew and employed the Apocalypse of John[61] and possibly also the *Fourth Book of Ezra*.[62] In the anti-Montanist criticism of Gaius there are also clear traces of anti-chiliastic tendencies, which suggest that his Montanist antagonists may have favored chiliastic eschatology (Eusebius, *Hist. eccl.* 3.28.2).

The linkage of Pepuza to the heavenly Jerusalem—either as a manifestation of the millenarian kingdom or the eternal, divine city according to the style of Rev 21—probably took place only after the early phase of Montanism or even after Tertullian. Montanus' idea of Pepuza as Jerusalem could no longer be concretely materialized in a small Phrygian town. Thus, its realization had to be elevated to another level and it became connected to an expectation of a divine transcendent interference. Belief in Pepuza as the place where the heavenly Jerusalem was expected to descend did not reach all Montanists, however, or all did not at least accept it. This is shown by the fact that many later anti-Montanist writers, such as Filastrius, Jerome, Augustine, and Praedestinatus, seemed to know nothing of this tradition. For them, Pepuza was simply known as the birthplace of the earliest Montanist prophets.

---

[60] Montanists were not the only Christians at the end of the second century among whom the expectation of the imminent end played a visible role. Hippolytus knows of two church leaders with similar views. One in Syria led his church to the desert to meet the returning Christ, and the other in Pontus predicted the coming of the day of the judgment and caused many of his Christian brothers to leave their lands and homes (*Comm. Dan.* 4.18–19).

[61] On this, see Antti Marjanen, "Montanism and the Formation of the New Testament Canon," in *The Formation of Early Christianity* (ed. Jostein Ådna; WUNT; Tübingen: Mohr Siebeck, forthcoming).

[62] This is argued by Trevett, *Montanism*, 25.

9. *Influential Women*

Montanism is one of those few second-century Christian movements in which women occupied a visible role.[63] It is clear that, together with Montanus, the movement can thank the two women prophets, Priscilla and Maximilla, for its existence. Although Montanus was the initiator and the first leader of the movement (Eusebius, *Hist. eccl.* 5.16.7; 5.18.2), the role women adopted in the movement seems no less influential. Their prominent role is underlined by the fact that when some mainstream Church leaders tried to meet the challenge of Montanism it was precisely the women prophets they encountered. The prophetic proclamation of both Priscilla and Maximilla often led to attempts by Catholic bishops or other ecclesiastical leaders to exorcize the spirit they believed to be effective in the women (*Hist. eccl.* 5.16.16; 5.18.13; 5.19.3). In every instance recorded by Eusebius or by his source the attempt ended without success since supporters of the women stopped the exorcists. That approximately half of the Montanist oracles preserved for posterity are attributed to the women prophets also demonstrates their crucial position in the New Prophecy.

The egalitarian character of the Montanist communities is further confirmed by the fact that Epiphanius states that among some Montanist groups women were ordained as clergy (*Pan.* 49.2.2), and women acted as bishops and presbyters (*Pan.* 49.2.5). According to the Montanists cited by Epiphanius, the practice finds its reason in a New Testament text: "In Christ there is neither male nor female" (cf. Gal 3:28). Another example of active Montanist women is provided by Firmilian, who, in his letter to Cyprian, tells about a Montanist prophetess who—to his great horror—baptized and administered the Eucharist (Cyprian, *Ep.* 75.10). The evidence for influential women church leaders among Montanists does not only depend on the remarks by the anti-Montanist writers. There are also inscriptions which speak of Montanist women presbyters and prophets.[64]

---

[63] On the role of women among Montanists, see Klawiter, "The Role of Martyrdom," 251–61; Trevett, *Montanism*, 151–97; Jensen, *God's Self-Confident Daughters*, 133–88.

[64] For the evidence, see Tabbernee, *Montanist Inscriptions and Testimonia*, 66–72, 80–82, 419–25, 518–25.

It is difficult to give any exhaustive answer as to why it was exactly in the Montanist movement that women had more open access to leadership roles than their fellow-sisters among mainstream Christians did. A partial explanation can be reasoned as follows: prophecy had a prominent position among Montanists, but prophecy was, at least in principle, a legitimate function for women according to traditional Jewish and Christian understandings as well.[65] Thus, a basic positive attitude toward women in Montanism could develop, which would then extend to all areas of ecclesiastical life and provide women with new possibilities to exercise influence. At any rate it is clear that the visible role women were allowed to have in Montanist communities contributed to the disfavor Catholic Christians began to show toward Montanism. This is well demonstrated by the criticisms of Firmilian and Epiphanius in the texts presented above.

10. *Ecclesiastical Organization of the Montanist Movement*

There is no firsthand information about the Montanist churches and their organization, and the anti-Montanist writers do not do very much to remedy this dearth. One interesting feature of the Montanist ecclesiastical life is nevertheless revealed by Apollonius in his description of the way the Montanist churches were operated. Apollonius states that Montanus paid a salary to those who proclaimed the word in the churches of the Montanist movement (Eusebius, *Hist. eccl.* 5.18.2; 5.18.7). According to Apollonius, the money for this purpose was collected as offerings by specially appointed tax gatherers from the supporters of the movement.

Apollonius is clearly indignant with the procedure adopted by the Montanists. It deviated from the practice which prevailed in main-

---

[65] As a matter of fact, it seems likely that the critical attitude of mainstream Christian theologians toward the visible role of women prophets develops as a protest against Montanism. Origen adduces a good example. In connection with his interpretation of 1 Cor 14:36 (*Fr. 1 Cor.* 14.36; for the text, see Labriolle, *Sources de l'histoire du Montanisme*, 55–56), he admits that there are references to women prophets both in the Old Testament and in the apostolic writings of the New Testament. Still, he claims, these women did not exercise their prophetic function in the public meetings of the church (the daughters of Philip) or they were only leaders of women (Miriam, the sister of Aron) or they did not address the whole nation in the way their male colleagues did but uttered their prophetic words privately (Debora and Huldah).

stream churches especially in Asia Minor. In those churches the leader of the congregation was often the one, in whose house the Christian group gathered and who was thus also responsible for the financial dimension of the activities. This meant that the spiritual and financial leadership were often linked and a person had to be wealthy in order to gain influential position in a Christian church. Failing this, he at least had to have a well-to-do patron who supported the activities he led. As Alistair Stewart-Sykes has pointed out, many bishops and church leaders in second-century Asia Minor were householders or individuals of relatively high social standing.[66]

The course of action Montanus chose may be due to the fact that during its earliest phase the Montanist leaders came from the poor countryside and did not have the resources to be financially responsible for the activities of their churches. In order to secure the best possible spiritual leaders for the churches Montanus reversed the traditional scheme. Instead of having church leaders who provided for their churches, he organized collections of offerings made by the adherents of the Montanist movement in order to provide financial support to those church leaders and visiting missionaries who could not do their work without a salary. This also meant a shift in church politics. In this way Montanist spiritual leaders and teachers as well as churches became independent of the outside (mainstream?) control and could thus ignore attempts to set boundaries on their prophetic activity.

Stewart-Sykes has argued that the new operations model created by Montanus was an aggravating challenge to large mainstream city churches which were led by wealthy individuals. It may even have been one of the main reasons why the Montanists incurred disfavor of Catholic Christianity.[67] That the question of a salary paid to a bishop, missionary or another spiritual leader was a matter of consequence is shown by the fact that it is not only the Montanists who were criticized because of this model. The adherents of Artemon, an approximate contemporary of Montanus, were also regarded as heretics since they, in addition to holding a false Christology, hired a bishop and paid him 150 denaries a month (Eusebius, *Hist. eccl.* 5.28.10).

---

[66] Stewart-Sykes, "The Original Condemnation of Asian Montanism," 18–20.
[67] Stewart-Sykes, "The Original Condemnation of Asian Montanism."

11. *Concluding Remarks*

Montanism did not deviate from mainstream Christinity in the central elements of Christian doctrine. Still, it was condemned as a heresy. It has been previously argued that the main reason for this was its chiliastic eschatology. Yet this was hardly the decisive reason for the repudiation of Montanism. Chiliasm was criticized but it was never completely rejected in the Christian church.[68] Therefore, albeit after hard resistance, even the Apocalypse of John, the primary source of early Christian chiliasm, was accepted into the New Testament canon.

The most significant reasons for denouncing Montanism as heretical were: the ecstatic nature of its prophecy, the claim of the Montanist prophecy for greater authority than that of the previous apostolic traditions, the visible role women had in the movement, and the salaries the Montanists paid to their spiritual leaders and teachers in Asia Minor, thus shaking the prevailing church-political power structures. An additional factor in anti-Montanist criticism was its rapid spread. Approximately twenty years after it originated in distant Phrygian villages, Montanism had reached Rome and Gaul, and somewhat later Cartahage in North Africa.

After the counterblow by mainstream Christians, aided by persecutions by Roman authorities, the spread of the Montanist movement was stopped in the course of the third century. In the following centuries Montanism began to die and received its final deathblow from the bishop of Ephesus in the sixth century. In the process the formative Catholic church increasingly distanced itself from Christian current that allowed women an active role in shaping Christian traditions and life. At the same time some leading Christians also set limits on forms of spirituality which it considered to be giving too much room for reevaluating old traditions and practices. Catholic Christians did not want challenge. Could direct revelation from God ever take precedence over the apostolic tradition and the written Scriptures as taught by the church? The answer from the church in power was no.

---

[68] Early supporters of chiliasm among early theologians were, e.g., Papias, Cerinthus, Justin Martyr, Irenaeus, Lactantius, and Commodianus.

Bibliography

Aland, Kurt. "Bemerkungen zum Montanismus und zur frühchristlichen Eschatologie." Pages 105–48 in *Kirchengeschichtliche Entwürfe: Alte Kirche, Reformation und Luthertum, Pietismus und Erweckungsbewegung*. Gütersloh: Gerd Mohn, 1960.

Ante-Nicene Fathers. Edited by Alexander Roberts and James Donaldson. 10 vols. 1885–1887. Repr., Peabody, Mass.: Hendrickson, 1994.

Bauer, Walter. *Rechtgläubigkeit und Ketzerei im ältesten Christentum*. 2nd revised edition by Georg Strecker. Tübingen: J. C. B. Mohr (Paul Siebeck), 1964.

Baus, Karl. *Von der Urgemeinde zur frühchristlichen Großkirche*. Vol. 1 of *Handbuch der Kirchengeschichte*. Edited by Hubert Jedin. Freiburg: Herder, 1962.

Bonwetsch, Nathanael. *Texte zur Geschichte des Montanismus*. Kleine Texte für Vorlesungen und Übungen 129. Bonn: A. Marcus und E. Weber, 1914.

Burkhardt, Walter. "Primitive Montanism: Why Condemned?" Pages 339–56 in *From Faith to Faith: Essays in Honor of Donald G. Miller*. Edited by Dikran Hadidian. Pittsburgh: Pickwick Publications, 1979.

Ehrman, Bart. *Lost Christianities: The Battles for Scripture and the Faiths We Never Knew*. Oxford: Oxford University Press, 2003.

Frend, W. H. C. *The Rise of Christianity*. Philadelphia: Fortress, 1984.

Grässer, Erich. *An die Hebräer: Zweiter Teilband (Hebr 7,1–10,18)*. Evangelisch-katholischer Kommentar 17/2. Zürich: Benziger; Neukirchen-Vluyn: Neukirchener Verlag, 1993.

Heine, Ronald E. *The Montanist Oracles and Testimonia*. Macon, Ga.: Mercer University Press, 1989.

——. "Montanus, Montanism." Pages 898–902 in vol. 4 of *The Anchor Bible Dictionary*. Edited by David Noel Freedman. 6 vols. New York: Doubleday, 1992.

——. "The Role of the Gospel of John in the Montanist Controversy." *The Second Century* 6 (1987/88): 1–19.

Jensen, Anne. *God's Self-Confident Daughters: Early Christianity and the Liberation of Women*. Translated by O. C. Dean, Jr. Louisville, Ky.: Westminster John Knox, 1996.

Klawiter, Frederick C. "The Role of Martyrdom and Persecution in Developing the Priestly Authority of Women in Early Christianity: A Case Study of Montanism," *Church History* 49 (1980): 251–61.

Kraft, Heinz. "Die altkirchliche Prophetie und die Entstehung des Montanismus." *Theologische Zeitschrift* 11 (1955): 249–71.

Labriolle, Pierre de. *Les sources de l'histoire du Montanisme: Textes Grecs, Latins, Syriaques*. Collecteanea Friburgensia 24. Fribourg: Librairie de l'université; Paris: Ernest Leroux, 1913.

Lampe, Peter. *From Paul to Valentinus: Christians at Rome in The First Two Centuries*. Translated by Michael Steinhauser. Minneapolis: Fortress, 2003.

Marjanen, Antti. "Montanism and the Formation of the New Testament Canon." In *The Formation of Early Christianity*. Edited by Jostein Ådna. WUNT. Tübingen: Mohr Siebeck, forthcoming.

McGinn, Sheila E. "The 'Montanist' Oracles and Prophetic Theology." Pages 128–135 in *Studia Patristica* 31. Edited by E. A. Livingstone. Leuven: Peeters, 1997.

Stewart-Sykes, Alistair. "The Original Condemnation of Asian Montanism." *Journal of Ecclesiastical History* 50 (1999): 1–22.

Strobel, August. *Das heilige Land des Montanisten: Eine religionsgeographische Untersuchung*. Religionsgeschichtliche Versuche und Vorarbeiten 37. Berlin: Walter de Gruyter, 1980.

Tabbernee, William. "Early Montanism and Voluntary Martyrdom." *Colloquium* 17 (1985): 33–44.

——. *Montanist Inscriptions and Testimonia: Epigraphic Sources Illustrating the History of Montanism*. North American Patristic Society: Patristic Monograph Series 16; Macon, Ga.: Mercer University Press, 1997.

——. "Portals of the Montanist New Jerusalem: The Discovery of Pepouza and Tymion." *Journal of Early Christian Studies* 11 (2003): 87–93.

——. "Remnants of the New Prophecy: Literary and Epigraphical Sources of the Montanist Movement." Pages 193–201 in *Studia Patristica* 21. Edited by E. A. Livingstone. Leuven: Peeters, 1989.

Trevett, Christine. "Eschatological Timetabling and the Montanist Movement." Pages 218–24 in *Studia Patristica* 31. Edited by E. A. Livingstone. Leuven: Peeters, 1997.

——. *Montanism: Gender, Authority and the New Prophecy*. Cambridge: Cambridge University Press, 1996.

Williams, Frank. *The Panarion of Epiphanius of Salamis: Books II & III (Sects 47–80, De Fide)*. Nag Hammadi and Manichaen Studies 36. Leiden: E. J. Brill, 1994.

Wright, D. F. "Why Were the Montanists Condemned?" *Themelios* 2 (1976): 15–22.

CERINTHUS

Matti Myllykoski

As many other so-called heretics,[1] Cerinthus is known to us only through the writings of those mainstream Christian teachers who had nothing good to say about him. Furthermore, none of these critics were contemporary with this disputed figure of early second-century Christianity in Asia Minor. In the hindsight of later centuries, Simon Magus and Nicolaus were considered the earliest enemies of orthodox Christianity since they were known by name from writings that were claimed to be apostolic (Acts 8:5–25; Acts 6:5; Rev 2:6, 14, 20–24). After them, together with Simon's disciple Menander, Cerinthus is the earliest heretic mentioned in sources outside the New Testament. Only a few decades after his death he was imagined to belong to the earliest period of the church. In the opening lines of the *Epistula Apostolorum*, which was written in the middle of the second century, Simon Magus and Cerinthus are mentioned as the main opponents of the apostles.[2] However, in *Ep. Apos.* there are no explicit references to the disputed teachings of Cerinthus.[3] We

---

[1] Here and elsewhere, I have left out the quotation marks that this term would deserve.

[2] Charles E. Hill has strengthened the case for locating the *Epistula Apostolorum* in Asia Minor (Hill, "The Epistula Apostolorum: An Asian Tract from the Time of Polycarp," *JECS* 7 (1993): 1–53). The reference to Cerinthus together with the arch-heretic Simon Magus is just one of arguments that favor such an assumption. The author of the *Epistula* relies strongly on the Gospel of John, bears witness to the Quartodeciman Easter (*Ep. Apos.* 15) and shows notable affinities with other contemporary Christian texts from Asia Minor. Furthermore, Hill demonstrates that the discourse that tells about earthquakes and plagues (*Ep. Apos.* 34–37) is much easier to locate in this geographical context than in Egypt or Syria. On the basis of references to these natural disasters, Hill assumes that *Ep. Apos.* was written "in the wake of one or more earthquakes of the 140's, any of which could have been attended by drought and followed by an outbreak of disease" (p. 49).

[3] There are some possible implicit references to Christological heresies that might include the Cerinthian type, notably the emphasis on the incarnation (*Ep. Apos.* 14), the idea that it was Lord Jesus Christ who was crucified in the days of Pontius Pilate (ch. 9; cf. ch. 8), and on the identity of the risen Jesus with the Savior (ch. 10). However, there is no indication of criticism against a separation between the highest God and the Creator God. The teaching on the resurrection of the flesh

can therefore assume that the storm around his heresy already belonged to a relatively distant past.

In our earliest sources, there are two different images of Cerinthus. In the west, Irenaeus, Hippoytus and Pseudo-Tertullian portrayed him as a heterodox teacher that proclaimed "knowledge falsely so called." The key passage of Irenaeus runs as follows (*Haer.* 1.26.1):

> A certain Cerinthus, then in Asia taught that the world was not made by the Supreme God, but by a certain Power highly separated and far removed from that Principality who transcended the universe, and which is ignorant of the one who is above all, God. He suggested that Jesus was not born of a virgin (because that seemed to him impossible), but that he was the son of Joseph and Mary, in the same way as all other men but he was more versed in righteousness, prudence and wisdom than other men. And after his baptism, Christ descended upon him from that Principality that is above all in the form of a dove. And then he proclaimed the unknown Father and performed miracles. But at last Christ flew again from Jesus; Jesus suffered and rose again while Christ remained impassible, being a spiritual being.[4]

In the east, Eusebius of Caesarea also placed Cerinthus in the apostolic times. He drew upon two earlier texts of the Roman Gaius and the Alexandrian bishop Dionysius, who vehemently opposed chiliastic expectations of Montanists and others in the first half of the third century. They both mocked Cerinthus as a man who cherished earthy chiliastic expectations. The passage of Gaius runs as follows (*Hist. eccl.* 3.28.2):

> But Cerinthus also, by means of revelations, said to be written by a great apostle, brings before us miraculous things in a deceitful way, saying that they were revealed to him by angels. And he says that after the resurrection the kingdom of Christ will be set up on earth, and that in Jerusalem the body will again serve as the instrument of desires and pleasures. And since he is an enemy of the divine Scriptures and sets out to deceive, he says that there will be a marriage feast lasting a thousand years.[5]

To begin with, this passage demonstrates that some Roman Christians at the beginning of the third century knew Cerinthus as a chiliast

---

with the soul, the healing of the flesh, and the eternal rest of the true believers (ch. 25–26) may be read as criticism directed against chiliasm. For a survey, see also Cristoph Markschies, "Kerinth: Wer war er und was lehrte er?" *JAC* (1998), 68–69.

[4] Translation by Klijn and Reinink, *Patristic Evidence for Jewish-Christian Sects.* (NovTSup 36; Leiden: E. J. Brill, 1973), 103, 105.

[5] Translation by Klijn and Reinink, *Patristic Evidence*, 141.

and not—at least not so much—as a spokesman for gnosis, as Hippolytus and others knew him. The testimony of Dionysius from Alexandria
is similar, but includes striking differences from the text of Gaius
(*Hist. eccl.* 3.28.4–5, identical with 7.25.3):

> For the doctrine which he taught was this: that the kingdom of Christ
> will be an earthly one. And as he dreamed that it would consist in
> these things he himself was devoted to, because he was a lover of the
> body and altogether carnal, namely delights of the belly and of the
> sexual passion, that is to say, in eating and drinking and marrying,
> and—because of this he thought he could provide himself with better
> reputation—in festivals and sacrifices and the slaying of victims.[6]

Thus in the late second and early third century, Cerinthus was
labelled as the progenitor of two quite different heresies—a gnostic
teacher and a hedonistically-oriented chiliast. In the following survey,
I shall first examine the later development of the tradition (1. section)
and the history of critical scholarship (2. section), in order to return
to the quest for the historical Cerinthus. I will look for the origins
of the Irenaean tradition and present some related christological texts
(3. section). After that I turn to the millenarian traditions of Eusebius
(4. section) and close with reflections on Cerinthus and Jewish Christianity (5. section).

1. *"Judaistic-Millennarian-Gnostic": Late Images of Cerinthus*

1.1. *Pseudo-Tertullian*

In the first half of the third century, the Pseudo-Tertullian heresiology portrayed Cerinthus in the vein of the Irenaean tradition. Its
author's main idea was to rework the information provided by Irenaeus
and present it in an abbreviated form. Since he already reported
that, according to Carpocrates, Christ suffered among the Jews and
that his soul was received in heaven, he left the teaching of the
descending and ascending Christ out of his passage on Cerinthus,
but added some new pieces of information (*Adv. omn. haer.* 3.2):

> After him [Carpocrates] broke out the heretic Cerinthus, teaching sim-
> ilarly. For he, too, says that the world was originated by those angels;

---

[6] Translation by Klijn and Reinink, *Patristic Evidence*, 143.

and sets forth Christ as born of the seed of Joseph, contending that
He was merely human, without divinity; affirming also that the Law
was given by angels; representing the God of the Jews as not the Lord,
but an angel.

There are two viable options for tracing the source of this passage,
and they do not necessarily exclude each other. Our first option is
Irenaeus' work. Excluding the humanity of Jesus, the image of
Cerinthus in this short passage deviates from that drawn by Irenaeus,
but all the other items stem from Irenaeus' presentation of Simon,
Menander, Saturninus, Basilides and Carpocrates. Pseudo-Tertullian
followed Irenaeus' order of presentation and modelled the image of
Cerinthus after these heretics that allegedly came before him. Irenaeus
portrayed Simon Magus as the arch-heretic who spread gnostic beliefs
among those who became known as teachers of gnosis in the second century. According to Irenaeus, Simon already taught basic gnostic doctrines. He was the first to claim that the world was set up
and the laws were given by the angels (*Haer.* 1.23.3) and he was followed by Menander (1.23.5). Saturninus added the idea that the
Jewish God was one of the angels, implying that the Law was given
by this particular angel (1.24.2). For Basilides, the Jewish God was
the leader of the angels and the giver of the Law (1.24.4, 5). If the
first option is correct, Pseudo-Tertullian brought Cerinthus closer to
other gnostics by adding these features to his short passage.

The second option is to assume that Pseudo-Tertullian used the
lost *Syntagma* of Hippolytus. We can safely assume that he knew from
Hippolytus' description that Cerinthus thought that the world was
created by an angelic power (Hippolytus, *Haer.* 10.21.1). It is possible that the other corresponding features in the passage of Pseudo-
Tertullian—that, according to Cerinthus, the Law was given by angels
and the God of the Jews was not the Lord, but an angel—stem
from Hippolytus' *Syntagma*'s passage on Cerinthus.

1.2. *Hippolytus*

It has indeed been assumed that Pseudo-Tertullian used the *Syntagma*
of Hippolytus as his source on Cerinthus.[7] The Hippolytean passage

---

[7] Gustave Bardy, "Cérinthe," *RB* 30 (1921): 353; Klaus Wengst, *Häresie und
Orthodoxie im Spiegel des ersten Johannesbriefes* (Gütersloh: Gerd Mohn, 1976), 29–30.

in question has been preserved in Syrian as a quotation by Dionysius bar-Salibi, who died in 1171:[8]

> Hippolytus the Roman says: A man named Gaius appeared, saying that the Gospel is not by John, nor the Apocalypse but that it is by Cerinthus the heretic. And against that Gaius the blessed Hippolytus stood up and showed that the doctrine of John in the Gospel and in the Apocalypse is one and that of Cerinthus is another. Cerinthus, then, taught circumcision and was enraged against Paul because he had not circumcised Titus and he called the apostle and his pupils in one of his letters false apostles and deceitful laborers. Further he taught that the world had been created by angels and that the Lord was not born of a virgin and about carnal food and drink and other blasphemies.

The latter part of this passage ("Cerinthus, then, taught circumcision . . .") consists of Jewish-Christian ideas, with the exception of attributing the creation of the world to the angels. If we assume that this passage stems from Hippolytus' *Syntagma*, we must also assume that Hippolytus erased all these Jewish features of Cerinthus from his account as he composed his *Refutatio omnium haeresium*. In this work he wanted to demonstrate the dependence of the heretics on the gentile philosophies, but it is hard to imagine that, in the case of Cerinthus, he simply replaced the previous Jewish-Christian features and confined himself to quoting Irenaeus alone (*Haer.* 7.33.1–2; 10.21.1–3). Furthermore, Pseudo-Tertullian, who used the work of Hippolytus, does not even hint at the Jewish-Christian elements mentioned in Dionysius' passage. The idea that the world was created by angels surely stems from Pseudo-Tertullian and Hippolytus who both developed the Irenaean idea that Cerinthus was a gnostic. Conclusion: the Jewish-Christian ideas attributed to Cerinthus in the quotation of Dionysius bar-Salibi probably do not stem from Hippolytus.

Dionysius' actual quotation from Hippolytus consists only of one sentence: "A man named Gaius appeared, saying that the Gospel is not by John, nor the Apocalypse but that it is by Cerinthus the heretic." After that Dionysios simply goes on to relate that Hippolytus refuted the thesis of Gaius. What follows about the doctrine of Cerinthus more probably stems from another source. These details are known from the following sources:[9]

---

[8] For text and translation, see Klijn and Reinink, *Patristic Evidence*, 272–73.

[9] Cf. the conclusion of Klijn and Reinink, *Patristic Evidence*, 18.

1) teaching of circumcision	Epiphanius
2) opposition to Paul	Epiphanius
3) world created by angels	Hippolytus, Pseudo-Tertullian
4) Lord was not born of a virgin	Irenaeus, Hippolytus, Pseudo-Tertullian
5) "carnal food and drink"	Eusebius

If we can rule out Hippolytus as the source of items 1 and 2, the earliest source for them is Epiphanius. From his discussion on the Alogi in *Panarion* 51, we know that he knew the defense of the Johannine literature by Hippolytus, and, as he mentions, he used both works of Hippolytus (*Pan.* 31.33.3). Epiphanius indeed portrays Cerinthus as a Jewish Christian, but in the light of the observations presented above, it is difficult to assume that the corresponding traits in his narrative stemmed from Hippolytus. He is himself more or less responsible for the Jewish-Christian image of Cerinthus.[10]

1.3. *Epiphanius*

As in the case of most deviant teachings in the early church, the voluminous heresiology of Epiphanius here also appears to be a melting pot of old tradition and a creative generator of new ideas. The bishop of Salamis dedicated a whole chapter (*Pan.* 28) to Cerinthus and Cerinthians and opened his presentation by drawing upon the passages of Pseudo-Tertullian and Irenaeus quoted above (*Pan.* 28.1.1–3 and 28.1.5–7). He obviously knew that ascribing the creation of the world and the scriptures to the angels is not in agreement with Judaism. However, he assumed that Cerinthus was an adherent of Judaism—even though "only partially" (28.1.3). He cleared the way for Cerinthus' Judaism by dividing his career in two and by locating his proclamation of the gnostic or un-Jewish doctrines in his later activities in Asia Minor (28.2.6). Guided by this idea, he directed his polemics against the obvious contradiction: it is stupid to claim that the giver of the Law is bad, but the Law itself is good (28.2.1–2).

What follows in *Pan.* 28.2 and 28.4 is description of Cerinthus' career before he moved to Asia Minor. Epiphanius identified him and his followers with the Jewish Christians who opposed the leading apostles and demanded the circumcision of gentiles:

---

[10] With Klijn and Reinink, *Patristic Evidence*, 6, 18.

against James the Just	*Pan.* 28.2.3	Acts 15:24;
		15:1
against Peter	*Pan.* 28.2.4–5	Acts 11:2–3
against Paul	*Pan.* 28.4.1–2	Acts 21:28

Some further details in the text of Epiphanius bring Cerinthus and Cerinthians close to the Ebionites. Obviously taking their rejection of the virgin birth of Jesus as his starting point, Epiphanius claimed that the Cerinthians used the Gospel of Matthew in the same way as they did, discarding the birth stories and founding their circumcision on Jesus' saying (Matt 10:25): "It is enough for the disciple to be like the teacher." Just like the Ebionites, they rejected Paul who did not believe in circumcision. Epiphanius derived all these details (*Pan.* 28.5.1–3) from his knowledge of traditions about the Ebionites (cf. especially 30.14.2; 30.26.1–2; 30.16.8–9). He further claimed that Cerinthus did not believe that Jesus is risen (28.6.1): "Christ suffered and was crucified, but has not yet risen again, but that he will rise, when the general resurrection of the dead takes place." Epiphanius did not notice that this was in contradiction with the Irenaean tradition he used (28.1.7: "Jesus suffered and rose again"). However, he certainly did not miss the opportunity to identify the Cerinthians as Paul's Corinthian opponents. It was their chaotic ideas that Paul had in mind as he wrote 1 Cor 15; they even baptized others for those who died young and unbaptized, so that these would not be punished by the creator of the world at the resurrection (28.6.4–5; cf. 1 Cor 15:29). Epiphanius assumed that Cerinthus had a prosperous school in Asia and Galatia (28.6.4) and that he maybe had a co-operator called Merinthus, or Cerinthus himself was called by that name as well (28.8.1–2).[11] Even though Epiphanius puts all kinds of Jewish-Christian teachings in the account of Cerinthus, he does not relate them and the chiliasm of Cerinthus at all, even though he was informed about the latter by Eusebius. The only reasonable starting point for his image of Cerinthus as a Jewish-Christian teacher seems to have been the statement of Irenaeus that the Ebionites taught about Jesus similarly to Carpocrates and

---

[11] Hill, "Cerinthus," 147, assumes that the story about Merinthus was related to the tradition that some baptized themselves for the dead and unbaptized (28.6.4) because Epiphanius says that both pieces of information have "come to us" from an unnamed source. However, Merinthus might as well be a misunderstanding just like Iexai, whom Epiphanius introduces as the brother of Elxai (*Pan.* 19.1.4).

Cerinthus (*Haer.* 1.26.2).[12] Epiphanius might also have been influenced by Pseudo-Tertullian's statement that Ebion was a successor of Cerinthus who seems to have agreed with him on almost everything, except that he did not attribute the creation and the giving of the Law to the angels.[13]

Epiphanius quite obviously followed earlier traditions as he located Cerinthus and Cerinthians in apostolic times.[14] He considered them contemporary with "Ebion" and the Ebionites (*Pan.* 31.2.1), and did not hesitate to tell about them such things that were previously told about Cerinthus and his followers; now the Ebionites also believed that Jesus was a mere man in whom Christ descended at the baptism in the form of a dove (30.14.3–4; 30.16.3), and it was Ebion whom John saw in the bath-house (30.24.1–7). Since Epiphanius thought that Ebion was a successor of Cerinthus (30.1.3), it is reasonable to assume that he was inclined to regard Cerinthus as an opponent of the apostles at an early stage, while Ebion was more likely to have opposed John who was active later.

The image, created by Epiphanius, of Cerinthus as a Judaistic gnostic was well received in later times. His account was already used in the 380's by Filastrius in Italy (*Diversarum haereseon liber* 36).[15] Augustine, in turn, combined the Judaistic Cerinthus of Epiphanius with the chiliast represented by Eusebius (*Haer.* 8). Throughout Late Antiquity, Cerinthus was known as a "Judaistic-Millennarian-Gnostic."[16] In

---

[12] With Hill, "Cerinthus," 146.

[13] Pseudo-Tertullian, *Adv. omn. haer.* 3 (translation of Klijn and Reinink, *Patristic Evidence*, 125): "His successor was Ebion, not in agreement with Cerinthus in every point, because he says that the world was made by God, not by angels, and because it is written, no disciple is above (his) master, nor a servant above (his) lord, he brings to the fore likewise the Law, of course for the purpose of excluding the gospel and vindicating Judaism." In the testimony of Pseudo-Tertullian, this reduces their similarities merely to the denial of Jesus' divinity, but for Epiphanius it seems to have meant more than that. In any case, Ebion as presented by him is a collector of heretical ideas (*Pan.* 30.1.1–3).

[14] Klijn and Reinink, *Patristic Evidence*, 10, assume that the warning against the "pseudo-apostles" Simon and Cerinhus in *Epistula Apostolorum* motivated Epiphanius to locate him among the opponents of the apostles in the New Testament. However, it is possible that the *Syntagma* of Hippolytus inspired him as well.

[15] Klijn and Reinink, *Patristic Evidence*, 14–15. Filastrius noted the Epiphanian contradiction between the adherence to circumcision and the doctrine of the creator-angel who gave the Law. He emphasized that Cerinthus thought that it was the God of the Jews who gave the Law to the children of Israel.

[16] I have borrowed this term from Klijn and Reinink, *Patristic Evidence*, 19.

the Middle Ages and later, Cerinthus was known as an antichrist—
particularly condemned by John the apostle—for denying the divinity and virgin birth of Christ. Cerinthus continued to be connected
with Johannine literature in critical scholarship, but his assumed chiliasm and Judaism seldom became a significant part of this discussion.

2. *Cerinthus in the History of Critical Scholarship*

Even though the critical scholarship of the 19th century was still
transmitting the traditional image of Cerinthus as a Judaistic gnostic, the modern discussion had some predecessors, too. The famous
historian Johannes Laurentius Mosheim doubted whether both the
chiliastic and gnostic image of Cerinthus can be maintained and
chose the latter as being more reliable.[17] In his extensive study on
the purpose of the Gospel and letters of John (*Ueber den Zweck der
evangelischen Geschichte und der Briefe Johannis*, Tübingen 1786) Gottlob
Christian Storr dated the polemics of the Alogi against Revelation
and the Gospel of John in times after Irenaeus in order to demonstrate that Cerinthus, whom they claimed to be the author of these
books, was no chiliast at all.[18] He further argued that the assumed
Judaism of Cerinthus originated in later sources and that Irenaeus
is our only reliable source on his original teaching.[19] According to
Storr, Cerinthus was an early gnostic who was vehemently opposed
by the apostle John. He read both the letters and the Gospel as
original works of the apostles written in Ephesus and directed against
two groups: the Jewish adherents of John the Baptist and the gentile gnostic Cerinthians.[20]

As far as I can see, Storr's analysis did not influence the 19th
century scholarship which mostly went on repeating the traditional
composite view on the teaching of Cerinthus. Ferdinand Christian
Baur thought that "the first known gnostic was the Jewish-Christian

---

[17] Johannes Laurentius Mosheim, *De rebus Christianorum ante Constantinum Magnum
commentarii* (Helmstedt: Friedrich Weygand, 1753), 197.

[18] Gottlob Christian Storr, *Ueber den Zweck der evangelischen Geschichte und der Briefe
Johannis* (Tübingen: J. F. Heerbrandt, 1786), 124–49.

[19] Storr, *Zweck*, 149–168.

[20] Storr, *Zweck*, 168–234. On the originality of the documents and the two groups
of opponents, see pp. 220–32. For the disciples of the Baptist see also pp. 1–27
and for Cerinthus pp. 43–54.

Cerinthus,"[21] and his disciple Adolf Hilgenfeld held Cerinthus to be "the first one with whom we find gnosis and Judaism bound together."[22] According to Adolf Harnack, Cerinthus maintained the idea that "the universal religion revealed by Christ was identical with undefiled Mosaism."[23] This view is still current in some presentations.[24]

The tide turned as the presentation of Epiphanius was discarded for the alternatives offered by Irenaeus and the traditions preserved by Eusebius. In an article published in 1904, Adolf Wurm asked whether Cerinthus was a gnostic or a Judaist and chose the latter option.[25] In 1914, Eduard Schwartz also argued for the latter alternative and claimed the image of Cerinthus as a gnostic docetist to be a creation of Irenaeus. According to Schwartz, Irenaeus himself created the image of John the Evangelist as a contemporary of Cerinthus, warning true Christians about this dangerous heretic.[26] In a more extensive article, Gustave Bardy further argued for the Jewish-Christian background of Cerinthus and against the gnostic one.[27] This trend continued in the works of Jéan Daniélou[28] and Oskar

---

[21] Ferdinand Christian Baur, *Das Christentum und die christliche Kirche der drei ersten Jahrhunderte* (2nd ed.; Tübingen: Fues, 1860), 190.

[22] Adolf Hilgenfeld, *Ketzergeschichte des Urchristentums* (1884; repr., Darmstadt: Wissenschaftliche Buchgesellschaft, 1963), 418. He characterized Cerinthus as an example of the intrusion of gnostic ideas into chiliastically oriented Jewish Christianity (pp. 418–21). In France, the composite view on Cerinthus was transmitted by Ernest Renan, *Les Évangiles et la seconde génération chrétienne* (Paris: Calmann Lévy, 1877), ch. 18. In England, F. J. A. Hort, *Judaistic Christianity* (London: Macmillan, 1894), 191, regarded Cerinthus as a Judaizing Christian who at the same time was a gnostic in the conventional sense.

[23] Adolf Harnack, *History of Dogma* (trans. Neil Buchanan; 7 vols.; New York: Dover, 1961), 1:247. Harnack considered Cerinthus advocated syncretism that utilized cosmological ideas and myths; he was one of those who made "peculiar attempts to elevate the Old Testament religion into the universal one", and therefore this opponent of Paul insisted on "a definite measure of Jewish national ceremonies" (1:303–4).

[24] See, e. g. Koester, *Introduction to the New Testament* (2 vols.; Philadelphia: Fortress, 1982), 2:204: "[Cerinthus] advocated Gnostic teaching, but seems to have been a Jewish Christian who insisted upon circumcision."

[25] Alois Wurm, "Cerinth—ein Gnostiker oder Judaist?" *TQ 87* (1904): 20–38.

[26] Eduard Schwartz, "Johannes und Kerinthos," *ZNW 15* (1914): 210–19, esp. 214.

[27] Bardy, "Cérinthe," 344–73.

[28] Jéan Daniélou, *The Theology of Jewish Christianity* (trans. John A. Baker; London: Darton, Longman & Todd, 1964), 68–69; Cerinthus advocated "materialist millenarianism," "carnal messianism" and some other sectarian Jewish-Christian ideas that go back to the testimony of Hippolytus and Epiphanius (world created by angels, rejection of the resurrection of Christ, baptism for the dead). For Daniélou,

Skarsaune.[29] However, there were many who now presented Cerinthus
as a gnostic teacher who was merely charged with chiliasm: Walter
Bauer,[30] Klaus Wengst,[31] Raymond E. Brown,[32] Georg Strecker,[33]
Martin Hengel,[34] and others. Many experts on Gnosticism still consider Cerinthus an early gnostic.[35] It has indeed become difficult to
choose between a gnostic and chiliastic Cerinthus. In their work on
Jewish-Christian sects (1973), A. F. J. Klijn and G. J. Reinink, after
a critical survey, reduced the historically reliable information to the
fact that "Cerinthus was a heretic operating in Asia."[36]

The pessimistic conclusion of Klijn and Reinink has not been well
received, but all the same, scholarship seems to be at an impasse.
Even though Gnosis and chiliasm are rather strange bedfellows,[37]

Cerinthus was "the most typical representative" of Jewish Christianity drawn into
the Jewish nationalist movement.

[29] Oskar Skarsaune, *The Proof from Prophecy: A Study in Justin Martyr's Proof-Text
Tradition: Text Type, Provenance, Theological Profile* (Leiden: E. J. Brill, 1987), 407–8,
esp. 408: "Irenaeus was a chiliast himself and would hardly find millenarian doctrine of Cerinth to be very offensive—if he had knowledge of it. But the sharp
rejection of Cerinth by John would naturally lead Irenaeus to suspect that Cerinth
was a Gnostic."

[30] Walter Bauer, *Orthodoxy and Heresy in Earliest Christianity* (ed. Robert A. Kraft
and Gerhard Krodel; trans. a team from Philadelphia Seminar on Christian Origins;
Philadelphia: Fortress), 85; see also p. 207.

[31] Wengst, *Häresie und Orthodoxie*, 35–36.

[32] Raymond E. Brown, *The Epistles of John* (AB 30; New York: Doubleday, 1982),
770. He rejects the thesis of Cerinthus' chiliasm particularly because "early antimil-
lenianists like Papias and Irenaeus show no awareness of Cerinthus' having a part
in that movement."

[33] Strecker, *Johannesbriefe* (KEK 14; Göttingen: Vandenhoeck & Ruprecht, 1989),
135, 138; on p. 336 he refers to the tradition that portrayed Cerinthus as a chiliast,
but does not evaluate it.

[34] Hengel, *Johannine Question* 60 assumes that Cerinthus was "a Judeo-Christian
teacher coming from outside with some popular philosophical learning of the kind
widespread in the Greek-speaking synagogue. He taught in a popular Platonic manner which spoke to the spirit of the time, seeing a fundamental difference between
the demiurge of the visible world and the supreme transcendent God."

[35] See, for instance, Kurt Rudolph, *Gnosis: The Nature and History of an Ancient
Religion* (trans. Robert McLachlan Wilson; Edinburgh: T&T Clark, 1983), 165;
Simone Pétrement, *A Separate God: The Christian Origins of Gnosticism* (trans. Carol
Harrison; San Francisco: Harper & Row, 1990), 308–11. However, Petrement doubts
that Cerinthus ever existed. She assumes that the "Cerinthians" was a deformation
of "Corinthians" and that a heretic called Cerinthus was derived from this name.
She also cautiously suggests that Cerinthus might have been a deformation of some
nickname given to Apollos.

[36] Klijn and Reinink, *Patristic Evidence*, 18.

[37] George W. MacRae, *Studies in the New Testament and Gnosticism* (Wilmington:
Michael Glazier, 1987), 247: "What is of course most distinctive of the apocalyptic

modern scholars routinely accept both Cerinthus traditions as historically trustworthy. After a thorough survey, Christoph Markschies
concludes that Cerinthus most likely was no early gnostic but that
his separation between God and Creator might be possible to locate
in a Jewish-Christian framework.[38] In a recent proposal, Charles E.
Hill has sought to find an affirmative interpretation for both teachings attributed to Cerinthus. He argues that Cerinthus was a predecessor of Cerdo and Marcion rather than of Valentinus and others.
His interesting theory will be discussed below in detail.

The scanty evidence we have is indeed difficult to assess. Excluding
Polycarp, mentioned by Irenaeus (*Haer.* 3.3.4), we have no references
to Cerinthus in documents that are relevant to understanding Christian
movements in early second-century Asia Minor. It might be just a
coincidence that Ignatius, Papias, Hegesippus, and Justin do not mention him in the texts that we now have in our hands. Unlike
Epiphanius, we cannot claim to know for sure whether there was a
major school of Cerinthus in Asia Minor, but his wide reputation
as a heresiarch certainly did not grow out of nothing. In the following survey, I will discuss the earliest evidence, which is tenden-
tious in various ways and therefore hard to accept as it is. However,
all attempts to uncover the historical Cerinthus behind this evidence
are particularly hypothetical and vulnerable—and so is the theory
presented in this article.

3. *Cerinthus, Gnosticism and Possession*[39] *Christology*

In spite of all obscurities and disagreements concerning the dubious
category called "Gnosticism," most scholars agree that the writings

---

eschatology of Gnosticism is the total absence of any new creation. Given its rad-
ically dualist perspective, expressed in the concept of creation as error, Gnosticism
can see the end time only as the dissolution of the created world." In Valentinian
and particularly Sethian theologies, it is possible to trace various Jewish apocalyptic elements that have been used for the purposes of anti-material eschatology; see
the survey of Harold W. Attridge, "Valentinian and Sethian Apocalyptic Traditions,"
JECS 8 (2000): 173–211.

[38] Markschies, "Kerinth," 76; "aber sicher ist das natürlich nicht."

[39] According to various forms of "possession Christology," Jesus in one way or
another came to possess a heavenly power that left him before he died. The term
"separation Christology" means practically the same, emphasizing the separation between Jesus and the power that came into him. Both terms are used in this
chapter.

and traditions that belong to this category have at least two common features. They make some kind of distinction between the highest transcendent deity and the creator(s) of the world, the latter
identified with angels or the creator God of biblical narrative.
Furthermore, they include a message sent from the higher realm,
which is intended to call humans to receive a saving knowledge,
according to which they may live and let the divine component
within them be saved from the world of matter.[40] Like all modern
abstractions of wider religious phenomena in Antiquity, the term
"Gnosticism" can be criticized as obscure and misleading. In an
important study, Michael Williams has proposed the replacement of
it with the designation "biblical demiurgical traditions,"[41] but the
problem is that no categorical designation can aptly describe the various sources and historical movements brought under the same
umbrella; used with caution, the expression Gnosticism is as good
as any other.[42] In this article, the term is interchangeable with such
expressions as gnosis and "false knowledge."

According to Irenaeus, Cerinthus separated the highest God from
the lower god that had created the material world. He denied the
virgin birth of Jesus and taught instead that Jesus was born like all
others, just being more righteous, prudent and wiser than anybody
else. Christ was a separate heavenly being who descended on Jesus
at baptism and left him before his death on the cross. This testimony has been preserved in Latin translation, but the Greek original can be recovered from Hippolytus (*Haer.* 7.33.1–2; 10.21.1–3)
who—as was already mentioned—copied Ireneaus' passage almost
word for word, adding that Cerinthus was "trained in the teaching
of the Egyptians" and that his creator was an angelic power.[43]

---

[40] Cf. M. A. Williams, *Rethinking "Gnosticism": An Argument for Dismantling a Dubious
Category* (Princeton: Princeton University Press, 1996), 26.

[41] Williams, *"Gnosticism,"* 261–66.

[42] Philip L. Tite ("Categorical Designations and Methodological Reductionism,"
Method and Theory in the Study of Religion 13 [2001]: 281–89) discusses Williams' theory critically and suggests that categorical designations like "Gnosticism" should be
used in terms of determinacy and indeterminacy. Categorical designations are deter-
minate, while cultural artefacts—texts and other physical objects—are indetermi-
nate. Tite proposes that "looking at the modes of relation as a relative analytical
basis for constructing and using categorical designations may help to ease the tension of this theoretical difficulty" (287).

[43] For the reconstruction of the Greek original of Irenaeus' text, see Markschies,
"Kerinth," 56–58.

I think that Irenaeus was not so well informed about the historical Cerinthus as many scholars are accustomed to assume. He had
an obvious and understandable tendency to draw various heretics
closer to his main target, Valentinian Gnosticism. Furthermore, his
presentation of the earliest heresies in *Haer.* 1.23–27 calls for a comment. The claim that it is based on a written source—Justin's *Syntagma*
or the like—does not go unchallenged.

As Irenaeus moves to his proof from the Scripture in the third
book of *Adversus haereses*, he tells the anecdote mentioned above (*Haer.*
3.3.4; quoted by Eusebius in *Hist. eccl.* 3.28.6): John the evangelist
is said to have run out of a bathhouse in Ephesus when he saw that
Cerinthus, "the enemy of the truth," was within. Later, as he treats
the testimony of each gospel in turn (*Haer.* 3.9–11), he mentions
(3.11.1) that, with his gospel, John "the disciple of the Lord" wanted
"to remove the error that by Cerinthus had been disseminated among
men, and a long time previously by those called Nicolaitans, who
are an outgrowth of the 'knowledge,' falsely so-called . . ." It is curious that Irenaeus here connects the Nicolaitans with the "false knowledge" as well; elsewhere he merely remarks that they taught fornication
to be a matter of indifference and that one should eat meat sacrificed
to idols (*Haer.* 1.26.3). He recalls that their master Nicolaus was
ordained to the deaconate by the apostles (Acts 6:5) and that their
true character was revealed in the Book of Revelation (2:6, 15).
Irenaeus followed the Nicolaus traditions known to him, but above
all he saw this dubious teacher and his followers as offspring of
Gnosticism.

Irenaeus clearly connects both Cerinthus and the Nicolaitans with
the "false knowledge," even though their role in his presentation of
the earliest heretics (*Haer.* 1.23–27) is marginal. In the frame of his
presentation, he characterizes these men as the "source and root"
of Valentinianism (1.22.2). On one hand, he aims to present the predecessors of Valentinus as proponents of false teaching on creation
and Christology. On the other hand, he emphasizes the complexity
and multiformity of his task (1.22.2), indicating that the heresies
themselves are far from uniformity.

In spite of the unevenness of the sections he devotes to each heretic
or schismatic group in 1.23–27, a somewhat clear line of thought is
visible. Irenaeus presented Simon Magus as the father of all "knowledge, falsely so-called" (*Haer.* 1.23.4), a conclusion that he drew on
the basis of earlier sources, most notably from information provided

by Justin (*1 Apol.* 26). He probably used Justin's lost *Syntagma* as a source, but we cannot know for sure which pieces of information stem from there. According to Irenaeus and his tradition, Simon the arch-heretic presented himself as the highest power and father over all, who descended in order to liberate his own from the world created by "angels and powers," appeared in seemingly human form and seemed to suffer in Judaea (*Haer.* 1.23.1–3). Menander, his follower, proclaimed the primary Power unknown to all and that he himself was sent "from the presence of the invisible beings as a savior, for the deliverance of men" (1.23.5). For Irenaeus, both Simon and Menander were immoral persons who misled their converts with magic.

Irenaeus says that Saturninus and Basilides drew upon the doctrines of these two men. Saturninus, like Menander, taught about the unknown Father and the creation of the world by angels, while Basilides[44] developed a complicated doctrine of the unbegotten Father and a chain of emanations flowing from him to the lower spheres. Their dependence on Menander is so meagre that it is questionable to regard them as immediate followers of Menander and so to date them early in the second century. The Christian reception of the Simonian gnosis in Syria and Egypt is safer to date closer to Marcion, Carpocrates and Valentinus. At least Justin lumps all these names together as he depicts the Christian heresies and their adherents in Rome (*Dial.* 35.6). Irenaeus portrays Saturninus and Basilides as teachers of thoroughly docetic Christology. Saturninus assumed the Savior (*Haer.* 1.24.2) "to be unbegotten, incorporeal, and without form, but appeared in semblance as a man." Basilides, in turn, presented Christ as the first-born Nous of the unoriginate and ineffable Father. He appeared on earth as a man and performed miracles. Through ignorance and error, Simon of Cyrene was crucified instead of him, while he took the form of Simon and laughed at his enemies. Since he was an incorporeal power, he could take any form he liked (*Haer.* 1.24.4).

Next, Irenaeus treats the teachings of Carpocrates even more thoroughly than those of Saturninus and Basilides. After a brief reference to the doctrine of the unbegotten father and the creation of the world by angels, Irenaeus describes his Christology. He taught

---

[44] For Basilides, see Pearson in this volume.

that Jesus was Joseph's son, but that he was more just than other human beings, having a strong and pure soul. He had memories of his past with the Father, from whom he had a special power to escape the evil powers that had made the world. His followers could also possess this power (*Haer.* 1.25.1). After arguing at length against the possession of power, the doctrine of reincarnation and assumed libertinism[45] among Carpocrates' followers, Irenaeus moves on to his short Cerinthus tradition, because this Asian heretic taught about Jesus in a similar manner. Then follow the Ebionites (1.26.2) whose "opinions with respect to the Lord are similar to those of Cerinthus and Carpocrates."[46] However, this does not mean more than denying the divinity of Jesus and taking him simply as a human being. There is no reference to the possession of power or to the baptism of Jesus, but it is likely that the tradition of Irenaeus linked the Ebionites with possession Christology.[47] Nicolaitans, whom Irenaeus elsewhere counts among the representatives of the "false knowledge," are described only briefly, focusing on their indifference to fornication and eating of meat offered to idols (1.26.3).[48] Then follows a short note on Cerdo who originated from the Simonians. He came to Rome under Bishop Hyginus and taught that "God proclaimed by the Law and the prophets is not the Father of our Lord Jesus Christ" (1.27.1). Irenaeus' treatment of Marcion, Cerdo's successor, is detailed (1.27.2–4).

In his treatment of different sects that followed these "heresies," Irenaeus mentions Encratites who were inspired by Saturninus and Marcion, and Libertines who followed Basilides and Carpocrates (1.28). The role of Cerinthus in Irenaeus' traditions can be clarified with the following table that presents different teachers/groups and their basic teachings:

---

[45] This latter claim is most likely based on Irenaeus' own prejudice rather than on historical facts; see Winrich A. Löhr, "Karpokratianisches," *VC* 49 (1995): 23–48.

[46] The Latin text reads *non similiter ut Cerinthus et Carpocrates*, but there is no doubt that the Greek original is preserved by Hippolytus; the word *non* is a scribal error.

[47] With Michael D. Goulder, *A Tale of Two Missons* (London: SCM Press, 1994), 109–10.

[48] Charles E. Hill ("Cerinthus, Gnostic or Chiliast? A New Solution to an Old Problem," *JECS* 8 [2000]: 157) assumes that Irenaeus mentions the Ebionites and the Nicolaitans after Cerinthus "as part of his general environment in Asia Minor in the time of John who wrote the Apocalypse."

Teacher/Group	separate God	docetic Christ	separate power in Jesus
Saturninus	x	x	—
Basilides	x	x	—
Carpocrates	x	—	x
Cerinthus	x	—	x
Ebionites	—	—	x(?)
Nicolaitans	—(?)	—	—
Cerdo	x	—	—
Marcion	x	—	—

Irenaeus starts with Saturninus and Basilides, the most obvious fore-runners of Valentinus, in order to next refute Carpocrates. From the Christology of Carpocrates, he takes the lead to introduce Cerinthus whose teaching already belonged to the past, just like that of the Ebionites, Nicolaitans and Cerdo. Cerdo and his follower Marcion are, in turn, different kind of heretics. Irenaeus wants to say that all these teachers and groups were ancestors of the "false knowledge." It is hardly likely that the whole passage in *Haer.* 1.23–27—includ-ing Simon and Menander—would stem from a written source.[49] Both the exhaustive treatments of Saturninus, Basilides, Carpocrates and Marcion and the order of presentation serve Irenaeus' own purposes. Some parts of the section may derive from Justin's *Syntagma*, but the short traditional passage on the Ebionites is in striking contradiction with Justin's permissive attitude to the Jewish Christians in *Dial.* 46–47. Obviously the tradition on Carpocrates was much shorter, and it is likely that the tradition drawn upon by Irenaeus was basi-cally interested in drawing a parallel between the Christologies of Carpocrates and Cerinthus (1.25.1; 1.26.1). In this case, Irenaeus might have drawn upon oral tradition.

Charles E. Hill attributes the main lines of Irenaeus' depiction in *Haer.* 1.26.1 to Polycarp of Smyrna because he thinks that the pres-byter mentioned by Irenaeus in 4.32.1 can be identified with him. He points to the testimony of "a presbyter, disciple of the apostles" presented in this passage, according to which there is only one God

---

[49] *Pace* Pheme Perkins, "Irenaeus and the Gnostics: Rhetoric and Composition in Adversus Haereses Book One," *VC* 30 (1976): 198, who argues that the cata-logue in *Haer.* 1.23–28 "treats all Gnostic heresies according to a set pattern" and that this pattern differs from that employed by Irenaeus. She assumes that the basic pattern may have derived from Justin's lost *Syntagma*.

and Creator and that the world was not created "by angels or a kind of power." Hill thinks that this testimony was not directed against the Valentinian doctrine, but against the heresies treated in 1.23–27 or 1.25–27. The idea that the world was created by "a kind of power" stems explicitly from Cerinthus, and therefore the whole Cerinthus tradition in 1.26.1 can be traced back to the presbyter and disciple of the apostles—who must be identical with Polycarp.

However, there are some problems with this suggestion. First of all, Irenaeus knows Polycarp as the bishop of the church of Smyrna, appointed by the apostles in Asia (*Haer.* 3.3.4) and also as a companion of Papias, who heard the preaching of John (5.33.4). However, Irenaeus does not name the presbyter whom he quotes six times in *Haer.* 4.27–32 (27.1; 27.2; 27.3; 30.1; 31.1; 32.1), even though he knew him as "a disciple of the apostles" (32.1). Irenaeus would hardly have left Polycarp unnamed on this occasion. It is more likely that the presbyter in question is a teacher that Irenaeus knew from his own time in Asia. He does not name him because his readers would not be able to identify him as a person with "ecumenical" authority. This presbyter most likely transmitted traditions concerning various Asian schismatic teachers.

Irenaeus clearly thought that, in his separation of Christ and Jesus in the Christology, Cerinthus was a forerunner of the Valentinians. Many of them thought that Christ was composed of four elements: the spiritual, the ensouled, the spiritual body, and the Savior, who at his baptism descended from above in the form of a dove (*Haer.* 1.7.2). Marcus the Magician taught similarly (1.15.3; cf. also 1.21.2): Jesus was generated by powers, came to the world through the womb of the virgin Mary, and the power from above, "the seed of the Father," descended on him in the form of a dove. The Ophites (1.30.12) taught that Jesus was to be the chosen pure basin in which the heavenly Christ descended from above, "through the seven heavens," as he was baptized. Like the followers of Cerinthus and Carpocrates, the Ophites also taught that Jesus "was wiser, purer, and more righteous than all other men." Later in his book (3.11.3), Irenaeus lumps these and other different "heterodox" Christological models together and states that none of them recognize the main point of orthodox teaching—that the Word of God was made flesh.

The Cerinthus tradition transmitted by Irenaeus in *Haer.* 1.26.1 is further related to several other pieces of information in his work. On some occasions, Irenaeus refers to the separation Christology of

Cerinthus without mentioning him by name. He quotes the story of Jesus' baptism according to Matt 3:16–17 and states again that "Christ did not at that time descend upon Jesus, neither was Christ one and Jesus another" (3.9.3). Later he states that the advocates of the false teaching about Jesus' baptism and death rely on the gospel of Mark (3.11.7). However, it is difficult to say whether this was already the case with Cerinthus and his followers.

The setting of Cerinthus' proclamation is, as Charles E. Hill notes, "very different from, and arguably earlier than, that of Valentinianism": he took Jesus as a natural offspring of Joseph and Mary.[50] Hill proposes that Cerinthus was a predecessor of Cerdo and Marcion, who also taught that the God who made the world was not the highest God, who was proclaimed by Jesus, and that the Creator was ignorant of this supreme and only good God. The Christologies of Cerinthus and Marcion differ notably, but Hill assumes that the adoptionism of Cerinthus was a different component of his thought that was not taken up by Marcion. According to Hill, the theology of Cerinthus was a coherent mixture of different ideas.[51]

I have some difficulties in accepting this stimulating theory. It is not quite clear how the revolutionary idea of a highest and good God versus the ignorant Creator God would have reached Cerinthus in early second-century Asia. Since all the teachers that make this sort of distinction are later than Cerinthus, it is difficult to perceive where it came from.[52] Furthermore, I find it difficult to imagine a process in which Cerinthus, as the first Christian teacher known to us, could have adopted a part of such drastic, novel and anti-Biblical worldview and made it a neat part of his own theology, which leaned on the primitive adoptionist Christology.

While not being able to disprove Hill's theory, I would make a different kind of proposal. As the presentation of Irenaeus makes

---

[50] Hill, "Cerinthus," 153.

[51] Hill, "Cerinthus," 154: "Thus the views attributed to Cerinthus by Irenaeus do not coalesce neatly or completely with any other person or group; one can speak of a coherent and distinctively Cerinthian combination of ideas."

[52] In his article on Valentinus in the present volume, Ismo Dunderberg points out that the fragments of Valentinus include "no references to the figure of Wisdom, to the demiurge, nor to the tripartition of humankind." Nevertheless, in one fragment "Valentinus describes the confusion of the creator angels arising from their observation that there was in Adam 'an essence from above' and the pre-existent human being." The historical Valentinus obviously proclaimed a far more simple doctrine than Irenaeus has made us believe.

clear, at his time and some two decades before him, various kinds
of teachings originating in deviant movements were likely connected
with the "false knowledge." There are some weighty reasons for
assuming that the Cerinthus tradition known to Irenaeus was interpreted within the theological framework of Valentinianism and other
similar movements.[53] Such a process might have been twofold: teachers like Valentinus were inspired by the idea of Christ or power
descending on Jesus at his baptism, known from teachers like Cerinthus,
and made it work in terms of their overall theological systems. The
"orthodox" polemists, in turn, could take such a connection for
granted, since they could easily believe that a heretic who separates
Jesus and Christ from each other also thinks that there is a separate, higher God in opposition to the Creator of the world. I suggest that all the so-called gnostic features in the Cerinthus tradition
of Irenaeus stem from such a twofold process.

This assumption is particularly supported by the strong testimonies
of Cerinthus' chiliasm. There is no other evidence of a combination
of the so-called Gnosticism and chiliasm among our traditions about
early Christian theologians.[54] Irenaeus himself presents the teaching
of Cerinthus as far more simple than that of the mid-second-cen-
tury "gnostics," without presupposing any complicated cosmological
speculations. It is hard to believe that Cerinthus was the *first* to pro-
claim a separation between the highest God and the Creator God,
if there was—on one hand—no tradition of the cosmological framework in which he would have placed his Christology and—on the
other hand—no corresponding later reputation as the father of such
ideas. Irenaeus names Cerdo as an immediate predecessor of Marcion,
but Cerinthus stands alone—too alone, I think, to be the first proponent of a Christology that is based on the idea of a separate higher

---

[53] See n. 51 above. Hill ("Cerinthus," 153–54) assumes that the idea of the ignorance of the Creator God common to Cerinthus and Marcion does not fit the
Valentinian system. However, Irenaeus clearly states that the Demiurge of Valentinus
was "ignorant of those things which were above him" (1.7.4). According to Irenaeus,
both Menander and Saturninus taught that the Father of all is unknown to all
(1.23.5–24.1).
[54] See also Pétrement, *Separate God*, 304: "It is not possible that a Jewish Christian
taught that the true God is not the creator of the world, and that this creator did
not know him. Only the idea that Jesus was at first a mere man like others could
have linked Cerinthus to Jewish Christianity." Pétrement considers the linkage of
Cerinthus to Jewish Christianity as a late creation because she finds evidence for
this only in the writings of Epiphanius and Filastrius (p. 305).

God. Furthermore, the first main gnostics presented in the same context as Cerinthus originated either in Syria (Menander and Saturninus) or in Egypt (Basilides and Valentinus). This might be the reason that Hippolytus located Cerinthus in Egypt instead of Asia as he otherwise faithfully transmitted the tradition of Irenaeus (*Haer.* 7.33.1–2; 10.21.1–3). Hippolytus mentions several times that the Hellenistic philosophy came from Egypt (*Haer.* 4.44.3; 6.21.3; 8.27.13; 9.27.3).[55]

There are three gnostic elements in the Irenaean passage on Cerinthus: 1) "the world was not made by the Supreme God, but by a certain Power highly separated and far removed from that Principality who transcended the universe, and which is ignorant of the one who is above all, God," 2) that Christ descended upon him "from that Principality that is above all, and then he proclaimed the unknown Father and performed miracles" and 3) that "Christ remained impassible, being a spiritual being." Without these elements, the tradition reveals a scheme that represents more simple, separation Christology (in *italics*):

> *A certain Cerinthus, then in Asia taught that* the world was not made by the Supreme God, but by a certain Power highly separated and far removed from that Principality who transcended the universe, and which is ignorant of the one who is above all, God. He suggested that *Jesus was not born of a virgin* (because that seemed to him impossible), *but that he was the son of Joseph and Mary, in the same way as all other men but he was more versed in righteousness, prudence and wisdom than other men. And after his baptism, Christ descended upon him* from that Principality that is above all *in the form of a dove. And then he* proclaimed the unknown Father and *performed miracles. But at last Christ flew again from Jesus; Jesus suffered and rose again* while Christ remained impassible, being a spiritual being.

The idea of the descent of "Christ" at the baptism of Jesus and its ascension before the death of Jesus originates in earlier tradition. Seen in tradition-historical light, the general background of this doctrine can be found in the possession Christology.[56] There is an ample

---

[55] With Bardy, "Cérinthe," 351. Benjamin G. Wright, "Cerinthus *Apud* Hippolytus: An Inquiry into the Traditions about Cerinthus's Provenance," *SecCent* 4 (1984): 103–15, assumes that Hippolytus has preserved the original tradition, while Irenaeus had replaced the original reference to Egypt with Asia Minor.

[56] For a thorough survey, see Goulder, *Tale*, 107–34. However, he connects Cerinthus' proclamation of the unknown Father and his miracles with the "Petrine good news," the Jewish-Christian message of the kingdom of God.

evidence for this Christological model in the early second-century traditions that refer to earlier developments. Justin's tradition of the baptism of Jesus refers in full to Ps 2:7 (below in *italics; Dial.* 88.8; cf. 103.6; 122.6):

> And when Jesus came to the Jordan, he was considered to be the son of Joseph the carpenter; and he appeared without comeliness, as the Scriptures declared; and he was deemed a carpenter (for he was in the habit of working as a carpenter when among men, making ploughs and yokes; by which he taught the symbols of righteousness and an active life); but then the Holy Spirit, and for man's sake, as I formerly stated, lighted on him in the form of a dove, and there came at the same instant from the heavens a voice, which was uttered also by David when he spoke, personating Christ, what the Father would say to him: '*You are My Son: today I have begotten you*'; [the Father] saying that his generation would take place for men, at the time when they would become acquainted with him: '*You are My Son; today I have begotten you.*'

The consequent use of Ps 2:7 as a witness for the birth of the Son of God on the day of his baptism can also be found in Luke 3:22 (D) and *1 Clem* 36.4. The scriptural combination of Ps 2:7 (LXX) and Is 42:1 (LXX) in the canonical gospels (Mark 1:11 parr.) seems to be an orthodox correction to this tradition.

The Akhmim fragment of the *Gospel of Peter* tells how "power" left the crucified Lord at the moment of his death (*Gos. Pet.* 19): "Then Lord exclaimed: 'My power, my power, you have left me!' As he had said this, he was taken above." The idea of the power leaving Jesus has replaced the citation of Ps 22:2 (Mark 15:34; Matt 27:46: "My God, my God, why have you forsaken me?"), which caused obvious difficulties for later Christian authors, starting with Luke and John. The power leaving Jesus might presuppose a power that once came into Jesus, most likely at his baptism.

The same possession Christology has been preserved in the Jewish-Christian gospel tradition transmitted by Epiphanius (*Pan.* 30.13.7):

> When the people had been baptized Jesus came also and was baptized by John. And when he ascended from the water the heavens were opened, and he saw the Holy Spirit in the form of a dove descending and entering into him. And there came a voice from heaven saying, 'You are my beloved Son, in you I am well pleased', and again, 'today I have begotten you'. And suddenly a great light shone round about the place. [. . .]

In contrast to the synoptic versions, the declaration in Ps 2:7 is quoted here in full, serving possession Christology. Moreover, it is notable that the Holy Spirit enters into Jesus and not only remains resting above him. This element has also been preserved in the earliest gospel (Mark 1:10). According to Irenaeus, those "who separate Jesus from Christ, alleging that Christ remained impassible, but that it was Jesus who suffered, preferred the Gospel by Mark" (*Haer.* 3.11.7).

The view of Cerinthus on the baptism of Jesus was clearly more developed than possession models, which described how the Holy Spirit or power entered into Jesus. *Gospel of Peter* tells us that the power left Jesus as he died, and it seems reasonable to assume that this was the case in the early possession model as well.[57] In other circles, this model was employed to serve the idea that the divine element in Jesus was impassible. It was not the Spirit or the power that came down upon Jesus at baptism, but the divine element "Christ" that made it possible for him to work miracles. Because this divine element that dwelled in the earthly Jesus could not suffer, it must have left him *before* his death. It is possible to flesh out some presuppositions of the Cerinthian model. Upon his resurrection, Jesus entered the divine realm, and he could be called Jesus Christ, the Lord, the Son of God and so on. But on the earth he was mere man, who was endowed with divine power. Those who called this man "Jesus Christ" made a mistake in assuming that a human being could be divine and that human and divine could be mixed in the earthly existence of a human being. It was also a mistake to believe that a divine being could suffer and die. However, Jesus was more than a man of God who had the Spirit. He was indeed "Jesus Christ," but in a particular way: it was precisely this "Christ" that descended upon him as he was baptized and influenced in him and left him just before his death.

---

[57] *Gos. Pet.* 19 runs as follows: "My power, [my] power, you have forsaken me! And having said this, he was taken up." This passage is disputed. In earlier scholarship, it was often interpreted in terms of docetic Christology. However, in recent studies these words have been taken as a simple euphemism for Jesus' death; see e.g. John D. Crossan, *The Cross That Spoke: The Origins of the Passion Narrative* (San Francisco: Harper & Row, 1988) 220–23.

The Christological model of Cerinthus has been portrayed as docetistic, but it would be better to reserve this category for teachings that totally deny the humanity of Christ.[58] Cerinthus did not deny it, but separated the divine element (Christ) from the human being (Jesus). The idea that the earthly Jesus or Christ was a human being only in appearance, but in reality no human being at all, presupposes a total denial of the humanity of the Savior, and of Jewish monotheism. Cerinthus, in turn, seems to have been a Jewish Christian who opposed the idea that Jesus was born as a being that was both human and divine at the same time. In their polemics against some unidentified teachers, the letters of Ignatius—and 1 John—offer ambiguous evidence for a deviant Christology. There is an ongoing debate whether these heretics in question were adherents of a separation Christology or docetists who denied that Jesus was a real person of real flesh.[59]

All this makes it possible to speculate with some developments among the Christians in Asia Minor. If both Cerinthus and the opponents of Ignatius were teachers of separation Christology, it is possible to see them as one source of inspiration for later teachers of the docetic Christology. The narrowly focused evidence on Cerinthus that includes chiliasm does not favor a hypothesis that he possessed a gnostic worldview. He was a teacher of the early second century; if he would have circulated a doctrine of the highest God, the lower Creator God, and everything that follows from this separation, his role as an arch-heretic would have been more remarkable in traditions known to Irenaeus and others.

4. *Cerinthus—a Chiliast*

Eusebius knew the work of Irenaeus and used it as his source. He quoted the bathhouse story of Irenaeus (*Hist. eccl.* 3.28.6), but hinted only vaguely at his main testimony that introduced Cerinthus as a representative of gnosis ("Irenaeus in Book 1 of his Adversus Haereses

---

[58] See Norbert Brox, "'Doketismus'—eine Problemanzeige," *ZKG* 95 (1984): 301–14.

[59] For the former theory, see particularly Michael D. Goulder, "Ignatius' 'Docetists,'" *VC* 53 (1999), 16–30, for the latter, the exhaustive study of Wolfram Uebele, *"Viele Verführer sind in die Welt ausgegangen": Die Gegner in den Briefen des Ignatius von Antiochien und in den Johannesbriefen* (BWANT 151; Stuttgart: Kohlhammer, 2001).

set out some of his more revolting errors"). The traditions which he quoted from other sources told him that this man was rather a chiliastic preacher than a gnostic. Being himself an Origenist and opponent of chiliasm, Eusebius presented Cerinthus as a representative of this heresy, while discarding the Irenaean image of a gnostic Cerinthus.

His first quotation, which can be dated to the turn of the third century, stemmed from the Roman antimontanist Gaius, who flourished in the time of Bishop Zephyrinus (198–217). In his disputation against Proclus, Gaius claimed that Cerinthus—a liar and deceiver—used the authority of John to promote his chiliastic doctrine (*Hist. eccl.* 3.28.2):

> But Cerinthus also, by means of revelations, said to be written by a great apostle, brings before us miraculous things in a deceitful way, saying that they were revealed to him by angels. And he says that after the resurrection the kingdom of Christ will be set up on earth, and that in Jerusalem the body will again serve as the instrument of desires and pleasures. And since he is an enemy of the divine Scriptures and sets out to deceive, he says that there will be a marriage feast lasting a thousand years.

Cerinthus seems to have proclaimed the coming of the wedding feast of the Lamb (Rev 19:7–9) and the idea that Christ will rule with the martyrs for thousand years (20:4) more or less in terms of the book of Revelation.[60] Gaius most definitely rejected this book, imagining that it was written by Cerinthus himself. In a passage quoted above, Dionysius bar-Salibi, a medieval teacher from Syria, has preserved a passage from Hippolytus that supports this piece of information. Hippolytus, being a contemporary and opponent of Gaius in the Church of Rome, knew the ideas of Gaius and responded to them. According to the passage quoted by Dionysius, Gaius claimed that both the gospel and the Revelation were not written by John the apostle, but by Cerinthus the heretic. Hippolytus opposed him and demonstrated that the doctrine of these works is one, while that of Cerinthus is another. It is conceivable that the idea of Cerinthus as the author of the Gospel of John is related to a misguided exegesis of John 1:14–34.[61] The opponents of the fourth Gospel known

---

[60] Markschies, "Kerinth," 59.
[61] Stuart G. Hall, "Aloger," *TRE* 2 (1978), 290–95.

as Alogi, were probably a rather small group since the information provided by the other source, Epiphanius, does not add anything to that of Dionysius bar-Salibi (*Pan.* 51.3.4). It has been assumed that Gaius was the only representative of the Alogi.[62]

The other tradition of Eusebius stems from Egypt. Dionysius was the bishop of Alexandria who died ca. 264/5, about the time Eusebius was born. In his lost work "On the Promises," Dionysius opposed the chiliastic movement in Egypt. Eusebius quoted him twice, first in a short passage on Cerinthus (*Hist. eccl.* 3.28.4–5) and later at length as he treated the authorship of the Book of Revelation (7.25). Dionysius claimed that the gospel and Revelation cannot have been written by the same person, but did not agree with those who claimed that Cerinthus wrote Revelation. He could not accept the apocalyptic descriptions of the book in concrete terms and was inclined to interpret its words in a deeper sense. Thus its author was for him a holy man, in spite of all the polemics against the book. In his specific description of Cerinthus and his sect, Dionysius is more detailed than Gaius (*Hist. eccl.* 3.28.4–5; identical with 7.25.3):

> For the doctrine which he taught was this: that the kingdom of Christ will be an earthly one. And as he dreamed that it would consist in these things he himself was devoted to, because he was a lover of the body and altogether carnal, namely delights of the belly and of the sexual passion, that is to say, in eating and drinking and marrying, and—because of this he thought he could provide himself with better reputation—in festivals and sacrifices and the slaying of victims.

According to Dionysius, Cerinthus did not write the Book of Revelation, but merely used it and the authority of the apostle John for his repulsive teachings. The Cerinthian imagery of the kingdom is portrayed quite similarly by both Gaius and Dionysius. They present the corresponding items in the same order:

---

[62] Schwartz, "Johannes," 213.

Gaius (Eusebius, *Hist. eccl.* 3.28.2)	Dionysius (Eusebius, *Hist. eccl.* 7.25.3; 3.28.3–5)
Revelations shown by angels	–
Resurrection	–
The earthly kingdom of Christ	The earthly kingdom of Christ
Jerusalem	–
Lusts and pleasures	Satisfaction of the belly and lower parts of the body
–	Eating and drinking
Wedding feast of thousand years	Wedding feast
–	Feasts, sacrifices, slaughtering of sacrificial animals

Both traditions portray Cerinthus as a heretic who delighted in the pleasures of the flesh. Just as in the Irenaean passages, there are no references to his followers, his school or community. It is reasonable to assume that the quarrel about Cerinthus was not current in either Rome or Alexandria at the time Gaius and Dionysius wrote their statements. Cerinthus was known as a heretic who was condemned by many, and whose teachings could be presented in a negative light and used against contemporary enemies. For both Gaius and Dionysius, these enemies were Montanists and other chiliasts. They could safely lean on a tradition in which Cerinthus already had a bad reputation.

The two accounts are similar, but differ in some interesting details. The tradition of Gaius draws directly upon the Apocalypse (marvellous things shown by angels, resurrection, Jerusalem, wedding feast of thousand years), while the text of Dionysius emphasizes throughout the earthly character of the Cerinthian kingdom of Christ and focuses much more sharply on the bodily manners and desires of Cerinthus himself. It is obvious that Gaius, or the anti-millenarian circles which he came from, interpreted the Cerinthian tradition in the light of the false assumption that this notorious man was the author of the Apocalypse. It is tempting to discard most of the Gaius tradition and trace the original proclamation of Cerinthus back to the items transmitted by Dionysius.[63] However, some scholars have

---

[63] Hill, "Cerinthus," 167–68, thinks that Gaius combined "elements from John's Apocalypse (the thousand years of 20:2–7; the marriage feast of 19:7, 9; the kingdom of 20:4–6 preceded by the resurrection) with what he thought he knew of Cerinthus' interpretations of the future."

concluded that Dionysius used the description of Gaius as his source on Cerinthus.[64] As Dionysius rejected the idea that the Apocalypse was written by Cerinthus and defended some hidden wisdom that he attributed to it, he distorted the evidence of Gaius and other Alogi by distancing the chiliasm of Cerinthus from the Apocalypse and drawing instead a caricature of him as a libertine Judaist.

Criticism against both sources is justified: neither Gaius nor Dionysius can be trusted. On the other hand, it is hardly enough to conclude with Klijn and Reinink that the supposed Asian background of Cerinthus was "sufficient reason for ascribing to him all Asian heretical phenomena."[65] Gaius and other critics of the Apocalypse certainly wanted to condemn this book by accusing it of more than could be read in its lines; they wanted to expose its true character by attributing it to the ill-reputed Cerinthus. Since the thousand-year rule of the martyrs with Christ is described quite moderately in Rev 20:4, one item of Gaius' witness is especially important: the earthly character of the kingdom of Christ.

Mutatis mutandis, the same can be said about the testimony of Dionysius. He also knew the moral reproach directed against Cerinthus' vision of the kingdom of Christ. He sharpened this critique in order to dissociate it totally from the Apocalypse, which he considered a book full of symbolic language that is difficult to understand correctly; obviously he was willing to read spiritually all such passages that were offensive to the Alexandrian theology. Dionysius believed that Cerinthus, in turn, certainly had no spiritual understanding of anything; he must have imagined that the kingdom of Christ was thoroughly physical. Therefore I find it likely that Dionysius, or the tradition known to him, was willing to add that Cerinthus also dreamt about feasts, sacrifices, and the slaughtering of sacrificial animals.[66]

---

[64] Bardy, "Cérinthe," 361; Klijn and Reinink, *Patristic Evidence*, 7–8.

[65] Klijn and Reinink, *Patristic Evidence*, 18.

[66] *Pace* Daniélou, *Theology*, 68: ". . . Cerinthus believed in the material restoration of the temple of Jerusalem and of the sacrifices. All this is a continuation of political Judaism, a temporal messianism, but with a Christian flavour." Skarsaune, *Proof*, 406–9, discusses this piece of the Cerinthus tradition in the light of Justin's warning against tendencies towards interpreting the sacrifices in concrete terms (*Dial.* 118.2). He thinks that Justin's passage "points to the existence of crude chiliasm of the type attributed to Cerinth" (p. 409). However, in *Dial.* 118.2 Justin is criticizing eschatological expectations of Jewish teachers and not those of heterodox Christians (cf. *Dial.* 80–81).

Charles E. Hill has made an alternative proposal to explain the evidence offered by Dionysius. He thinks that Cerinthus was a gnostic, but that it is at the same time possible to explain why he was accused of chiliasm. Hill assumes that Cerinthus was the first to introduce the idea that, in spite of the salvation of the Christians who believe in the higher God revealed by Jesus, the Jews will have their earthly Messiah sent by the lower Demiurge. This idea was adopted by Marcion (Tertullian, *Marc.* 4.6; 3.21). He thinks that this teaching stemmed from Cerinthus who therefore was later falsely accused of being a chiliast himself.[67] Instead, he belonged to certain Christian circles in Asia Minor influenced by dualistic and docetic tendencies. According to Hill, Cerinthus rejected the disputed writings of the Old Testament and left their materialistic expectations and war-loving God to the Jews. Thus he was one of the first Christians of this kind and Marcion was reaping in fields prepared by these people.[68] Hill's main argument for this theory is that Cerinthus could not have been a lover of "festivals and sacrifices and the slaying of victims," since this was a feature quite uncommon to all Christians, including all known branches of the so-called Jewish Christianity.[69] This explanation seeks to explain, how the "gnostic" Cerinthus could have been involved with chiliast theories. However, if Cerinthus was no gnostic, an explanation of this kind is not necessary. It is obvious that Dionysius drew a caricature of Cerinthus' teaching, and it is rather difficult to explain this detail as correct piece of information. Furthermore, if Cerinthus were such a pre-Marcionite innovator as Hill assumes, I find it difficult to imagine how he could have been remembered for a subsidiary view that was completely misunderstood.

In spite of the blatant bias in the traditions of Gaius and Dionysius, I think that there is a seed of truth in both of them: according to Cerinthus, the kingdom of Christ was an earthly one. It was commonplace for Origen and his followers to criticize excessive eating, drinking and sexual pleasures.[70] Even though the idea of eating and drinking in the kingdom of God is transmitted only by Dionysius, it

---

[67] Hill, "Cerinthus," 159–70.
[68] For the full discussion, see Hill, "Cerinthus," 159–70.
[69] Hill, "Cerinthus," 164–65.
[70] Markschies, "Kerinth," 60.

is important to see that it goes back to the Jewish-Christian tradition and ultimately to the teaching of Jesus himself (Matt 8:11–12;
Luke 13:28–29; cf. Matt 11:19; Luke 7:34). It is reasonable to conclude that Dionysius did not draw upon Gaius or his source, but
leaned on a similar, but independent tradition. Both traditions were
polemical and twisted the self-understanding of Cerinthus and his
vision of the kingdom of Christ. We might assume that Cerinthus
was a pious and sincere chiliast, just like Papias and Irenaeus, but
his Christological heresy made him a suitable weapon in later struggle against millennial ideas.

I suggest that it is possible to reconstruct a profile of the millennial kingdom of God imagined by Cerinthus from four details mentioned by Gaius and Dionysius:

1) kingdom of Christ on earth
2) Jerusalem as its center
3) marriage of Christ with the faithful
4) eating and drinking in the kingdom

If this rather broad reconstruction is correct, the chiliastic vision of
Cerinthus consisted of a primitive Jewish-Christian imagination nour-
ished by the synoptic gospel traditions and such holy texts as Isa 65.
His chiliasm seems to have been passed over in silence among the
second-century mainstream Christians who shared this basic conviction with him. Irenaeus was a chiliast who was devoted to polemics
against the "false knowledge." He either did not know or—more
probably—kept silent about traditions that presented Cerinthus as
an earthy and despised chiliast. In the last book of his work, he cites
an allegedly reliable Jesus tradition about the miraculous growth of
vines and grain in the kingdom. He emphasized the authority of the
transmitters of this tradition: the elders, who relied on John, the disciple of the Lord, and Papias, who was in the audience of John and
a companion of Polycarp (*Haer.* 5.33.3–4). Even though the tradition cannot be traced back to the apostle John himself, the presbyter John mentioned by Papias has probably been one of the key
proponents of the chiliast tradition. He belonged to mainstream
Christianity and therefore was a reliable source, at least in the eyes
of Irenaeus.

If Cerinthus would have proclaimed—like Polycarp, Papias and
Irenaeus—the incarnation Christology of mainstream Christianity,
his chiliasm probably would not have made him a target of later

orthodox polemics. There were several chiliasts, whose naïve eschatology was pardonable if they otherwise maintained the sound doctrine. Even though Eusebius is not a contemporary witness of the
battle against the Montanists, his words on Papias and Irenaeus
reflect this kind of attitude (*Hist. eccl.* 3.39.11–13):[71]

> The same author also gives other accounts which he says came to him
> through unwritten tradition, as certain strange parables and teachings
> of the Savior, and some other more mythical things. To these belong
> his statement that there will be a period of some thousand years after
> the resurrection of the dead, and that the kingdom of Christ will be
> set up in material form on this earth. I suppose he got these ideas
> through a misunderstanding of the apostolic accounts, not perceiving
> that the things said by them were spoken mystically in figures. For he
> appears to have been of very limited understanding, as one can see
> from his discourses. However, it was due to him that so many of the
> Church Fathers after him adopted a similar opinion, urging in their
> own support the antiquity of the man; as, for instance, Irenaeus or
> any one else that may have adopted similar views.

I think that it is possible to see the teaching of Cerinthus reconstructed above as a historically plausible unity. It was—though much
is unknown to us—an original combination of primitive chiliasm and
primitive Christology, and both of these views were heretical among
those of his fellow Christians who were driven by "higher" Christological and eschatological visions. He was probably a sincere Christian
who lived in the wrong place at the wrong time. Both in his Christology
and chiliasm, he was closer to the theological heritage of Judaism
and Jewish Christianity than many Christian teachers of his time.
Could he be characterized as a Jewish Christian?

5. Cerinthus and the Jewish Christianity

The manifold ambiguities in the second- and third-century evidence
on Cerinthus provide opportunities for various interpretations. This
early second-century theologian in Asia Minor might have been a
gnostic who was one of the very first Christians who taught the separation between the highest God and the lower Creator God. He

---

[71] Bardy, "Cérinthe," 356–57, finds this parallel convincing; cf. also Skarsaune,
Proof, 406–7. Cf. also the words of Dionysius of Alexandria on the millenarian
Bishop Nepos cited by Eusebius in *Hist. eccl.* 7.24.

did so in order to ascribe the miraculous power ("Christ") that was
active in Jesus to the former. According to an alternative interpretation, he was no gnostic, but a chiliast who proclaimed an earthly
kingdom of Christ. Or perhaps—to follow a third theory—he, in
one way or another, was both, a sort of gnostic chiliast. It is also
possible that he was neither a gnostic nor a chiliast, and all traditions
about him were created in the heat of polemics against later heterodox teachers.

In the present chapter, I have argued for the view that Cerinthus
was not an early gnostic, but a spokesman for a traditional possession or separation Christology. Correspondingly, he embraced the
early Christian idea of the kingdom of Christ on earth. If this reconstruction is correct, it is tempting to imagine him as a "Jewish
Christian." However, if Jewish Christianity can be identified on the
basis of commitment to the most important Jewish practices—circumcision, Sabbath, food laws—there is no early evidence for the
Jewish-Christian identity of Cerinthus.[72] The later evidence provided
by Epiphanius cannot be taken at face value, even though its ker-
nel might go back to a much earlier tradition.[73] Epiphanius is well
known for much confusion in his treatment of different sects, and it
is most likely that he has simply mixed Ebionite ideas in his presentation of Cerinthus and Cerinthians or Merinthians, as he called
his followers.

The second-century evidence of Jewish Christianity in Asia Minor
does not document the presence of the central Jewish practices in
Christian communities. However, in the letters of Ignatius there is
clear evidence of Gentile Judaizers. The bishop of Antiochia says
that "it is better to hear Christianity from a man who is circumcised than Judaism from a man who is uncircumcised" (*Phld.* 6.1).
In addition to the separation Christology and chiliasm, we have evidence of the Quartodeciman Passover that many Christians celebrated according to the Jewish custom on the 14. Nisan. This practice
was perhaps brought to Asia by Palestinian and/or Syrian Jewish-
Christian refugees who fled the consequences of the Jewish War after

---

[72] For such a practical definition of Jewish Christianity, see Marcel Simon,
"Réflexions sur le Judéo-Christianisme," in *Christianity, Judaism, and Other Greco-Roman
Cults: Studies for Morton Smith at Sixty* (ed. Jacob Neusner; 4 vols.; SJLA 12; Leiden:
E. J. Brill, 1975), 2:55–57.
[73] See also Skarsaune, *Proof*, 409.

70 C.E. It is reasonable to ask, whether the success of chiliasm and possession Christology in Asia was related to this immigration and whether Cerinthus can be better located in such an environment.

It is not necessary to assume that Cerinthus was a Jew or Jewish Christian by birth or that he was a member of a Jewish-Christian community. He and teachers like him might have developed Jewish-Christian traditions in dualistic terms. Christ descending on Jesus, departing from him and ascending back to heaven is a model comparable to the heavenly Jerusalem descending on earth. This image was current among Jewish Christians and Christians particularly influenced by Judaism in Asia Minor (Rev 21:2; Irenaeus, *Haer.* 5.35.2; cf. also Justin, *Dial.* 80.5), and it survived up to the days of Montanism (Tertullianus, *Marc.* 3.24). It is not unfounded to assume that the economy of separation between the heavenly and earthly realm as well as their timely union structured both Cerinthus' Christology and his eschatology. Whether Cerinthus can be called a Jewish Christian or not, he adhered to Jewish traditions and the basic tenets of the Hebrew Bible: no human being is God or from heaven, but all righteous human beings who believe in the correct way—that of Cerinthus and believers like him—can have their share in the kingdom God on earth, eating and drinking, celebrating the heavenly wedding of God and humans, Christ and his faithful.

Bibliography

Attridge, Harold W. "Valentinian and Sethian Apocalyptic Traditions." *Journal of Early Christian Studies 8* (2000): 173–211.

Bardy, Gustave. "Cérinthe." *Revue biblique* 30 (1921): 344–73.

Bauer, Walter. *Orthodoxy and Heresy in Earliest Christianity.* Edited by Robert A. Kraft and Gerhard Krodel. Translated by a team from the Philadelphia Seminar on Christian Origins. Philadelphia: Fortress, 1971.

Baur, Ferdinand Christian. *Das Christentum und die christliche Kirche der drei ersten Jahrhunderte.* 2nd ed. Tübingen: Fues, 1860.

Brown, Raymond E. *The Epistles of John.* Anchor Bible 30. New York: Doubleday, 1982.

Brox, Norbert. "'Doketismus'—eine Problemanzeige." *Zeitschrift für Kirchengeschichte* 95 (1984): 301–14.

Crossan, John D. *The Cross That Spoke: The Origins of the Passion Narrative.* San Francisco: Harper & Row, 1988.

Daniélou, Jéan. *The Theology of Jewish Christianity.* Translated by John A. Baker. London: Darton, Longman & Todd, 1964.

Goulder, Michael D. *A Tale of Two Missions.* London: SCM Press, 1994.

———. "Ignatius' 'Docetists'." *Vigiliae christianae* 53 (1999): 16–30.

Hall, Stuart G. "Aloger." Pages 290–95 in *Theologische Realenzyklopädie 2* (1978).

Harnack, Adolf. *History of Dogma*. Translated by Neil Buchanan. 7 vols. New York: Dover, 1961.

Hilgenfeld, Adolf. *Ketzergeschichte des Urchristentums*. 1884. Repr. Darmstadt: Wissenschaftliche Buchgesellschaft, 1963.

Hill, Charles E. "The Epistula Apostolorum: An Asian Tract from the Time of Polycarp," *Journal of Early Christian Studies* 7 (1999): 1–53.

———. "Cerinthus, Gnostic or Chiliast? A New Solution to an Old Problem." *Journal of Early Christian Studies* 8 (2000): 135–72.

Hort, F. J. A. *Judaistic Christianity*. London: Macmillan, 1894.

Klijn, A. F. J., and G. J. Reinink. *Patristic Evidence for Jewish-Christian Sects*. Supplements to Novum Testamentum 36. Leiden: E. J. Brill, 1973.

Koester, Helmut. *Introduction to the New Testament*. 2 vols. Philadelphia: Fortress, 1982.

Löhr, Winrich A. "Karpokratianisches." *Vigiliae christianae* 49 (1995): 23–48.

MacRae, George W. *Studies in the New Testament and Gnosticism*. Wilmington: Michael Glazier, 1987.

Markschies, Christoph. "Kerinth: Wer war er und was lehrte er?" Pages 48–76 in *Jahrbuch für Antike und Christentum* 41 (1998).

Mosheim, Johannes Laurentius. *De rebus Christianorum ante Constantinum Magnum commentarii*. Helmstedt: Friedrich Weygand, 1753.

Perkins, Pheme. "Irenaeus and the Gnostics: Rhetoric and Composition in Adversus Haereses Book One." *Vigiliae christianae* 30 (1976): 193–200.

Pétrement, Simone. *A Separate God: The Christian Origins of Gnosticism*. Translated by Carol Harrison. San Francisco: Harper & Row, 1990.

Renan, Ernest. *Les Évangiles et la seconde génération chrétienne*. Paris: Calmann Lévy, 1877.

Rudolph, Kurt. *Gnosis: The Nature and History of an Ancient Religion*. Translated by Robert McL. Wilson. Edinburgh: T&T Clark, 1983.

Schwartz, Eduard. "Johannes und Kerinthos." *Zeitschrift für die neutestamentliche Wissenschaft* 15 (1914): 210–19.

Simon, Marcel. "Réflexions sur le Judéo-Christianisme." Pages 53–76 in vol. 2 of *Christianity, Judaism, and Other Greco-Roman Cults: Studies for Morton Smith at Sixty*. Edited by Jacob Neusner. Studies in Judaism in Late Antiquity 12. Leiden: E. J. Brill, 1975.

Skarsaune, Oskar. *The Proof from Prophecy: A Study in Justin Martyr's Proof-Text Tradition: Text Type, Provenance, Theological Profile*. Leiden: E. J. Brill, 1987.

Storr, Gottlob Christian. *Ueber den Zweck der evangelischen Geschichte und der Briefe Johannis*. Tübingen: J. F. Heerbrandt, 1786.

Strecker, Georg. *Die Johannesbriefe*. Kritisch-exegethischer Kommentar über das Neue Testament 14. Göttingen: Vandenhoeck & Ruprecht, 1989.

Tite, Philip L. "Categorical Designations and Methodological Reductionism." *Method and Theory in the Study of Religion* 13 (2001): 269–92.

Uebele, Wolfram. *"Viele Verführer sind in die Welt ausgegangen": Die Gegner in den Briefen des Ignatius von Antiochien und in den Johannesbriefen*. Beiträge zur Wissenschaft vom Alten und Neuen Testament 151. Stuttgart: Kohlhammer, 2001.

Wengst, Klaus. *Häresie und Orthodoxie im Spiegel des ersten Johannesbriefes*. Gütersloh: Gerd Mohn, 1976.

Williams, M. A. *Rethinking "Gnosticism": An Argument for Dismantling a Dubious Category*. Princeton: Princeton University Press, 1996.

Wright, Benjamin G. "Cerinthus Apud Hippolytus: An Inquiry into the Traditions about Cerinthus's Provenance." *The Second Century* 4 (1984): 102–15.

Wurm, Alois. "Cerinth—ein Gnostiker oder Judaist?" *Theologische Quartalschrift* 87 (1904): 20–38.

———. *Die Irrlehrer im ersten Johannesbrief*. Biblische Studien 8.1. Freiburg: Herder, 1903.

EBIONITES

Sakari Häkkinen

1. *Introduction*

According to Patristic texts, Ebionites are Christians who observe Jewish customs and, for the most part, reject the virgin birth of Jesus, holding him only as a common man. All the ancient authors describing the Ebionites consider them heretics.

The name Ebionites (Greek *ebiōnaioi*, Latin *ebionaei, ebionitae, hebionitae*) is derived from the Hebrew word *'ebyon*, which means "poor." The church fathers use either the title Ebionites for a group or mention Ebion, the fictive leader of the movement.[1] The name probably comes from the tradition of Jewish piety. Naturally, the word occurs quite often in the Hebrew Bible[2] and other Jewish Literature but it is not at all clear whether it is used as a specific title or only as a general reference to poor people. The image of the poor having a special relationship with God had been prominent in Judaism for centuries. Pious Jews often considered themselves poor and humble before God (see, for example, Psalms 9–10, 12 and 14). However, there are no clear cases in Hebrew writings where a group would have explicitly called itself "The Poor"—excluding one example from Qumran.[3]

---

[1] The earliest accounts of the Ebionites, such as Irenaeus and his source (see below pp. 250–51), do not mention that the movement was founded by Ebion. This information appears for the first time in the texts of Tertullian and Hippolytus. Therefore, Ebion is to be regarded as a fictive figure, created to give the impression that, like many other "heretical" movements, also the Ebionites had a known historical founder.

[2] The word *'ebyon* occurs 58 times in the Hebrew Bible, 22 of these occurrences are in Psalms. See, for example, Ps 9:19, 12:6, 35:10, 40:18 and 107:41.

[3] The only Hebrew text where the word *'ebyonim* is clearly used as a title of a group is a part of a commentary to Psalm 37 found in Qumran (4QpPs37):

> Then the meek will inherit the earth and enjoy all the abundance that peace brings. This refers to all of the company of the poor [*'adath ha'ebyonim*] who endure the time of error but are delivered from all the snares of Belial. (*The Dead Sea Scrolls: A New Translation* [trans. M. Wise, M. Abegg, Jr., and E. Cook; San Francisco: HarperSanFrancisco, 1996], 221.)

In this article, I shall discuss the basic information about the Ebionites. First, I shall present the most important early sources that refer to the Ebionites. The reliability of these sources must be evaluated before presenting the practices of the Ebionites. Having done that, I will offer some conclusions concerning the Ebionite theology and try to locate them in an ancient geographical and religious setting.

2. *The Sources*

One of the problems with the research on the Ebionites is the strong polemical tone of the sources where the Ebionites are mentioned. Only fragments of the texts produced or used by the Ebionites have been preserved and even they have been selected by the church fathers who quote them for polemical purposes. Therefore, it is quite impossible to draw a clear and historically trustworthy picture of the Ebionite theology. However, some distinctive features of the movement can be defined on the basis of these texts, especially when it is possible to compare them with parallels from other early Christian movements.

The earliest references to the Ebionites are to be found in catalogues of heresies that were composed by several church fathers. The catalogues were written for Christian congregations in order to warn them against deviant movements. Usually they were composed in a way that formed a *successio haereticorum*, a series of heretics beginning from Simon Magus—the very first heretic, who was already mentioned in Acts—and continuing through some known heretics until the time of the author. The last name in the catalogue was the name of the main adversary of the author. The earliest known catalogues of heresies were Justin Martyr's *Syntagma against Heresies* (now lost)[4] and a

---

The text is probably referring to the Qumran community itself. It would, however, be a mistake to argue that the Ebionites in patristic writings were related to Qumran since the Qumranites also used other titles for themselves derived from Jewish piety, like "Children of Light," "The Way," etc. Furthermore, the word *'ebyon* occurs several times in the Dead Sea Scrolls meaning simply "poor" without referring to any movement. It is quite clear that the same term can be used both as a general term as well as a specific title.

[4] Justin himself refers to the *Syntagma* in his *First Apology* (26.8), written around 150 C.E.: "I have a treatise against all the heresies that have existed (*Syntagma kata pasōn tōn gegenēmenōn haireseōn*) already composed, which, if you wish to read it, I will give you." In the same chapter, Justin mentions some persons who could have been among the heretics described in the *Syntagma*. According to the reconstruction of the *Syntagma* by A. Hilgenfeld, *Die Ketzergeschichte des Urchristenthums: urkundlich dargestellt*

catalogue composed by Hegesippus that has been preserved as a part of Eusebius' *Ecclesiastical History*.[5]

Justin's *Syntagma* probably did not mention the Ebionites since, in his other work *Dialogue with Trypho*, Justin did not consider Jewish Christians to be heretics, even though they obeyed the Torah and practiced circumcision (46–47), and confessed Jesus to be the Messiah without believing in his divine origins (48). According to his own words, Justin regarded these Jewish Christians as "his own kinsmen and brothers" though he did not share their opinions. For Justin, they were an acceptable part of Christianity as long as they did not demand that Gentile Christians become Jews. Justin's description even gives the impression that there were two types of Jewish Christians in one congregation: those who demanded that Gentile Christians become Jews and those who accepted Gentile Christians as they were, without demanding circumcision and strict observance of the Torah. Justin obviously knew Jewish Christians but did not consider them heretics nor did he call them Ebionites.[6] In Hegesippus' catalogue, the Ebionites are not mentioned.

The catalogues were continuously updated and enlarged. New authors based their own works on earlier catalogues, especially targeting their own adversaries. Usually a catalogue of heretics culminated in a teacher active in the author's lifetime. If the author was able to point out how his adversary derived his[7] opinions from earlier heretics, it was easy to reject him. The influence of Justin's *Syntagma* was especially far-reaching since many church fathers formed their own heresiological works according to this model.

(Leipzig: Fues, 1884), 23–26, the catalogue of heresies began with Simon Magus and Menander and ended with Marcion, who lived at the same time as Justin. These three men were the chief heretics (Hauptketzer) for Justin. The other heretics described in the *Syntagma* were, according to Hilgenfeld, Saturninus, Basilides, Valentinus, and some other heretics earlier than Valentinus.

[5] *Hist. eccl.* 4.22.4–6.

[6] Jerome writes in *Helv.* 17: "Ignatius, Polycarp, Irenaeus, Justin Martyr and many other apostolic and eloquent men, who hold these same views, write volumes full of wisdom against Ebion, Theodotus of Byzantium and Valentinus." From this general reference, it cannot be concluded that Justin would especially have written against the Ebionites. Jerome's comment gives the impression of being a note based on his own memory. Therefore, it cannot be regarded as very reliable.

[7] All the writers of the heresiologies and almost all the heretics in patristic writings were men!

It is interesting to note that the Ebionites first appear in the catalogues in the latter half of the second century. The earliest reference to the Ebionites was included in a catalogue used by Irenaeus
in his *Refutation and Subversion of Knowledge Falsely So-Called*, usually
called and better known with the title *Against Heresies*. The section
on the Ebionites is in the first book of his five-volume work. In
the first book, Irenaeus briefly presents the heresies to be rejected. The
brief note on the Ebionites (*Haer.* 1.26.2) probably came from the
source Irenaeus was using and he did not correct it or add anything
to it. This can be deduced by comparing the whole section on the
Ebionites to the sections dealing with other heresies that have been
clearly enlarged by Irenaeus. The reason for such enlargements is
his own acquaintance with some heresies. He lengthens descriptions
of heresies with which he is personally acquainted. Such enlargements are found especially in the description of his main adversary,
Valentinus and his adherents, and in the accounts of Carpocrates
(1.25) and the Cainites (1.31). Irenaeus also edited the description
of Marcion (1.27). The description of Tatian (1.28.1), the disciple of
Justin, is possibly totally written by Irenaeus himself since it cannot
have been taken from Justin's *Syntagma*.[8]

The brief notes on the Ebionites in the other books of Irenaeus'
work (*Haer.* 3.11.7, 3.21.1, 4.33.4 and 5.1.3) do not add anything to
the information already given in the catalogue of the first book.
Thus, Irenaeus did not have further knowledge of the Ebionites except
the catalogue he used in the first book. Nowhere does he describe
the type of Jewish Christianity that could be connected to the Ebionites.
For him, the Ebionites were only a heresy known from his source.

If Justin's *Syntagma* did not yet rank the Ebionites among heretics,
from where did Irenaeus get the catalogue? There is no unambiguous
answer. A link is missing between Justin's *Syntagma* and Irenaeus' *Against
Heresies*. The fact is that the Ebionites were added to the catalogues
of heresies in the latter half of the second century. Why and by
whom this was done remains unsolved because of the lack of evidence.
As the best solution, I would suggest that Irenaeus used an updated

---

[8] Hilgenfeld, *Ketzergeschichte*, 8–9. According to G. Lüdemann, *Heretics: The Other
Side of Early Christianity* (trans. John Bowden; Louisville, Ky.: Westminster John Knox,
1996), 19, the section on the Nicolaitans (*Haer.* 1.26.3) was also added by Irenaeus.

version of Justin's *Syntagma*, written sometime after the original work.[9] The updated heresiology might be the same that was used by Hippolytus in his *Refutation*, a heresiology that was written—according to the author—already "a long time ago" and called "*Syntagma*." The work is lost but it is referred to in several patristic texts.[10]

Hippolytus' *Syntagma* must have listed the Ebionites—or probably Ebion—among the heretics. This is to be concluded from the fact that Pseudo-Tertullian's *Against All Heresies*,[11] which was probably based on Hippolytus' *Syntagma*, mentions Ebion (3). In his larger heresiological work called *Refutation of All Heresies*, Hippolytus writes about both the Ebionites (*Haer.* 7.34) and Ebion (7.35).[12] Deviating from

---

[9] S. Häkkinen, *Köyhät kerettiläiset: Ebionit kirkkoisien teksteissä* (Suomalaisen Teologisen Kirjallisuusseuran julkaisuja 223; Helsinki: Suomalainen Teologinen Kirjallisuusseura, 1999), 84–85, 125, 129. An interesting theory was already offered in 1694 by John Deacon. Glen W. Menzies, "Interpretive Traditions in the *Hypomnestikon Biblion Ioseppou*" (Ph.D. diss., University of Minnesota, 1994), 208 n. 152, summarizes Deacon's theory. According to the theory, the addition of the Ebionites was connected to the Trinitarian schism. The Unitarians accused Justin of inventing the Trinitarian doctrine which is based on Greek philosophy and not on apostolic teaching. The Trinitarians responded to these accusations by adding to the first Christian catalogue of heresies, Justin's *Syntagma*, two heresies that are clearly based on Judaism: Cerinthians and the Ebionites. Both of these were condemned, at least in the beginning, only because they rejected the virgin birth and the divinity of Jesus, which were of great importance to the Trinitarian doctrine.

[10] Eusebius, *Hist. eccl.* 6.22; Jerome, *Vir. ill.* 61; Photius, *Bibliotheca* 121; *Chronicon Paschale* 12.22.

[11] The work, written in Latin, offers a good example of the history of the catalogues of heresies. It was based on an earlier Greek heresiology, probably Hippolytus' *Syntagma*, which was translated into Latin and updated. The work was counted among the writings of Tertullian who cannot, however, have composed it because the work also ranks the Cataphrygians among the heretics. The Cataphrygians were Montanists like Tertullian himself. The work is impossible to date accurately but it had to exist before the middle of the fourth century when Filastrius' heresiology, based on it, was written. The last heresy described in this work is not the same as in its source. According to Photius (*Bibliotheca* 121), the last heretic in Hippolytus' *Syntagma* was Noëtus but in Pseudo-Tertullian's catalogue, the last heretic is Praxeas.

[12] The work was written after 222 C.E. and consists of ten books. Books 2–3 and the beginning of Book 4 are lost and Books 4–10, which were found in 1841, are severely damaged. First, the work was thought to have been written by Origen and therefore the first edition had Origen's name on it. Ten years later, the work was recognized as a lost work of Hippolytus, but even in 1947, Hippolytus as the author of the work was questioned by P. Nautin, *Hippolyte et Josipe: contribution a l'histoire de la littérature chrétienne du troisième siècle* (Études et textes pour l'histoire du dogme de la Trinité 1; Paris: Cerf, 1947), 85–88. Nowadays, it is scholarly consensus that Hippolytus was the author of the work. See M. Marcovich, "Introduction," in Hippolytus, *Refutatio omnium haeresium* (ed. M. Marcovich; Patristische Texte

his mentor Irenaeus and his own *Syntagma*, Hippolytus does not derive the heresies from the arch-heretic Simon Magus but from the Greek philosophy that was practiced in schools of philosophy.[13] His information about the Ebionites is, however, clearly derived from Irenaeus. Hippolytus' section on the Ebionites (*Haer.* 7.34) is based on the description of the Ebionites by Irenaeus (*Haer.* 1.26.2) supplemented with what Irenaeus said about the Christology of Cerinthus and Carpocrates because, according to Irenaeus, their Christology was similar to the Ebionites' Christology.

Having presented the Ebionites, Hippolytus writes about a person called Theodotus, a native of Byzantium (*Haer.* 7.35), who was excluded from the church by Bishop Victor in Rome (Eusebius, *Hist. eccl.* 5.28.6). When Hippolytus describes this contemporary of his, he refers to "the school of the Gnostics, and of Cerinthus and Ebion," where Theodotus learned his wrong opinions. Such a school probably never existed. By presenting Theodotus as belonging to that school, Hippolytus only wanted to point out that Theodotus was to be counted among the heretics. It is doubtful that Theodotus had any connections to the Ebionites.[14]

The influence of Irenaeus' and Hippolytus' descriptions of the Ebionites can also be seen in the works of Tertullian. Tertullian never discusses the Ebionites but several times mentions the leader of the sect, Ebion. The earliest passages can be found in *De praescriptione haereticorum* (10; 33.3–5 and 33.20) but there Ebion is mentioned only in passing and always in the company of at least one other heretic. No new data is given concerning the Ebionites. However, in *De carne Christi* 14, Tertullian deals with the Christological view according to which Jesus was an ordinary human being possessed by an angel. This view would be suitable for Ebion, Tertullian writes, but does not

---

und Studien 25; Berlin: De Gruyter, 1986), 1–17 esp. 7; M. Marcovich, "Hippolyt von Rom," *TRE* 15:381–87, esp. 384; Menzies, "Interpretive Traditions," 178–250; A. Brent, *Hippolytus and the Roman Church in the Third Century: Communities in Tension before the Emergence of a Monarch-Bishop* (Supplements to Vigiliae Christianae 31; Leiden: E. J. Brill, 1995), 127–44.

[13] A "school" seems to have been a negative concept for Hippolytus. He even calls the church led by Pope Callistus a philosophical school (*didaskaleion*) to make a distinction between it and the true church led by himself (*Haer.* 9.7.3).

[14] Hippolytus also mentions Theodotus in *Contra haeresin Noeti* (3), which is difficult to date, but in this passage he does not connect him to the Ebionites. Furthermore, no other Church father mentioning Theodotus connects him to the Ebionites.

exclusively claim that Ebion would have thought in this way. The view is quite close to the Christology of Cerinthus as it is presented by Irenaeus and Hippolytus, and, according to Irenaeus, Cerinthus' Cristology was similar to the Ebionite view. Thus, the Ebionites became connected with the debate on angelomorphic Christology because of the comparison made by Irenaeus in *Against Heresies* 1.26.2. However, the target of Tertullian's criticism is not Ebion but the advocates of angelomorphic Christology he has met.[15] He opposes them but reminds the reader of Ebion who—according to Irenaeus and Hippolytus—taught similarly. Thus, Tertullian does not give any data that could not be derived from his predecessors Irenaeus and Hippolytus.[16]

A survey of all the patristic works that mention the Ebionites or Ebion would go beyond the confines of this article.[17] It suffices to note that the influence of Irenaeus and Hippolytus was so strong that for centuries most of the church fathers' descriptions of the Ebionites were based solely on these early catalogues of heresies. Especially in the Western part of the Roman Empire, the church fathers seem to have had no personal contacts with Jewish-Christian Ebionites or any information about them that could not be derived from earlier literature. Most of them do not even write about the Ebionites. They only write about a fictive leader of the sect, Ebion, often in passing and as one of heretics. For these authors, Ebion was merely a heretic among others. His greatest—some would say only—fault was wrong Christology. Research on the history of the Ebionites cannot be based on the lists of heresies, excluding the description of the Ebionites by Irenaeus.

In addition to the tradition based on early catalogues of heresies, there is also other information about the Ebionites. In Alexandria, sometime between 220 and 230 C.E., Origen wrote a work entitled *First Principles*, which also has a note on the Ebionites:

---

[15] On angelomorphic Christology in Tertullian's works, see C. A. Gieschen, *Angelomorphic Christology: Antecedents and Early Evidence* (AGJU 42; Leiden: E. J. Brill, 1988), 193–94.

[16] Tertullian also refers to the Ebionites in *De virginibus velandis* 6.1 and *De carne Christi* 18 and 24.

[17] All such passages up to the beginning of the fifth century have been analyzed in my *Köyhät kerettiläiset*.

If what has been said to us about Israel, its tribes and families, is meant
to impress us, when the Saviour says, "I was sent only to the lost sheep
of the house of Israel," we do not understand this like the Ebionites,
poor of understanding, so-called after their poverty of understanding
(because Ebion signifies "poor" with the Hebrews) so that we should
suppose that Christ especially dwelt among the carnal Israelites, for
"the children of the flesh are not the children of God." (*Princ.* 4.3.8)[18]

Origen presents the Ebionites as an example of persons whose interpretation of the Scriptures is literal and "poor" because the Ebionites
regarded Jesus as having come only for the Jews. Origen's enormous
literary production includes several references to the Ebionites[19] but,
at least in his preserved works, he never used the proper name
Ebion[20] and indicates no dependency on the early catalogues of
heretics.[21] Origen considered the Ebionites as Christians poor in reason and thought that they err because of their simplicity. Origen
seems to have called all Jewish Christians Ebionites. An Ebionite is,
for him, an abusive term used of Jewish Christians who are poor in
understanding. Unlike Irenaeus and the church fathers who followed
him, Origen also seems to have had personal acquaintance with
Jewish Christians, whom he called Ebionites.[22] He may have gotten

---

[18] Translated from the Greek by A. F. J. Klijn and G. J. Reinink, *Patristic Evidence
for Jewish-Christian Sects* (NovTSup 36; Leiden: E. J. Brill, 1973), 125. The Latin version translated by Rufinus is somewhat different but the note on the origin of the
name of the Ebionites is similar. Unless otherwise indicated, all the translations in
this article—excluding minor corrections—are derived from Klijn and Reinink,
Patristic Evidence.

[19] *Princ.* 4.3.8; *Comm. Matt.* 11.12; 16.12; *Comm. ser. Matt.* 79; *Hom. Luc.* 17; *Hom.
Gen.* 3.5; *Hom. Jer.* 19.12; *Hom. Luc.* 14.18; *Ep. Rom.* 3.11; *Ep. Tit* (ed. Lommatzsch
5, pp. 285–286); *Cels.* 2.1; 5.61 and 5.65. In his last writing that has been preserved,
Contra Celsum, an aged Origen seems to be more tolerant towards the Ebionites and
claims that the Ebionites got their designation from "the poverty which comes from
the law" (*Cels.* 2.1, translation mine).

[20] To be sure, in *Ep. Rom.* 3.11, Ebion is mentioned but probably only in Rufinus'
translation. He probably replaced the term Ebionites with Ebion. Cf. Häkkinen,
Köyhät kerettiläiset, 152.

[21] A fragment of Irenaeus' *Against Heresies*, P. Oxy. 405, has been dated around
the year 200 C.E. Thus, it was read in Egypt before Origen's literary activity.
Naturally, Origen may have had quite a lot of knowledge about the ideas of the
church fathers in Rome because he travelled to Rome before finishing *De Principiis*.
He at least met Hippolytus there (Eusebius, *Hist. eccl.* 6.14.10).

[22] N. R. M. De Lange, *Origen and the Jews: Studies in Jewish-Christian Relations in
Third-Century Palestine* (Cambridge: Cambridge University Press, 1976), 9: "If there
were Jewish communities in Egypt in Origen's time we might expect him to know
something about them; we might even assert that they are the source of his early
information about Judaism, including the knowledge of the Halakhah which he displays in the *de Principiis*."

the name from heresiological catalogues[23] but otherwise his information about the Ebionites seems to be trustworthy, in spite of the polemics.

Eusebius of Caesarea (ca. 263–340 C.E.) knew all the treatises of Origen, which understandably influenced his own views. Following Origen, he describes the Ebionites as poor in understanding (*Hist. eccl.* 3.27.6 and *Eccl. theol.* 1.14)[24] and does not use the personal name Ebion. However, he clearly derives his view of the Ebionites not only from Origen but also from Irenaeus' description of the Ebionites in *Against Heresies*.[25] Eusebius also gives such information about the Ebionites that is not based on any known literary sources. For example, information about the Ebionites' practice of observing both the Sabbath and the Day of the Lord (*Hist. eccl.* 3.27.5), the piece of data that Symmachus belonged to the Ebionites (*Hist. eccl.* 6.17; *Dem. ev.* 7.1),[26] and knowledge of the hometown of the Ebionites (*Onom.* p. 172.1–3). However, it should be noted that Eusebius seems to

---

[23] There is no consensus concerning Origen's competence in Hebrew. He composed the *Hexapla* largely on the basis of an already existing work by Jewish Scribes, as E. Ulrich, "Origen's Old Testament Text: The Transmission History of the Septuagint to the Third Century C.E.," in *Origen of Alexandria: His World and His Legacy* (ed. C. Kannengiesser and W. L. Petersen; Christianity and Judaism in Antiquity 1; Notre Dame: University of Notre Dame Press, 1988), 4, has pointed out. Nevertheless, in the *Hexapla*, the Hebrew word *'ebyon* is transliterated in Greek and translated with the word *ptōchos*, just like in the *Septuagint*. Thus, Origen had the information about the name by the time he was composing the *Hexapla* together with his pupils in Alexandria.

[24] In *Hist. eccl.* 3.27.1 and 6, Eusebius wrote that the Ebionites "held poor and mean opinions concerning Christ" and "in consequence of such a way of life, they received the name Ebionites, which signified the poverty of their understanding. For, this is the name by which a poor man is called among the Hebrews." Eusebius also refers to the Ebionites in *Eccl. theol.* 1.14: "The first preachers of our Saviour himself called them by a Hebrew name Ebionites, indicating them to be poor of understanding. They say they know one God and do not deny the body of the Saviour, but they do not recognise the divinity of the Son."

[25] Cf. Häkkinen, *Köyhät kerettiläiset*, 159–60. Klijn and Reinink, *Patristic Evidence*, 25, claim that Eusebius' source in the section on the Ebionites in *Ecclesiastical History* would have been Hippolytus' *Refutation of All Heresies* but they do not provide any evidence for the theory. R. A. Pritz, *Nazarene Jewish Christianity: From the End of the New Testament Period until Its Disappearance in the Fourth Century* (Leiden: E. J. Brill, 1988), 25–26, (followed by A. F. Segal, "Jewish Christianity," in *Eusebius, Christianity and Judaism* [ed. H. W. Attridge and G. Hata; StPB 42; Leiden: E. J. Brill, 1992], 326–51, esp. 342) holds that Eusebius' sources were both Irenaeus and Hippolytus. H. W. Attridge and G. Hata, "Introduction," in *Eusebius, Christianity and Judaism* (ed. H. W. Attridge and G. Hata), 37, provide a lengthy list of the church fathers cited by Eusebius. Hippolytus is not among them; Irenaeus is included. Their comment that Eusebius knew some of Tertullian's works in Greek translations is also interesting.

[26] In *Demonstratio Evangelica* 7.1 the piece of data is most probably an interpolation based on *Ecclesiastical History*.

have called all Jewish Christians Ebionites. The section that deals
with the Ebionites in *Ecclesiastical History* is located in the third book
of the work, which describes the years 69–117 C.E. Eusebius clearly
places the Ebionites in the past (*Hist. eccl.* 3.27.6; *Eccl. theol.* 1.14 and
1.20). Geographically, he locates them in the far north-east, where
he knew Jewish Christians to have lived.

At the turn of the fourth century, the information about the
Ebionites seems to have been channelled into two different lines of
tradition. A very influential one was based on an early description
of the Ebionites which was used by Irenaeus in his *Against Heresies*,
probably originating from an updated version of Justin Martyr's
Syntagma. The other line of tradition stemmed from Origen and was
more clearly based on some intercourse with Jewish Christians whom
Origen called Ebionites. These two lines of tradition converged during the fourth century, in part already in Eusebius' works. However,
at the end of the fourth century, the amount of data on the Ebionites
was dramatically increased when Epiphanius of Salamis composed
his lengthy treatise on heresies, *Panarion*. It is based on several sources,
including some books used by the heretics.

In order to evaluate the information provided by Epiphanius, it
is important to know something about his personal history. His work
is not solely based on known literary sources because he may also have
had some knowledge based on his own observations and personal
experiences of Jewish Christianity.[27] Epiphanius was born in Judaea
and educated in the monasteries of the area. He continued his studies in Egypt. At the age of about 20, he returned to Palestine and
founded there a monastery which he led for some 30 years until he
was elected the bishop of Salamis in Cyprus in 367 C.E.

Epiphanius said that he used Irenaeus' *Against Heresies*, Hippolytus'
Syntagma (now lost) and *Refutation of All Heresies*, and Eusebius' *Ecclesiastical
History* in the *Panarion*. In addition to these, he utilized some works
used by the heretics themselves. In the section where he deals with the
Ebionites (*Panarion* 30), he refers to the following works: The *Book of
Elchasai*, the gospel used by the Ebionites (the *Gospel according to the
Hebrews*), *Periodoi Petrou*, *Anabathmoi Iakobou* (= the *Ascents of James*) and
a version of the *Acts of the Apostles*, which was different from the

---

[27] This was suggested already by R. A. Lipsius, *Zur Quellenkritik des Epiphanios*
(Wien: W. Braumüller, 1865), 149–50, and especially J. B. Thomas, *Le Mouvement
Baptiste en Palestine et Syrie* (Gembloux: J. Ducolot, 1935), 263.

canonical one. He also notes that the Ebionites had some other books.

Epiphanius also used the *Book of Elchasai*[28] in other sections of the *Panarion*[29] while the other works are referred to only in the section dealing with the Ebionites (*Panarion* 30). The work, named after the leader of the Elchasaites, is now lost but it was cited by both Hippolytus and Epiphanius. It was in Greek except a short Aramaic formula cited by Epiphanius. Usually the work is dated to the last years of the reign of Trajan (98–117). In contrast to Epiphanius, Hippolytus used the work solely in his description of the Elchasaites. Because Hippolytus makes no connections between the Ebionites and the *Book of Elchasai*, it is probable that Epiphanius connected the *Book of Elchasai* to the Ebionites only on the basis of his own reasoning.

Many parallels with the *Pseudo-Clementines*[30] prove that Epiphanius knew Pseudo-Clementine texts and used them especially when he was describing the Ebionites. Epiphanius is the first author to connect the Pseudo-Clementine writings to the Ebionites. However, because the Ebionites are not mentioned by name in the *Pseudo-Clementines*, the connection between the two must be based on Epiphanius' own conclusions. He either got these writings from the Ebionites themselves or he thought them to be Ebionite writings because they so closely resembled the theology of the Ebionites.

Epiphanius provides the largest amount of data on the Ebionites. Despite all the difficulties connected to Epiphanius' works, *Panarion* 30 is the most remarkable source for research on the Ebionites because it also provides material independent of Irenaeus' description.

Epiphanius' contemporary and friend, Jerome, also mentioned the Ebionites several times in his writings. Jerome lived most of his life in the eastern parts of the Roman Empire: Antioch, Constantinople and Bethlehem.[31] He had some contacts with Jewish Christians and he knew at least one Jewish-Christian gospel.

---

[28] For the *Book of Elchasai*, see G. Luttikhuizen's article in the present volume.

[29] In *Panarion* 19.5.4, Epiphanius connects the *Book of Elchasai* to the Nasareans, Ossaeans and Nazarenes, and according to *Panarion* 53.1.3, the book was used, in addition to the Elchasaites, by the Ossaeans, the Nazarenes, the Ebionites and the Sampsaeans. Of these sects, the Ossaeans and the Sampsaeans are known solely from the works of Epiphanius, who may have invented these sects.

[30] For the Pseudo-Clementine literature, see F. S. Jones' article in the present volume.

[31] On Jerome's life, see H. von Campenhausen, *The Fathers of the Latin Church* (trans. Manfred Hoffman; London: Adam & Charles Black, 1963), 129–82, and P. Nautin, "Hieronymus," *TRE* 15:304–15, esp. 304–9.

258   SAKARI HÄKKINEN

Jerome's comments on the Ebionites clearly prove that he knew
quite well what the church fathers had written about them. He considered the Ebionites as a past phenomenon but compared some
contemporary movements and teachers to the Ebionites and Ebion.
He does not have any new information about the Ebionites but his
works are an excellent indication of the construction of the tradition
about the Ebionites in the late fourth century. At first, Jerome seems
to have used the title "the Ebionites" of all Jewish Christians as
Origen and Eusebius had done before him. However, in his *Commentary
on Matthew* from 392 C.E., he began to cite a Jewish-Christian gospel
that he claimed to have received from the Nazarenes. This work was,
according to Jerome, used by both the Nazarenes and the Ebionites
who to him were one and the same movement (*Comm. Matt.* 12.13).
Later he may have made a distinction between the two, considering
the Ebionites heretics and simple-minded Jews (*Comm. Isa.* 1.3, 1.12
and 66.20)[32] and the Nazarenes as believers in Christ, albeit obser-
vant Jews (*Comm. Isa.* 8.11–15, 19–22; 11.1–3 and 19.17–21).[33] The
history of the Ebionites cannot be reconstructed on the basis of
Jerome's writings. After Epiphanius, there was no further new information about the Ebionites; later authors base their views on earlier writings.

3. *The Literature Used by the Ebionites*

We have already seen that all information about the practices and
theology of the Ebionites comes from patristic writings. The same
holds true concerning our knowledge about the literature used by
the Ebionites. According to Irenaeus (*Haer.* 1.26.2), the Ebionites
observed the Torah and practiced the Jewish way of life. On the
other hand, Epiphanius states that the Ebionites "do not accept the
whole Pentateuch of Moses but leave certain passages aside" (*Pan.*

---

[32] In *Comm. Isa.* 66.20, Jerome calls the Ebionites "Jews and heirs of Jewish heresy"
and claims that they were millenarians. More than giving historical information
about the millenarian faith of the Ebionites, this comment illuminates Jerome's own
views according to which the Ebionites were literalists and poor in reason (this he
derived from Origen). As a matter of fact, in Jerome's view, everyone who understands
the Scriptures "just as they were written" is a Jewish Ebionite lacking reason.
[33] A. F. J. Klijn, *Jewish-Christian Gospel Tradition* (Supplements to Vigiliae christianae
17; Leiden: E. J. Brill 1992), 18–19. For the distinction, see also P. Luomanen's
article in this volume.

30.18.7). As examples, he presents disputes about eating meat and sacrificing. However, Epiphanius' information is not very trustworthy since it is derived from the *Book of Elchasai*, which may not have had anything to do with the Ebionites.[34]

According to Irenaeus, the Ebionites also read the Prophets although they interpreted them "in a curious way" (*curiosius exponere*). This theme is never again dealt with in Irenaeus' work and the meaning remains a bit unclear.[35] Irenaeus' note may also have appeared obscure to the church fathers who based their descriptions of the Ebionites on Irenaeus' work since this particular theme is not cited by them. According to Methodius of Olympos (ca. 300 C.E.; *Symposium* 8.10), the Ebionites "say out of contentiousness that the prophets spoke of their own accord." The passage is the only one where Methodius mentioned the Ebionites. The brief comment may indicate that the Ebionites did not value the prophets very much. Unfortunately, not much can be said about the sources of this polemical comment and about its trustworthiness. Epiphanius notes (*Pan.* 30.15.2 and 30.18.9) that the Ebionites detest Elia, David, Samson, and all the prophets. Probably Epiphanius quotes here the Pseudo-Clementine literature, which seems to cohere very well with Irenaeus' comment about the Ebionites' way of reading the prophets in a curious way. *Homilies* deals with the "error of the prophets" (*Hom.* 3.53), and in *Hom.* 3.25.5 it is said that the "the prophecy of his [Cain's] descendants

---

[34] Epiphanius states in *Panarion* 18.1 and 19.5 that the Nasareans and the Ossaeans used a Pentateuch that did not include the sacrificial laws. His source for this is also the *Book of Elchasai*.

[35] Maybe Irenaeus has understood the saying to have referred to the interpretation of Isa 7:14, which was much disputed in early Christianity. Irenaeus himself refers to the passage in the third book of *Against Heresies* (3.21.1) and says how the Ebionites follow a Jewish translation that translates the Hebrew word ʿalmah by the Greek word *neanis*, which means "young woman," and not by the word *parthenos*, which can also mean a virgin (but not necessarily) and was used in the Septuagint. Another possibility for understanding the concept *curiosius exponere* is to compare it with a similar concept in Tertullian's work *Praescr.* 8–12, 14, where *curiositas* is seen as the motive for the continuous questioning typical of Greek philosophy and, as such, leading to heresy. Whatever the original expression in Greek was, at least the person who translated Irenaeus' work into Latin could have understood the expression he translated as *curiosius exponere* to have referred to Greek philosophical interpretative tradition. H.-J. Schoeps, *Theologie und Geschichte des Judenchristentums* (Tübingen: J. C. B. Mohr [Paul Siebeck], 1949), 159, 166 and 466, and G. Lüdemann, *Paulus, der Heidenapostel: Band II. Antipaulinismus im frühen Christentum* (FRLANT 130; Göttingen: Vandenhoeck & Ruprecht, 1983), 259, interpret the expression *curiosius exponere* as a criticism towards the prophetic writings.

being full of adulterers and of psalteries, secretly by means of pleasures excites to wars." The Pseudo-Clementine literature also criticizes the Old Testament, holding some passages to be false although
the prophets are not explicitly mentioned (*Hom.* 2.51 and 18.19).
Epiphanius notes that the Ebionites regarded Jesus as the "true
prophet" and that, for them, the prophets were only "prophets of
reason and not of truth" (*Panarion* 30.18.5).

According to Irenaeus, the Ebionites used only the "Gospel according to Matthew" (*Haer.* 1.26.2 and 3.11.7).[36] He does not give any
hint that the gospel would have deviated from the Gospel of Matthew
that he himself used. Indeed, because Irenaeus thought that the main
error of the Ebionites was the rejection of the virgin birth, he probably
would have referred to the birth and childhood narratives or to their
absence in the gospel used by the Ebionites if he had had access to
the work.[37] It is unlikely that Irenaeus had first hand knowledge
about the gospel used by the Ebionites. The church fathers, who
based their information about the Ebionites on Irenaeus' work, did
not show any interest in the Ebionites' use of the Gospel of Matthew.

Origen also implies that the Ebionites used the Gospel of Matthew.
He writes (*Princ.* 4.3.8) that the Ebionites understand literally the
words of Jesus in Matt 10:6: "I was sent only to the lost sheep of
the house of Israel." The passage occurs only in the Gospel of
Matthew. Origen does not explicitly refer to the gospel used by the
Ebionites but he seems to have known that the Ebionites understood
this particular passage to mean that Jesus came only for the Jews.

Origen also mentioned the *Gospel according to the Hebrews* and even
cites it (*Comm. Jo.* 2.12; *Hom. Jer.* 15.4 and *Comm. Matt.* 15.4) but he
never connects it to the Ebionites. Eusebius, who based his infor-

---

[36] Klijn, *Jewish-Christian Gospel Tradition*, 4, thinks that this is only Irenaeus' own
conclusion. In my opinion, this piece of data has probably come from the source
used by Irenaeus. According to Klijn, Irenaeus would also have thought that the
Gospel of Matthew was originally written in Hebrew because it was meant for
Jewish Christians. However, Irenaeus does not deal with the language of the gospel
that the Ebionites used. He seems to suppose that it was written in Greek and did
not deviate from his own Gospel of Matthew. Irenaeus writes (*Haer.* 3.1.1) that the
Gospel of Matthew was originally written in "Hebrew dialect" but he never connects this Hebrew version of the gospel to the Ebionites. According to Irenaeus, it
was not written for Christians but for Jews.
[37] At least he might have noticed the citation in Matt 1:23 of Isa 7:14 "a virgin will conceive." He seems to suppose that it was also included in the gospel used
by the Ebionites!

mation about the Ebionites on both Origen and early heresiologies, argues: "They used only the so-called *Gospel according to the Hebrews* and made small account of the rest" (*Hist. eccl.* 3.27.4). Obviously, Eusebius himself did not know the *Gospel according to the Hebrews*, since he never cited it.[38] Yet, he seems to have thought that the Ebionites used precisely that gospel. On the other hand, he states (*Hist. eccl.* 6.17) that Symmachus, whom Eusebius considered an Ebionite, "appears to support this heresy by attacking[39] the Gospel of Matthew." The incoherence of Eusebius' comments is understandable because Eusebius called all Jewish Christians Ebionites.

Obviously influenced by Eusebius, Epiphanius stated (*Pan.* 30.3.7): "They accept the Gospel according to Matthew. For they too use only this like the followers of Cerinthus and Merinthus.[40] They call it 'according to the Hebrews' which name is correct since Matthew is the only one in the New Testament who issued the Gospel and the proclamation in Hebrew and with Hebrew Letters." On the one hand, Epiphanius believed—probably due to having read Irenaeus' *Against Heresies*—that the Gospel according to Matthew was written in Hebrew and that the Ebionites used the same gospel, calling it the *Gospel according to the Hebrews*. On the other hand, Epiphanius possessed the gospel used by the Ebionites and it was in Greek as can be seen from his quotations from it. Thus, Epiphanius had a problem: his patristic sources stated that the Ebionites used only the Hebrew Gospel of Matthew, which Epiphanius had never seen (probably no one had), but the gospel he possessed and regarded as used by the Ebionites was in Greek.[41] Epiphanius solves the problem in

---

[38] In *Hist. eccl.* 3.25.5 he includes the *Gospel according to the Hebrews* in the list of disputable writings. In 3.39.16–17, he cites Papias and in 4.25.1, he says that Hegesippus used the *Gospel according to the Hebrews*. In none of these passages does he connect this gospel to the Ebionites.

[39] Translation by Klijn and Reinink, *Patristic Evidence*, 147. The Greek word is *apoteinomenos*, which normally means "stretching out" or "lengthening." Eusebius probably thinks that Symmachus made some alterations to the text of the Gospel of Matthew. The translation "attacking" is not the best possible since the Ebionites seem to have accepted the Gospel of Matthew but perhaps in a different version. By "lengthening," Eusebius may even refer to a gospel harmony that bore the title of the Gospel of Matthew, like the gospel that Epiphanius cites as the gospel used by the Ebionites.

[40] Cerinthus and Merinthus were presented in *Pan.* 28. Probably they were one person, although Epiphanius seems to be unsure. Cf. Hilgenfeld, *Ketzergeschichte*, 417.

[41] The strongest evidence on that, that the gospel was not a translation from

Panarion by relating—right after having mentioned the gospel—a lengthy story about Joseph of Tiberias who had told Epiphanius that he found Hebrew Christian literature in a secret Jewish treasury (geniza) in Tiberias: the Gospel according to John, the Acts of the Apostles and the Gospel according to Matthew. Thus, the fact that almost no one had ever seen these works in Hebrew was to be explained by the secrecy of the treasury in Tiberias.[42]

Epiphanius claims that the Ebionites used the Gospel according to Matthew "which is not complete but falsified and distorted" (*Pan.* 30.13.2).[43] The quotations clearly indicate that the gospel was a harmony that was based on the synoptic gospels.[44] It includes remarkably close parallels to all the synoptic gospels and especially to the material only used in Luke's gospel. The gospel does not differ very much from the synoptic gospels but it reflects the theology of the Ebionites very well. The gospel begins with the work of John the Baptist (*Pan.* 30.13.6 and 14.3) and it does not have any birth or childhood narratives. Instead of locusts, John the Baptist ate honey cakes (30.14.4), which was more suited to the Ebionites who avoided meat. In the passage about Jesus' baptism, the gospel cites a clause from the psalms that better fits with the Ebionite theology than the one in the synoptic gospels: "Today I have concieved you." However, the clause cited by the synoptics also is presented: "In you I

Hebrew to Greek, is Epiphanius's redaction critical notice on the Greek negative that was added into the text (*Pan.* 30.22.3), but also other quotations make it clear that the gospel was based on the synoptic gospels.

[42] Naturally, the lengthy story about Joseph, which has nothing to do with the Ebionites, also had other motives. Cf. Häkkinen, *Köyhät kerettiläiset*, 200–204. On the story of Joseph: G. A. Koch, "A Critical Investigation of Epiphanius' Knowledge of the Ebionites: A Translation and Critical Discussion of *Panarion* 30" (Ph.D. diss., University of Pennsylvania, 1976), 374–83; S. J. Goranson, "Joseph of Tiberias Episode in Epiphanius: Studies in Jewish and Christian Relations" (Ph.D. diss., Duke University, 1990).

[43] The text includes only a probable interpolation "they call it the Hebrew Gospel."

[44] D. A. Bertrand, "L'Evangile des ébionites: une harmonie évangélique antérieure au Diatessaron," *NTS* 26 (1979): 548–63, holds that the gospel used by the Ebionites was a harmony comparable to the *Diatessaron*. This view is dealt with by G. Howard, "The Gospel of the Ebionites," *ANRW* 25.5: 4034–53 esp. 4037–39, who gives a good description of early Christian gospel harmonies. According to Howard, the "tendency [of the gospel used by the Ebionites] to harmonize must be viewed as a normal technique of composition widely used in the early patristic period" (4039). P. Vielhauer and G. Strecker, "Jewish-Christian Gospels," in *New Testament Apocrypha* (ed. W. Schneemelcher; trans. and ed. R. McL. Wilson; 2 vols.; Cambridge: James Clarke & Co., 1991), 1:140, also hold the gospel used by the Ebionites to be a harmony based on the synoptic gospels.

am pleased." The passages cited by Epiphanius are common to the synoptic gospels except one saying of Jesus (30.16.5): "I have come to abolish sacrifices and if you do not stop sacrificing, the wrath will not cease from you."

The gospel quoted by Epiphanius is usually dated to the second century. The use of the synoptic gospels (and possibly also Acts) indicates that the gospel used by the Ebionites probably did not yet exist in the first century. On the other hand, the fact that, according to Irenaeus—who wrote at the end of the second century—the Ebionites only used the Gospel of Matthew, indicates that the source used by Irenaeus probably knew that the Ebionites accepted only one gospel that was called by them the Gospel according to Matthew. If this gospel was not the one that was later canonized but the gospel cited by Epiphanius two centuries later, the gospel used by the Ebionites could be dated to the first half of the second century.[45]

Epiphanius also presents other books that he thought the Ebionites used (*Pan.* 30.15–16). *Periodoi Petrou* which Epiphanius used as a source in *Panarion* 30, had the name of Clement of Rome attached to it but he was not the real author. Obviously, Epiphanius did not know any other version of the work except the one used by the Ebionites, which he believed had been falsified because the contents of the book deviated so much from Clement's proclamation. The work used by Epiphanius has not been successfully reconstructed although there are clear parallels to his quotations in the Pseudo-Clementine literature. For this reason, it is also impossible to date the work.

According to Epiphanius, the Ebionites "also mention other Acts of Apostles in which is much that is full of impiety" (*Pan.* 30.16.6). The comment indicates that the Acts mentioned by the Ebionites was not the same work that was known to Epiphanius. Indeed, keeping in mind the Ebionites' opposition to Paul, it would have been strange if they had used the canonical Acts. Epiphanius says next to

---

[45] According to S. C. Mimouni, *Le judéo-christianisme ancien: essais historiques* (Paris: Cerf, 1998), 260, the lack of parallels to the fourth gospel proves that the *terminus ad quem* of the Ebionite gospel must be around 150 C.E. Mimouni also holds it possible that Justin Martyr cited the gospel in 135 C.E. Furthermore, the comparable gospel harmonies of Justin and Tatian point to the middle or the latter half of the second century. Bertrand, "L'Evangile des ébionites," 548–63; Howard, "The Gospel of the Ebionites," 4037–39.

nothing of the book and he does not even claim to have seen it.[46]
However, it is interesting that a little bit further along *Panarion* (30.6.8),
Epiphanius states that the Ebionites quoted a passage from the canonical Acts (21:39). The explanation of the poverty of the Ebionites was,
according to them, derived from the story told in *Acts* (*Pan.* 30.17.2):
"But they themselves are obviously proud of themselves saying that
they are poor because they say, they sold their belongings in the
time of the apostles and laid the money at the feet of the apostles
and because they looked for poverty and the abolition of worldly
goods. And, therefore, they say, everyone calls us poor ones." The
connection to Acts 4:34–35 is obvious. It is clear that the Ebionites
were committed to poverty and traced their origin back to the first
Christian community in Jerusalem. For them, Acts 4:32–35 was a
foundation story. Was the Acts used by the Ebionites an abbreviated
version of the canonical Acts of the Apostles? The connections between
the gospel used by the Ebionites and Acts are also noteworthy. The
Acts used by the Ebionites may have been based on the canonical
Acts which was edited by the Ebionites.

Epiphanius notes that the Ebionites "bring a charge against Paul . . .
they declare that he is of Greek descent . . . He is a Greek, the child
of a Greek mother and a Greek father; that he went up to Jerusalem
and stayed there for a time; that he desired to marry the daughter
of a priest and therefore became a proselyte and that he had himself
circumcised and that, since he could not receive such a girl as his wife,
he became angry and wrote against circumcision, the Sabbath and
the legislation" (*Pan.* 30.16.8–9). Because the story is not known from
any other source, it may have belonged to the Acts used by the
Ebionites.

According to Epiphanius (*Pan.* 30.16.7), the Ebionites also used a
work called *Anabathmoi Iakobou*. As regards the contents of the book,
he notes: "In the *Anabathmoi Iakobou* they accept some 'steps' and stories for example that he preaches against the temple and the sacrifice,
against fire on the altar and they accept many other things full of
empty talk." Some scholars have thought that the work is to be

---

[46] Schoeps, *Theologie*, 437–38, 453–54, made a reconstruction of the Acts used by
the Ebionites on the basis of the Pseudo-Clementine literature. He suggested that
the *Anabathmoi Iakobou* mentioned by Epiphanius was originally an independent source
of the Ebionite Acts.

found in the Pseudo-Clementine *Recognitiones* 1.27–71[47] but that idea has not been unreservedly accepted.[48] Epiphanius does not cite *Anabathmoi Iakobou* but he has clearly known the work that was used in *Recognitiones* 1.27–71 because, when he describes the death of James in *Panarion* 78.13–14, he clearly alludes to *Rec.* 1.70.

4. *The Theology of the Ebionites*

The earliest available description of the Ebionites, Irenaeus' *Against Heresies* 1.26.2, was especially concerned with the theology of the Ebionites:

> Those who are called Ebionites, then, agree that the world was made by God; but their opinions with regard to the Lord are similar[49] to those of Cerinthus and Carpocrates. They use the Gospel according to Matthew only and repudiate the apostle Paul, saying that he was apostate from the Law. As to the prophetical writings, they do their best to expound them diligently; they practice circumcision, persevere in the customs which are according to the Law and practice a Jewish way of life, even adoring Jerusalem as if it were the house of God.

According to Irenaeus, the Ebionites were monotheists, which sounds self-evident when speaking of Jewish Christians. However, in the catalogue of heresies presented by Irenaeus, there are also such movements

---

[47] Hilgenfeld, *Ketzergeschichte*, 45–52, and Lipsius, *Zur Quellenkritik*, already thought that *Rec.* 1.27–71 is based on one of the sources of the *Recognitiones*. The first scholar who made the connection between *Anabathmoi Iakobou* and *Rec.* 1.27–71 was G. Uhlhorn, *Die Homilien und Recognitionen des Clemens Romanus nach ihrem Ursprung und Inhalt dargestellt* (Göttingen: Dieterich, 1854) 367. Van Voorst has written a monograph on the subject: R. E. Van Voorst, *The Ascents of James: History and Theology of a Jewish Christian Community* (SBLDS 112; Atlanta, Ga.: Scholars Press, 1989).

[48] F. S. Jones, *An Ancient Jewish Christian Source on the History of Christianity: Pseudo-Clementine Recognitions 1:27–71* (SBLTT 37; Christian Apocrypha Series 2; Atlanta, Ga.: Scholars Press, 1995), 35: "Though Epiphanius evidently did know an actual writing entitled *Anabathmoi Iakobou* (contra Schmidtke), there is no sufficient reason to bring this writing into an unusually close relationship with R 1.27–71."

[49] According to the early Latin translation of *Against Heresies*, the Ebionites' Christology was not similar to Cerinthus' and Carpocrates' Christology: "ea autem quae sunt erga Dominum non similiter ut Cerinthus et Carpocrates opinantur." However, the negative is not original for the following reasons: 1) the passage has also been preserved in a Greek fragment where the negative is absent. 2) Hippolytus, who used *Against Heresies* as a source for his *Refutation*, seemed not to have been aware of the negative (*Haer.* 7.34). 3) If the negative was original, the reader would wait to be told something about the deviating Christology of the Ebionites. This does not happen.

that believed in several gods in addition to the Supreme God. One
of these lower gods was the Creator God (or a spirit, in some movements), who had created the world. Cerinthus—whose heresy was
described just before the Ebionites in the catalogue—also had a belief
like this. Therefore, it was necessary to point out that the Ebionites
believed in one God who was also the creator of the world.

According to Irenaeus, the greatest mistake of the Ebionites was
their Christology. In the latter parts of his work, Irenaeus especially
takes the wrong opinions of the Ebionites on Christ as the reason
for condemning them.[50] This feature is significant in all heresiologies written after Irenaeus. In Irenaeus' catalogue, the Ebionites'
views were identified with Cerinthus' and Carpocrates' Christologies.
According to Cerinthus, "Jesus was not born of a virgin, but he was
the son of Joseph and Mary, an ordinary man, though more versed
in righteousness, prudence and wisdom than other men." After his
baptism, a spirit named Christ descended upon him from the Supreme
God in the form of a dove. Possessed by this spirit, Jesus proclaimed
the unknown Father and performed miracles. At last, the Christ-
spirit flew away from Jesus before his passion and resurrection
(Irenaeus, *Haer.* 1.26.1). The Christology of Carpocrates was similar
to that of Cerinthus (1.25.1). Early Christian authors understood
almost without exception that the Christology of the Ebionites was
similar to that of Cerinthus, whose disciple Ebion was considered to
have been.[51] In contrast, Origen, whose data on the Ebionites is not
based on the catalogues, never connected the Ebionites or Ebion to
Cerinthus. Still, Origen also maintains that the Ebionites err in denying the virgin birth (*Hom. Luc.* 17; *Ep. Tit.*). Following him, Eusebius
presented a general view, according to which the Ebionites claimed
that Christ was born of Joseph and Mary (*Hist. eccl.* 5.8.10 and 6.17).
On the other hand, both Origen (*Comm. Matt.* 16.12; *Cels.* 5.61) and

---

[50] In *Haer.* 5.1.3, Irenaeus writes about the virgin birth and condemns the Ebionites
who do not accept it. He uses here the expression taken from the liturgy of his
church: *commixtio.* Just like water and wine are mixed in the chalice, the human
and divine nature are mixed in Jesus: "[the Ebionites] do not receive by faith into
their soul the union of God and man ... [and] reject the commixture of the heavenly wine and wish it to be water of the world only, not receiving God so as to
have union with Him." Epiphanius (*Pan.* 30.16) already thought, however, that
Irenaeus is writing on the Ebionite way of celebrating the Eucharist only with water.
This is not expressed by Irenaeus.

[51] Hippolytus, *Haer.* 7.35.1; Pseudo-Tertullian, *Adversus omnes haereses* 3; Victorinus
of Pettau, *Comm. Apoc.* 9.1; Filastrius, *Diversarum haereseon liber* 37.

Eusebius (*Hist. eccl.* 3.27.2–3) claimed that some of the Ebionites accepted the virgin birth.[52] It is worth remembering that both of these church fathers called all Jewish Christians Ebionites.

Epiphanius also has a lot of information about the Christology of the Ebionites. He also knows that the Ebionites had two different views about Jesus' birth (*Pan.* 30.3.1–2). Epiphanius interprets the inconsistent data of his sources so that the doctrine of the Ebionites must have changed under the influence of Elchasai.[53] Epiphanius describes the Christology of the Ebionites as many as four times. The description is similar to the one given by Irenaeus (*Haer.* 1.26.1) of the Christology of Cerinthus:

> For some of them even say that Adam is Christ—the man who was formed first and infused with God's breath. But others among them say that Christ is from above; that he was created before all things; that he is a spirit, higher than the angels and ruler of all; that he is called Christ, and the world there is his portion. But he comes here when he chooses, as he came in Adam and appeared to the patriarchs with Adam's body on. And in the last days the same Christ who had come to Abraham, Isaac and Jacob came and put on Adam's body, and he appeared to men, was crucified, rose and ascended. (*Pan.* 30.3.3–6)
>
> This is because they mean that Jesus is really a man, as I said, but that Christ, who descended in the form of a dove, has entered him— as we have found already in other sects—<and> been united with him. Christ himself <is from God on high, but Jesus> is the product of a man's seed and a woman. (*Pan.* 30.14.4)
>
> And they say that this is why Jesus was begotten of the seed of a man and chosen, and thus named Son of God by election, after the Christ who had come to him from on high in the form of a dove. (*Pan.* 30.16.3)
>
> They say, however, that Christ is prophet of truth and Christ; <but> that he is Son of God by promotion, and by his connection with the elevation given to him from above.[54] ... He alone, they would have it, is prophet, man, Son of God, and Christ—and yet a mere man, as I said, though owing to virtue of life he has come to be called the Son of God. (*Pan.* 30.18.5–6)[55]

---

[52] Obviously, Theodoret of Cyrrhus (*Compendium haereticorum fabularum* 2.1) and the writer of *Hypomnestikon* (140.5–6), derived their descriptions of the Ebionites from Origen or Eusebius.

[53] See also *Pan.* 30.34.6.

[54] The passage is translated differently by Klijn and Reinink: "Christ they call the prophet of truth and 'Christ, the Son of God' on account of his progress (in virtue) and the exaltation which descended upon him from above."

[55] Translations from *The Panarion of Epiphanius of Salamis: Book I (Sects 1–46)* (trans. F. Williams; NHS 35; Leiden: E. J. Brill, 1987).

It seems like Epiphanius had difficulties in understanding the Ebionite Christology. The difficulties were caused by the differences in his sources: the descriptions of the Ebionites by Irenaeus and Hippolytus, and the *Book of Elchasai*.[56] The view of Adam as Christ and Christ as a spirit above all others who appears to the world whenever it chooses can also be found in the *Pseudo-Clementines*.[57]

The gospel used by the Ebionites also reflects the type of Christology presented above. Naturally, it did not include the birth- and child-hood narratives (*Pan.* 30.14.2). The narrative about the baptism of Jesus (*Pan.* 30.13.7) told how the Spirit descended into Jesus in the form of a dove. A heavenly voice proclaimed: " 'Thou art my beloved Son, in thee I am well pleased,' and again 'This day I have begot-ten thee.' "

Traditionally, the Ebionites' Christology is characterized as adop-tionistic. Its basic idea is that God adopted Jesus as His son at the moment of Jesus' baptism. However, Goulder has also characterized the Ebionites Christology as "possession Christology."[58] The title crys-tallizes the Ebionite view of what happened to Jesus when he was baptized: God's Spirit possessed him and he was possessed of that Spirit until his death. This Spirit was called Christ by the Ebionites.[59] The Christ-spirit left Jesus, though, on the cross. The words in the Gospel of Matthew connected to Jesus' death, *aphēken to pneuma*, can be understood in two ways: either Jesus "gave his [last] breath" or "the Spirit left him." Obviously, the Ebionites understood the expres-sion in the latter way.

Interestingly, similar Christology can already be found in the oldest parts of the New Testament: Paul's letters and the Gospel of Mark. Although the canonical Scriptures mainly present the views of the "orthodox" church (i.e., those who "won the battle"), which rejected the Ebionite Christology, an older, possessionist Christology can be seen in the background of several New Testament books. Goulder

---

[56] Cf. Hippolytus, *Haer.* 9.14.1, which is derived from the *Book of Elchasai*.

[57] *Homilies* 3.19–21; 8.10; *Recognitiones* 1.32.4–33.2; 1.45–47; 1.52 (Armenian and Latin translations); 4.9. Jones, *Ancient Jewish Christian Source*, 123, believes that Epiphanius used here *Recognitiones* 1.32.4–33.2.

[58] M. D. Goulder, *St. Paul versus St. Peter: A Tale of Two Missions* (Louisville, Ky.: Westminster John Knox Press, 1995), 99–106.

[59] The formula "Jesus is Christ" used in the Pauline congregations could also be understood as rejecting the view of the Ebionites that Jesus was "only" possessed by the Spirit. See Goulder, *St. Paul versus St. Peter*, 121–27.

even thinks that this is the oldest known Christology.[60] Goulder connects the "possessionist Christology" especially to Jerusalem, and to
Peter,[61] but I can see no reason why "possessionist Christology" would
have expressly developed in Jerusalem. In any case, the Ebionites
seem to have preserved a view of Christ that preceded the New
Testament.

Sometimes the church fathers also connect other Christological
models to the Ebionites. For example, Tertullian connects the Ebionite
Christology he knew from the literature to an angelomorphic Christology of which he had better knowledge. According to him, the Ebionites
believed that an angel was in Jesus (*Carn. Chr.* 14).[62] Angelomorphic
Christology was indeed quite close to the Ebionite Christology if the
spirit in Jesus is understood as an angelic being. Epiphanius, for his
part, related a Christological model he found in the *Book of Elchasai*
to the Ebionite Christology, and claimed that the Ebionites believed,
like Elchasai, that Christ was a gigantic figure whose measures were
known to them (*Pan.* 30.17.5–7). Since the description is clearly

---

[60] Goulder, *St. Paul versus St. Peter*, 128–34. On page 134, Goulder writes: "So
the 'Ebionite' christology, which we found first described in Irenaeus about 180 is
not the invention of the late second century. It was the creed of the Jerusalem
church from early times. It underlies the earliest Pauline Gospel, Mark, and is evi-
denced from the middle 50s in Paul's first letter to Corinth, where people sometimes cursed Jesus in church. . . . The Paulines became the church, and in time they
called the Jerusalem mission Ebionites, and made them a heresy." Goulder's work
does not include a bibliography but his views fit quite well to those of G. W. H.
Lampe, "The Holy Spirit and the Person of Christ," in *Christ, Faith and History* (ed.
S. W. Sykes and J. P. Clayton; Cambridge: Cambridge University Press, 1972),
117: "The category of Spirit-possession was used to some extent in early Christian
thought to interpret not only Christ's present relationship to believers but also his
relationship to God. If believers are sons of God through the indwelling of God's
spirit, possessing their souls and reshaping their lives according to the pattern of
Christ, can Christ's own sonship be interpreted in the same terms? The gospel suggests this possibility. In the synoptists Spirit-possession and messianic sonship are
linked together in the narrative of Christ's baptism. The Spirit descends upon him
and he receives the divine assurance that he is Son of God. . . . The early church
felt constrained to interpret Jesus in terms of deity 'coming down' to the human
sphere in his person. It might be expected that the most appropriate concept for
the expression of this image would be Spirit-possession." For a similar view, see
also S. L. Davies, *Jesus the Healer: Possession, Trance and the Origins of Christianity* (New
York: Continuum, 1995), 18–21.

[61] M. D. Goulder, "The Pre-Marcan Gospel," *SJT* 47 (1994): 454–55; Goulder,
St. Paul versus St. Peter, 134.

[62] Angelomorphic Christology in Tertullian's works is dealt with by Gieschen,
Angelomorphic Christology, 193–94.

derived from the *Book of Elchasai*, it is not at all certain that the Ebionites shared this view, although Epiphanius so argued.[63]

Although their Christology was regarded as the greatest heresy of the Ebionites, Irenaeus' description also contains some other deviant views. Among other things, the Ebionites repudiated Paul whom they considered an apostate. This piece of data is confirmed by a brief note in Origen's *Cels.* 5.65.[64] Origen also writes that "up to the present day the Ebionites strike the Apostle of Jesus Christ with shameful words incited by the unlawful word of the high priest" (*Hom. Jer.* 19.12). With the expression "shameful words," Origen may have referred to the story about Paul's Greek origin, unhappy attraction to the priest's daughter and the following anger that was poured out in writing against the law—the story possibly derived from the Ebionites' "other Acts" (*Pan.* 30.16.8–9; see above).[65]

From Paul's own letters, we know that he had several opponents in almost all the provinces of Asia and Achaea, even in the congregations he had founded himself. Supposedly, most of the opponents were Jews who strictly held to the observance of the Torah.[66] According to Galatians 2:11–14 and Acts 21:21, Paul also had opponents in Jerusalem.[67] In early Egyptian Christianity, Paul was criticized for abandoning the Torah.[68]

---

[63] Close parallels are also attested in the *Pseudo-Clementines: Rec.* 1.24.5; *Hom.* 20.2–3; *Rec.* 2.42.5.

[64] "For there are some heresies like the Ebionites, both groups, and the so-called Enkratites, which do not accept the letters of Paul." Following Irenaeus and Origen, the same thing is also stated by Eusebius, *Hist. eccl.* 3.27.4, and Jerome, *Comm. Matt.* 12.2, and Theodoret of Cyrrhus, *Compendium haereticorum fabularum* 2.1.

[65] The same story is also referred to by Epiphanius in *Pan.* 30.25.1. It is noteworthy that in Origen's brief note the high priest is also mentioned.

[66] This is emphasized by Mark Nanos in *The Irony of Galatians: Paul's Letter in First-Century Context* (Minneapolis, Minn.: Fortress, 2002), 143–52.

[67] Many scholars see here a clear allusion to the pre-70 Jerusalem Christianity, since the opponents of Paul came chiefly from Jerusalem until 70 C.E. See, for example, E. Käsemann, "Die Legitimität des Apostels," *ZNW* 41 (1942): 33–71; G. Friedrich, "Die Gegner des Paulus im 2. Korintherbrief," in *Abraham unser Vater: Festschrift für O. Michel* (ed. O. Betz, M. Hengel, and P. Schmidt; Leiden: E. J. Brill 1963), 181–215; D. Georgi, *Die Gegner des Paulus im 2. Korintherbrief: Studien zur religiösen Propaganda in der Spätantike* (WMANT 11; Neukirchen-Vluyn: Neukirchener Verlag, 1964), 58; C. K. Barrett, *A Commentary on The First Epistle to the Corinthians* (2nd ed.; BNTC; London: Adam & Charles Black, 1971), 251; G. Theissen, *Social Setting of Pauline Christianity: Essays on Corinth by Gerd Theissen* (ed. and trans. and with an Introduction by John H. Schütz; Philadelphia: Fortress, 1982), 50, and Lüdemann, *Heretics*, 53.

[68] A. F. J. Klijn, "Jewish Christianity in Egypt," in *The Roots of Egyptian Christianity* (ed. B. A. Pearson and J. E. Goehring; SAC; Philadelphia: Fortress, 1986), 174.

The repudiation of Paul by the Ebionites was connected to the observance of the Torah, including the practice of circumcision. A close adherence to Judaism is also attested by Irenaeus' comment that the Ebionites were "adoring Jerusalem as if it were the house of God." The expression means the typical prayer orientation towards Jerusalem[69] and it cannot be used as evidence of the origins of the Ebionites in Jerusalem.[70] As the Ebionites were committed to Jewish traditions, it was natural that they also prayed like Jews.

Most of the church fathers after Irenaeus do not have any information about the Ebionites' theology besides their Christology. An exception is Epiphanius, whose lengthy report includes several descriptions of the Ebionites' theological views and religious practices. According to Epiphanius, the Ebionites strictly obeyed different kinds of purity rules and rites (*Pan.* 30.2.3–5), forbade virginity and celibacy (*Pan.* 30.2.6–7; 30.15.2; 30.18.2–3),[71] were vegetarians (*Pan.* 30.15.3) and recited spells (*Pan.* 30.17.4).[72] According to Epiphanius (*Pan.* 30.18.2), their congregational life was arranged the same way as in Jewish communites: "Ebionites have elders and heads of synagogues, and they call their church a synagogue, not a church." In addition to daily purifying baptisms, they also accepted the Christian baptism and celebrated the Eucharistic meal once a year (*Pan.* 30.16.1).[73]

The Ebionites emphasized their heritage was from the earliest Christianity in Jerusalem. However, this was done by teachers in almost all Christian movements of the time, including the church fathers.

---

[69] Originally, all Christians probably prayed towards Jerusalem. The position was later changed to the east. Cf. F. J. Dölger, *Sol Salutis: Gebet und Gesang im christlichen Altertum: Mit besonderer Rücksicht auf die Ostung in Gebet und Liturgie* (2nd ed.; Liturgiegeschichtliche Quellen und Forschungen 16–17; Münster: Aschendorff, 1925), 170.

[70] In contrast to G. Lindeskog, *Das jüdisch-christliche Problem: Randglossen zu einer Forschungsepoche* (Acta Universitatis Upsaliensis; Historia Religionum 9; Stockholm: Almqvist & Wiksell, 1986), 58; Goulder, *St. Paul versus St. Peter*, 109; and Lüdemann, *Heretics*, 53.

[71] While claiming that the Ebionites forbade virginity (*Pan.* 30.2.6), Epiphanius clearly used the *Book of Elchasai*. Cf. Häkkinen, *Köyhät kerettiläiset*, 192–93. In the same passage, Epiphanius refers to some other sects of the same kind, by which he means probably the sects (invented by himself?) that used the *Book of Elchasai*.

[72] The spell cited is derived from the *Book of Elchasai*; cf. Hippolytus, *Haer.* 9.13.2–3 and Epiphanius, *Pan.* 19.4.1–2 and 53.1.9. There is a close parallel for the spell also in Pseudo-Clementine literature: *Contestatio* 2.1 and 4.1.

[73] Similar stories can also be found in the Pseudo-Clementine Literature. Peter's daily baptisms: *Hom.* 1.10 and 11.1.1; *Rec.* 4.3.1; 4.36.3 and 8.1.1. Peter abstaining from meat: *Hom.* 8.15.4 and 12.6.4; *Rec.* 7.6.4.

A claim of "apostolic heritage" cannot be denied to any of the movements that are called Christian. Jerusalem was regarded as the place
of birth of Christianity and the home of the first Christians. Many
scholars have suggested that the Ebionites preserved the early traditions
and ideas more faithfully than any other Christian movement.[74] This
suggestion is based on a hypothesis that there are more or less clear
parallels between the Ebionite religion and the early Jerusalem
Christianity. The problem is that the former is known only through
texts that opposed the Ebionites from late second century onwards,
and the latter mostly from post-70 writings, now part of the New
Testament.

5. Where Did the Ebionites Live?

The earliest references to the Ebionites do not include any hint of
the areas where the Ebionites lived. Irenaeus' description of the
Ebionites (Haer. 1.26.2), probably written in Lyons, suggests that
Irenaeus himself did not have any personal experiences of the Ebionites,
neither in Rome nor in Lyons. The same can be said of the other
church fathers active in Rome. They knew the Ebionites exclusively
from literature.

In contrast to Irenaeus, Origen, who mainly lived in Alexandria
and Caesarea Maritima, wrote about the Ebionites and often implied
that he had had at least some personal contacts with such Jewish
Christians he called Ebionites. By the time of Origen, quite a lot of
Jewish Christians lived in Alexandria.[75] The gentile Christian the-

---

[74] In Jewish-Christian studies, the article by F. C. Baur, "Die Christuspartei in
der korinthischen Gemeinde, der Gegensatz des petrinischen und paulinischen
Christenthums in der ältesten Kirchen, der Apostel Petrus in Rom," Tübinger Zeitschrift
für Theologie (1831/4): 61–206; repr. in vol. 1 of Ausgewählte Werke in Einzelausgaben
(ed. K. Scholder; Stuttgart – Bad Cannstatt: Friedrich Frommann [Günther Holzboog],
1963) 1:1–146, was epoch-making. In the article, Baur called Paul's Jewish-Christian
opponents Ebionites. He also published already a monograph on the Ebionites the
same year. According to Baur, all early Christianity was nothing but Ebionite. In
recent scholarship, the connections between the Ebionites and Jerusalem Christianity
have been emphasized, especially by James D. G. Dunn, Unity and Diversity in the
New Testament: An Inquiry into the Character of Earliest Christianity (London: Westminster
John Knox Press, 1977), 242–63; Goulder, St. Peter versus St. Paul, 70, 141; and
Lüdemann, Heretics, 52–53.

[75] Such Jewish-Christian works as the Letter of Barnabas, Epistula Apostolorum, Sibylline
Oracles, the Testament of Truth, and the Apocalypse of Peter were probably written in
Alexandria. In these works, Paul is either not mentioned or he is treated with great
suspicion or totally rejected. Cf. Segal, "Jewish Christianity," 337–39.

ologians of Alexandria knew the *Gospel according to the Hebrews*, but never connected it to the Ebionites. In his preserved writings, Clement of Alexandria never mentioned the Ebionites.[76]

In Caesarea Maritima, Palestine, Eusebius continued the work of Origen. His information about the Ebionites seems to be totally based on literary sources, especially the works of Origen. There is only one piece of information in his writings that is not known from any earlier sources. It deals with the Ebionites keeping both the Sabbath and the Day of the Lord (*Hist. eccl.* 3.27.5). This interesting detail is in the section of *Ecclesiastical History* that is based on Origen's *Against Celsus* and Irenaeus' *Against Heresies*. Neither of these writings contains this detail, which cannot be traced to any other source either. Archaeology does not confirm the hypothesis that some Jewish Christians might have lived in Caesarea at the time of Eusebius,[77] and there are no traces of personal contacts with the Ebionites in Eusebius' works. Thus, it seems probable that Eusebius—who called all Jewish Christians Ebionites, like Origen—concluded on his own that the Ebionites kept both the Sabbath and Sunday.

However, Eusebius is the first Church father who explicitly writes about the hometown of the Ebionites (*Onom.* 172.1–3):

> Choba. "This is to the left of Damascus." There is also a village Choba in the same region in which live those of the Hebrews who believed in Christ, called Ebionites.

Unfortunately, Eusebius does not reveal where he got this information. From Eusebius' angle, the Ebionites lived in the far north-east,[78] beyond Damascus. Eusebius does not mention the village elsewhere but in his *Hist. eccl.* 1.7 he writes about a village in Galilee called Kokhaba, which was inhabited by some relatives of the Savior. Although Eusebius does not make any connection between these two villages and their inhabitants, many scholars—beginning from Epiphanius (*Pan.* 30.2.8)—have embraced the supposition that Choba and Kokhaba are one and the same village and concluded from that that the Ebionites were relatives of Jesus.[79]

---

[76] Alexander of Alexandria (died either in 311 or 326) mentioned the sect-leader Ebion (*Ep.* 9), but did not deliver any historical data on the sect.

[77] J. E. Taylor, *Christians and the Holy Places: The Myth of Jewish-Christian Origins* (Oxford: Clarendon, 1993), 64.

[78] The Greek *aristera* in the Septuaginta means both "left" and "north."

[79] E.g., T. Zahn, *Forschungen zur Geschichte des neutestamentlichen Kanons und der altkirch-*

Following Eusebius, Epiphanius first locates the Ebionites (*Pan.* 30.2.8) in Kokhaba (Kokabe),

> Their origin goes back to the time after the capture of Jerusalem. For, after all those who believed in Christ had generally come to live in Perea, in a city called Pella of the Decapolis, of which it is written in the Gospel that it is situated in the neighbourhood of the region of Batanaea and Basanitis, Ebion's preaching originated here after they had moved to this place and had lived there. Initially he lived in some village called Kokabe not far from the region of Karnaim and Asteroth in the region of Basanitis; this is according to the contents of information which has reached us. From there he began his vicious teaching, from the same place where the Nazoraeans originated, of whom I gave an account above. (*Pan.* 30.2.7–8)

A bit later Epiphanius also notes (*Pan.* 30.18.1) that their roots were "mostly from Nabatea and Banias, Moabitis, and Cocabe in Bashanitis beyond Adrai—in Cyprus as well."

Epiphanius's information about the geography of the Ebionites is detailed. The source analysis of *Panarion*, however, is revealing. The "Pella-legend" is derived from Eusebius' *Ecclesiastical History* (3.5), where the Ebionites are not mentioned.[80] Epiphanius also claims that the leader of the movement, Ebion, preached in Asia and Rome. He may have drawn conclusions concerning the destinations of the missionary journeys of Ebion from the fact that his literary sources were mainly from these areas. The note on Cyprus may instead imply that on that island where Epiphanius was a bishop, there were such Jewish Christians whom Epiphanius considered Ebionites. Maybe

---

lichen Literatur (10 vols.; Erlangen: A. Deichert, 1881–1929), 1:333–36; Klijn and Reinink, *Patristic Evidence*, 27; Lüdemann, *Ketzer: Die andere Seite des frühen Christentums* (Stuttgart: Radius-Verlag, 1995), 40. The hypothesis is convincingly opposed by Taylor, *Christians and Holy Places*, 32–38, 225, who argues that there is no evidence of Jewish Christians in Kokhaba and nearby Nazareth (which is also mentioned by Eusebius in the same passage). There is evidence only of Jews who belonged to the ancestry of King David. Cf. Häkkinen, *Köyhät kerettiläiset*, 165–267.

[80] The historicity of the "Pella-legend" is disputable. Some scholars consider it only as a fiction derived from the foundation story of a Christian community at Pella; cf. G. Strecker, *Das Judenchristentum in den Pseudoklementinen* (2d ed.; TUGAL 70.2; Berlin: Akademie-Verlag, 1981), 229–31; G. Lüdemann, "The Successors of Pre-70 Jerusalem Christianity: A Critical Evaluation of the Pella-Tradition," in *The Shaping of Christianity in the Second and Third Centuries* (Vol. 1 of *Jewish and Christian Self-Definition*; ed. E. P. Sanders; London: SCM Press, 1980), 161–73; and Lüdemann, *Heretics*, 28–30. S. G. Wilson, *Related Strangers: Jews and Christians 70–170 C.E.* (Minneapolis: Fortress, 1995), 145–48, considers the legend partly trustworthy.

he even obtained some of his information from these local Jewish Christians. Nabatea to the south and to the east of the Dead Sea is a large district; Paneas (Banias, Caesarea Philippi) is located in the north close to the springs of the Jordan River. It is important to remember that Epiphanius was born in Palestine and lived there long enough to have at least some knowledge of Jewish Christians in the vicinity. On the other hand, besides Cyprus, all the other districts have been mentioned in connection with some other sects either in Epiphanius' *Panarion* or Eusebius' *Onomasticon*, which was known to Epiphanius.

The area where the Ebionites lived remains unclear. They probably lived in the eastern parts of the Roman Empire, plausibly in Alexandria but especially in the region of Transjordan.

6. Why Were the Ebionites Heretics?

The Ebionites were Christians who wanted to be faithful to Judaism and therefore they continued to practice Jewish customs and had some difficulties with gentile thinking. They could be said to have been conservative Christians who were more faithful to a Palestinian-type of Christianity in the first century than was Paul and the authors who later condemned the Ebionites in their writings.[81]

The Ebionites were poor. Thanks to Epiphanius, we know that the Ebionites called themselves by the name that was derived from their poverty. It was not just a scornful nickname given by outsiders. Used by the Ebionites, the name referred to Jewish piety, where poor people had an especially high esteem in the eyes of God. We do not know the reasons for their poverty. It may have been fidelity to early Christian tradition that was influenced by the ideal of poverty. It might as well have been their destiny, caused by some crisis or economic injustice in the society. In any case, poverty was also a reason for their being disregarded and for their gradual disappearance from the map of Christianity. They had no opportunities defending themselves and their way of life and faith.

---

[81] So argues Dunn, *Unity and Diversity*, 266.

Bibliography

Attridge H. W., and G. Hata, "Introduction." Pages 27–49 in *Eusebius, Christianity and Judaism*. Edited by H. W. Attridge and G. Hata. Studia Post-Biblica 42. Leiden: E. J. Brill, 1992.

Barrett, C. K. *A Commentary on the First Epistle to the Corinthians*. 2d ed. Black's New Testament Commentaries. London: Adam & Charles Black, 1971.

Baur, F. C. "Die Christuspartei in der korintischen Gemeinde, der Gegensatz des petrinischen und paulinischen Christenthums in der alten Kirche, der Apostel Petrus in Rom." *Tübinger Zeitschrift für Theologie* 1831/4: 61–206. Repr. pages 1–146 in vol. 1 of *Ausgewählte Werke in Einzelausgaben*. Edited by K. Scholder. Stuttgart – Bad Cannstatt: Friedrich Frommann [Günther Holzboog], 1963.

Bertrand, D. A. "L'Evangile des ébionites: une harmonie évangélique antérieure au Diatessaron." *New Testament Studies* 26 (1979): 548–63.

Brent, A. *Hippolytus and the Roman Church in the Third Century: Communities in Tension before the Emergence of a Monarch-Bishop*. Supplements to Vigiliae christianae 31. Leiden: E. J. Brill, 1995.

Campenhausen, H. von, *The Fathers of the Latin Church*. Translated by Manfred Hoffman; London: Adam & Charles Black, 1963.

Davies, S. L. *Jesus the Healer: Possession, Trance and the Origins of Christianity*. New York: Continuum, 1995.

De Lange, N. R. M. *Origen and the Jews: Studies in Jewish-Christian Relations in Third-Century Palestine*. Cambridge: Cambridge University Press, 1976.

Dölger, F. J. *Sol Salutis: Gebet und Gesang im christlichen Altertum: mit besonderer Rücksicht auf die Ostung in Gebet und Liturgie*. 2d ed. Liturgiegeschichtliche Quellen und Forschungen 16–17. Münster: Aschendorff, 1925.

Dunn, James D. G. *Unity and Diversity in the New Testament: An Inquiry into the Character of Earliest Christianity*. London: Westminster John Knox Press, 1977.

Friedrich, G. "Die Gegner des Paulus im 2. Korintherbrief." Pages 181–215 in *Abraham unser Vater: Festschrift für O. Michel*. Edited by O. Betz, M. Hengel, and P. Schmidt. Leiden: E. J. Brill, 1963.

Georgi, D. *Die Gegner des Paulus im 2. Korintherbrief: Studien zur religiösen Propaganda in der Spätantike*. Wissenschaftliche Monographien zum Alten und Neuen Testament 11. Neukirchen-Vluyn: Neukirchener Verlag, 1964.

Gieschen, C. A. *Angelomorphic Christology: Antecedents and Early Evidence*. Arbeiten zur Geschichte des antiken Judentums und des Urchristentums 42. Leiden: E. J. Brill, 1988.

Goranson, S. J. "Joseph of Tiberias Episode in Epiphanius: Studies in Jewish and Christian Relations." Ph.D. diss., Duke University, 1990.

Goulder, M. D. "The Pre-Marcan Gospel." *Scottish Journal of Theology* 47 (1994): 453–71.

————. *St. Paul versus St. Peter: A Tale of Two Missions*. Louisville, Ky.: Westminster John Knox Press, 1995.

Häkkinen, S. *Köyhät kerettiläiset: Ebionit kirkkoisien teksteissä*. [Poor Heretics: The Ebionites in the Texts of the Church Fathers.] Suomalaisen Teologisen Kirjallisuusseuran Julkaisuja 223. Helsinki: Suomalainen Teologinen Kirjallisuusseura, 1999.

Howard, G. "The Gospel of the Ebionites." *ANRW* 25.5:4034–53. Part 1, *Principat*, 25.5. Edited by Wolfgang Haase. New York: Walter de Gruyter, 1988.

Jones, F. S. *An Ancient Jewish Christian Source on the History of Christianity: Pseudo-Clementine Recognitions 1:27–71*. SBL Texts and Translations, 37: Christian Apocrypha Series 2. Atlanta, Ga.: Scholars Press, 1995.

Käsemann, E. "Die Legitimität des Apostels." *Zeitschrift für die Neutestamentliche Wissenschaft* 41 (1942): 33–71.

Klijn, A. F. J. *Jewish-Christian Gospel Tradition*. Supplements to Vigiliae christianae 17. Leiden: E. J. Brill, 1992.
———. *Jewish Christianity in Egypt*. Pages 161–75 in *The Roots of Egyptian Christianity*. Edited by B. A. Pearson and J. E. Goehring. Studies in Antiquity and Christianity. Philadelphia: Fortress, 1986.
Klijn, A. F. J., and G. J. Reinink. *Patristic Evidence for Jewish-Christian Sects*. Supplements to Novum Testamentun 36. Leiden: E. J. Brill, 1973.
Koch, G. A. "A Critical Investigation of Epiphanius' Knowledge of the Ebionites: A Translation and Critical Discussion of *Panarion*, 30." Ph.D. diss., University of Pennsylvania. 1976.
Kraue, G. and G. Müller, eds. *Theologische Realenzyklopädie*. New York: Walter de Gruyter, 1977–.
Lampe, G. W. H. "The Holy Spirit and the Person of Christ." Pages 111–30 in *Christ, Faith and History*. Edited by S. W. Sykes and J. P. Clayton. Cambridge: Cambridge University Press, 1972.
Lindeskog, G. *Das jüdisch-christliche Problem: Randglossen zu einer Forschungsepoche*. Acta Universitatis Upsaliensis. Historia Religionum 9. Stockholm: Almqvist & Wiksell, 1986.
Lipsius, R. A. *Zur Quellenkritik des Epiphanios*. Wien: W. Braumüller, 1865.
Lüdemann, G. *Heretics: The Other Side of Early Christianity*. Translated by J. Bowden; Louisville, Ky.: Westminster John Knox, 1996.
———. *Paulus, der Heidenapostel: Band II. Antipaulinismus im frühen Christentum*. Forschungen zur Religion und Literatur des Alten und Neuen Testaments 130. Göttingen: Vandenhoeck & Ruprecht, 1983.
Luttikhuizen, G. F. *The Revelation of Elchasai: Investigations into the Evidence for a Mesopotamian Jewish Apocalypse of the Second Century and its Reception by Judeo-Christian Propagandists*. Texte und Studien zum Antiken Judentum 8. Tübingen: J. C. B. Mohr (Paul Siebeck), 1985.
Marcovich, M. "Introduction." Pages 1–17 in *Hippolytus, Refutatio omnium haeresium*. Edited by M. Marcovich. Patristische Texte und Studien 25. Berlin: de Gruyter, 1986.
Menzies, Glen W. "Interpretive Traditions in the *Hypomnestikon Biblion Ioseppou*." Ph.D. diss., University of Minnesota, 1994.
Mimouni, S. C. *Le judéo-christianisme ancien: essais historiques*. Paris: Cerf, 1998.
Nanos, M. *The Irony of Galatians: Paul's Letter in First-Century Context*. Minneapolis, Minn.: Fortress, 2002.
Nautin, P. *Hippolyte et Josipe: contribution a l'histoire de la littérature chrétienne du troisième siècle*. Études et textes pour l'histoire du dogme de la Trinité 1. Paris: Cerf, 1947.
Pritz, R. A. *Nazarene Jewish Christianity: From the End of the New Testament Period until Its Disappearance in the Fourth Century*. Leiden: E. J. Brill, 1988.
Schoeps, H.-J. *Theologie und Geschichte des Judenchristentums*. Tübingen: J. C. B. Mohr (Paul Siebeck), 1949.
Segal, A. F. "Jewish Christianity." Pages 326–51 in *Eusebius, Christianity and Judaism* Edited by H. W. Attridge and G. Hata. Studia Post-Biblica 42. Leiden: E. J. Brill, 1992.
Strecker, G. *Das Judenchristentum in den Pseudoklementinen*. 2d ed. Texte und Untersuchungen zur Geschichte der altchristlichen Literatur 70.2. Berlin: Akademie-Verlag, 1981.
Taylor, J. E. *Christians and the Holy Places. The Myth of Jewish-Christian Origins*. Oxford: Clarendon, 1993.
Theissen, G. *The Social Setting of Pauline Christianity: Essays on Corinth by Gerd Theissen*. Edited and translated and with an Introduction by J. H. Schütz. Philadelphia: Fortress, 1982.
Thomas, J. B. *Le Mouvement Baptiste en Palestine et Syrie*. Gembloux: J. Ducolot, 1935.

Uhlhorn, G. *Die Homilien und Recognitionen des Clemens Romanus nach ihrem Ursprung und Inhalt dargestellt.* Göttingen: Dieterich, 1854.

Ulrich, E. "Origen's Old Testament Text: The Transmission History of the Septuagint to the Third Century C.E." Pages 3–33 in *Origen of Alexandria: His World and His Legacy.* Edited by C. Kannengiesser and W. L. Petersen. Christianity and Judaism in Antiquity 1. Notre Dame: University of Notre Dame Press, 1988.

Van Voorst, R. E. *The Ascents of James: History and Theology of a Jewish Christian Community.* Society of Biblical Literature Dissertation Series 112. Atlanta, Ga.: Scholars Press, 1989.

Vielhauer, P., and G. Strecker, "Jewish-Christian Gospels." Pages 134–77 in Vol. 1 of *New Testament Apocrypha.* Edited by W. Schneemelcher. English translation edited by R. McL. Wilson. 2 vols. Cambridge: James Clarke, 1991.

Wilson, S. G. *Related Strangers: Jews and Christians 70–170 C.E.* Minneapolis: Fortress, 1995.

Wise, M., M. Abegg, Jr., and E. Cook, *The Dead Sea Scrolls: A New Translation.* San Francisco: HarperSanFransisco, 1996.

NAZARENES

Petri Luomanen

1. *Introduction*

The Jewish-Christian "heresy" of the Nazarenes was first discussed by Epiphanius, the fourth-century bishop of Salamis. Although Epiphanius dates the origin of the heresy to the first century, it is striking that none of his predecessors refers to a heretical sect called Nazarenes whereas the Ebionites are often described by earlier heresiologists, starting with Irenaeus. By the end of the fourth century, the only church father besides Epiphanius who knows something about the Nazarenes, is his contemporary and friend Jerome.

Scholars have explained this gap in the recorded history of the Nazarenes in various ways. The explanations can be roughly divided into three categories, each connected to a particular view of the overall development of early Christianity.

1) *The Nazarenes were later, more tolerant Jewish Christians.* F. C. Baur argued—in contrast to early heresiologists—that the Ebionites were not originally a heretical sect but successors of the very first Jewish Christians in Jerusalem. The Nazarenes, for their part, represented a later phase of Jewish Christianity, which had developed from its strictly anti-Pauline stance to a more lenient attitude towards the Gentiles.[1]

---

[1] Baur thought that the teaching and the practices of the Ebionites were so close to the very first Jewish Christianity that, in general, one could call the early Jewish Christianity Ebionism. However, he also notes that it is more common to restrict the name Ebionites to those Jewish Christians who excluded themselves from the Catholic Church because they were not able to keep up with the development of the Christian consciousness ("Bewusstsein") that moved from Jewish Christianity towards Catholicism. See, F. C. Baur, *Das Christentum und die christliche Kirche der drei ersten Jahrhunderte* (2nd ed.; Tübingen: L. Fr. Fues, 1860; repr. in vol. 3 of *Ausgewählte Werke in Einzelausgaben*; ed. K. Scholder; Stuttgart – Bad Cannstatt: Friedrich Frommann [Günther Holzboog], 1966), 174, 174 n. 1. Among contemporary scholars, for instance, G. Lüdemann and M. D. Goulder have argued that the Jewish Christians described as Ebionites by Irenaeus were an offshoot of the earliest Jerusalem community. See G. Lüdemann, *Heretics: The Other Side of Early Christianity* (trans. J. Bowden; Louisville, Ky.: Westminster John Knox, 1996), 52–56; M. D. Goulder, *A Tale of Two Missions* (London: SCM Press, 1994), 107–13.

2) *The Nazarenes were early "orthodox" Jewish Christians*. A. Ritschl argued—in contrast to Baur—that strict Jewish Christianity with its anti-Paulinism cannot be considered as the dominant current in first-century Christianity because the Nazarenes, who accepted the apostle Paul, were the successors of the early Jerusalem community.[2] R. A. Pritz presents a similar interpretation in his 1988 monograph. According to Pritz, the history of the Nazarenes can be traced back to the early Jerusalem community and the Ebionites came out of a split among the Nazarene ranks around the turn of the first century. The split was possibly caused by disputes concerning Christology. The doctrine of the Nazarenes was "orthodox" although they still followed the Jewish law. Thus, the Nazarene Jewish Christians existed from the first century onwards but they were mistakenly called as Ebionites by such church fathers as Origen and Eusebius. Justin, who wrote in the middle of the second century, possibly also had knowledge of the Nazarenes although he did not explicitly name them. The earliest heresiologists may have failed to name the Nazarenes simply because they were not heretical enough.[3]

3) *The Nazarenes were later, local "Catholic" Jewish Christians*. A. Schmidtke argued in the beginning of the 20th century that the Nazarenes in Beroea were a purely local phenomenon which had no connection to the early Jerusalem community. The Catholic Church in Beroea had originally consisted of members that were of both

---

[2] A. Ritschl, *Die Entstehung der altkatholischen Kirche: Eine kirchen- und dogmengeschichtliche Monographie* (2nd ed.; Bonn: Adolph Marcus, 1857), 152–54. Ritschl also argued that Origen and Eusebius erroneously identified the Nazarenes with the more heretical Ebionites (p. 156) and that the separation of Gentile and Jewish Christians was caused by the growing intolerance of the strict Jewish Christians toward the Gentile Christians and by the Bar Kochba war (pp. 250, 252–58, 266). Although Ritschl originally belonged to the Tübingen school, he wrote the second edition (1857) of *Die Entstehung*, where he rejects Baur's construction, after the breakdown of his relationship with Baur. For the Tübingen school see, for instance, R. Morgan, "Tübingen school," in *A Dictionary of Biblical Interpretation* (ed. R. J. Coggins and J. L. Houlden; 3rd impression; London: SCM Press, 1994), 710–13.

[3] R. A. Pritz, *Nazarene Jewish Christianity: From the End of the New Testament Period until Its Disappearance in the Fourth Century* (Leiden: E. J. Brill, 1988), 28, 82, 108–10. Similarly S. C. Mimouni, *Le judéo-christianisme ancien: essais historiques* (Paris: Cerf, 1998), 82–86; F. Blanchetière, *Enquête sur les racines juives du mouvement chrétien (30–135)* (Paris: Cerf, 2001), 145, 183, 238–39, 521; R. Bauckham, "The Origin of the Ebionites," in *The Image of the Judaeo-Christians in Ancient Jewish and Christian Literature* (ed. P. J. Tomson and Doris Lambers-Petry; WUNT 158; Tübingen: Mohr Siebeck, 2003), 162–81, esp. 162.

Gentile and Jewish pedigree. During the first half of the second century, the Jewish members had formed a community of their own in order to be better able to follow their national customs. Nevertheless, the Nazarenes still felt themselves as part of the worldwide ekklesia.[4] H. J. Schoeps followed Schmidtke, emphasizing that Epiphanius was responsible for the heretical reputation of the Nazarenes because he connected these "Catholic" Jewish Christians with the heretical sect of the Ebionites, the real offshoot of the early Jerusalem church.[5]

All the above interpretations agree that, although Epiphanius' description of the genesis of the Nazarenes cannot be trusted as such, it is clear that by the second half of the second century, at the latest, the Nazarenes had formed a community of their own with its own peculiar theology. Opinions differ, however, as regards the question of how closely the Nazarenes were integrated with the other forms of Christianity and whether the Nazarenes represented the theology and practice of the early Jerusalem church or were a group that had only later on broken away from Gentile Christians.

Because the ancient writers that explicitly deal with the Nazarenes, Epiphanius and Jerome, are from the fourth century and are known for often allowing their polemical interests and personal ambitions to dictate the contents of their presentations, it is no wonder that the role of the Nazarenes in second-century Christianity has been open to various interpretations. The aim of the present article is to introduce the evidence provided by Epiphanius and Jerome and to assess its character and reliability. Critical analysis of Epiphanius' and Jerome's presentations leaves us with very little material that could be connected to the heresy of the Nazarenes—if the Nazarenes are understood as a separate, historically definable group or movement. Therefore, instead of being a description of a concrete "heresy" that once existed, the following presentation reads more like a pathology of heresiologial writing, a story of how Christian identity is created and supported by cultivating stereotypes of "the other side."

---

[4] A. Schmidtke, *Neue Fragmente und Untersuchungen zu den judenchristlichen Evangelien: Ein Beitrag zur Literatur und Geschichte der Judenchristen* (TUGAL 3.7; Leipzig: J. H. Hinrichs'sche Buchhandlung, 1911), 41–42, 105, 124–25, 301–2.

[5] H. J. Schoeps, *Theologie und Geschichte des Judenchristentums* (Tübingen: J. C. B. Mohr [Paul Siebeck], 1949), 19–20.

2. Who Were Called Nazarenes?

Epiphanius discusses the correct spelling of the term Nazarenes (*Nazōraioi*) in *Pan.* 29.5.6–29.6.1, emphasizing that the name does not refer to nazirites or to the pre-Christian heresy of the Nasarenes (cf. *Pan.* 18) but is derived from the name of Jesus' hometown. In the NT, Jesus is called Nazarene using the Greek words *Nazōraios* (in Matt, Luke, John and Acts) and *Nazarēnos* (in Mark and Luke) which are rendered in English translations either as Nazorean or Nazarene. Accordingly, in English the present "heretics" are known either as the Nazoreans or the Nazarenes.[6]

In addition to the fact the Jesus himself is called Nazarene several times in the canonical gospels and Acts, Paul is accused in Acts of being a leader of the "sect of the Nazarenes" by the high priest Ananias' attorney, Tertullus: "We have, in fact, found this man a pestilent fellow, an agitator among all the Jews throughout the world, and a ringleader of the sect of the Nazarenes" (Acts 24:5 NRSV).

Obviously, the early followers of Jesus were named after their leader, Jesus of Nazareth.[7] Two of Epiphanius' predecessors in the formative Catholic tradition still used the term Nazarenes in this general sense. Tertullian noted in his *Against Marcion:* "Christ had to be called Nazarene according to the prophesy of the Creator. Therefore also by this very name the Jews call us Nazarenes because of Him" (*Marc.* 4.8).[8] Furthermore, Eusebius' *Onomasticon* has the following description: "Nazareth. From this name Christ was called Nazarene

---

[6] For the term Nazarene in general, see S. J. Goranson, "Nazarenes," *ABD* 4:1049–50; H. H. Schaeder, "Ναζαρηνός Ναζωραῖος," *TDNT* 4:874–79.

[7] To be sure, other hypotheses about the origin of the term have also been discussed in connection with the interpretation of Matt 2:23 or based on speculations about Jesus' being a nazirite or a former member of the allegedly pre-Christian sect of the Nasarenes, the "observants." See Schaeder, "Ναζαρηνός," 874–75. Pritz argues that the very first Christians used the term Nazarenes as a self-designation on the basis of a messianic interpretation of Isa 11:1, which refers to the shoot (*netser* in Hebrew) of Jesse. See Pritz, *Nazarene Jewish Christianity*, 12–14. Although Isa 11:1 may be the passage that the writer of Matthew's gospel had in mind when writing Matt 2:23—but which he did not explicate (!)—the interpretation is too speculative to constitute a basis for the naming of the first Christians in general.

[8] If not indicated ofthterwise, the translations of patristic passages are based on A. F. J. Klijn and H. J. Reinink, *Patristic Evidence for Jewish-Christian Sects* (NovTSup 36; Leiden: E. J. Brill, 1973), 109. However, minor corrections and modifications, like the spelling of the name Nazarenes, have been made. My own translations are indicated by the initials PL.

and we being now called Christians received in the past the name Nazarenes" (*Onom.* p. 138, 24–25).

Eusebius' information that the term Nazarenes was used of Christians in the past is correct only concerning Greek and Latin literature, since Syrians, Arabs, Persians and Armenians used the cognates of the term Nazarenes to designate Christians in general even after Eusebius' time.[9] In addition, Talmudic tradition includes some references to *notsrim*,[10] and some versions of the Jewish *Eighteen Benedictions* include a curse against the *notsrim*, which seems to refer to Christians in general.[11]

The assumption that *notsrim* in the *Eighteen Benedictions* refers to Christians in general is in harmony with Jerome's references to this practice. In his *Commentary on Amos*, Jerome writes: "Until today they blaspheme the Christian people under the name of Nazarenes" (*Comm. Am.* 1.11–12). Epiphanius also knows about the versions of the *Eighteen Benedictions* that refer to *notsrim* but he connects the curse only to the heretical sect of the Nazarenes he is describing in *Panarion* 29.

Overall, among early Christian and Jewish writers there are only two men, Epiphanius and Jerome, and some later writers who depend on them, who clearly used the term Nazarenes to designate a specific Jewish-Christian group. Furthermore, of these two writers, it is mainly Epiphanius who condemns the Nazarenes as heretics. For Jerome, the Nazarenes provided useful information from Hebrew writings. For the majority of writers before and after Epiphanius and Jerome, the term Nazarenes referred to (Jewish) Christians in general.

---

[9] See, Schaeder "Ναζαρηνός," 874–75; Goranson, "Nazarenes," 1049. In Syriac, a Christian is *natsraya*.

[10] *b.>Abod. Zar.* 6a; *b. Ta>an.* 27b.

[11] Thus, for instance, W. Horbury, "The Benediction of the Minim and Early Jewish Christian Controversy, " *JTS* 33 (1982): 19–61, esp. 59–61, in contrast to R. Kimelman, "Birkat ha-Minim and the Lack of Evidence for Anti-Christian Jewish Prayer in Late Antiquity," in *Aspects of Judaism in the Greco-Roman Period* (ed. E. P. Sanders, A. I. Baumgarten, and A. Mendelson; vol. 2 of *Jewish and Christian Self-Definition*; ed. E. P. Sanders; London: SCM Press, 1975), 226–44, and M. C. de Boer, "The Nazoreans: Living at the Boundary of Judaism and Christianity," in *Tolerance and Intolerance in Early Judaism and Christianity* (ed. G. N. Stanton and G. A. G. Stroumsa; Cambridge: Cambridge University Press, 1998), 250. The different versions are discussed by P. Schäfer, "Die sogenannte Synode von Jabne: Zur Trennung von Juden und Christen im ersten/zweiten Jh. n. Chr.," *Judaica* 31 (1975): 54–64, 116–24, esp. 57–61, who suggests that *notsrim* were included in the prayer in localities where the "Nazarenes" had become a problem. In most cases, the "benediction" refers only to the *minim*.

3. *Epiphanius' View of the Nazarenes*

3.1. *An Overview of the Main Sources and Composition of Pan. 29*

Eusebius' *Ecclesiastical History* and Acts provided the backbone for the information Epiphanius collected in *Panarion* 29. Most of the information that Epiphanius used from Eusebius' *Ecclesiastical History* can be found between *Hist. eccl.* 2.16 and 3.5, which covers the time from Mark's alleged preaching in Egypt to the disciples' flight from Jerusalem, as is shown by the following table:

Mark's preaching in Egypt	*Hist. eccl.* 2.16	→	*Pan.* 29.5.4
Philo's Therapeutae	*Hist. eccl.* 2.17	→	*Pan.* 29.5.1–3
James as the first bishop	*Hist. eccl.* 2.23	→	*Pan.* 29.4.1–4
The flight from Jerusalem	*Hist. eccl.* 3.5.3	→	*Pan.* 29.7.8

Epiphanius explicitly refers to Acts concerning the following points:

Jesus was called a Nazarene	Acts 2:22	→ *Pan.* 29.5.6
		→ *Pan.* 29.6.7
Quote from the Apostolic degree	Acts 15:28–29	→ *Pan.* 29.8.6
The "leader" of the Nazarenes	Acts 24:5	→ *Pan.* 29.6.2
Paul's "Nazarene confession"	Acts 24:12–14	→ *Pan.* 29.6.4

In addition, the wording of Acts influenced Epiphanius' diction in several places, and he drew on Galatians and several other New and Old Testament passages in his refutation of the Nazarenes, as will be shown in the course of the following discussion.

3.2. *The Genesis of the Heresy of the Nazarenes*

When Epiphanius lists the heresies in *Panarion*, one of his main concerns is to show how they developed from each other. Therefore, the opening lines of each chapter usually link the heresy to be treated with the one that has been refuted in the previous chapter. A model for this composition was already provided by Irenaeus who traced the heresies he discussed back to the activity of Simon Magus. Heresiologists who preceded Epiphanius—Irenaeus, Hippolytus and Pseudo-Tertullian—had presented the heresies of Cerinthus and Ebion in that order. Epiphanius inserts the Nazarenes between these two, arguing that the Nazarenes came after, or were contemporary with, the Cerinthians and that the Ebionites were founded by a certain Ebion who came from the Nazarenes' school.

In the beginning of *Panarion* 29, Epiphanius still admits that he is
not sure whether the Nazarenes followed the Cerinthians or vice
versa. This does not prevent him from trying to locate stories in his
sources that would tell about the genesis of the Nazarenes with the
result that *Panarion* 29 now contains three different and partly incompatible explanations of the genesis of the Nazarenes.

First, in the beginning of *Panarion* 29, Epiphanius states that he does
not know when the Nazarene heresy began. According to Epiphanius,
after the Cerinthians

> come Nazoreans, who originated at the same time or even before, or
> in conjunction with them or after them. In any case they were con-
> temporaries. I cannot say more precisely who succeeded whom. For,
> as I said, these were contemporaries with each other, and had simi-
> lar notions. (*Pan.* 29.1.1)[12]

If the Nazarenes originated at the same time or even before the Cerin-
tians, they must—using Epiphanius' time line—have been a pre-70
movement since Epiphanius argues that Cerinthus was among those
conservative Jewish Christians who, according to Acts, had gone from
Jerusalem to Antioch and caused confusion there (Acts 15:24), and
who also had opposed Peter (Acts 11:2–3).

Second, Epiphanius makes an attempt to determine the beginning
of the heresy more exactly. He states that, in the period of time
when Christians

> were called Jessaeans,[13] for a short time after the Saviors ascension and
> after Mark had preached in Egypt, some again seceded (*tines exelēlythasi*

---

[12] Trans. by F. Williams, in *The Panarion of Epiphanius of Salamis: Book I (Sects
1–46)* (trans. F. Williams; NHS 35; Leiden: E. J. Brill, 1987), 112.

[13] Jessaeans as the title of the first Christians is not discussed by other church
fathers. However, in Syraic, Christians are called not only *natsraye*, as was indicated
above, but also *yeshuaye*, and a cognate title is to be found in Arabic as well (I owe
this observation to Prof. Heikki Räisänen; see also Blanchetière, *Enquête*, 144).
Therefore, it is possible that these titles were in fact known to Epiphanius from
Syriac traditions but he connected them—or better, their appropriate use—only to
the very first followers of Jesus. According to Jerome (*Ruf.* 2.22; 3.6), Epiphanius
was versed in Syriac and Hebrew (in addition to Egyptian, Latin and Greek) but
because Jerome listed Epiphanius' language skills in order to ridicule Rufinus, who
knew only two languages, he may have been slightly exaggerating. In any case,
Epiphanius was trained in Egypt and wrote mainly in Greek. If his knowledge of
Semitic languages was limited and he did not converse with orthodox Syriac-speaking Christians, that would explain why he thought that the terms Nazarenes and
Jessaeans belonged only to the past in the history of "orthodox" Christianity.

palin). They were called the followers of the apostles, indeed, but I think that they were the Nazarenes whom I am describing here. They are Jews by birth and they dedicate themselves to the law and submit to circumcision. (*Pan.* 29.5.4; trans. PL)

Epiphanius is clearly using here a source (or sources) that refer to "some people" who "went out" (*exelēlythasi*) and were called the followers of the apostles, and draws a conclusion of his own that these must have been the Nazarenes. What is Epiphanius' source and how does he date this event?

The timing, "a short time after the Savior's ascension and after Mark preached in Egypt," shows that Epiphanius still has in mind Eusebius' account. There the conversion of Egyptian Therapeutae, which Eusebius falsely identifies with Christians, is said to be caused by Mark's preaching in Alexandria (*Hist. eccl.* 2.13,16).[14] Epiphanius has quoted this description in the preceding lines of *Panarion* 29 where he discusses the Jessaeans (= Eusebius' Therapeutae). Eusebius does not say anything about "some people" who "again went out/seceded." Therefore, it is clear that Epihanius either is using here an additional source that has not survived[15] or is drawing his own inferences from Eusebius' account and the New Testament writings.[16]

Be that as it may, it is clear that Epiphanius describes the appearance of these "some" in terms similar to Acts 15:24 where the *"apostles"* and presbyters write: "Since we have heard that some (*tines*) of us have come (*exelthontes*, literally "went out"; the same Greek term as

---

[14] The expression "after the Savior's ascension" seems to be based on *Hist. eccl.* 2.13 where Eusebius quotes Justin's *First Apology* (*1 Apol.* 26). Epiphanius' wording follows Eusebius (*meta tēn analēpsin* instead of Justin's *meta tēn aneleusin*).

[15] For instance, F. Williams suggests that Epiphanius may have known Justin's lost *Syntagma*. See "Introduction" in *The Panarion of Epiphanius of Salamis: Book I (Sects 1–46)* (trans. F. Williams; NHS 35; Leiden: E. J. Brill, 1987), IX–XXVII, esp. XX.

[16] The description in Acts 15 of the envoys that come from Jerusalem and cause problems in Antioch is not entirely compatible with Paul's description of similar events in Gal 2. Therefore, Epiphanius—or the writer of the source he is using— may have concluded that the church in Antioch must have been attacked twice by Jerusalem conservatives: first before the Apostolic council (described in Acts 15) and then again after it (as suggested by Gal 2). As was shown above, Epiphanius claims in *Pan.* 28 that Cerinthus was among those men who came from Jerusalem, and in this connection, he explicitly quotes Acts 15. If he counted two invasions from Jerusalem, it is natural to assume that he made the Nazaranes responsible for the second one because the Nazarenes are refuted after the Cerinthians in the *Panarion*. In any case, Epiphanius consulted both Acts and Gal for *Pan.* 29 since he quotes Acts 15:28–19 and Gal 3:10; 5:2, 4 when he later on moves on to refute the Nazarenes (*Pan.* 29.8.1; 29.8.6–7).

in the *Panarion*!) and confused you. . . ." Notably, the majority of Greek manuscripts also include a summary of the message of these envoys. They came "saying that one has to be circumcised and keep the law." Thus, the content of the message of these envoys is the same as the "doctrine" of the Nazarenes that Epiphanius quotes in this connection: "They are Jews by birth and they dedicate themselves to the Law and submit to circumcision" (*Pan.* 29.5.4). Furthermore, the description of Simon's conversion in Acts has clearly inspired Epiphanius' description of the Nazarenes' "conversion":

> When they heard Jesus' name and *saw the* divine *signs that happened through the hands of the apostles they* also *believed* in Jesus. (*Pan.* 29.5.6; trans. PL)
> *Simon* also *believed* and was baptized . . . and when *he saw the signs* and great miracles *that happened* he was amazed . . . and when he saw that *through* the laying on *the hands of the apostles.* . . . (Acts 8:13, 18)

It is clear that Eusebius' reference to the genesis of the Nazarenes draws heavily on Acts. Even if Epiphanius made use of a traditional description of the activities of early Jewish Christians, it is clear that he was himself responsible for identifying these with the Nazarenes. When he made this identification, he was mainly concerned with criticizing the Nazarenes and he did not pay much attention to the timing of the incidents described. In Eusebius' time line, which Epiphanius basically follows, Mark's preaching in Egypt happened well before 70 C.E., whereas Epiphanius' third reference to the genesis of the sect, which will be discussed next, is clearly a post-70 event.

> This heresy of the Nazarenes exists in Beroea in the neighbourhood of Coele Syria and Decapolis in the region of Pella and in Bashan in the so-called Kokaba (*en tē Kōkabē*), Chochaba (. . . *Chōchabē*) in Hebrew. For from there it took its beginning after the exodus from Jerusalem when the disciples went to live in Pella because Christ had told them to leave Jerusalem and to go away since it would undergo a siege. Because of this advice they lived in Perea after having moved to that place, as I said. There the Nazarene heresy had its beginning. (*Pan.* 29.7.7–8)

Epiphanius' source for the story about the exodus from Jerusalem is again Eusebius (*Hist. eccl.* 3.5) but, in contrast to the two earlier descriptions, he now dates the genesis of the Nazarene heresy after the fall of Jerusalem. There are two obvious reasons for this. First, in this connection, Epiphanius presents a list of villages where the Nazarenes supposedly lived in his time and the list also includes Pella, which connects it with the tradition about the disciples' flight from Jerusalem. Second, the timing after the fall of Jerusalem provides a very good starting point for the following refutation of the Nazarenes where Epiphanius argues that it is impossible to fulfill the law because access to Jerusalem is denied.

Overall, Epiphanius' remark in the beginning of *Panarion* 29 that he does not really know when the Nazorean heresy begun, coheres with his contradictory descriptions about its beginning. Epiphanius ends up locating the genesis of the heresy after the fall of Jerusalem because it provides a good starting point for his refutation but he has no historical data about the origins of this movement.

3.3. *The Summary of the Nazarenes' Practices and Doctrine: Pan. 29.7.2–8, 29.9.2, 4*

In Williams' English translation, *Panarion* 29 covers approximately 7.5 pages but a relatively small number of lines describe the beliefs and practices of the Nazarenes. On the first five pages, Epiphanius discusses the reasons why all Christians were, for a short while, called Jessaeans and Nazarenes before they began to be called Christians in Antioch. In practice, this long "introduction"—which contains several digressions typical of Epiphanius' style—does not reveal anything more about the Nazarenes except that, in Epiphanius' view, these "heretics" adopted the name that once was common to all Christians. The actual description of the Nazarenes' practices and doctrines is to be found in *Pan.* 29.7.2–7:

> *Pan.* 29.7.2: (1)They used not only the New but also the Old Testament, confessing everything (2) as the Law proclaims it.
>
> *Pan.* 29.7.3: They "acknowledge both (3) the resurrection of the dead, and (4) the divine creation of all things, and declare that (5) God is one, and that (6) his Son/servant (*pais*) is Jesus Christ."
>
> *Pan.* 29.7.4: (7) They read the Law, the Prophets and the Writings in Hebrew.
>
> *Pan.* 29.7.5: The position of the Nazarenes is summarized: They disagree with the Jews only because of their belief in Christ and they are not in accord with the Christians only because they are still fettered by the Law.
>
> *Pan.* 29.7.6: Epiphanius "confesses" that he does not know whether or not the Nazarenes believed in the virgin birth.
>
> *Pan.* 29.7.8: (8) List of the locations of the Nazarenes and their connection to the Pella tradition.

This concise description of the Nazarenes is followed by the refutation which begins in *Pan.* 29.8.1. Epiphanius quotes several passages from the Old and New Testament, including Acts and Galatians, in order to show that the Jewish law no longer binds the Christians. The refutation culminates in a description which also gives more information about the Nazarenes' relation to the Jews. Epiphanius' point is that the Nazarenes who try to be Jews are also cursed by the Jews themselves:

> *Pan.* 29.9.2: (9) The Jews "stand up at dawn, at midday, and toward evening, three times a day when they recite their prayers in the synagogues, and curse and anathematize them. Three times a day they say, 'God curse the Nazarenes.'"

Finally, before moving on to deal with the next sect, the Ebionites, Epiphanius reveals one more detail about the Nazarenes.

> *Pan.* 29.9.4: (10) The Nazarenes have Matthew's gospel in its entirety in Hebrew.

However, Epiphanius does not know whether or not they have removed the genealogies from Abraham to Christ.

3.4. *The Locations of the Nazarenes*

As already noted, Epiphanius locates the Nazarenes in Syrian Beroea, as well as the areas of Bashan (Kokaba/Chochaba) and Decapolis (Pella). Because Jerome, who spent some time near Beroea,[17] also locates the Nazarenes there, it is clear that, by the time of Epiphanius and Jerome, Beroea had some Christian inhabitants who were called Nazarenes.

Because Epiphanus had himself lived in Palestine in Eleutheropolis (Beth Guvrin), one can also assume that he had some knowledge about the areas where Jewish Christians were living in his time. Epiphanius locates his Kokaba/Chochaba in the area of Bashan, near Karnaim and Ashtaroth (*Pan.* 29.7.7 and *Pan.* 30.2.8–9). Kokaba/Chochaba has been identified with the remains of a town some twenty-seven kilometers east of the Sea of Galilee.[18] In the nearby village of Farj,

---

[17] Jerome first tried to fulfill his ascetic goals around 374–377 C.E. in Syria, near Chalcis, which was located 88 km east-southeast of Antioch and 27 km southwest of Beroea. J. N. D. Kelly, *Jerome: His Life, Writings, and Controversies* (New York: Harper & Row, 1975), 46.

[18] J. E. Taylor, *Christians and the Holy Places: The Myth of Jewish-Christian Origins* (Oxford: Clarendon Press, 1993), 37.

there has also been found some archaeological evidence which may suggest the presence of a Jewish-Christian community: inscriptions including both menorahs and Christian symbols. The inscriptions are dated between the latter part of the fourth century and the early fifth, which makes them roughly contemporary with Epiphanius.[19] Eusebius has also located Ebionites in a village called Choba (*Chōba*),[20] which might be the same village as Epiphanius' Kokaba/Chochaba.[21] In any case, it seems that Epiphanius indentified these villages with each other because he locates the genesis of the sect of the Ebionites in his Kokaba/Chochaba (*Pan.* 30.2.8–9).

The tradition about the disciples' flight to Pella before the conquest of Jerusalem, as it is transmitted by Eusebius in his *Ecclesiastical History* (*Hist. eccl.* 3.5), is hardly historical as such. Nevertheless, G. Lüdemann has shown that the story can be understood as a foundation legend of a Jewish-Christian community that was living in Pella.[22] If the Pella-tradition was transmitted by Aristo of Pella, as Lüdemann suggests, then it is clear that the Jewish-Christian community had settled in Pella in 135 C.E., at the latest.[23] In any case, it is clear that, by the time of Epiphanius, Pella was known as a local center of Jewish Christians who claimed to be the successors of the early Jerusalem community.

---

[19] Taylor, *Christians*, 39–41.

[20] Eusebius, *Onomasticon*. Quoted by Klijn and Reinink, *Patristic Evidence*, 150–51.

[21] Thus Klijn and Reinink, *Patristic Evidence*, 27 and Taylor, *Christians*, 38. If the village is not the same, Eusebius' Choba must have been closer to Damascus because the biblical Hobah (Gen 14:15)—in connection with which Eusebius mentions the Choba of the Ebionites—is located to the north of Damascus.

[22] G. Lüdemann, "The Successors of Pre-70 Jerusalem Christianity: A Critical Evaluation of the Pella-Tradition," in *The Shaping of Christianity in the Second and Third Centuries* (ed. E. P. Sanders; vol. 1 of *Jewish and Christian Self-Definition*; ed. E. P. Sanders; London: SCM Press, 1980), 161–73, 245–54, esp. 165. An even more critical view is presented by J. Verheyden who argues that Eusebius fabricated the whole story. For a summary of Verheyden's book (which was not available to the present author), see W. L. Petersen, review of J. Verheyden, *De vlucht van de christenen naar Pella: Onderzoek van het getuigenis van Eusebius en Epiphanius*, *SecCent* 8 (1991): 186–88.

[23] Lüdemann, "The Successors," 248, n. 19, argues that the emigration must have happened before 135 C.E. I agree with Lüdemann that, if the Pella tradition was transmitted by Aristo of Pella, who wrote around 140–150 C.E., the Bar Kochba war (135 C.E.) cannot have been the disaster that gave rise to the legend. Later on Lüdemann (*Heretics*, 29) has suggested that the legend could also be rooted in the flight of some members of the Jerusalem community to Pella in the wake of the execution of James the Just, which happened a couple of years before the disaster of 70 C.E. If there were only a few members from Jerusalem, it is perfectly possible that they survived when the Jews raided the town in revenge for the killing of their compatriots in Caesarea (Josephus, *Bell.* 2.458).

Another question is whether or not the Jewish Christians living in Kokaba/Chochaba and Pella were called Nazarenes. At least Epiphanius' predecessors in the formative Catholic tradition presumably called the Jewish Christians of Pella, who understood themselves as the successors of Jerusalem community, Ebionites. Irenaeus already knew that the Ebionites were "adoring Jerusalem as if it were the house of God." Epiphanius himself also testifies that the Ebionites traced their name—'ebyon means "poor" in Hebrew—back to the time of the Apostles by claiming that they sold their properties and laid the money at the Apostles' feet (*Pan.* 30.17.2). Epiphanius' own interpretation of the pre-history of the Ebionites is in sharp contrast with this explanation since he traces the genesis of the Ebionites back to the activity of Ebion, a former member of the sect of the Nazarenes.

Although one cannot exclude the possibility that there were Jewish Christians who were generally called Nazarenes in Pella and Kokaba/Chochaba in Epiphanius' time, it is more likely that Epiphanius is responsible for connecting the Nazarenes to these environs. Because Epiphanius' *Panarion* depicts the Nazarenes as the first representatives of heretical Jewish Christianity, they had to be connected to the places where Jewish Christians were traditionally thought to be living.

3.5. *The Nazarenes' Use of the Scriptures*

Because Jewish Christians were generally thought to be competent in the Hebrew language[24] and obedient to the Jewish law, there is no need to assume that Epiphanius must have used a source where it was stated that the Nazarenes used both the New and the Old Testament. On the contrary, the context where Epiphanius presents this information indicates that the reference to the Nazarenes' use of the scriptures only serves to exemplify his accusation that Nazarenes are "complete" Jews. Unlike the representatives of the Jewish sects that Epiphanius has discussed in the beginning of his work, the Nazarenes did not repudiate any parts of the Old Testament but were representatives of "orthodox" Judaism since they accepted the Law, the Prophets and the Writings. In Epiphanius' view, the Nazarenes were blameless as regards Judaism—except for their belief in Christ.

---

[24] See, Eusebius, *Hist. eccl.* 3.25.5; 3.39.16–17; 5.8.2.

The Nazarenes' use of the Gospel of the Matthew in Hebrew is referred to at the very end of *Panarion* 29, as if it were a sort of appendix to the discussion. Obviously, Epiphanius has added this note in view of his following treatment of the Ebionites. In the next chapter (*Pan.* 30), he presents several quotations from a gospel that was used by the Ebionites saying that the Ebionites call their writing the "Gospel according to the Hebrews." Epiphanius admits that Matthew, indeed, wrote his gospel in Hebrew (*Pan.* 30.3.7). However, it is clear that the "Gospel of the Ebionites" was a Greek document since the quotations that Epiphanius presents are in Greek and they include word plays that are understandable only in Greek.[25] According to Epiphanius, the "Gospel of the Ebionites" was "corrupt and mutilated" (*Pan.* 30.13.1) and a quotation from the beginning of their gospel shows that it opened with the description of the baptism of John. Thus, it did not include the birth narratives (*Pan.* 30.13.6; 30.14.3). With this kind of evidence about the writings of the Ebionites in his hands, Epiphanius must have been faced with the dilemma of how to explain the information he found in his sources which stated that the Ebionites used only Matthew's Gospel (Irenaeus, *Haer.* 1.26.2) or the "Gospel According to the Hebrews" (Eusebius, *Hist. eccl.* 2.27.4). An easy solution was that the Gospel of Matthew in Hebrew was used by the Nazarenes who preceded the Ebionites. However, Epiphanius was not able to decide if the birth narratives were already cut from the version that was used by the Nazarenes, or only from the Greek version that was used by their successors, the Ebionites.

The gospel (or some passages of it) that Epiphanius had in his hands was not the only information that was at odds with the characterization of the Ebionites that Epiphanius found in his sources. Epiphanius reports that the Ebionites were using *Periodoi Petrou, Anabathmoi Iakobou* (30.15.1; 30.16.6), that obviously were sources for Pseudo-Clementine writings,[26] and "other Acts of the Apostles." Furthermore, Epiphanius seems to have ascribed to the Ebionites views that were typical of the *Book of Elchasai*.[27]

---

[25] For instance, the Ebionites, who were vegetarians, had introduced changes to John the Baptist's diet by replacing locusts (*akrides*) with honey cakes (*enkrides*).

[26] For the sources of the Pseudo-Clementine writings, see the article of F. Stanley Jones in this volume.

[27] For the *Book of Elchasai*, see the article of G. Luttikhuizen in this volume.

The reason why Epiphanius understood these documents to be Ebionite is unknown but it is clear that, because he did do so, he was faced with the problem of how to deal with the "traditional" picture of the Ebionites. Furthermore, had Epiphanius dealt only with the "Pseudo-Clementine" and "Elchasaite" Ebionites, he would have left open the possibility that Jewish Christianity in its more traditional, "pure" form was not so corrupt after all. My hypothesis is that, because this is not what he wanted to say, he created a picture of an earlier Nazarene heresy which made it possible for him to refute all attempts to try to be both a Jew and a Christian at the same time.

3.6. *The Doctrines of the Nazarenes*

As regards the Christology of the Nazarenes, Epiphanius confesses that he does not know whether or not the Nazarenes followed the Cerinthians in regarding Christ as a mere man (*Pan.* 19.7.6). This statement is revealing in two respects. First, since Epiphanius did not know the Nazarenes' stance on such a burning Christologial issue, it is unlikely that he had any personal contact with them. Second, Epiphanius' ignorance also shows that, by his time, the Nazarenes were not generally known as "those believing Jews who do believe in the virgin birth."

In the light of Epiphanius' ignorance, it is surprising that modern scholars usually characterize the Nazarenes' theology by pinpointing their belief in the virgin birth. One argument presented in favor of this view is that, although the Nazarenes were not mentioned by Epiphanius' predecessors, they were already known to Origen (*Contra Celsum* 5.61) and Eusebius (*Hist. eccl.* 3.27.1–3) who make a distinction between two groups of Ebionites: some Ebionites did believe in the virgin birth (= "Nazarenes"), while others did not (= the "real" Ebionites).[28] However, this distinction may itself be based on an early textual corruption of Irenaeus' heresiology.[29] In any case, it is clear

---

[28] See, Pritz, *Nazarene Jewish Christianity*, 28, 108–9; Stephen G. Wilson, *Related Strangers: Jews and Christians 70–170 C.E.* (Minneapolis: Fortress Press, 1995), 155–57; Mimouni, *Le judéo-christianisme*, 82, 86; Bauckham, "The Origin," 162–63.

[29] On the one hand, the extant manuscripts of Irenaeus' heresiology read that the Ebionites *did not* think of Christ *the same way* (*non similiter*) as Cerinthus and Carpocrates (*Haer.* 1.26.2). On the other hand, Hippolytus' version—which follows Irenaeus almost word for word—reads that the Ebionites *did* think of Christ the same way (*similiter*) as Cerinthus and Carpocrates (*Haer.* 7.34.1). Irrespective of which

that Epiphanius, the "inventor" of the Nazarenes, did not identify the Nazarenes with these "more orthodox" Ebionites. Further evidence of the Nazarenes' belief in the virgin birth has been found in Jerome's letter to Augustine (*Ep.* 112) but, as will be shown below, the reference to the Nazarenes in this letter is extremely problematic from a historical point of view.

If Epiphanius' did not know the stance of the Nazarenes on the virgin birth, how is it possible that he was able to present some other details about their doctrines? Where did he get his information?

Everything that Epiphanius reveals about the doctrines of the Nazarenes can be read in *Pan.* 29.7.3. Therefore, the passage will be repeated here, with the numbering of the information about the Nazarenes' doctrines that was used above:

> They acknowledge both (3) the resurrection of the dead, and (4) the divine creation of all things, and (5) declare that God is one, and that (6) his Son/servant (*pais*) is Jesus Christ.

According to Pritz, one indication of the fact that the Nazarenes were the successors of the earliest Jerusalem Church is that Epiphanius' information in *Pan.* 29.7.3 about the doctrines of the Nazarenes coheres with Acts' information about the early Jerusalem Church:

> One need make only a quick comparison with the opening chapters of Acts to see that these basic doctrines had a place in the teaching of the earliest Jerusalem church: the resurrection of the dead (Acts 2:24,32; 3:15; 4:10); God is the creator of all things (4:24); and belief in one God and his child (παῖς) Jesus Christ (3:13,26; 4:27,30). To this point we do not have anything that would differentiate the Nazarene church from the primitive church.[30]

---

version is original—I agree with those who opt for Hippolytus' text—it is clear that there were two versions of Irenaeus'/Hippolytus' heresiology in circulation: One version claimed that the Christology of the Ebionites was similar to the Cerinthians, that is, they did not accept the virgin birth, while the other version made the opposite claim. Origen seems to have come across both of these traditions, concluding that there must be two groups of Ebionites who had different views about Jesus' birth. Thus, the distinction that was made between the two types of Ebionites may only reveal the zeal of Origen and others for classifying groups on the basis of Christological distinctions. It may have nothing to do with the way the Ebionites themselves defined their in-group or intergroup boundaries. Cf. Klijn and Reinink, *Patristic Evidence*, 25–26.

[30] Pritz, *Nazarene Jewish Christianity*, 44. Similarly de Boer, "The Nazoreans," 246.

Pritz finds here substantial evidence for his thesis according to which the Nazarenes were successors of the early Jerusalem community and that their doctrine was "orthodox" from the very beginning. However, this line of thought is problematic in two respects. First, from a historical point of view, it is clear that Acts presents Luke's interpretation of the life and doctrines of the early Jerusalem community. Therefore, if there is a perfect match between *Pan.* 29.7.3 and Acts, it is questionable how much this reveals about the Nazarenes' relation to the early Jerusalem community. Second, as was shown above, at least some connections between *Panarion* 29 and Acts can be traced back to Epiphanius' use of Acts as a source in *Panarion* 29, which raises the question if that is the case also in *Pan.* 29.7.3.

Because the *belief in resurrection* does not play any role in other parts of Epiphanius' discussion of the Nazarenes, it is somewhat surprising to find it listed among the Nazarene doctrines. This reference becomes understandable in the light of Epiphanius' use of Acts since the resurrection is one of the main points of contention between Paul and his Jewish accusers in Acts.[31] For the sake of his own rhetoric, Paul—who is accused of being the leader of the Nazarene heresy—"confesses" the main points of the "Nazarene doctrine" in Acts 24:14–15:

> However, I admit that I worship the God of our fathers as a follower of the Way, which they call a heresy (*hairesis*). I believe everything that agrees with the Law and that is written in the Prophets, and I have the same hope in God as these men, that there will be a resurrection of both the righteous and the wicked.

A couple of verses later Paul's defense culminates in his recalling of the earlier events in Jerusalem:

> Or these who are here should state what crime they found in me when I stood before the Sanhedrin—unless it was this one thing I shouted as I stood in their presence: "It is concerning *the resurrection of the dead* that I am on trial before you today." (Acts 24:20–21)

Pritz correctly notes that Acts often connects resurrection to Jesus' position as *God's servant*. Notably, Epiphanius uses here the same Greek word (*pais*) that is also used in Acts 3:13–15, 26.[32] Because

---

[31] Cf. Schmidtke, *Neue Fragmente*, 122–23.
[32] *Pais* appears 24 times in the NT: Matt 8, Luke 9, John 1, Acts 6.

Epiphanius argued that the Nazarenes were mimicking the early
Jerusalem church, it is easy to understand why he spiced up his
description of the Nazarenes by borrowing these details from Acts.

However, Epiphanius did not need to consult Acts in order to
state that the Nazarenes believed in the *divine creation of all things*—
though one can find this belief in Acts 4:24—or that the Nazarenes
declared *belief in one God*. These characteristics were traditionally connected to Jewish Christians ever since Irenaus' heresiology, which
emphasized that, in contrast to the Cerinthians, the Jewish Christians
(Ebionites) did not believe that the world was created by a power
(demiurge) that was separate from the supreme God (Ireneaeus, *Haer.*
1.26.1–2).

4. Jerome's View of the Nazarenes

4.1. Jerome's Letter to Augustine

When assessing Jerome's references to the Nazarenes, it should be
kept in mind that he wrote after Epiphanius' *Panarion* was composed
and after he had been in contact with Epiphanius several times,
especially during their common journey to Rome in 382 C.E. Although
Jerome does not explicitly quote the *Panarion*, it is probable that,
when he moved to Palestine and started to refer to the Nazarenes,
he was already influenced by Epiphanius' interpretation of the
Nazarenes as "heretics."

As compared to Epiphanius, Jerome's attitude towards Christians
called Nazarenes is much more positive. Most of Jerome's references
are to be found in contexts where he quotes the writings that were
used by the Nazarenes: a gospel that they used and a commentary
on Isaiah. Jerome's critical comments are usually aimed at Ebion
and the Ebionites but on one occasion he also mentions the Nazarenes.
This is in his letter to Augustine in 404 C.E., where Jerome defends
his interpretation of Paul's and Peter's conflict in Antioch (cf. Gal 2).

In order to understand Jerome's critical reference to the Nazarenes
correctly, it is important to know something about the history of
Jerome's correspondence with Augustine. Almost two decades earlier (386/7), Jerome had argued in his *Commentary on Galatians*—following Origen and other Greek commentators—that in reality Paul
and Peter did not have any disagreement concerning the Christians'
obedience to the law. The conflict in Antioch (cf. Gal 2:11–14) was

staged only for didactical purposes: Peter pretended to obey the law in order to win Jews to his side and Paul pretended to reprimand him in order to make it clear that the Gentile Christians were not obliged to obey the law.

Augustine was offended by Jerome's interpretation because it seemed to indicate that the Bible was not trustworthy. He sent his own interpretation of the incident followed by some critical remarks and questions to Jerome. Jerome did not get Augustine's first letter and Augustine had to resend his inquiries. The original of the second letter also failed to reach Jerome and when Jerome was finally informed about Augustine's critical remarks through an abbreviated copy of the letter that was circulated around, he refused to answer. However, the dispute had become widely known and in 404 Jerome could no longer postpone his answer.[33] Jerome pushes Augustine's case to the extreme, claiming that Augustine obviously wants all the Jews who have become Christians to continue to obey the law. This would lead into the heresy of Cerinthus and Ebion:

> If this is true, we shall fall into the heresy of Cerinthus and Hebion, who believe in Christ and for this only have been anathematized by the fathers, because they mixed the ceremonies of the Law with the Gospel of Christ and in this way they confess new things while they did not cut loose from the old. What shall I say of the Ebionites who claim to be Christians? Until now a heresy is to be found in all parts of the East where Jews have their synagogues; it is called "of the Minaeans" and cursed by Pharisees up to now. Usually they are named Nazoreans. They believe in Christ, the Son of God born of Mary the virgin, and they say about him that he suffered and rose again under Pontius Pilate, in whom also we believe, but since they want to be both Jews and Christians, they are neither Jews nor Christians.

Jerome comes back to the same argument a bit later (112.16) but then he refers only to the Ebionites. Clearly, Jerome is not giving an objective account of the Nazarenes' doctrines here. The name of the Nazarenes is mentioned only in passing, as a synonym for the Ebionites, whose heresy Augustine is propagating, in Jerome's opinion. Jerome is making exactly the same point here as Epiphanius does at the

---

[33] For the conflict between Augustine and Jerome, see Kelly, *Jerome*, 217–20, 263–72; R. Hennings, *Die Briefwechsel zwischen Augustinus und Hieronymus und ihr Streit um den Kanon des Alten Testaments und die Auslegung von Gal. 2,11–14* (Supplements to Vigiliae christianae 21; Leiden: E. J. Brill, 1994), 274–91.

end of *Panarion* 29: If you try to be both a Jew and a Christian at the same time, you end up being neither Jewish nor Christian and you will become anathematized.

I think it is not too far-fetched to assume that Jerome owed this argument to Epiphanius. The reason why the name of the Nazarenes is taken up in this context is that the Pharisees were not known for cursing the Ebionites in their synagogues but the "Mineans" and the "Nazarenes"—obviously corresponding to the two forms of the *Eighteen Benedictions* that were in use in Jewish synagogues. Since no curse against the Ebionites was known, Jerome had to bring in the "Mineans" and the "Nazarenes" in order to show that Augustine's position was anathematized both by Jewish and Christian "fathers." Furthermore, Epiphanius' description of the Nazarenes'/Ebionites' beliefs is all but a quote from early Christian creeds: "They believe in Christ, the Son of God born of Mary the virgin, and they say about him that he suffered and rose again under Pontius Pilate, in whom also we believe . . ." The "fact"[34] that some of the Ebionites believed in the virgin birth was certainly known to Jerome from Origen's and Eusebius' writings. By reciting an early Christian creed, Jerome demonstrates that correct doctrine does not help if one still adheres to the Jewish law. Because Jerome lumps the Nazarenes together with the Ebionites and this serves so well his case against Augustine, one should refrain from drawing any conclusions about the Nazarenes' doctrine on the basis of this reference.

4.2. *The Gospel Used by the Nazarenes*

The first references to the gospel used by the Nazarenes are to be found in Jerome's eulogy of Christian teachers and writers, *Illustrious Men*, which was completed in 392.[35] Jerome wrote *Illustrious Men* in order to provide a Christian counterpart for the chronicles of secular authors. Jerome's inspiration for writing becomes clear in the last paragraph of his introduction to the book:

---

[34] As was noted above, the distinction between two kinds of Ebionites is historically unreliable.

[35] Jerome's first reference to the translation from a Hebrew gospel is to be found in his *Commentary on Micah* (7.6), completed in 391 C.E. However, in this connection Jerome does not refer to the Nazarenes. The same passage can also be found in Origen's writings (see below).

Let Celsus, then, learn, and Porphyri and Julian, those rabid dogs barking against Christ; let their followers learn—those who think that the church has had no philosophers, no orators, no men of learning; let them learn the number and quality of the men who founded, built and adorned the church, and let them stop accusing our faith of such rustic simplicity, and recognize their own ignorance.[36]

At the end of this list of illustrious, noble men there is none other than Jerome himself. Nevertheless, the reader of the book does not have to wait until the last lines of this noble collection before he/she gets a glimpse of the skills of its author. Second in the list, after Peter, is James, the brother of the Lord. Some information about him is also to be found in the "Gospel according to the Hebrews,"

> which I have recently translated into Greek and Latin and of which also Origen often makes use. (*Vir. ill.* 2)

After James follows Matthew, who, according to Jerome, composed a gospel in Hebrew, which was later on translated into Greek by an unknown author.[37] However,

> the Hebrew itself has been preserved until the present day in the library at Caesarea which Pamphilius the martyr so diligently collected. From the Nazarenes who use this book in Beroea, a city of Syria, I also received the opportunity to copy it. (*Vir. ill.* 3)

At first glance, these references to the gospel used by the Nazarenes seem to give an eyewitness' report of a Hebrew gospel. However, the number of quotations Jerome actually presents in his writings is very limited, had he really possessed a copy of the complete Gospel of Matthew in its original language. For instance, Jerome's *Commentary on Matthew* includes only six possible references to the Nazarenes' gospel, and of these, four are minor text critical notes. In some connections, Jerome says that the same gospel was used by Origen (*Vir. ill.* 2) and he quotes three times the same passage that is also known from Origen's writings (*Comm. Mich.* 7.6; *Comm. Isa.* 40.9–11; *Comm. Ezech.* 16.13). Furthermore, sometimes he claims that he translated the gospel into Greek (*Vir. ill.* 2, 3; *Comm. Matt.* 12.13) as well, and

---

[36] Trans. by T. P. Halton in Jerome, *On Illustrious Men* (trans. T. P. Halton; FC 100; Washington, D.C.: Catholic University of America, 1999).
[37] This information is obviously derived from Eusebius *Hist. eccl.* 3.24.6; 3.39.16; 5.8.2.

he refers to the translators in the first person plural (*Comm. Mich.* 7.5–7; *Comm. Matt.* 12.13).[38] Based on these observations, scholars have long thought that, in practice, Jerome was working with fragments of Jewish-Christian gospels which were partly gleaned from the writings of other authors.[39]

By the time that Jerome started to refer to the Hebrew Gospel of Matthew used by the Nazarenes, he was also promoting his program according to which the Latin translation should not be based on the Septuagint but on the original Hebrew bible (*Hebraica veritas*). The reason why Jerome began to mention that he had translated the gospel that was used by the Nazarenes must be connected to the fact that in *Illustrious Men*—which was published by the time he started to refer to the Nazarenes—his own list of publications also included the entire New and Old Testaments. However, he never completed the translation of the New Testament and the translation of the Old Testament was to be completed only about a decade later.[40] It seems that the fact that he had started the work and was looking forward completing the translation justified the inclusion of these accomplishments in his list of publications. Jerome wanted to be remembered as a man who had translated the entire Bible from Greek and Hebrew. Obviously, he also wanted to give the impression that he had access to the Hebrew original of Matthew's gospel. By the time he was writing *Illustrious Men*, he may also have thought that it might be possible to get a complete copy and translate it.[41]

In spite of the fact that Jerome got some of his quotations from other authors he also seems to have recorded some genuine passages from the writings of the Nazarenes. Therefore, scholars have tried

---

[38] Notably, the first person plural appears in the passages where either Origen or Greek language are also mentioned which suggest that in these cases the plural is not a stylistic device but implies some other (Greek) authors in addition to Jerome.

[39] This has been clear since Schmidtke's *Neue Fragmenten*.

[40] Cf. Kelly, *Jerome*, 161–62.

[41] During the years preceding the writing of *Illustrious Men*, Jerome prepared several works that required much collecting and compiling. In addition to Eusebius' work, he collected information from various Christian and rabbinical sources for his *Hebrew Names*, *Biblical Places* and *Hebrew Questions*. He also prepared a small exegetical work on Psalms (*Commentarioli*). This was based on Origen's *Enchiridion*, which Jerome had supplemented with the remarks that Origen had made on the Psalms in his larger works. See, Kelly, *Jerome*, 153–59. Thus, it is quite conceivable that, along with these projects, he also planned a translation of the "Gospel according to Hebrews" and was collecting material for that.

to reconstruct the gospel that the Nazarenes used by excluding the quotations that Jerome must have derived from other authors. A widely accepted reconstruction makes a distinction between the Greek "Gospel of the Hebrews" that was known to Origen and other Alexandrian writers (Clement, Didymus the Blind) and the Semitic "Gospel of the Nazarenes." Although the contents of these reconstructed gospels are presented in several collections of apocryphal gospels,[42] it is far from certain if it is possible to define valid criteria on the basis of which a distinction can be made between the "Gospel of the Hebrews" and the "Gospel of the Nazarenes," and if indeed such a distinction is justified.[43]

Because of all the uncertainties connected to the reconstruction of the gospel that was used by the Nazarenes, Jerome's alleged quotations from it do not provide a very fruitful starting point for a discussion about the Nazarenes' doctrine and practices. Furthermore, since many of Jerome's quotations from "the gospel that the Nazarenes used" do not reveal very much about the theology and practices of its supposed composers and transmitters, it is irrelevant to the present discussion to which gospel the quotations are to be ascribed.

4.3. *The Nazarenes and the Rabbis*

A much more reliable source for information about the Nazarenes is the Nazarenes' explanation of Isaiah, quoted by Jerome in his *Commentary on Isaiah*, written around 408/410. Jerome's commentary contains five quotations from the Nazarenes' explanation. Three of these are to be found in one block, at the end of Isaiah 8 and in the beginning of Isaiah 9. The remaining two are in Isa 29:17–21

---

[42] For instance, P. Vielhauer and G. Strecker, "Jewish-Christian Gospels," in *New Testament Apocrypha* (ed. W. Schneemelcher; trans. and ed. R. McL. Wilson; 2 vols.; Cambridge: James Clarke & Co., 1991), 1:134–77; A. F. J. Klijn, *Jewish-Christian Gospel Tradition* (Supplements to Vigiliae Christianae 17; Leiden: E. J. Brill, 1992).

[43] For critical views, see Mimouni, *Le judéo-christianisme*, 209–11, 215–16. W. L. Petersen, *Tatian's Diatessaron: Its Creation, Dissemination, Significance and History in Scholarship* (Supplements to Vigiliae Christianae 25; Leiden: E. J. Brill, 1994), 29–31, 39–41; P. Luomanen, "Where Did Another Rich Man Come From? The Jewish-Christian Profile of the Story About a Rich Man in the 'Gospel of the Hebrews' (Origen, *Comm. in Matth.* 15.14)," *Vigiliae christianae* 57 (2003), 243–75, esp. 245–46, 262–65; P. Luomanen, "Let Him Who Seeks Continue Seeking: The Relationship Between Jewish-Christian Gospels and the *Gospel of Thomas*," in *Thomasine Traditions in Antiquity: The Gospel of Thomas and Its Relatives* (ed. J. Ma. Asgeirsson, A. DeConick, and R. Uro; forthcoming).

and 31:6–9. All these quotations exemplify the Nazarenes' highly critical attitude towards the early Rabbis and their tradition. Because Jerome does not draw on the Nazarenes' commentary in any other connection or even refer to the work in any of his writings, he probably did not have the entire explanation available. More likely, he was only using a Nazarene collection of prophetic testimonies against the "scribes and the pharisees" that he had either received from the "Nazarenes" or that was connected to them for some other reason.[44]

4.4. The "Scatterer" and the "Unholy"

In the beginning of the first quotation, Jerome introduces the Nazarenes as the ones "who accept Christ in such a way that they do not cease to observe the old Law." The quoted explanation itself concerns two houses mentioned in Isaiah 8:14:[45]

According to Jerome,

> the Nazarenes . . . explain the two houses as the two families, viz. of Shammai and Hillel, from whom originated the Scribes and the Pharisees. Akiba who took over their school is called the master of Aquila the proselyte and after him came Meir who has been succeeded by Joannes the son of Zakkai and after him Eliezer and further Telphon, and next Ioseph Galilaeus and Josua up to the capture of Jerusalem. Shammai then and Hillel were born not long before the Lord, they originated in Judea. The name of the first means scatterer and of the second unholy, because he scattered and defiled the precepts of the Law by his traditions and δευτερώσεις. And these are the two houses who did not accept the Saviour who has become to them destruction and shame. (*Comm. Isa.* 8.11–15)

The passage gives the impression of being a combination of information based on the Nazarenes' explanation and Jerome's own comments to the reader. Other quotations indicate that the Nazarenes' explanation quite faithfully repeated the original sentences and images of Isaiah's passage but interpreted them as predictions of the actions

---

[44] Schmidtke, "Neue Fragmente," 63–90, argued that Jerome had received the information about the Nazarenes' Isaiah exegesis from his teacher Apollinaris. The assumption is a part of Schmidtke's—generally dismissed—hypothesis that both Jerome and Epiphanius (in *Pan.* 29) derived their information about the Nazarenes from Apollinaris.

[45] Isaiah 8:14: ". . . but for both houses of Israel he will be a stone that causes men to stumble and a rock that makes them fall. And for the people of Jerusalem he will be a trap and a snare."

of "the Scribes and the Pharisees" and the future's judgment of them. Thus, the scornful explanations of the names of Hillel and Shammai as well as the list of Rabbis may very well have been derived from elsewhere.[46]

Nevertheless, even if the passage was enlarged with some critical notes, the mere fact that Shammai's and Hillel's schools are identified with the two houses of Israel, which are to face the judgment, indicates that the Nazarenes' own explanation must already have been directed against the Rabbinic tradition.

The interpretation of the name of Hillel indicates that the one who was responsible for it was working with the Hebrew script since Hillel becomes "unholy" if one reads the root as *hll* instead of *khll*. Pritz has also pointed out that Telphon in Jerome's quotation most likely refers to Tarphon who was one of Akiba's students. This mistake, too, is understandable only in an unpointed Hebrew text where vowels are not indicated and a defective *l* may resemble *r*. A third indication of Hebrew/Aramaic being the original language of the exposition is to be found in the passage that is quoted below. There it is stated that the "preaching became more dominant, that means the preaching was multiplied" (*ingrauata est, id est multiplicata praedecatio*). However, neither "becoming more dominant" or "multiplied" fits the context very well. Obviously, Jerome has here had difficulties in translating the Hebrew root *kbd* which can mean (in Hiphil) both "make heavy" and "make honored." Jerome's Vulgate opted for the first meaning in Isa 8:23 and that was also his starting point when he was translating the Nazarene's exposition. However, the original meaning in the context of the Nazarenes' expositions must have been "made honored," which Jerome did not realize. Klijn has also pointed out several connections between the Nazarenes' expositions and Targumic traditions,[47] which is a further indication of the fact that

---

[46] For instance, the explanation of the name Shammai has clear connections to Jerome's Latin translation of the Old Testament and it is not impossible that Jerome himself was responsible for that. See Pritz, *Nazarene Jewish Christianity*, 61. In the Vulgate, *dissipare* ('to scatter') is often used to translate the Hebrew root *shmm*. Furthermore, the sequence of the Rabbis is incorrect since Meir should be the last one on the list. This may indicate that the list was later on enlarged with Yohanan ben Zakkai and his students and the revisor did not know the real sequence of the Rabbis, or that the one who added the reference to the Rabbis was not too well versed in the Rabbinic tradition in the first place. Cf. Schmidtke, "Neue Fragmente," 123; Pritz, *Nazarene Jewish Christianity*, 59.

[47] A. F. J. Klijn, "Jerome's Quotations from a Nazorean Interpretation of Isaiah,"

the passages Jerome quoted were derived from Aramaic-speaking Christians.

In addition to the connection with Hebrew and Aramaic scriptures, the quoted passages reflect the wordings of the Vulgate.[48] Because the exposition often paraphrases Isaiah's passages, it is natural that Jerome drew on his own Latin translation instead of preparing an independent direct translation from the Nazarenes' exposition.

4.5. Did Jerome's Nazarenes Still Observe the Old Law?

The criticism of the Scribes and the Pharisees is so obvious in the Nazarenes' expositions that there is no doubt that the Nazarenes totally rejected the early Rabbis and their teaching. However, at some points the criticism goes so far that it becomes questionable if the excerpts really were derived from people "who accept Christ in such a way that they do not cease to observe the old Law," as Jerome claimed in the introduction to the first quotation.

> The Nazoreans whose opinion I have set forth above, try to explain this passage in the following way: When Christ came and his preaching shone out, the land of Zebulon and the land of Naphtali first of all were freed from the errors of the Scribes and the Pharisees and he shook off their shoulders the very heavy yoke of the Jewish traditions. Later, however, the preaching became more dominant, that means the preaching was multiplied, through the Gospel of the apostle Paul who was the last of all the apostles. And the Gospel of Christ shone to the most distant tribes and the way of the whole sea. Finally the whole world which earlier walked or sat in darkness and was imprisoned in the bonds of idolatry and death, has seen the clear light of the gospel. (*Comm. Isa.* 9.1)

According to this quotation, the Nazarenes fully accepted Paul's mission to the Gentiles. Thus, their stance was totally different form the Ebionites and from the Jewish-Christianity of the *Pseudo-Clementines*.[49]

---

in *Judéo-Christianisme: Recherches historiques et théologiques offertes en hommage au Cardinal Jean Daniélou*, *RSR* 60 (1972): 241–55. In addition to connections that Klijn has pointed out, it is to be noted that the translation *vectigales* (see below *Comm. Isa.* 31:6–9) reflects later Hebrew meaning of the root *sm* and the language of Targums. See BDB, סם (pp. 586–87).

[48] For instance, the following expressions are paralleled in the Vulgate: *stridunt in incantationibus suis* (Isa 8:19), *qui peccare faciebant homines in verbo* (Isa 29:21).

[49] Cf. S. Häkkinen's and F. S. Jones' articles in this volume.

Even though it might be possible to interpret the clause "were freed from the errors of the Scribes and the Pharisees" so that only the Rabbinic tradition was dismissed by Christ, in the following sentence the "heavy yoke of Jewish traditions" (*grauissimum traditionum Iudaicarum iugum*) is discarded altogether. Notably, the image of the "yoke"—which in Judaism is often connected to covenant loyalty in general—cannot be found in those verses of Isaiah that the passage paraphrases (Is 8:23; 9:1). It is deliberately brought into the exposition in order to make it clear that Jesus' preaching did not comply with the "Jewish traditions."

The total rejection of Jewish traditions can also be seen in the following passage which equates the following of the traditions with a nation's worship of idols:

> For the rest the Nazarenes explain the passage in this way: When the Scribes and the Pharisees tell you to listen to them, men who do everything for the love of the belly and who hiss during their incantations in the way of the magicians in order to deceive you, you must answer them like this. It is no wonder if you follow your traditions since every nation consults its own idols.[50] We must not, therefore, consult your dead about the living ones. On the contrary God has given us the Law and the testimonies of the scriptures. If you are not willing to follow them you shall not have light, and darkness will always oppress you. (*Comm. Isa.* 8.19–22)

The last passage that Jerome quotes also targets the Israelites as whole, not just to the Scribes and the Pharisees as their leaders:[51]

> The Nazarenes understand this passage in this way: O sons of Israel who deny the Son of God with the most vicious opinion, turn to him and his apostles. If you will do this, you will reject all idols which to you were a cause of sin in the past and the devil will fall before you, not because of your powers but because of the compassion of God. And his young men who a certain time earlier fought for him, will be tributaries of the Church and any of its power and stone will pass. Also the philosophers and every perverse dogma will turn their backs to the sign of the cross. Because this is the meaning of the Lord that his will take place, whose fire or light is in Sion and his oven in Jerusalem. (*Comm. Isa.* 31.6–9)

---

[50] In Latin: *Non mirum si uos uestras traditiones sequamini, cum unaquaque gens sua consulat idola.*

[51] Klijn, "Jerome's Quotations," 253–54, thinks that the Nazarenes' exposition only attacks the Jewish leaders but it is hard to find such a distinction in the texts.

The passage reveals a viewpoint that is nothing short of the formative Catholic view: The Jews are expected to convert and accept the
apostolic faith. In order to do so they will have to abandon their
worship of idols, which—as was shown above—is the same as following Jewish traditions. Consequently, the young men of Israel, who
earlier had fought with the devil against the Christians, will become
the tributaries of the Church. Finally, the conclusion of the passage
also indicates that, despite its sharp criticism of the Scribes and the
Pharisees, the Nazarenes' exposition was also attacking the "philosophers" and other "perverse dogmas." Thus the Nazarenes guarded
their dogmatic frontiers much like the church fathers themselves.

A remarkable parallel to the Nazarenes' position can be found in
the *Didascalia Apostolorum* (*DA*), which confirms that the Nazarene's
interpretation exemplified a typically Syrian attitude towards the early
Rabbis. *Didascalia Apostolorum* makes a clear distinction between the
First Law that binds the Christians (Moses' Ten Commandments)
and the Second Legislation (*deuterōsis*; cf. *deuterōseis* in Jerome, *Comm.
Isa.* 8.11–15) with which the Jews were bound after they had fallen
into idol worship (Ex 32). Consequently, obedience to this Second
Legislation is equated with *idol worship* and is described as a *heavy
burden* and a *hard yoke* in contrast to the First Law which is described
as a *light yoke* and equated with the *"Law and the Prophets"* that Jesus
has come to fulfill according to Matt 5:17.[52] Obviously, Jerome's
Nazarenes and the *Didascalia Apostolorum* had a similar view of the
Second Legislation. The *Didascalia Apostolorum* is usually dated to the
third century but it was still used in Syria in the latter half of
the fourth century since Epiphanius found it in the hands of Audians
who were Syrian Christians and "heretics" to Epiphanius (*Pan.*
70.10.1–4; cf. *DA* XXI; Lagarde, pp. 91–92).

In the light of Jerome's passages and similar views presented in
the *Didascalia Apostolorum*, it is difficult to picture Jerome's "Nazarenes"
as a strict, law-observant sect separated from the formative Catholic
Church. The Christians from whom Jerome received the expositions
unreservedly accepted Paul and his mission to the Gentiles. Their

---

[52] See, *DA* II/Lagarde, pp. 4–5; *DA* IV/Lagarde, p. 12; *DA* XIX/Lagarde, p. 79
and *DA* XXVI/Lagarde, pp. 107–9, 111–12, 115). For *DA*'s use of the term δευτέρωσις,
see C. E. Fonrobert, "The *Didascalia Apostolorum*: A Mishnah of the Disciples of
Jesus," *JECS* 9 (2001): 483–509, esp. 495–99.

criticism was also targeted at the Jewish nation and people as a whole. The Jews were required to repent/convert and this did not presuppose the maintenance of a particular Jewish identity or aim at the re-establishment of a traditional Jewish covenantal relationship, as one would expect if the repentance was announced by a person who still had a Jewish self-understanding. Instead, the Jews were expected to adopt a Christian identity by becoming subjects of the Apostles.

On the basis of the Rabbis named in the quotations, the passages cannot be dated earlier than the mid-second century. However, since the exposition indicates that the *deuterōtai*—the church fathers' standard expression for early Rabbis—have passed away[53] and argues that these dead teachers should not be consulted, it is to be assumed that the writer(s) of the exposition were confronted with Jewish teachers who already had the Mishnah in their hands, and that the Mishnah had also been established as authoritative teaching.[54] If this is correct, then the most likely time of composition for the expositions would be the late third or early fourth century. Because the comments were written in Hebrew script and the writer was acquainted with Targumic traditions, the writer must have been a Jewish convert.

5. *Who Were the "Nazarenes?"*

Epiphanius' description of the "heresy" of the Nazarenes in *Panarion* 29 is first and foremost a refutation of an idealized, stereotyped picture of people who try to be both Jews and Christians at the same time. The refutation of this standard type of Jewish Christianity needed to be included in the *Panarion* because—as it seemed from Epiphanius' point of view—the Ebionites who were known to him had adopted all kinds of strange ideas from Elchasite and Pseudo-Clementine writings. Epiphanius did not have any Nazarene texts

---

[53] Jerome, *Comm. Isa* 29.17–21: "What we understand to have been written about the devil and his angels, the Nazoreans believe to have been said against the Scribes and the Pharisees, because the δευτερωταὶ passed away, who earlier deceived the people with very vicious traditions. And they watch night and day to deceive the simple ones who made men sin against the Word of God in order that they should deny that Christ was the Son of God."

[54] Cf. Fonrobert, "The *Didascalia Apostolorum*," 496, who argues that the *Didascalia's* use of the term δευτέρωσις presumes the consolidation of mishnaic traditions.

or any sources describing the Nazarenes available, but on the basis of Eusebius' *Ecclesiastical History*, Acts and his own conclusions, he was able to create a picture of the genesis, doctrines and practices of the heresy of the Nazarenes that was easy for him and his fellow Christians to refute. The heresy of the Nazarenes as it is depicted in *Panarion* 29 is pure fiction.[55]

Nevertheless, three pieces of information with some historical credibility can be inferred from Epiphanius' story. First, by Epiphanius' time in some Jewish synagogues in Palestine and Syria the prayer of *Eighteen Benedictions* included a curse on the Nazarenes, that is Aramaic/Syriac-speaking Christians. Second, areas to the east and north-east of the Jordan river and especially the villages of Kokaba and Beroea were known as places where Christians adhered to the Jewish law. Third, in Syriac "Nazarenes" was a common title for all Christians and it seems that, in the Latin/Greek-speaking Christian communities of Antioch, the term Nazarenes was especially used for some Christians who lived in Beroea. This, together with the fact that for the Latin and Greek fathers, Syriac-speaking Christians, the "Nazarenes," had a reputation for being heretical,[56] may have been a good enough reason for Epiphanius to call the "standard" Jewish Christians, who were not yet influenced by Ebion's and Elchasai's weird doctrines, Nazarenes.

In principle, Jerome shared Epiphanius' view of the Nazarenes as Jewish-Christian heretics but in practice, except for some general ref-

---

[55] If the "heresy" of the Nazarenes is fictional, as is argued in this article, it probably is not the only fictional group in Epiphanius' long list of heresies. An interesting point of comparision is the Alogi, whom Epiphanius discusses in *Pan.* 51. In the case of the Alogi, Epiphanius explicitly states that he himself invented the term to be used for those who reject the Gospel of John and Revelation. For the Alogi, see A. Marjanen, "Montanism and the Formation of the New Testament Canon," in *The Formation of the Early Church* (ed. Jostein Ådna; WUNT; Tübingen: Mohr Siebeck, forthcoming). According to Frank Williams, "(w)e cannot assume that, because Epiphanius refers to a given group as a 'sect' and gives it a name, it was necessarily an organized body ... Epiphanius says that he himself coined the names, 'Alogi,' 'Antidicomarians,' and 'Collyridians,' and he may have done the same in other cases. Certainly some of his 'sects' are simply persons who take a particular position; ... An Epiphanian 'sect,' then, may represent anything from an organized church to a school of thought, or a tendency manifested by some exegetes." ("Introduction," XVIII).

[56] This is especially reflected in their earlier history up to the time of Ephrem and the bishop Rabbula. See, J. B. Segal, *Edessa: The Blessed City* (Oxford: Oxford University Press, 1970; repr., Piscataway, N.J.: Gorgias Press, 2001), 87–93.

erences, he did not polemicize against them. Obviously, some Christians who were called Nazarenes had provided Jerome useful information about the Hebrew scriptures which he was able to use to back up his program of *Hebraica veritas*. Jerome may also have been reluctant to criticize the Nazarenes because the excerpts from the Nazarenes' writings he had received did not evince heretical ideas or practices. Instead, they provided him with a powerful weapon to be used in his anti-Rabbinic polemics. As a matter of fact, the fragments in Jerome's writings that are likely to be derived from some Christians called Nazarenes—instead of testifying to the existence of a group of heretics—indicate that the term Nazarenes was also connected to Syriac/Aramaic-speaking Christians whose views hardy differed from mainstream Catholicism.

Overall, there is no historically reliable evidence which would justify an assumption that, among Syriac/Aramaic-speaking Christians, there would have been a more or less organized faction with borders defined by characteristically "Nazarene" doctrines, practices or self-understanding, distinct from other Syriac/Aramaic-speaking Christians. Even for the church fathers who lived in Palestine, Syriac/Aramaic-speaking Christianity was by and large an unmapped territory of which they had gained knowledge more by hearsay than through personal experience.

6. Christian Identity in the Making:
The "Genesis" of the Heresy of the Nazarenes

Why did Epiphanius create the picture of the Nazarene heresy practically out of nothing? I have suggested above that this was because the sources that Epiphanius had in his hands, and which he connected to the Ebionites, did not match the traditional information about the Ebionites and because Epiphanius still wanted to refute Jewish Christianity also in its "pure form." Thus, in line with his basic conviction that heresies sprung from each other, he painted a picture of the development of Jewish-Christian heresies where the Nazarenes, placed between the Cerinthians and the Ebionites, played the role of imitators of the early Jerusalem church, pure in their "Christian doctrine" as the early Jerusalem community was pure in Epiphanius' mind, and erring only in their adherence to the Jewish law. With such a clear picture, it was easy to refute all the attempts to connect Christianity with the practicing of the Jewish law. Epiphanius' comment at the end of *Panarion* 29 is revealing: "People like these are easy to catch and refute—they are nothing but Jews" (*Pan.* 29.9.1).

Stereotypes are very powerful tools in creating and maintaining boundaries. According to social identity theory, stereotyping often accompanies ingroup/outgroup categorization.[57] Fredrick Barth has modeled the formation of (ethnic) identity on three levels: 1) the micro level which focuses on personal and interpersonal interaction, 2) the median level which focuses on the formation of collectives, and 3) the macro level which is connected to the apparatus of the state. According to Barth, the "median level is needed to depict the processes that create collectivities and mobilize groups. . . . This is the field of entrepreneurship, leadership and rhetoric; here stereotypes are established and collectives are set in motion. . . . Processes on this level intervene to constrain and compel people's expression and action on the micro level; package deals and either-or choices are imposed, and many aspects of the boundaries and dichotomies of ethnicity are fashioned."[58]

Although Barth is mainly interested in the formation of ethnic identity, it is clear that the median level of his analysis can also be applied to illuminate the role of heresiologies in the formation of Christian identity, especially as far as this identity is formed in relation to an ethnic group such as the Jews. Epiphanius—and other heresiologists—can be seen as social entrepreneurs who create stereotypes and collectives in order to control the actions of individual Christians and their relation to outsiders.

One central aspect in the formation of social identities is the patterning of time by highlighting significant events in the history and future of the people whose collective identity is being created. The concept of "social time" refers to the recording of events of social

---

[57] See, for instance, M. A. Hogg and D. Abrams, *Social Identifications: A Social Psychology of Intergroup Relations and Group Processes* (London: Routledge, 1988), 77–78; P. F. Esler, *Conflict and Identity in Romans: The Social Setting of Paul's Letter* (Minneapolis: Fortress, 2003), 21–22.

[58] F. Barth, "Enduring and Emerging Issues in the Analysis of Ethnicity," in *The Anthropology of Ethnicity: Beyond "Ethnic Groups and Boundaries"* (ed. H. Vermeulen and C. Govers; Amsterdam: Het Spinhuis, 1994), 11–32, esp. 20–22. For a summary of Barth's approach, see Esler, *Conflict*, 42–49. According to Esler, the median level of Barth's modelling "corresponds to what Paul is attempting to achieve in Romans."

change which a group finds significant. Those who have the power to impose their interpretation of significance of events on others largely determine which events will become significant within a group. Consequently, when power relations change within the group or when new events call forth restructuring of the social time, the history of the community needs to be rewritten. Philip Esler has aptly described this process: "Thus, as power relations in society at large or within a particular group change, modifications are made to the patterning of social time. Those in power rewrite the meaning of some events, erase some, and *invent* others."[59]

In the case of early Christian heresiologies, one can clearly see that the heresiologists not only aimed at refuting undesirable doctrines and practices, but also imposed their interpretation of the history of the "heresies" they were discussing. The history of the early Catholic Church was purified and all ties to "heretic" groups cut by claiming that the heresies were sprouting from one single root separate from the Church. The heresiologists, who were writing mainly for their own community, had full power to create a pre-history for the groups and doctrines they were refuting. At some points, where the writers were involved with polemics, glimpses of the way in which their opponents themselves viewed their own earlier history come to the surface, as can be seen in Epiphanius' note about the Ebionites who traced their origins back to Apostolic times. Yet it was easy for Epiphanius to place the Ebionites in the history created for the heretics by claiming that the Ebionites originated with a certain Ebion—who had already been invented by Epiphanius' predecessors[60]—and that Ebion got his "poor" name from his parents by prophecy. All this is nonsense from the viewpoint of present standards of critical history, but its value for building up the sense of doctrinal purity of the church cannot be underestimated.

The parallel story of the heresies was already there when Epiphanius started to write his *Panarion*.[61] He only needed to update the story to incorporate more recent heresies as well. In the case of Jewish Christians, he was able to anchor the genesis of this branch of heresy

---

[59] Esler, *Conflict*, 24 (italics added).
[60] The name Ebion probably appeared for the first time in Hippolytus' *Syntagma*. See S. Häkkinen's article in this volume.
[61] Irenaeus had traced the heresies back to Simon Magus, and Hippolytus back to Greek philosophies.

more firmly in history when he came up with the idea that the
Nazarenes started to imitate the Christians who had escaped to Pella.
By doing this, Epiphanius argued that people who mixed Jewish
practices with their Christian way of life were not descendants of the
early Jerusalem community. Instead, they were people who had misunderstood the true character of Christianity from the very beginning.

The stereotyped picture of the Nazarenes that was created by
Epiphanius has proved to be very pervasive. In the light of the above
assessment, this persistence is hardly based on the weight of historical evidence about their existence. Yet even present critical scholarship usually takes it for granted that there once existed a group
of Christians who were not just called Nazarenes (as all Christians
were in Syriac) but who were also distinguishable from other Christians
in respect of their doctrine, practices and the literature that they
used.[62] One reason for this might be that once a very clear picture
of a historical entity is created, it may be easier for the human mind
to try to define its "true" character and place it in the history than
to discard the idea altogether. There may be other explanatory factors as well. One cannot help asking if the image of the Nazarenes
has been so pervasive in scholarly discourse because it still has a
positive role in legitimizing the present Christian identity. For instance,
by showing that to the extent that Christians continued to regard
the Jewish law binding, this was done in full accord with the earliest Christian community in Jerusalem, whose Christology was "orthodox" in character.

Bibliography

Barth, F. "Enduring and Emerging Issues in the Analysis of Ethnicity." Pages 11–32
in *The Anthropology of Ethnicity: Beyond "Ethnic Groups and Boundaries."* Edited by
H. Vermeulen and C. Govers. Amsterdam: Het Spinhuis, 1994.
Bauckham, R. "The Origin of the Ebionites." Pages 162–81 in *The Image of the
Judaeo-Christians in Ancient Jewish and Christian Literature.* Edited by P. J. Tomson
and Doris Lambers-Petry. Wissenschaftliche Untersuchungen zum Neuen Testament
158. Tübingen: Mohr Siebeck, 2003.
Baur, F. C. *Das Christentum und die christliche Kirche der drei ersten Jahrhunderte.* 2d ed.
Tübingen: L. Fr. Fues, 1860. Repr. in vol. 3 of *Ausgewählte Werke in Einzelausgaben.*
Edited by K. Scholder. Stuttgart – Bad Cannstatt: Friedrich Frommann (Günther
Holzboog), 1966.

---

[62] J. E. Taylor, "The Phenomenon of Early Jewish-Christianity: Reality or Scholarly
Invention?" *VC* 44 (1990): 313–34, esp. 326; Bauckham, "The Origin," 162; De
Boer, "The Nazoreans," 239.

Blanchetière, F. *Enquête sur les racines juives du mouvement chrétien* (30–135). Paris: Cerf, 2001.

Brown, F., S. R. Driver, and C. A. Briggs, *A Hebrew and English Lexicon of the Old Testament.* Oxford: Clarendon, 1907.

De Boer, M. C. "The Nazoreans: Living at the Boundary of Judaism and Christianity." Pages 239–62 in *Tolerance and Intolerance in Early Judaism and Christianity.* Edited by G. N. Stanton and G. A. G. Stroumsa. Cambridge: Cambridge University Press, 1998.

Esler, P. F. *Conflict and Identity in Romans: The Social Setting of Paul's Letter.* Minneapolis: Fortress, 2003.

Fonrobert, C. E. "The *Didascalia Apostolorum*: A Mishnah of the Disciples of Jesus." *Journal of Early Christian Studies* 9 (2001): 483–509.

Freedman, D. N., ed. *Anchor Bible Dictionary.* 6 vols. New York: Doubleday, 1992.

Goulder, M. D. *A Tale of Two Missions.* London: SCM Press, 1994.

Häkkinen, S. *Köyhät kerettiläiset: Ebionit kirkkoisien teksteissä.* Suomalaisen Teologisen Kirjallisuusseuran julkaisuja 223. Helsinki: Suomalainen Teologinen Kirjallisuusseura, 1999.

Hennings, R. *Die Briefwechsel zwischen Augustinus und Hieronymus und ihr Streit um den Kanon des Alten Testaments und die Auslegung von Gal. 2,11–14.* Supplements to Vigiliae christianae 21. Leiden: E. J. Brill, 1994.

Hogg, M. A., and D. Abrams. *Social Identifications: A Social Psychology of Intergroup Relations and Group Processes.* London: Routledge, 1988.

Horbury, W. "The Benediction of the Minim and Early Jewish Christian Controversy." *Journal of Theological Studies* 33 (1982): 19–61.

Kelly, J. N. D. *Jerome: His Life, Writings, and Controversies.* New York: Harper & Row, 1975.

Kimelman, R. "Birkat ha-Minim and the Lack of Evidence for Anti-Christian Jewish Prayer in Late Antiquity." Pages 226–44 in *Aspects of Judaism in the Greco-Roman Period.* Edited by E. P. Sanders. Vol. 2 of *Jewish and Christian Self-Definition.* Edited by E. P. Sanders, A. I. Baumgarten, and A Mendelson. London: SCM Press, 1975.

Kittel, G., and G. Friedrich, eds. *Theological Dictionary of the New Testament.* Translated by G. W. Bromiley. 10 vols. Grand Rapids: Eerdmans, 1964–1976.

Klijn, A. F. J. "Jerome's Quotations from a Nazorean Interpretation of Isaiah." Pages 241–55 in *Judéo-Christianisme: Recherches historiques et théologiques offertes en hommage au Cardinal Jean Daniélou. Recherches de science religieuse* 60, 1972.

———. *Jewish-Christian Gospel Tradition.* Supplements to Vigiliae christianae 17. Leiden: E. J. Brill, 1992.

———. *Patristic Evidence for Jewish-Christian Sects.* Novum Testamentum Supplements 36. Leiden: E. J. Brill, 1973.

Luomanen, P. "Let Him Who Seeks Continue Seeking: The Relationship Between Jewish-Christian Gospels and the *Gospel of Thomas.*" *Thomasine Traditions in Antiquity: The Gospel of Thomas and Its Relatives.* Edited by J. Ma. Asgeirsson, A. De Conick and R. Uro, forthcoming.

———. "Where Did Another Rich Man Come From? The Jewish-Christian Profile of the Story About a Rich Man in the 'Gospel of the Hebrews' (Origen, *Comm. in Matth.* 15.14)." *Vigiliae christianae* 57 (2003): 243–75.

Lüdemann, G. *Heretics: The Other Side of Early Christianity.* Translated by J. Bowden. Louisville, Ky.: Westminster John Knox, 1996.

———. "The Successors of Pre-70 Jerusalem Christianity: A Critical Evaluation of the Pella-Tradition." Pages 161–173 in *The Shaping of Christianity in the Second and Third Centuries.* Vol. 1 of *Jewish and Christian Self-Definition.* Edited by E. P. Sanders. London: SCM Press, 1980.

Marjanen, A. "Montanism and the Formation of the New Testament Canon." In *The Formation of Early Christianity.* Edited by Jostein Ådna. WUNT. Tübingen: Mohr Siebeck, forthcoming.

Mimouni, S. C. *Le judéo-christianisme ancien: essais historiques*. Paris: Cerf, 1998.

Morgan, R. "Tübingen school." Pages 710–13 in *A Dictionary of Biblical Interpretation*. Edited by R. J. Coggins and J. L. Houlden. 3d impression. London: SCM Press, 1994.

Petersen, W. L. Review of J. Verheyden, *De vlucht van de christenen naar Pella: Onderzoek van het getuigenis van Eusebius en Epiphanius*. *Second Century*, 8 (1991): 186–88.

———. *Tatian's Diatessaron: Its Creation, Dissemination, Significance and History in Scholarship*. Supplements to Vigiliae christianae 25. Leiden: E. J. Brill, 1994.

Pritz, R. A. *Nazarene Jewish Christianity: From the End of the New Testament Period Until Its Disappearance in the Fourth Century*. Leiden: E. J. Brill, 1988.

Ritschl, A. *Die Entstehung der altkatholischen Kirche: Eine kirchen- und dogmengeschichtliche Monographie*. 2d ed. Bonn: Adolph Marcus, 1857.

Schäfer, P. "Die sogenannte Synode von Jabne: Zur Trennung von Juden und Christen im ersten/zweiten Jh. n. Chr." *Judaica* 31 (1975): 54–64, 116–24.

Schmidtke, A. *Neue Fragmente und Untersuchungen zu den judenchristlichen Evangelien: Ein Beitrag zur Literatur und Geschichte der Judenchristen*. Texte und Untersuchungen zur Geschichte der altchristlichen Literatur 3.7. Leipzig: J. H. Hinrichs'sche Buchhandlung, 1911.

Schoeps, H. J. *Theologie und Geschichte des Judenchristentums*. Tübingen: J. C. B. Mohr, 1949.

Segal, J. B. *Edessa: The Blessed City*. Oxford: Oxford University Press, 1970. Repr., Piscataway, N.J.: Gorgias, 2001.

Taylor, J. E. *Christians and the Holy Places: The Myth of Jewish-Christian Origins*. Oxford: Clarendon, 1993.

———. "The Phenomenon of Early Jewish-Christianity: Reality or Scholarly Invention?" *Vigiliae christianae* 44 (1990): 313–34.

Vielhauer, P., and G. Strecker. "Jewish-Christian Gospels." Pages 134–77 in Vol. 1 of *New Testament Apocrypha*. Edited by W. Schneemelcher. English translation edited by R. McL. Wilson. 2 vols. Cambridge: James Clarke, 1991.

Williams, F. "Introduction." Pages IX–XXVII in *The Panarion of Epiphanius of Salamis: Book I (Sects 1–46)*. Translated by F. Williams. Nag Hammadi Studies 35. Leiden: E. J. Brill, 1987.

Wilson, S. G. *Related Strangers: Jews and Christians 70–170 C.E.* Minneapolis: Fortress, 1995.

JEWISH CHRISTIANITY OF
THE *PSEUDO-CLEMENTINES*

F. Stanley Jones

Around 220 C.E. a Syrian Jewish Christian composed a fascinating novel about the origins of Christianity. Set in the year that encompasses the death of Christ, the novel is a first-person account by Clement of Rome (Peter's successor as bishop), whose family was scattered by a tragedy when he was a child. Clement relates not only how he came to accompany Peter through Syria and eventually to convert to Christianity but also how he unexpectedly regained his family through a series of delightfully surprising "recognitions." The larger purpose of this novel is to illustrate how Christian rebirth (baptism) can overcome astrological determination (a bad horoscope), which in this case lay at the root of the disruption of the family.[1]

This original novel evidently bore the title *Periodoi Petrou, Circuits of Peter*, though scholarship often calls it simply the Basic Writing or the *Grundschrift*. It has unfortunately been lost to the modern world in its original form, doubtless in part because of its "heretical" Jewish-Christian perspective—which is precisely what this chapter intends to recapture. The remarkable novelistic creativity of the author, however, did lead two later writers independently to adopt the essentials of the novel in reworkings at the time of the early fourth century Christological debates. It is from these two later redactions, the *Homilies* (*Hom.*, preserved in two Greek manuscripts) and the *Recognitions* (*Rec.*, preserved only via ancient Latin and Syriac translations of the original Greek), that the *Circuits of Peter* can be recovered. The two later redactions agree verbatim in many large segments. Wherever they agree (par. = parallel passages), the material is assured to have stood in the *Circuits of Peter*.

---

[1] For presentation and discussion of the Pseudo-Clementine novel of recognitions, with attention to its relationship with novellistic literature of antiquity, see F. Stanley Jones, "Eros and Astrology in the Περίοδοι Πέτρου: The Sense of the Pseudo-Clementine Novel," *Apocrypha* 12 (2001): 53–78.

The Jewish-Christian perspective of the *Circuits of Peter* has rarely been studied. Much more effort has been expended on the restitution of supposed Jewish-Christian sources of the *Circuits*. Some of these hypothetical sources are turning out to be fantasies of scholarly imagination. This is the case with a supposed source called the *Kerygmata Petrou*, the "Preachings of Peter." Other of these suggested sources seem to have been real and are worthy of independent study. In particular, *Recognitions* 1.27–71 draws from a source that was a Jewish-Christian refutation of Luke's Acts of the Apostles and blamed Paul not only for the failed mission to the Jewish nation, which was on the way to be baptized, but also apparently for the death of James the brother of Jesus. This fascinating source material has been studied elsewhere.[2] The present study will focus on the actual novel, the *Circuits of Peter*, which apparently did not use Luke's Acts at all but which contains even more rare and neglected evidence for ancient Jewish-Christian beliefs and practices.

The framework of the *Circuits* is the distinctive doctrine that the history of the present world is dominated by ten pairs of figures, called "syzygies":

Rec. 3.61.1	*Rec.* 3.61.1	*Hom.* 2.16.1
Latin	Syriac	
There are therefore ten of what we have called *pairs*, destined for this world from the beginning of the age.	Therefore there are ten *pairs* that are from Adam:	As in the beginning God, though one, so to speak as right hand and left first made heaven and then earth, even so he thereafter established all the

---

[2] For *Recognitions* 1.27–71, see my study and translations of the Latin and Syriac in F. Stanley Jones, *An Ancient Jewish Christian Source on the History of Christianity: Pseudo-Clementine "Recognitions" 1.27–71* (Texts and Translations 37, Christian Apocrypha Series 2; Atlanta, Ga.: Scholars Press, 1995; paperback reprint, Atlanta, Ga.: Society of Biblical Literature, 1998). Further details on the refutation of Acts are found in "An Ancient Jewish Christian Rejoinder to Luke's Acts of the Apostles: Pseudo-Clementine *Recognitions* 1.27–71," in *The Apocryphal Acts of the Apostles in Intertextual Perspectives* (ed. Robert F. Stoops, Jr.; *Semeia* 80; Atlanta, Ga.: Scholars Press, 1997), 223–45.

		syzygies. With humans, however, he does not proceed thus but rather inverts all the syzygies. (2) For as from him the first things are better and the second worse, with humans we find the inverse: the first things are worse and the second better. (3) For example, from Adam, who came into being in accord with the image of God, the first one who came into being was the
Cain and *Abel* were one pair;	*Cain* and *Abel*;	unrighteous *Cain*, while the second was the righteous *Abel.* (4) Again,
the second was of the giants and Noah;	the second, the one in the days of Noah;	from the one who among you is called Deucalion two types of spirits—I mean the unclean and the clean—were sent out: the black raven and, as second, the
the third was of Pharaoh and *Abraham*; the fourth of the Philistines and *Isaac*;	the third of Pharaoh and *Abraham*; the fourth of the Philistines and of *Isaac*;	white dove. (5) From the founder of our race, *Abraham*, there were also two principals: first Ishmael, then *Isaac* who had been blessed by God. (6) Similarly, there were again two from this Isaac: the
the fifth of *Esau* and *Jacob*;	the fifth of *Esau* and of *Jacob*;	impious *Esau* and the pious *Jacob.* (7) Even so first in order, as firstborn in

(2) the sixth of the magi and the *legislator* Moses;	(2) the sixth of John and of the *lawgiver*;	the world, was the high priest, then the *lawgiver.* (2.17.1) Similarly—for the member corresponding to Elijah, who ought to follow, was willingly left for another time since it desired for itself to receive its part appropriately at another time—(2) therefore, the first one among the offspring of women came, then the second one among the *sons of men* arrived. (3) Following this order it should be possible to understand of which sort *Simon* is, who as first went before me to the gentiles, and of which sort *I* happen to be, who have come after him and have entered as light upon darkness, as knowledge upon ignorance, as healing upon sickness. (4) Even thus it is necessary, as the true prophet has said to us, for there first to be a false gospel by a certain deceiver and thus *then after the destruction of the holy place for the*
the seventh of the tempter and the *Son of Man*;	the seventh of the tempter and the *Son of Man*;	
the eighth of *Simon* and *myself*, Peter;	the eighth of *Simon* and of *myself*, Peter;	
the ninth of all the nations and the one who *will be sent* to sow the seed among the nations;	the ninth of the seed of tares and of *the gospel sent for* conversion *when the holy place has been uprooted* and	

	they will set up the desolation of abomination; and	true *gospel to be* secretly *sent forth for correction of the heresies that will be.* (5) And after these things, towards the end, again as first *Antichrist* must come and then the real *Christ,* our Jesus, will appear. And after this, when the eternal light has arisen, all the things of darkness will disappear."
the tenth of the *Antichrist* and *Christ.*	the tenth of the *Antichrist* and of *Christ* himself.	
(*Rec.* 1.64.2) . . . *the temple will be destroyed* and the abomination of desolation will be set up in the holy place. *Then the gospel will be proclaimed* to the nations as a testimony of you, so that your unbelief might be judged on the basis of their belief.	(*Rec.* 1.64.2) . . . *the temple will be destroyed,* and they will erect the abomination of desolation in the holy place. *Then, the gospel will be made known* to the nations as a witness *for the healing of the schisms that have arisen* so that also your separation will occur.	

This table of ten syzygies that rule over the present world clearly distinguishes between Simon, who is the evil part of the eighth syzygy that includes Peter as the good part, and a ninth syzygy that consists of the seed of tares or a false gospel by a certain deceiver and the gospel made known after the destruction of the holy place. The seed of tares or a false gospel by a certain deceiver apparently stands in reference to Paul; the gospel that is made known for the healing of the schisms after the destruction of the temple would seem to correlate with the message of the *Circuits*.

This rudimentary framework seems to indicate that the author is writing primarily for non-Jews and/or non-Jewish Christians. He wants to correct a false gospel that has already been spread among the gentiles. His corrections of gentile Christianity disclose the remarkable Jewish-Christian perspective of this author and the community or communities he represents.

One of the things that the author is conscious of correcting is the lack of attention to the requirement not to approach one's wife when she is in separation. The *Homilies* and the *Recognitions* both document the *Circuits'* statement that this is "the law of God":

Rec. 6.10.5	*Hom.* 11.28.1
The care of purity, I say, of which there are many sorts, but first of all that everyone should observe not to be joined in intercourse with a menstruating woman. For the law of God considers this accursed.	I mean keeping pure: Not to have intercourse with one's own wife when she is in menstruation, for the law of God commands this.

While the author is aware that some of the nations keep this law (*Rec.* 8.48.5; cf. *Rec.* 1.33.5), this practice seems to support the view that the author is a Jewish Christian (a category best defined, incidentally, primarily through evidence of known Jewish practices—to a degree that sets a group apart from other Christian groups—in combination with a genetic relationship to the early ethnically Jewish Christians).[3] This practice of menstrual separation is found also among the Jewish Christians in the *Didascalia* 26 (p. 242.6–8 Connolly), which seems to derive from broadly the same region and which describes such people as "you who have been converted from the People" (p. 216.1 Connolly).

A second correction the author wishes to make to the known gospel is the necessity to bathe:

Rec. 6.11.1	*Hom.* 11.28.2
But it is good and contributes to purity even to wash the body with water.	Wash the body with a bath.

There are several types of bathing that occur in the *Circuits*: bathing before meals (*Rec.* 4.3.1 par. *Hom.* 8.2.5; *Rec.* 5.36.3 par. *Hom.* 10.26.2) as well as morning bathing before prayer (*Rec.* 8.1.1 par. *Hom.* 14.1.2). Washing after intercourse is actually found only in the *Homilies* (*Hom.* 7.8.2; 11.30.1; 11.33.4) and thus cannot be assumed for the *Circuits*.

---

[3] See my *An Ancient Jewish Christian Source on the History of Christianity*, 164 n. 21.

Yet even with the lack of specificity, the *Circuits'* special command-ment "to bathe" seems to point in a Jewish-Christian direction. In ancient Christianity, it is only among the Jewish Christians, such as the Elchasaites, that prescriptions for various baths are found.

Next, there are food regulations in the *Circuits*. The author teaches that the Christian should refrain from "the table of demons," i.e., food offered to idols, blood, carrion, and what has been strangled:

Rec. 4.36.4	*Hom.* 7.8.1
Now the things that pollute both the body and the soul are these: to participate in the table of the demons, that is, to eat food sacrificed to idols or blood or carrion which has suffocated and if anything is something that has been offered to demons.	Not to partake of the table of demons, I mean, of things offered to idols, of carrion, of suffocated animals, of animals killed by beasts, of blood.

If, as a number of scholars have argued,[4] the Basic Writer is not dependent here on Acts, then the *Circuits* presents a living indepen-dent transmission of the commands generally referred to as the Apostolic Decree. It is at least possible to interpret this fact as sup-porting the Jewish Christianity of the *Circuits*.[5] In any event, the posi-tion of the *Circuits* that the baptized should not eat with the non-baptized (*Rec.* 1.19.5 par. *Hom.* 1.22.5; *Rec.* 7.29.3–5 par. *Hom.* 13.4.3–5; *Rec.* 7.36.4 par. *Hom.* 13.11.4; cf. *Rec.* 2.71.2) points clearly in the Jewish-Christian direction:

Rec. 7.29.3	*Hom.* 13.4.3
But we also observe that: Not to have a common table with gentiles unless they should believe and, when truth has	In addition to these things, we do not live indiscriminately and do not partake of the table of gentiles, just as we are not able

---

[4] So, e.g., A. F. J. Klijn, "The Pseudo-Clementines and the Apostolic Decree," *NovT* 10 (1968): 312, and Einar Molland, "La circoncision, le baptême et l'autorité du décret apostolique (Actes XV, 28 sq.) dans les milieux judéo-chrétiens des Pseudo-Clémentines," *ST* 9 (1955): 28 (reprinted in idem, *Opuscula Patristica* [Bibliotheca Theologica Norvegica 2; Oslo: Universitetsforlaget, 1970], 25–59, esp. 48).

[5] See, however, Tertullian, *Apol.* 9, and Origen, *Comm. Rom.* 2.13, for gentile Christian observance of such regulations.

322 F. STANLEY JONES

been received, should be
baptized and consecrated
through the trine invocation
of the blessed name, and then
we eat with them.

to eat with them since they live
impurely. Yet whenever we
persuade them to consider and
do the matters of the truth,
being baptized in a certain
thrice blessed invocation, then
we eat with them.

Related with the food regulations is the latent vegetarianism in the
Circuits of Peter. The description of Peter's diet as consisting of "bread
alone, with olives and rarely vegetables" (*Rec.* 7.6.4 par. *Hom.* 12.6.4)
fairly clearly presents vegetarianism as an ideal. Other passages in
either the *Homilies* or the *Recognitions* could be cited to support the
view that the *Circuits* was more than latently vegetarian,[6] but the
Homilist might be responsible for the stronger statements. Still, there
may well be a link between the *Circuits'* vegetarianism and the author's
documented rejection of sacrifices (*Hom.* 3.45.2; *Rec.* 1.36–37). Both
vegetarianism and rejection of sacrifices can serve to support the
Jewish Christianity of the *Circuits,* though not so much because these
are Jewish practices as because these attitudes and practices are witnessed elsewhere for Jewish Christians: the vegetarian diet of James
according to Hegesippus (Eusebius, *Hist. eccl.* 2.23.5), the vegetarian
and anti-sacrificial attitude of the *Gospel of the Ebionites,* the vegetarians of the Jewish Christians of the *Didascalia* 23 (p. 202.15–17
Connolly),[7] and statements by Epiphanius about anti-sacrificial and
vegetarian attitudes among the Jewish Christians (*Pan.* 30.16.7; 30.15.3;
19.3.6). The connection between vegetarianism and an attitude against
sacrifices here makes it unlikely that the vegetarianism should be
explained as a result of the difficulty of getting meat that was kosher.[8]
It is more likely that these characteristics reflect a strongly Hellenized
(Pythagorean) mentality among the Jews and Jewish Christians.

---

[6] *Hom.* 8.15.2–16.2; *Rec.* 1.30.1.

[7] With Hans Achelis and Johannes Flemming, *Die ältesten Quellen des orientalischen
Kirchenrechts: Zweites Buch: Die syrische Didaskalia* (TUGAL NS 10.2; Leipzig: J. C.
Hinrichs, 1904), 356, contra Georg Strecker in Walter Bauer, *Orthodoxy and Heresy
in Earliest Christianity* (trans. a team from the Philadelphia Seminar on Christian
Origins; ed. Robert A. Kraft and Gerhard Krodel; Philadelphia: Fortress, 1971), 253.

[8] Contra the implication of John T. Townsend, "The Date of Luke-Acts," in
Luke-Acts: New Perspectives from the Society of Biblical Literature Seminar (ed. Charles H.
Talbert; New York: Crossroad, 1984), 47–62, esp. 51–52.

Next, there is the issue of circumcision in the *Circuits of Peter*. Advocacy of circumcision is not clearly documented in parallel passages in the *Homilies* and the *Recognitions*. Nevertheless, the statement of the *Adjuration* (attached to the *Homilies*) that the books should be passed on only to a faithful circumcised person does find something of a parallel in *Rec.* 1.33.5, which speaks positively of circumcision in the context of purifications. If these two passages are combined, one can view the *Circuits* as considering circumcision a desired purification, particularly for teachers (a historical perspective is being expressed in the requirement of *Adjuration* 1.1). The author, it must be assumed, was circumcised. While the *Circuits* did not demand circumcision of fellow Christians, the *Circuits* wished that they listen to circumcised Christians and to others in this tradition of the true gospel.

The requirements and oath for teachers in the *Adjuration* furthermore have noticeable parallels to the *Book of Elchasai*. A few other passages found in both the *Recognitions* and the *Homilies* also bear similarities with the *Book of Elchasai*, a known Jewish-Christian work. In particular, *Rec.* 6.8–9 par. *Hom.* 11.24–26 has the opposition between water and fire also witnessed in the *Book of Elchasai* (Epiphanius, *Pan.* 19.3.7; cf. also *Rec.* 1.48.3–5). This passage contains furthermore a type of mystical veneration of water as having made all things and as perhaps the first-born, along with the command, "Flee to the waters"—again both with Elchasaite similarities (cf. Epiphanius, *Pan.* 19.3.7, and the well-known stories in the Manichaean *On the Origin of His Body* 94–96). While it would be too much to say that the author of the *Circuits* was an Elchasaite, as Hort and others have done (the term is non-historical to begin with),[9] characterization of the reception of the *Book of Elchasai* in the *Pseudo-Clementines* as farcical, as suggested by others,[10] is not appropriate, either. Use of the

---

[9] Fenton John Anthony Hort, *Notes Introductory to the Study of the Clementine Recognitions: A Course of Lectures* (London: Macmillan, 1901), 131.

[10] Cf. Wilhelm Brandt, *Elchasai, ein Religionsstifter und sein Werk: Beiträge zur jüdischen, christlichen und allgemeinen Religionsgeschichte* (Leipzig: J. C. Hinrichs, 1912), 20, who maintained "daß der Verfasser von elchasäischen (oder elchasäisch beeinflußten ebionäischen) Bräuchen gewußt und sie bei diesem schriftstellerischen Scherze sich zum Muster genommen hat." John Chapman, "On the Date of the Clementines," *ZNW* 9 (1908): 21–34, 147–59, esp. 148, stated regarding the *Epistula Petri* and the *Adjuration*: "the writer is romancing." Cf. Georg Strecker, *Das Judenchristentum in den Pseudoklementinen* (2d rev. ed.; TUGAL 70; Berlin: Akademie-Verlag, 1981), 144.

Book of Elchasai again indicates that the *Circuits* stands at the cross-roads of Jewish-Christian traditions.

Finally, the *Circuits* displays an attitude toward the Pharisees that has been considered remarkable in the Christian tradition. The author can affirm that the Pharisees and scribes received the key of the kingdom of heaven, that is, knowledge, from Moses, though the *Circuits* also states that they have hidden it (*Rec.* 1.54.7; 2.30.1; 2.46.3 Syriac; *Hom.* 3.18.2–3 18.15.7–16.2). It has been noticed that this affirmation that Pharisaic tradition derives from Moses reflects "a Pharisaic point of view on a particularly sensitive issue."[11] Even though Matt 23:2 ("the scribes and the Pharisees sit on the chair of Moses") might have influenced these texts,[12] it could possibly be the case that the Jewish life known by the *Circuits* was dominated by the rabbis.[13] The *Circuits* is also noteworthy for stating that Jesus, in his saying regarding inward and outward purity (Matt 23:25–26), did not condemn all of the scribes and the Pharisees, but only some of them, namely, the hypocrites among them:

Rec. 6.11.2–3	*Hom.* 11.28.4–29.2
For so even our teacher thus criticized certain of the Pharisees and scribes—who seem to be better than the rest and are separate from the multitude—calling them hypocrites because they were purifying only the things that were seen by humans but the hearts, which only God sees, they were leaving polluted and filthy. (3) To certain of them, therefore, not to all, he said,	For even our teacher immediately rebuked some of the Pharisees and scribes among us—those who are separate and, as scribes, know the laws better than others— because they were purifying only the things that appear to humans but were neglecting the pure things of the heart seen only by God. (11.29.1) Therefore he used this famous saying truly for the hypocrites

---

[11] Albert I. Baumgarten, "Literary Evidence for Jewish Christianity in the Galilee," in *The Galilee in Late Antiquity* (ed. Lee I. Levine; New York and Jerusalem: The Jewish Theological Seminary of America, 1992), 39–50, esp. 42.

[12] This verse is connected with a similar statement in *Hom.* 3.18.2–3 and perhaps also with the statement in *Hom.* 11.29.1. It is only in the *Homilies* that stronger statements about obedience to some Pharisees and scribes are found: *Hom.* 11.29.1; 3.70.2; 3.18.2.

[13] So Baumgarten, "Literary Evidence for Jewish Christianity in the Galilee," 46 n. 37. One problem with this argument, however, is that the early rabbis (the Tannaites) did not consider themselves heirs of the Pharisees.

"Woe to you scribes and
Pharisees, hypocrites, because
you clean what is outside on
the cup and the plate, but
inside they are full of filth."

among them and not for all,
for he said to listen to some of
them because they were
entrusted with the chair of
Moses. (2) Yet to the
hypocrites he said, "Woe to
you, scribes and Pharisees,
hypocrites, because you
cleanse the exterior of the cup
and the plate, but inside it is
full of filth."

Though another parallel to this sentiment is found in the Syriac of
Rec. 2.30.1, only the parallel passages just cited assuredly preserve
the original context of this statement in the *Circuits*. This context is
an argument in favor of the necessity of bathing. This passage per-
mits the conclusion that in the perspective of the *Circuits* (or of the
Christians the *Circuits* is trying to correct), the bathing practices being
advocated were related to bathing practices prescribed by the Pharisees
(or at the very least, outwardly similar to them).

In sum of the observations so far, there are sufficient reasons to
view the *Circuits* as Jewish-Christian. This conclusion can be drawn
not only by observing that the *Circuits* advocates particularly Jewish
practices but also by correlating the *Circuits* with what is known elsewhere of Jewish Christians. To the degree that the *Circuits* can be
positively identified in the parallels of the *Homilies* and the *Recognitions*,
this author displays a fairly clear, consistent profile. The *Circuits* can
no longer be dismissed as merely a compiler whose views either cannot be studied[14] or should be understood as literary playfulness and
not be taken seriously.[15] What one gains, hereby, is a new witness
to early third century Syrian Jewish Christianity, many times more
secure than any conjectured *Kerygmata Petrou*, which have repeatedly
been used as the mainstay for presentations of Jewish Christianity
of this period. When taken together with the *Didascalia* and other
late second and early third century sources such as Hippolytus's
information on the Apamaean Elchasaite Alcibiades, Julius Africanus,
Hegesippus, and the source of *Recognitions* 1.27–71, the *Circuits* should

---

[14] Hans Joachim Schoeps, *Theologie und Geschichte des Judenchristentums* (Tübingen:
J. C. B. Mohr [Paul Siebeck], 1949), 41.
[15] Strecker, *Das Judenchristentum in den Pseudoklementinen*, 257.

allow the field to rewrite the history of later Jewish Christianity, this time on a secure basis.

In the context of this chapter, one further step may be taken to advance knowledge of later Jewish Christianity. The features of the *Circuits of Peter* studied so far have revealed that this writing derives from a Jewish-Christian milieu. Since "Jewish Christian" is a modern analytical historical term (and a hotly disputed one), it will be helpful for the study of Jewish Christianity to ask about the *Circuits'* self-definition: How does the *Circuits* define its own group?

One passage that is revelatory of the author's self-understanding is *Recognitions* 4.5 and its parallel *Homilies* 8.5–7. The context of this passage is Peter's arrival in Tripolis and Simon's consequent and immediate departure for Syria. A great crowd of people is impatient to hear Peter. Peter sees in this situation the fulfilment of the saying of Jesus, "Many shall come from the east and from the west, the north and the south, and shall recline on the bosoms of Abraham, and Isaac, and Jacob" (cf. Matt 8:11 and Luke 13:29). Peter then appends an explanation:

Rec. 4.5.1
"For thus it was also given to *the Hebrews* from the beginning to love *Moses* and to *believe* his word. Hence it is also written, 'The people believed God and his servant Moses.' (2) What therefore was of special gift *from God* toward the nation of *the Hebrews* we now see to have been given also to *those who are called* to the faith *from the nations*. (3) But the means of *works* is entrusted to the power and will of *each one*, and this is unique for them. But *to have a desire toward a teacher of truth is a gift from the heavenly father*. (4) But salvation is in this: that you do the will of the one for whom you have conceived love and desire through the grace of God, lest that word of his

Hom. 8.5.1
"For *the Hebrews* who believe *Moses* and do not observe the things spoken through him are not being saved unless they observe the things spoken to them (2) because even their *believing* Moses has occurred not of their will, but *of God*, who said to Moses, 'Behold I am coming to you in the column of a cloud in order that the people might hear me speaking to you and might believe you forever.' (3) Since then *belief in teachers of truth has come from God* to both *the Hebrews* and *those called from the nations*, while good *deeds* have been left for *each one* to do by their *individual judgment*, the reward is justly given to those who do well. (4) For there would not have been a need for the coming of either

should be said to you which he spoke: 'But *why do you say to me "Lord, Lord" and do not do what I say?'* (5) Therefore, it is of the distinctive gift granted by God to *the Hebrews* that they should believe *Moses*, but to the nations, that they should love *Jesus*.

For the *Lord* also indicated this where he *said, 'I praise you, Father,* Lord *of heaven and earth, because you have hidden these things from the wise* and prudent *and have revealed them* to children.' (6) By this it is declared, at any rate, that the people of the *Hebrews*, educated out of the Law, did *not recognize* him, but the people of the gentiles recognized Jesus and venerate him, because of which it will also be saved, not only recognizing him but also doing his will. (7) But the *one who is from the gentiles* and has it from God to love Jesus should have it of his *own undertaking* to believe also *Moses*. (8) And again the Hebrew who has it from God to believe *Moses* should have it of his own undertaking to believe in Jesus, so that each of them, having in themselves something of divine gift and something of their own industry,

Moses or Jesus if they had desired of themselves to understand what is reasonable. Nor does salvation occur through belief in teachers and calling them lords. (8.6.1) For this reason Jesus is hidden from *the Hebrews* who have taken *Moses* as a teacher, but Moses is hidden from those who have believed *Jesus.* (2) For since there is one teaching through both, God accepts the one who has believed one of these. (3) But believing a teacher occurs for the sake of doing the things spoken by God. (4) Since this is so, our *Lord* himself *says, 'I praise you, Father of heaven and of earth, because you have hidden these things from the wise* presbyters *and you have revealed them to* nursing babes.' (5) Thus, God himself hid the teacher from those who already knew what to do, but revealed [him] to those who did not know what to do. (8.7.1) Therefore, because of the one who hid, neither are *Hebrews* condemned for their ignorance of Jesus, if doing the things of Moses they do not hate the one they have *not recognized*, (2) nor again are the *ones from the nations* condemned who, because of the revealer, have not recognized *Moses*, if they too do the things spoken through *Jesus* and do not hate the one they have not recognized. (3) And some will not profit from calling teachers lords but not doing the things of servants. (4) For this reason, our Jesus

(Cf. 4.5.4)

said to someone who often called him lord but did nothing of the things he had commanded, 'Why do you say, "Lord, Lord," and do not do what I say?' For saying will not profit anything, but rather doing. (5) Thus, in every respect there is need for good works, but if someone should be deemed worthy to

might be perfect from *both*. (9) For our Lord spoke of such a rich man who brings forth from his treasures *new things* and *old*."

recognize *both* as of one teaching proclaimed by them, this man has been deemed rich in God, having understood *old* things to be new in time and *new things* to be old."

This passage must be carefully compared in the *Homilies* and the *Recognitions*. Only the material common to both was assuredly in the *Circuits* (the material in italics in the translation). The following ideas can thus be attributed to the *Circuits*: Believing in teachers of truth is something that comes from God. The Hebrews have it from God to believe in Moses. The gentiles have it from God to believe in Jesus. In addition to believing, which comes from God, some individual human action is necessary for salvation. This action, according to Peter, is the recognition of the other teacher. Peter connects this thought with a reference to the rich person who understands new and old things (cf. Matt 13:52).

Peter does not go on to explain at this point exactly what one gains from the other teacher, but broader knowledge of the *Circuits* can leave little doubt about the essential elements. The Hebrews, on the one hand, must be baptized under the thrice blessed invocation to be saved (*Rec.* 6.8–9 par. *Hom.* 11.25–26). Gentile believers, on the other hand, must observe regulations regarding purity (*Rec.* 6.10 par. *Hom.* 11.28)—items mentioned above.

An important point to note is that the *Circuits* does not define its own group either as Hebrews or as gentile believers in Jesus. This author can state that the goal is to restore the original form of religion that was committed to humanity (*Rec.* 4.32.1 par. *Hom.* 9.19.2). While the *Circuits* does assert that the god who is to be worshiped is the God of the Jews (*Rec.* 2.44.1 par. *Hom.* 16.7.1), the *Circuits* apparently does not place its own group among either the Jews or the believing gentiles. Without defining what its group is here, the *Circuits* is apparently setting its group apart as a *tertium quid*, though perhaps not quite in the same way that others of the time are speaking of the Christians as a "third race":[16] the *Circuits* is defining its group as a *tertium quid* not between Hebrews and gentiles, but rather between Hebrews and believing gentiles. Such people would seem to qualify as Jewish Christians, but it is worth investigating if there is any further evidence for the *Circuits'* self-definition.

A further passage helpful in this regard is *Rec.* 5.34 par. *Hom.* 11.16:

Rec. 5.34.1	*Hom.* 11.16.2
"*But someone will say, 'These sufferings* sometimes *happen even to those who worship God.'* It is not true. For we say that that one is a *worshiper of God* who does the will of God and keeps the precepts of the law. (2) For with God not the one who *is called* a Jew among humans is a Jew, nor is the one who is called a gentile a gentile, but the one who, *believing in God, has fulfilled the law* and has done his will, even if he is not circumcised, is the *true worshiper of God.* (3) This person is not only himself free of sufferings but even makes others free of them, even though they should be *heavy* to the extent of being equal to *mountains.* (4) *Through the faith* by which he believes in God, he removes them. But he removes by faith even mountains with their trees if it is necessary. (5) But the one who appears to be	"*But someone* perhaps *will say,* 'Certain of *the worshipers of God also fall* under *such sufferings.'* I say that this is impossible. For this is the *worshiper of God* who I am talking about, the true worshiper of God, not who only is called such: the one who is actually such fulfills the commandments of the law given to him. (3) If someone acts impiously, he is not pious. In the same way, if the person of another race practices the law, he is a Jew, but when he has not done it, he is a Greek. (4) For the Jew, *believing in God, does the law.* *By that faith* he takes away also the other sufferings that resemble *mountains* and are *heavy.*
	But it is clear that the one who does not do the law is a

---

[16] See, e.g., H. Karpp, "Christennamen," *RAC* 2:1114–38, esp. 1124–25.

someone who worships God, but is supported neither by complete faith nor by the deeds of the commandments, being rather *a sinner*, has *consequent upon the sins* given place in himself for *sufferings* which have been *established by God for the punishment of sinners* so that they might exact from them the debts of sins through introduced tortures and might lead them cleaner to that general *judgment of all*, if only faith does not abandon their punishment. (6) For the <pleasure> of the nonbelievers in the *present life* is a judgment by which they begin to be alien to future *good things*. But the chastisement of those who worship God, which is introduced for the sins that happen to them, exacts from them the debt so that anticipating the judgment in the present world, they take care of the debt of sin and might be set free, at least by half, from the *eternal punishments* that are prepared there."

deserter for not believing in God and thus as *a sinner*, not a Jew, is subject *because of sin* to the *sufferings* that are *established to punish the sinners by* the will of *God* justly decreed from the beginning. (5) For those who worship him, punishment comes because of transgressions, which happens so that when it has demanded back through anguish the sin as a debt, those who repent might be pure in the coming *judgment of all*. (6) For just as luxury *here* will lead to loss of eternal *good things* for the evil,

so punishments are sent to the transgressing Jews for retribution so that having taken back the transgression they might escape the *eternal torture beyond*."

Again, a careful focus on only the material witnessed by both the *Recognitions* and the *Homilies* reveals the following: the *Circuits* is engaged in a discussion of who, in God's sight, is or is not actually a Jew and who is or is not actually a gentile or a Greek. It is apparent that for the author truly being a Jew is good, while being a gentile is not so good. This attitude is readily understandable as part of the Jewish-Christian perspective that has been explored so far. What is distinctive, however, is that the author's ultimate concern is not who is actually a Jew; this concern is rather the way the Homilist tweaked the passage. The Homilist, by the way, also does not require baptism for Jews to be saved (*Hom.* 8.6.2; cf. also *Hom.* 13.20.2 where the Homilist allows chastity to be sufficient for salvation).

The *Circuits'* concern, in contrast, is not actually with who should be called a Jew. This writer wants rather to know who is a "worshiper of God" (*theosebēs*). This term apparently presents the author's self-understanding, and it is notable again (in agreement with the previous passage) that the author does not struggle to be clearly included in the category "Jew."

At first glance, the *Circuits'* self-definition might seem to be generically Hellenistic. *Theosebēs* as one who practices true piety is found in Greek literature from the time of Herodotus and Sophocles onwards. The *Circuits* would be choosing a term for its group and other Jewish Christians from the vocabulary of Hellenistic piety. Upon closer inspection however—and here benefit can be gained from the large debate about "god-fearers" in ancient Judaism evidently without getting wrapped up in the more controversial points—*theosebēs* as a choice self-designation for these Jewish Christians discloses some interesting contours.

First, the use of this term by Hellenistic Jews already reveals the desire to make a universalistic claim for their religion; it fits in with other terms such as *kyrios, pantokrator,* and *theos hypsistos,* which served to transcend narrower nationalistic vocabulary.[17] Second, however, by the time this Hellenistic legacy reaches the third century of the common era, *theosebēs* seems to have gone through a phase in which groups of Jews had made the word something of their own. These groups preferred *theosebeia* and cognates over *eusebeia* and cognates apparently because *theosebeia* and cognates "pointed more directly to Jewish worship of the one God and rejection of idolatry."[18] Usage of the term *theosebēs*, for example on gravestones and inscriptions in the place of the usual word *eusebēs*, could indicate Jewish ties.[19] A third relevant contour to the usage of *theosebēs* by the *Circuits* is that there is evidence that Jews and Christians of this time vied over the

---

[17] G. Bertram, "θεοσεβής, θεοσέβεια" in *TDNT* 3:123–28, esp. 125.
[18] J. M. Lieu, "The Race of the God-Fearers," *JTS* 46 (1995): 483–501, esp. 496.
[19] So Folker Siegert, "Gottesfürchtige und Sympathisanten," *JSJ* 4 (1973): 109–64, esp. 156. Lieu, "The Race of the God-Fearers," 493, writes: "Whereas pagan inscriptions are apt to celebrate their honorand as 'pious' (εὐσεβής), the claim that he or she was θεοσεβής seems to have been monopolized by the Jews."

claim to the word *theosebēs*. It has been noticed, for example, that Justin uses the word *theosebeia* and its cognates in his *Dialogue* with the Jew Tryphon but never in his *Apologies*.[20]

The *Circuits'* self-definition for the Jewish Christian is thus *theosebēs* ("worshiper of God"), a word derived from Hellenistic piety but carrying heavy Jewish overtones and simultaneously being adopted by gentile Christians.

In sum then, the *Circuits of Peter* was written by a Jewish Christian who, on the one hand, apparently consciously avoids a self-definition as a Jew or a Hebrew.[21] The *Circuits* is aware of being distinct from the Jews primarily on the basis of baptism under the thrice blessed invocation and belief in Jesus. On the other hand, the *Circuits* also rejects an identification with plain gentile believers. The *Circuits* is aware of being distinct from plain gentile believers on the basis of purity regulations and belief in Moses. Thus, while the *Circuits'* use of the self-designation *theosebēs* does fit in with broader Christian adoption of this term during this period, the *Circuits* seems to be more aware of the word's Jewish overtones. *Theosebēs* encapsulates the self-definition of a group of Jewish Christians in early third century Syria. In their mode of life, these Jewish Christians were characterized by observance of menstrual separation, avoidance of "the table of demons" (food offered to idols, blood, carrion, and what has been strangled), not sharing meals with the non-baptized, circumcision as a desired purification, religious bathing, latent vegetarianism, and an express anti-Paulinism.

Bibliography

Achelis, Hans, and Johannes Flemming. *Die ältesten Quellen des orientalischen Kirchenrechts: Zweites Buch: Die syrische Didaskalia*. Texte und Untersuchungen zur Geschichte der altchristlichen Literatur NS 10.2. Leipzig: J. C. Hinrichs, 1904.
Bauer, Walter. *Orthodoxy and Heresy in Earliest Christianity*. Edited by Robert A. Kraft and Gerhard Krodel. Translated by a team from the Philadelphia Seminar on Christian Origins. Philadelphia: Fortress, 1971.

---

[20] Lieu, "The Race of the God-Fearers," 497–98; see Edgar J. Goodspeed, *Index Apologeticus sive Clavis Iustini Martyris Operum Aliorumque Apologetarum Pristinorum* (Leipzig: J. C. Hinrichs, 1912), 133.

[21] The evidence thus does not support the second part of the following sentence by Daniel Boyarin, "Justin Martyr Invents Judaism," *CH* 70 (2001): 427–61, esp. 459: "The 'authors' of the Pseudo-Clementines, then, considered themselves at least fellow travelers of the Rabbis, if not orthodox rabbinic Jews for Jesus."

Baumgarten, Albert I. "Literary Evidence for Jewish Christianity in the Galilee." Pages 39–50 in *The Galilee in Late Antiquity*. Edited by Lee I. Levine. New York and Jerusalem: The Jewish Theological Seminary of America, 1992.

Boyarin, Daniel. "Justin Martyr Invents Judaism." *Church History* 70 (2001): 427–61.

Brandt, Wilhelm. *Elchasai, ein Religionsstifter und sein Werk: Beiträge zur jüdischen, christlichen und allgemeinen Religionsgeschichte*. Leipzig: J. C. Hinrichs, 1912.

Chapman, John. "On the Date of the Clementines." *Zeitschrift für die neutestamentliche Wissenschaft* 9 (1908): 21–34, 147–59.

Connolly, R. Hugh. *Didascalia Apostolorum: The Syriac Version Translated and Accompanied by the Verona Latin Fragments*. Oxford: Clarendon, 1929.

Frankenberg, Wilhelm. *Die syrischen Clementinen mit griechischem Paralleltext: Eine Vorarbeit zu dem literargeschichtlichen Problem der Sammlung*. Texte und Untersuchungen zur Geschichte der altchristlichen Literatur 48.3. Leipzig: J. C. Hinrichs, 1937.

Goodspeed, Edgar J. *Index Apologeticus sive Clavis Iustini Martyris Operum Aliorumque Apologetarum Pristinorum*. Leipzig: J. C. Hinrichs, 1912.

Hort, Fenton John Anthony. *Notes Introductory to the Study of the Clementine Recognitions: A Course of Lectures*. London: Macmillan, 1901.

Jones, F. Stanley. "An Ancient Jewish Christian Rejoinder to Luke's Acts of the Apostles: Pseudo-Clementine *Recognitions* 1.27–71." Pages 223–45 in *The Apocryphal Acts of the Apostles in Intertextual Perspectives*. Edited by Robert F. Stoops, Jr. *Semeia* 80. Atlanta, Ga.: Scholars Press, 1997.

———. *An Ancient Jewish Christian Source on the History of Christianity: Pseudo-Clementine "Recognitions" 1.27–71*. Texts and Translations 37, Christian Apocrypha Series 2. Atlanta, Ga.: Scholars Press, 1995. Paperback reprint, Atlanta, Ga.: Society of Biblical Literature, 1998.

———. "Eros and Astrology in the Περίοδοι Πέτρου: The Sense of the Pseudo-Clementine Novel." *Apocrypha* 12 (2001): 53–78.

Karpp, H. "Christennamen." Columns 1114–38 in vol. 2 of *Reallexikon für Antike und Christentum*. Edited by Theodor Klauser, Ernst Dassman, and Georg Schöllgen. Stuttgart: Anton Hiersemann, 1954.

Kittel, Gerhard, and Gerhard Friedrich, eds. *Theological Dictionary of the New Testament*. Translated by G. W. Bromiley. 10 vols. Grand Rapids: Eerdmans, 1964–1976.

Klauser, Theodor, Ernst Dassman, and Georg Schöllgen, eds. *Reallexikon für Antike und Christentum*. Stuttgart: Anton Hiersemann, 1950–.

Klijn, A. F. J. "The Pseudo-Clementines and the Apostolic Decree." *Novum Testamentum* 10 (1968): 305–12.

Lieu, J. M. "The Race of the God-Fearers." *Journal of Theological Studies* 46 (1995): 483–501.

Molland, Einar. "La circoncision, le baptême et l'autorité du décret apostolique (Actes XV, 28 sq.) dans les milieux judéo-chrétiens des Pseudo-Clémentines." *Studia theologica* 9 (1955): 1–39. Reprinted in idem, *Opuscula Patristica*. Bibliotheca Theologica Norvegica 2. Oslo: Universitetsforlaget, 1970.

Rehm, Bernhard. "Zur Entstehung der pseudoclementinischen Schriften." *Zeitschrift für die neutestamentliche Wissenschaft* 37 (1938): 77–184.

Rehm, Bernhard, and Georg Strecker, eds. *Die Pseudoklementinen I: Homilien*. 3d rev. ed. Die griechischen christlichen Schriftsteller der ersten Jahrhunderte 42. Berlin: Akademie-Verlag, 1992.

———. *Die Pseudoklementinen II: Rekognitionen in Rufins Übersetzung*. 2d rev. ed. Die griechischen christlichen Schriftsteller der ersten Jahrhunderte 51. Berlin: Akademie-Verlag, 1994.

Schoeps, Hans Joachim. *Theologie und Geschichte des Judenchristentums*. Tübingen: J. C. B. Mohr (Paul Siebeck), 1949.

Siegert, Folker. "Gottesfürchtige und Sympathisanten." *Journal for the Study of Judaism* 4 (1973): 109–64.

Smith, Thomas, and Peter Peterson, and James Donaldson, trans. "Pseudo-Clementine Literature." Pages 67–346 in *The Twelve Patriarchs, Excerpts and Epistles, the Clementina, Apocrypha, Decretals, Memoirs of Edessa and Syriac Documents, Remains of the First Ages*. Vol. 8 of *The Ante-Nicene Fathers: Translations of the Writings of the Fathers down to A.D. 325*. Edited by Alexander Roberts and James Donaldson. American reprint revised by A. Cleveland Coxe. 10 vols. Reprint ed. Grand Rapids: Eerdmans, 1978.

Stoops, Robert F. Jr., ed. *The Apocryphal Acts of the Apostles in Intertextual Perspectives*. Semeia 80. Atlanta, Ga.: Scholars Press, 1997.

Strecker, Georg. *Das Judenchristentum in den Pseudoklementinen*. 2d rev. ed. Texte und Untersuchungen zur Geschichte der altchristlichen Literatur 70. Berlin: Akademie-Verlag, 1981.

———. *Die Pseudoklementinen III: Konkordanz zu den Pseudoklementinen*. Die griechischen christlichen Schriftsteller der ersten Jahrhunderte. Berlin: Akademie-Verlag, 1986–89.

Townsend, John T. "The Date of Luke-Acts." Pages 47–62 in *Luke-Acts: New Perspectives from the Society of Biblical Literature Seminar*. Edited by Charles H. Talbert. New York: Crossroad, 1984.

ELCHASAITES AND THEIR BOOK

Gerard P. Luttikhuizen

1. *Origen's Helkesaites*

In a sermon on Psalm 82 delivered between 240 and 250 C.E., the famous patristic theologian Origen warned his audience in Caesarea against the doctrine of "the Helkesaites." The very brief summary of this sermon in Eusebius' *Ecclesiastical History*[1] suggests that Origen was referring to religious propagandists who had recently appeared in the Christian churches of Palestine. Origen reported that the Helkesaites made selective use of the whole Old Testament and the Gospels but that they rejected the apostle Paul entirely. What is more, he reported that they claimed to possess a book that had fallen from heaven, and that they promised remission of sins to all those who listened to the reading of this book and believed in it. Unfortunately, it is not clear from this report what was the exact connection between the Helkesaite book and the issue of remission of sins.

According to Origen, the Helkesaites declared that, in case of emergency, denial of one's faith is permitted, provided that one only denies with the lips and not in one's heart. It is possible that they derived this message from their book.[2]

The summary of Origen's report gives rise to several questions. First of all: who were these Helkesaites? What was their religious background? We are also interested in their book. When and where was it written? Why did the Helkesaite missionaries refer to this book in connection with remission of sins?

---

[1] Eusebius, *Hist. eccl.* 6.38. This report and all other relevant sources are collected, translated into English, and commented in Gerard Luttikhuizen, *The Revelation of Elchasai: Investigations into the Evidence for a Mesopotamian Jewish Apocalypse of the Second Century and Its Reception by Judaeo-Christian Propagandists* (TSAJ 8; Tübingen: J. C. B. Mohr [Paul Siebeck], 1985).

[2] Especially because this idea is also attributed to the book by Epiphanius (*Pan.* 19.1.8–19.2.1; cf. 19.3.2–3; discussed below).

2. *Alcibiades of Apamea and the Elchasaite Book*

Some of these questions can be answered when we consider the more detailed information about an earlier manifestation of basically the same missionary movement in the Christian church of Rome. This information is provided in the *Refutation of All Heresies,* an anti-heretic work that Hippolytus, the Roman presbyter and leader of a schismatic community, composed in about the year 230 C.E., i.e. some ten to twenty years before Origen held his sermon on Psalm 82.

Hippolytus does not attach the name "Helkesaites," or any other name, to the missionary movement under discussion, and he rarely refers to the group as a whole.[3] Instead, he focuses on the activities and the teachings of a certain Alcibiades, no doubt because he regarded him as the leader of the group.

In the opening section of his report, Hippolytus informs us that Alcibiades came from Apamea in Syria (*Haer.* 9.13.1). In basic agreement with Origen, he points to a Jewish or Christian-Jewish element in Alcibiades' teachings. Origen stated that the Helkesaites rejected the apostle Paul, and Hippolytus reports that according to Alcibiades, Christian believers ought to be circumcised and to live according to the (Mosaic) Law.[4] This allows the conclusion that the missionaries active in the churches of Rome and Palestine at the time of Hippolytus and Origen had a background in some form of Jewish Christianity in Syria.

In Hippolytus' report, we also find more detailed information about the book. According to this report, Alcibiades claimed that the book was revealed by an angel of huge dimensions who was accompanied by a female angel of the same size:

> It had been revealed by an angel whose height was 24 *schoeni*—that is 96 miles—and whose girth was 4 *schoeni*; from shoulder to shoulder he was 6 *schoeni*; his footprints were three and a half *schoeni* long— that is fourteen miles—, the breadth being one and a half *schoenus*. With him was a female whose dimensions, he said, accorded with those mentioned, the male being the Son of God and the female was called 'Holy Spirit.' (*Haer.* 9.13.2–3)

---

[3] In *Haer.* 9.14.2–3 and 10.29, the third person plural is used to denote co-religionists or followers of Alcibiades.

[4] *Haer.* 9.14.1.

Alcibiades also stated that "a certain righteous man, Elchasai," had received the book (from the angel?) somewhere in Parthia.[5] Elchasai transmitted it to "someone called Sobiai" (or rather to the *Sobiai* or baptists?).[6]

The name "Elchasai" recalls the name of Origen's "Helkesaites."[7] This is an additional indication that the reports by Hippolytus and by Origen-Eusebius speak of basically the same phenomenon. The connection between the two names is made manifest in the usual scholarly designation of this religious group as "Elchasaites" or "Elkesaites." But it should be observed that these forms of the name are not found in the ancient sources.

Note that it is not clear from Hippolytus' account what Elchasai's role in the origin of the book was: were its contents dictated by the angel and written down by Elchasai, or did he receive the book in its finished material form? The latter possibility would be in accordance with the claim of Origen's Helkesaites that the book had fallen from heaven.

According to Hippolytus, Alcibiades stated that the huge angel had proclaimed a new remission of sins.[8] This information is compatible with the brief report about the Helkesaites in Origen-Eusebius. But Hippolytus adds that Alcibiades appointed a *baptism* for the remission of sins, in fact a second baptism as far as Christians were concerned: baptized Christians who had committed a grave sin (a so-called "deadly sin") could receive remission, Alcibiades declared, if they listened to the book and believed in it *and thereupon were baptized a second time*.[9] Hippolytus' report does not give us any reason to assume

---

[5] That the book originated in Parthia is confirmed by another important detail in Hippolytus' report. In what might be a quotation from the book (*Haer.* 9.16.3–4, discussed below), mention is made of a third year in connection with Trajan's campaign against the Parthians.

[6] The meaning of the name "Sobiai" will be discussed in the conclusion of this chapter.

[7] But note that in the Greek texts, the names are spelled differently; the most important deviation is that the opening vocal of "Elchasai" is an *ēta*, that of "Helkesaites" an *epsilon*.

[8] He added that this message was proclaimed "in the third year of Trajan's reign." This chronological information might be an error caused by a misunderstanding of the other mention of a third year in connection with Emperor Trajan; cf. above, n. 5.

[9] *Haer.* 9.13.4: "and he (Alcibiades) appoints a baptism ... saying that those who have been involved in any lasciviousness, pollution, and lawlessness—even if he be a believer—when he has repented and listened to the book and believed in it, he will receive remission of sins by means of a baptism."

that this baptism was part of the message of the book. Rather, Hippolytus suggests that the rebaptism of Christian sinners was an innovation introduced by Alcibiades in Rome.

At the time when Alcibiades arrived in Rome, the Roman church did not yet have an institutionalized method for the remission of grave sins committed by baptized Christians (the sacrament of penance). In the previous chapters of book 9 in *Refutatio omnium haeresium*, Hippolytus speaks at length of a controversy about the position of Christian sinners in the Roman church.[10] Alcibiades' promise of remission of sins even to notorious sinners was seized upon by Hippolytus as an opportunity to carry on his controversy with Bishop Callistus, his former rival in the See of Rome. In his refutation of Callistus, Hippolytus tries to explain why the church of the Catholic bishop had so many members as compared with his own community. He charges Callistus with having admitted sinners into his 'school' by promising them remission of their sins. In the subsequent refutation of Alcibiades, Hippolytus states that the idea of a baptism for the remission of grievous sins was suggested to this heretic by the teachings of Bishop Callistus. In this way, Hippolytus made the Catholic bishop accountable for what he considered the most objectionable aspect of Alcibiades' heresy. Actually, the report of Alcibiades' heresy is nothing more than an appendix to Hippolytus' bitter polemics against Bishop Callistus.

The continuation of Hippolytus' report (*Haer.* 9.15–16) might give a clue to the question of why the Elchasaites referred to the book in connection with the issue of remission of sins. In this part of his report, Hippolytus quotes passages from a written account of Alcibiades' instruction of his pupils and followers.[11] The first quotations relate to baptismal rites which Alcibiades prescribed for various purposes. Hippolytus' selection of these sayings focuses on the treatment of

---

[10] Apparently Alcibiades' second baptism was a condition for forgiveness demanded exclusively from baptized Christians who had committed a so-called "deadly sin." Although Alcibiades' message of remission of sins was directed to sinners, we cannot assume that he was particularly interested in this category of Christians. He may have considered all Roman Gentile Christians sinners inasmuch as they did not live according to the Mosaic Law (cf. *Haer.* 9.14.1).

[11] Hippolytus refers to this record as "his written words." Cf. Gerard Luttikhuizen, "The Book of Elchasai: A Jewish Apocalyptic Writing, Not a Christian Church Order," *SBL Seminar Papers, 1999* (SBLSP 38; Atlanta, Ga.: Society of Biblical Literature, 1999), 405–25, esp. p. 410, n. 17.

Christians who committed grave sins (notably sexual sins such as incest, adultery, homosexuality, fornication, bestiality) and on sufferers from rabies (a metaphor for sexual desire?). Hippolytus concludes this selection of Alcibiades' sayings with a summary of the repeated immersions which he prescribed for consumptive patients and for people possessed of demons.

In his prescriptions for Christian sinners and for sufferers from rabies, Alcibiades referred explicitly to the book. Among other things, he stated that there would be peace and a share with the righteous *also* for sinners who wished to be converted and to be freed from their sins, if, after having heard the reading of the book, they let themselves be baptized a second time. Before their rebaptism, they should purify and cleanse themselves and call to witness the seven witnesses *written in the book*. Alcibiades also mentioned the names of the seven witnesses. One of the prescriptions discloses what the function of the witnesses was. The person in question should call them to witness and say:

> I call to witness the heaven and the water and the holy spirits and the angels of prayer and the oil and the salt and the earth. I call these seven witnesses to witness that I shall sin no more, I shall not commit adultery, I shall not steal, I shall not do injustice, I shall not be greedy, I shall not hate, I shall not break faith, nor shall I take pleasure in any evil deeds. (*Haer.* 9.15.5–6)[12]

We are dealing with an abjuration of all sins to be pronounced before seven non-human witnesses. It is important to know, that according to Epiphanius, our third main source (discussed below), the seven witnesses were mentioned in the book as witnesses to an "oath" (*Pan.* 19.1.6a and 19.6.4). This allows us to surmise that not only the list of the seven witnesses but also the text of the formula to be pronounced before these witnesses was "written in the book." If so, we are able to understand why the Elchasaites referred to the book in connection with remission of sins: the book (perhaps the angel who granted the revelation of the book?) promised the addressees that they could be sure of their future bliss if they were prepared to declare before the seven witnesses that they would not sin any more.

---

[12] Note that we do not find the usual focus on sexual transgressions in this list; cf. the sins mentioned by Alcibiades in *Haer.* 9.15.1.

Another saying of Alcibiades quoted by Hippolytus deserves our special interest because it might disclose the original purpose of the book as well as the historical circumstances in which it was written. In this saying, Alcibiades cautioned his followers against the influences of 'the wicked stars': they should not baptize or take any other initiative on the Sabbath and on Tuesday, the third day of the week. His ban on beginning activities on Tuesday is motivated in the following way:

> Beware also of undertaking anything on the third day of the week, for when again three years of Emperor Trajan are completed, from the time he reduced the Parthians to his own sway, when three years have been completed, the war among the impious angels of the North breaks out. Thereby all impious kingdoms are troubled. (*Haer.* 9.16.3–4)[13]

This passage refers to Trajan's Parthian war of 114–117 C.E. It has the literary form of a prophecy or prognostication. For some reason, it was connected with an astrological caution (it is possible that this connection was made in a later stage of the transmission of the text, see below).

Needless to say, the war did not end with an apocalyptic catastrophe, if this is what is meant by the war among the impious angels and the troubles in all impious kingdoms. In fact, the Parthian war resulted in the withdrawal of the Roman armies from Parthia and the reversion of the conquered territory to the Parthians. For this reason, the relevant prediction must be dated to the time before the cessation of the war. The clause, "when again three years of Emperor Trajan are completed, from the time he reduced the Parthians to his own sway" enables us to date this prognostication more exactly to the autumn of 116 C.E., three years after the beginning of the war according to the ancient mode of inclusive counting.[14] At that time, the combined efforts of Mesopotamian Jews and Parthians to shake off the Roman yoke were violently suppressed. It seems that the author of the book expected that, after the completion of another period of three years of Roman occupation, a new war of much larger dimensions would break out. This cosmic war would cause trouble in the Roman Empire and in all godless kingdoms.

---

[13] Cf. the discussion in the section "The Original Message of the Book and the Greek Version," and Luttikhuizen, *The Revelation of Elchasai*, 79, 190–94.

[14] See, e.g., F. A. Lepper, *Trajan's Parthian War* (London: Oxford University Press, 1948), 207–213; Luttikhuizen, *The Revelation of Elchasai*, 190–92.

Although Alcibiades did not explicitly state that he derived this prognostication from the book, as he did when he referred to the seven witnesses, there can be little doubt that the passage under discussion stems from this text. In his quotation, the focus is not on the imminent cosmic war among the impious angels but on the warning against baptizing and taking other initiatives on the Sabbath and on the third day of the week.[15]

We shall see below that, in one of the quotations from the book in Epiphanius' *Panarion*, reference is made to the imminent "Day of the Great Judgement." This confirms the suspicion that the original book reckoned with apocalyptic events in the near future. The hearers could be sure of "peace and a share with the righteous" (Hippolytus, *Haer.* 9.15.3) on the imminent Judgement Day if they fulfilled the conditions stipulated in the book. It is quite remarkable that reference was still made to the book in connection with remission of sins more than a century after the expected apocalyptic events.

3. *Other Elements of Alcibiades' Teachings: Baptismal Rites and Christological Speculations*

What about the other elements of the teachings of Alcibiades reported by Hippolytus? Here we have to pay attention to the water rites prescribed by Alcibiades and to his christological speculations (*Haer.* 9.15.1–16.1 and 14.1b, respectively).

As far as the baptismal rites are concerned, it is important to recall that the source excerpted by Hippolytus in *Haer.* 9.15–17 was not the Elchasaite book but a written account of Alcibiades' instructions designated by the heresiologist as "his written words." Only two or three times in the selected passages does Alcibiades quote the book, for example, where he speaks of the seven witnesses "written in this book." We have no reasons to attribute the whole text of the water rites to the Elchasaite book. This leaves room for the hypothesis that he was familiar with these baptismal rites from his Jewish-Christian background in Syria.

---

[15] Apparently the cosmic war was associated with the warlike Mars, the supposed ruler of the third day. We do not know for certain if this astrological idea was part of the original book; cf. below "The Original Message of the Book and the Greek Version."

Alcibiades' ideas about Christ are summarized in *Haer.* 9.14.1 (cf. 10.29.2). The most specific feature of this christology is the idea that Christ was born and manifested himself many times before he appeared in Jesus. There is nothing in Hippolytus' report to suggest that Alcibiades derived this christological speculation from the Elchasaite book. This aspect of his teaching might also be explained by his Jewish-Christian background. Below I shall mention some other sources that attribute baptismal practices and speculations about the many manifestations of Christ to Jewish-Christian groups resident on the eastern side of the river Jordan and in Syria.

4. *Elchasai*

On the basis of Hippolytus and Origen-Eusebius, we can state that the Elchasaites were missionary representatives of a particular form of Jewish Christianity who possessed a post-biblical book to which they referred in connection with remission of sins. Did they also appeal to a religious authority called Elchasai?

Unfortunately, Hippolytus' report is rather vague and cryptic about Alcibiades' relationship to Elchasai; Hippolytus is much more interested in his relationship to Bishop Callistus. The opening passage of his report (*Haer.* 9.13.1, discussed above) suggests that Alcibiades regarded Elchasai as a "righteous man" who had received the book— the complete book or its contents—from the huge angel. For the rest, Hippolytus usually mentions the name of Elchasai just to emphasize the allegedly strange character of Alcibiades' teaching. He speaks of Alcibiades' activities in Rome as "the recent appearance of the strange demon Elchasai" (*Haer.* 9.4), as if Alcibiades were inspired by a demon called Elchasai. Elsewhere he depicts Alcibiades as "the most amazing interpreter of the wretched Elchasai" (*Haer.* 9.17.2).[16] He also speaks of the "mysteries of Elchasai" which Alcibiades would have transmitted to his followers (*Haer.* 9.15.2). We cannot be sure that Alcibiades referred to the teachings of Elchasai as something different from the contents of the book. It is possible that, for him, "Elchasai" coincided with the message of the book. From *Haer.*

---

[16] Here he also makes the ironical remark that it would not have been necessary for the Greek philosophers to learn wisdom from the Egyptian priests, had Elchasai lived in their time.

10.29.1, "... a strange book called after a certain Elchasai," it is apparent that the name Elchasai was mentioned in the title of the book (The Book of Elchasai?). It remains to be seen whether our other sources are more specific about Elchasai.

5. *The Contents of the Book According to Epiphanius*

In his *Panarion* ("*Medicine Chest*"), an extensive anti-heretic work, which was completed ca. 377 C.E., Bishop Epiphanius of Salamis (Cyprus) supplies some valuable details about the mysterious book. The relevant reports deviate so strikingly from Hippolytus' account of the teachings of Alcibiades that we cannot possibly assume that Epiphanius is dependent on Hippolytus. Epiphanius makes a clear distinction between pre-Christian (pagan and Jewish) and Christian heresies (*Pan.* 1–20 and 21–80, respectively). What is striking is that he introduces the book in the part of his work that is devoted to the pre-Christian "heresies," to wit in his short report of the Jewish Ossaeans (*Pan.* 19). This is remarkable because Epiphanius dates its composition to the time of Emperor Trajan, "after the advent of the Saviour" (*Pan.* 19.1.4), and because he identifies the author of the book with the teacher of a fourth-century sect of Sampsaeans or "Elkeseans" (*Pan.* 53). Why did he not speak more extensively about the book in connection with the Sampsaeans (the only specific information about the book in *Pan.* 53 will be discussed below) or with another heresy after Christ and after the time of the Emperor Trajan?

A plausible answer to this question is that Epiphanius understood from his source for the book that it was a Jewish rather than a Christian writing. This is confirmed by what the heresiologist writes in *Pan.* 19.1.4: "he [the author of the book] was of Jewish origin and his ideas were Jewish." The survey below of the preserved contents of the book suggests that, on this point, Epiphanius is right.

Epiphanius is also correct in dating the book to the time of the Emperor Trajan. This is in accordance with the relevant information from Hippolytus. Another possible point of agreement with Hippolytus is Epiphanius' statement that the book was "ostensibly based on a prophecy or inspired by divine wisdom" (*Pan.* 19.1.4). This is not inconsistent with Hippolytus' observation that, according to Alcibiades, the book was revealed by an angel.

The description of the enormous male angel and his female companion, which we already know from Hippolytus, can be found in

three places in Epiphanius: not only does he mention it in his report
of the Jewish Ossaeans (*Pan.* 19.4.1–2), but also in his reports of the
Ebionites and the Sampsaeans (*Pan.* 30.17.6–7 and 53.1.9).[17] In *Pan.*
19.3.4 he adds that the male angel was designated as "the great
King."[18] Sometimes Epiphanius calls the male angel "Christ," but in
the last-mentioned passage, he states explicitly that he doubts that
"our Lord Jesus Christ" is meant. Epiphanius assumes that the author
of the book meant or expected someone else. Just as in Hippolytus'
report, the female companion of the male angel is designated as
"Holy Spirit."[19]

The three parallel accounts agree in substance, but each of them
supplies information which we do not find elsewhere. Peculiar to the
account in *Pan.* 19.1.4 is the statement that the male angel was
described as a "power." In *Pan.* 30.17.6–7, Epiphanius reports that
the two angelic figures were "invisible to men."[20] Interestingly, in
Pan. 19.2.2, Epiphanius writes that the name "Elxai" means "hidden
power." It is possible indeed to recognize in the name Elxai/Elchasai
the Aramaic *hayil kesai*, "hidden power." But was "Hidden Power"
the name of the Transjordanian teacher and the supposed author
of the book, as Epiphanius claims, or the name of the huge, manlike angel of the book? It is worthwhile noting that Epiphanius' own
statements that the male angel was regarded as a "power" who was
"invisible to men" come quite close to a circumscription of the name
or title "Hidden Power."

Likewise, the non-human witnesses recur three times in Epiphanius,
although not always exactly the same ones. The list which he gives
in *Pan.* 19.1.6b is identical to the one in Hippolytus, *Haer.* 9.15.2;
9.15.5; different lists occur in *Pan.* 19.1.6a and *Pan.* 30.17.4. The
reports of Hippolytus and Epiphanius also agree with respect to the
function of the witnesses: according to Epiphanius, they were prescribed as witnesses to an oath (*Pan.* 19.1.6; 19.6.4), while accord-

---

[17] It is clear from *Pan.* 19.3.4 that Epiphanius found this description in the book:
with reference to this passage about the huge angel, he writes, among other things,
"I have not fully understood from his (the author's) deceitful and false formulation
in the book filled with his nonsense, whether he spoke about our Lord Jesus Christ."
[18] Cf. Hippolytus, *Haer.* 9.15.1. According to *Haer.* 9.15.3, Alcibiades also designated the angel as the son of God.
[19] Note that in Semitic languages the word for "spirit" is feminine.
[20] It is plausible, therefore, that the author of the book claimed that he had
received a *vision* of the two angels.

ing to Hippolytus, they should be called upon as witnesses to a for-
mal abjuration of all sins (*Haer.* 9.15.5–6).

We already observed that Epiphanius mentions a passage of the
book in which reference was made to the great Judgement Day.
However, this reference is not immediately clear. With a view to
exposing the allegedly "deceitful and empty talk" of the author of
the book, the heresiologist states that he said the following words:

> Let nobody search for the meaning but only speak in prayer the fol-
> lowing words: "*Abar anid moib nochile daasim ane daasim nochile moib anid*
> *abar selam.*" (*Pan.* 19.4.3)

Epiphanius makes an attempt to decipher the cryptic words but his
solution is far from convincing. Not before 1858 did two scholars
(I. Stern and M. A. Levy, apparently working independently of each
other) succeed in unravelling the logogriph. When the first six words
are read from right to left they reveal a Greek transcription of an
Aramaic sentence: *ena misaad elichon biom dina raba*, or: "I bear witness to you (plur.)[21] on the Day of the Great Judgement." I shall
return to this quotation from the book below.

In Epiphanius, we also find an interesting parallel with Origen's
brief account of the teaching of the Helkesaites. Origen reported
that, in their opinion, outward denial of one's faith is permitted in
case of emergency. In Epiphanius, we read that the author of the
book stated:

> it is not a sin if someone happens to have worshipped idols in the
> face of imminent persecution, if only he does not do so from convic-
> tion. (*Pan.* 19.1.8; cf. 19.3.2–3)

To this Epiphanius adds (*Pan.* 19.2.1) that the book referred to a
priest who lived during the Babylonian Exile, and who was a descen-
dant and namesake of Phinehas, the ancient hero of faith (Num
25:6–15). By worshipping the Artemis of Susa, this Phinehas is said
to have escaped death under King Darius. The agreement between
the two sources suggests that the book contained a message to the
effect that outward denial of one's faith is permitted under pressure.

In a few other cases it is more difficult to ascertain whether or
not Epiphanius refers to the contents of the book. In *Pan.* 19.1.7,

---

[21] It is also possible to translate "I will intercede on your behalf."

the heresiologist states that the author of the book "detested" virginity, that he "hated" continence, and "forced" people into marriage. When we read this report without Epiphanius' value judgements, it says that marriage was recommended by the book while virginity and continence were disallowed. Is it possible that we have here an expression of the ancient Jewish view of marriage as an institution for avoiding fornication (cf., e.g., Paul's argument in 1 Cor 7:2–9)?[22]

Finally, Epiphanius reports that the book prescribed that when praying one should turn towards Jerusalem from all directions. This precept induced the heresiologist to point to a supposed contradiction in the book: on the one hand, the author insisted that one should pray in the direction of Jerusalem ("where the altar and the sacrifices were"), on the other hand, he "cursed" sacrifices and temple services, saying that water is agreeable and fire alien to God. The last words introduce a somewhat enigmatic statement in which water is opposed to fire:

> Children, do not go towards the sight of fire, for you shall err. This is an error because you see it quite near but it is far away. Do not go towards the sight of it but rather go towards the voice of water. (*Pan.* 19.3.7)

One wonders why Epiphanius does not adduce more unequivocal evidence for the book's alleged rejection of the temple services in Jerusalem and, consequently, for the inconsistency of its contents. It will become increasingly clear below that Epiphanius' opinion about the book's rejection of sacrifices and temple services was not based on his knowledge of the book's contents but on a combination of very different source data. The words about water and fire quoted above may indeed stem from the book. What this metaphoric statement means, however, is far from clear.[23]

---

[22] Cf. also the *Pseudo-Clementines* (*Ep. Clem. ad Jac.* 7; *Hom.* 3.68), where marriage is recommended because it was supposed to prevent people from committing sexual sins.

[23] Some authors (Ritschl, Bousset, Rudolph) assume that it was directed against the Parthian fire cult. But the warning against the sight of fire may just as well mean a rejection of martyrdom or an allusion to sexual desire (cf. *Ps.-Clem. Hom.* 11.26.4).

6. *The Original Message of the Book and the Greek Version*

I will now bring together the various source data about the book's contents and about its message and purpose. The prediction of a war among the impious angels, "when again three years of Emperor Trajan are completed, from the time he reduced the Parthians to his own sway," quoted in Hippolytus, *Haer.* 9.16.4, enables us to date and locate the book rather precisely in the autumn of 116 C.E. when the Parthian revolt against Trajan, in which Mesopotamian Jews played an active part, ended in disaster. During the Roman reprisals, the Jews of Mesopotamia were massacred. We can imagine that the book was written shortly after these events. At that time, the author could not yet have known that the Roman army would soon withdraw from Parthia. That happened in the summer of 117 C.E.

Apparently, the author of the book expected that, after the completion of another period of three years of Roman dominion, a new war would rage, this time of much greater dimensions. Thereby all impious kingdoms would be troubled. Although this prediction did not come true, the book continued to be read and transmitted. Here it should be noticed that we have several reasons to assume that the original language of the book was Aramaic but that the information in our sources relates to Greek versions which were quoted between one and two and a half centuries later.[24] Is it possible that, in the course of time, the message of the original Aramaic book was reinterpreted? I shall mention two instances where a more or less thorough revision of the text can be suspected.

In the version of the book cited by Alcibiades, the prediction of a war among the impious angels and the attendant troubles in all impious kingdoms is embedded in a warning against the evil influence of the war-like Mars, the ruler of the third day of the week: "beware of undertaking anything on the third day of the week too, for when again three years of Emperor Trajan are completed . . ." Was the prognostication of an imminent war of apocalyptic character given a new meaning in the Greek version?

---

[24] That the book was originally written in Aramaic can be gathered from the intended audience (Jews living in northern Mesopotamia), from the Aramaic logogriph, and also from the name or title "Elchasai."

We come across a comparable phenomenon in Epiphanius. In the fragment of the book quoted in *Pan.* 19.4.3 the words, "I will bear witness to you (or: I will intercede on your behalf) on the Day of the Great Judgement," are left untranslated, which turned them into an incomprehensible formula. The introductory prohibition is in the same vein: "Let nobody search for the meaning but only speak in prayer the following words, '*abar anid moib . . .*'" But it is almost self-evident that the relevant words were supposed to be wholly understandable to the originally intended audience, and that the message was highly relevant to them. In Epiphanius' Greek source, this quite important assurance of the book was disguised and therefore unrecognizable to a Greek-speaking audience or readership.

In view of these uncertainties, any investigation of the book's contents and message must necessarily remain tentative and hypothetical. Was the book written in order to encourage the Jews who had survived the Roman massacre in northern Mesopotamia in 116 C.E.? Was the huge angel who was designated as the "the Great King" and possibly as "Hidden Power" expected to defend and to protect them?

Not only did the book announce a cosmic catastrophe and the Day of the Great Judgement, it also stipulated how the hearers should prepare themselves for the imminent eschatological events: they were summoned to formally declare before seven non-human witnesses that they would no longer commit any sins. It must have been of vital importance to the people who made this vow that they avoided further trespasses. Was this the background to the idea that, in times of persecution, outward denial of one's faith is not a trespass? After the massacre of Jews in northern Mesopotamia in the summer and autumn of 116 C.E., there was every reason for the surviving Jews to fear that the Romans would soon put an end to the religious liberty they had enjoyed under the Parthians. The passage under discussion may mean that denying one's faith under coercion is not a violation of the vow made before the seven witnesses.

The Greek version of the book, at least the version used by the Elchasaite missionaries in Palestine and Rome, still purported to reveal how the hearers could be freed from their sins and be sure of their future bliss. Apparently, it was this message that induced Syrian Jewish Christians to visit the churches of Palestine and Rome. With reference to their book, they proclaimed a new remission of sins ("a remission other than Jesus Christ has given," Origen, in Eusebius). The second baptism for Christians who had committed grave (or "mortal") sins was not part of the book's contents. Hippolytus states correctly that this baptism was introduced by Alcibiades who—still according to the heresiologist—in his lenient attitude towards sinners was inspired by the Roman Bishop Callistus.

7. Epiphanius' View of the Influence of the Book on Transjordanian Sects (Elkeseans, Ebionites)

There can be little doubt that the book connected with the name Elchasai/Elxai originated in Parthia, more specifically in northern Mesopotamia, the part of Parthia which, in 114–116 C.E., was occupied by Trajan's armies. Why, then, did Epiphanius believe that it was written by a Transjordanian teacher?

The Transjordanian connection would be more understandable if reference was made to the book in at least one of Epiphanius' sources of Transjordanian sects. This is, however, highly questionable, in spite of all Epiphanius' contentions. Epiphanius states, for instance, that the Sampsaeans "had their origin in the book" (*Pan.* 53.1.3) and that several other Transjordanian sects, notably the Ebionites, were influenced by the author of the book.

Let us first consider his brief report of the Sampsaeans or Elkeseans. According to Epiphanius, the name "Sampsaeans" means "Solar Ones." This may be correct although there is no indication in his report that their religion was related to the sun in any particular way. The second name, Elkeseans, is not explained by the heresiologist. We might take it for granted that this name was derived from the name of their teacher[25]—Epiphanius states that they "prided themselves on having Elxai as their teacher" (*Pan.* 53.1.2)—but this derivation is not as self-evident as it may seem to be because, in the Greek text, the name Elxai begins with the vowel *ēta*, while the name Elkeseans begins with *epsilon*.

Epiphanius adds that Elxai had a brother, called Iexai, who also wrote a book, and that two female descendants of Elxai, Marthus and Marthana, still lived and were venerated by the Sampsaeans in his own days. Apart from these biographical details, the heresiologist has not much to say about the sect. He reports that they believed

---

[25] But compare the names "Ebion" and "Ebionites." In this case, the name of the putative founder was derived by early heresiologists from the name of the sect.

in one God, that they rejected the apostles as well as the prophets, and that they were baptists and revered water.

His report is more detailed with respect to their ideas about Christ. Epiphanius states that, according to the Sampsaeans, the Holy Spirit is Christ's sister and that both of them are ninety-six miles long, etc. Of course the description of Christ and the Holy Spirit derives from the book. But this does not necessarily mean that he found the book's description of the two angelic figures in his source for this Transjordanian sect. We will see presently that he may have had another reason for attributing this idea to the Sampsaeans.

If we are right in suspecting that Epiphanius' source for the Sampsaeans did not refer to the book, why, then, did the heresiologist believe that the book was composed by the teacher and founder of this sect? Epiphanius' reasonings are often inscrutable.[26] It is not impossible that this idea occurred to him just because the name of the book reminded him of the name of the teacher of the Transjordanian Sampsaeans.[27]

Epiphanius' opinion that the book was written by a Transjordanian teacher had far-reaching consequences for his reports of Transjordanian sects, in particular for his views on the history of the Ebionites. In addition, his ideas lie at the root of many scholarly discussions of the teaching of Elchasai, the Elchasaites and the Ebionites, Transjordanian baptist sects and Jewish Christianity in general.[28]

Epiphanius' views on the connection between Elxai and the Ebionites require special attention. For his extensive report on the Ebionites (*Pan.* 30), Epiphanius used two different sets of sources: earlier heresiological reports (Irenaeus, Eusebius), and later documents which for some reason or other he believed to have been composed (or

---

[26] Ever since the beginning of the 18th century, Epiphanius has been characterized as "doctor confusus." Cf. F. Stanley Jones, "The Genre of the Book of Elchasai: A Primitive Church Order, Not an Apocalypse," in *Historische Wahrheit und theologische Wissenschaft: Gerd Lüdemann zum 50. Geburtstag* (ed. A. Özen; Frankfurt am Main: Lang, 1996), 87–104.

[27] Epiphanius may not have known that the book originated in Parthia. Cf. the conclusion of this chapter.

[28] See the survey of past scholarship in Luttikhuizen, *The Revelation of Elchasai*, 2–37; and more recently R. Merkelbach, "Die Täufer, bei denen Mani aufwuchs," in *Manichaean Studies: Proceedings of the First International Conference on Manichaeism* (ed. P. Bryder; Lund: Plus ultra, 1988), 105–33, esp. pp. 110 and 129; K. Rudolph, "The Baptist Sects," in *The Early Roman Period* (vol. 3 of *The Cambridge History of Judaism*; ed. W. Horbury, W. D. Davies, and J. Sturdy; Cambridge: Cambridge University Press, 1999), 471–500, esp. pp. 485–92.

rewritten) by the Ebionites, in particular the *Periodoi Petrou* and the *Anabathmoi Iakobou*, lost writings which, according to modern scholarship, were closely related to the surviving Pseudo-Clementine texts.[29] Since the christological ideas contained in the new documents differed from those in his heresiological sources, Epiphanius guessed that the Ebionites had changed their opinions about Christ in the course of time. As the heresiologist states explicitly, he "supposed" that they had done so under the influence of Elxai, the teacher of the neighbouring Sampseans. This induced him to believe that the "later Ebionites" were familiar with the contents of the book supposedly written by this teacher, notably with "Elxai's fantasy about Christ" as a manlike figure of enormous dimensions:

> At first this Ebion (the supposed founder of the Ebionites) determined for himself that Christ was born from the seed of man, that is from Joseph. But from a certain time up to now among his followers different things are told about Christ since they have turned their minds to chaotic and impossible things. I suppose that after Elxaios had joined them, the false prophet <whom I mentioned before> in connection with the so-called Sampsenes and Ossenes and Elkeseans, they started to tell some fantastic ideas about Christ and the Holy Spirit . . . For some of them say that Christ is also Adam, the first man created and breathed into by God's inspiration . . . Others say . . . that he came in Adam and appeared to the patriarchs clothed with a body. (*Pan.* 30.3.2–5)
>
> I have already explained above that Ebion did not yet know these matters (viz. the invocation of seven non-human witnesses) but that after some time, when his followers had joined Elxai, they retained from Ebion circumcision and the Sabbath and the customs, but from Elxai the phantasy, so as to suppose that Christ is some manlike figure, invisible to men, ninety-six miles long. (*Pan.* 30.17.5–6)

---

[29] Georg Strecker, *Das Judenchristentum in den Pseudoklementinen* (2nd ed.; TUGAL 70; Berlin: Akademie Verlag, 1981), 265. For a recent discussion of the complicated source-critical problems of the *Pseudo-Clementines*, see J. Wehnert, "Abriss der Entstehungsgeschichte des pseudoklementinischen Romans," *Apocrypha* 3 (1992): 211–35; cf. F. Stanley Jones, *An Ancient Jewish Christian Source on the History of Christianity: Pseudo-Clementine Recognitions 1.27–71* (SBLTT 37 and Christian Apocrypha 2; Atlanta, Ga.: Scholars Press, 1995); P. Geoltrain, "Le roman pseudo-Clémentin depuis les recherches d'Oscar Cullmann," in *Le Judéo-Christianisme dans tous ses états* (ed. Simon C. Mimouni and F. Stanley Jones; Paris: Cerf, 2001), 31–38. The question of why Epiphanius regarded the relevant documents as Ebionite is examined by Glenn A. Koch, "A Critical Investigation of Epiphanius' Knowledge of the Ebionites: A Translation and Critical Discussion of 'Panarion' 30" (Ph.D. diss., University of Pennsylvania, 1976); cf. also A. F. J. Klijn and G. J. Reinink, *Patristic Evidence for Jewish-Christian Sects* (NovTSup 36; Leiden: E. J. Brill, 1973), 28–38.

Epiphanius "supposed" that Elxai was responsible for Ebionite ideas which were not reported in his standard sources of this Jewish-Christian sect. For Epiphanius, this implied that the reverse must also be true: just as the "later Ebionites" shared the ideas of the Sampsaean teacher, so the Sampsaeans shared the ideas of the "later Ebionites." After all, in Epiphanius' opinion, Elxai was the teacher of both groups. Now, Epiphanius' relatively detailed report of the christological ideas of the Sampsaeans, already mentioned briefly above, becomes more understandable:

> They (the Sampsaeans/Elkeseans) confess Christ in name, believing that he is a creature, and that he appears time and again, and that for the first time he was formed in Adam and puts on and off Adam's body, whenever he wishes. He is called Christ, and the Holy Spirit, with a female shape, is his sister. Both of them . . . are ninety-six miles long. (*Pan.* 53.1.8)

We have here the same combination of quite different ideas about Christ as in the earlier report of the Ebionites (*Pan.* 30.3.2–5, quoted above). While it is obvious that the second idea—the view of Christ as an angel of gigantic size—stems from the book, we may safely assume that Epiphanius found the first-mentioned idea about the repeated manifestations of Christ in his new sources for the Ebionites.

To conclude: we have no reasons to attribute the Adam-Christ speculations mentioned by Epiphanius in his reports of the Ebionites and the Sampseans to the Mesopotamian-Jewish book, no more than we can trace the somewhat similar christological ideas of Alcibiades to this book. Rather, these ideas developed in Jewish-Christian circles somewhere in the Transjordan or in Syria.

This hypothesis is the more plausible since we find very comparable christological ideas in the *Pseudo-Clementine Homilies* and *Recognitions*. Here, Christ is regarded as the "true prophet" who manifested himself many times, first of all in Adam, before he appeared in Jesus.[30] There is a broad consensus in recent scholarship that these ideas were already expressed in early sources or versions of the *Pseudo-Clementines*. It is also generally accepted that these lost basic texts originated in a Jewish-Christian environment in Western Syria and in Transjordan, and that they were related to the texts which Epi-

---

[30] Cf. *Ps.-Clem. Hom.* 3.17–26, esp. 3.20.2.

phanius used for his report of an allegedly later form of Ebionism, in particular the *Periodoi Petrou* (*Pan.* 30.15.1–3).[31]

We surmise that Alcibiades' christological speculations and the ideas about the many manifestations of Adam-Christ which Epiphanius attributed to his Sampseans/Elkeseans as well as to the Ebionites had a common background in a particular form of Jewish-Christianity in Western Syria. Interestingly, the ideas of Mani, the founder of the Manichaean religion, about repeated appearances of the apostle of Light are reminiscent of the above speculations.

8. *Baptismal Rites*

Epiphanius makes Ebion, the putative founder of the Ebionites, responsible for the purification rites of this Transjordanian sect. According to *Pan.* 30.2.4–5, Ebion said:

> that a man has to wash himself with water every day, after he had intercourse with a woman and left her, if there is enough water available either of the sea or of other water. And likewise, when he meets somebody when he comes up from the immersion and the baptism with water, he returns to wash himself in the same way, several times and fully clothed. (cf. *Pan.* 30.15.3; 30.16.1 and 30.21)

Epiphanius' attribution of these ritual immersions to Ebion is notable because it is virtually certain that he found information about similar water rites in the early Pseudo-Clementine sources which he used for his report of a later form of Ebionism.[32] His connection of these rites with Ebion and not with Elxai suggests that he did not find a similar tradition in his source for the book.

His statements that the Sampsaeans used "certain baptisms" and that they revered water (*Pan.* 53.1.4 and 7) can probably be explained in the same way as his attribution of Ebionite (Pseudo-Clementine) ideas about many manifestations of Christ to this sect. At any rate, Epiphanius is more detailed about baptist ideas and rites in his report of the Ebionites than in that of the Sampsaeans.[33]

---

[31] Cf. the studies mentioned in n. 29, and Robert E. Van Voorst, *The Ascents of James: History and Theology of a Jewish-Christian Community* (SBLDS 112; Atlanta, Ga.: Scholars Press, 1989).

[32] Cf. *Hom.* 7.8; 11.1 and 33.

[33] For the veneration of water, see also *Pan. anaceph.* 2.30.3–4: the Ebionites "consider water to be divine . . . They baptize themselves continually in running water, summer and winter."

From his new sources about the Ebionites, Epiphanius concluded that the water rituals of the Ebionites went together with a critical attitude towards sacrifices and temple services. According to the gospel which the Ebionites used, Jesus said:

> I came to abolish sacrifices, and unless you cease sacrificing, the wrath will not cease from you. (*Pan.* 30.16.5)

A similar tradition is expressed in the surviving Pseudo-Clementine writings. Here it is explicitly stated that Jesus introduced a baptism for the remission of sins to substitute for the sacrifices in the Temple in Jerusalem (see esp. *Rec.* 1.39 and 48). It was already questioned above whether Epiphanius is right in claiming that Elxai "cursed" sacrifices and temple services (*Pan.* 19.3.6–7) and noted that the only proof text adduced by Epiphanius is a rather enigmatic saying in which water is contrasted with fire. It is possible that he understood this obscure saying in the light of the aforementioned Pseudo-Clementine opposition of water (the baptism) vs. fire (the sacrificial cult in Jerusalem).

In *Pan.* 30.17.4, Epiphanius reports that the Ebionites also used immersions for therapeutical purposes:

> whenever one of them falls ill or is bitten by a snake, he goes down into running water and invokes the names which are in Elxai, *viz.* of the heaven and the earth and the salt and the water and the winds and angels of righteousness, as they say, and the bread and the oil, and he begins to say, "Help me and remove the pain from me." (*Pan.* 30.17.4)

Several features of this report deserve attention. Note, first of all, that Epiphanius ascribes this allegedly magical practice to the Ebionites. Were immersions for therapeutical purposes mentioned in one of his lost sources on the Ebionites? We do not find traces of this "magical" rite in the surviving *Pseudo-Clementines*. But in these writings, more precisely in one of the introductory letters, we do come across a prescription to go down into running water and to call upon four non-human witnesses (heaven, earth, water, air) in connection with a vow (a promise to be careful with the information in the secret texts).[34]

---

[34] *Contestatio Jacobi* 2.1 and 4.1. This introductory writing must have formed part of one of the lost basic texts of the *Pseudo-Clementines*. Cf. Strecker, *Das Judenchristentum*, 137–45; Jones, *An Ancient Jewish Christian Source*, 125–38.

It should also be noted that the list of "names" in *Pan.* 30.17.4 differs from the two lists of witnesses given in the earlier report of the Ossaeans (*Pan.* 19.1.6, mentioned above), and, furthermore, that eight names are listed in *Pan.* 30, although it is stated explicitly in *Pan.* 19 that the author of the book appointed seven witnesses. Did Epiphanius, in *Pan.* 30.17.4, combine the seven witnesses of the book with the four Pseudo-Clementine elements?[35]

Alcibiades was also familiar with therapeutical immersions (Hippolytus, *Haer.* 9.15.4–16.1). If we assume, as most commentators do, that Epiphanius was informed about the therapeutical water rites of *Pan.* 30.17.4 by his early Pseudo-Clementine sources, the agreement between these Pseudo-Clementine rites and Alcibiades' therapeutical immersions confirms us in our assumption that Alcibiades' Syrian background was related to the early type of Jewish Christianity recorded in the Pseudo-Clementine writings.

A few more words about Epiphanius' Elkeseans or Sampsaeans are in order. Although the Elkeseans referred to a teacher called Elxai, it is questionable whether they were familiar with the book that, according to Epiphanius, was written by this teacher. The only piece of information in his report that certainly goes back to the book is the description of the two huge angels. Epiphanius mentions this supposedly christological idea in connection with a speculation about repeated manifestations of Christ in Adam's body (*Pan.* 53.1.8–9). It is rather suspicious that a very similar combination of christological ideas occurs in Epiphanius' report on the Ebionites. The most plausible explanation is that the heresiologist guessed that the Sampsaeans shared the ideas about Christ of the "later Ebionites" because he (wrongly) supposed that they were influenced by the same teacher.

If we leave the description of the two angelic figures aside, there is nothing in Epiphanius' report to suggest that the Sampsaeans/ Elkeseans had any knowledge of the book. This has consequences for the question of the relationship between the Elkeseans and the Elchasaite missionaries of the earlier sources. I proposed to define Elchasaites as missionary representatives of a particular form of Jewish Christianity who possessed a post-biblical book to which they referred in connection with a new remission of sins. Epiphanius' "later

---

[35] Koch, *A Critical Investigation*, 272–73.

Ebionites" may indeed have been related to the Elchasaite missionaries in the churches of Palestine and Rome, not so, however, because
they possessed the relevant book but because both the Pseudo-
Clementine Christians (Epiphanius' "later Ebionites") and the Elchasaite
missionaries originated in a form of Jewish Christianity resident in
Western Syria. Distinct features of this form of Jewish Christianity
were speculations about repeated manifestations of Christ and various baptist practices.[36]

It is, however, very unclear if also Epiphanius' Sampseans/Elkeseans
were related to this Jewish Christianity. His very brief and rather
confused report of this sect gives us little to go on.

9. The Jewish-Christian Baptists of Mani's Youth

We will now turn to a brief examination of two documents of a
quite different nature, the Cologne Mani Codex (CMC) and the Fihrist
of al-Nadim, an Islamic encyclopaedia of the tenth century. These
writings report that Mani (216–276 C.E.), the founder of the
Manichaean Church, spent his youth among southern Babylonian
baptists, to wit in the cloistral community where his father Pattikios/
Futtuq lived. The baptists of Mani's youth regarded "Alchasaios"
(CMC) or "al-Hasih" (Fihrist) as their spiritual leader (or as the founder
of their community?).

Are Alchasaios and al-Hasih other forms of the name Elchasai/Elxai?
Is there any reason to assume that the Babylonian baptists had any
relations to the type of Jewish Christianity discussed above? Is it
possible that Mani borrowed some of his ideas from this type of
Jewish Christianity? Answers to these questions will mainly be based
on the CMC.

The CMC is a miniature parchment (4,5 × 3,5 cm) of the fourth
or fifth century, found near Assiut in Egypt. It is now part of the
manuscript collection of the University of Cologne. The tiny codex
was opened and deciphered in 1969. A preliminary overview of its

---

[36] But whereas the Elchasaite missionaries possessed the mysterious book, we have
no reason to surmise that the Syrian Jewish Christians of Epiphanius' Pseudo-
Clementine sources had any knowledge of this book or that they were influenced
by its ideas in any way. In the surviving Pseudo-Clementines, there is no mention of
Elxai/Elchasai nor do we find in these texts clear traces of the book's contents. Cf.
Koch, A Critical Investigation, 273.

contents was published a year later by Albert Henrichs and Ludwig Koenen, who introduced the designations *CMC* and *Mani Codex*.[37]

The original title of the manuscript is "Concerning the Origin of His Body," which is likely to refer to the earliest history of the Manichaean Church (cf. Paul's speaking of the Christian community as the body of Christ). As to its literary character, the *CMC* is a collection of fragments from the writings of Manichaean authorities, apparently Mani's immediate followers. An unknown editor arranged the excerpts in a more or less chronological order: in the opening sections, we are informed about Mani's childhood among the baptists and about his first revelations; the middle part relates his break with the baptists; the last sections speak of revelations and missionary activities after Mani's exclusion from the baptist community.

Three aspects call for our attention: the references to Alchasaios, the water rites of the Babylonian sect, and recent hypotheses about the christological ideas of the sect (note, however, that the *CMC* and the *Fihrist* are completely silent about this last issue).

In *CMC* 94–97, four legendary stories about a baptist leader Alchasaios are put into the mouth of Mani. The first two stories tell how the spirit of a spring appeared to Alchasaios when he was about to wash himself. The spirit ("the image of a man") protests against its ill-treatment caused by the pollution of the water. In the third narrative, Alchasaios is addressed by a voice from the earth which he is about to plough. It reproaches the baptist for making his living from the earth. The fourth story tells how Alchasaios saw his disciples when they were baking bread. The bread talked to Alchasaios, although we are not informed of what it actually said. Thereupon Alchasaios prohibited further bread-baking.

These narratives about Alchasaios (just like those about two other baptist leaders in *CMC* 97–99) are primarily illustrations of a fundamental Manichaean tenet: they are supposed to show that particles of divine Light are imprisoned in the darkness of the material world, in water, in the earth, in trees and vegetables, in bread, and so on. The Manichaeans believed that such human activities as washing with water, ploughing the earth, baking bread, were injurious to

---

[37] Albert Henrichs and Ludwig Koenen, "Ein griechischer Mani-Codex," *ZPE* 5 (1970): 97–216. English translation of pp.1–99 of the codex: *The Cologne Mani Codex (P. Colon. inv. nr. 4780): Concerning the Origin of His Body* (trans. Ron Cameron and Arthur J. Dewey; SBLTT 15; Missoula, Mont.: Scholars Press, 1979).

this divine substance. In effect, the stories relate the conversion of prominent baptists to Manichaean insights. It is possible to detect polemical overtones: Manichaeans could use these stories in their controversies with the baptists and claim that they were the true followers of the baptist authorities, while, in contrast, the baptists deviated from the teaching of their own leaders.

In the opening sentence of the first narrative, Alchasaios is introduced as the *archegos* of the baptist sect.[38] I propose that we understand this term in the light of Mani's own designation as the *archegos* of the Manichaean Church. Mani was not called *archegos* because he was the founder of the Church but as its head or leader. This is clear from the fact that his successors also bore this title.[39] In addition, the *CMC* refers to more baptist authorities as *archegoi* of the sect.[40] The term is further used to designate the leaders of other religious groups.[41] Thus a comparison with other occurrences of the title in the *CMC* as well as the possible analogy to Mani's designation as the *archegos* of the Manichaean Church indicates that reference is made to Alchasaios as a (past) leader of the baptists. There is no conclusive evidence for the assumption, advocated by Henrichs and Koenen, that Alchasaios is presented as the founder of the baptist sect in which Mani was reared in the *CMC*.

In the *Fihrist* as well as in the *CMC*, the members of the sect are called "baptists." This is an adequate appellation for they are reported to have washed themselves daily, apparently for ritual purposes.[42] They also used to wash all their food. Some passages suggest that they only ate agricultural products which they had cultivated and prepared for consumption themselves. The ritualistic piety of the

---

[38] Not only does the *Fihrist* report that al-Hasih was known as the "head" of the baptists (*Mughtasila*), but also that he was the one who had instituted their sect. I do not believe that this addition to the *CMC* carries us five centuries back to a tradition behind the Greek Mani biography. It is more plausible that we are dealing with a later comment, perhaps just with an interpretation of the imprecise term *r'is*, "head." Cf. Luttikhuizen, *The Revelation of Elchasai*, 171, 185.

[39] The definite article before *archegos* denotes that Alchasaios is presented as a well-known leader. Cf. *CMC* 74.12: "Sitaios, the *presbyteros* of their council."

[40] *CMC* 9.2ff.; 85.13–24.

[41] *CMC* 104.1ff.

[42] From Mani's argumentation in *CMC* 80.22–85.12, we may gather that physical purity was important to the baptists because of their belief in the resurrection of the body.

baptists seems to have developed from Jewish roots.[43] But they also referred to "the commandments of the Saviour (i.e., Jesus)" and it is significant that they were addressed by Mani with arguments taken from the New Testament.

While it is evident that, according to the *CMC* and the *Fihrist*, Mani spent his youth in a community of Jewish-Christian baptists, it remains doubtful whether these baptists were Elchasaites. First of all, we do not find any allusion to the Elchasaite book in the two documents. Do their water rites give us a reason to assume that they were Elchasaites? This is likewise doubtful. We could not trace Alcibiades' water rites and those of Epiphanius' Ebionites to the Elchasaite book. Apart from that, the differences between Alcibiades' water rites, those of Epiphanius' Ebionites and his Sampsaeans/ Elkeseans, and the ritual customs of the Babylonian baptists are conspicuous: Alcibiades prescribed repeated immersions for therapeutical purposes and a second baptism for the remission of grievous sins; Epiphanius' Ebionites were also familiar with therapeutical immersions (at least according to *Pan.* 30.17.4), furthermore they used water rites after ritually impure acts and contacts, notably after sexual intercourse, while the baptists of Mani's youth (probably celibate men) washed themselves daily. If we consider the general spread of all kinds of water rites in the ancient world and elsewhere, we can hardly hypothesize a specific connection between the continual immersions of the Babylonian baptists, the therapeutical water rites prescribed by Alcibiades for outsiders and the ritual purifications of Epiphanius' Ebionites.

It is necessary to return to the issue of christology. The editors of the *CMC* reason in the following way. Mani saw himself as the apostle of Light and as the last one in a series of incarnations of the prophet. With reference to Alcibiades' christological speculations and the ideas about Christ of Epiphanius' Ebionites and Sampsaeans/ Elkeseans, Henrichs and Koenen state that the Elchasaites believed in repeated incarnations of Christ. Their conclusion is that Mani borrowed this idea from the supposedly Elchasaite baptists of his

---

[43] The religion of the baptists is frequently designated as their "Law." In addition, the *CMC* points to the ancestral traditions of the baptists, cf., e.g., 91.6–9: "the washing of our Law and that of the fathers, in which we have walked from of old."

youth.[44] For the greater part, this reasoning is correct. Alcibiades of Apamea and the authors of Epiphanius' early Pseudo-Clementine texts indeed speculated about repeated manifestations of Christ. But the source of these speculations was not the Elchasaite book.

Mani may have borrowed his ideas about recurring incarnations of the prophet from the Jewish-Christian baptists of his youth. But if the baptists held such ideas, they did not do so because they were influenced by the Elchasaite book but because they were distant relatives of the Syrian type of Jewish Christianity represented by the Elchasaite missionaries in Palestine and Rome, and attested by the sources which Epiphanius used for his report of a later development in the history of the Ebionites. Actually, the agreement between the christological speculations of Alcibiades and the *Pseudo-Clementines* on the one hand, and the ideas of Mani and early Manichaeans about recurring incarnations of the prophet on the other, is more specific than the partial agreement in baptist matters.

However, we should be aware that in their reports, the *CMC* and the *Fihrist* are silent about the christology of the Babylonian baptists. It is quite possible to imagine more direct connections—historical or merely literary—between early Manichaeans, the Syrian Jewish Christianity of the Elchasaite missionaries, and Epiphanius' Ebionites.

10. *Conclusions*

Who were the Elchasaites? Our earliest sources, Hippolytus and Origen-Eusebius, speak of missionary representatives of a (Syrian?) form of Jewish Christianity. Two features mark the identity of this missionary movement: the possession of a post-biblical book that, according to the leader of the group in Rome, Alcibiades of Apamea, was revealed by an angel somewhere in Parthia (Origen's 'Helkesaites' claimed that it had fallen from heaven) and the proclamation of remission of sins for all those who listened to the reading of this book.

Apart from the contents of the book, we could not detect teach-

[44] Henrichs and Koenen, "Ein griechischer Mani-Codex," 139–40. Cf. A. Henrichs, "Mani and the Babylonian Baptists. A Historical Confrontation," *HSCP* 77 (1973): 24–59, esp. pp. 54–55. R. Merkelbach ("Die Täufer, bei denen Mani aufwuchs," 116–22) traces the relevant speculations to the Elchasaite book. Cf. my response, "The Baptists of Mani's Youth and the Elchasaites," in Luttikhuizen, *Gnostic Revisions of Genesis Stories and Early Jesus Traditions*. Nag Hammadi and Manichaean Studies 58. Leiden: E.J. Brill, forthcoming 2005.

ings that in some way or another were associated with the name of a religious authority Elchasai. As far as our earliest sources are concerned, it therefore does not make much sense to define Elchasaitism in terms of the influence of a teacher 'Elchasai'.

The book's message of remission of sins may have induced Elchasaite Jewish Christians in Syria to undertake missionary activities in Rome and Palestine. That it is absent in reports that do not speak of the religious propaganda of Elchasaite missionaries may therefore not be surprising. The possession of the book is a different matter. Only if we can ascertain that a religious group was acquainted with the Elchasaite book and/or was influenced by its contents does it make sense to label its members Elchasaites.

In this respect, the relevant reports by Epiphanius are very problematic for we did not find any indication that either the Sampsaeans/Elkeseans or the Ebionites (or for that matter the authors of the early Pseudo-Clementine texts used by Epiphanius for his description of the Ebionites) were acquainted with the Elchasaite book. There is, therefore, no textual basis for the assumption that Epiphanius' Sampseans/Elkeseans and/or his "later Ebionites" were Elchasaites in the above sense.

Epiphanius' report of the Sampsaeans/Elkeseans gives rise to two serious problems. First of all, this report does not disclose anything of the teaching of Elxai, the supposed teacher of the sect. Secondly, we have reasons to doubt that Epiphanius is right in maintaining that the Elchasaite book was composed by a Transjordanian teacher Elxai. It is in itself possible to follow Epiphanius and to designate the members of this Transjordanian sect as Elkeseans because of their appeal to a teacher Elxai, but this designation is void of meaning since we know nothing of the character of this teaching.

Epiphanius was well informed about the contents of the book. But, how he came into possession of his source for the book remains completely unclear. At any rate, it is highly doubtful that he owed his knowledge of the book to an Elchasaite community.[45] It is likewise unclear what prompted him to believe that the teacher of the Transjordanian Sampseans had composed the book.[46]

---

[45] In that case, he would have dealt with the book in connection with the sect in question and not with the Jewish Ossaeans.

[46] A possibility, mentioned above, is that the name of the Sampsaean teacher reminded Epiphanius of the name of the book.

Apparently Epiphanius' source did not inform him of the origin and the authorship of the book. We surmise that the connection with a Transjordanian teacher and, through him, with various Transjordanian sects was made by the heresiologist himself. Oddly enough, this connection helped him to explain a supposed development in the religious history of the Ebionites and, more particularly, the occurrence of diverse christological ideas in the sources he used for his extensive report of this Jewish-Christian sect. This is quite remarkable, indeed, for we concluded that the only relevant detail of the book mentioned by Epiphanius in connection with the christology of the Ebionites is the description of the huge male angel. But the heresiologist states explicitly that he has his doubts about the identity of this angelic figure. In fact, he surmises that somebody was meant other than the Christian Saviour (*Pan.* 19.3.4).

It is likewise questionable whether we should regard the Babylonian baptists, reported in the *CMC* and the *Fihrist*, as Elchasaites. The only information that reminds us of the Elchasaites of Hippolytus and Origen-Eusebius is the name of a baptist authority (not necessarily the founder of the community), Alchasaios. Neither source mentions the Elchasaite book and we cannot trace any of the reported ideas and customs of the baptists to this book.

In a way, the Babylonian baptists can be compared with Epiphanius' Sampsaeans/Elkeseans. While the Sampsaeans referred to a teacher Elxai, the baptists may have acknowledged a teacher Alchasaios. But, in both cases the name of the teacher is an empty shell. In the *CMC*, the baptist authority Alchasaios is the protagonist of legendary stories. In these stories, he is presented as a champion of the universal Manichaean truth.

Nevertheless, we assume that the baptists of Mani's youth, the Elchasaite missionaries in Rome and Palestine, and the early Jewish Christianity attested in the *Pseudo-Clementines* were remote relatives and may have had a common background in a form of Jewish Christianity originally resident in Western Syria and in regions beyond the river Jordan. Characteristic features of this religious tradition were speculations about repeated manifestations of the true prophet Adam-Christ and various water rites for ritual and therapeutic purposes. It is possible that Mani borrowed his idea of recurring incarnations of the prophet of Light from this type of Jewish Christianity. The possible relations between the Jewish Christianity of the Elchasaites and the basic texts of the *Pseudo-Clementines* on the one hand, and the earliest stages of Manicheism on the other, deserve a more searching examination.

According to Hippolytus (*Haer.* 9.13.2), Alcibiades stated that the book had been transmitted from Parthia to someone called "Sobiai." Several authors detect in the name Sobiai a Greek transcription of the plural passive participle of the Aramaic verb "to wash" or "baptize."[47] This suggestion involves Hippolytus misunderstanding Alcibiades, who would have stated that the book was transmitted to the *Sobiai,* "the baptized" or "baptists." If we follow this suggestion, we are able to recognize the history of the book in his statement: it originated in Parthia, then it was transmitted to Jewish-Christian baptists (in Syria?);[48] the possession of the book, notably its message of "a new remission of sins" (Origen), prompted some Syrian Jewish Christians to undertake missionary activity in the Gentile-Christian churches of Rome and Palestine. In Rome they were confronted with the distressing situation of baptized Christians who had committed grave sins.

In conclusion, three phenomena can be distinguished:

1. The Mesopotamian-Jewish book, its message and its surviving contents, attested by Alcibiades-Hippolytus and by Epiphanius; in more general terms also by Origen-Eusebius.

2. Several groups of Jewish-Christian baptists originally resident in Western Syria and in the Transjordan, attested by Hippolytus, by some of the hypothetical sources of the *Pseudo-Clementines* (freely used by Epiphanius for his reports of the Ebionites and the Sampsaeans), and by the *CMC* and the *Fihrist.*

3. The missionary activity of some Syrian Jewish Christians in Gentile-Christian churches. They possessed a Greek version of the Mesopotamian-Jewish book and proclaimed a new possibility of forgiveness based on this book. This is reported by Hippolytus and, more generally, by Origen's brief account in Eusebius' *Ecclesiastical History.*

---

[47] Cf. esp. W. Brandt, *Elchasai: Ein Religionsstifter und sein Buch* (Leipzig, 1912; repr. Amsterdam: Philo, 1971), 42.

[48] The mixture of ideas in Alcibiades' teaching (Jewish-Christian traditions, aspects of pagan learning, reference to a Parthian book and to the wisdom of the Egyptian priests) becomes more understandable if we bear in mind that Alcibiades' home town, the Syrian city of Apamea, was a well-known centre of syncretistic learning.

Bibliography

Brandt, W. *Elchasai: Ein Religionsstifter und sein Buch.* Leipzig, 1912. Repr. Amsterdam: Philo, 1971.

Cameron, R. and Dewey, A. J. *The Cologne Codex (P. Colon. inv. nr. 4780): Concerning the Origin of His Body.* Society of Biblical Literature Texts and Translations 15. Missoula, Mont.: Scholars Press, 1979.

Geoltrain, P. "Le roman pseudo-Clémentin depuis les recherches d'Oscar Cullmann." Pages 31–38 in *Le Judéo-Christianisme dans tous ses états.* Edited by Simon C. Mimouni and F. Stanley Jones. Paris: Cerf, 2001.

Henrichs, Albert. "Mani and the Babylonian Baptists. A Historical Confrontation." *Harvard Studies in Classical Philology* 77 (1973): 24–59.

Henrichs, Albert, and Ludwig Koenen. "Ein griechischer Mani-Codex." *Zeitschrift für Papyrologie und Epigraphik* 5 (1970): 97–216.

Jones, F. Stanley. *An Ancient Jewish Christian Source on the History of Christianity, Pseudo-Clementine Recognitions 1.27–71.* Texts and Translations 37, Christian Apocrypha 2; Atlanta, Ga.: Scholars Press, 1995.

———. "The Genre of the Book of Elchasai: A Primitive Church Order, Not an Apocalypse." Pages 87–104 in *Historische Wahrheit und theologische Wissenschaft: Gerd Lüdemann zum 50. Geburtstag.* Edited by A. Özen. Frankfurt am Main: Lang, 1996.

Klijn, A. F. J., and G. J. Reinink. *Patristic Evidence for Jewish-Christian Sects.* Leiden: E. J. Brill, 1973.

Koch, G. A. "A Critical Investigation of Epiphanius' Knowledge of the Ebionites: A Translation and Critical Discussion of 'Panarion' 30." Ph.D. diss., University of Pennsylvania, 1976.

Lepper, F. A. *Trajan's Parthian War.* London: Oxford University Press, 1948.

Luttikhuizen, Gerard P. "The Book of Elchasai: A Jewish Apocalyptic Writing, Not a Christian Church Order." Pages 405–25 in *SBL Seminar Papers, 1999.* Society of Biblical Literature Seminar Papers 38; Atlanta, Ga.: Society of Biblical Literature, 1999.

———. *The Revelation of Elchasai: Investigations into the Evidence for a Mesopotamian Jewish Apocalypse of the Second Century and its Reception by Judaeo-Christian Propagandists.* Texte und Studien zum antiken Judentum 8. Tübingen: J. C. B. Mohr (Paul Siebeck), 1985.

———. "The Baptists of Mani's Youth and the Elchasaites," in G. Luttikhuizen, *Gnostic Revisions of Genesis Stories and Early Jesus Traditions.* Nag Hammadi and Manichaean Studies 58. Leiden: E.J. Brill, forthcoming 2005.

Merkelbach, R. "Die Täufer, bei denen Mani aufwuchs." Pages 105–33 in *Manichaean Studies: Proceedings of the First International Conference on Manichaeism.* Edited by P. Bryder. Lund: Plus ultra, 1988.

Rudolph, K. "The Baptist Sects." Pages 471–500 in *The Early Roman Period.* Vol. 3 of *The Cambridge History of Judaism.* Edited by W. Horbury, W. D. Davies and J. Sturdy. Cambridge: Cambridge University Press, 1999.

Strecker, Georg. *Das Judenchristentum in den Pseudoklementinen.* 2nd ed. Texte und Untersuchungen zur Geschichte der altchristlichen Literatur 70. Berlin: Akademie Verlag, 1981.

Van Voorst, R. E. *The Ascents of James: History and Theology of a Jewish-Christian Community.* Society of Biblical Literature Dissertation Series 112. Atlanta, Ga.: Scholars Press, 1989.

Wehnert, J. "Abriss der Entstehungsgeschichte des pseudoklementinischen Romans." *Apocrypha* 3 (1992): 211–35.

NOTES ON CONTRIBUTORS

Nicola Denzey received her Ph.D. from Princeton University (1998). She has taught at Bowdoin College (2002–present) and Harvard Divinity School (2004–5). Denzey's recent publications include "'Enslavement to Fate,' 'Cosmic Pessimism' and other explorations of the Late Roman psyche," *Studies in Religion* 33 (3/4; 2005): 277–299, and "A New Star on the Horizon: Astral Christologies and Stellar Debates in Early Christian Discourse," in *Prayer, Magic and the Stars*, eds. S. Noegel and J. T. Walker (Pennsylvania State Press, 2003). She is currently completing a book on women and death in Rome.

Ismo Dunderberg received his Dr. theol. from the University of Helsinki (1994). He is currently Professor of New Testament Studies at the University of Helsinki. He is the author of *Johannes und die Synoptiker* (Finnish Academy of Sciences and Letters, 1994) and the editor (together with C. Tuckett and K. Syreeni) of *Fair Play: Diversity and Conflicts in Early Christianity* (Brill, 2002). In addition, he has published several articles on relationship between the Gospel of John and the *Gospel of Thomas*. He is currently working on a book about the School of Valentinus.

Sakari Häkkinen received his Dr. theol. from the University of Helsinki (2000). His Dr. theol. dissertation on the Ebionites was published in Finnish in 1999 (*Köyhät Kerettiläiset: Ebionit kirkkoisien teksteissä* [Suomalainen teologinen kirjallisuusseura, 1999]) and he is currently preparing an English monograph on the same subject.

F. Stanley Jones received his Dr. theol. from the University of Göttingen and Ph.D. from Vanderbilt University. He is Professor of Religious Studies at California State University, Long Beach. He has published *"Freiheit" in den Briefen des Apostels Paulus* and has edited (with S. Mimouni) *Le judéo-christianisme dans tous ses états*. He is currently at work on a new critical edition and English translation of the Syriac *Pseudo-Clementines* for the series Corpus Christianorum, Series Apocryphorum.

Petri Luomanen, received his Dr. theol. from the University of Helsinki (1996). He is Docent of New Testament Studies at the University of Helsinki and Research Fellow of the Helsinki Collegium for Advanced Studies. He is the author of *Entering the Kingdom of Heaven: A Study on the Structure of Matthew's View of Salvation* (Mohr Siebeck, 1998) and the editor of *Luke-Acts: Scandinavian Perspectives* (Vandenhoek & Ruprech, 1991). Recently he has published articles on Jewish-Christian gospels and his current research focuses on the socio-cognitive basis of hatred towards early Jewish Christians.

Gerard P. Luttikhuizen received his Ph.D. with a dissertation on the book of Elchasai and the Elchasaites at the University of Groningen, the Netherlands (1984), where he now holds the chair of Early Christian Literature and New Testament Studies. His present research centers on the interpretation of biblical texts and traditions in Gnostic Christian literature. His book *Gnostic Revisions of Genesis Stories and Early Jesus Traditions* will be published by Brill in 2005.

Antti Marjanen received his Dr. theol. from the University of Helsinki (1996). He is Docent of New Testament Studies at the University of Helsinki and Research Fellow of the Academy of Finland. He is the author of *The Woman Jesus Loved* (Brill, 1996) and a translator and co-editor of a collection of Finnish translations of the Coptic Nag Hammadi Library (2001). His current research projects deal with influential women in Early Christianity and social-historical issues among second- and third-century Christians, traditionally called Gnostics.

Matti Myllykoski received his Dr. theol. from the University of Helsinki (1991). He is Docent of New Testament Studies at the University of Helsinki and currently Research Fellow in the Formation of Early Jewish and Christian Ideology Research Unit (Centre of Excellence of the Academy of Finland). His publications include *Die Letzten Tage Jesu*. Vols. 1–2 (Finnish Academy of Sciences and Letters, 1991–1994). His current research projects deal with Jewish Christianity, Christianity and anti-Semitism, and the *Gospel of Peter*.

Birger A. Pearson received his Ph.D. from Harvard University in 1968 and Dr. h.c. from Uppsala University in 2002. He is Professor Emeritus of Religious Studies at the University of California, Santa Barbara. His latest books are *The Emergence of the Christian Religion*

(1997) and *Gnosticism and Christianity in Roman and Coptic Egypt* (2004). He is currently participating in a project to publish a new English translation of the Nag Hammadi Codices.

William L. Petersen received his Dr. theol. from Utrecht University in the Netherlands (1984). He is currently Professor of New Testament and Christian Origins at The Pennsylvania State University (University Park, PA, USA). Among his books are *Tatian's Diatessaron* (Brill, 1994), and he recently published his study "The Genesis of the Gospels" in *New Testament Textual Criticism and Exegesis* (Festschrift J. Delobel), ed. A. Denaux (Peeters, 2002). He is presently working on a commentary on *Second Clement* (for Hermeneia) and a monograph on Judaic Christianty.

Heikki Räisänen is Professor of New Testament Studies at the University of Helsinki, and Academy Professor at the Academy of Finland. He received Dr. theol. from the University of Helsinki in 1969, Dr. theol. h.c. from the University of Edinburgh in 1990, and Dr. theol. h.c. from Uppsala University in 2002. His recent publications include *Marcion, Muhammad and the Mahatma* (SCM Press, 1997) and *Challenges to Biblical Interpretation* (Brill, 2001). He is currently working on an overall account of early Christian thought.

Michael A. Williams is Professor of Comparative Religion and Chair of the Department of Near Eastern Languages and Civilization at the University of Washington (Seattle). He received his M.A. from Miami University, Oxford, Ohio, and his Ph.D. from Harvard University. He is the author of *The Immovable Race: A Gnostic Designation and the Theme of Stability in Late Antiquity* (Brill, 1985), and *Rethinking "Gnosticism": An Argument for Dismantling a Dubious Category* (Princeton, 1996).

INDEX OF MODERN AUTHORS

Abegg, Jr., M., 247, 278
Abrams, D., 310, 313
Achelis, H., 322, 332
Ådna, J., 206, 211, 308, 313
Aland, B., 102, 103, 104, 105, 122
Aland, K., 185, 186, 203, 211
Algra, K., 139, 156
Amand de Medieta, D., 177, 183
Arnim, H. von, 167, 183
Asgeirsson, J. Ma., 73, 97, 301, 313
Attridge, H. W., 24, 29, 31, 71, 87, 97, 98, 136, 157, 224, 245, 255, 276, 277

Bacon, E., 176, 184
Baker, J. A., 115, 122, 222, 245
Barb, A. A., 16, 29
Bardy, G., 128, 131, 132, 133, 153, 156, 216, 222, 233, 240, 243, 245
Barnard, L. W., 131, 156
Barnes, J., 139, 156
Barrett, C. K., 270, 276
Barry, C., 44, 45, 61
Barth, F., 310, 312
Bauckham, R., 280, 293, 312
Bauer, W., 119, 122, 138, 156, 198, 211, 223, 245, 322, 332
Baumgarten, A. I., 283, 313, 324, 333
Baur, F. C., 222, 245, 272, 276, 279, 312
Baus, K., 203, 211
Baynes, C., 49, 61
Beck, E., 160, 183
Bertram, G., 331
Bertrand, D. A., 262, 263, 276
Betz, O., 270, 276
Bianchi, U., 125, 158
Blackman, E. C., 108, 120, 122
Blanchetière, F., 280, 285, 313
Blasi, A. J., 80, 97
Blatz, B., 21
Böhlig, A., 37, 61
Bonner, C., 16, 29
Bonwetsch, N., 187, 211
Bowden, J., 103, 279, 313
Boyarin, D., 332, 333
Brandt, W., 323, 333, 363, 364

Brent, A., 252, 276
Briggs, C. A., 313
Brock, S., 165, 183
Broek, R. van den, 12, 13, 14, 29
Bromiley, G. W., 313, 333
Brooks, E. W., 163, 184
Brown, F., 313
Brown, P., 125, 155, 157
Brown, R. E., 223, 245
Brox, N., 236, 245
Bryder, P., 350, 364
Buchanan, N., 246
Buell, D. K., 58, 61
Burkhardt, W., 195, 211

Cameron, R., 357, 364
Campenhausen, H. F. von, 115, 122, 257, 276
Casey, R. P., 76, 81, 97
Ceresa-Gastaldo, A., 132, 143, 157
Chabot, J.-B., 125, 143, 157, 163, 164, 172, 183, 184
Chadwick, H., 125, 139, 148, 157
Chapman, J., 323, 333
Chase, M., 88, 97
Cirillo, L., 178, 184
Clayton, J. P., 269, 276
Coggins, R. J., 280, 314
Connolly, R. H., 320, 333
Cook, E., 247, 278
Corrigan, K., 56, 61
Coxe, A. C., 334
Crossan, J. D., 235, 245
Cureton, W., 159, 183

Dahl, N. A., 17, 29, 40, 61
Daniélou, J., 222, 240, 245
Dassmann, E., 157, 333
Davies, S. L., 269, 276
Davies, W. D., 350, 364
Deacon, J., 251
Deakle, D. W., 104, 122
Dean Jr., O. C., 186
De Boer, M. C., 283, 294, 312, 313
De Conick, A. D., 67, 73, 74, 97, 301, 313
De Lange, N. M. R., 254, 276

Delobel, J., 114, 123
Denaux, A., 152, 157
Denzey, N., 80, 97, 177, 183
Desjardins, M. R., 70, 84, 97
Detmers, A., 116, 121, 123
Dewey, A. J., 357, 364
Dihle, A., 178, 183
Dillon, J. J., 82, 83
Dillon, J. M., 166, 183
Di Nola, A. M., 15, 30
Dölger, F. J., 271, 276
Donaldson, J., 197, 211, 334
Donfried, K. P., 94, 98
Doresse, J., 33, 61
Dornseiff, F., 15, 30
Doutreleau, L., 10, 131, 132, 135,
  142, 144, 158, 177
Draguet, R., 172, 183
Drewermann, E., 119
Drijvers, H. J. W., 156, 157, 160, 161,
  162, 164, 169, 171, 173, 174, 175,
  181, 182, 183, 184
Driver, S. R., 313
Droge, A. J., 128, 157
Duhaime, J., 80, 97
Dummer, J., 133, 157
Dunderberg, I., 72, 73, 90, 91, 95, 97,
  98, 164, 231
Dunn, J. D. G., 272, 274, 276

Ehrman, B., 203, 211
Elze, M., 129, 157
Esler, P. F., 310, 311, 313
Evans, E., 101, 124

Flemming, J., 322, 332
Foerster, W., 2, 5, 7, 10, 13, 15, 16, 18,
  19, 20, 21, 24, 25, 26, 27, 29, 30
Fonrobert, C. E., 306, 307, 313
Förster, N., 82, 83, 96, 98
Frankenberg, W., 333
Freedman, D. N., 211, 313
Frend, W. H. C., 139, 157, 189, 211
Frenschkowski, M., 101, 123
Friedrich, G., 270, 276, 313, 333
Früchtel, L., 128, 143, 148, 149, 153,
  158
Funk, W.-P., 44, 47, 61

Gager, J., 118, 123
Garsoian, N., 162, 184
Geoltrain, P., 351, 364
Georgi, D., 270, 276

Gesché, A., 164, 183
Gianotto, C., 47, 61
Gieschen, C. A., 253, 269, 276
Giversen, S., 11
Godman, S., 257, 276
Goehring, J. E., 270, 276
Goodspeed, E. J., 131, 157, 332, 333
Goranson, S. J., 262, 276, 282, 283
Goulder, M. D., 228, 233, 236, 245,
  268, 269, 271, 272, 276, 279, 313
Goulet, R., 5, 31
Govers, C., 310, 312
Grant, R. M., 3, 12, 13, 30, 139, 143,
  149, 157
Grässer, E., 204, 211
Greene, W. C., 167, 184
Greschat, K., 101, 102, 105, 107, 116,
  119, 122, 123, 124
Griffiths, J. G., 14, 30
Gronewald, M., 164, 183
Guidi, I., 163, 184

Hadidian, D., 195, 211
Hadot, P., 88, 97
Häkkinen, S., 251, 253, 254, 255, 262,
  271, 274, 276, 304, 311, 313
Hall, S. G., 237, 245
Halton, T. P., 299
Harmon, A. M., 129, 157
Harnack, A. von, 101, 103, 105, 108,
  111, 114, 115, 119, 120, 121, 123,
  222, 246
Harrison, C., 3, 52, 62, 71, 99, 223, 246
Hata, G., 136, 157, 255, 276, 277
Hedrick, C. W., 46, 61, 71, 97, 98
Hegedus, T., 177, 184
Heine, R. E., 186, 187, 198, 203, 211
Hella, M., 87
Helm, R., 1, 30, 132, 157
Hengel, M., 223, 270, 276
Hennings, R., 297, 313
Heinrichs, A., 357, 360, 364
Hilgenfeld, A., 2, 3, 30, 222, 246, 248,
  249, 250, 261, 265
Hill, C. E., 213, 219, 220, 228, 229,
  230, 231, 232, 239, 241, 246
Hodgson, R., 71, 97
Hoek, A. van den, 11, 30
Hoffmann, R. J., 104, 105, 123
Hogg, M. A., 310, 313
Hoheisel, K., 19, 30
Holl, K., 133, 157
Holzhausen, J., 149, 157

Horbury, W., 283, 313, 350, 364
Hort, F. J. A., 222, 246, 323, 333
Houlden, J. L., 280, 314
Howard, G., 262, 263, 276

Isenberg, W. W., 89, 90, 95

Jackson, H. M., 45, 61
Jedin, H., 203, 211
Jensen, A., 186, 188, 202, 203, 204, 207, 211
Johnson, M. D., 77, 98
Jones, F. S., 162, 178, 179, 184, 257, 265, 268, 276, 304, 315, 316, 320, 333, 350, 351, 354, 364

Kannengiesser, C., 255, 278
Karpp, H., 329, 333
Käsemann, E., 270, 276
Kelly, J. N. D., 289, 297, 300, 313
Kimelman, R., 283, 313
King, C. W., 16, 30
King, K. L., 34, 49, 60, 61, 62, 149, 157
Kinzig, W., 102, 121, 123
Kittel, G., 313, 333
Klauser, Th., 157, 333
Klawiter, F. C., 203, 207, 211
Klijn, A. F. J., 34, 35, 62, 214, 215, 217, 218, 220, 223, 240, 246, 254, 255, 258, 260, 261, 267, 270, 274, 276, 277, 282, 290, 294, 301, 303, 304, 305, 313, 321, 333, 351, 364
Knox, J., 115, 123
Koch, G. A., 262, 277, 351, 355, 364
Koenen, L., 357, 360, 364
Koester, H., 222, 246
Koivisto, M., 100, 122
Koschorke, K., 91, 92, 96, 97, 98
Kraft, H., 190, 211
Kraft, R. A., 119, 122, 138, 156, 223, 245, 322, 332
Krause, G., 122, 124, 277
Krause, M., 62, 96, 98
Krodel, G., 119, 122, 138, 156, 223, 245, 322, 332
Kroll, W., 139, 140, 158
Kuula, K., 110, 123

Labahn, M., 72, 98
Labriolle, P. de, 185, 187, 189, 190, 194, 198, 208, 211
Lagarde, P. de, 306

Lambers-Petry, D., 280, 312
Lampe, G. W. H., 269, 277
Lampe, P., 77, 95, 98, 194, 211
Lane, W. L., 94, 98
Langerbeck, H., 19, 20, 21, 30
Layton, B., 2, 3, 4, 5, 6, 9, 11, 16, 17, 18, 19, 20, 22, 24, 25, 26, 27, 29, 30, 33, 34, 40, 51, 61, 62, 63, 73, 75, 76, 85, 87, 98
Le Boulluec, A., 66, 98
Leloir, L., 144
Lepper, F. A., 340, 364
Levenson, J., 111, 123
Levi della Vida, G., 168, 184
Levine, L. I., 324, 333
Lieu, J. M., 331, 332, 333
Lieu, S. N. C., 6
Lindeskog, G., 271, 277
Lipsius, R. A., 256, 265, 277
Livingstone, E. A., 56, 62, 102, 186, 203, 211
Logan, A. H. B., 38, 52, 62, 71, 98
Löhr, W. A., 1, 2, 3, 4, 5, 6, 7, 8, 9, 10, 11, 12, 13, 16, 17, 18, 19, 20, 23, 24, 25, 26, 27, 28, 29, 30, 228, 246
Lüdemann, G., 72, 77, 79, 98, 103, 123, 250, 259, 270, 271, 272, 274, 277, 279, 290, 313
Luomanen, P., 258, 301, 313
Luttikhuizen, G., 257, 277, 335, 338, 340, 350, 358, 360, 364

MacDermot, V., 49, 62
MacRae, G. W., 40, 62, 223, 246
Mahé, A., 12, 30
Mahé, J.-P., 12, 30, 47, 61
Mai, A., 126, 157
Mairet, P., 33, 61
Majercik, R., 46, 56, 61
Mansfeld, J., 139, 156
Marcovich, M., 133, 142, 157, 177, 251, 252
Marjanen, A., 1, 30, 90, 98, 206, 211, 308, 313
Markschies, C., 9, 30, 70, 72, 73, 74, 79, 98, 107, 123, 214, 224, 225, 237, 241, 246
Martin, D. B., 92, 98
May, G., 8, 30, 101, 102, 103, 105, 107, 115, 116, 119, 122, 123, 124
McGinn, S. E., 186, 211
McGuire, A. M., 56, 62, 72, 98

McLean, N., 153
Méhat, A., 17, 24, 30
Ménard, J.-É., 12, 76
Mendelson, A., 283, 313
Menzies, G. W., 251, 252, 277
Merkelbach, R., 350, 360, 364
Mimouni, S. C., 263, 277, 280, 293, 301, 313, 351, 364
Mitchell, C. W., 160, 164, 166, 169, 174, 175, 184
Mitchell, M. M., 91, 98
Molland, E., 321, 333
Mommsen, Th., 143
Morgan, R., 280, 314
Mosheim, J. L., 221, 246
Müller, G., 122, 124, 277
Musurillo, H., 131, 157

Nagel, P., 34, 62
Nanos, M., 270, 277
Nau, F., 143, 156, 172, 179, 184
Nautin, P., 18, 30, 251, 257, 277
Neusner, J., 246
Newbold, W. R., 164, 184

Otto, J. C. Th., 128, 157
Oulton, J. E. L., 148, 157

Pagels, E. H., 64, 81, 82, 83, 87, 92, 97, 98
Painchaud, L., 34, 62, 84, 99
Parrott, D. M., 14, 30
Pasquier, A., 10, 30, 34, 62, 84, 99
Pearson, B. A., 1, 11, 12, 22, 30, 31, 45, 47, 62, 64, 227, 270, 276
Peel, M. L., 24, 31, 87, 98
Perkins, P., 229, 246
Petersen, W. L., 114, 122, 126, 127, 128, 129, 133, 136, 138, 144, 145, 152, 154, 155, 157, 158, 163, 255, 278, 290, 301, 314
Peterson, P., 334
Pétrement, S., 3, 12, 15, 31, 52, 62, 71, 99, 223, 232, 246
Pilhofer, P., 128, 158
Plooij, D., 144
Poirier, P.-H., 44, 61
Preisendanz, K., 16, 31
Pritz, R. A., 255, 277, 280, 282, 293, 294, 303, 314
Puech, H.-C., 21, 30, 31

Quasten, J., 131
Quispel, G., 125, 148, 158, 175, 184

Rackham, H., 140, 158
Räisänen, H., 78, 79, 99, 116, 124, 163, 285
Regul, J., 103, 112, 113, 119, 122, 123
Rehm, B., 333
Reinink, G. J., 214, 215, 217, 218, 220, 223, 240, 246, 254, 255, 261, 267, 274, 282, 290, 294, 351, 364
Renan, E., 222, 246
Richardson, P., 94, 98
Riedinger, O., 177, 184
Riley, G., 22, 23
Rist, J., 167, 184
Ritschl, A., 280, 314
Rizzerio, L., 11, 31
Roberts, A., 197, 211, 334
Robinson, J. M., 32, 62, 146, 148, 158
Rousseau, A., 10, 131, 132, 135, 142, 144, 158, 177
Rudolph, K., 223, 246, 350, 364

Sagnard, F., 149, 158
Sanders, E. P., 274, 283, 290, 313
Schaeder, H. H., 282, 283
Schäfer, P., 283, 314
Schenke, H.-M., 34, 51, 62
Scher, A., 165, 184
Schmid, U., 113, 114, 124
Schmidt, C., 49, 62
Schmidt, P., 270, 277, 295
Schmidtke, A., 281, 300, 302, 303, 314
Schneemelcher, W., 4, 21, 31, 116, 124, 148, 158, 262, 278, 301, 314
Schoene, A., 1, 31
Schoeps, H.-J., 259, 264, 277, 281, 314, 325, 333
Scholder, K., 279, 312
Schöllgen, G., 157, 333
Scholten, C., 125, 128, 149, 158
Schüngel, P., 26, 31
Schütz, J. H., 270, 277
Schwartz, E., 128, 143, 153, 158, 222, 238, 246
Scott, A. B., 62
Segal, A. F., 255, 272, 277
Segal, J. B., 176, 184, 308, 314
Sevrin, J.-M., 34, 57, 62
Sieber, J., 44, 62
Siegert, F., 331, 333
Simon, M., 110, 124, 244, 246
Skarsaune, O., 223, 240, 243, 246
Smith, T., 334
Snyder, H. G., 66, 99

Stählin, O., 128, 142, 143, 148, 149, 153, 158
Stanton, G., 283, 313
Steinhauser, M., 77, 98, 194, 211
Stewart-Sykes, A., 194, 209, 211
Stoops, Jr., R. F., 316, 333, 334
Storr, G. C., 221, 246
Stough, C., 167, 184
Strecker, G., 198, 211, 223, 246, 262, 274, 277, 278, 301, 322, 323, 325, 333, 334, 350, 354, 364
Strobel, A., 190, 211
Stroumsa, G. A. G., 35, 62, 283, 313
Strutwolf, H., 93, 99
Strycker, E. de, 146, 158
Sturdy, J., 350, 364
Sykes, S. W., 269, 276
Syreeni, K., 90, 98

Tabbernee, W., 186, 187, 189, 190, 191, 193, 194, 205, 207, 211, 212
Talbert, C. H., 322, 334
Talley, T. J., 29, 31
Taylor, J. E., 273, 274, 277, 289, 290, 312, 314
Tardieu, M., 5, 23, 31, 62
Thackeray, H. St. J., 140, 158
Theissen, G., 270, 277
Thelwall, S., 199, 201, 202
Thomas, J. B., 256
Thomassen, E., 85, 99
Tite, P. L., 225, 246
Tomson, P. J., 280, 312
Tongerloo, A. van, 178, 184
Townsend, J. T., 322, 334
Trakatellis, D., 12, 13, 15, 31
Treu, U., 142, 143, 149, 158
Trevett, C., 186, 188, 192, 193, 196, 198, 200, 201, 203, 205, 206, 207, 212
Trumbower, J. A., 80, 99
Tuckett, C. M., 90, 98
Turcotte, P.-A., 80, 97
Turner, J. D., 33, 44, 46, 49, 51, 52, 53, 54, 56, 61, 63, 72, 91, 98

Uebele, W., 236, 246
Uhlhorn, G., 265, 277

Ulrich, E., 255, 277
Unger, D. J., 82, 83
Uro, R., 73, 97, 301, 313

Van Voorst, R. E., 265, 278, 353, 364
Verheyden, J., 290, 314
Vermes, M., 6, 15, 31
Vermeulen, H., 310, 312
Vieillefond, J. R., 163, 184
Vielhauer, P., 262, 278, 301, 314
Vogels, H. J., 144, 145
Völker, W., 2, 5, 31, 73
Vööbus, A., 125, 144, 146, 155, 156, 158

Waldstein, M., 9, 31, 42, 63, 173, 184
Wallis, E., 197
Wehnert, J., 350, 364
Wengst, K., 216, 223, 246
White, L. M., 34, 62
Whittaker, M., 128, 129, 130, 131, 134, 135, 137, 143, 148, 150, 151, 158
Williams, D. S., 114, 124
Williams, F., 14, 31, 137, 158, 192, 204, 212, 267, 285, 286, 308, 314
Williams, M. A., 1, 31, 54, 56, 59, 60, 63, 69, 70, 99, 107, 124, 225, 246
Wilson, R. McL., 4, 30, 148, 158, 246, 262, 278, 301, 314
Wilson, S. G., 101, 107, 118, 119, 120, 124, 274, 278, 293, 314
Wise, M., 247, 278
Wisse, F., 9, 23, 31, 33, 37, 42, 61, 63, 173, 184
Wissowa, G., 139, 140, 158
Worrall, A. S., 8, 30
Wright, B. G., 233, 246
Wright, D. F., 195, 212
Wright, W., 153, 158
Wucherpfennig, A., 70, 79, 99
Wurm, A., 222, 246

Yarbrough, O. L., 34, 62

Zahn, T., 273
Zangenberg, J., 72, 98
Zazoff, P., 16, 31

GENERAL INDEX

The transliteration convention of the names in ancient languages adopted in this volume follows the rules of general-purpose styles presented in *The SBL Handbook of Style for Ancient Near Eastern, Biblical, and Early Christian Studies* (Peabody, Mass.: Hendrickson, 1999), 25–31.

'Abd Iso' bar Berika, 125, 154
Abel, 32, 35, 93, 317
Abgar VII bar Isates (king of Edessa), 162
Abgar VIII the Great (king of Edessa), 163
Abgarus (son of Bardaisan), 164
Abraham, 35, 106, 114, 317, 326
Abrasax, 15, 16, 39
abstinence from wine, 140, 142, 143, 145, 152, 266
'Abu'l Hasan bar Bahlul, 154
Achamoth (inferior Wisdom), 68, 88, 89
Acta Archelai, 4, 6, 7, 15, 20, 21
Acts of the Apostles, 295, 316
Acts of the Apostles (Ebionites), 256, 263, 264
Acts of the Apostles (Hebrew), 262
Acts of Thomas, 164
Adam, 18, 32, 35, 36, 49, 58, 69, 75, 142, 143, 146, 149, 150, 151, 152, 155, 268
Adam-Christ speculations, 352, 353, 355, 362
Adamas, 39, 40, 41, 42, 43, 45, 48, 58, 61
Addai, 90, 165
Adelphios, 55
Adiabene, 133, 162
adoptionistic Christology, 268
adultery, 339
aeons, 67, 142, 146, 175
Aeschines (Montanist), 194
Agapius of Hierapolis (Mabbug), 131, 154, 160, 164, 173
Agabus, 195
Agrigento (Sicily), 142
Agrippa Castor, 4, 5
Akiba, 302, 303
Albinus, 166, 169
Alchasaios (al-Hasih), 356–358, 362
Alcibiades (Apamea), xii, 325,

336–342, 347, 349, 352, 355, 359–363
Alcibiades (Montanist), 197
Alexander of Alexandria, 273
Alexander of Libya, 55
Alexander the Great, 135
Alexandria, 3, 4, 12, 27, 28, 119, 130, 138, 139, 141, 154, 192, 272, 273, 275
Alexandrian Christianity, Alexandrian theology, 1, 3, 4, 13, 27–29, 240, 272–273
allegory, 105, 108
Allogenes, 48, 50, 51, 53, 54, 55, 60, 61
Allogenes, 49, 51, 55, 60
Alogi, 218, 221, 238, 240
Ambrose (bishop of Milan), 96, 97
Ammia, 195
Anabathmoi Iakobou (see *Ascents of James*)
Ananias (Jewish high priest), 282
Anatolia, 139
Androcydes, 142
angelomorphic Christology, 252, 253, 269–270, 352
angelology, 149
angels, 147, 336, 343, 344
Anicetus (bishop of Rome), 72, 136, 156
Ankyra (Galatia), 191
anointing, 89, 174
anthropogony, 18–21, 147, 149
anthropology, 18–21, 75, 80, 81, 85, 86, 107, 147, 150, 173–175, 181
anti-Canaanite passages of the Old Testament, 122
Antichrist, 319
anti-Paulinism, 219, 270–271, 279, 304, 319, 332, 335
Antioch of Daphne, 133
Antioch (on the Orontes), 3, 9, 27, 28, 130, 191, 257, 285, 286, 289, 296, 308

anti-semitism, 116, 121, 122
Antitheses (Marcion), 101, 105
Antoninus Pius, 4, 27, 104, 159, 192, 205
Apamea, 166, 336
Apelles, 119, 120
Aphrahat, 127
Apocalypse of Adam, 49–50, 53
Apocalypse of John (Audius), 173
Apocalypse of Peter, 272
Apocalypse of Peter (Nag Hammadi), 23
Apocalyptic features, 224
Apocryphon of John, 9, 10, 14, 18,
    42–44, 45, 46, 47, 50, 51, 52, 53,
    71, 75, 170, 206
apokatastasis, 17, 24
Apollinaris, 302
Apollonius, 186, 187, 189, 196, 198,
    199, 200, 201, 205, 208
Apollos, 223
Apostles, 304, 306, 307
Apostolic Decree, 284, 321
Aquila (co-worker of Paul), 102
Aquila (proselyte, Old Testament
    translator), 102, 302
Aquilinus, 55
Aramaic Christianity, 125
Arbela, 133
Archelaus, 6, 7
Archon (demiurge), 15, 16, 17, 20, 21,
    23, 24
Archontics, 53, 55, 57
Ardabau (Ardat, Ardab), 188, 190
Aristippus, 135
Aristo of Pella, 290
Aristotle, Aristotelian philosophy, 3, 135
Armenia, Armenian, 161, 162, 165
Armenian mountains, 129
Arnobius of Sicca, 44
Artemis of Susa, 345
Ascents of James (*Anabathmoi Iakobou*),
    256, 264, 265, 292, 351
asceticism, ascetics (see also Encratism,
    Encratites), xii, xiii, 56, 102, 106,
    107, 125, 139, 140, 151, 152, 155,
    156, 164, 346
Ashtaroth, 289
Asia Minor, x, 4, 83, 103, 133, 190,
    191, 193, 194, 205, 206, 208, 213,
    218, 219, 223, 224, 230, 241, 244,
    245, 274
Assyria, Assyrian, 129, 130, 132, 133,
    153
Asterius Urbanus, 187
astral fatalism, astrological determination,
    159, 167, 180, 315

astrology, 159, 167, 175–180, 182, 183
Atargatis, 162
Athens, 130
Attis, 162
Audians, 163, 306
Augustine, 136, 187, 206, 294, 296,
    297, 298
Avircius Marcellus, 190
Awida (pupil of Bardaisan), 159, 179,
    181
Azazel, 83

Baal, 162
Babylon, 162, 176
Babylonian Talmud, 162
Banias (Paneas, Caesarea Philippi),
    274, 275
baptism, 27, 37, 42, 47, 49, 50, 52,
    54, 57, 61, 89, 219, 271, 315, 330,
    331, 341, 353–356, 359
baptism for the dead, 222
baptism of Jesus (Christ), 23, 29, 214,
    220, 230, 231, 232, 233, 234, 235,
    262, 269, 292
baptists of Babylonia, 356–360
Bar Hebraeus, 154
Bar Jamna, 181
Bar Kochba war, 280, 290
Barbelo, 38, 43, 45, 46, 47, 48, 50, 52
Barbeloites, 52
Bardaisan (Bardesanes), ix, x, 156,
    159–183
Barkabbas, 5
Barkoph, 5
Bashanitis (Bashan), 274, 289
Basilides, ix, x, xi, 1–29, 52, 152, 177,
    216, 227, 229, 233, 249
bathing practices, 320, 325, 332
Belial, 247
Beroea, 280, 287, 289, 299, 308
Bethlehem, 257
Bithynia, 103
body, 18, 24
Book of the Chaldeans (Bardaisan), 167
Book of Elchasai, xii, 256, 257, 259,
    268, 269, 270, 292, 323, 324,
    335–363
book fallen from heaven (see *Book of
    the Elchasaites*), 335, 337
Book of Jubilees, 35
Book of the Laws of the Countries, ix,
    159–183
Book of Revelation, ix, xiii, 204, 206,
    210, 217, 221, 226, 237, 238, 239,
    240

Book about the Signs of the Zodiac
(Bardaisan), 167
Book of Zoroaster, 14
Borborites, 53
Brahmanic customs, 178
bridal chamber, 69, 89, 90, 174, 175
Bruce Codex (*Untitled Text*), 49, 50, 51,
55

Caesarea Maritima, 138, 272, 273,
290, 299
Cain, 32, 35, 93, 106, 317
Cainites, 250
Callinicum, 96
Callistus (bishop of Rome), 252, 338,
349
Calvin, Calvinism, 120, 121, 136
Canaanites, 109
Canon Muratori, 4
Caracalla (emperor of Rome), 165
Carchar, 6
carnal pleasures, 214, 215, 238, 239
Carpocrates, 215, 216, 219, 227, 229,
230, 250, 252, 265, 266, 294
Carthage, 138, 191, 210
catalogues of heresies, 248–253
Cataphrygians (see Montanists)
celibacy, 140, 142, 143, 145, 146,
200–202, 271
Celicia, 133
Celsus, 139, 196
Cerdo, 103, 104, 228, 229, 231, 232
Cerinthus, Cerinthians, ix, x, xi, xii,
23, 210, 213–245, 251, 252, 253,
261, 265, 266, 267, 284, 285, 286,
293, 294, 296, 297, 309
certainty of salvation, 69
Chalcis (Syria), 289
Chaos, 40, 59
charismatic gifts, 91
chastity, 139, 164
children, 144
chiliasm, chiliasts, x, xii, 203–206, 210,
214, 215, 219, 220, 221, 222, 223,
232, 236–243, 244, 245, 258
China, 127
Choba, 273, 290
Chochaba (Kokaba, Kokabe), 273,
274, 287, 289, 290, 308
Christ, Christology, 21–24, 32, 37, 42,
43, 44, 46, 47, 48, 51, 64, 68, 73,
74, 78, 80, 85, 90, 105, 106, 108,
109, 110, 114, 118, 125, 138, 152,
154, 155, 170–172, 175, 180, 194,

213, 214, 220, 225, 227, 229, 235,
252, 265–270, 280, 282, 284, 288,
293, 294, 304, 319, 342, 344, 350,
351, 352, 353, 359, 360
Chronicle of Se'ert, 154
Chronicon Edesseneum, 163
Chronicon (of Georgius Hamartolus), 178
Chrysippus, 167
Church, 86
Circuits of Peter (Grundschrift of
Pseudo-Clementines), xi, 315–332, 351
circumcision, 110, 113, 118, 217, 219,
220, 244, 249, 286, 323, 329, 332,
336
Clement of Alexandria, 3, 4, 5, 10,
11, 16, 17, 18, 19, 20, 23, 25, 26,
28, 29, 33, 71, 73, 74, 76, 79, 104,
141, 142, 148, 149, 153, 187, 273
Clement of Rome, 263, 315
Codex Fuldensis (Victor of Capua's
preface), 131, 153
Cologne Mani Codex (*CMC*), 356–360,
362, 363
Commodianus, 210
Commodus (emperor of Rome), 206
concord (*homonoia*) speech, 91
Constantine the Great, 96, 101
Constantinople, 257
Corinthian opponents of Paul (see also
anti-Paulinism), 219
cosmogony, 9, 13–17, 67, 71, 92, 171
cosmology, 9, 13–17, 60, 150,
168–170, 183
creator-angels, 14, 15, 22, 37, 40, 75,
215, 216, 217, 218, 220, 222, 225,
227, 230
Crescens, 131
criticism toward Old Testament
prophets, 259–260
cross, 305
crucifixion of Christ, 85, 106
Ctesiphon, 129
cult society, 83
Cybele, 189
Cyprus, 73, 274, 275
Cyril of Jerusalem, 119, 185, 187

Daisan, 163
Damascus, 273, 290
Darius (king of Persia), 345
daughters of Philip, 195, 208
Davithe, 39, 43, 45, 47, 48, 49
Day of the Great Judgment, 341, 345,
348

Day of the Lord (Sunday), 255, 273
Dea Syria, 162
Death, 47
death-bed ritual, 83, 89
Debora, 208
Decalogue, 78
demiurge, 52, 60, 66, 68, 69, 75, 78, 80, 83, 85, 86, 89, 93, 120, 146, 148, 170, 223, 232, 241
Democritus, 169
demons, 149
Demostratos, 55
denial of one's faith, 335, 345
descent of a divine revealer, 53
destruction of the temple, 319
determinism, 20, 21, 25, 58, 167, 180
Deucalion, 317
deuterōtai, 307
Devil, 68, 69, 78, 112, 188, 306
Dialogue of a Montanist and an Orthodox, 187
Dialogue of the Savior, 174
Dialogue with Trypho (Justin Martyr), 77, 249
Diatessaron, ix, xii, 125, 126, 127, 133, 138, 139, 144, 145, 152, 154, 155, 262
Didascalia Apostolorum, 306, 320, 322, 325
Didymus the Blind (Alexandria), 164, 187, 197
Dikaiosyne (justice), 11, 13
Diodorus of Tarsus, 178
Diogenes (cynic philosopher), 102
Diogenes Laërtius, 74
Dionysius, 135
Dionysius (bishop of Alexandria), 214, 215, 238, 239, 240, 241, 242
Dionysius bar Salibi, 131, 154, 217, 237, 238
divine creation of all things, 288, 294, 296
divorce, 77, 78
docetism, 22, 74, 85, 90, 91, 106, 172, 222, 227
Dositheos, Dositheans, 45, 140
dualism, 6, 7, 8, 60, 75, 149, 214, 224, 241, 245
Dynamis (power), 10, 13

Eastern Valentinianism, 76
eating meat sacrificed to idols, 25, 69, 144, 228, 321, 332
Ebion, Ebionites, x, xi, xii, 140, 141, 219, 220, 229, 244, 247–275, 279,

280, 281, 289, 291, 292, 293, 294, 296, 297, 298, 304, 307, 308, 309, 311, 350–356, 359
ecstatic prophecy, 196, 210
Edessa (modern Sanliurfa), x, 90, 133, 156, 161–165, 166, 168, 176, 178, 182
Egypt, Egyptians, 3, 9, 14, 16, 24, 28, 49, 56, 57, 72, 73, 79, 106, 127, 179, 213, 225, 227, 233, 254, 256, 285
Eighteen Benedictions, 283, 298, 308
Eirene (peace), 11, 13, 39
Elchasai (Elxai), Elchasaites (Helkesaites, Elkesaites), Elchasaite writings, 219, 257, 307, 308, 323, 335–363
elders, 271
elect, 19, 21, 24
Eleleth, 39, 43, 45, 47, 48, 49, 59
Eleutheropolis (Beth Guvrin), 289
Eleutherus (bishop of Rome), 191, 193
Eliezer, 302
Elijah, 318
Emmacha Seth, 45
Empedocles, 141, 142, 143
Encratism, Encratites, xii, 125, 137, 139, 141, 142, 143, 144, 145, 154, 155, 156, 228
Ennoia (thought), 13, 38
Enosh, 32
Enthymesis (reflection), 13
epagomenal days, 14
Ephesus, 226
Ephrem Syrus, 127, 145, 160, 164, 167, 171, 172, 175, 176, 181, 182
Epimenides, 74
Epiphanius of Salamis, xi, 2, 3, 6, 9, 14, 16, 28, 33, 48, 49, 53, 55, 56, 57, 59, 64, 73, 76, 102, 114, 133, 134, 137, 140, 141, 149, 150, 153, 160, 167, 182, 186, 192, 194, 197, 201, 204, 207, 208, 218–221, 222, 224, 232, 234, 244, 256–257, 259, 261–265, 267, 268, 271, 274, 275, 279, 281, 282, 283, 284–296, 298, 306, 307–312, 339, 341, 343–346, 349–356, 359–363
Epiphany, 29
Epistle of Barnabas, 13, 272
Epistle to the Hebrews, 111
Epistula Apostolorum (*Epistle of Apostles*), 213, 220, 272
Er, 44
error, 85

Esau, 317
Esephech (child of the child), 38
esoteric and exoteric teaching, 71–72
Essenes, 140
Eternal Life, 38, 39
ethical theories, ethics, 24–27, 167
Ethics (Isidore), 28
eucharist, 54, 89, 193, 207, 266, 271
Eugnostos the Blessed, 10, 12, 13, 14, 15, 28
Euphrates, 161
Eusebius of Caesarea, xi, 1, 131, 132, 133, 134, 141, 143, 153, 154, 159, 160, 164, 182, 186, 187, 188, 192, 194, 196, 197, 200, 207, 214, 215, 219, 220, 222, 236, 237, 238, 243, 249, 255, 256, 258, 260, 261, 266, 267, 273, 274, 275, 280, 282, 283, 284, 286, 290, 292, 293, 308, 335, 337, 348, 350, 360, 362, 363
Eutaktos, 55
Eve, 32, 35, 36
evil, 25, 32, 47, 59, 60, 69, 78, 83, 147, 148, 167
Excerpts from Theodotus, 76, 81
Exegetica (Basilides), 5, 7, 8, 10, 13, 17, 26, 28
Expositions of the Prophet Parchor (Isidore), 28

faith, Faith, 67, 107
family, 144
Farj, 289
fasting, 106, 107, 199–200
Fate, 60, 159, 166, 167, 174, 175, 177, 179, 180
Father (unoriginate, unbegotten, self-begotten; see also God [supreme, transcendent, unknown]), 10, 11, 13, 17, 23, 38, 39, 44, 46, 67, 68, 80, 83, 86, 146, 148, 171, 172, 175, 227
Felix (a Roman governor in Alexandria), 141
Fihrist (Islamic encyclopaedia), 356–360, 362, 363
Filastrius, 2, 187, 206, 220, 232, 251
fire, 169
Firmilian (bishop of Caesarea in Cappadocia), 187, 196, 197, 199, 207, 208
First Apocalypse of James, 84, 90–91
First Book of Enoch, 35
firstborn angel, 147
First Epistle of John, 236

five seals (see also baptism), 38, 39, 42, 43, 47, 57
Flavia Neapolis (Sechem), 132
Flavia Sophe, 174
Flora, 77
Florinus, 95
food regulations, 111, 244, 321
Fourth Book of Ezra, 190, 204
free will, 20, 166, 175, 179

Gabriel, 39
Gaius, 186, 191, 193, 206, 214, 215, 217, 237, 238, 239, 240, 241, 242
Galatia, 219
Gamaliel, 39
Gaul, 191, 192, 194, 210
gemstones, 16
Genesis, 32, 34, 35, 41, 75, 89, 93, 168
genethlialogy, 178, 180
geniza in Tiberias, 262
Gentile Christians, 249, 279, 280, 281, 319, 327, 329, 363
Ger-Adamas, 45, 48
Germans, 177
gladiator shows, 69
Glaukias, 4
Gnostics, Gnosticism, gnosis, x, 1, 9, 12, 13, 16, 17, 19, 27–29, 107, 146, 147, 148, 149, 152, 154, 156, 214, 215, 216, 220, 221, 222, 223, 224–236, 241, 244, 252
good, Good, 32, 59, 166, 167, 170, 175
God of the Old Testament (Creator), 14, 26, 28, 43, 52, 104, 105, 106, 108, 109, 112, 117, 118, 120, 214, 216, 225, 231, 241, 243
God (supreme, transcendent, unknown; see also Father), 20, 78, 104, 105, 106, 108, 109, 110, 112, 117, 146, 186, 214, 223, 225, 231, 241, 243, 266
gospel, 318
Gospel according to Basilides, 5
gospel harmonies, 127, 262
"Gospel of the Ebionites," 256, 261–263
Gospel of the Hebrews (*Gospel according to the Hebrews*), 126, 127, 148, 256, 260, 261, 273, 292, 298–301
Gospel of John, ix, 12, 52, 112, 115, 126, 149, 194, 198, 213, 217, 221, 226, 237
Gospel according to John (Hebrew), 262
Gospel of Luke, 101, 113, 114, 115, 126, 262

Gospel of Mark, 115, 126, 268, 269
Gospel according to Matthew (Ebionite), 261–263, 292
Gospel according to Matthew (Hebrew), 261, 262, 289, 292, 299
Gospel of Matthew, 73, 79, 115, 126, 219, 260
"Gospel of the Nazarenes" (Semitic), 298–301
Gospel of Peter, 234, 235
Gospel of Philip, 84, 88–90, 91, 95, 174
Gospel of Thomas, xi, xii, 19, 20, 73, 88, 115
Gospel of Truth, 73, 84–86, 90
Grace, 39, 67
Gratus (proconsul of Asia), 196
"Great Church," 139
Greece, Greek, 129, 130, 138, 153, 162
Greek Christianity, 125

Hades, 40, 44, 59, 106
Hadrian, 1, 4
Harmonius (son of Bardaisan), 164
Harmozel (Armozel), 39, 43, 45, 47, 48, 49
Hasdu (son of Bardaisan), 164
heads of synogogues, 271
heavens (365), 14, 15
Hebrews, 326, 327
Hegemonius, 4, 5, 6, 7, 8
Hegesippus, 224, 249, 261, 325
Helkesaites (see Elchasaites)
Heracleon, 70, 76, 79–81, 94
Hermetic writings, 95
Hexapla, 255
"Hidden Power," 344
Hierapolis, 129, 191
Hillel, 302, 303
Hinduism, 155, 177
Hippolytus, 2, 3, 4, 8, 16, 17, 33, 48, 64, 71, 73, 76, 79, 92, 96, 133, 141, 142, 143, 153, 177, 187, 194, 206, 214, 215, 216–218, 233, 237, 247, 251–253, 254, 257, 265, 284, 293, 294, 336, 337, 338, 339, 340, 341, 342, 343, 344, 345, 347, 349, 360, 362, 363
Hippo Regius, 138
Holy Book of the Great Invisible Spirit (Gospel of the Egyptians), 36–42, 43, 44, 45, 47, 50, 51, 52, 53, 61
holy kiss, 89
Holy Spirit (female angel), 336, 344
Homer, 128

homosexual behavior, 144, 339
Hope, 67
Horus, 14
Huldah, 208
Humanity, 40, 41
Hyacinthus, 202
Hyginus (bishop of Rome), 72, 228
Hymn of the Pearl, 164
hypocrites, 324, 325
Hypostasis of the Archons, 49, 53

Ialdabaoth (Yaldabaoth), 43, 47, 49, 69, 71
Iao, 16
idol worship, 306
Iexai, 219, 349
Ignatius of Antioch, 224, 236, 244, 249
Illuminator, 49
Illustrious Men (Jerome), 300
image and likeness of God, 147, 150, 151, 152
imminent end, 195, 203–206
impious angels, 347
incarnation, 74, 230
incest, 339
Incorruptibility, 38
India, Indians, 162, 164, 165, 177
Interpretation of Knowledge, 84, 91–92, 93
Invisible Spirit, 38, 40, 43, 45, 59
Iolaos, 44
Ioseph Galilaeus, 302
Irenaeus of Lyons, 2, 3, 4, 8, 9, 10, 12, 13, 14, 15, 18, 19, 21, 22, 23, 24, 26, 27, 28, 43, 50, 51, 56, 64, 65, 66, 67, 69, 70, 71, 75, 76, 77, 80, 82, 83, 84, 85, 89, 91, 93, 94, 95, 96, 129, 131, 132, 133, 134, 135, 137, 138, 139, 141, 142, 143, 146, 151, 152, 153, 154, 177, 187, 193, 194, 210, 214, 215, 216, 218, 219, 221, 222, 224, 226, 227, 228, 229, 230, 231, 232, 233, 236, 237, 242, 243, 247, 249, 250–253, 254, 255, 256, 257, 258–260, 261, 263, 265, 266, 267, 268, 270, 271, 272, 273, 279, 284, 292, 293, 294, 350
Isaac, 35, 317, 326
Ishmael, 317
Isho' bar Ali, 154
Isho'dad of Merv, 131, 154
Isidore, 4, 11, 12, 28
Isidore of Pelusium, 188
Isis, 14
Islam, 183

Israel, Israelites, 108, 109, 114, 305, 306
Italian Valentinianism, 76, 79, 93
Iwannis of Dara, 171

Jacob (patriarch), 35, 317, 326
Jacob of Edessa, 183
James the Just (bishop of Jerusalem), 219, 284, 290, 299, 316
Jerome, 1, 142, 143, 153, 182, 187, 189, 206, 249, 257, 258, 279, 281, 283, 285, 294, 296–307, 308, 309
Jerusalem, 141, 203, 204, 205, 206, 214, 237, 239, 242, 245, 269, 271, 279, 280, 284, 285, 286, 287, 290, 291, 305, 346, 354
Jerusalem church, 280, 281, 296, 309, 312
Jessaeans, 285, 286, 288
Jesus (see Christ, Christology)
Jewish Christianity of the *Pseudo-Clementines*, 304, 315–332
Jewish Christians, Jewish Christianity, x, xi, xii, 125, 140, 163, 217, 218, 219, 221, 222, 223, 224, 236, 242, 243, 244, 245, 249, 250, 253, 254, 256, 257, 258, 272, 279, 280, 281, 283, 285, 287, 290, 311, 316, 336, 342, 355, 356, 362, 363
Jewish rabbis, 95, 302, 303, 304, 307, 309, 324
Jewish revolt in Alexandria (115–117), 28
Jewish traditions, 304, 305, 306
Jewish War, 244, 287–288, 290, 302
Jews, 80, 102, 105, 108, 110, 113, 116–119, 122, 162, 177, 215, 249, 282, 286, 298, 306, 307, 310, 331, 343, 344, 347, 348
Joannes, the son of Zakkai (Yohanan ben Zakkai), 302, 303
John (disciple of Jesus), 43, 220, 222, 226, 237, 242, 318
John the Baptist, 140, 221, 262
John of Ephesus, 187, 194
Jordan River, 126, 275
Joseph, 214, 216, 228, 231, 266
Joseph of Tiberias, 262
Josephus, 35, 36, 45
Josua, 302
Judaism, 111, 140, 155, 163, 218, 222, 245, 275
judgment according to deeds, 114
Julius Africanus, 163, 182, 325
Julius Cassianus, 12

Junius Rusticus, 131, 132
Justin Martyr, 2, 9, 10, 27, 77, 95, 104, 113, 131, 132, 137, 141, 142, 180, 210, 224, 227, 229, 234, 240, 248, 249, 250, 286
Justinian I (emperor of Rome), 193

Karnaim, 289
Kerygmata Petrou ("Preachings of Peter"), 316, 325
kingdom of Christ, kingdom of God, 20, 214, 215, 237, 238, 239, 240, 241, 242, 243, 244, 245
knowledge, 24, 59, 85, 86, 107, 151, 214, 225, 226
Korah, 106

Lactantius, 210
Latin, 162
Latin Christianity, 125
laughing Jesus, 22, 23
law, Law (biblical, Jewish, Mosaic), 78, 106, 110, 111, 112, 118, 148, 286, 288, 289, 305, 306, 309, 310, 312, 336
Lazarus, 7, 20
Lesser Armenia, 55, 57
Letter to Flora (Ptolemy), 70, 71, 76, 77, 79, 87, 94, 108
libertinism, 106, 228, 240
licentious practices, 25, 69, 70, 228, 339
Life of Adam and Eve, 36
light, 169
logogriph, 345, 347
Logos (Word), 10, 13, 38, 39, 46, 86, 148, 171
Logismos (reasoning), 13
Love, 39, 67
Lucian, 129
lust for power, 86
Lydos, 55
Lyons, 193, 194, 272

Man, Human, 17, 40
Mani, 6, 8, 181, 182, 353, 356–360, 363
Manichaeism, 8, 182, 353, 356, 357
manifestations of Christ, 342
Ma'nu IX, 165
Marcion, Marcionites, ix, x, xii, 72, 78, 79, 94, 100–122, 125, 132, 141, 142, 143, 152, 154, 155, 163, 170, 181, 182, 202, 227, 228, 229, 231, 232, 241, 249, 250

Marcus Aurelius, 104, 159, 205, 206
Marcus the Magician, Marcosians,
    82–83, 89, 91, 95, 96, 177, 230
Marilaha, 162
Mark (evangelist), 4, 284, 285, 286
marriage, 144, 200–202, 346
Mars, 341
Marsanes, 55, 60
Marsanes, 55
Marsianos, 55
Marthana, 349
Marthus, 349
Martiades, 55
Martyrdom of Perpetua and Felicitas, 186
martyrs, martyrdom, 26, 106, 107, 193
Mary (mother of Jesus), 172, 214, 231,
    266
material human beings, 68, 69, 80, 86
matter, 169
Matthias, 4
Maximilla, 187, 188, 189, 192, 197,
    199, 200, 201, 203, 204, 207
Mazareus, 50
Media, Medes, 129, 177
Meir, 302
Melchizedek (Nag Hammadi), 47–48
Melchizedek (11QMelch), 47
Melchizedek, Melchizedekians, 47, 48
Melito (bishop of Sardis), 202
Memory, 39
Menander, 2, 3, 9, 213, 216, 227,
    232, 233, 249
menstrual separation, 320, 332
Merinthus, 219, 261
Mesopotamia, Mesopotamian, 133,
    160, 163, 347, 348, 349
Messiah, 108, 111, 116, 117, 172, 241,
    249
Messos, 51, 55
metempsychosis, 18
Methodius of Olympos, 259
Michael the Syrian (Syrus), 125, 154,
    160, 164, 172, 173, 187, 189
Michar, 47, 50
Micheus, 47, 50
Middle Platonism, Middle Platonists,
    166, 167, 169, 174
Miltiades, 196
Mind, 38, 67
Mineans, 298
Miriam (sister of Aron), 208
Mirothoe (Mirothea), 39, 47
Mishnah, 307
Mithras, 15

Mnesinous, 47, 50
Moabitis, 274
modalist Christology, 44, 105, 194
monism, 170
Monomoirai, 177
monotheism, 236, 265, 266, 288, 294
Montanism, Montanists, ix, x, xii, 4,
    185–210, 214, 239, 243, 245, 251
Montanus, 187, 188, 189, 190, 192,
    196, 197, 198, 199, 200, 201, 205,
    207, 209
Moses, 77, 78, 100, 109, 112, 120,
    128, 318, 326, 327
Moses bar Kepha, 154, 171
Mother (transcendent), 38, 39, 43, 44,
    46, 48, 83, 171, 172
Mysia, 188
mystical ascent through supernal
    realms, 53, 54, 55, 61

Nabatea, 274, 275
Nag Hammadi texts, xi, 11, 32, 33, 34,
    36, 37, 44, 45, 46, 47, 48, 49, 53, 54,
    55, 56, 57, 65, 70, 84, 170, 174
Nasareans, 257, 259
Nasarenes, 282
nature (*physis*), Nature, 8, 20, 166,
    174, 178
Nazarene collection of testimonies
    against scribes and pharisees, 302
Nazarenes (Nazoraeans), 257, 258,
    274, 279–312
Nazarenes' explanation of Isaiah, 301
Nazirites, 140
Nebo, 162
Nebruel, 40
Necessity, 180
Nephthys, 14
Nepos, 243
New Testament, 20, 32, 64, 89, 114,
    115, 121, 122, 140, 143, 167, 181,
    203, 208, 286, 288, 291, 359
Nicolaus, Nicolaitans, 213, 226, 228,
    229, 250
Nikotheos, 51, 55
Nisibis, 156
Noah, 35, 106, 317
Noetus, 194, 251
nomina barbarika, 177
non-human witnesses, 354, 355
Norea, 49
North Africa, 193, 200, 210
notsrim, 283
Nous, 10, 13, 21, 23, 29, 171, 227

observance of the Torah, 111, 249, 258, 270, 271, 304, 307
Odes of Solomon, 162, 164
Of Domnus (Bardaisan), 166
Ogdoad, 11, 12, 13, 38
Old Testament (Hebrew Bible, Jewish scripture), xii, 20, 25, 67, 77, 78, 79, 100, 102, 105, 107, 108, 109, 110, 113, 115, 118, 120, 121, 122, 139, 148, 167, 181, 198, 199, 208, 241, 245, 247, 260, 288, 291, 335
On the Face of the Moon (Plutarch), 169
On Fate (Alexander of Afrodisias), 179
On the Grown Soul (Isidore), 28
On the Origin of His Body (Manichaean; see *Cologne Mani Codex*), 323, 356–360
On the Origin of the World, 170
Ophites, 146, 230
opposition between water and fire, 323
Oratio ad graecos (Tatian), ix, 128, 129, 130, 131, 144, 146, 147, 148, 149, 150, 151, 152, 153
Origen, 5, 6, 18, 28, 79, 95, 120, 138, 141, 156, 187, 208, 237, 241, 251, 253–256, 258, 260–261, 266, 267, 270, 272, 273, 280, 293, 294, 299, 335, 336, 337, 345, 348, 360, 362, 363
Oroiael, 39, 43, 45, 47, 48, 49
Orphism, 142
Osiris, 14
Osrhoene, 161
Ossaeans, 140, 257, 259, 343, 344, 355, 361

pagan festivals, 69
pagans, 80, 177
Palestine, 55, 57, 139, 256, 273, 336, 348, 360, 362
Pantheism, 60
Papias, 4, 210, 223, 224, 230, 242, 243
Paraclete (Holy Spirit), xii, 186, 198, 199, 202
Parthia, Parthians, 161, 162, 178, 181, 205, 337, 340, 347, 348, 349, 363
Parthian revolt against Trajan (116 C.E.), 340, 347
particles of divine Light, 357
Passing of Peregrinus (Lucian), 129
Pattikios (father of Mani), 356
Paul (apostle), xii, 18, 21, 25, 52, 78, 91, 92, 101, 106, 107, 109, 110, 114, 118, 136, 140, 174, 181, 187, 194, 217, 219, 222, 264, 269, 270, 282, 284, 286, 295, 296, 297, 303, 306, 316, 348, 357
Pauline epistles, 12, 108, 109, 110, 113, 114, 115, 116, 268
Pelagianism, 150
Pella, 287, 288, 289, 290, 291, 312
penance, 338
Pentateuch, 258
Pepuza, 187, 190, 191, 203, 205, 206
Peratae, 177
Perception 39
Perea, 287
Periodoi Petrou, 256, 263, 292, 351, 353
persecution, 25, 37, 41, 101, 182, 193, 194
Persia, Persian, 4, 162, 182
Peter (apostle), 4, 114, 219, 269, 285, 296, 297, 299, 315, 318, 326
Peter (an archontic monk), 55
Pharisees, 140, 298, 302, 303, 304, 305, 306, 307, 324
Phibionites, 53, 177
Philip, 88
Philippus (pupil of Bardaisan), ix, 159, 160, 171, 174, 177, 178, 179, 181
Philistines, 317
Philo of Alexandria, 27, 35, 179
Philokomos, 55
Philoxenus of Mabbug, 172
Phinehas, 345
Photius, 73, 251
Phronesis (prudence), 10, 13, 39
Phrygia, Phrygians, x, 186, 190, 193, 206, 210
physics, 167, 168, 169
Pisidia, 133
Pius (bishop of Rome), 72
Plato, Platonism, 9, 17, 18, 20, 26, 27, 44, 52, 53, 54, 55, 56, 66, 74, 94, 135, 164, 166, 167, 169, 170, 171, 180, 182, 223
Pleasure, 67
pleroma, 24, 38, 67, 68, 82, 93, 181
Plesithea, 39
Pliny, 103
Plotinus, 50, 51, 53, 54, 55, 56, 59, 95
Plutarch, 14
pneumatics (spiritual), 66, 68, 69, 70, 80, 82, 86
Polycarp of Smyrna, 136, 156, 224, 229, 230, 242, 249
Pontus, 101, 102, 103

"Poor," 247, 248, 254, 291
Porphyry, 51, 55
Posidonius, 166, 173
possession Christology, xii, 220, 224–236, 244, 245, 266–269
Power of the Great Light, 39
Praedestinatus, 206
Praxeas, 193, 195, 251
prayer, 271, 346
Prayer of the Apostle Paul, 84
predestination, 150
Preexistent One, 45
Priscilla, 187, 188, 189, 197, 199, 200, 201, 203, 204, 205, 207
Proclus (Montanist), 191, 193, 194, 237
Prognosis (foreknowledge), 13, 38
prognostication, 178, 180
prophecy, (Christian) prophets, 185, 188, 189, 195, 196–199, 208
Protennoia (first thought), 46, 47
Protevangelium Iacobi (*Protevangelium of James*), 146
Providence, 24–27, 43, 59, 179, 180
Pseudo-Anthimus, 73
Pseudo-Clementines (*Homilies* and *Recognitions*), xi, 162, 257, 260, 263, 264–265, 268, 270, 271, 292, 307, 315, 352, 353, 354, 355, 356, 360, 361, 363
Pseudo-Dionysius of Tell-Mahrē, 189
Pseudo-Tertullian, 2, 16, 33, 48, 103, 187, 194, 214, 215–216, 217, 218, 220, 251, 284
psychics, 66, 68, 69, 70, 80, 82, 86, 87
Ptolemy, 70, 76–79, 94, 103
purifying baptisms, 271
purity rules and rites, 271, 328
Pythagoras, Pythagoreanism, 5, 74, 139, 141, 142, 173, 322

Q, 115
Quadratus, 195
Quaestiones (of Caesarius), 178
Quartodecimans, 136, 138, 213, 244
Quinisextine (Trullan) Synod (692 C.E.), 138
Quintilla, 197, 204, 205
Qumran, 47, 140, 247, 248
Quqites, 163

Rabbula of Edessa, 139, 155, 183
race of the Perfect Human, 58, 59
Recognitions 1.27–71 (*Pseudo-Clementines*), 316, 325

redemption, 83, 89, 91
refusal to eat with the non-baptized, 321, 332
Refutation of All Heresies (Hippolytus), 251
regula fidei, 64, 198
reincarnation, 18, 26, 44, 228
rejection of sacrifices and temple services, 322, 346, 354
rejection of virgin birth of Jesus, 214, 219, 221, 225, 247, 260, 266
relatives of Jesus, 273
remission of sins, 335, 337, 338, 348, 354, 359, 361, 363
repudiation of Paul, 270, 271, 335
resurrection of Christ, 219, 222
resurrection of the dead, 87, 88, 147, 174, 214, 219, 288, 294
retaliation, 78, 105, 117
Rheginus, 87
Rhodon, 132, 134
rituals, 54
Rome, Romans, Roman Christians, ix, x, xii, 72, 73, 77, 79, 94, 95, 96, 103, 104, 105, 113, 119, 130, 131, 132, 133, 134, 138, 140, 153, 154, 155, 156, 161, 162, 175, 176, 177, 178, 191, 193, 194, 205, 210, 214, 227, 254, 272, 274, 336, 338, 342, 348, 360, 362, 363
Rufinus, 285
Rule of the Community (1QS), 140

Sabbath, 109, 244, 255, 273, 340, 341
Sabellius, 194
sacrificial laws, 259
Sakla, 40, 41, 49, 59
Salamis (Cyprus), 256
salary of church leaders, 208–209, 210
salvation, 18, 24, 47, 53, 69, 87, 88, 90, 107, 111, 113, 150, 152, 225, 330, 331
Samael, 49
Samlo, 39
Samosata, 129
Sampsaeans (Elkeseans), 257, 343, 344, 349–353, 355, 356, 359, 361–363
Samson, 140
Satan, 83, 101, 122
Saturninus (Satornilos), 3, 9, 12, 14, 15, 18, 21, 22, 27, 28, 52, 125, 133, 141, 142, 143, 216, 227, 229, 232, 233, 249
Savior, 87, 227
"scatterer," 302

Scribes, 140, 302, 303, 304, 305, 306, 307, 324
Scythianus, 6, 7, 8
Second Apology (Justin Martyr), 77
second baptism, 337, 338, 339, 349, 359
Second Legislation, 306
second marriage, 201
second repentance, 202
Second Treatise of the Great Seth, 22, 174
Secret Gospel of Mark, 115
seed (separated/superior), 81
Seleucos I Nicator, 161
separation Christology (see possession Christology)
Septuagint, 130, 131
Serapion of Antioch, 186, 191, 193, 196
servant of God, 295
Seth, 32, 34–36, 37, 38, 39, 40, 41, 42, 43, 44, 45, 48, 49, 52, 55, 58, 60, 61
Seth-Typon, 14
Sethians, Sethianism, x, xi, 9, 32–61, 69, 71, 75, 76, 94, 146
Sethites, 52
Seth's offspring, 35, 37, 39, 41, 42, 45, 48, 52, 58
seven planets, seven planetary beings, 169, 170, 173
seven witnesses (*Book of Elchasai*), 339, 341, 344, 348, 355
Severus Sebokt, 179
sexual intercourse, 164, 359
sexual sins, 339
Shammai, 302, 303
Sibylline Oracles, 272
Silence, 67
Silk Road to China, 161
Simon of Cyrene, 21, 22, 227
Simon Magus, Simonians, 2, 3, 4, 9, 213, 216, 226, 227, 248, 249, 252, 318, 326
sin, sinfulness, 26, 27, 110, 111, 337, 338, 339, 348
Sinope, 102, 103
Sobiai, 337, 363
social identity theory, 310–312
Sodomites, 106
solar year, 14
Son, 38, 39, 44, 46, 105, 171, 172, 175, 186, 234, 294
Son of God, Christ (male angel), 336, 344, 348
Son of Man, 17, 318

Sophia, 10, 13, 35, 40, 43, 45, 47, 49, 67, 68, 75, 79, 81, 85, 86, 181
Sophia of Jesus Christ, 13
sorcery, 25
soteriology, 21–24, 175
soul, 18, 24, 150, 151, 170, 172, 173, 175, 180, 182, 215, 228
spirit, Spirit, 148, 151, 171, 173
Stoicism, Stoics, 9, 21, 25, 27, 75, 163, 166, 167, 169, 170, 178, 180
sufferers from rabies (sexual desire?), 339
suffering, 25, 26, 27, 329
suffering of Jesus, 26, 214, 215, 235
Sumatar Harabesi, 176
Symmachus, 255, 261
synagogue (church), 271
Syntagma (Hippolytus), 2, 103, 216, 220, 251, 252, 311
Syntagma (Justin Martyr), 2, 10, 226, 227, 229, 248, 249, 250, 251, 286
Syria, Syriac, 89, 139, 161, 162, 163, 205, 213, 227, 233, 326, 336
Syriac Didascalia, 162
Syrian (Jewish) Christianity, x, xii, 133, 139, 153, 155, 156, 160, 173, 183, 308, 309, 325, 348, 360, 363
syzygy, 316

tares, 318
Targumic traditions, 303, 307
Tascodrugians, 186
Tatian, ix, x, xii, 125–156, 163, 164, 182, 202, 250
Teachings of Silvanus, 174
Telphon (Tarphon), 302
Temenouthyrai, 191
Tertullian, Tertullianists, 64, 72, 101, 103, 109, 112, 113, 114, 116, 117, 137, 153, 186, 188, 191, 193, 194, 197, 198, 200, 201, 205, 247, 251, 252, 253, 282
Tertullus, 282
Testament of Truth, 272
Testimony of Truth, 5, 11, 12
Themiso, 187, 199
theodicy, 166
Theodore bar Koni, 154, 160, 164, 171, 173
Theodoret of Cyrrhus (Cyrus), 139, 155, 181
Theodosius (emperor of Rome), 96, 97
Theodotus (the money-changer), Theodotians, 48

Theodotus (Montanist), 197
Theodotus (Valentinian), 76, 81–82, 149
Theodotus of Byzantium, 249, 252
theogony, 10–13, 147, 148
Theophilus of Antioch, 152
theosebēs, 331, 332
Therapeutae (Philo), 284, 286
third race (*tertium genus*), 80
Thomasine Christians, xi, xii,
Thrace, 191
Three Steles of Seth, 45–47, 48, 50, 53,
    54, 55
Tiberius, 29, 105
Tigris, 129
Timaeus (Plato), 169, 170, 173, 180
Titus, 217
Trajan, 103, 257, 337, 340, 343, 347
transcendental realm (see also
    Pleroma), 44, 47, 48
Transjordan, 275
Transjordanian Jewish-Christian circles
    (see Sampsaeans/Elkeseans),
    349–353, 361, 362
*Treatise on the Resurrection (Letter to
    Rheginus)*, 84, 87–88
Trimorphic Protennoia ("First Thought in
    Three Forms"), 46–47, 50, 52, 53
Trinitarian schism, 251
Tripartite Tractate, 71, 84, 86–87
Tripolis, 326
Trulla, 97
Truth, 67
Tuesday, 340, 341
Tymion, 190, 191, 205
typology, 108

Understanding, 39
"unholy," 302
Union, 67
universal religion revealed by Christ, 222
Urbicus (prefect of Rome), 77

Valentinian Exposition, 84, 92–93
Valentinus, Valentinianism, ix, x, xi, 5,
    9, 11, 12, 20, 24, 28, 40, 52, 56,
    64–97, 103, 107, 125, 142, 146,
    149, 152, 154, 155, 164, 165, 169,
    172, 174, 175, 180, 181, 226, 227,
    230, 231, 232, 233, 249, 250
vegetarianism, 139, 142, 143, 271,
    292, 322, 332, 358
Victor (bishop of Rome), 95, 193,
    252
virgin birth of Jesus, 267, 288, 293,
    294, 297
Virgins of Vesta, 140
Vulgate, 155, 303, 304

water, 169
wicked spirits, 47
wicked stars, 340
Will, 38
wind, 169
Wisdom (see also Sophia), 83, 88, 89,
    171
women, 82, 83, 144, 196, 197, 199,
    207–208, 210
Word (celestial; see also Logos), 147,
    148
world-rejection, 75

Yaldabaoth (see Ialdabaoth)
Yessedekeus, 50
Yesseus, 50
YHWH, 16
yoke, 304–306
Youel (thrice-male child), 38

Zeno, 148
Zephyrinus (bishop of Rome), 191,
    193, 237
Zeus Latiaris, 130
Zoroaster, 51, 55
Zoroastrianism, 155
Zostrianos, 44–45, 47, 48, 50, 51, 53,
    54, 55, 58
Zostrianos (son of Iolaos), 44, 45, 51,
    55